STATECRAFT

Canadian Prime Ministers and Their Cabinets

Statecraft delves into the intricate relationships between Canadian prime ministers and their cabinets since Confederation. Through twenty critical essays, leading scholars systematically analyse the challenges and decisions faced by individual prime ministers, from Sir John A. Macdonald to Justin Trudeau. The essays explore essential questions: What influenced cabinet appointments? How and why were ministers shuffled or dismissed? How did the drive for re-election shape the leadership styles employed by prime ministers?

At its core, the book examines statecraft – the art of decisive leadership in the face of shifting social, economic, and cultural realities. Statecraft involves the balancing act of maintaining government cohesion, prioritizing urgent issues, and navigating the relentless pursuit of political survival. Even the most seasoned leaders can master statecraft one day and falter the next.

Drawing on extensive research, *Statecraft* bridges history and political science, offering fresh perspectives on the strategies, decisions, and leadership techniques that have defined twenty prime ministers. This comprehensive volume sheds light on the evolving art of governance and its enduring challenges.

(IPAC Series in Public Management and Governance)

STEPHEN AZZI is a professor of political management, history, and political science at Carleton University.

PATRICE DUTIL is a professor in the Department of Politics and Public Administration at Toronto Metropolitan University.

IPAC IAPC

The Institute of
Public Administration of Canada

L'Institut d'administration
publique du Canada

THE INSTITUTE OF PUBLIC ADMINISTRATION OF CANADA
SERIES IN PUBLIC MANAGEMENT AND GOVERNANCE

Editors:
Peter Aucoin, 2001–2
Donald Savoie, 2003–7
Luc Bernier, 2007–9
Patrice Dutil, 2010–18
Luc Juillet, 2018–

This series is sponsored by the Institute of Public Administration of Canada as part of its commitment to encourage research on issues in Canadian public administration, public sector management, and public policy. It also seeks to foster wider knowledge and understanding among practitioners, academics, and the general public.

For a list of books published in the series, see page 501.

EDITED BY STEPHEN AZZI AND PATRICE DUTIL

Statecraft

Canadian Prime Ministers and Their Cabinets

IPAC **IAPC**
The Institute of
Public Administration of Canada
L'Institut d'administration
publique du Canada

UNIVERSITY OF TORONTO PRESS
Toronto Buffalo London

ISBN 978-1-4875-5896-3 (cloth)   ISBN 978-1-4875-5899-4 (EPUB)
ISBN 978-1-4875-5897-0 (paper)   ISBN 978-1-4875-5898-7 (PDF)

Library and Archives Canada Cataloguing in Publication

Title: Statecraft : Canada's prime ministers and their cabinets /
   edited by Stephen Azzi and Patrice Dutil.
Other titles: Statecraft (Toronto, Ont.)
Names: Azzi, Stephen, 1965– editor | Dutil, Patrice A., 1960– editor
Description: Includes bibliographical references and index.
Identifiers: Canadiana (print) 20250142155 | Canadiana (ebook) 20250142163 |
   ISBN 9781487558970 (paper) | ISBN 9781487558963 (cloth) |
   ISBN 9781487558994 (EPUB) | ISBN 9781487558987 (PDF)
Subjects: LCSH: Cabinet system—Canada. | LCSH: Cabinet officers—Canada. |
   LCSH: Prime ministers—Canada. | LCSH: Canada—Politics and government—
   Decision making.
Classification: LCC JL97 .S73 2025 | DDC 320.471—dc23

Cover design: Heng Wee Tan
Cover image: (top) John A. Macdonald's cabinet, 1878. Library and Archives Canada,
C-126574; (middle) Prime Minister Justin Trudeau, pictured with his Cabinet at Rideau
Hall on Nov. 4. The *Hill Times* photograph by Steve Garecke; (bottom) Laurier's
Cabinet of All the Talents, 1896. Library and Archives Canada, item 3000508.

We wish to acknowledge the land on which the University of Toronto Press
operates. This land is the traditional territory of the Wendat, the Anishnaabeg, the
Haudenosaunee, the Métis, and the Mississaugas of the Credit First Nation.

This book has been published with the help of a grant from the Federation for the
Humanities and Social Sciences, through the Awards to Scholarly Publications
Program, using funds provided by the Social Sciences and Humanities Research
Council of Canada.

University of Toronto Press acknowledges the financial support of the Government
of Canada, the Canada Council for the Arts, and the Ontario Arts Council, an
agency of the Government of Ontario, for its publishing activities.

Canada Council   Conseil des Arts
for the Arts   du Canada

ONTARIO ARTS COUNCIL
CONSEIL DES ARTS DE L'ONTARIO
an Ontario government agency
un organisme du gouvernement de l'Ontario

Funded by the   Financé par le
Government   gouvernement   Canada
of Canada   du Canada

For our students. May you find within these pages knowledge and insights that will long outlive this book's contributors.

Study history, study history!
In history lies all the secrets of statecraft.

— Winston Churchill

Contents

Images

Tables

Acknowledgments

Over the enormous time that it takes to make a book, authors and editors incur many debts. Our first thanks go to Daniel Quinlan of the University of Toronto Press. He responded to our book proposal with the enthusiasm that all writers hope to hear. The process of transforming the manuscript to a book occupied many others at UTP, particularly Antonia Pop, vice president for publications; Ryan Pidhayny, production coordinator; and Simon Coll, who carefully copyedited these widely differing texts. Cheryl Lemmens expertly prepared the index. We are grateful to them all.

Carleton University's Faculty of Public and Global Affairs and Toronto Metropolitan University's Faculty of Arts provided essential funding that helped defray some of the publication costs. We are also grateful for the support of the Assistance to Scholarly Publications Program of the Federation for the Humanities and Social Sciences and to the Institute of Public Administration of Canada. The project's genesis can be found in a grant to Stephen Azzi from the Social Sciences and Humanities Research Council of Canada for a project on prime ministerial leadership in Canada.

Our contributors, an impressive group of experts on prime ministers and cabinet governance, generously contributed their research and insights. They delighted us by submitting work on time, responding quickly to queries, and sharing our excitement for this project. It is said that editors of academic collections make many enemies. We count ourselves lucky to have assembled twenty-one scholars who were a joy to work with right to the end. We strengthened old friendships and made new ones along the way.

Not least, we are grateful to our spouses, Adriana Gouvêa and Maha Dutil, who remained unwavering in their support as the book ate up more and more of our time.

We dedicate this volume to our students, those individuals who sign up for our courses, who are the first to hear our theories and who give us feedback on our approaches. Their eager quest for knowledge has kept us motivated to create and complete this work. We hope they are aware of the important place they have on the reflections of all of us who have contributed to this book.

Stephen Azzi and Patrice Dutil
17 December 2024

STATECRAFT

Introduction: The Idea of Cabinet Government

PATRICE DUTIL AND STEPHEN AZZI

"How little people really know of what is really going on in a Cabinet," Prime Minister Wilfrid Laurier confided to his old friend John S. Willison, the editor of the Liberal Toronto *Globe*.[1] It was mid-October 1899, and Laurier was experiencing his first cabinet crisis. The prime minister's colleagues were split over Canada's involvement in the Boer War and unhappy with his proposed compromise of sending a detachment of Canadian volunteers at minimal cost to the government (a one-way ticket to South Africa). Some saw it as an insufficient, quasi-insulting response to Great Britain's call for Imperial defence. Others interpreted it as nothing less than a precedent-setting abandonment of Canadian sovereignty. Laurier's lament did not entail notable revelations; he treasured cabinet confidence far too much. All the same, his observation is still valid 125 years later: what really goes on in cabinet is still a mystery. Certainly, there are clues, and the historical record can point to significant outcomes, but we know practically nothing about lost opportunities, false starts, and hesitations, or how cabinets lose momentum. The endless phases of scepticism, confusion, and frustration are rarely documented.

Thinking back to his days in Lester Pearson's government, Pierre Trudeau recounted in his memoirs how "agendas were hastily slapped together" and how "cabinet wasted an inordinate amount of time discussing insignificant topics, and then had to whisk through questions of major importance, often without arriving at any conclusions." Trudeau complained that decisions had been made elsewhere – typically by Pearson himself and a "handful of our colleagues."[2] It was a complaint that could have been uttered by any minister since 1867, but few have had Trudeau's candour – not that he learned many lessons himself. Indeed, it was as his government took its first steps that the cry of "presidentialization" was levelled in Canada. It was not his fault: the denunciation, as readers of this book will soon discover, could have been made one hundred years before. Trudeau's government continued in the tradition of maintaining the prime minister at the centre of authority and, like all its predecessors, added new dimensions to that control, as government grew more complex and was increasingly called to intervene at unprecedented degrees in policy areas that were unimaginable a generation before.

The prime minister's position of authority in Canada is unequalled in Westminster systems. In part, this is because the system itself is structured to favour a strong core – prime ministers are vested with the powers of a monarch in their ability to set the agenda and in their powers to nominate people to a vast range of authoritative positions, including the highest advisory board: the cabinet. More importantly, in Canada, individuals who acceded to the position had proven that they saw the country "whole" and had a magic touch in rallying various regions of the country and in showing that they could win elections. The ability to win, or to at least carry the illusion of being able to win, has given most prime ministers a capacity to command. But to win, a prime minister needs a cabinet that works. And for this to happen, the first minister must select individuals who will provide reliable advice, perform their administrative and political tasks, act with probity, and be effective translators of what the public favours and what the government aspires to accomplish. The hard task of aligning ideas with individuals in cabinet and in top public sector positions, structures, and, not least, electoral support is called *statecraft*. The study of statecraft goes beyond a study of personal character and reveals that prime ministers must meet three difficult tests: political management, collegial management, and state management. Statecraft also refers commonly to managing a country's foreign relations, but this volume focuses on the first three elements.[3]

Maintaining popularity with the electorate is the crucial test of statecraft. This can be done through personal appeal, but charisma is a perishable commodity. Popularity can also be achieved through clever policy innovations. But it inevitably means activating the cabinet team to deliver the right messages at the right time and to the right audiences. Collegial management – the management of cabinet – draws on personal appeal equally, but on a smaller and perhaps a far more vital scale. It entails appointing the right people to the right posts, keeping them there, and creating supportive coalitions so that ministers remain motivated. It also means removing individuals who are no longer valuable to the government. Prime ministers know that the most effective challenges to their authority always come from cabinet. Statecraft finally relates to the prime minister's structural changes to the administrative state: the creation of new departments and agencies (or the elimination or fusion of others).

Cabinet members in Canada have favoured strong prime ministerial governments. Since 1867, ministers have buried their own private agendas, at least temporarily, to taste the fruits of power (there were exceptions, but they only proved the rule). They turned to the source of light at the centre, investing their political futures in the prime minister's ability. Over the past twenty years, ministers have even allowed the Prime Minister's Office to have the last say on appointments to their personal staff, a remarkable turn of authority. That said, there has always been a tension between the personal clout of the prime minister and the collegial requirements of cabinet government. Herman Bakvis's *Regional Ministers* stands out as an exceptional study of this tension, but the focus of this work was on ministers, not the prime minister. Our purpose with this book is different.[4]

One might call it a troubled heliotropism, but that has not been a popular subject because it is notoriously difficult to qualify and to quantify. In 1964, the journalist Bruce Hutchison published a first study of prime ministers to uncover the alchemy that led to success. In *Mr. Prime Minister, 1867–1964*, he called the Prime Minister's Office a "listening post" and an "engine room" but focused his stylish essays on personal portraits of the various men and their key decisions. "Cabinet" as a subject was never raised. Hutchison's worthy successor was Michael Bliss's *Right Honourable Men: The Descent of Canadian Politics from Macdonald to Chrétien*, a book that first came out in 1994 and was republished with an update ten years later. Bliss's study was more comprehensive than Hutchison's and clearly benefited from thirty years of accumulated scholarship, but even he scarcely paid attention to the mechanisms by which Canadian prime ministers imposed their authority on cabinets and the state.

The work of prime ministers as government executives is as complex as it is undefined. The cabinet system assumes that the individual who sits at the head of the table is suitably educated, has the intelligence necessary to manage numerous policy issues competently, and is deeply experienced and clear in the priorities that are to be pursued, even if they have to be delegated. The persons who have been successful in the position were able to convince colleagues that they could be trusted. They showed confidence, decisiveness, and intelligence in interpreting events of the past and in anticipating developments. Most showed their competence with long hours spent in study and in thoughtful consultation. The best ones had a sense of humour.

Cabinet doctrine can work well only if ministers are highly collaborative, willing to compromise while pursuing some of their own personal objectives. It accepts that the ministers share roughly the same political agenda. It presumes that the bureaucracy is at the ready and firmly in control of available policy and program instruments. It hopes that the public service can also be creative when need be. The system is based on the understanding that all players are governed by the ethical prerogative of putting their personal interests far down the list and that the institutional culture will asphyxiate corruption. Not least, it depends on a collegiality that welcomes and debates a variety of ideas freely, frankly, unafraid of being revealed at the least opportune times.

Cabinet government is not directed by any provisions in the written constitution. Nor are its functions.[5] Cabinet privileges and habits have been derived from ill-defined royal prerogatives borrowed from British practices whose origins are not easily traced. Not surprisingly, cabinet government has over time been altered to meet changing circumstances. Yet from a theoretical perspective, the role of the prime minister and the idea of cabinet government has been a great deal more difficult to interpret. Jean Blondel considered it almost impossible in his famous *Thinking Politically*, but that has not deterred many from trying.[6]

Cabinet management is the essence of statecraft because without it nothing can happen or be executed correctly. The choices made in selecting some individuals over others can have lasting, and sometimes damaging consequences on the success of a ministry. Cabinet members can enable or disable policy alternatives long before they can be noticed.

This book is an attempt to capture answers to key questions about governance in Canada's Westminster system: What were the key features of prime ministerial approaches to cabinet and how did they translate into a craft of governing? What were their preferred methods of politics – of persuading and, if need be, of forcing – and policymaking? To what degree have they assumed control, and under what circumstances, and to what extent, did they delegate the work of governing? What can history teach about the evolution of prime ministerial government?

The chapters that constitute this book explore how various prime ministers managed government and department structures, engineered policy changes, and gave personal direction to their cabinet by expressing their personal styles. The first chapter captures the efforts made by theoreticians of all sorts to capture how prime ministers have been successful and have failed. Patrice Dutil then examines the evolution of cabinet governance by Sir John A. Macdonald, who, legend has it, once checked into a hotel by indicating that "cabinetmaker" was his profession. Macdonald was highly successful to the point where he was often called an "autocrat," and his imprint on Canadian governance can be felt to this day. His first successor, Alexander Mackenzie, was not so skilled. In chapter 3, Ben Forster examines Mackenzie's cabinet governance and concludes that the most important lessons about cabinet management had not been learned. The coalition created by the first Liberal prime minister was unable to overcome its weaknesses. Macdonald's later successors, a varied group of four, could not replicate their master's success either. Ted Glenn recounts in chapter 4 how the Tory cabinet under John Abbott, John Thompson, Mackenzie Bowell, and Charles Tupper was unable to follow a single vision, which led to a cabinet revolt – vivid evidence of a failed statecraft. In chapter 5, J.P. Lewis takes another look at Laurier's famed "cabinet of all talents" and highlights how Laurier wisely crafted his government by relying on a few critical individuals to sustain a government that seemed to be constantly in motion. In chapter 6, John English revisits the Robert Borden cabinet, noting that his management was always hamstrung by his sense of being an outsider.

Borden showed that cabinet government is not easy, and the post-First World War governments proved the notion. Mary Janigan and Tom Kierans in chapter 7 take an unprecedented look at Arthur Meighen's attempts to pull together a coalition that might have worked but find that his personal intransigence on various policy challenges made the task almost impossible and impaired his statecraft. In part, the quality of talent was not there, something Robert Wardhaugh also uncovers in his treatment of the Mackenzie King governments of the 1920s (see chapter 8). Richard B. Bennett came to office in 1930, probably the worst time for any new government in the history of Canada, and although he worked endlessly to bring about change, his government also failed the test of statecraft. In chapter 9, Larry Glassford scrutinizes Bennett's practice, again highlighting the tension between a know-it-all and do-it-all prime minister and his cabinet. Mackenzie King's tenure between 1935 and 1948 brought about a revolution in cabinet management. The prime minister's staff was the first and most important locus of reform, but King also placed enormous importance on having the right kind of person at the ministerial table and won the allegiance of most of his ministers (there were exceptions) as Canada was at war with Nazi Germany and Imperial Japan, as Robert Bothwell argues in chapter 10.

Stephen Azzi then examines Louis St-Laurent's approach to cabinet management and documents a system that is both highly efficient and effective: a case study in statecraft. In chapter 11, he shows how St-Laurent led by providing the unquestioned centre of gravity. Was this also the seed of arrogance and contentment? The experience of the succeeding governments showed the mastery of St-Laurent's practice of statecraft. In chapter 12, Patricia McMahon concludes that John Diefenbaker's deep experience as a small-practice lawyer did not particularly suit him to the tasks of statecraft. P.E. Bryden's study of the Pearson government in chapter 13 shows a leader eminently capable of statecraft, regardless of what Pierre Trudeau must have thought as he sat at the cabinet table. Asa McKercher in chapter 14 and Frédéric Boily in chapter 15 both examine Pierre Trudeau, but in separate times, using separate styles. McKercher captures Trudeau's statecraft in the 1970s, focused on massive expansions of the state. Boily examines Trudeau in his last mandate focused on constitutional change and agrees that there certainly was a presidentialization of the office, but likens it much more to the French presidency than any emulation of the American republic.

In chapter 16, Raymond Blake focuses on Brian Mulroney's unique management style and his comprehensive approach to statecraft. Lori Turnbull explores the leadership of Jean Chrétien in chapter 17 and observes how centralization of operations took another leap, but also notes that his thrusts in that direction led to his downfall after ten years. Chapter 18, by Patrice Dutil and Stephen Azzi, examines the short-lived Paul Martin ministry and brings to light the prime minister's efforts to roll back the centralization trend and involve more cabinet members in the decision-making process. The consequence of his reforms may have contributed to that government's reputation for hesitation (which was not wrong). Those difficulties might have been sorted out had the government lasted longer, but there is no doubt that the prime minister's worst management habits were compounded by the cabinet structure he adopted.

In chapter 19, Paul Wilson's treatment of Stephen Harper's prime ministership shows how detached cabinet had become and how messaging assumed the prime focus of activity. That strategy worked until it no longer did in 2015. The final chapter, by Jeni Armstrong, Alex Marland, and Dan Arnold, examines Justin Trudeau's claim that cabinet government was back and concludes that this objective was not met. The statecraft displayed by both Harper and Trudeau, two vastly different personalities, show that success and failure go far beyond character.

We have not covered the cabinets of three prime ministers: Joe Clark, John Turner, and Kim Campbell. Each was in office for less than one year and had little time to develop a distinctive approach to statecraft. Clark's government was defeated in the Commons after only six months, before it had found its footing. Campbell was in office for only seventy-five days before an election campaign began. During that period, she undertook a transformation of the cabinet, but it was one that had been designed in the dying days of the Mulroney regime and would be completed under Jean Chrétien. Turner launched an election campaign in his second week as prime minister.

This book combines the views of historians and political scientists who have kindly lent their time and erudition to this project, combing through the record and the many interpretations of cabinet government as it has evolved through time. This volume was not intended to provide a consistent lens through which to view all the ministries but to demonstrate how various approaches could yield insight and even new interpretations of statecraft. All the contributors, however, accepted the notion that time can be revealing of how institutions like the cabinet can evolve in certain directions, shaped as they are by succeeding first ministers and their colleagues. They followed Churchill's dictum that, notwithstanding the introduction of new techniques of analysis, an appreciation of statecraft can be obtained only with a careful study of its history. It may even occasionally pierce the screen and give Canadians an idea of what really goes on in the cabinet.

NOTES

1 Library and Archives Canada, John Stephen Willison fonds, MG 30 D 29, Laurier to Willison, 14 October 1899.

2 Pierre Elliott Trudeau, *Memoirs* (Toronto: McClelland and Stewart, 1993), 108. Jody Wilson-Raybould has probably disclosed more about the functioning of the

Justin Trudeau cabinet than has been revealed about any other. See *Indian in the Cabinet: Speaking Truth to Power* (Toronto: HarperCollins, 2021); and Patrice Dutil, "Crisis of Cabinet Government," *Dorchester Review*, Summer 2022, 42–51.

3 See Patrice Dutil, ed., *Statesmen, Strategists and Diplomats: Canadian Prime Ministers and Their Foreign Policies* (Vancouver: University of British Columbia Press, 2023).

4 Herman Bakvis, *Regional Ministers: Power and Influence in the Canadian Cabinet* (Toronto: University of Toronto Press, 1991).

5 See Christopher Foster, "Cabinet Government in the Twentieth Century," *Modern Law Review* 67, no. 5 (2004): 743–71.

6 Jean Blondel, *Thinking Politically* (London: Pelican Books, 1978), 15.

1 Statecraft: Theory and the Thirst for History

PATRICE DUTIL AND STEPHEN AZZI*

Cabinet government is now three hundred years old, and theorists have engaged in a diligent search over the past half-century to better understand its mystifying logic. There seems to be an appetite for insights into the black box of cabinetry not just because its rules seem so plastic but because the forces behind them are often very difficult to discern. To its credit, the government of the United Kingdom has recently tried to define the responsibilities of prime minister and cabinet as part of its efforts to modernize its operations, but somehow its labours have never been complete.[1] In 2010, Sir Peter Hennessy produced a comprehensive listing of the roles and powers of the prime minister that remains the clearest statement.[2] There has been no equivalent in Canada.

The subtleties and limits of a Westminster system have been evolving since Robert Walpole shaped the position and practice of prime minister in the Great Britain of the 1720s and 1730s.[3] It took 130 years before the erudite journalist Walter Bagehot placed it in theoretical terms in his landmark *The English Constitution* (1867). Bagehot famously described the prime minister as the *primus inter pares* ("first among equals") to capture the notion that the individuals who held the title were not necessarily more talented or more intelligent than their peers but instead had been supported by their colleagues for a variety of political or administrative reasons. Power was shared, the product of a constant exchange between ministers. The prime minister's role was to act as interpreter and spokesman of the cabinet's mood and policy inclinations. Their success was attributed to their ability to compromise, to capture a "middle road" that was acceptable to most, at least for a time. Politics mattered to Bagehot, as he described the cabinet as the "near fusion" of the executive and legislature, "a hyphen which joins ... a buckle which fastens." For him, it was the "efficient secret" of the British political system. He described cabinet as "the executive: a board of control chosen by the legislature, out of persons it trusts and knows, to rule the nation."[4]

The key principles of Bagehot's model were notably updated and commented on by Sir Ivor Jennings in his *Cabinet Government* (1959), but it was

Richard Crossman, a Labour MP at Westminster (and later a minister in Harold Wilson's cabinet), who transformed how students of politics viewed the prime minister and cabinet. In his introduction to the 1963 version of Bagehot's classic work, Crossman declared that things had changed dramatically. The prime minister had assumed a far greater influence than Bagehot could have ever imagined, Crossman wrote, even alluding to an American-style presidentialization of British politics. His observations of real-life politics (captured in the three-volume work *Diaries of a Cabinet Minister*, which was published after his death in 1974), showed vividly how prime ministers had risen far above the rank of their peers. Prime ministers were now extending the authority of their offices to the farthest reaches of the state, robbing colleagues of authority and voice in the making of both key and minor decisions.

The notion of presidentialization seemed confirmed by the way Margaret Thatcher conducted her government (1979–90) as Michael Foley described it in *The Rise of the British Presidency* (1993). Foley argued that structural developments, changing leadership styles and new power sources had transformed the prime minister's position to the point where it looked like the American government's executive branch. It had its own identity, its own independence vis-à-vis cabinet as well as the legislature and the courts. Prime ministers now campaigned like American presidents (alone, and often against parties and institutions) and seemed to govern separately from cabinet and the House of Commons. Their power was not derived from the support of their colleagues but instead came from the ability of their personal staffs to manipulate the media. They even seemed to dominate cabinet members – people who had actually been *elected* to represent the citizens. Foley could easily point to Thatcher's successful removal of the "wets" from her cabinet during the early 1980s, until it was entirely dominated by people loyal to her.

Of course, this theory crashed into the brick wall of reality when Thatcher's cabinet colleagues forced her to resign years later, and her successor John Major seemed willing to roll back the clock to give cabinet collegiality a new vitality. At that point, political scientists in the United Kingdom and Australia launched a search for new insight into the mysteries of power. Patrick J. Dunleavy and Roderick A.W. Rhodes championed a model of leadership that went beyond the prime minister as an individual, focussing their work on "the court," the assemblage of advisers that surrounded the chief executive.[5] It was composed of elected members of the legislature, or cabinet ministers, obviously, but Dunleavy and Rhodes also included key advisers in the bureaucracy as well as personal influencers who worked in the prime minister's office.

The theme of presidentialization was revived by Tony Blair's prime ministership as he notably overrode cabinet concerns about issues as diverse as the Iraq War, foxhunting, and the Millennium Dome exhibition facility. Blair was said to be a particularly adept practitioner of "sofa politics" to deal with the worries of his colleagues, choosing to meet them individually instead of confronting issues at the cabinet table. Foley updated his thinking in *The British Presidency: Tony Blair and the Politics of Public Leadership* (2000).

In Canada, cabinet government was first described by John George Bourinot in his *How Canada Is Governed* (1895) and *Canada under British Rule, 1760–1900* (1900). Bourinot was more interested in the structures borrowed from Great Britain than in analysing how policy was made. He gave far more space to the roles of the governor general than to the prime minister, which hardly received more than a page's attention. The first real effort to theorize and explain the practice of cabinet government were made by Norman McLeod Rogers, a professor of political science at Queen's University until he became private secretary to prime minister Mackenzie King in 1927. He was elected to the House of Commons in 1935 and served as minister of labour and then briefly as minister of national defence before he was killed in a plane crash in 1940.[6] Rogers patterned his studies of cabinet government (all published in 1933) in part on Bagehot's theories and in part on what he witnessed personally. His first essay on the roots of cabinet government in Canada examined British practices. A second article focused on the impact of federalism on cabinet, explaining the imperative of regional and bicultural representation in the Canadian case.[7] His third piece examined the evolution of the cabinet since 1867, emphasizing the evolution of portfolios. Rogers was not particularly impressed. "It cannot be said," he declared, "that the changes in the Canadian Cabinet, as indicated in this study of its growth, were adopted in accordance with any deliberate plan of increasing its efficiency."[8] Rogers proposed that a cabinet secretariat be established and that more ministers without portfolio be appointed to take on special tasks. Mackenzie King adopted those suggestions during the Second World War.

More than thirty years after Rogers, the temptation to declare the prime ministership in Canada as presidential as it had become in the UK was impossible to resist,[9] but the best effort to theorize the office and the cabinet came from University of Toronto political scientist J. Stefan Dupré.[10] He observed that cabinet government had developed in three phases. The first phase, dating from Confederation, was labelled the "unaided cabinet." In this system, the prime minister held multiple portfolios and the only cabinet committee was the Treasury Board, which was focused on controlling expenses. No records were kept and the few aides in the Privy Council Office were truly clerks. The expertise was localized in government departments.

The period of "departmentalized cabinet" followed as departments expanded significantly in the first half of the twentieth century. This period favoured portfolio loyalty for both ministers and senior public servants, and they enjoyed a good measure of decision-making autonomy. Cabinet solidarity was dependent on the confidence in colleagues, not information-sharing or shared decision-making. Dupré saw the "institutionalized cabinet" emerge during the Second

World War. The example in Ottawa was clearly a case in point, but Dupré also argued that the T.C. Douglas government in Saskatchewan was particularly innovative (1944–60). Again, it was the first minister who structured cabinet, but he no longer held other portfolios. As government grew more complex, multiple cabinet committees and subcommittees were spawned and the Cabinet Office attracted increasingly sophisticated permanent staff, who in turn began to argue for more sophisticated policy and planning apparatus. To simplify administration, super-ministries were created in the 1970s.

Herman Bakvis echoed Rogers's early treatment of regionalization of cabinet with his *Regional Ministers: Power and Influence in the Canadian Cabinet* (1991). For him, the trick of cabinet government in Canada was not simply a notion of appointing key allies and even friends (who would remain loyal) to important positions. Success also depended on ensuring that regions had a voice at the cabinet table. Other imperatives had been added as new categories of representativeness were included in the equation of making sure that cabinet was as good a mirror of the Canadian population as possible. It would include women and, increasingly, other sectors of the population.

The most notable explorations of the contemporary primacy of the Canadian prime minister in Canada were performed by Donald Savoie in his many books. His 1999 *Governing from the Centre: The Concentration of Power in Canadian Politics* had an explosive impact as he challenged long-established conventions about how Canada's cabinet worked. Savoie did not use the term *presidentialization*, but his arguments certainly pointed to prime ministerial dominance. He argued that Parliament had been bypassed and that cabinet government had been effectively sidelined since the day of Pierre Trudeau. Borrowing heavily from Australian and British scholars, he pointed to the realities of a government directed by a prime minister and "a small group of carefully selected courtiers rather than with the prime minister acting in concert with his elected Cabinet colleagues."[11] Savoie's thesis has been tested ever since, with countless observers confirming that this trend of cabinet governance had been perpetuated by Paul Martin, Stephen Harper, and Justin Trudeau, leaving some observers to ask whether cabinet government in Canada still existed.[12]

At the same time, a new school of thought emerged, one emphasizing that prime ministerial authority was not automatic and certainly open to political challenge even within the court. Two particularly eloquent scholars, Martin Burch and Ian Holliday, concluded that the "UK has neither a presidential institutional structure nor presidential institutional capacity." They argued that although there were times when prime ministers dominated their cabinets, their position simply could not be sustained, because the structures to buttress their power did not exist. Yet they did discern a system under constant tension between prime ministers and their colleagues. Even when it came to discussing Blair, their conclusion was that "while there has clearly been substantial change, there has not been a revolution." Instead, they saw changes that were consistent with "traditions and practice" in the UK.[13]

The experiences of Gordon Brown and David Cameron further showed that negotiating with disgruntled factions and the other parties necessary for coalition government required a cabinet system that properly distributed executive functions. In Canada, Jean Chrétien was effectively forced out of office as caucus support melted after the turn of the millennium; the same fate awaited Justin Trudeau twenty years later.

Others have raised serious objections to the presidentialization thesis in Canada. Among the more persuasive was Graham White of the University of Toronto, who pointed out that evidence beyond anecdote was lacking.[14] Herman Bakvis issued similar reservations.[15] Conducting a survey of politicians to test their perceptions of centralization in the prime minister or premier's office, J.P. Lewis did not find that this attitude prevailed.[16] In Australia, it was Patrick Weller who challenged the idea that prime ministers had grown too powerful in 2003, arguing that the trend towards centralization was not particularly telling: "It was unrealistic to expect the style of the 19th century to survive war and economic development, so the modern cabinet too has to evolve to meet the pressures on it."[17] "The tests are political, not constitutional," he reminded his readers, "the argument that prime ministerial government has replaced cabinet government presents a false dichotomy as prime ministers work through cabinet as often as they act individually."[18] Weller also insisted that prime ministers had not been relieved of the need to gain support from ministers who had real authorities and that cabinet was still a "vital forum." Acknowledging that cabinet was not an entirely effective conduit of decision-making, Weller argued that it was still important because it constituted a "working set of arrangements, not a set of rules or a given distribution of power."[19]

The theoretical framework of the prime minister's office was thus at an impasse, yet again – and, arguably, as it had always been. Taking a new look at Margaret Thatcher's governance, British scholar James Bulpitt was not convinced by the idea of "presidentialism" and instead roughly sketched out an idea of "statecraft" in 1985 to re-emphasize the importance of politics in cabinet management and to show that it was still highly malleable. He reminded his readers that structures of power were not necessarily inherited by prime ministers (unlike the American presidency) and that they had to literally redefine their powers over time. Not least, their efforts in convincing their colleagues that they should remain in the central seat had to be unrelenting in order to maintain power. To achieve successful statecraft, leaders had to demonstrate competence in office, of course, but also had to develop winning electoral strategies and carefully manage their colleagues in order to protect their place at the apex of power.[20]

Bulpitt's perspective was not greeted enthusiastically, because it raised many more questions than it resolved. Bulpitt stressed individual styles of power politics when most scholars were looking for systemic explanations, and he extended his ideas on a historical plane. He conceptualized party leaders as self-interested, rational, and cohesive actors who used different "governing codes" to stay in power.[21] Furthermore, Bulpitt emphasized support mechanisms such as party management, electoral strategies, and most importantly, governing competence.[22] Leaders operated within a structural context that Bulpitt called a "natural rate of governability," which affected their ability to achieve successful statecraft.[23] Jim Buller, another British scholar, offered qualified support in 1999, but emphasized that the theory was being suffocated by a lack of grounded evidence.[24]

That evidence could come only from a study of history. Toby James, a professor of politics and public policy at the University of East Anglia in Norwich, updated Bulpitt's notions by developing a "neo-statecraft" theory. In it, he emphasized that prime ministers had to be evaluated on how well they ensured the proper functioning of their parties and crafted platforms to attract partisans and funding in order to win elections.[25] After all, history had shown repeatedly that prime ministers could be dethroned by an internal coup. Perhaps more controversially, James also insisted that prime ministers had to be willing to "bend the rules of the game" in order to win. He saw the occasional super-primacy of the prime minister as sometimes necessary to win, but not always essential.

The thinking around statecraft also revived the foci on the imperatives of electoral politics as a source of change as well as individual styles. James pointed to the premiership of John Major (1990–7), who revived collective thinking and adopted a more consensual style of leadership. Notwithstanding his centralized style, Tony Blair imitated Major by appointing John Prescott (a figure from "Old Labour") as deputy prime minister (1997–2007) to harden the link between the cabinet and the party. David Cameron appointed Nick Clegg as his deputy prime minister to keep the Liberal Democrats onside during the coalition era (2010–15). James noted that both of these prominent deputies chaired many important cabinet committees, which can only be viewed as an important strategic role. More than anything, James emphasized that history mattered, and that the evolution of power had to be seen both in its continuities and changes. In other words, for all the merits of political science modelling, the understanding of power as it is articulated by those in and around the prime ministers demanded a grounding in history. No one could get to the bottom of things unless the tools of history – the picks and shovels used to mine archives, data, and testimony – were applied. More recently, the statecraft approach was applied to the prime ministership of Theresa May (2016–19) by examining party management, electoral success, and government competence.[26]

The study of prime ministers in Canada has come to an impasse. Models of character-driven governments, of governments managed by regional reconciliation or by courts that suddenly developed in the 1980s have lost their steam and the interest of readers. This is why we turn to the teachings of statecraft.

It is a given that prime ministers in Canada have been allowed to play an outsized role in shaping policy and politics. This was assumed by the historians who tended to cast aside the theoretical junkets launched by political scientists. Historians accepted the essential impact of prime ministers in Canada in shaping statecraft, and studies in this country have focused more on demonstrating thoughts and actions instead of theorizing them. In his *Prime Ministerial Power in Canada*, Patrice Dutil demonstrated that John A. Macdonald, Wilfrid Laurier, and Robert Borden had created a distinct culture of power in Ottawa in how they structured departments, made key appointments in cabinet and in the senior ranks of the bureaucracy, prioritized budgets, managed factions and dissent, and set the general tone of the administration of their governments. In other words, the prime ministership in Canada, and even "the court" to use another expression, has been cardinal in importance since 1867 – certainly far more than the courts, the legislature, or the bureaucracy. It was also clear that prime ministers could be challenged from outside and inside: the press, tribunals, provinces, and even colleagues have tried to undermine Canada's chief elected officials repeatedly, consistently, and often successfully.[27]

Those who did examine prime ministers showed that they accepted the need to delegate to trusted loyalists so as to get things done, but historians and political scientists with a sympathy for the past have seldom had a chance to probe cabinet management as a central act of statecraft. It has emerged in discussions of crises, such as when Mackenzie Bowell faced a cabinet revolt, or when Robert Borden's idea of giving the United Kingdom a grant to fund the building of battleships was blocked by the Liberal-dominated Senate, or when his unconditional support of the British government's declarations of war on the German-Austrian alliance in 1914 cost him the support of cabinet ministers from Quebec. Many of Bennett's ministers were upset by his one-man show, and one minister started his own party, earning almost nine percent of the vote in 1935, most of it from former Conservative voters. Mackenzie King faced considerable cabinet discontent during the Second World War. The travails of John Diefenbaker in keeping peace in his cabinet have long been common knowledge. Lester Pearson often got an earful from cabinet colleagues, and many (like Pierre Trudeau) were privately disappointed. Pierre Trudeau himself faced dissent (notably from the "blue" Liberals) to the point where John Turner resigned as minister of finance in 1975. The chapters that follow revisit the instances when statecraft was particularly controversial, but also examine the remarkable stability of Canada's more than 150 years of cabinet government, a story that has mostly remained veiled.

NOTES

* We are very grateful for the research help provided by Ali Akbar for this chapter.

1 In 1948, the Cabinet Office prepared a paper titled "Function of the Prime Minister and His Staff"; in 2011, the same office published *The Cabinet Manual*, setting out the main laws, rules, and conventions affecting the conduct and operation of government, including a description of the role of the prime minister; and in 2014 the Political and Constitutional Reform Select Committee produced a final report to their inquiry, titled *Role and Powers of the Prime Minister*.

2 Peter Hennessy, "The Role and Powers of the Prime Minister" (presentation to Select Committee on Political and Constitutional Reform, 21 February 2011), https://publications.parliament.uk/pa/cm201012/cmselect/cmpolcon/writev/842 /pm04.htm. See also Martin Burch and Ian Holliday, "The Blair Government and the Core Executive," *Government and Opposition* 39, no. 1 (Winter 2004): 1–21. Notably, Canada's Commission of Inquiry into the Sponsorship Program and Advertising Activities (the Gomery Commission) of 2004–6 avoided the topic.

3 See Anthony Seldon, *The Impossible Office? The History of the British Prime Minister* (Cambridge: Cambridge University Press, 2021).

4 Bagehot, as cited in William H.P. Clement, *The Law of the Canadian Constitution* (Toronto: Carswell, 1916), 340.

5 See P. Dunleavy and R.A.W. Rhodes, "Core Executive Studies in Britain," *Public Administration* 68, no. 1 (1990): 3–28; R.A.W. Rhodes, "From Prime Ministerial Power to Core Executive," in *Prime Minister, Cabinet and Core Executive*, ed. R.A.W. Rhodes and P. Dunleavy (London: Macmillan, 1995), 11–37; and R.A.W. Rhodes, "Core Executives, Prime Ministers, Statecraft, and Court Politics: Towards Convergence," in *The Craft of Governing*, ed. Glyn Davis and R.A.W. Rhodes (Sydney: Allen & Unwin, 2014), 53–72.

6 Norman McLeod Rogers, "The Introduction of Cabinet Government in Canada," *Canadian Bar Review* 11, no. 1 (1933): 1–17.

7 Norman McLeod Rogers, "Federal Influences on the Canadian Cabinet," *Canadian Bar Review* 11, no. 2 (1933): 103–21. It is worth underlining the important studies carried out by the Royal Commission on Bilingualism and Biculturalism on regional representation in Canadian cabinets. See Frederick W. Gibson, ed., *Cabinet Formation and Bicultural Relations: Seven Case Studies* (Ottawa: Queen's Printer, 1970). On Rogers, see the forthcoming entry in the *Dictionary of Canadian Biography* by Stephen Azzi and Norman Hillmer.

8 Norman McLeod Rogers, "Evolution and Reform of the Canadian Cabinet," *Canadian Bar Review* 11, no. 4 (1933): 235.

9 Denis Smith was the first to use the expression in Canada in 1969. See the reprint of his paper in Thomas A. Hockin, ed., *Apex of Power: The Prime Minister and Political Leadership in Canada* (Toronto: Prentice Hall, 1977). For a general discussion of the presidentialization thesis, see Patrice Dutil, *Prime Ministerial*

Power in Canada: Its Origins under Macdonald, Laurier and Borden (Vancouver: University of British Columbia Press, 2017), ch. 1.

10 Stefan J. Dupré, "The Workability of Executive Federalism in Canada," in *Federalism and the Role of the State*, ed. Herman Bakvis and William M. Chandler (Toronto: University of Toronto Press, 1987), 236–58.

11 See Donald Savoie, *Governing from the Centre: The Concentration of Power in Canadian Politics* (Toronto: University of Toronto Press, 1999).

12 Donley T. Studlar and Kyle Christensen, "Is Canada a Westminster or Consensus Democracy? A Brief Analysis," *PS: Political Science and Politics* 39, no. 4 (October 2006): 837–41.

13 Burch and Holliday, "Core Executive," 20–1.

14 Graham White, "The 'Centre' of the Democratic Deficit: Power and Influence in Canadian Political Executives," in *Imperfect Democracies: The Democratic Deficit in Canada*, ed. Richard Simeon and Patti Tamara Lenard (Vancouver: University of British Columbia Press, 2006), 226–47.

15 Herman Bakvis, "Prime Minister and Cabinet in Canada: An Autocracy in Need of Reform?," *Journal of Canadian Studies* 35, no. 4 (2000), 60–79; and Herman Bakvis and Steven B. Wolinetz, "Canada: Executive Dominance and Presidentialization," in *The Presidentialization of Politics: A Comparative Study of Modern Politics*, ed. Thomas Poguntke and Paul Webb (Oxford: Oxford University Press, 2005), 199–220.

16 J.P. Lewis, "Elite Attitudes on the Centralization of Power in Canadian Political Executives: A Survey of Former Canadian Provincial and Federal Cabinet Ministers, 2000–2010," *Canadian Journal of Political Science* 46, no. 4 (2013): 799–819.

17 Patrick Weller, "Cabinet Government: An Elusive Ideal?," *Public Administration* 81, no. 4 (2003): 720.

18 Patrick Weller, "'The Modern Autocrat': Myths and Debates about the Power of Prime Ministers," *Social Alternatives* 36, no. 3 (2017): 5.

19 Weller, "Cabinet Government."

20 See Jim Bulpitt, "The Discipline of the New Democracy: Mrs. Thatcher's Domestic Statecraft," *Political Studies* 34, no. 1 (March 1986): 19–39.

21 Jim Bulpitt, "Historical Politics: Leaders, Statecraft and Regime in Britain at the Accession of Elizabeth II," in *Contemporary Political Studies 1996*, ed. Iain Hampsher-Monk and Jeffrey Stanyer (Oxford: Blackwell, 1996), 2:1093–106.

22 Bulpitt, "Historical Politics."

23 Jim Bulpitt, "Rational Politicians and Conservative Statecraft in the Open Polity," in *British Foreign Policy under Thatcher*, ed. Peter Byrd (Oxford: Philip Allan, 1988), 214–56.

24 Jim Buller, "A Critical Appraisal of the Statecraft Interpretation," *Public Administration* 77, no. 4 (1999): 691–712.

25 Toby S. James, "Neo-statecraft Theory, Historical Institutionalism and Institutional Change," *Government and Opposition* 51, no. 1 (2016): 84–110;

Toby S. James, "Political Leadership as Statecraft? Aligning Theory with Praxis in Conversation with British Party Leaders," *British Journal of Politics and International Relations* 20, no. 3 (2018): 555–72; and Jim Buller and Toby James, "Statecraft and the Assessment of National Political Leaders: The Case of New Labour and Tony Blair," *British Journal of Politics and International Relations* 14, no. 4 (2012): 534–55.

26 Andrew S. Roe-Crines and David Jeffery, eds., *Statecraft: Policies and Politics under Prime Minister Theresa May* (London: Palgrave Macmillan, 2023).

27 Patrice Dutil, *Prime Ministerial Power in Canada: Its Origins under Macdonald, Laurier and Borden* (Vancouver: University of British Columbia Press, 2017).

2 Sir John A. Macdonald and His Cabinets: The "Autocrat" in Power

PATRICE DUTIL

Six months before the birth of Confederation, Hector Langevin, a former mayor of Quebec City and a delegate from Canada-East sent to London to negotiate the terms of Confederation, surveyed the best talent the British Northeast American colonies had mustered. The Nova Scotia delegation, he thought, was a mixed bag. Charles Tupper was "speculative, ambitious, divisive." Jonathan McCully was "impetuous but good hearted" and William A. Henry was "tall, popular," and had "good talents." But he was "ugly." He did not have many kind things to say about New Brunswick's people either. While the former premier Leonard Tilley was "clever, upstanding," Charles Fisher was "mediocre." Robert D. Wilmot was "better than Fisher, but mediocre" and, to boot, "very ugly." Peter Mitchell was "verbose," and possessed of a "big head, constantly aware of his own importance." John Mercer Johnson was "brusque [but] fun-loving." The Ontarians were not impressive. William Pearce Howland was "2nd class" and "slow"; William McDougall was "capable [but] lazy, dissembling."

When it came to Quebec, he described Alexander Galt as "impetuous, unstable." He considered George-Étienne Cartier and himself, the "2nd and 3rd" most important men of the conference. The best delegate was without question John A. Macdonald: "a smart fox, educated, ingratiating, able and very popular." He summed it up neatly: "He's *the man* of the conference."[1] (Emphasis in the original.)

Langevin could exaggerate for effect in his private correspondence, but he was not too far off the mark. Alexander Cameron, a good friend of John A. Macdonald, shared many of Langevin's views. He thought that Tilley was "without influence" and that Howland had no talent. McDougall was indeed lazy, and Galt was mischievous.[2] Cameron, a man more forgiving than Langevin, had nothing to say about appearances; Macdonald would have to decide on his own how put the best faces forward for the Canadian government's inaugural cabinet. Langevin's view of Macdonald was further confirmed by Frederick Rogers of the Colonial Office in London. Macdonald was "the ruling genius" of the meeting, he observed: "I was very much struck by his powers of management and adroitness."[3]

It was always expected, but Macdonald was formally commissioned by Governor General Lord Monck, on 24 May 1867, to form the first government under Confederation.[4] Upon his return to Canada, Macdonald had to think of how to transition what had been a floppy cabinet of Ontarians and Quebeckers in the United Province of Canada to a steady, purposeful one that would include the Maritimers.

The crushing pressure to create a cabinet of national unity that could actually work and succeed as a government stressed Macdonald to the maximum, prompting to him to drink to the point of breaking. Galt wrote to his wife, alarmed at the situation in Ottawa, and described the prime minister designate as "in a constant state of partial intoxication."[5] Tupper speculated in his memoirs that Macdonald might have even asked Lord Monck to summon George Brown to form a government, but this could not have been more than an idle threat meant to scare the Conservatives to fall in line.[6] Even his marriage to Agnes Bernard in February could not sustainably bolster the new prime minister's mood. Macdonald seized himself against all odds to execute the difficult arithmetic of cabinet composition.

Over the next twenty-five years, and through nearly twenty more years in power, Macdonald would think about his cabinet a great deal: it was central to his statecraft. As the years wore on, it grew older, a little less Catholic, and much less hybrid in political orientation. Macdonald did insist on talent and experience, not simply representativeness. Most of his cabinet ministers were successful in private business and could, for the most part, be trusted in administration. Canada's first "cabinetmaker" thought he was assembling a good government, though he grew increasingly concerned by the aging of his team. "Give me better wood," he apparently once said, "and I will make you a better cabinet."[7]

Macdonald as Prime Minister and the First Cabinet

Macdonald was a logical choice to head the government, both politically and administratively. In the province of Canada, he had used his administrative skills and his experience in various cabinet positions to spread his influence.[8] His extraordinary reputation, to say nothing of his personal abilities, made him the logical candidate to head the government. No member of the Conservative Party over the next twenty-five years thought otherwise.

Macdonald was successful as a government executive because of his confident personality. As Sir Richard Cartwright put it, "He was 'John A.,' and there was no other like him." Though he could be very severe towards Macdonald (Cartwright later said that he "degraded the whole tone of public life and of political morality in Canada") he noted what gave Macdonald an almost natural command over his cabinet: "He was well read, and he had had an immense experience of men and things, and he had also a curious philosophic streak in him, which showed out occasionally at a certain stage in the evening. Many of his remarks were not only shrewd but far-seeing."[9]

The demands for representation came from all regions, religious denominations, ethnicities and, not least, political corners. On top of all that were the exigencies of competence. It was probably the hardest cabinet to put together and to justify in the history of the country. Tupper, it was widely expected, would take his place;[10] same with Tilley – it was assumed that the tireless, battling former premier would quit Fredericton in order to join the government of Canada.[11] George-Étienne Cartier insisted that at least three members (almost a quarter) of the cabinet be French-speaking Catholic Quebeckers.[12] Macdonald agreed: Cartier himself was owed a cabinet seat as was Langevin. On the English side, Galt's experience and importance commanded respect. Thomas D'Arcy McGee, the hard-drinking Irish convert to the Conservative cause and fiery promoter of Confederation certainly deserved a seat, but there was no room for him (it is the stuff of legend that Macdonald famously quipped that there was only room for one drunk in cabinet, and that he was destined to occupy that seat). The Ontario reformers also tormented Macdonald, demanding a ransom of at least three positions for their support. Negotiations were at an impasse until 23 June, a week before the birth of a new Canada, when Macdonald finally gave in: Howland as minister of inland revenue, Blair as president of the Privy Council, and McDougall as minister of public works would represent the "Liberal" element of the cabinet. From New Brunswick, Tilley would go to Customs, while Mitchell, the premier since April 1866, would serve as minister of marine and fisheries. Nova Scotia was more problematic. Tupper, who had fought so hard to sell Confederation to the sceptical Maritimers, deserved a seat, but his piece did not fit the puzzle. Macdonald felt he needed a Liberal representative as well as a Catholic Irishman.

He picked Adams Archibald as well as Edward Kenny who would pull the double-duty of representing Nova Scotia and Irish Catholics across Canada (as a one-time mayor of Halifax, he could also be seen as representing municipalities). It was a tour de force. It was only as 1 July approached that the first prime minister was able to conclude the effort, thanks to the generosity of friends like Thomas D'Arcy McGee and Charles Tupper who both relinquished their legitimate claims to a cabinet seat.[13] Macdonald's first cabinet was sworn in on Canada's first day with every province well represented.

The prime minister also ensured that some minorities could be seen around the table. Galt represented Anglo-Protestant Quebeckers and the business community. No thought was given to representing Acadians and the French minority in Ontario was still much too small to warrant consideration. The most important feature of Macdonald's cabinet was its hybrid nature: seven of the ministers were Macdonald Conservatives, while six were reformers or former "Liberals." It was a cabinet of rivals, but one dedicated to the cause of legitimizing the Confederation project.

1 Agriculture: Jean-Charles Chapais, 55, Merchant, Quebec, Catholic (senator)
2 Customs: Samuel Leonard Tilley, 48, Pharmacist, New Brunswick, Protestant, *Liberal*
3 Finance: Alexander Tilloch Galt, 50, Quebec, Protestant
4 Inland Revenue: William Pearce Howland, 56, Businessman, Ontario, Protestant, *Liberal*
5 Justice and Attorney General: Sir John A. Macdonald, 52, Lawyer, Ontario, Protestant
6 Marine and Fisheries: Peter Mitchell, 42, Lawyer, New Brunswick, Protestant, *Liberal* (senator)
7 Militia and Defence: Sir George-Étienne Cartier, 58, Lawyer, Quebec, Catholic
8 Postmaster General: Alexander Campbell, 50, Lawyer, Ontario, Catholic (senator)
9 President of the Privy Council: Fergusson Blair, 52, Lawyer, Ontario, Protestant, *Liberal* (senator)
10 Public Works: William McDougall, 45, Lawyer, Ontario, Protestant, *Liberal*
11 Receiver General: Edward Kenny, 67, Businessman/banker, Nova Scotia, Catholic (senator)
12 Secretary of State of Canada: Hector-Louis Langevin, 40, Editor/Lawyer, Quebec, Catholic
13 Secretary of State for the Provinces: Adams G. Archibald, 53, Lawyer, Nova Scotia, Protestant, *Liberal*

It proved to be one of the youngest cabinets in the history of Canada, average age 51, a few months junior to Macdonald. Edward Kenny, 67, was the eldest by far; Hector Langevin the youngest at age 40. Five of the thirteen around the table were Catholic. Four of the thirteen – almost a quarter – were senators, one from each province. Though Ontario constituted half the population of Canada, only five of the thirteen ministers came from that province, including the prime minister. McDougall was a Toronto lawyer, a pillar of the Clear Grit movement that demanded universal male suffrage, representation by population, inexpensive government, free trade with the United States and the abolition of clergy reserves. An ardent defender of the Union cause south of the border, he held the distinction of probably being the only Canadian to have heard Abraham Lincoln deliver his Gettysburg address in person in 1863.[14]

Howland, born in the United States, had served as minister of finance, receiver general, and postmaster general in the Province of United Canada.[15] Both Howland and McDougall were denounced for joining Macdonald's cabinet at a Reform Convention held in Toronto four days before Dominion Day. The third Reformist was Adam Fergusson Blair, like Macdonald a Scot born in 1815 and a lawyer from Canada West with deep political experience. Alexander Campbell rounded out the count for the Ontario component of cabinet. The former dean of the Faculty of Law at Queen's University was a very close friend of Macdonald's.[16]

French Quebec would be represented by Cartier (as minister of militia and defence), Langevin (secretary of state and superintendent general of Indian affairs in a few more months), and Jean-Charles Chapais (a very successful farmer and merchant and former Mayor of Saint-Denis-de-La-Bouteillerie) in agriculture.[17] All of them were *bleus*, distinguished in business as well as political management. From English Quebec, Macdonald named Galt (another Quebecker, but one who was also the director of the British American Land Company and of the St. Lawrence and Atlantic Railway) as minister of finance. The two New Brunswick representatives were also accomplished administrators. Leonard Tilley, long a Reformer, had long been a leading businessman and railway promoter in addition to defending Confederation. Tilley, in turn, convinced Macdonald to include Peter Mitchell, the New Brunswick premier, in cabinet. Mitchell had been, since 1864, a chief proponent of Confederation. Trained as a lawyer, he was a prosperous lumberman and shipbuilder from Miramichi. He had a reputation as an able administrator; that was enough for Macdonald who named him to the Senate.[18] Nova Scotia brought a lot less administrative talent to the table. It would be represented by Adams Archibald and Senator Edward Kenny. The real surprise was the absence of two of Macdonald's best political friends: Charles Tupper of Cumberland County, Nova Scotia, and Thomas D'Arcy McGee from Montreal, who had served in cabinet since 1863. Tupper would eventually find his place in cabinet. D'Arcy McGee, who would have represented the Catholic Irish vote (and, arguably, the vote of men who enjoyed alcohol immensely), had to wait. His turn would not come, however, as he was murdered on Sparks Street in Ottawa nine months later.

This cabinet lasted long enough to survive the first election in September 1867.[19] Archibald was actually defeated in Nova Scotia, but Macdonald kept him in office (anyone can serve in cabinet; and while it is especially convenient to also serve in the legislature in a democracy, it is not required) for seven months. Then, in early November, the capital was shaken by the news that Macdonald effectively fired Galt over a grave disagreement on banking regulation.[20] Macdonald first approached Howland to replace Galt – a sign of faith in the coalition – but was turned down.[21] He then approached John Rose, an old friend based in Montreal and London who had won election in Huntingdon

(Quebec) as a Conservative, and he occupied the post for almost two years. Blair died suddenly in late December 1867 and Howland retired in the summer of 1868 due to illness. Macdonald made slight changes at that point. When Archibald finally retired at the end of April 1868 as secretary of state for the provinces, Macdonald left the post vacant. He needed an elected member of Parliament from Nova Scotia in his cabinet and feared that naming Tupper would only inflame the affairs in that province. So, he waited.

Macdonald felt it important that cabinet not be too large – and surely the temptation to make it broader so as to easily accommodate the myriad demands made the task all the more difficult. But Macdonald also wanted to have a lean and efficient team. To that end, through an order-in-council passed on 2 July 1867, Macdonald established a "Board of Treasury," the first and only formal subcommittee of the executive council. It was designed to monitor systematically the revenue and expenses of the government, to review submissions of duties, and more generally to approve all departmental regulations as they related to public accounts. It was an innovative decision. Macdonald, who was genuinely devoted to following British government practices, plucked out of the past an institution that had been all but abandoned in London. While the British "Commission of Treasury" had not actually met since the 1820s, Macdonald thought it could be very useful in Ottawa to help cabinet focus on priorities.[22] Two years later, in April 1869, the government tabled a bill to officially create a small bureaucracy to underpin it. A secretary was named to prepare an agenda and to keep records of decisions. His tasks were to keep a sharp eye on revenue and expenditures, to review proposals and field queries from other departments who might be affected by it, and to inspect departmental rules and regulations that could affect revenue or expenditures in the government. The Treasury Board would also receive the reports of the Board of Audit.[23] There is no evidence of any other formal cabinet committees. In the British tradition, if Macdonald did ask for ministers to examine questions in some sort of subcommittee structure, but they were kept informal and secret. This practice would endure until the maximum pressures for organization of the war against the Nazis forced Macdonald's successors to build on his methods.

The 1869 Shuffle

Macdonald ran a tight ship. Smith conceded publicly in early January 1868 that ministers were "utterly powerless." "We are under the controlling power of Messrs McDonald [*sic*] and Cartier," he declared, adding that "The interests of Ontario were entirely distinct and at variance with all other provinces."[24] Macdonald worked with this cabinet for about eighteen months, deeply committed to find a way to defeat the anti-Confederation sentiment in Nova Scotia and determined to show that Canada could work. He needed to create a bi-partisanship and focused his attentions on the genial Sir Joseph Howe, the formerly anti-Confederation journalist, Liberal prime minister of Nova Scotia (1860–3) and newspaper owner who had been elected to represent Hants in the House of Commons. Less than fifteen months after bitterly campaigning against Confederation in the 1867 election, Howe accepted to cross the floor and in January 1869 was named president of the Privy Council. To make room for him, Macdonald named Senator Kenny to a vague position of "administrator" in Nova Scotia. The symbolism was right: what more eloquent testimony to solidarity than to have a former "anti" now act on behalf of the federal government? It was all the more urgent as it sought to deliver on its promise of consolidating the territory to the West and to finish the job in the Maritimes by finally bringing Prince Edward Island into the fold (and perhaps Newfoundland!).

Just as importantly, Macdonald knew Howe was a workhorse, even at age sixty-eight (making him the cabinet elder). As secretary for the provinces and superintendent of Indian affairs, Howe cast aside for good his doubts about the merits of Confederation, dived into his work with characteristic enthusiasm, and took advantage of working with William Meredith, a very able deputy minister.[25] A year later, Macdonald reached out to his old friend and another Nova Scotia workaholic, Dr. Charles Tupper, and made him president of the Privy Council. Tupper and Howe, once bitter rivals over the future of their province in Canada, learned to work amiably for the next three years. Macdonald had created a new national project for naturally ambitious builders.

In the summer of 1869, John Rose informed Macdonald that he would be returning to Britain and thus would resign the portfolio of finance. Richard Cartwright, the MP for Lennox and a good friend of Macdonald's, believed the job should be his. But Macdonald thought otherwise and tapped Francis Hincks, now sixty-five years old, a veteran Reformer who had been a commanding force in Upper Canadian politics. Cartwright, angry and insulted, quit the party and crossed the floor to join the Liberals, vowing to be a piercing thorn in the prime minister's side (Cartwright served as minister of finance in the Mackenzie government and later in the Laurier cabinet).[26] A month later, Alexander Morris, a Scottish Tory Eastern Ontarian who had once articled with Macdonald, was named minister of inland revenue.[27] That November, Senator Jean-Charles Chapais was moved out of agriculture in favour of Christopher Dunkin, a colourful lawyer who once provoked a student riot at Harvard with his spectacularly mediocre teaching methods. In December 1869, Howe was promoted to secretary of state for the provinces as well as superintendent general of Indian affairs.

Macdonald respected his engagement to Reform/Liberals in his coalition, but it could not last permanently. As indicated above, Blair's death and

Howland's retirement had made things easy. The last one standing was William McDougall, and Macdonald asked him to serve as lieutenant governor of the new province of Manitoba. McDougall was out of cabinet by 27 September 1869 and the Department of Public Works was entrusted to Hector Langevin. Langevin's post as secretary of state of Canada was passed to Senator James Cox Aikins, a highly respected and prosperous farmer from Peel County, Ontario (and a former Clear Grit as well).

The thirteen-man cabinet Macdonald had created when the legislature was dissolved on 20 July 1872 was a broad mixture, but it was mostly "Tory" and had accomplished a great deal, including the expansion of the country from coast-to-coast. The average age was fifty-four, younger than Macdonald, and it featured four Quebeckers, four Ontarians in addition to Macdonald, as well as two New Brunswickers, and two Nova Scotians. Five were Catholics, eight were Protestant. Francis Hincks, who had always been an Upper Canadian, was designated as the British Columbia representative (and was elected there by acclamation). Six were lawyers, two were farmers. The cabinet included a journalist, a doctor, and a pharmacist. The other two were businessmen by profession.

1 Agriculture: John Henry Pope, 53, Quebec, Farmer, Protestant
2 Customs: Samuel L. Tilley, 54, Pharmacist, New Brunswick, Protestant
3 Finance: Sir Francis Hincks, 65, Businessman, British Columbia, Protestant
4 Secretary of State for the Provinces; Superintendent General of Indian Affairs: Joseph Howe, 68, Journalist, Nova Scotia, Protestant
5 Inland Revenue: Charles Tupper, 45, Nova Scotia, Physician, Protestant
6 Justice and Attorney General: Sir John A. Macdonald, 57, Lawyer, Ontario, Protestant
7 Marine and Fisheries: Peter Mitchell, 48, Lawyer, New Brunswick, Protestant (senator)
8 Militia and Defence: Sir George-Étienne Cartier, 58, Lawyer, Quebec, Catholic
9 Postmaster General: Alexander Campbell, 50, Lawyer, Ontario, Catholic (senator)
10 President of the Privy Council: John O'Connor, 48, Lawyer, Ontario, Catholic
11 Public Works: Hector-Louis Langevin, 46, Editor/Lawyer, Quebec, Catholic
12 Receiver General: Jean-Charles Chapais, 61, Merchant, Quebec, Catholic (senator)
13 Secretary of State of Canada: James Cox Aikins, 49, Farmer, Ontario, Protestant (senator)

The more purely Conservative government was elected but lost its second-in-command temporarily when Cartier was defeated in Montreal-East (he soon ran in a by-election in St. Boniface, Manitoba, the seat that was vacated by Louis Riel, and won it).[28] It is interesting to note that Macdonald's personal success in 1872 was also diminished. In 1867, he had been elected with almost 84 per cent of the vote in Kingston. That majority was sliced down to just under 55 per cent in 1872.

The Heat of Battle of 1873

The cabinet would change dramatically a year later, while Macdonald experienced one of the most trying years of his career. The first accusations of wrongdoing in the 1872 election were levelled by Lucius Seth Huntington, the MP for Shefford (Quebec) on 2 April 1873. On the exterior, Macdonald was unflustered and confident, but the revelations in the spring and summer that CPR president Hugh Allan had been sending money to a number of cabinet members in order to influence the vote, rocked him to his core. His drinking again grew out of hand, and he urgently felt a need to make changes.

Macdonald had already decided to make changes to his ministerial team. It started in late January, months before the Huntington revelations, when he asked for Senator Jean-Charles Chapais's resignation as receiver general.[29] Chapais was not performing to his liking, and Macdonald assigned the portfolio to the much younger Théodore Robitaille, thirty-nine, a loyal friend, the MP for Bonaventure (Quebec), and man of wealth and stature. Francis Hincks, in finance, retired a few weeks later for reasons that are unclear, and Macdonald tapped Tilley, who had loyally served since 1867 but who often expressed the wish to assume a bigger portfolio, to replace him.[30] At the same time, Charles Tupper was named to take Tilley's place in Customs (moving him from inland revenue) on 21 February.

What became known as the "Pacific Scandal" was in full swing when Macdonald was prompted to make two other important changes. The first was to deal with the resignation of Joseph Howe as secretary of state for the provinces and superintendent-general of Indian affairs in the first week of May, again for reasons that are unclear. Macdonald decided to change the name and created a new portfolio of minister of the interior (who would also act at superintendent-general of Indian affairs) and appointed Senator Alexander Campbell to the portfolio. Campbell was asked to give up the postmaster general portfolio, and it was given to John O'Connor, the MP for Essex (Ontario) on 1 July.

But the most important shock that month was the news of the death of his old and loyal friend George-Étienne Cartier. Hector Langevin was moved into Cartier's portfolio as minister of militia and defence as a placeholder. Hugh

McDonald, the MP for Antigonish, was named to the post on Dominion Day, assuming at the same time the post of president of the Privy Council.

The portfolios most affected were involved in money management: customs, receiver general, inland revenue, and finance. The net result was a cabinet that was a little less French-speaking, and much younger, but in the end, the shuffle made little difference. The Macdonald government resigned in November 1873 and Alexander Mackenzie was asked by the Governor General to form a new ministry. It held by a thread and Mackenzie asked that the legislature be dissolved on 7 January. A very brief campaign of two weeks saw the Conservatives lose thirty-five seats, with barely 30 per cent of the popular vote. Remarkably, none of the ministers were defeated. Macdonald's own victory in Kingston was ensured by 51.2 per cent of the vote but was declared void later that year. A by-election was held on 29 December and Macdonald was re-elected, but with a bare majority of 50.5 per cent of the vote.

Macdonald's cabinet from 1867 to 1873 included twenty-five people. Four ministers held the same and only portfolio through these years: Macdonald himself at justice and as attorney general, George-Étienne Cartier as minister of militia and defence, Senator Peter Mitchell at marine and fisheries, and Alexander Campbell in charge of the Post Office. Hector-Louis Langevin held the record for portfolios, occupying five posts in the six years of the first mandate. Four people held the finance portfolio; three held agriculture; six people occupied the position of minister of inland revenue. The same for the post of president of the Privy Council over the six years, though the post was vacant for all of 1868 and much of 1873. Five people occupied the post of superintendent general of Indian affairs. The position of secretary of state for the provinces changed hands four times, and the receiver general three times. Such instability ensured that Macdonald's views would set the agenda and dominate discussion. Whatever impact the turnover may have had on administration was minimized. Macdonald could rely on the steadiness of his deputy minister corps to carry out his preferences on policy matters.[31]

Macdonald's Second Mandate (1878–91)

Macdonald's party won a crushing victory on Election Day, 17 September 1878. The Mackenzie government resigned on 8 October and within twenty-four hours Macdonald promptly beat his way back to the East Block to assume his office and announce his new cabinet. For Macdonald, the win came with a bitter taste. Sensing perhaps that his local popularity was running low, he ran in three ridings during that election: Kingston, Marquette (Manitoba), and Victoria (B.C.) (the practice was disallowed in 1919).[32] He lost Kingston to Alexander Gunn by a margin of almost 8 per cent. He won handily in Victoria, beating Amor de Cosmos (the former premier of the province) and was acclaimed in

Marquette. He chose to represent British Columbians. Within ten days, Macdonald had eleven of his cabinet ministers sworn in; the other three would be in place by 8 November.

Macdonald found the East Block practically as he had left it in 1873. Macdonald's second ministry, from October 1878 until his death in June 1891 was, like his first, remarkably stable. There were minor shuffles in 1879, 1882, and 1888. The most important one was in the hectic year of 1885, following the suppression of the second Riel insurrection.

Macdonald moved slowly and carefully in choosing ministers. Joseph Pope, his closest aide during the 1880s, made a note of it:

> Rather was it the outcome of his quality of caution, which regulated his life, and ever prompted him to weigh all the circumstances of a case before taking action thereon. This was illustrated in many ways; for example, in his choice of colleagues and in his administration of patronage. It is very easy for a prime minister to invite a man to enter his Cabinet, but it is very difficult to repair a hasty selection. It is equally easy to fill a vacant office, but the step once taken is practically irrevocable.... He preferred, as a general rule, to "hasten slowly," to weigh well all the circumstances, to keep his hand free as long as possible and to act only in the light of the fullest knowledge he could gather. Such a course, he has observed, often saved him from the disastrous consequences of hasty and ill-considered action. He was a firm believer in the efficacy of time as a solvent of many difficulties which beset his path, and his wisdom in this regard has time and again been exemplified.[33]

The most important change was that Macdonald abandoned justice and instead designated himself minister of the interior. It telegraphed the critical priority of his government that had become developing Western Canada by ensuring the building of the transcontinental railroad and in dealing with the multitude of crises that beset the Indigenous people on the prairies.[34] Leonard Tilley was named minister of finance with the added responsibilities of the functions of the receiver general. The very able John Henry Pope was reappointed to agriculture.[35] James Cox Aikins returned as secretary of state and Hector Langevin returned as postmaster general for a few months while Macdonald sorted out a strategy for the railway and then resumed his command of public works. Senator John O'Connor was back this time as president of the Privy Council and later as secretary of state (the registrar general). Including Macdonald himself, six cabinet ministers in this government were already battle-worn.

There were new faces. James McDonald, from Nova Scotia, was made minister of justice and attorney general. Mackenzie Bowell, from Ontario, was appointed to Customs. James C. Pope, once a Liberal prime minister of Prince Edward Island, was named minister of marine and fisheries. Two new young Quebec members were brought in: Georges Baby, a lawyer and former mayor

Image 2.1. John A. Macdonald's cabinet, 1878

Source: Library and Archives Canada, C-126574.

of Joliette, was named to inland revenue and Louis-Rodrigue Masson (who, like Baby, had been a protégé of George-Étienne Cartier) to Militia and Defence.

It was fairly young cabinet. The average age of the ministers was just over fifty-five (see image 2.1). The deputy corps had closed the gap – their average age was now just over 53; much older, relatively speaking, than they had been when Macdonald had formed his first administration in 1867. If there was weakness in the ranks, it was in French Canadian representation. Neither Baby nor Masson – who was particularly popular in the press of the time[36] – cared much for administrative matters, and both grew irritated at the inexorably growing importance Hector Langevin was assuming in cabinet. Baby and Masson quit within two years. Macdonald's inability to refresh the French Canadian representation in his cabinet would dog him to his last days.

With its weaknesses and strengths, the cabinet remained relatively stable through the mandate that would last until 1882. Its hard, administrative core of gravitated around Tupper, Tilley, John Henry Pope, and Hector Langevin. Within a year, Baby was appointed to the Quebec court and was replaced by James Cox Aikins, and he in turn eventually gave way to Sir Adolphe Caron. James McDonald lasted three years as minister of justice and was succeeded by Senator Alexander Campbell. The job of postmaster general changed no fewer than five times, until Macdonald settled with John Carling, who would actually hold the job for three years. The post of president of the Privy Council also changed every year. To ensure consistency and reliability, Macdonald counted on the senior leadership of the public service, as he had in his first mandate.

When the House of Commons was dissolved on 6 June 1882, Macdonald's cabinet had grown older to an average age of fifty-seven, with Macdonald himself the eldest member, now ten years older than the average. It had grown by one member, a minister without portfolio but needed to represent the government in the Senate (Macdonald otherwise had eliminated senators from active ministries, abandoning the principles of his 1867 cabinet). The youngest was Adolphe Caron, from Quebec. It included:

1 Agriculture: John Henry Pope, 63, Quebec, Farmer, Protestant
2 Customs: Mackenzie Bowell, 59, Ontario, Printer/Editor, Protestant
3 Finance; Receiver General: Sir Samuel L. Tilley, 64, Pharmacist, New Brunswick, Protestant
4 Interior and Superintendent-General of Indian Affairs: Sir John A. Macdonald, 67, British Columbia, Protestant
5 Inland Revenue: John Costigan, 47, Judge, New Brunswick, Catholic
6 Justice and Attorney General: Sir Alexander Campbell, 60, Lawyer, Ontario, Catholic
7 Marine and Fisheries: James Colledge Pope, 56, Shipbuilder, Prince Edward Island, Protestant
8 Militia and Defence: Adolphe Caron, 39, Lawyer, Quebec, Catholic
9 Postmaster General: John O'Connor, 58, Lawyer, Ontario, Catholic
10 President of the Privy Council: Archibald Woodbury McLelan, 58, Shipbuilder, Nova Scotia, Protestant
11 Public Works: Hector-Louis Langevin, 56, Editor/Lawyer, Quebec, Catholic
12 Railways and Canals: Sir Charles Tupper, 61, Physician, Nova Scotia, Protestant
13 Secretary of State of Canada: Joseph-Alfred Mousseau, 44, Lawyer, Quebec, Catholic
14 Minister without Portfolio: David Lewis Macpherson, 64, Contractor, Ontario, Protestant (senator)

Again, Macdonald's cabinet was shaped by six Catholics and eight Protestants. The number of Quebeckers had dropped to four, and the Ontarians were reduced to four also. There were two Nova Scotians and a pair of New Brunswickers. One only was from Prince Edward Island. Macdonald, elected in Victoria in 1878, was the sole British Columbian in this cabinet.

The Macdonald Tories won handily. Macdonald ran in two neighbouring ridings in Ontario: Carleton and Lennox. He won both constituencies and chose to represent Carleton. None of the ministers were defeated.

The Shuffle of 1885

Macdonald strategically put himself at the centre of a small but strategically important shuffle in October 1883. He resigned his portfolio of minister of the interior but kept the superintendence general of Indian affairs and took the president of the Privy Council position, which had been left vacant since the election sixteen months earlier. Macdonald had clearly presided over the Privy Council during this time; it was simply a matter of making it official. The posting had a small perk: he was now working closely with John James D'Arcy McGee, the young half-brother of his old friend, and together they would make the Privy Council a clearing house of information.[37] Macdonald gave this office even more importance and made it politically aware when he brought in Joseph Pope in the fall of 1889 as assistant clerk of the Privy Council. Macdonald's move to the presidency of the Privy Council veiled the many changes he brought to the Department of the Interior that fall. He gave the portfolio to Senator David Lewis Macpherson, a man not known as an effective administrator but who, by virtue of his place in Parliament, would also be spared the exigencies of defending his department in the House of Commons.

Macdonald also came to an arrangement with Charles Tupper by appointing him High Commissioner for Canada in the United Kingdom. Strangely, the arrangement was made whereby Tupper would serve without salary. He continued to hold the portfolio of minister of railways and canals until 28 May 1884, when a new commission was issued to him granting him a salary as high commissioner, at which time the always dependable John Henry Pope was given the mantle of critical infrastructures. Richard Cartwright's interpretation, even thirty years after the fact, was telling. The departure of Charles Tupper, he argued, "left Sir John absolute dictator in his Cabinet, and he availed himself of this position to the full."[38]

Macdonald would have agreed with his old nemesis Cartwright that his government was growing old. In reality, the average age of his ministers was now over fifty-eight years old, while his corps of deputies had also grown older, now reaching an average age of almost fifty-six. More problematically, Macdonald did not see successors and did next to nothing to cultivate the men with the right jelly. Dalton McCarthy, for instance, was considered by many to be in line, but Macdonald was not particularly impressed. McCarthy had refused to join cabinet as minister of justice, choosing to remain in Toronto and to keep his law practice.[39]

The only other changes would wait until 1885 when the government's mettle was tested as never before by the second Métis uprising and a "most harassing and disagreeable" parliamentary session. "Now is the time for me to retire," Macdonald told Tupper. "I have finished my work. Everything that I proposed to do from Confederation down to the present time has been completed."[40]

But Macdonald could not resist staying in the game and instead sought to renew the strength of the cabinet as a top priority. Everybody was old and tired, not least him: "We were awfully weak last session," he said to Campbell, "I would not wittingly go through another session like it. Just think!"[41] But he had to make changes and Nova Scotia, now that it was led by the separatist William S. Fielding, was especially urgent. He needed to rebuild in time for an election in 1887. The idea of a minister of justice sitting in the Senate, such as Senator Campbell, did not sit well with Macdonald, particularly given the Riel situation.

Leonard Tilley (finance), now sixty-seven and in Great Britain waiting for surgery, had given notice that he wanted to retire at home in New Brunswick as lieutenant governor, and David Macpherson (interior), also sixty-seven, was ill and had been flabby in dealing with the Métis.[42] Pope (railways) was also repeatedly ill. "The work all fell unto me, and much of it of necessity was ill done, and our friends grumbled," said the prime minister. Macdonald knew that colleagues fell silent only because they felt a "compassionate sympathy" for him, "but everyone said I must reconstruct [the cabinet] before Parliament met again."

Macdonald needed new tenors and decided that Macpherson had to go as he had proved himself "over cautious and deliberate in his methods" but in the view of Joseph Pope, could hardly be blamed for the Riel uprising.[43] Macdonald's first move was to name Thomas White in his place, and he was sworn in by the governor general on 5 August. White, fifty-five, an old friend of the prime minister, had been an ardent supporter of Macdonald's since the days of Confederation and had singled himself out all through his career with good cheer and, in the words of P.B. Waite, his biographer, "a tremendous capacity for work, a great span of knowledge, and a thick seam of common sense." He would bring to the front bench the talents of "a graceful, polished, indeed telling speaker, [giving] the impression, usually a correct one, that he was master of his subject." Politically, he seemed perfect: a Montrealer who sat in the Ontario riding of Cardwell. White was sworn in and immediately set out for the West to speak with the Métis to find a quick way to settle their claims.[44]

Campbell had indicated earlier in the year that he wished to retire, which was good news, but could never seem to let himself out. He was, apparently, consistently sceptical of the CPR's claims and was not afraid to let Macdonald know. With two Nova Scotia seat to fill, potentially, and with Tupper in London, the need to find a man of quality from Nova Scotia became paramount. Tupper indicated in February that he would be ready to return to Ottawa.[45] "There are great jalousies among the Nova Scotians as they stand on an equality of unfitness," he observed.[46] "We want new blood badly," Macdonald told Tupper in February 1885.[47] John Thompson's name had been on the list of many already, and he had been approached by intermediaries, but he had pushed back in 1883 and 1884, not eager to leave either Halifax or his comfortable lifestyle. A Catholic convert, he was only forty years old, but already had sat for three years on the Nova Scotia Supreme Court. First elected to the Nova Scotia Assembly in 1877, he was named attorney general for the province in 1878 and actually served as premier for two months in 1882. As such, he had met Macdonald twice in the early 1880s.

Macdonald put out feelers in the spring, but Thompson resisted. The first day after the House of Commons ended its work on 20 July, Macdonald put pen to paper and wrote out his own appeal, flattering Thompson on his administrative abilities and by alluding to the position of minister of justice "as the highest in Canada." He was offering prestige and influence. "Hoping to hail you as a colleague," Macdonald concluded. Thompson, despite his wife Annie's urgings, resisted.[48] He simply did not feel up to the "active political work," but he was in Ottawa by the end of September and met with Macdonald in the East Block. Privately, Macdonald said, "If we don't get Thompson, I don't know what to do." He had never spent so much time and effort in wooing a man to cabinet, but the stakes were high, and the prime minister wished to strengthen the government team as his top priority. Macdonald probably raised the matter in cabinet, because two days later, he confirmed to Thompson that the Department of Justice was his, and the Nova Scotian was sworn in on 26 September.[49] Thompson reported that Macdonald was "light as a bird."[50]

The French seemed divided against each other. Langevin consistently had Macdonald's support, and there is evidence that the prime minister easily saw him as his successor.[51] Caron also remained close to the prime minister. They had met when Caron was elected to the House of Commons in 1873 and particularly distinguished himself in setting up a bipartisan drinking club in his house that boasted a French chef (a refugee of the Paris Commune, no less).[52] Over time, and especially during the Riel crisis, Macdonald appreciated Caron's many talents, but thought him "too much influenced by his hates – a fatal mistake in a public man, who should have no resentments," Macdonald reportedly said to a journalist.[53] Chapleau, an undeniably able man, was not dependable. He felt sick from overwork and left for France as soon as the parliamentary session of 1885 was over. Langevin seemed to twin with Caron against Chapleau; sometimes he seemed to work with Chapleau against Caron. "There was absolutely no difference between those three men in respect of public policy, but the personal jealousy and suspicion with which they regarded one another was amusing," wisely observed P.B. Waite: "Sir John had no pleasant time keeping the peace among them."[54]

There were other changes. John Carling, the member for London (Ontario) was named minister of agriculture, thus relieving John Henry Pope of that added responsibility. Archibald McLelan was moved to Finance, now that Tilley had retired; George Foster was sent to Marine and Fisheries. Pope could thus focus on Railways and Canals. McLelan's marine and fisheries portfolio was given to George Foster, the MP for King's (New Brunswick). Those final changes would be effective in December.[55] As was the custom, all the new ministers had to refresh their mandates in by-elections, and all were handily re-elected and confirmed.

It was, for Macdonald, the most important and significant cabinet shuffle of his career as prime minister. It had only involved five departments, but the result was telling. There were two new entries to cabinet, both from the Maritimes (Thompson and Foster). There were still two cabinet seats for Nova Scotians, but they were both in key portfolios: finance and justice. Robert Borden would later say that the 1885 Rebellion had done more than any other event to unite Nova Scotia and Canada.[56] New Brunswick had two seats also. As before, five of the thirteen ministers were from Ontario, four from Quebec (three francophones and one anglophone). There was no representation from Prince Edward Island. Macdonald himself had made no changes to his own position. He remained president of the Privy Council and minister responsible for Indian affairs. He was older than his ministers overall, but the entry of Foster and Thompson reassured him that some youthful vitality had been injected in the cabinet. Thompson impressed him immensely and Macdonald may have thought of him as a possible successor. The prime minister increased the Treasury Board's membership, and six ministers were specifically designated as members, including the secretary of state, the minister of justice, and the auditor general. In effect, Thompson and Chapleau were thus given more prominence in decision-making. Treasury Board was also charged to approve departmental plans for any reorganizations before securing the concurrence of the cabinet. Macdonald had all sorts of reasons to think that the management adjustments he had conceived through the summer of 1885 left him in a stronger position to govern.

Macdonald waited as long as he could after the Riel rebellion to call an election. The government had a fairly solid record: The completion of the Trans-Canada railway, the Fisheries Act of 1883 and 1886 (which were bolstered by British promises to provide naval protection should the United States not respect international boundaries), the dramatic expansion of the right to vote, and the Railway Acts of 1885 had settled long-festering issues. To appeal even more to the Maritimes, Macdonald asked Charles Tupper to resign his position as High Commissioner to the Court of St. James and to enter cabinet as minister of finance. He did so on 27 January, three weeks before Election Day.[57]

When the House of Commons was dissolved on 22 February 1887, the Macdonald cabinet members averaged fifty-eight years old and Macdonald now a full fourteen years older. There were eight Protestants and six Catholics. Ontario had six members (Macdonald, the thorough Upper Canadian, now represented the riding of Carleton in cabinet) while Quebec only had three. There were two New Brunswickers but three Nova Scotians. No representatives came from Prince Edward Island or British Columbia.

1 Agriculture: John Carling, 59, Brewer, Ontario, Protestant
2 Customs: Mackenzie Bowell, 64, Printer, Ontario, Protestant
3 Finance; Receiver General: Sir Charles Tupper, 66, Physician, Nova Scotia, Protestant
4 Interior; Superintendent General of Indian Affairs: Sir John A. Macdonald, 72, Lawyer, Ontario, Protestant
5 Inland Revenue: John Costigan, 52, Judge, New Brunswick, Catholic
6 Justice and Attorney General: Sir John Thompson, 42, Lecturer/Lawyer, Nova Scotia, Protestant
7 Marine and Fisheries: George Eulas Foster, 40, Professor, New Brunswick, Protestant
8 Militia and Defence: Sir Adolphe Caron, 44, Lawyer, Quebec, Catholic
9 Postmaster General: John O'Connor, 63, Lawyer, Ontario, Catholic
10 President of the Privy Council: Sir John A. Macdonald, 72, Lawyer, Ontario, Protestant
11 Public Works: Hector-Louis Langevin, 61, Editor/Lawyer, Quebec, Catholic
12 Railways and Canals: Sir Charles Tupper, 66, Physician, Nova Scotia, Protestant
13 Secretary of State of Canada: Joseph Adolphe Chapleau, 47, Lawyer and Professor, Quebec, Catholic
14 Minister without Portfolio: Frank Smith, 65, Grocer, Ontario, Catholic (senator)

The Conservatives won again; none of the ministers were defeated. Macdonald again ran in two districts: Carleton and Kingston. He won both, and chose to return to his political home, Kingston. Liberal leader Edward Blake resigned.

The last important shuffle took place in 1888, when Macdonald moved many chairs. It was prompted by Charles Tupper who, despite his long-standing friendship and respect for Macdonald, saw two choices before him: either becoming prime minister or returning to Britain. Either way, he was not interested in staying on as minister of finance. Macdonald would not leave but accepted that Tupper could. As a compensation, Macdonald allowed Tupper's 33-year-old son, Charles "Charley" Hibbert Tupper, to enter cabinet as minister of marine and fisheries. Edgar Dewdney, the former superintendent for the North-West, would assume the position of minister of the interior in September

Image 2.2. J.W. Bengough, "Sir John A.'s New Marionettes," 1878

Source: McCord Museum, M994X.5.273.203.

1888. Macdonald kept the presidency of the Privy Council. His cabinet was to his liking, it seemed, to the point where he could dominate it completely, something the cartoonist J.W. Bengough could always mock (see image 2.2).

John Henry Pope announced his retirement a few months later in 1889, and, not finding a suitable successor, Macdonald kept the portfolio of railways and canals. He kept a watchful eye on his key concern especially as various interests clamoured to see Ottawa involved in regulating this form of transportation. The Report of the Royal Commission on Railways that he had formed in 1886 had recommended that the Railway Committee of the Privy Council become responsible for enforcing the laws, and Macdonald had accepted to have this provision included in the 1888 Railway Act.[58] In his biography of Macdonald, Donald Creighton emphasized that the prime minister decided to keep the portfolio to himself because the only person clamouring for it was Adolphe Chapleau, a man Macdonald still did not trust. Eventually, he relented. "I was very unwilling to do this," he told Tupper, "but could not avoid it without a *crise ministérielle*."[59] There was a much better reason. As president of the Privy Council, he would keep an eye on the entire issue. Creighton is undoubtedly correct in perceiving him as "still interested in general ideas rather than administrative detail. He had a young man's zest for new constructive policies and a young man's impatience with mere competent routines."[60]

This was not the best of cabinets, Macdonald knew, but he did little to bring remedy to the situation. Dewdney was not popular among the Quebec members of the caucus, most likely because his administration in the West had ignited Métis resentment. Frank Smith and John Costigan, the two "Irish" representatives, were politicians and little else – men of little vision and administrative ability. It this particular context, it is not surprising that he was often remembered for pleading for better parliamentarians."[61] "I am a good deal discouraged as to our future," Macdonald had written to Charles Tupper in June 1890, enumerating the physical frailties of his colleagues: "Not that the country has gone or is going against us, but because our ministry is *too old* and *too long* in office."[62] Macdonald was half-right. His government was nearing its twelfth anniversary, but his more recent appointments had rejuvenated the cabinet somewhat with the addition of Charles Hibbert Tupper, who brought the average age down. Charles Colby would be sixty-two when he was appointed in 1889. Whereas the age of his ministers in 1882 hovered around fifty-eight, in 1887 they averaged just above fifty-six.

When the House of Commons was dissolved in January 1891, the Macdonald cabinet was older than ever, now averaging age fifty-seven. There were five representatives from Ontario, four from Quebec, two from New Brunswick, two from Nova Scotia, and one from the Northwest Territories. There were again eight protestants and six Catholics. There were now two ministers without portfolio, both senators.

1 Agriculture: John Carling, 63, Brewer, Ontario, Protestant
2 Customs: Mackenzie Bowell, 68, Printer, Ontario, Protestant
3 Finance; Receiver General: George Eulas Foster, 44, Professor, New Brunswick, Protestant
4 Interior; Superintendent General of Indian Affairs: Edgar Dewdney, 56, Civil Engineer Northwest Territories, Protestant
5 Inland Revenue: John Costigan, 56, Judge, New Brunswick, Catholic
6 Justice and Attorney General: John Thompson, 46, Lecturer/Lawyer, Nova Scotia, Catholic
7 Marine and Fisheries: Charles Hibbert Tupper, 36, Lawyer, Nova Scotia, Protestant
8 Militia and Defence: Sir Adolphe Caron, 48, Lawyer, Quebec, Catholic
9 Postmaster General: John Haggart, 55, Mill Owner, Ontario, Protestant
10 President of the Privy Council: Vacant
11 Public Works: Hector-Louis Langevin, 65, Editor, Quebec, Catholic
12 Railways and Canals: Sir John A. Macdonald, 76, Lawyer, Ontario, Protestant
13 Secretary of State of Canada: Joseph Adolphe Chapleau, 51, Lawyer and Professor, Quebec, Catholic

14 Minister without Portfolio: Frank Smith, 69, Grocer, Ontario, Catholic (senator)
15 Minister without Portfolio: John Abbott, 70, Professor, Quebec, Protestant (senator)

Macdonald campaigned on the slogan of "The old flag, the old policy, the old leader" in 1891.[63] It was telling of the government's policy, but also spoke volumes about the administration that was completely centred on an old leader. Government was focused on the man, a recognition that had been as central to the management of the administration as it was to its politics. The government managed to eke out yet another victory, but the margin of victory had eroded. Remarkably, none of the ministers were defeated. Macdonald this time only ran in Kingston, confident that his neighbours would support him, and they did, giving him a margin of almost 16 percentage points over Alexander Gunn, the man who had defeated him in 1878. Macdonald would end his days satisfied that his hometown had forgiven him.

Conclusion

Was Macdonald an autocrat? There's no real evidence of it. He clearly tolerated dissent over the Riel issues, the National Policy, the CPR, foreign involvements, and budgets, but there were few disputes. What his extensive stay in the prime minister's chair showed was a real command of statecraft. In his creation and manipulation of departments and of cabinet posts, in his choice of men and in his campaigns, and finally in making hard decisions, Macdonald demonstrated the rarest of skills: to surmount crisis, to hear the demands of the electorate and to win both hearts and minds to the causes of state building.

Macdonald could rationalize the expansion of prime ministerial influence by claiming that he borrowed from past practices, but he deliberately shaped government management according to his own wishes and inclinations. First, he created a cabinet structure in which the prime minister played the central role, not only in commanding the agenda but in ensuring that policies and programs were implemented with as much likelihood of success as possible. He also crafted a cabinet that could paper over the vast regional, linguistic, religious, and cultural differences that constituted the new country. Nothing less than the legitimacy of Canada was in his hands. His cabinet had to win confidence not just for the process it represented but to win a crucial upcoming election in September 1867 where opposition and "anti-Confederation" candidates would be popular. Macdonald felt this was his duty for the rest of his career in post-Confederation Canadian politics.

Secondly, he personally played a dominant role inside cabinet by consistently occupying a number of sensitive and far-reaching portfolios at a time when cabinet itself assumed a great deal of detailed decision-making. With

Confederation, Macdonald held four key positions in cabinet: first minister, attorney general, chief police officer, and de facto minister of external affairs. That file alone kept him heavily involved in negotiations with the UK over the Northwest Territories, and particularly on issues related to the United States that led to the negotiation of the Washington Treaty of 1871.

Macdonald initially chose to head the Department of Justice. His choice of portfolio reflected the importance he personally attached to the file, and it deeply marked his mandate. It started with a reorganization. In this role, he earned a salary of $5,000 as minister of justice and attorney general, the same as any other minister; importantly, he was not paid as prime minister because the position was not officially recognized. He was, financially, among *pares*, not drawing an additional sum to serve as premier.[64] He then held the vitally important portfolio for the interior, which included Indian affairs. At other times, he held the presidency of the Privy Council and railways and canals. His relevance was strengthened by his assuming the leadership on foreign affairs. In part, this was natural. As the prime minister, he would be the key interlocutor between the government of Canada and the British authorities – first the governor general, then the secretary for the colonies, and then, of course, the British prime minister. It was in effect a third portfolio for Macdonald that tied itself to his roles as minister of justice and prime minister. Macdonald set a far-reaching precedent in assuming the role of a minister of external relations. Except for a few short years in the early 1910s, that role would be filled by the prime minister of Canada until 1946.

Thirdly, he cemented the prime minister's ability to name deputy ministers (or deputy heads, as they were commonly known then), and thereby installed individuals who were friendly to him and his administration, but who were also remarkably able managers. In this, Macdonald ensured that he had almost as much control on patronage in the "outside" civil service, the term used for the three thousand non-permanent employees that were hired by the state to implement Ottawa's policies in the regions.

Macdonald bought a lot of support for much of his time in governance by naming a lot of Catholics to cabinet, though their numbers diminished somewhat at the end. The only PEI representative was James C. Pope. No one from BC ever sat in a Macdonald cabinet – instead, two Ontarians represented that province: himself and Francis Hincks. He allowed dissidents to sit in cabinet: both Howe and McLelan, who had opposed Confederation, were invited. Galt was chosen for finance but was soon out of a job. There was evidence of some opposition to his unquestioned support for the CPR in the 1880s, but in all cases the dissent was relatively easily managed. At times, Macdonald grew weary of some members of his cabinet and disposed of them quietly as they were ushered into retirement. Macdonald's cabinet grew older, more English-speaking, and more Protestant as the years wore on. It was always very centrally Canadian-focused.

Macdonald attracted opposites to his cabinet from the very beginning. Inevitably, hardened opponents of any given policy would cancel each other out. He made sure he was always in touch with his ministers by meeting them daily and keeping his finger on the political pulse of the party. Not surprisingly, there were no challenges to his leadership. Not least, Macdonald succeeded in statecraft because he was a careful listener of the public views. He knew how to set priorities and managed to convince people that these were the right ones. He was consistent, predictable and, when he needed to, he was decisive. In building Canada, and in defending it both from outside influence as from internal violence, he managed to keep the coalition of the willing strong enough to survive. Richard Cartwright, a Kingston friend until he bolted from the party because he was denied a cabinet position in 1869 and joined the Liberal Party, endlessly called Macdonald an "autocrat," a designation the *New York Times* adopted.[65] There was some of that in Macdonald's management of cabinet over the first twenty-five years of Confederation, but it seems that the Conservative Party – including cabinet ministers, caucus members, and ordinary partisans – was quite happy to live with it. As one writer observed in a completely different context in observing leadership, as he moved, "centre stage moved with him."[66] Macdonald's collegiality, his ability to conceive and implement policy, and his extraordinary statecraft justified it.

NOTES

1 H. Langevin to J. Langevin, 4 December 1866, Archives Publiques du Québec, Fonds Hector Langevin, 4, cited in Andrée Désilets, *Hector Langevin, un père de la confédération canadienne* (Quebec: Presses de l'Université Laval, 1969), 159.

2 Alexander Cameron to Macdonald, 2 January 1867, Library and Archives Canada (hereafter "LAC"), J.A. Macdonald Fonds, 340.

3 Cited in Donald Creighton, *The Road to Confederation* (Toronto: Macmillan, 1964), 420.

4 Macdonald was told sometime in March 1867 that he would be tapped as the first prime minister. See his letter to Louisa Macdonald, 21 March 1867, repr. in J.K. Johnson, *Affectionately Yours: The Letters of Sir John A. Macdonald and His Family* (Toronto: Macmillan, 1969), 104.

5 A.T. Galt to wife, 23 June 1867, LAC, A.T. Galt fonds, vol. 7, 001174.

6 Sir Charles Tupper, *Recollections of Sixty Years in Canada* (London: Cassells, 1914), 53.

7 This well-known quotation has been brought down by legend, but captured in George R. Parkin, *Sir John A. Macdonald* (Toronto: Morang, 1908), 140. (My thanks go to Stephen Azzi for locating it.) The first cabinet created by Macdonald

has been covered elsewhere. See W.L Morton, "The Cabinet of 1867," in *Cabinet Formation and Bicultural Relations: Seven Case Studies*, ed. Frederick W. Gibson (Ottawa: Queen's Printer, 1970), 1–17, which focuses mostly on regional representation. A useful update is J.P. Lewis, "'The Lion and the Lamb Ministry': John A. Macdonald and the Politics of the First Canadian Federal Cabinet" (MA thesis, University of Guelph, 2004). My own treatment examines the first cabinet in light of its administrative abilities; see Patrice Dutil, "Macdonald, His 'Ottawa Men' and the Consolidation of Prime Ministerial Power (1867–1873)," in *Macdonald at 200: New Reflections and Legacies*, ed. Patrice Dutil and Roger Hall (Toronto: Dundurn, 2014), 282–310.

8 J.E. Hodgetts, *Pioneer Public Service: An Administrative History of the United Canadas, 1841–1867* (Toronto: University of Toronto Press, 1956), 83. See also J.K. Johnson, "John A. Macdonald," in *The Pre-Confederation Premiers: Ontario Government Leaders, 1841–1867*, ed. J.M.S. Careless (Toronto: University of Toronto Press, 1980), 207; and Patrice Dutil, *Prime Ministerial Power in Canada: Its Origins under Macdonald, Laurier and Borden* (Vancouver: University of British Columbia Press, 2017).

9 Richard Cartwright, *Reminiscences* (Toronto: William Briggs, 1912), 302.

10 Macdonald himself assumed this. See letter from Macdonald to Archibald, 30 May 1867, cited in Creighton, *Road to Confederation*, 433.

11 Exchange of letters from Tilley to Macdonald and vice-versa, 30 May 1867, cited in Creighton, *Road to Confederation*, 433.

12 It is rumoured that Lady Macdonald took exception to Cartier because he maintained a clearly romantic relationship with Luce Cuvillier, a wealthy Montreal woman of substance. See Alastair Sweeny, *George-Etienne Cartier: A Biography* (Toronto: McClelland & Stewart, 1976), 169–72.

13 Tupper claims the credit for convincing McGee, in fact for bringing the cabinet together. No doubt he must have been influential in solidifying the consensus. See Tupper, *Recollections*, 52–5.

14 McDougall was often of object of real scorn among Conservatives and was burned in effigy in Whitby, Ontario, in 1861 by a riot of Macdonald supporters. See Robin Winks, *Canada and the United States: The Civil War Years*, 4th ed. (Montreal: McGill-Queens University Press, 1998), 59–60.

15 Donald Creighton, *John A. Macdonald: The Old Chieftain* (Toronto: Macmillan, 1955), 36.

16 Creighton, *Old Chieftain*, 12.

17 Andrée Désilets, "Chapais, Jean-Charles," in *Dictionary of Canadian Biography*, vol. 11, accessed 23 August 2024, https://www.biographi.ca/en/bio/chapais_jean _charles_11E.html.

18 W.A. Spray, "Mitchell, Peter," in *Dictionary of Canadian Biography*, vol. 12, , accessed 23 August 2024, https://www.biographi.ca/en/bio/mitchell_peter_12E .html.

19   See Patrice Dutil, *Ballots and Brawls: The 1867 Canadian Election* (Vancouver: University of British Columbia Press, 2025).

20   See my treatment in Dutil, *Prime Ministerial Power*.

21   190 Parl. Deb. (3d ser.) (1867) col. 90.

22   See Hodgetts, *Canadian Public Service*, 242–4.

23   Robert B. Bryce, *Maturing in Hard Times: Canada's Department of Finance through the Great Depression* (Montreal: McGill-Queen's University Press, 1986), 4.

24   *Morning News*, 3 January 1868.

25   See J. Murray Beck, *Joseph Howe*, vol. 2, *The Briton Becomes Canadian, 1848–1873* (Montreal: McGill-Queens University Press, 1983), 257–69. See also George F.G. Stanley, *The Birth of Western Canada: A History of the Riel Rebellions* (1936; repr., Toronto: University of Toronto Press, 1961). On William Meredith, see Sandra Gwyn, *The Private Capital: Ambition and Love in the Age of Macdonald and Laurier* (Toronto: McClelland & Stewart, 1984).

26   Donald Swainson, "Richard Cartwright Joins the Liberal Party," *Queen's Quarterly*, no. 75 (1968): 124–34; "Richard Cartwright's Tory Phase," Lennox and Addington Historical Society, *Papers and Records* (Napanee, ON), no. 15 (1976): 11–27; P.B. Waite, *Canada, 1874–1896: Arduous Destiny* (Toronto: McClelland & Stewart, 1971); P.B. Waite, *The Man from Halifax: Sir John Thompson, Prime Minister* (Toronto: University of Toronto Press, 1985); and Cecilia Morgan and Robert Craig Brown, "Cartwright, Sir Richard John," in *Dictionary of Canadian Biography*, vol. 14, accessed 23 August 2024, https://www.biographi.ca/en/bio /cartwright_richard_john_14E.html.

27   See Robert J. Talbot, *Negotiating the Numbered Treaties: An Intellectual and Political Biography of Alexander Morris* (Saskatoon: Purich, 2009), ch. 2.

28   See Brian J. Young, "The Defeat of George-Etienne Cartier in Montreal-East in 1872," *Canadian Historical Review* 51, no. 4 (1970): 386–406.

29   Andrée Désilets argues that Macdonald himself sought the change, but that Chapais insisted he had resigned over the dispute over French-language schools in New Brunswick (Désilets, "Chapais, Jean-Charles").

30   See Carl M. Wallace, "Sir Leonard Tilley: A Political Biography" (PhD thesis, University of Alberta, 1972), 278–80.

31   See Dutil, "'Ottawa Men.'"

32   The passage of a private bill in 1919 disallowed the practice; see 10 Geo. 5, c. 18. I am grateful to Barbara Messamore for this detail.

33   Joseph Pope, ed., *Correspondence of Sir John Macdonald* (Toronto: Oxford University Press, 1921), 653.

34   See Dutil, *Prime Ministerial Power*, 72–8, 203–5.

35   P.B. Waite, "John Henry Pope," in *Dictionary of Canadian Biography*, vol. 11, accessed 23 August 2024, https://www.biographi.ca/en/bio/pope_john_henry_11E.html.

36   Donald Creighton, "The Cabinet of 1878," in Gibson, *Cabinet Formation and Bicultural Relations*, 29.

37 See Dutil, *Prime Ministerial Power*, ch. 10.

38 Richard Cartwright, *Reminiscences* (Toronto: William Briggs, 1912), 236.

39 Creighton, *Old Chieftain*, 389–90.

40 Macdonald to Charles Tupper, 27 July 1885, in Creighton, *Old Chieftain*, 427.

41 Macdonald to Sir A. Campbell, 12 September 1885, in Pope, *Correspondence of Sir John Macdonald*, 358.

42 Waite, *Arduous Destiny*, 146–7.

43 Waite, *Arduous Destiny*, 144.

44 P.B. Waite, "White, Thomas," in *Dictionary of Canadian Biography*, vol. 11, accessed 23 August 2024, https://www.biographi.ca/en/bio/white_thomas_1830 _88_11E.html.

45 Stephen to Macdonald, 12 March 1885, in Pope, *Correspondence of Sir John Macdonald*, 337.

46 Cited in Waite, *Man from Halifax*, 132.

47 Waite, *Man from Halifax*, 128.

48 Macdonald to Thompson, 21 July 1885, in Pope, *Correspondence of Sir John Macdonald*, 351–2.

49 Macdonald to Justice Thompson, 17 September 1885, in Pope, *Correspondence of Sir John Macdonald*, 361. (P.B. Waite is certain it was raised in cabinet.)

50 See Waite, *Man from Halifax*, 128–33.

51 Waite, *Man from Halifax*, 132.

52 P.B. Waite, *Macdonald: His Life and World* (Toronto: McGraw-Hill Ryerson, 1975), 51.

53 J.S. Willison, *Reminiscences, Political and Personal* (Toronto: McClelland & Stewart, 1919), 194.

54 Waite, *Arduous Destiny*, 143.

55 According to Foster's very friendly biographer, he turned out to "one of the best departmental heads who have ever taken the oath of office." See W. Stewart Wallace, *The Memoirs of the Rt. Hon. Sir George Foster* (Toronto: Macmillan, 1933), 56.

56 *Robert Laird Borden, His Memoirs*, ed. Henry Borden (Toronto: Macmillan, 1938), 1:25.

57 See Patrice Dutil, *Sir John A. Macdonald and the Apocalyptic Year of 1885* (Toronto: Sutherland House, 2024).

58 See Ken Cruikshank, *Close Ties: Railways, Government and the Board of Railway Commissioners, 1851–1933* (Montreal: McGill-Queens University Press, 1991), 57.

59 Creighton buys this line (*Old Chieftain*, 523).

60 Creighton, *Old Chieftain*, 522.

61 Parkin, *Macdonald*, 140.

62 Macdonald to Tupper, June 1890, in Creighton, *Old Chieftain*, 545.

63 See Christopher Pennington, *The Destiny of Canada: Macdonald, Laurier and the Election of 1891* (Toronto: Penguin Books, 2011).

64 *Sessional Papers of the Dominion of Canada*, 1st parl., 1st sess., 1867–8, 26, vol. 1, 1.

65 See "An Autocrat in Power," *New York Times*, 10 March 1888, 3.

66 The famed baseball writer Roger Kahn observed this about Jackie Robinson. See *The Boys of Summer* (New York: Signet, 1973) 169.

3 Alexander Mackenzie's Statecraft: Looking for Stability Ex-centrically

BEN FORSTER

In November 1873, Alexander Mackenzie, the first Liberal prime minister of Canada, hammered together his cabinet with some difficulty. He and his party were asked to form the government after Macdonald faced defeat in Parliament in light of the revelations of the Pacific Scandal. Mackenzie was pleased with the resulting cabinet: he thought it was at least thoroughly representative. The quiet satisfaction showed in the bland summary William Buckingham, his biographer, later provided: "As between the House of Commons and the Senate the number of Ministers was eleven to three, and although Ontario held six seats in the Cabinet, two of them were without portfolio. Quebec held three, Nova Scotia and New Brunswick two each, and Prince Edward Island one." Mackenzie, sensitive to the religious divisions that spiced this sectional mixture, added that "there are five Catholics, three members of the Church of England, three Presbyterians, two Methodists, one Congregationalist and one Baptist [himself]."[1] He further extolled the many virtues of individual cabinet members, though with the passage of time after 1873 and in private, he was less complimentary.

While the construction of cabinets with some consideration for regional and group representation was and is common in Canada, it was critically central to Mackenzie's efforts to frame his, as the above quotes suggests. The cabinet – the core political and policy-making edifice of his government – was to a very large degree *fashioned to meet the needs and demands of regions and groups* – even individuals as it turned out – rather than to function in terms of broad national policy defined by Mackenzie's leadership. The cabinet was implicitly ex-centric. In practice, this ex-centrical system, which developed in the very way Mackenzie ascended to leadership, proved quite detrimental to his statecraft. Forceful leadership was further made difficult by Mackenzie taking on the heavy Public Works Department. That sharply reduced his capacity for planning and strategic manoeuvring. The problems of an ex-centrical cabinet structure were mitigated in some degree by Mackenzie's sometimes successful efforts to control his party, and by the Liberal belief in the values of late nineteenth-century liberal ideas.[2] Still, leadership – and statecraft – were hard to accomplish in this ex-centric political world.

In discussing the making of the cabinet, both Buckingham and Mackenzie left out one important consideration: an imbalance in the representation of business and economic interests. It would have been divisive to formally discuss that in a Liberal party that publicly prided itself on egalitarianism.[3] Such lofty ideals, however, crashed against the hard realities of this government's time in power. Canada suffered a debilitating economic downturn for much of the Liberals' time in power, robbing the government of revenue, and smothering possible initiatives. More precisely, the government, at the end of its mandate and in the face of depression, was trapped into policy inaction by its liberal ideals and by ex-centric divisions. As a result, it was routed at the polls on 17 September 1878.

There has been some dispute as to what caused the defeat. Some, like P.B. Waite in his excellent survey of the period, have argued that the deep economic depression of the 1870s would have defeated any government.[4] Some point out the latent political positions and strategic strengths of Macdonald and his party.[5] Others have pointed to Mackenzie's policy failures.[6] These few treatments only seem to underline the fact that Mackenzie's government has not attracted much attention. Typical of this is Michael Bliss's survey of prime ministers, *Right Honourable Men*, which barely mentions the first Liberal prime minister of Canada.[7] In what follows, I emphasize the weaknesses of Mackenzie's leadership of a fractionated party, particularly as they were manifested in his structuring and management of cabinet.

Alexander Mackenzie's Leadership

Leadership among the Reformers had been fluid for many years and remained so after Confederation, as it was limited to rule by a committee consisting of Alexander Mackenzie, Luther Holton, Antoine-Aimé Dorion, and Edward Blake.[8] George Brown, for many the very inspiration of Liberalism, begged off from the leadership role after 1867, though there remained residual yearning for him in Ontario ranks. Other potential leaders had flaws that made them difficult choices, and the best, Edward Blake, had commitments in the Ontario Reform party and to provincial government. Only with the abolishment of dual provincial and federal representation in 1873 was that issue laid to rest.[9] Mackenzie, in this context from Confederation to 1873, could be hardly more than a parliamentary party manager.

The Liberals were also bedevilled by old ethnic and religious tensions between Quebec and Ontario, fostered by the divisive Canada West (Ontario) leadership of George Brown, editor and owner of the *Globe* newspaper. There were also divisions between moderate Liberals and more radical Clear Grits in Ontario. Yet in the years following Confederation the Ontario Liberals/ Reformers increasingly posed a threat to Conservative political power. In Quebec, the Rouge (Liberal) element, despite its anti-clerical tinge, and its anti-confederate bias before 1867, formed a robust political group in the Montreal and Quebec City regions. They had some important links to their Ontario counterparts. Yet the Maritimes were much more uncertain. There, many of the leading Liberal figures had been anti-confederates: thereafter they partially aligned themselves with the Macdonaldian Liberal-Conservatives for political and patronage advantage.

Despite uncertainties and divisions, the Reformers/Liberals/Rouges in all the provinces shared a general ideological position, in their egalitarian tendencies, their notions of strong provincial rights, their demands for the separation of church and state, their desire for a wider franchise, their inclination towards free trade, their rejection of concentrated economic power, and their emphasis on a liberal individualism deeply rooted in the North American ethos.[10] Alexander Mackenzie fitted well into this perspective. He also added much energy and an obsessive work ethic, a vigorous debating style, and talent as an efficient party organizer. With his lack of venality and the support of George Brown, he emerged as the key Reform figure among the federal Liberals in Ontario.

And he had an eye on the national scene. The jaunt Mackenzie and some others took to the Maritimes in the summer of 1870 was intended to consolidate a potential alliance with Liberal-leaning MPs from the region. Mackenzie knew that the Maritimers were not easily convinced, as they liked the possibility of patronage and other benefit from the Macdonald government. This kowtowing by nominally independent MPs repulsed Mackenzie. "The general disposition to go with the powers that be in all soil was never so strong as at present," he wrote in 1869. "It's very disgusting."[11] So getting the Maritimers on board was a delicate business. Still, the trip to the Maritimes met with modest success, and as the election of 1872 approached, the Liberals fondly hoped they might gain power. Though disappointed by the election results, the rumours that afterwards swirled on the subject of Conservative corruption and the Pacific railway had the Liberals panting on the leash.

Yes, the election had disappointed. The Liberals had done better than in 1867, earning 34.7 per cent of the votes and increasing the size of the parliamentary delegation by thirty-four seats, including fifteen in Ontario. All the same, the Conservatives kept 100 seats and even increased their harvest of votes by over four percentage points, to 38.7 per cent. The good news for the Liberals was that the Macdonald government was returned with a majority of only six seats. And Mackenzie was clearly the federal leader in Ontario, despite Blake's provincial premiership. Mackenzie had played an important role on the hustings, speaking in nearly twenty Ontario constituencies in addition to his own during the election. Afterwards, given the hopes the Liberal caucus had about perhaps becoming the governing party, it was critical that a national leader be chosen; leadership teams and their uncertainties were no longer possible. A committee to select a leader was formed: Antoine-Aimé Dorion, Luc Letellier de Saint-Just, Luther Holton, Blake, and Mackenzie – a round table of leadership candidates. Blake and Dorion were serious contenders and Mackenzie favoured his friend Blake. There was much to-and-froing, but despite Mackenzie's hesitations (he stubbornly continued to urge Blake's name) leadership was thrust upon him by way of compromise, officially on 6 March 1873. Nonetheless, in the years that followed, Mackenzie was to face episodic challenges not only from the much-admired Blake (bedevilled though the Ontario lawyer and politician was by his own psychological uncertainties) but also in the form of stubborn resistance from various parliamentary elements.[12]

Mackenzie stands as an oddity in the list of Canadian prime ministers, especially because of his class origins as a stone worker – a hard-scrabble man of working-class background, sprung from poverty. He was born in Logierait (Perthshire) in 1822 into a family led by a father who had difficulty finding good work and was increasingly ill. Mackenzie started working full-time in Scotland at the age of thirteen after his father's death, along with two older brothers, in a surviving family of eight. He took on an apprenticeship in masonry at age sixteen; he was an independent journeyman within a few years. Marked by strong religious belief and rigid moral underpinnings, he moved from a stony Calvinist Presbyterianism to a more convivial and hopeful Baptist faith once he left his family to work in Irvine, Scotland, at age nineteen.[13] With the surrogate family he adopted in Irvine, he emigrated to Canada in 1842. In due course he made a name for himself in Sarnia, Ontario, displaying considerable organizational talents and a certain ability to chivvy people along. He was not a particularly attractive figure, dressed indifferently, and smiled only sporadically. He let his weather-beaten face tell his story – a tale that seemed to justify his Clear Grit view of life. He grew prosperous in the construction business and pursued a career in politics almost simultaneously, starting in the early 1850s. He was elected to the legislature as the member for Lambton (Canada West) in 1861. His organizational skills, combined with an ability to moderate his views for political gain, proved critical in drawing together a Liberal party from disparate sectional elements.

Mackenzie was a tough man, but he frequently pushed himself to his limits, and as prime minister he did so regularly – emotionally, physically, and mentally. It showed on his face: tight-lipped and austere (though there was a touch of humour and goodwill around the eyes). He broke his voice with public speaking in Parliament and out; Mackenzie could hardly be heard when he spoke in the Commons after the election of 1878. Utilitarian and unsparing, he did not brook fools. When Mackenzie dumped one Nova Scotian cabinet member (William Ross) he thought to be unworthy, he told the man he "needed brains and hands that could work."[14] One commentator said of his oratory that it was "generally moderate in tone, but when aroused and excited, he spoke with a rapid and nervous utterance. His dry caustic wit was only noticeable in his ordinary speeches. On great occasions he carried his points by storm and relied more on denunciation and invective."[15] This was the individual the Liberals had chosen to lead: clear in his beliefs, forceful in their enunciation, dedicated to the point of self-corrosion.

The 1873 Cabinet

Macdonald lost the confidence of the House of Commons on 5 November 1873, and Alexander Mackenzie was asked to form a government a few days later. It was not an easy task, and the results were viewed by many Conservatives, and others, with disparagement.[16] The Liberals were ill-prepared to form government because of weaknesses in their groupings, and because so few of them had held ministerial power before. The array of experienced political individuals from whom Mackenzie had to choose was constrained. Equally limiting was the paramount need for regional or sectional balance in the structure of the cabinet, driven by Mackenzie implicit ex-centric perspectives, shared widely in the party. Moreover, it was necessary to find men who had a relatively high level of administrative, electoral, and parliamentary competence, and had a strong policy orientation.

In terms of portfolios, meeting habits (almost daily), and the maintenance of a Treasury Board, Mackenzie adopted the cabinet structure Macdonald had established. It included two former provincial premiers and several former Conservatives, including Senator Alexander Campbell, Macdonald's former law partner. Was Mackenzie intent on showing that he could match Macdonald's ability to organize a government by creating a coalition with former adversaries? It might seem so.

As with Sir John A. and other early prime ministers, Mackenzie was willing to take on a cabinet post in addition to his leadership. But where Macdonald had chosen justice, essentially a patronage-rich central agency of government, Mackenzie chose public works. This was natural because of his construction background.[17] However, public works was a geographically dispersed portfolio, not only demanding ferocious attention to detail with attendant heavy time commitments but also evidencing intense regional patronage demands. It was a big-spending department rife with sleaziness; Mackenzie wished to clean these Augean stables.[18] Richard Cartwright knew the trouble the prime minister's commitment to this department created. "Time and time again, scores of times in fact, I can remember having gone over to his office in the afternoon and finding him completely done up with his long day's work, and time and time again I have had to say to him 'You are not fit to discuss important matters now. Take a rest and I will come and see you at some Christian hour – tomorrow morning.'"[19]

Mackenzie was deeply committed to reform in patronage practices, though not systemically through policy. Appropriate patronage – the appointment of able and trustworthy Liberals – was quite allowable. Mackenzie told Charles Brydges, the man he appointed general superintendent of railways, that hiring good Liberals was fine, but that Brydges should not appoint incompetents. Alfred Gilpin Jones, a leading voice in Nova Scotia Liberal politics and a sometime believer in less discriminating patronage, vehemently protested. Mackenzie held firm, telling Jones, "It is impossible to fill the Railway offices on political grounds; they must have experience, and if we cannot get experienced men among our friends we must take them elsewhere."[20] And Jones was the man that Mackenzie wanted to lead the Maritime Liberals! Still, Mackenzie faced attacks on purported corruption in public works. He was accused of nepotism in awarding a contract in 1875 to a firm in which his brother was involved. The transaction was above board, but that did not stop the accusations. He nonetheless defended his public works remit with courage and persistence. The constant barrage of office seekers there led him to do two things: first, build a secret staircase in the West Block of Parliament so he could escape the desperate demands of favour-seekers, and secondly to ponder creating civil service exams to weed out the unworthy.[21] He also kept close watch on the qualifications of the inside service of the Public Works Department.[22] Taking on the immense workload of that department seriously weakened Mackenzie's efforts as leader; he was urged to, and sometimes he did, consider giving it up, though in the end he proved too stubborn to do so.

Public Works was a difficult, time-consuming line ministry; Mackenzie sacrificed himself on that altar. The cabinet choices that followed were more difficult, though a path could be seen. The Liberal parliamentarians knew each other through reputation, acquaintanceship, enmity, friendship, and collegial beliefs. Individuals among them, from days well before Confederation, formed loose networks that extended beyond the political core of the House of Commons and Senate, forming multiple overlapping areas of action, policy development, representation of economic interests, and patronage. These characteristics were vital to Mackenzie in making hard choices.

Mackenzie knew only too well that the cabinet had to represent the weight of the various sections of the new country. He knew from the beginning of his mandate what it took Richard Cartwright some two more years to realize: "I am every day more and more convinced that no stable govt. is possible except in one of two ways, i.e. either by securing a decisive majority in Ontario and Quebec taken together, *or by deliberately purchasing the smaller provinces from time to time*."[23] This indeed bound Mackenzie's hands in cabinet selection.

Ontario's weight in cabinet was a good place to start. It was Mackenzie's backyard; he knew the Liberal political players intimately having campaigned for many of them prior to Confederation and then again forcefully in 1867 and 1872. He was always considered something of a Clear Grit, which gave him standing among the more radical elements. It was in Ontario that his leadership was first acknowledged, with the uncertain exception of Edward Blake and his supporters. In Ontario, as well, Mackenzie had a broad selection of individuals to call upon as cabinet members, given the dominance of Liberals/Reformers in the province.

First, there was the issue of George Brown. Mackenzie appointed him to the Senate as soon as he could, but Brown had little interest in direct government activity. Then there was Edward Blake, the Liberal premier of Ontario who had resigned in October 1872 to focus his efforts on Ottawa. Blake was a person of great competence – George Brown at one time thought he was the best public man in the country, a view widely shared. He was certainly one of the finest lawyers. He was forensically intense in debate, sometimes expounding for eye-glazing hours. Deeply insecure and sensitive, often open to severe mental strain, Blake was concurrently ambitious and arrogant.[24] Richard Cartwright thought him "constitutionally incapable of serving loyally under anybody."[25] Blake was certainly highly independent: his lucrative legal practice made him worth more than $100,000 at age thirty-three (a millionaire multiple times over in modern terms).[26] He had widespread support among Ontarian Liberal MPs, and in forward-looking circles in Toronto and throughout the province. His inclusion in the cabinet was thus of the utmost necessity. Yet he was difficult to bring in, and to keep. Mackenzie had served in Blake's cabinet in Ontario: the former subordinate was now in charge federally, which complicated matters.[27] Blake often thought that he, rather than Mackenzie, should be leading the party and should be prime minister. Blake could have likely claimed any portfolio, but he accepted the post of minister without portfolio in November 1873. He went in and out of cabinet over the next few years, vacillating, challenging Mackenzie, retreating, and re-entering, and in the process undermining the prime minister and even the party's government.

The finance portfolio went to Ontario, but only after Quebec's Luther Holton refused it. Mackenzie wanted a man of clear financial competence and experience, and that led him to Richard Cartwright, the disaffected former Conservative. Cartwright's business and political power base was in Kingston and Eastern Ontario generally – John A. Macdonald's own backyard. There were many grudges between the two men. Macdonald's pre-Confederation government had allowed Cartwright's chief financial instrument, a bank, to fail, which created a distance between Macdonald and his putative follower. Macdonald then brought on Sir Francis Hincks as finance minister to replace John Rose, much to Cartwright's disgust. Enraged, Cartwright moved first to the cross-benches (a contemporary term signifying independent opposition) and then to the Liberals. His undeniable abilities, particularly his parliamentary speaking skills, and his hankering for power and prestige – one businessman called him "a vain, pedantic creature"[28] – did not disappoint Mackenzie, and his attitudes about free trade and sectionalism made him a Liberal fit.[29] Donald A. Macdonald (the brother of Sandfield Macdonald, Ontario's first premier) was appointed postmaster general. A successful businessman, he was thought to be quite capable of using his considerable mortgage holdings to pressure voters. He was a strong ally to Mackenzie, a Clear Grit, both sharing the view that "the brother" had not been sufficiently reformist.

David Christie was a representative of agricultural south-western Ontario. He was a successful (and model) farmer in the Brantford area, and his involvement in agricultural associations gave him an entrée to politics. He favoured elective institutions and universal male suffrage – Clear Grit radicalism. Christie was appointed to the Senate at Confederation, which removed him as a troublesome activist from the House of Commons, to John A.'s pleasure.[30] Christie was given the innocuous posting of secretary of state, and thereafter was named speaker of the Senate.[31]

The religious interests of Irish Catholics in Ontario, the lumbering interests in the province, and the political and economic interests of the Ottawa area, found excellent representation in Richard Scott. A lawyer and one-time mayor of Ottawa, he undertook to elevate the concerns of anglophone Catholics before Confederation. He was one of the founders of the Ontario Catholic League when most Reformers of Canada West/Ontario were well known for their anti-Catholic bias, alarmingly so in the controversy over Louis Riel in 1870.[32] Scott pushed hard for separate Catholic schools, finally winning the cause in 1863. That success led Edward Blake to name Scott as the commissioner of Crown lands in the Ontario government. In that office, Scott displayed his support of the lumber interests: he was lavish in opening up territories for lumbering – it was patronage as policy. With Scott representing both religious and business interests, Mackenzie asked him to sit as minister without portfolio in 1873, forcing Scott to give up the provincial post. Mackenzie made Scott secretary of state a few months later. In that post, Scott originated the local option for temperance, which relieved the government of dealing with that troubling issue. Mackenzie would use him as a jack of all trades, as an interim minister in five different positions.[33] The Ontario representation in cabinet thus achieved a rough balance between old Clear Grits and moderates.

Obtaining appropriate ministers from the Maritimes gave Mackenzie particular problems. Here his difficulties in occupying the centre of the government were most evident. Nova Scotia was a case in point, exhibiting the ex-centric impact of sectionalism, and how patronage played a critical centripetal role. Mackenzie targeted Alfred Gilpin Jones, a successful Halifax businessman who had strongly opposed Confederation on commercial principles. Jones's stance against raising tariffs and his desire to limit government expenditures, as well as a tendency towards provincial rights, made him a Mackenzie ally in 1869. To Mackenzie's chagrin however, Jones had been defeated in the election of 1872, and the Nova Scotian consequently could resist efforts to ensnare him as regional leader and adviser (he did eventually join the ministry in its last year, as minister of militia and defence).

Mackenzie was subjected to intense pressure from the Nova Scotian Liberal caucus, which insisted on pushing forward two of its members for cabinet postings that offered rich potential for patronage. Mackenzie felt he could not withstand this pressure: "My real trouble has been the result of sectional representation forcing upon [me] men of so inferior calibre as to be utterly useless."[34] The two men in question were Thomas Coffin and William Ross, neither of whom was particularly effective in advancing their province's interests.[35] Ross, apparently something of a blabbermouth and undiscerning with patronage appointments, was made minister of militia and defence. Coffin, who had not shown much ability in his political career in Nova Scotian politics prior to Confederation, was appointed receiver general. He proved innocuous at best ("neither talent, tongue or sense," wrote the prime minister, never sparing in his private assessments of his ministers).

New Brunswickers offered less collective difficulty than Nova Scotians, though here too the Pacific Scandal worked some wonders. Isaac Burpee, the very successful St. John businessman who was involved in a variety of interests from merchandising, to railways, to manufacturing, was elected to Parliament in 1872. Of some independence, though with hope for benefit, he supported Sir John A. until the Pacific Scandal, when he threw in his lot with the Liberals. His mercantile world view, his emphasis on individual accomplishment, and his notions of limited government accorded with the Liberal ethos. As a businessman from the free trade–oriented Maritimes, Mackenzie appointed him minister of customs, the post he occupied for the rest of the regime.[36] He busied himself with departmental matters and never spoke much.[37]

Albert Smith from New Brunswick was a coup for Mackenzie. A wealthy man by inheritance and effort, Smith nonetheless had an egalitarian streak, a hostility to established privilege, and he demanded electoral reform and a broader franchise.[38] A lawyer as well as businessman, and deeply conversant with marine law, he became a seasoned politician and fierce debater before Confederation. He had been premier of New Brunswick and was opposed to Confederation. He nevertheless ran for seat in the House of Commons and was elected the MP for Westmorland. In the eyes of Mackenzie, the Department of Marine and Fisheries was a natural fit for him, and he was successful, wringing substantial benefit from the United States in resolving some of the outstanding marine issues created by the 1871 Treaty of Washington.[39]

British Columbia received no representation in Mackenzie's cabinet, but Prince Edward Island, newly in the Canadian fold in 1873, was critical to the making of the Liberal government, and so was deemed deserving. Mackenzie travelled east to soften the politicians there as well as in Nova Scotia and New Brunswick. David Laird of PEI, though his commitment to the Liberal Party was not fully clear until the Macdonald government faced imminent collapse in 1873, was an important recruit, as he brought five of six Island MPs with him.[40] Laird, a former premier of PEI, was a competent man with appropriate late nineteenth-century liberal individualist leanings. His family had a long political legacy on the Island. Mackenzie rewarded Laird's adherence with the post of minister of the interior, a position for which Laird had no experience. Still, Mackenzie could trust Laird with pursuing the business of the department, directly and in Parliament. Thus, when the Indian Act, largely a consolidation of existing legislation, was presented to the House of Commons in 1876, Mackenzie felt no need to intervene in the debates, though he did frequently for other ministers. The major change the Liberal government saw fit to introduce with the act was a pathway to full citizenship and voting rights for Indigenous band members – by them giving up their Indian Act rights.

Quebec presented its own set of challenges in both competence and ideological outlooks. Many of the Liberal/Rouge politicians were well acquainted with their Ontario counterparts from before Confederation and, despite tensions on ethnic and religious lines (though both desired the separation of church and state), there was considerable overlap in basic ideological perspectives. As in all regions, it was necessary to get individuals with political sway into the cabinet, even if they were of dubious character.

It was vital to find some cabinet members from the anglophone minority in Quebec. Mackenzie's first preference, Luther Holton, a Montreal businessman engaged in trade and transportation, had broad connections within the emerging Liberal/Reform/Rouge coalition.[41] Mackenzie initially offered him finance, but Holton declined for vague "personal considerations."[42] Mackenzie thus turned away from the Montreal business nexus (had Holton accepted, Quebec quite likely would have had five cabinet appointments, and Ontario four).

Mackenzie's other choice to represent Quebec anglophone community was Lucius Seth Huntington. The choice was made easy because of his vital role in revealing and doggedly pursuing the evidence of the Pacific Scandal. Moreover, he did to some degree represent Montreal business and business/legal activity and certainly business and anglophone interests in the Eastern Townships. These considerations, despite the narrow scope of his abilities and his penchant for getting into trouble by voicing his Protestant-Anglocentric views, made the presidency of the Privy Council a useful spot for him. Not a politically active posting, it nonetheless gave Huntington prestige and a voice in cabinet.

Mackenzie had somewhat easier choices to make among French-Canadians. The circles of such Liberal politicians in Quebec – an elite dominated by lawyers – were firmly established by Confederation.[43] Melded through diverse organizations such as the Institut Canadien, the (mostly anglophone) annexationist movement of 1849, the Reform Association of Lower Canada, the Parti National, and interlocking journalistic and legal endeavours, these men shared perspectives of liberal individualism and a desire for the separation of church and state. Here there were complex networks of political relationships that generated a pool of politicians from which Mackenzie could choose ministers. Many of them had significant contacts with the anglophone business world in Montreal, and politically, with important Reformers in Canada West (Ontario).

The leading choice among these was obvious: Antoine-Aimé Dorion, a man who had declared his liberal sympathies in the early 1850s. He and his fellows were "democrats in conscience and French Canadian in origin," supporting "education of the masses, [free] trade, and universal suffrage."[44] His subsequent political career in the Union of the Canadas included a cabinet position held for some two years. His leadership, which in Quebec stretched from 1854 to beyond Confederation, and his earlier willingness to find compromise with the difficult George Brown, made him necessary as a member of Mackenzie's cabinet. Dorion had considerable connections with the Montreal anglophone mercantile elite, where he counted among his friends Luther Holton, as well as the businessman William Molson. His inclusion in the cabinet was essential in the hopes for the development of a cohesive Liberal front in Parliament after the union; he worked closely with Mackenzie.

Dorion's political circle, which made him of such importance to Mackenzie, was replicated elsewhere among liberal elements in Quebec, and was manifested in Mackenzie's cabinet. Another obvious choice was Luc Letellier de Saint-Just, who was assigned the agriculture portfolio. The Quebec historian Robert Rumilly identified Letellier de Saint-Just as a core organizer by as early as 1847: "the local elite [of Rivière-Ouelle], the Letelliers, Casgrains, Chapais and Dionnes supported the Reform group … Luc Letellier de Saint-Just assembled these families in his [law] office to form an electoral organizing committee."[45] As a lawyer, Letellier de Saint-Just was involved in real estate and mortgage arrangements, which gave him a position of influence. At Confederation he was appointed to the Senate, and from that position he saw success directing the Liberal electoral machinery on the Quebec South Shore. He, with Richard Scott, became a leader of the Liberals in the upper house.

Mackenzie also turned to Télesphore Fournier, a third figure in the French Canadian Rouge/Liberal pantheon, in part because of Blake's encouragement.[46] Fournier was closely connected to Dorion and was named minister of inland revenue. He shared with Mackenzie and Blake an intense hostility to political corruption and lax patronage. A lawyer and active in Quebec provincial politics both prior and after Confederation, he built his reputation primarily as a jurist.[47]

Confident that he had made the right choices, Mackenzie asked that the House of Commons be dissolved, and an election was called for 22 January 1874. His cabinet had barely ten weeks of experience. It was composed of fourteen men (David Laird held two portfolios) who averaged forty-eight years of age, with the prime minister slightly older:

1 Prime Minister; Public Works – Alexander Mackenzie, Ontario, 51, Protestant, Ontario
2 Agriculture – Luc Letellier de St-Just, 53, Catholic, Quebec (senator)
3 Customs – Isaac Burpee, 48, Protestant, New Brunswick (Conservative)
4 Finance – Richard Cartwright, 38, Protestant, Ontario (Conservative)
5 Indian Affairs – David Laird, 40, Protestant, Prince Edward Island
6 Interior – David Laird, 40, Protestant, Prince Edward Island
7 Inland Revenue – Télesphore Fournier, 50, Catholic, Quebec
8 Justice and Attorney General – Antoine-Aimé Dorion, 55, Catholic, Quebec
9 Marine and Fisheries – Albert J. Smith, 51, Protestant, New Brunswick
10 Militia and Defence – William Ross, 49, Protestant, Nova Scotia
11 Postmaster General – Donald Alexander Macdonald, 57, Ontario, Catholic
12 President of the Privy Council – Lucius Seth Huntington, 46, Protestant, Quebec
13 Receiver General – Thomas Coffin, 56, Protestant, Nova Scotia (Conservative)
14 Secretary of State of Canada – Richard W. Scott, 48, Catholic, Ontario (senator, soon after cabinet appointment)
15 Minister without Portfolio – Edward Blake, 40, Protestant, Ontario

It seemed like a workable coalition, and it gained favour among the voters. The results of the election favoured the Liberals, who took 129 seats and 39.5 per cent of the popular vote. Macdonald's Conservatives were reduced to sixty-five seats and barely 30 per cent of the vote. All of his ministers were re-elected; Mackenzie thus had a solid mandate.

The Shuffles

Five ministers served the entirety of the five-year Liberal mandate: Isaac Burpee in customs, Richard Cartwright in finance, Albert J. Smith in marine and fisheries, Thomas Coffin as receiver general, and Mackenzie himself in public works. Richard William Scott also served throughout the ministry, but in multiple portfolios. Changes had to be made in the months that followed the election.

Possibly stimulated by Edward Blake's abrupt resignation from the cabinet, Mackenzie adjusted the corps of ministers from Quebec in the spring of 1874. Dorion decided to retire from justice as a result of his anticipated appointment to the Quebec judiciary. He was replaced by Télesphore Fournier, whose place in inland revenue was assigned to Félix Geoffrion, a notary from Varennes who had represented the area since 1863 and who was also an old friend of Dorion's.[48] Geoffrion had played a role in obtaining amnesty for most of those involved in the Northwest problems in 1869–70. He was highly thought of, and even Blake recommended him for inclusion in the cabinet.[49] Fournier's focus was on the establishment of the Supreme Court of Canada. (While the plan for such a court had been pressed by John A. Macdonald, it had failed because of French Canadian opposition.) Fournier displayed leadership capacity in steering the bill in the House of Commons, but unfortunately displayed no sense of his place in the world when he engaged in a tavern brawl in late 1874. There was talk of his being forced out of justice as a result, but he was critically important in the cabinet coalition, and until an appropriate post was found for him, he remained.[50]

In the spring and summer of 1875, further adjustments were made, again focusing on Quebec ministers. Fournier, with his extensive legal experience (and despite his pugilistic tendencies!), was expected to take a place on the Supreme Court. Mackenzie then invited the troublesome Edward Blake to return to cabinet and assume the Department of Justice.[51] To make sure that Ontario was not overly represented, Mackenzie removed Donald Alexander Macdonald as postmaster general and appointed him lieutenant governor of Ontario. These moves stabilized Mackenzie's leadership, and calmed party divisions, though the negotiations to bring Blake back were strenuous, involving not only Blake, but in adjunct Luther Holton and Alfred Gilpin Jones.

The postmaster general portfolio also changed hands multiple times in 1875, finally landing in Lucius Huntington's lap in October. The post demanded only adherence to international and British norms, while offering a great many patronage possibilities, but Huntington had faded as a parliamentarian once in office, having shot his oratorical bolt with the Pacific Scandal.[52]

To fill the position of president of the Privy Council vacated by Huntington, Mackenzie turned to another Quebecker, the magnificently bearded Joseph-Édouard Cauchon, whose power in the Quebec City area was legitimized by his newspaper, Le journal de Quebec.[53] Swaddled in privilege from birth, Cauchon engaged in municipal, provincial (his role as minister of public works in 1861 gave him a rich source of patronage and venality), and then federal politics. Cauchon was widely seen as grasping and self-centred, "enamoured of money, honours and luxury, [and] lacking in scruples." Cauchon was generally viewed as a Conservative, but he was a very stubborn and independent one, often baffling his friends by supporting Liberal causes. He had been mayor of Quebec City at the time of Confederation and nearly became premier of the province. Macdonald appointed him to the Senate and its speakership under intense demands from the man, but that chamber did not prove the centre of power Cauchon anticipated. He resigned, became a Conservative parliamentary candidate, and won the seat of Quebec-Centre for the Commons in 1872. He then actively pursued becoming lieutenant governor of Quebec through the Conservatives, but without success. With Cartier's death in 1873, Cauchon conceived of becoming the leader of French Canadian Conservatives. Again denied, he opportunistically used the Pacific Scandal to shift his allegiance to the Liberals.[54] His good relations with the clergy in Quebec, and his involvement in resolving the difficult question of Louis Riel's holding a seat in the Commons, led Mackenzie to proffer him the presidency of the Privy Council in 1875. He was the prime example of Mackenzie's need to recruit at least some individuals without consideration of Liberal political orthodoxy.

Mackenzie again tinkered with his cabinet at the midpoint of the mandate. In October 1876, David Laird was moved out of interior and Indian affairs and David Mills assumed the portfolio within weeks. In November, Mackenzie reluctantly decided to part ways with Geoffrion, who was not well, exhibiting signs of memory loss (perhaps as a result of typhoid), which necessitated cutting short that ministerial career. Geoffrion was moved out of inland revenue and replaced by Rodolphe Laflamme, another unconditional Rouge Montreal-based lawyer who also had enjoyed an association with Dorion reaching back to the late 1840s.[55] Active in the Institut Canadien, Laflamme had worked on the brother Eric Dorion's newspaper, *L'avenir*.[56] The connections went further, as Laflamme, the leading member of a legal firm in which Lucius Seth Huntington was also partner, had recruited Wilfrid Laurier to the Institut.[57] Laurier had been a law student of Laflamme's at McGill, and had furthered his legal career at Laflamme's law office (as did Louis Riel). In December, Luc Letellier de St-Just was moved out of agriculture and replaced by Charles-Pantaléon Pelletier, the MP for Kamouraska, a fairly moderate Liberal.

The fall of 1876, the midpoint of the mandate, also forced changes to the Ontario representation in cabinet. The agrarian heartland of south-western Ontario, where the Liberals had much strength and where Mackenzie was at home, required cabinet representation. David Mills stepped to the fore here, sitting for the riding of Bothwell. Mills had well-honed debating skills and strong attachment to the Liberal belief system. His American legal training enhanced his constitutional acumen and his democratic tendencies rendering him capable of arguing his position from basic principles.[58] His ability to argue the case for provincial powers (second only to Edward Blake's among the leading Liberals – Mills was key in bringing about the end of dual representation[59]) gave him a cause that led to his intervention in a broad range of debates. These skills, and his chairing the Committee on Causes of the Present Depression, which sharply defined the free-trade outlook of the party in 1876, clearly marked him as ministerial material. The prime minister appointed him minister of the interior, replacing the more pedestrian David Laird, who did not often rise in the House except on his department's business.[60] Mills, an intense liberal with a wide-ranging intellect, was a better all-rounder in Parliament.[61] Laird, though somewhat dismayed by his concurrent patronage elevation as lieutenant governor of the Northwest and as the western superintendent of Indian affairs, was a good soldier and went without much protest. In the Northwest, he had to struggle with Mills in trying secure budgets to respond to the ravaging disaster for First Nations of bison destruction in prairie Canada.[62]

Preparing for the Election

Mackenzie continued to have problems with his Maritimes wing – and others – in cabinet. He reported to his brother in early 1877 that "Smith is lazy, Burpee knows his own business, nothing more. Vail I cannot let loose. Coffin has neither talent, tongue or sense. Mills and Cartwright are always willing and effective, Cauchon no use. Scott is not always near me and often blunders in the Senate in spite of all my posting him daily."[63] Looking at faces at the cabinet table, he might have remembered what he had said about Albert J. Smith, whom he considered "fat and easy" by 1877, a view apparently widely shared.[64] When Richard Cartwright proposed to increase the tariff to get more revenue in 1876 (the government was in deficit and the tariff was the chief source of government income), he ran head first into regional interests: "The Islanders and New Brunswickers and also the Nova Scotians were most determined of all. They waited upon me to warn me that an increase would be fatal to them and indeed said that they would not promise to support the govt if such an increase should be proposed."[65] The finance minister, and Mackenzie, backtracked in the face of such intransigence. Sectionalism remained rampant despite Mackenzie's efforts to tame it.

As the final year of the mandate approached, Mackenzie made a few more changes to the cabinet, though he found no way to replace Smith. William Vail in Militia and Defence had been lacklustre and spoke only rarely in the House of Commons to defend the government – "never of any use to me," wrote Mackenzie sourly. When it was revealed that Vail might have been personally profiting from a government printing contract, Mackenzie ordered him to resign as an MP. Vail pleaded to remain, without success. Mackenzie did however trigger a by-election to allow Vail to legitimize himself.[66] Vail lost, and Alfred Gilpin Jones, another Nova Scotian, was asked to take the portfolio in January 1878. It was unfortunate that Mackenzie did not have much time to enjoy this new-found pillar of strength. Jones was an acute businessman and parliamentary debater, and was a knowledgeable figure in militia matters, but the general election later that year brought this potential to an end.

Quebec's poor showing in cabinet was another important matter that needed fixing. Mackenzie, who perhaps relied too much on Dorion's Rouge nexus, had consistently appointed such men, and word was that their views were likely to harm the party in the upcoming election. The changes started in January 1877, when Charles-Pantaléon Pelletier was named to the Senate and appointed minister of agriculture. Pelletier, a lawyer whose first wife was a Casgrain, had an established place in the militia, which gave him substantial prestige; he dabbled in business as well and had signed up as a member of the Parti National in 1872. In 1869, he won a federal seat, which he retained until early 1877, when he was appointed a senator, following in Letellier Saint-Just's footsteps. Known for his ruthless use of patronage particularly in the Quebec region, Pelletier possibly furthered personal interests as well as those of the party.[67]

Mackenzie grew impatient with Cauchon. Andrée Désilets, Cauchon's biographer, described him as "invariably peremptory, surly and argumentative," a view the prime minister no doubt would have shared. It was in this context that Wilfrid Laurier, the MP for Drummond–Arthabaska, gave a speech in Quebec City in June 1877 that proclaimed that the Quebec Liberals had turned their backs on the old radicalism and that their views of politics were nothing more than an expression of British Liberal traditions.[68] Laurier had always been associated with the Dorion-Letellier-Laflamme-Pelletier brand of Rouge Liberalism, so the speech was explosive. Mackenzie immediately saw the opportunity to elevate the obscure thirty-five-year-old. Mackenzie made room for him in the cabinet by providing Joseph Cauchon with the lieutenant governorship of Manitoba and appointed Laurier as minister of inland revenue in October 1877.[69] It was good riddance, Mackenzie told George Brown: "I told Cauchon that I could not maintain him any longer, that his advent had done us harm everywhere; and whether just or unjust the feeling was so strong and universal against him that I had resolved not to go to the elections with him."[70]

By 1877–8, Mackenzie had created an uneasy but effective balance in his cabinet (see image 3.1). He had limited the Nova Scotian caucus's collective powers with Alfred Gilpin Jones; he had found effective structure in the choice of cabinet members from Quebec by inviting Laurier in; he had to some degree managed Blake to seal a formidable grouping in Ontario (Blake did leave justice in 1877 because of his illness).

Mackenzie had thus gone far to forge a political party with national presence. In the process, the cabinet he so frequently disparaged had served relatively well, and had he given his ministers more room to grow in debate, he might have been more pleased with them. As it was, the leading members of the cabinet did their jobs effectively in the debating struggle.[71] His efforts to stem dubious

THE POLITICAL JONAH; or, SAVING THE SHIP.

Image 3.1. "The Political Jonah; or Saving the Ship," 1877. Joseph Cauchon is removed from cabinet in the hopes of saving the Mackenzie government.

Source: *Grip*, 22 September 1877, repr. in J.W. Bengough, *A Caricature History of Canadian Politics: Events from the Union of 1841 as Illustrated by Cartoons from* Grip *and Various Other Sources* (Toronto: Grip Print and Publishing, 1886), 361.

patronage, as well as corruption, had its limits. He refused to involve himself in the patronage activities of departments other than his own, so his perspective remained incomplete. His mild attempts to change the appointment system in the public service did not really alter matters: he knew that patronage was essential if there was to be any hope of keeping his party together and in power.

Mackenzie called for an election on 17 September 1878 with a very different cabinet of only twelve men (the presidency of the Privy Council being vacant since January that year). There were no representatives from Prince Edward Island or British Columbia, and two cabinet members were senators.

1 Agriculture: Charles-Pantaléon Pelletier, Catholic, Quebec (senator)
2 Customs: Isaac Burpee, Protestant, New Brunswick
3 Finance: Richard Cartwright, Protestant, Ontario

4   Indian Affairs: David Mills, Protestant, Ontario
5   Interior: David Mills, Protestant, Ontario
6   Inland Revenue: Wilfrid Laurier, Catholic, Quebec
7   Justice and Attorney General: Rodolphe Laflamme, Catholic, Quebec
8   Marine and Fisheries: Sir Albert J. Smith, Protestant, New Brunswick
9   Militia and Defence: Alfred Gilpin Jones, Protestant, Nova Scotia
10 Postmaster General: Lucius Seth Huntington, Protestant, Quebec
11 President of the Privy Council: vacant
12 Public Works: Alexander Mackenzie, Ontario, Protestant, Ontario
13 Receiver General: Thomas Coffin, Protestant, Nova Scotia
14 Secretary of State of Canada: Richard W. Scott, Catholic, Ontario (senator)

The Liberal government could point to a variety of accomplishments. It had established a governing council in the Northwest, the Royal Military College, and the Supreme Court. It had seen to the completion of the Intercolonial Railway and had forwarded the construction of the Pacific railway. It had run a government largely free of scandal. It had signed numerous treaties with the Indigenous peoples in the Northwest, though distress and starvation among them was significantly ignored. It had limited the potentially dangerous fallout from Riel and the making of Manitoba. It had settled the New Brunswick school dispute. It had held its line in rejecting protectionism. "I have nothing to regret in looking back at my course," Mackenzie told the governor general, Lord Dufferin.[72] Canadians thought differently. The government was badly defeated, with the distressed economy as the central issue. Smith and Coffin (the two former Conservatives from the Maritimes) were beaten. In Ontario, Cartwright, himself a former Tory, lost his seat, and Edward Blake also lost. Mackenzie himself won by only 146 votes. In Quebec, Laflamme was defeated.

Mackenzie's government served only one term because it could not find adequate responses to the grave policy challenges engendered by the economic depression. But within that, his statecraft was flawed. Mackenzie had little time for developing or managing his political team because his energies were sapped by public works, divisive cabinet members, and the tensions of sectional politics. Despite the strong set of liberal beliefs held by many in his cabinet and caucus, he was unable to provide the leadership to shape those beliefs in creating a unified Liberalism and party, though that surely should and probably was his aim. Mackenzie had hoped to fashion a broader coalition by inviting Conservatives into cabinet, but he had none of Macdonald's charm to carry it off. Worse, his efforts engendered a good deal of distrust, as with Cauchon and others. "I have a horde of spies round me in the office," the prime minister complained about senior public servants that had been appointed by his predecessor, and there may have been suspicions that some cabinet members occasionally and injudiciously blabbered. Mackenzie probably lost support in

Quebec because of difficulties in developing effective leadership in the provincial wing of the party. He did not include talent from either British Columbia throughout or Prince Edward Island at the end – two provinces that largely abandoned the Liberals in the 1878 election. There is no doubt that Mackenzie had difficulty in recruiting reliable talent. Time and again he complained about the mediocrity of his ministers. The constant hesitations of Edward Blake highlighted Mackenzie's difficulties in maintaining a confident leadership. Mackenzie's gravest mistake was in holding for himself the demanding public works portfolio, as that sharply limited the time to consider the wider questions of shaping his party and his government. On this, Richard Cartwright was categorical: "It was a fatal error."[73] As a result, Mackenzie was unable to fully respond to political pressures – threats of sectionalism, endless demands for patronage, or the consequences of weak administration by ministers. Combined, they undermined his leadership and this, in turn, made it difficult to forge a cabinet that could act fully under his direction. For him and his cabinet, it was quite difficult to govern from the centre. Mackenzie worked ex-centrically, and his party demanded that. He would be the last prime minister to allow this mistake.

The Macdonald Conservatives roared back to power, taking 134 seats (sixty-nine more than in 1874) and just over 42 per cent of the vote. The Liberals won sixty-three seats, less than half the Conservative haul, having lost sixty-six. A third of voters had favoured them. The Conservatives beat the Liberals in every province except New Brunswick. Mackenzie was humiliated and resigned the leadership of his party, likely under some pressure. One would be rightly tempted to conclude it was a profoundly felt vote: the Liberals were condemned to the political wilderness for the next eighteen years.

NOTES

1 William Buckingham and George W. Ross, *The Hon. Alexander Mackenzie: His Life and Times* (Toronto: Rose, 1892), 354.

2 Those ideas were hardly foreign to their Conservative counterparts, of course, though there less explicitly fostered. That permitted Mackenzie to recruit erstwhile Conservatives into the cabinet.

3 See *The Globe*, 1 April 1872: "It can hardly be said that in this country there is such a thing as a capitalist class, much less, like that of England, a capitalist class socially separated from the working-man." This was specious, though ideologically happy.

4 P.B. Waite, *Canada, 1874–1896: Arduous Destiny* (Toronto: McClelland & Stewart, 1971), 92. The whole of Dale C. Thomson's biography could be read as a defence of Mackenzie's policies. See *Alexander Mackenzie: Clear Grit* (Toronto: Macmillan, 1960).

5 See Donald Creighton, *John A. Macdonald: The Old Chieftain* (Toronto: Macmillan, 1955), 213–42.

6 See Bruce Hutchinson, *Mr. Prime Minister, 1867–1964* (Don Mills: Longmans Canada, 1964), 48–74.

7 Michael Bliss, *Right Honourable Men: The Descent of Canadian Politics from Macdonald to Chrétien*, 2nd ed. (Toronto: HarperPerennial Canada, 2004).

8 Richard J. Cartwright, *Reminiscences* (Toronto: William Briggs, 1912), 121. One might consider George Brown as well, as Mackenzie consulted him often.

9 "An Act to Render Members of the Legislative Councils and Legislative Assemblies of the Provinces Now Included, or Which May Hereafter Be Included within the Dominion of Canada, Ineligible for Sitting or Voting in the House of Commons of Canada," S.C. 1873, c. 2.

10 W.R. Graham, "The Alexander Mackenzie Administration, 1873–78: A Study of Liberal Tenets and Tactics" (MA thesis, University of Toronto, 1944), 1–2. See also F.H. Underhill, "Political Ideas of Upper Canada Reformers, 1867–1878," *C.H.A. Report* (1942): 104–15. For the same trends in French Canada, the *Manifeste du Club National Démocratique* (n.p., 1849) is instructive.

11 Thomson, *Clear Grit*, 111. Similar sentiments about the Maritimers were shared with George Brown: "They are without exception the meanest lot of plundering rascals ever known." See Library and Archives Canada (hereafter "LAC"), Brown Papers, vol. 8, 1828–31, Mackenzie to Brown, 30 March 1871; and Mackenzie to Jones, 3 March 1870, in *Report of the Board of Trustees of the Public Archives of Nova Scotia, for the Year 1952* (Halifax: Queen's Printer, 1953), appendix B, "Letters of Hon. Alexander Mackenzie to Hon. A.G. Jones, 1869–85," 14–66.

12 J.M.S. Careless, *Brown of the Globe: Statesman of Confederation, 1860–1880* (Toronto: Dundurn, 1989), 174–5; and Careless, *Brown of the Globe: Statesman of Confederation, 1860–1880* (Toronto: Macmillan, 1963), 270–1.

13 The Baptist Church in Irvine (Ayr), where he converted, had some 600 congregants in 1841, in a town with a population of 8,377. See *New Statistical Account of Scotland*, cited in "Irvine, Ayrshire, Scotland Genealogy," FamilySearch, last modified 15 July 2024, https://www.familysearch.org/en/wiki/Irvine,_Ayrshire,_Scotland_Genealogy. His youthful involvement with the Irvine-based Neil family with whom he chose to emigrate to Canada, and whose daughter Helen became his first wife, was a critical matter. The Neils had income from three working men in a well-to-do town. The daily involvement with a forward-looking and relatively prosperous family let Mackenzie peer into a more hopeful life.

14 Thomson, *Clear Grit*, 220.

15 George Stewart Jr., *Canada under the Administration of the Earl of Dufferin* (Toronto: Rose-Belford, 1878), 242.

16 Creighton, *Old Chieftain*, 187–91.

17 For a discussion of the impact of Macdonald's choice of ministry, see Patrice Dutil, "Macdonald, His 'Ottawa Men' and the Consolidation of Prime Ministerial

Power (1867–1873)," in *Macdonald at 200: New Reflections and Legacies*, ed. Patrice Dutil and Roger Hall (Toronto: Dundurn, 2014), 282–310.

18 B. Forster, "Mackenzie, Alexander," in *Dictionary of Canadian Biography*, vol. 12 (Toronto: University of Toronto Press, 1990), 647–58; and Buckingham and Ross, *Hon. Alexander Mackenzie*, 430–1. See also Albert Breton, "Patronage and Corruption in Hierarchies," *Journal of Canadian Studies* 22, no. 2 (1987): 19–33.

19 Cartwright, *Reminiscences*, 124.

20 Thomson, *Clear Grit*, 319–20.

21 There was a certain desire among Liberals to professionalize the civil service through exams to avoid the potential horrors of the "American system." See Parliament of Canada, Debates, 3rd parl., 2nd sess., vol. 1 (1875) 708–11; and Thomson, *Clear Grit*, 179.

22 LAC, Mackenzie Papers, MG 26 B, vols. 10–11. The "inside service," a contemporary term, referred to departmental civil servants working in Ottawa.

23 Archives of Ontario, Blake Papers, vol. 19, Cartwright to Edward Blake, 12 May 1875 (my emphasis).

24 J.D. Livermore, "The Personal Agonies of Edward Blake," *Canadian Historical Review* 56, no. 1 (1975): 45–58.

25 Cartwright, *Reminiscences*, 134.

26 Ben Forster and Jonathan Swainger, "Blake, Edward," in *Dictionary of Canadian Biography*, vol. 14 (Toronto: University of Toronto Press, 1998), 75.

27 Careless, *Brown of the Globe*, 325.

28 LAC, Macdonald Papers, MG 26 A, vol. 348, 159954-7, G. Dustan to Sir J.A. Macdonald, 2 March 1878. Cartwright also accepted a knighthood, while Mackenzie's and Brown's egalitarianism led them to reject similar offers. Sir Francis Hincks had been a moderate Reformer, inspector general (finance minister), and party leader during the pre-Confederation period. See W.G. Ormsby, "Hincks, Sir Francis," in *Dictionary of Canadian Biography*, vol. 11, accessed 25 August 2024, https://www.biographi.ca/en/bio/hincks_francis_11E.html.

29 Cecilia Morgan and Robert Craig Brown, "Cartwright, Sir Richard John," in *Dictionary of Canadian Biography*, 14:200–5; and LAC, Buckingham Papers, MG 27 II 3, J. Young to W.E. Buckingham, 25 May 1892.

30 Creighton, *Old Chieftain*, 187–91.

31 J.M.S. Careless, "Christie, David," in *Dictionary of Canadian Biography*, vol. 10 (Toronto: University of Toronto Press, 1972), 168–72.

32 Henry James Morgan, *The Canadian Men and Women of the Time: A Hand-book of Canadian Biography* (Toronto: William Briggs, 1898), 921–2. See also R.W. Scott, *Some Incidents in the Public Life of Hon. R.W. Scott* (Ontario: n.p., [1908?]).

33 Brian Clarke, "Scott, Sir Richard William," in *Dictionary of Canadian Biography*, 14:913–16.

34 LAC, Mackenzie Papers, MG 26 B, Letterbooks, vol. 1 [vol. 19, photocopy], 689, Mackenzie to Holton, 14 October 1876. Cabinet posts were apparently worth

some $7,000 a year (Thomson, *Clear Grit*, 220) at a time when a very well-paid skilled working man employed year-round would be fortunate to make 10 per cent of that, and ordinarily would more likely draw some $500.

35 J. Murray Beck, "Jones, Alfred Gilpin," in *Dictionary of Canadian Biography*, vol. 13 (Toronto: University of Toronto Press, 1994), 525–9.

36 William M. Baker, "Burpee, Isaac," in *Dictionary of Canadian Biography*, vol. 11 (Toronto: University of Toronto Press, 1982), 133–5. The Department of Customs was one of the three largest departments of the government, along with the Post Office and Agriculture. It was thus a rich area for patronage. See James Ross Hurley, "Highlights of the History of the Public Service," Government of Canada (website), last modified 18 January 2021, https://www.canada.ca/en/privy-council/services/highlights-history-public-service.html.

37 Burpee stuck to New Brunswick matters for the most part in the 1875 debates and did not engage in the broader array of subjects of debate. See House of Commons Debates, 3rd parl., 2nd sess., vol. 1 (1875), index, 3.

38 He did take a knighthood in May 1878.

39 Charles Callan Tansill, *Canadian-American Relations, 1875–1911* (Toronto: Ryerson Press, 1943), 11–12. The Department of Marine and Fisheries developed the Canadian arguments under the direction of Smith, for the Commission appointed to consider the award to be given to Canada for the American use of Canadian inshore fisheries. The award amounted to $5,500,000 – enough, as Richard Cartwright thought, to cover the Mackenzie government's deficits.

40 Thomson, *Clear Grit*, 157, 160, 167; and Cartwright, *Reminiscences*, 118.

41 Holton undertook to bring Antoine-Aimé Dorion into the coalition, had strong links with Huntington, and was a trusted political confidant of Mackenzie's, as well as a frequent correspondent of Edward Blake.

42 H.C. Klassen, "Holton, Luther," in *Dictionary of Canadian Biography*, 10:354–8.

43 My perspectives on what follows, as I have realized with the passage of time, have been influenced by Fernand Ouellet, who taught me as an MA student and allowed me to read and comment on an early draft of his *Le Bas-Canada, 1791–1840: Changements structuraux et crise*.

44 Jean-Claude Soulard, "Dorion, Sir Antoine-Aimé," in *Dictionary of Canadian Biography*, vol. 12, accessed 25 August 2024, https://www.biographi.ca/en/bio/dorion_antoine_aime_12E.html.

45 Robert Rumilly, "Letellier de Saint-Just, Luc," in *Dictionary of Canadian Biography*, 11:519–21.

46 Thomson, *Clear Grit*, 219.

47 George Maclean Rose, *A Cyclopedia of Canadian Biography: Being Chiefly Men of the Time* (Toronto, Rose, 1888), 481–2.

48 Jean-Paul Bernard, *Les Rouges: Libéralisme, nationalisme et anticléricalisme au milieu de xixe siècle* (Montreal: Presses de l'Université du Québec, 1971), 225–6.

49 Blake had gained political notoriety in Ontario for his condemnation of Louis Riel and Riel's leadership cohort in Manitoba.

50 LAC, Mackenzie Papers, MG 26 B, Letterbooks, vol. 1 [vol. 19, photocopy], Mackenzie to Fournier, 7 December 1874, 243–4; and Sister Teresa Avila Burke, "Mackenzie and His Cabinet 1873–1878," *Canadian Historical Review* 41, no. 2 (1960): 141. Burke's article, though now dated, is of importance and offers excellent discussion of Blake's role in the machinations of the cabinet.

51 Michèle Brassard and Jean Hamelin, "Fournier, Télesphore," in *Dictionary of Canadian Biography*, 12:323–6.

52 William Smith, "The Post Office," in *Canada and Its Provinces: A History of the Canadian People and Their Institutions by One Hundred Associates*, ed. Adam Shortt and Arthur G. Doughty (Toronto: Publishers' Association, 1913), 7:629, 633–4, shows that more than 3,600 post offices existing in the country after 1873. This made the postmaster general an individual who could provide widespread low-level appointments. The suggestion that there were 2,660 civil service positions at Confederation in Ontario and Quebec combined seems uncertain from a patronage perspective. See J.E. Hodgetts, *Pioneer Public Service: An Administrative History of United Canada, 1841–1867* (Toronto: University of Toronto Press, 1955), 36. There were 3,011 *post offices alone* in the country with Ontario, Quebec, New Brunswick, and Nova Scotia after the union in 1867, and many ports of entry (Customs) to boot. PEI added 180 post offices, and British Columbia 30, though there was a distribution system there that was not counted. See also J.L. Little, "Huntington, Lucius Seth," in *Dictionary of Canadian Biography*, 11:437–9.

53 Maximilien Bibaud, *Le panthéon canadien: Choix de biographies* (Montreal: Jos M. Valois, 1891), 49–50.

54 Andrée Désilets, "Cauchon, Joseph-Eduard," in *Dictionary of Canadian Biography*, 11:159–65. Cartwright made considerable efforts to rehabilitate Cauchon's reputation (Cartwright, *Reminiscences*, 144–5; and Thomson, *Clear Grit*, 156).

55 LAC, Mackenzie Papers, MG 26 B, Letterbooks, vol. 1 [vol. 19, photocopy], 636, Mackenzie to Luther Holton, 26 October 1876; and Marcel Caya, "Geoffrion, Felix," in *Dictionary of Canadian Biography*, 12:362–3.

56 Bernard, *Les Rouges*, devotes an entire chapter to the newspaper, in a study examining les Rouges through their newspaper voices.

57 "Lucius Seth Huntington (1827–1886)," Assemblée Nationale du Québec, last modified April 2021, https://www.assnat.qc.ca/fr/deputes/huntington-lucius-seth-3679/biographie.html.

58 Morgan, *Canadian Men and Women*, 634–5.

59 See his desire that Senate appointments be a provincial prerogative, "to protect the Provinces against the encroachment of the House of Commons" (Buckingham and Ross, *Hon. Alexander Mackenzie*, 388).

60 Robert C. Vipond, "Mills, David," in *Dictionary of Canadian Biography*, 13:707–12; and Thomson, *Clear Grit*, 278.

61 House of Commons Debates, 3rd parl., 2nd sess., vol. 1 (1875), index, 11, 15. Laird intervened in debates fourteen times, almost entirely on Indian matters. Mills intervened twenty times on thirteen different subjects.

62 Laird's addition to the Indian Act was a liberal individualist one that had little meaning in the Northwest of the 1870s. Laird was not utterly ignorant of the native west, as he apparently went to Fort Qu'Appelle in 1874 for treaty-making purposes (Duncan C. Scott, "Indian Affairs 1867–1912," in Shortt and Doughty, *Canada and Its Provinces*, 7:597). See also Forster, "Mackenzie, Alexander"; and Andrew Robb, "David Laird," *Dictionary of Canadian Biography*, 14:578–81. For the grim circumstances of Saskatchewan throughout the 1870s, see Bill Waiser, *A World We Have Lost: Saskatchewan before 1905* (Markham: Fifth House Books, 2016), 497, 498, 500, 503, 505. Laird complained that the Government House there could be so cold that the residents feared for their lives (Waiser, *World We Have Lost*, 493).

63 Thomson, *Clear Grit*, 301.

64 See Graham, "Mackenzie Administration," 59, for a general statement on the Rouges in Quebec. As for Mackenzie's similar perspectives, see *Sarnia Observer*, 9 December 1859.

65 Cartwright, *Reminiscences*, 157–8; and J.J.B. Forster, *A Conjunction of Interests: Business, Politics, and Tariffs, 1825–1879* (Toronto: University of Toronto Press, 1986), 143–58.

66 Stephen J. Harris, "Vail, William Berrian," in *Dictionary of Canadian Biography*, 13:1045–6.

67 Jean-Guy Pelletier, "Pelletier, Sir Charles-Alphonse Pantaléon," in *Dictionary of Canadian Biography*, 14:833–5.

68 See Wilfrid Laurier, "On Political Liberalism," in *Canada Always: The Defining Speeches of Sir Wilfrid Laurier*, ed. Arthur Milnes (Toronto: McClelland & Stewart, 2016), 53–82.

69 Réal Bélanger, "Laurier, Sir Wilfrid (baptized Henry-Charles-Wilfrid)," in *Dictionary of Canadian Biography*, 14:611–28.

70 Cited in Andrée Désilets, "Cauchon, Joseph (baptized Joseph-Édouard)," in *Dictionary of Canadian Biography*, vol. 11, accessed 25 August 2024, https://www.biographi.ca/en/bio/cauchon_joseph_edouard_11E.html.

71 Stewart, *Canada under the Administration*, 242–3, provides snapshots of the skills of the Liberal front bench; in his judgment, it was as effective and powerful as anything the Conservatives could offer.

72 Mackenzie to Dufferin, 19 September 1878, cited in Thomson, *Clear Grit*, 340.

73 See Patrice Dutil, *Prime Ministerial Power in Canada: Its Origins under Macdonald, Laurier and Borden* (Vancouver: University of British Columbia Press, 2017), 65–7.

4 The Cabinet in Chronic Crisis: The Lessons of Abbott, Thompson, Bowell, and Tupper

TED GLENN

John A. Macdonald died on the morning of 6 June 1891, "at 10:15 without pain and in peace," in the words of Joseph Pope, his faithful secretary. Macdonald, at age seventy-six, had been feeling very sick since February and suffered a stroke on 29 May. The prognosis was not a good one, though Macdonald did recover consciousness. Cabinet assembled for six hours on the next day, according to press reports, though no official record exists. "A crisis in political circles is imminent," reported the *New York Times*.[1] On 5 June, a second stroke felled Macdonald. He would be the first Canadian prime minister to die in office. There followed, in short order, the last four Conservative administrations to govern Canada until 1911: John Abbott's Fourth Ministry (June 1891 to November 1892), John Thompson's Fifth Ministry (December 1892 to December 1894), Mackenzie Bowell's Sixth Ministry (December 1894 to April 1895), and Charles Tupper's Seventh Ministry (May 1896 to July 1896). Often overlooked in the literature, these administrations nevertheless offer useful insight into key elements of prime ministerial statecraft in Canada, namely: carrying out the duties and responsibilities of office; maintaining the support of caucus; keeping cabinet colleagues in harness; and winning elections. The Macdonald succession is especially noteworthy in that it suffered a rare cabinet revolt under Mackenzie Bowell.

The Abbott Ministry

Macdonald's death left Governor General Lord Stanley in a bind: for the first time since Confederation, it was unclear who should be called upon to form a ministry. The Conservatives held a twenty-seven-seat majority in the Commons, but Macdonald had not signalled any preference for a successor and the three most able Conservatives were out of the running. Charges of bribery and corruption had derailed the chances for public works minister Hector Langevin, Macdonald's long-time Quebec lieutenant. Charles Tupper, the High

Commissioner to Great Britain who had been key in helping the Conservatives clinch victory in previous general elections, pulled his name from the running the day after Macdonald died. "Nothing would induce me to accept the position," he said, uncertain of how far his support extended beyond a loyal core. Tupper himself thought John Thompson, the forty-six-year-old justice minister and former puisne justice of the Supreme Court of Nova Scotia, was the best choice. "His great ability, high legal attainments, forensic powers and above all his personal character all render his choice one of which our party and country should be proud."[2] Many Conservatives agreed with Tupper – "the best thing I ever invented" Macdonald himself had once supposedly said of Thompson.[3] There was just one problem: Thompson was a Roman Catholic – a convert no less – which many Conservatives believed would impair his ability to win elections. As Sam Hughes put it (in his typical fashion), "Sir John is the right man but it is a d— pity he is a 'pervert.'"[4]

Thompson was Lord Stanley's first choice as well. Meeting with him and Senate Leader John Abbott Friday morning, 12 June 1891, Stanley pressed his point, but Thompson held firm that he was the wrong man for the job. He and Abbott had canvassed party members extensively and were convinced that a Roman Catholic could not command the confidence needed across the party to form and maintain a government. And besides, the last thing anyone wanted was to squander the majority the Conservatives had just secured only a few months before and give the Liberal opposition an "opportunity which might lead to disaster."[5] Thompson suggested a better option was for seventy-one-year-old Abbott to lead a caretaker government for the balance of the legislative session and then have the party conduct a more orderly transition to a more permanent administration.

Abbott was a good choice for caretaker. He had represented Argenteuil County off and on since 1860 and been a member of cabinet since 1887. He was a highly respected and successful commercial lawyer, the second dean of McGill Law School,[6] senior counsel for the Canadian Pacific Railway for the previous decade, and a two-term mayor of Montreal. And besides, as Abbott himself said, he was not "particularly obnoxious to anybody. Something like the principle on which it is reported some men are selected as candidates for the Presidency of the United States … that they are harmless and have not made any enemies."[7]

Stanley agreed to the proposition and Abbott and Thompson began work that afternoon gauging how many of Macdonald's former cabinet ministers would agree to serve with Abbott in Canada's Fourth Ministry. On Tuesday 17 June, Canada's third prime minister – and first native-born – told Parliament that he had received his colleagues' consent to remain in cabinet and had "submitted to His Excellency my recommendation that they should be continued in their present positions, of which His Excellency was pleased to approve."[8]

There was tension in the air of the Tory camp, and Agnes Macdonald decided it was time to call for party unity. "I appeal to the Conservative party with all the power of my words can convey to do now and in the future what they and I know would be my husband's ... wish ... to stand side by side, shoulder to shoulder, regardless of irritation, self-interest, or seeming reverses, with no goal but Canada's welfare and Canada's success."[9]

At the outset, the structure of Abbott's ministry was identical to Macdonald's last, with regional, religious, and linguistic representation dictating the terms of organization. Ontario had five representatives (Mackenzie Bowell, John Carling, John Haggart, and Senator Frank Smith; Macdonald's replacement had yet to be determined), Quebec had four (Hector Langevin, Adolphe Caron, Joseph-Adolphe Chapleau, and John Abbott), Nova Scotia and New Brunswick each had two (John Thompson, Charles Hibbert "Charlie" Tupper [the son of Sir Charles Tupper], George Foster, and John Costigan), and the West had one (Edgar Dewdney). Three of Quebec's seats went to French-speaking Québécois (Caron, Chapleau, and Langevin), one went to an English-speaking Protestant (Abbott), one represented Irish Catholics (Smith), and one spoke unofficially for the Orange Order in Ontario (Bowell). PEI continued without representation, as had been the case since James Pope had left cabinet after becoming incapacitated in 1882. The representative character of the Dominion cabinet was as strong in 1891 as when Macdonald put his first cabinet together back in 1867.[10]

The only difference between the structure of Abbott and Macdonald's ministries came with the exercise of leadership duties in Parliament. Both Macdonald and Alexander Mackenzie had managed their government's affairs in the Commons as part of their leadership duties (a practice continued until King created a separate office of government House leader in 1944), while duties in the Senate were assumed by the government leader there, a position accorded the rank of cabinet minister since 1867. With Abbott staying in the Senate (and retaining his role as government leader), Thompson took over leadership duties in the Commons. It was a relationship, as MP Duncan Cameron Fraser put it, in which "Abbott was the Mikado, the ruler *de jure*, but Thompson was the Taikun, the leader *de facto*."[11]

Abbott's government hit the ground running. On 26 June 1891, the Commons Committee on Privileges and Elections began hearings into the corruption charges against Hector Langevin and MP Thomas McGreevy. The charges (brought by Conservative-turned-Liberal MP Israël Tarte) were that a Quebec construction firm had paid McGreevy and his brother, Robert, over $200,000 for providing confidential information on bids for Dominion-funded construction projects, which the company would use to either underbid or buy off competitors. It was also alleged that as the minister responsible for these projects, Langevin not only had knowledge of the corruption but had even received kickbacks. In the first six weeks of hearings, the committee turned up evidence to implicate McGreevy in the scheme (enough for Thompson as justice minister to initiate legal proceedings against them and the contractors for defrauding the Dominion government) but nothing concrete against Langevin. Undeterred, the Conservative government struck back. On 3 August, Abbott had the Senate launch hearings into corruption connected with the Baie des Chaleurs Railway in Quebec, where it was alleged that $175,000 out of a $280,000 Dominion payment towards construction of the Gaspé-area railway "had disappeared in a mysterious way for the benefit" of at least one of the developers closely associated with the Quebec government of Liberal Premier Honoré Mercier.[12] The Senate investigation eventually triggered Mercier's resignation in November; the more immediate effect, though, was to take the wind out of the McGreevy-Langevin investigation. Laurier admitted privately on 17 August that "there was not much hope any more of making any serious breaches in the government majority,"[13] and Tarte himself declined to appear before the committee.

The final report on the McGreevy-Langevin affair was presented to Parliament on 26 September 1891. Authored by Thompson, it recommended that criminal prosecutions begin against Larkin, Connolly and Company and McGreevy but also declared that the evidence that Langevin either knew of the conspiracy or actively took part in it was insufficient. Langevin was not directly implicated, but the odious headlines were enough to force his resignation. The response proved Abbott and Thompson were serious about cleaning up corruption in the Conservative government and thinning out its ranks. Thompson in particular earned wide acclaim from Conservative backbenchers and the press for his handling of the committee investigation. Sam Hughes told Thompson, "Your best friends are more than pleased while your most bitter partisan opponents are dumb.... The 'pervert cry' is vanishing."[14]

Parliament prorogued on 30 September, and Abbott set about reconstructing cabinet as promised. With Langevin gone, Joseph-Adolphe Chapleau considered himself French Canada's senior representative in cabinet and demanded the railways and canals portfolio as "recognition of French-Canadian influence at Ottawa" and his own "personal prestige."[15] Few liked or trusted him by this point. Since Macdonald appointed Chapleau to cabinet in 1882, he had developed a reputation for an "innate want of loyalty" and making "sordid demands" for promotion that were nothing more than bald plays for "more influence or patronage or material advantage."[16] Ontario MP (and future lieutenant governor of Manitoba) James Patterson told Thompson that among "our most stalwart Conservatives ... there is not one in favour of his promotion from his present portfolio. The feeling is universal."[17] To move him out, Abbott offered Chapleau the lieutenant governorship of Quebec once its current occupant, Auguste-Réal Angers, retired at the end of 1892. Until then, Chapleau agreed to serve as minister of customs, and Abbott agreed to appoint Chapleau's protégé, forty-four-year-old Montreal lawyer and former Commons speaker, Joseph-Aldéric Ouimet, as minister of public works.

As for filling Macdonald's spot in cabinet, many believed the appointment of a "strong Protestant lieutenant from Ontario" would allow Thompson to shore up support for eventual leadership of the party.[18] Ontario Conservatives had in mind their provincial leader, William Meredith. In June, Abbott asked Meredith to join his cabinet, but Meredith said he could not "consent to abandon" his principles, namely that separate schools be publicly governed bodies free from "the control or dictation of any church" and that "outside the Province of Quebec the English language is the language of the country."[19] Under pressure from Ontario's Roman Catholic clergy, Abbott chose to eschew star power and enhance the government's electioneering capacity by appointing veteran machine politician and Ontario Conservative party president James Patterson as Ontario's new representative in cabinet.

Abbott's reconstructed Fourth Ministry was announced on 25 January 1892, one month before the 2nd Session of the 7th Parliament began. That session was unremarkable, save for two achievements: the introduction and passage of Canada's first Criminal Code (arguably Thompson's crowning achievement as justice minister), which sought to bring "order out of what at the time was a rather chaotic tangle of Common Law precedents";[20] and the referral of corruption and bribery charges against Postmaster General Adolphe Caron to an arms-length, independent commission. Once again, Thompson and Abbott were lauded for their ability to manage the government's agenda. As the Conservative-friendly *Montreal Gazette* put it, "To the sagacity, the experience, and the great ability of Sir John Abbott and Sir John Thompson the country owes no small debt of gratitude for the wise and prudent administration of public affairs during the past year, and the Conservative party owes profound thankfulness for much of the political successes achieved."[21] Voters agreed: in a remarkable string of by-elections held between June 1891 (when Abbott's ministry began) and July 1892 (when Parliament was prorogued), sixteen Conservative challengers wrested seats away from either Liberal or Independent incumbents and eighteen of twenty Conservative incumbents retained their seats.[22] The ability to win at the ballot box put wind back into Conservative sails – and gave Thompson the authority needed to succeed Abbott as prime minister.

Thompson's Government

John Abbott suffered a severe bout of dizziness in a House of Commons washroom on 3 August 1892. His doctors diagnosed the problem as "cerebral congestion and consequent exhaustion of the brain and nervous system" but could not identify the cause. Two weeks later, he and his wife Mary left for Britain in hopes that the long sea voyage would provide rest and that London specialists could better diagnose the problem. It turned out to be stomach cancer (Abbott would succumb to it the following autumn). In early November, Abbott wrote Thompson saying he had to resign immediately for the sake of his health and that it was time he – Thompson – take over as prime minister. In typical fashion, Thompson demurred. "Mr. Bowell has the respect of all of us and that any of us would follow him while we could agree with his policy." Abbott disagreed. "I do not think the choice you suggest would be to the advantage of the country, and I am convinced also it would cause great difficulty in the Cabinet.... In fact, I am convinced not only that the feeling of the party points directly and unmistakeably to yourself, but that the interest of the country will be best served by your assuming power."[23] Governor General Lord Stanley "heartily concurred"[24] and asked Thompson to form a government on 23 November. Thompson finally agreed, but not before completing one last piece of business: hearing an appeal from Manitoba's Roman Catholic minority to reclaim their rights to separate schools.

It was an issue that continued to dog the Conservatives. In March 1890, the Manitoba government abolished the province's separate school system and replaced it with a single, non-denominational regime.[25] Roman Catholics denounced the Act as a violation of their constitutional right to denominational schooling as stipulated in the Manitoba Act 1870. The Archbishop of St. Boniface, Alexandre Taché, demanded that Ottawa disallow the legislation, but Prime Minister Macdonald refused, arguing that the best place to settle the question was in the courts. As then justice minister Thompson put it, if the legislation were *ultra vires*, it did not need to be disallowed. If it were *intra vires*, it should not be disallowed. And if the case of the minority failed in the courts, then it would be time for the Dominion cabinet to consider the appeals that had been lodged under the Manitoba Act.[26] Thompson was no doubt sensitive to the political risk of a Catholic prime minister revoking a democratically-elected Protestant legislature's actions.

Manitoba's Roman Catholics lost their first case – *Barrett* – in July 1892. On appeal, Britain's Judicial Committee of the Privy Council (JCPC), which functioned as Canada's highest court, ruled that while denominational schools may have existed when the Manitoba Act was passed in 1870, Roman Catholics technically had no legal rights or privileges to denominational schooling at that time and thus no rights or privileges were protected in section 22 of the Act. The only way the 1890 legislation could have prejudicially affected Roman Catholic rights or privileges would have been if the province had compelled Roman Catholic children to attend the public school system. But it did not, so minority rights were not prejudicially affected.[27] It was a tortured logic, at best.

The courts tossed the political football back to the politicians. As promised, Thompson struck a cabinet subcommittee (himself, Bowell, Chapleau, and Ouimet – three Catholics and an Orangeman) to hear the appeal from Roman

Catholics on 27 November 1892. The conversation there focused on three main questions: had *Barrett* "disposed of or concluded" the issue? Were grounds for an appeal well founded (i.e., did section 22 of the Manitoba Act confer a right to denominational schooling)? And did the Dominion have the power to remediate the situation through legislation? Like Macdonald, Thompson tried to avoid answering these questions directly and punted the issue back to the courts in a reference case known as *Brophy*.[28]

The vacancies created by the departures of Chapleau and Abbott gave Thompson a window to put his stamp on cabinet. The first step was easy: Thompson replaced Chapleau with Auguste-Réal Angers (the former lieutenant governor was appointed to the Senate and named minister of agriculture) and filled Abbott's spot with a prominent Eastern townships businessman, William Ives (promoted from the backbench to president of the Privy Council).

The need to inject some "young and vigorous stock" into the "old and shopworn"[29] cabinet Thompson had inherited was a more complex challenge, which the Senate Committee on Machinery of Government later described like this:

> The freedom of selection which a Prime Minister can exercise in the choice of his colleagues is most seriously hampered by demands for Cabinet representation based on grounds of race, region, and religion. So uniformly ever since Confederation have these claims, not directly connected with sagacity in council or administrative skill, been recognized, that they have attained (particularly among Parliamentarians considering themselves of cabinet rank) almost the force of a constitutional principle. Any marked change would excite a hostile disposition, before the good effects of a new system could become apparent.[30]

Thompson skirted the issue with some innovation. First, he completed Macdonald's efforts to create a Department of Trade and Commerce in December 1892 and appointed Mackenzie Bowell as minister responsible.[31] Bowell was also designated as the government leader in the Senate. Thompson then created three new positions within the ministry but not part of cabinet: solicitor general (responsible for managing Crown prosecutions),[32] controller of customs (responsible for customs revenue), and controller of inland revenue (responsible for non-customs revenue). Thompson maintained collective responsibility by having the positions report to cabinet through other senior ministers (the solicitor general through the minister of justice, the controllers through the new minister of trade and commerce). Modelled after the British undersecretary position, the innovation was intended to give "younger members of Parliament" the opportunity to serve a "period of probation" and thereby "prove eligible for promotion" to the rank of full cabinet minister.[33] The positions also allowed Thompson to add regional representation to his government without making the fifteen-member cabinet itself any more unwieldy as a decision-making body than it already was. Montreal Centre lawyer John Curran was appointed solicitor general, Vaughan MP (and Orange Lodge grand master) Nathaniel Clarke Wallace was made controller of customs, and Brockville lawyer (and former deputy speaker) John Wood became controller of inland revenue. In all, Thompson brought five new men into his government, increased Ontario's representatives to seven members, and Quebec to six.

Thompson then left the country. He spent half of 1893 – March to September – in Paris as Canada's representative on the Bering Sea Arbitration. While he kept up with paperwork while away (as both prime minister and minister of justice), Thompson trusted the day-to-day management of his government to acting Prime Minister Mackenzie Bowell and the other ministers. One example of the kinds of issues they managed – and the level of trust Thompson had in his cabinet – was tariff reform, arguably one of his government's most important policy achievements. During the summer of 1893, Finance Minister George Foster led a commission that included Bowell, Wood, and Wallace on a cross-country tour to hear from manufacturers on how to reform the tariff structure. Based on what they heard, Foster put together a far-reaching reform package as part of the 1894 budget that saw increased duties on "tobacco, spirits and wines, and manufactures of iron and steel," and substantial reductions in a long list of raw materials used in manufacturing, including coal and coke, puddled bar, iron and steel bar, sheet steel, and flat iron. Farmers were also offered a variety of breaks, including a reduction in duties on carriages, live animals, and agricultural implements (from 35 to 20 per cent).[34] The 1894 reforms were the most comprehensive changes to the tariff structure since the National Policy was introduced in 1879 and became the Conservatives' counter to Liberal proposals for free trade with the United States.

The breakthroughs on trade, particularly as Canada sank into a deep continental depression, and the hosting of the 1894 Colonial Conference in Ottawa, gave momentum to the Conservatives, now fourteen years in office, but it did not last long. Thompson travelled to London after unveiling the Macdonald statue on the tip of Queen's Park in Toronto to be sworn in to the Imperial Privy Council at Windsor Castle. The reception took place on 12 December. One hour later, he died of a heart attack while lunching in the Octagon Room. Thompson, who had just turned 49, was the second prime minister to die in office in just 42 months.

Bowell's Ministry

Thompson, like Macdonald, did not name a successor. Governor General Lord Aberdeen (who had succeeded Stanley in September 1893) thought the best option was to appoint another caretaker administration until spring when voters could provide a fresh mandate to either a reconstructed Conservative party or

Wilfrid Laurier's Liberals. Aberdeen's choice was Mackenzie Bowell. At the time, some Conservatives still held out hope that Sir Charles Tupper would return to lead the party, but he had been out of cabinet, out of Parliament, and largely out of the country since 1887. Tupper's case was not helped by the fact that Aberdeen and his wife, Ishbel, did not like him. As for members of Thompson's ministry, scandals of various sorts disqualified its three most able candidates – finance minister George Foster,[35] railways minister John Haggart,[36] and Postmaster General Adolphe Caron. And that left Bowell. He had been elected to Parliament (Belleville) in 1867, helped hold the fort while the Conservatives were out in the wilderness during the Mackenzie administration, and held five cabinet posts thereafter – customs (1878–92), railways and canals (acting, 1891), militia and defence (1892), trade and commerce (1892–4), and government leader in the Senate (1892–4). He had foreign affairs experience, having negotiated a settlement with Great Britain for the Royal Navy dockyard at Esquimalt in 1892, and organized the 1894 Colonial Conference in Ottawa. And, unlike anyone else in cabinet, Bowell had actual experience in the Big Chair. He had served as acting prime minister for both Abbott (three months in 1892) and Thompson (five months in 1893 and six weeks in 1894).[37]

Just one issue dogged Bowell: his long-time association with the Orange Order (he had even served as grand master). Late Thursday afternoon (13 December), Aberdeen asked long-time Irish Catholic power broker, Senator Frank Smith, if Bowell's Orange past would affect his ability to gain the support of and deal fairly with Roman Catholics. Smith said he had known Bowell for years and had "never known him to say an offensive word about Catholics, or to do anything which they could regard as offensive." As he told a reporter after the meeting, "Mr. Bowell has been so careful in the administration of his cabinet duties that he has never to my knowledge offended a single Catholic." That was good enough for Aberdeen. At ten o'clock Thursday evening, the governor general invited Mackenzie Bowell to form Canada's Sixth Ministry.

The process of forming government was swift. By Friday evening, twelve of Thompson's ministers had agreed to stay on and serve under Bowell. By Monday, the remaining two (Ives and Tupper had been out of town) also agreed to stay put, and Arthur Dickey agreed to fill Thompson's Nova Scotia seat in cabinet as secretary of state. The only significant changes were the addition of two more ministers without portfolio to round out regional balance: Senator Donald Ferguson was appointed to represent PEI (James Pope's old role) and John Haggart's protégé, Dr. Walter Montague (Haldimand), was added for Ontario. (Haggart was successful in arguing Ontario was entitled to a fifth full member of cabinet; the two controllers did not suffice). Once again, the basic representative structure established by Macdonald remained intact.

On Friday, 21 December, Bowell travelled to Montreal where he and the five ministers who assumed new portfolios were sworn into office by Lord

Aberdeen in the study of the governor general's residence – the old Abbott House – on Sherbrooke. Asked about his government's new program at dinner later that evening, Bowell told *The Empire's* Fred Cook, "The old party will carry out the old policy and follow the lines laid down by Sir John Thompson. I have every confidence the country will support the Conservative party in the future just as it has done in the past."[38]

Bowell never got the chance to sell "the old party" or "the old policy" to voters in a spring election. On 29 January 1895, the JCPC ruled on *Brophy*, the case Thompson had referred to the Supreme Court two years earlier. The court said that Manitoba had violated Roman Catholics' constitutional right to denominational schooling when it abolished the province's separate school system in 1890. The court also held that Manitoba's Roman Catholics had a constitutional right to appeal to the Dominion cabinet for remediation and Parliament had the power to grant it.

The historic appeal of Manitoba's Roman Catholic minority took place in the Railway Committee room of Parliament beginning 4 March, and the four-day cabinet meeting to decide on how to proceed began on 17 March.[39] The compromise which Bowell was able to achieve there had two parts. First, the Dominion cabinet would issue an order-in-council directing Manitoba to pass legislation to "restore to the Roman Catholic minority the rights and privileges." Failure to do so would trigger the second part of the deal – "confer upon Parliament authority to pass such a law" before prorogation of the current parliamentary session on 20 July 1895.[40]

On 14 June, the Manitoba Premier Thomas Greenway announced that it would not "accept the responsibility of carrying into effect the terms of the remedial order," but it might be interested in participating in a "full and deliberate investigation of the whole subject" in order to "furnish a substantial basis of fact" upon which a future course of action "could be formed with a reasonable degree of certainty."[41]

The announcement put Bowell's feet to the fire: he had committed his government to remedial action in the 18 April Throne Speech; he had told the Senate as part of his maiden speech on 22 April that "the present administration is quite prepared to assume the responsibility which may fall upon them, no matter what the results may be;"[42] and he had made private assurances to his French-speaking ministers that he had put remedial legislation before Parliament if Manitoba failed to act before the current session prorogued. But on 3 July, thirty-nine of Ontario's fifty-one Conservatives signed a pledge circulated by the whip George Taylor saying that they would refuse to support the legislation. Protestant voters in their ridings had made it crystal clear that anyone who did so would suffer electoral retribution at the coming election.

The threatened revolt forced the prime minister to back down. Bowell announced at a 4 July cabinet meeting that "amicable settlement" was the best possible outcome and Greenway's 14 June reply to the remedial order had to be read as leaving

THE BOLT AMONGST THE BOLTERS!

Image 4.1. J.W. Bengough, "The Bolt amongst the Bolters!" In a speech in Perth, Ontario, Mackenzie Bowell denounces the ministers who had bolted from his cabinet.

Credit: Library and Archives Canada, item 4322036.

the door open to it. Bowell's three French-speaking cabinet ministers – Angers, Caron, and Ouimet – disagreed. Angers said Manitoba's response gave no reasonable hope for the kind of compromise or settlement Bowell hoped for and the anti-remediation pressure then being aroused would only intensify. He told Bowell he had the power and the strength to push forwards and do the right thing, right now, but that power and strength could – and would – vanish tomorrow. For all of this, Angers said he could not remain as a member of the cabinet and would tender his resignation immediately. (In solidarity, Caron and Ouimet followed him out the door. While Bowell was able to convince these two to rescind their resignations over the following week, Angers would not budge; see image 4.1.)

On 27 July, Bowell left on a seven-week tour of reserves and residential schools along the Pacific coast and across the Prairies. He hoped while there to "ascertain by friendly negotiations" if "a middle course will commend itself" between the Manitoba and Dominion governments "so that Federal action may become unnecessary."[43] The mission fell flat. Asked by a reporter at the train station in Winnipeg on 15 September if he had spoken with anyone in Manitoba on the Schools Question, Bowell replied, "No, not a word."[44]

***

Preoccupation with the Manitoba Schools Question and his seven-week Western tour impaired Bowell's ability fill vacancies, one of his basic duties as prime minister. By the time the prime minister returned to Ottawa on 17 September 1895, these included Angers's spot in cabinet; three seats in the House of Commons; sixteen seats in the Senate; one seat on the Supreme Court; six deputy minister appointments; customs collectors in Montreal, Sherbrooke, and Winnipeg; and a post office inspector in Montreal. Three more Commons seats opened in early October. John Curran's Montreal Centre riding opened when Bowell appointed him to the Quebec Superior Court. Cardwell (in Ontario) became vacant when Bowell appointed Robert White as Montreal customs collector. And the riding of Jacques-Cartier became vacant when Bowell appointed Désiré Girouard to the Supreme Court.

Angers's cabinet seat was arguably the most critical and the most difficult to fill. Bowell tried first to lure Chapleau back to Ottawa, but Chapleau said that Ontario Protestants like Haggart, Montague, and Clarke Wallace would have to promise that they would agree to passing remedial legislation immediately. In November, Bowell approached Louis-Philippe Pelletier, then provincial secretary to Conservative Quebec Premier Louis-Olivier Taillon. Pelletier told Bowell his long-term plans were to remain in Quebec. In late December, Bowell tried to draft Senator Alphonse Desjardins, but to no avail.[45] Bowell made more progress setting up the by-elections, although it took until the end of November to set dates and confirm Conservative candidates for Jacques-Cartier (30 November), Ontario North (12 December), Caldwell (24 December), and Montreal Centre (27 December).

On 18 November, Manitoba told Ottawa how far it would be willing to compromise on the Schools Question. Greenway said his government would make every effort to ensure the provincial public school system was completely nonsectarian by removing "any tinge of Protestantism that may have worked into the system." In addition, priests would be allowed into the schools after three o'clock to "give any religious teachings to the children that they see fit." The "compromise" fell far short of the terms set out in the March order-in-council, and representatives of Manitoba's Roman Catholic minority rejected it outright – "We cannot even entertain the idea of adopting such a poor scheme," said Archbishop Adélard Langevin, who had recently succeeded Taché at St. Boniface.[46]

On 30 November, confidence in Bowell's leadership took another hit when news reached Ottawa that the Conservatives had lost the by-election in Jacques-Cartier. Customs controller Nathaniel Clarke Wallace asked Bowell a week later if he still intended to pursue remedial legislation. Bowell said it was his duty to do so, and as long as Clarke Wallace remained in the ministry, he had a responsibility to support the policy as well. Clarke Wallace said he could not, in all good conscience, do that, and Bowell told him the only honourable course left to him was to resign.[47] Clarke Wallace did so on Thursday, 12 December. And then later that same day, results came in from the Ontario North by-election: The Conservative candidate had won handily but refused to pledge his support to the government's remedial policy.

Five days later, British Columbia's six Conservatives announced that they were set to bolt on the government's remedial policy as well. In a panic, Bowell wired Lieutenant Governor Edward Dewdney, asking him to "Kindly ascertain from [E.G.] Prior" – the nominal head of the BC caucus – "if he will accept a controllership with a seat in the cabinet. This would give British Columbia [its first] voice in the council." But Prior would not be bought so easily. He told a Conservative party meeting that as British Columbia's sole ministry representative he was "thoroughly entitled to a seat in the cabinet" and would not accept a mere controllership. "If Sir Mackenzie Bowell made a mistake, and does not mean a seat in the cabinet, I shall tell him that he can't get E.G. Prior to represent British Columbia in that way." Bowell wired Prior on 17 December, assuring him that "Governor Dewdney wires me there is a misunderstanding as to your status in the Government. You are Controller of Inland Revenue, Privy Councillor, and a member of Cabinet, and have just as much voice in affairs of the Dominion as I have. I would have offered you nothing less." In the interests of fairness, Bowell promoted John Wood (the other controller) to cabinet one week later.[48]

Prior's appointment quelled the threatened caucus revolt, but it was a messy fix. The controllers were cabinet appointments reporting to the minister of trade and commerce. Neither the prime minister nor the governor general could alter the terms of their appointment or their reporting relationship without amending the governing legislation. That legislation was not amended. More significantly, inviting the controllers to sit at the same table as their boss was functionally untenable: the controllers would have the same vote as the individuals who appointed them. As the *Globe* said, "A controller cannot be a cabinet minister, because there are not two classes of cabinet ministers, one inferior to the other, liable to be dismissed from office by the other, and in receipt of less salary than the other."[49]

On 21 December, the Greenway government issued its formal response to the Dominion, declaring that "so far as the Government of Manitoba is concerned, the proposal to establish a system of Separate Schools, in any form, is positively and definitely rejected."[50] In short order, the Conservatives lost the by-elections in Cardwell (24 December) and Montreal Centre (27 December). For seven members of Bowell's cabinet, these were the final straws.

The movement to replace Bowell had been gathering steam as he struggled through the fall of 1895. In November, Militia and Defence Minister Arthur Dickey wrote Charles Tupper in London that the task of governing had grown "too heavy" for Bowell. "He does his best and is not afraid of work but in every direction, public affairs show the want of a firm hand at the helm." Dickey implored Tupper to "come out as first minister," refresh the Conservative ranks, and "form a powerful government that would sweep the country" with popular policies like preferential tariffs and the fast Atlantic steamship service.[51] Charlie Tupper followed up a week later, telling his father, "It seems a downright shame to follow tamely an old man to the slaughter when if we were up and doing with a real leader we could march on to victory.... I verily believe if you could visit Canada on some excuse the party would run up and form under you."[52]

Sir Charles, in fact, came up with two excuses: the fast Atlantic steamship service and the Pacific Cable projects. On 14 November, Tupper wired Bowell to tell him British Prime Minister Neville Chamberlain had agreed to provide an annual mail subsidy worth $75,000 to the fast steamship service and that the Imperial government was "on the verge" of announcing support for the Pacific Cable as well. "Shall I come out consult you about these two matters?" Tupper asked Bowell. "Think you could render material assistance," Bowell replied on 2 December 1895: "Regarding fast line, come out to consult. Get all information possible."[53]

Tupper arrived in Ottawa on 16 December and immediately met with Dickey, Haggart, Ives, Montague, Wood, and Charlie Tupper, to confirm their support for dumping Bowell.[54] George Taylor, the government whip, told Tupper the Ontario caucus was behind him as well, as did party leaders from Nova Scotia and New Brunswick.

The next step in the coup took place on 3 January. Haggart and Montague were sent to meet Bowell in his East Block office and inform him that he did not have the majority needed to pass his proposed remedial legislation.[55] After accounting for illnesses, absences, resignations, and by-election outcomes, Haggart said the government's majority in the Commons stood at forty-five. And with at least forty Ontario Conservatives on record as opposed to remediation, Bowell's majority now hung with cabinet. Montague said seven ministers were ready to side with the anti-remedialists and force Bowell to resign. Bowell railed Friday night but agreed Saturday morning to meet with old Tupper in the afternoon. Whatever progress the two made, though, was scuttled when George Foster's private secretary entered the room and laid a manila envelope on Bowell's desk. It contained a letter of resignation signed by Dickey, Haggart, Foster, Ives, Montague, Charlie Tupper, and Wood. And there the meeting ended. Bowell would not resign with "a pistol to his head," especially one put there by the likes of Haggart, Foster, and Montague.[56]

The drama kept Ottawa – and the country – on tenterhooks for the next ten days. Bowell tried a couple of times to reconstruct his cabinet, and Tupper upped the pressure by going on public record about his interest in the job.[57] Finally, on Sunday 13 January, the prime minister relented. Senator Frank

Smith (and other party officials) convinced Bowell that the Conservatives' best shot at winning the 1896 election was to face voters with a new leader (Tupper), a reconstructed administration, and an alternative, more conciliatory approach on the schools issue. To give Tupper and party time to reorganize, Bowell agreed to stay on as prime minister until the end of the parliamentary session (set for 24 April). Tupper, meanwhile, would enter cabinet as secretary of state (and de facto government leader in the Commons) along with six of the conspirators – Dickey, Foster, Haggart, Ives, Montague, and Wood – as a show of party solidarity.[58] Tupper would also seek re-election in the House of Commons where he would be best positioned to orchestrate the death of Bowell's remedial bill and prepare the groundwork for launching a new policy. The final version of Canada's Sixth Ministry was announced in Parliament on 15 January 1896.

Tupper deployed as much red tape and filibuster as he could to kill the remedial bill. Even though the new parliamentary session began 2 January, Tupper insisted that Bill 58 not be introduced until after the Cape Breton by-election on 4 February. Other delays – securing the approval of the bill's wording from John Ewart and the "friends of Manitoba," completing French translation, etc. – pushed the start of Second Reading to 3 March. Debate in principle then dragged on for another two and a half weeks, with seventy-five members speaking for a combined 140 hours over the course of seven long sittings. On 6 April, the House moved Bill 58 to committee review by a majority of eighteen – the same number of (mostly Ontario) Conservatives who voted against it.

Tupper might have lost the vote entirely had he not promised earlier in March that Sir Donald Smith would "conference with Mr. Greenway's government with a view to arriving at a settlement of this question." This was Tupper's effort to begin laying the groundwork for an alternative approach to the schools issue. Based loosely on the system Tupper had implemented long before as premier in Nova Scotia in 1865, Smith proposed that religious instruction take place within the framework of the public school system "where numbers warranted."[59] Laurier and the Manitoba Liberals, however, had already decided there was no way a negotiated settlement would be reached with the Dominion – despite what Smith had to offer. After three days of negotiations, Attorney General Clifford Sifton told reporters that "we are precluded from accepting the proposition which has been made. Such acceptance would ... be a direct breach of faith with the people of our province."[60]

The final act of the remedial bill drama began with committee review of Bill 58 on 6 April. As with debate on principle, Tupper charged the House with sitting day and night. "I, for one, am prepared to exhaust every physical power I possess by staying here night and day in order to carry this measure through committee.... And failing that, to go to the intelligent electorate of this country to decide between the conduct of the Government in regard to this important measure and the public business of this country, and the unparliamentary means adopted by hon. gentlemen opposite to obstruct the public business." And exhausted the House became. The first sitting of clause-by-clause review lasted 129 hours, from Monday, 6 April, until Saturday, 11 April. The second lasted 56 hours, from Monday, 13 April, until Wednesday, 15 April, when the bill was withdrawn with only 15 of 112 clauses passed.[61]

Tupper's Ministry

As promised, Canada's fifth prime minister, Mackenzie Bowell, resigned on 27 April 1896. Later that day, Governor General Lord Aberdeen asked seventy-four-year-old Sir Charles Tupper to form Canada's Seventh Ministry. It took him a week, the bulk of which was spent trying to add star power to his cabinet from Quebec and the West. Tupper tried to lure Chapleau back into cabinet by offering him "the leadership of Quebec" and the freedom to pick its cabinet representatives.[62] Chapleau turned him down.[63] Rebuffed, Tupper cobbled together a slate of Ultramontanes, that included Auguste-Réal Angers; Senator Alphonse Desjardins; the then premier of Quebec, Louis-Olivier Taillon; and former Quebec premier and current speaker of the Senate John Jones Ross. As for the West, Tupper was able to persuade Hugh John Macdonald – Sir John A.'s son – to return to Ottawa from Winnipeg and assume Thomas Daly's spot in cabinet.[64] The rest of Tupper's ministry remained much the same as the last iteration of Bowell's government: Foster and Costigan from New Brunswick; Dickey and (Charlie) Tupper (now solicitor general) from Nova Scotia; Ferguson from PEI; Ives from (English-speaking) Quebec; and Haggart, Smith, Wood, and newcomer David Tisdale from Ontario. Tupper did not seek to adjust the regional balance in any way. The only structural change of note was the re-establishment of the two controller functions and the demotion of Prior and Wood into those positions. Tupper and his ministers were sworn into office on 1 May 1896.

Tupper went into the election with a cabinet that had two more people than in the last election of 1891 under Sir John A. Macdonald. In fact, the cabinet had been entirely overhauled since then, with only Foster and Haggart surviving in their original roles. It was a slightly older cabinet (with an average age of fifty-four), including one member as young as forty-one and two (including Tupper himself) as old as seventy-four. Six were Catholics; three were francophones from Quebec.

1 Prime Minister; Secretary of State of Canada – Charles Tupper, 74, Physician, Nova Scotia, Protestant
2 Agriculture – Walter Montague, 37, Physician, Ontario, Protestant
3 Customs – John Wood, 43, Lawyer, Ontario, Protestant

4 Finance and Receiver General – George Eulas Foster, 48, Professor, New Brunswick, Protestant

5 Inland Revenue – Edward Prior, 43, Land Surveyor, Merchant, British Columbia, Protestant

6 Interior; Indian Affairs – Hugh John Macdonald, 46, Lawyer, Manitoba, Protestant

7 Justice and Attorney General – Arthur Dickey, 41, Lawyer, Nova Scotia, Protestant

8 Leader of the Government in the Senate – Mackenzie Bowell, Publisher, Ontario, Protestant (senator)

9 Marine and Fisheries – John Costigan, 61, Judge, New Brunswick, Catholic

10 Militia and Defence – David Tisdale, 61, Soldier/Businessman, Ontario, Protestant

11 Postmaster General – Louis-Olivier Taillon, 55, Lawyer, Quebec, Catholic

12 President of the Privy Council – Auguste-Réal Angers, 59, Lawyer, Quebec, Catholic (senator)

13 Public Works – Hector Alphonse Desjardins, 41, Editor, Quebec, Catholic (senator)

14 Railways and Canals – John Haggart, 59, Mill Owner, Ontario, Protestant

15 Trade and Commerce; Customs – William Ives, 54, Businessman, Quebec, Protestant

16 Without Portfolio – Donald Ferguson, 57, Farmer, Prince Edward Island, Protestant (senator)

17 Without Portfolio – John Jones Ross, 69, Physician, Quebec, Catholic (senator)

18 Without Portfolio – Frank Smith, 74, Grocer, Ontario, Catholic (senator)

Canada's Seventh Ministry never faced Parliament. Without that constitutional authority, Tupper and his administration could only "carry on the necessary business of the State."[65] The caretaker status did not stop Tupper from consolidating the power of his office *vis-a-vis* cabinet, though, perhaps as a bulwark against the kind of coup that he had just orchestrated. On 1 May, Tupper set out the "Special Prerogatives of the Prime Minister" in one of his first orders-in-council. These included the exclusive right to call cabinet meetings and make key appointments, like cabinet ministers, lieutenant governors, senators, members of key committees like the Treasury Board, Railway, and Internal Economy, deputy ministers, and other key departmental positions. The powers themselves were hardly new (previous prime ministers had exercised them) but the codification was. As such, the 1896 order-in-council represents a major milestone in the centralization of prime ministerial authority in Canada and an important precedent: Laurier's cabinet issued a similar Order in Council in 1896, Borden in 1911, Meighen in 1920, Bennett in 1930, and King in 1935.[66]

Tupper and his ministry spent forty-eight of the fifty-three days between installation and the 23 June election on the campaign trail; the old Ram of Cumberland County himself delivered forty-two stump speeches in Ontario between 8 June and 22 June.[67] The Conservatives did well, collecting 46.3 per cent of the vote overall, while the Liberals took 45.1 per cent. Nothing, however, could stem the Liberal haul of districts. Of the 213 seats up for grabs on 23 June, 118 went Liberal, 88 went Conservative, and 7 other. Four ministers were defeated, including the young newcomer Dickey from Nova Scotia and, tellingly, three francophones from Quebec: Taillon, Angers, and Desjardins.

On 24 June, Tupper admitted defeat – but then did everything in his power to stave off the inevitable. Beginning 25 June, he chaired almost daily cabinet meetings to settle Conservative party accounts before leaving office, including efforts to make 453 appointments.[68] By 4 July, Lord Aberdeen had had enough. In a memo to Tupper and his ministers, Aberdeen said Canada's Seventh Ministry had never held the confidence of Parliament and did not have any powers beyond "the transaction of all necessary public business," including the reappointment of the Angers and Desjardins to the Senate (they had resigned their Senate seats to run for the Commons in the 1896 election) and the appointment of seventeen Conservatives to "new offices or appointments."

On 5 July, Tupper met with Aberdeen at Rideau Hall to plead his case. Tupper argued his ministry had a right to face Parliament and would resign only if it failed to secure Parliament's confidence. In the meantime, Tupper's government had the right "carry on the public business until their successors are appointed, and to fill any vacancies that may exist." Aberdeen refused to budge. He "insist[ed] that popular sovereignty must replace parliamentary sovereignty where the electorate has granted one party an absolute majority of seats in the House of Commons."[69] On these grounds, Aberdeen rejected 17 of 453 submissions from the Privy Council that involved "the creation of new offices or appointments," filling vacancies "for which no provision has been by Parliament," and "superannuations (and the consequential appointments)." These included recommendations to reappoint Angers and Desjardins to the Senate. Tupper finally acknowledged defeat on Tuesday, 8 July 1896, and resigned. Three days later, Aberdeen called upon Wilfrid Laurier to form Canada's Eighth Ministry.

Conclusion

The Abbott, Thompson, Bowell, and Tupper administrations offer useful insight into key elements of prime ministerial statecraft in Canada.

The first element of successful statecraft requires prime ministers to carry out the duties and responsibilities of office in a timely and efficient manner.

The root of Abbott's success was his ability to manage (with Thompson's help) the day-to-day affairs of government, including cleaning up the series of scandals left over from Macdonald and forcing Macdonald's Quebec long-time lieutenant Hector Langevin to resign. By contrast, Bowell's inability to perform basic duties like filling cabinet, parliamentary, and bureaucratic vacancies in a timely manner, let alone more complex ones like negotiating a settlement of the Manitoba Schools Question, served to undermine both caucus and cabinet confidence in his ability to lead.

A second element of successful statecraft requires prime ministers to maintain the support of caucus. Abbott was successful here because he was able to convert his anti-corruption platform into by-election victories for thirty-four caucus members, while Bowell faced caucus revolts in British Columbia and Ontario over his pursuit of a controversial and unpopular policy.

Keeping cabinet colleagues in harness is a third and much more complex requirement of prime ministerial statecraft in Canada. Not only are the stakes higher (as Bowell found out), but the process is complicated by having to heed the rigid conventions of racial, regional, and religious representation. Abbott ran up against these when he was prevented from appointing William Meredith to cabinet because Meredith's brand of ultra-Protestantism would have upset the religious balance then in cabinet. Thompson appeared to get around the conventions when he created three non-cabinet controller positions to infuse new blood into his cabinet. Bowell, however, was forced to scuttle the experiment when British Columbia balked at having anything less than a full seat at the federal cabinet table. Tupper made perhaps the most enduring contribution to managing cabinet personnel during this period despite serving in office for only seventy-eight days. His codification of key powers like calling cabinet meetings and making high-level appointments was a milestone in the consolidation of prime ministerial power in Canada, a precedent followed by five subsequent prime ministers.

A fourth element of prime ministerial statecraft is the ability to win elections. The key to Abbott's success was his ability to translate his government's anti-corruption record into electoral victories. These increased the Conservative majority in the Commons and paved the way for Thompson's ascension by proving that his religious affiliation was not a liability at the ballot box. Bowell's pursuit of remedial legislation, by contrast, produced a handful by-election losses in late 1895. While these did not threaten the legislative majority Abbott had built up, the prospect of losing that majority in the coming general election because of an unpopular policy position precipitated the coup that forced Bowell from office.

Bowell's experience underscores a final lesson about prime ministerial statecraft from the 1891–6 period: there is no single element to success. Satisfying the competing claims and interests of caucus and cabinet requires diligent

management of the day-to-day affairs of government and the pursuit of electorally successful policies all at the same and in real time. It is a complicated and
delicate act in which one misstep can result in disaster.

NOTES

1 *New York Times*, 1 June 1891, 4.
2 Tupper to Charles Hibbert Tupper, 4 June 1891, repr. in E.M. Saunders, *The Life and Letters of the Rt. Hon. Sir Charles Tupper, Bart., K.C.M.G.* (Toronto: Cassell, 1916), 2:154–6.
3 Library and Archives Canada (hereafter "LAC"), Thompson Papers, T.C. Patteson to Thompson, 3, 9 June 1891.
4 LAC, Thompson Papers, 135, Sam Hughes to Thompson, 15 August 1891.
5 This was the advice both Senator C.A. Boulton and T.C. Patteson had given Thompson just before Macdonald died. See LAC, Thompson Papers, 130, Senator Boulton to Thompson, 1 June 1891; and T.C. Patteson to Thompson, 3, 9 June 1891.
6 Two of Abbott's students at McGill were Wilfrid Laurier and Adolphe Caron.
7 *Debates and Proceedings of the Senate of Canada*, 7th parl., 1st sess., 17 June 1891, 96–7.
8 *Debates and Proceedings of the Senate of Canada*, 7th parl., 1st sess., 17 June 1891, 89.
9 *New York Times*, 21 June 1891, 15.
10 See the chapter in this volume by Patrice Dutil. Early appreciations of the topic were done by Norman Rogers: "Federal Influences on the Canadian Cabinet," *Canadian Bar Review* 11, no. 2 (February 1933): 103–21; and "Evolution and Reform of the Canadian Cabinet," *Canadian Bar Review* 11, no. 4 (April 1933): 227–44.
11 Quoted in P.B. Waite, *The Man from Halifax: Sir John Thompson, Prime Minister* (Toronto: University of Toronto Press, 1985), 304.
12 *Debates and Proceedings of the Senate of Canada*, 7th parl., 1st sess., 3 August 1891, 387.
13 Waite, *Man from Halifax*, 308.
14 LAC, Thompson Papers, 135, Sam Hughes to Thompson, 15 August 1891, quoted in Lovell Clark, "A History of the Conservative Administrations, 1891 to 1896" (PhD thesis, University of Toronto, 1968), 61.
15 H. Blair Neatby and John T. Saywell, "Chapleau and the Conservative Party in Quebec," *Canadian Historical Review* 37, no. 1 (March 1956): 16.
16 Joseph Pope, *Memoirs of the Right Honourable Sir John A. Macdonald* (Ottawa: J. Durie and Son, 1894), 2:48–9.
17 LAC, Thompson Papers, 138, Patterson to Thompson, 14 October 1891, quoted in Clark, "Conservative Administrations," 70.
18 LAC, Thompson Papers, W.H. Montague to Foster, 12 June 1891, quoted in Clark, "Conservative Administrations," 62.

19 LAC, Abbott, 1, W.R. Meredith to Abbott, 24 June 1891, quoted in Clark, "Conservative Administrations," 65.

20 Clark, "Conservative Administrations," 106.

21 Editorial, *Montreal Gazette*, 6 June 1892, quoted in Clark, "Conservative Administrations," 107.

22 See "Elections and Candidates," Parliament of Canada, ParlInfo, accessed 30 August 2024, https://lop.parl.ca/sites/ParlInfo/default/en_CA/ElectionsRidings /Elections. Both Waite and Clark provide analyses of these results.

23 LAC, Thompson Papers, 166, Abbott to Thompson, 10 November 1892, quoted in Clark, "Conservative Administrations," 117.

24 LAC, Thompson Papers, 167, Lord Stanley to Thompson, 24 November 1892, quoted in Clark, "Conservative Administrations," 117.

25 The Manitoba government argued that the numbers no longer warranted the separate system: in 1870, there were roughly the same number of French-speaking Roman Catholics as English-speaking Protestants in the province. By the late 1880s, Roman Catholics made up just 13 per cent of the provincial population; French speakers were down to 7 per cent. The legislation – accompanied by a companion piece making English the sole official language – was popular, playing to anti-French and anti-Catholic sentiment on the rise not only in Manitoba but across the country since the Northwest Rebellion in 1885 and the Jesuit Estates Act in 1888.

26 Back in August 1890, Manitoba's Catholic clergy and 4,000 laity had petitioned the Dominion government for remediation under section 22 of the Manitoba Act; a second appeal, organized by Archbishop Taché, was lodged in September 1892; a third, signed by all but one of Canada's Roman Catholic bishops and archbishops, was submitted in November 1892.

27 Said the JCPC, "It is not the law that is in fault. It is owing to religious convictions that everyone must respect, and to the teachings of their Church, that Roman Catholics and members of the Church of England find themselves unable to partake of advantages which the law offers to all alike."

28 Chapleau was not happy. Even though he was set to become lieutenant governor of Quebec in a few days' time, he told Thompson that he could not "consent to shelter the final responsibility of the Council behind a mere judicial interpretation of the statute," and that he would be "missing in my duty if I were to sign any document which would in any way affect my freedom of action in that great and delicate question" (LAC, Thompson Papers, Chapleau to Thompson, 29 December 1892, quoted in Neatby and Saywell, "Chapleau and the Conservative Party," 17).

29 Waite, *Man from Halifax*, 347.

30 Special Senate Committee on Machinery of Government, *Journals of the Senate*, vol. 60 (1919): 343.

31 The office of minister of trade and commerce was created by Macdonald and assented to on 23 June 1887, but was left unproclaimed until 3 December 1892.

32 The role of solicitor general had existed in the old United Province of Canada;
     John Abbott had served as solicitor general for Lower Canada from 1862 to 1863.

33 *Debates of the House of Commons of the Dominion of Canada*, 6th parl., 1st sess.,
     10 June 1887, 863.

34 Clark, "Conservative Administrations," 190.

35 Foster was married to a woman named Addie Chisholm, whose first husband
     had deserted her. Unable to pay for a divorce in Canada, Chisholm had moved
     to Chicago in 1887 to meet that state's requirements for uncontested divorce.
     The couple married in 1889 but were shunned in Ottawa's notoriously catty and
     conservative social circles as many – including Agnes Macdonald and Lord and
     Lady Stanley – judged the divorce illegal and Chisholm a bigamist. See Robert
     Craig Brown, "Foster, Sir George Eulas," in *Dictionary of Canadian Biography*,
     vol. 16, accessed 30 August 2024, https://www.biographi.ca/en/bio/foster_george
     _eulas_16E.html.

36 Haggart had lived apart from his wife since 1872 and maintained a rather
     "Bohemian" life in Ottawa, including having an affair with a former secretary
     whom he had kept on the payroll for months after she had quit. In 1892, Haggart
     had also approved the construction of a new supply canal for the Rideau system –
     the Tay – which just happened to provide a new and enhanced supply to his flour
     mill operation at Perth. See "Bohemian – John Graham Haggart (1836–1913),"
     Perth & District Historical Society, accessed 30 August 2024, https://www
     .perthhs.org/documents/Bohemian-John-Haggart.pdf.

37 Make no mistake: there was nothing daring nor dashing about Mack Bowell.
     No one ever mistook him for a brilliant orator or anything other than a plodding
     and punctilious administrator. But everyone in Ottawa's rarified social circles
     liked his easy manner – and everyone respected him. Thompson, remember, had
     recommended Bowell succeed Abbott in 1892. Even Lady Aberdeen, who judged
     Bowell "rather fussy, & decidedly common place," also admitted that he was "a
     good & straight man and he has great ideas about drawing together of the colonies
     and the Empire, as was evidenced by all the trouble he took about getting up that
     Conference" (Ishbel Gordon, *The Canadian Journal of Lady Aberdeen, 1893–1898*
     [Toronto: Champlain Society, 1960], 166). The Aberdeen outlook is well
     examined in Veronica Strong-Boag, *Liberal Hearts and Coronets: The Lives and
     Times of Ishbel Marjoribanks Gordon and John Campbell Gordon, the Aberdeens*
     (Toronto: University of Toronto Press, 2015).

38 "To Be Sworn in Today," *The Empire*, 21 December 1894, 1.

39 Two good newspaper summaries of the cabinet meetings are "The Order Made,"
     Globe, 20 March 1895, 1; and "School Question," *Daily Mail and Empire*, 22
     March 1895, 1.

40 Charlie Tupper did not see it this way. He said cabinet had settled on the first point
     but had agreed to go to the polls to secure a "direct mandate from the people"
     before proceeding with remediation. In a series of letters, he charged Bowell

with going "behind my back" and getting his "English-speaking colleagues" – that "pack of political micawbers" – to agree to the new session instead. Tupper ended the exchange by resigning, the fifth time he had done so since 1891. It took convincing by party elders Donald Smith and Senator George Drummond to reel Tupper back in. See LAC, Bowell Papers, C.H. Tupper to Bowell, 21 March 1895; Bowell to Tupper, 23 March 1895; Tupper to Bowell, 25 March 1895. Tupper's previous resignations are documented in Clark, "Conservative Administrations," 52, 144, 146, 168.

41 See "The Answer," *Globe*, 14 June 1895, 1; and "At the Capital," *Globe*, 14 June 1895, 5.

42 *Debates of the Senate of the Dominion of Canada*, 7th parl., 5th sess., 22 April 1895, 16.

43 Memorandum of 27 July, in sessional paper no. 39, *Sessional Papers of the Dominion of Canada*, 7th parl., 5th sess., 1895, vol. 11.

44 "The Premier Departs," *Daily Nor'Wester*, 14 September 1895, 1.

45 On this point, see Paul Crunican, *Priests and Politicians: Manitoba Schools and the Election of 1896* (Toronto: University of Toronto Press, 1974), esp. chs. 4, 5; and Neatby and Saywell, "Chapleau and the Conservative Party."

46 See Crunican, *Priests and Politicians*, esp. ch. 4.

47 See "Clarke Wallace," *Globe*, 12 December 1895, 1; "Resist Coercion," *Globe*, 19 December 1895, 8; "Wallace at Home," *Globe*, 20 December 1895, 5; and "Hon. N.C. Wallace," *Evening Star*, 30 December 1895, 1.

48 On the BC caucus revolt and Prior's appointment, see "A New Minister," *Mail and Empire*, 16 December 1895, 1; "At the Capital," *Globe*, 17 December 1895, 1; "Col. Prior's Position," *Daily Colonist*, 18 December 1895, 1–2; "Col. Prior's Standing," *Globe*, 19 December 1895, 1; and "At the Capital," *Globe*, 1 January 1896, 1. The Bowell-Dewdney correspondence is included in "Col. Prior's Standing."

49 "At the Capital," *Globe*, 20 December 1895, 8.

50 Manitoba's 21 December response to the 27 July Order is in Clark, "Conservative Administrations," 422.

51 LAC, Tupper Papers, Dickey to Tupper, 1 November 1895. Reprinted in various sources.

52 The telegrams are included in Saunders, *Life and Letters of the Rt. Hon. Sir Charles Tupper*, 187.

53 Saunders, *Sir Charles Tupper*, 187.

54 On Tupper's 16 December meetings in Ottawa, see his 6 January 1896 letter to Van Horne, included in Saunders, *Sir Charles Tupper*, 190. For additional background, see A.W. Macintosh, "The Career of Sir Charles Tupper" (PhD thesis, University of Toronto, 1960), 413. Tupper would meet with Finance Minister George Foster later in the week.

55 This account is based on "One to Smash," *Globe*, 6 January 1896, 1.

56   The timing of events on Saturday 4 January is from "Cabinet Crisis," *Daily Mail and Empire*, 6 January 1896, 1–2, 8; "One to Smash," *Globe*, 6 January 1896, 1; and George Foster's memorandum to Governor General Aberdeen, included in Wallace Stewart, *The Memoirs of the Rt. Hon. Sir George Foster* (Toronto: Macmillan, 1933), 92–5. The 4 January meeting between Tupper and Bowell is based on "Cabinet Crisis," 1–2.

57   See "Cabinet Crisis," 1–2.

58   Charlie Tupper agreed to sit out for the time being, the logic being one Tupper in cabinet was enough at any given time.

59   The Smith Commission proposed that religious instruction take place within the framework of the public school system established in the Public School Act 1890. Where numbers warranted (at least twenty-five Roman Catholic children in a town or village, fifty in a city), local school boards would provide a schoolhouse or a room where a Roman Catholic teacher could provide religious instruction. Textbooks would have to meet the educational standards of the provincial advisory board and not "offend the religious views of the minority." Catholics would be given representation on the advisory board and on the board of examiners, which certified all teachers. Catholics would be given provincial assistance to maintain a normal school for their teachers. And existing Catholic teachers would be given two years to qualify for credentials. These proposals were similar to those Laurier and Greenway agreed to in November 1896.

60   "No Settlement," *Globe*, 2 April 1896, 1.

61   Lord Aberdeen had sent a note to cabinet the day before, warning that "Parliament had but a week more to run and the Supplementary Estimates had yet to be passed." Many government employees, including parliamentary staff, had not been paid in over a month.

62   Neatby and Saywell, "Chapleau and the Conservative Party," 20.

63   Neatby and Saywell, "Chapleau and the Conservative Party," 21.

64   The courting had begun in January, but Hugh John was not comfortable with Tupper's views on the schools question or a number of specific provisions of the recent remedial bill. Macdonald finally agreed to come aboard on the condition that "the particulars of future remedial legislation" remain an open question to be settled as a later date (Clark, "Conservative Administrations," 495).

65   "At the Capital: Governor-General's Present Authority," *Globe*, 4 May 1896, 7.

66   See James W.J. Bowden, "1896: 'Tu Perds,'" *Dorchester Review* (Autumn/Winter 2019): 32.

67   Not surprisingly, there were only two cabinet meetings in this period – in Ottawa on the morning of 6 May and in Montreal on the afternoon of 5 June. The 6 May meeting focused on firming up plans for the election, while Tupper used the occasion of the Montreal meeting to announce that the Dominion government would assume possession of the Baie des Chaleurs Railway and a number of other local railways in New Brunswick and add them to the Intercolonial system – a

bald play for shoring up Conservative support in eastern Quebec. See "Laurier, Mowat and Victory," *Globe*, 8 June 1896, 7.

68 Said the *Globe*, "Claims for appointments are blowing in from all parts of the Dominion, and even from outside. There are men here from all parts of the country with axes to grind and schemes to put through and appointments to secure. After eighteen years of patronage the hungry crowd are not yet appeased. The Ministers are filching favors right and left. They are trying to create vacancies by superannuation in order to fill the mouths of the greedy" ("Will Resign at Once," *Globe*, 30 June 1893, 2).

69 Bowden, "1896," 38.

5 Pillars and Posts: Wilfrid Laurier's Cabinet Management

J.P. LEWIS

Wilfrid Laurier's management versatility was put to the test in 1907 in dealing with Henry Emmerson, the minister of railways and canals. Born and raised in Maugerville, New Brunswick, Emmerson was as smart as he was entrepreneurial. He took a law degree from Boston University and launched himself in a wide variety of business ventures before he fell into the political game. At age thirty-five, he was elected to the New Brunswick legislative assembly as a Liberal. Within three years he was named chief commissioner for public works in Andrew Blair's government – and he impressed. Blair resigned to join the Laurier government in 1897, and Emmerson was named premier of New Brunswick the following year. He was elected to the House of Commons in 1900, and a few months after Blair was dismissed from his job as minister of railways and canals over serious policy disagreements in 1903, Laurier rather unimaginatively tapped yet another New Brunswick premier to succeed him.

Emmerson, fifty-one, was amiable and dedicated. He was an innovative man and a progressive – promoting women's suffrage with a resolution in the New Brunswick legislature in 1899, when few dared to speak about it. But he had a problem: he drank to excess and had developed a reputation as a womanizer, notably after his wife died in 1901. Time and again, he caused real embarrassment to his colleagues, and Laurier grew weary of him. As a protection, Laurier made him sign the following undertaking: "I hereby pledge my word to Sir Wilfrid Laurier that I will never again taste wine, beer or any other kind of intoxicating liquors, in token of which engagement I place in Sir W.L.'s hands my resignation as a member of the cabinet and minister ———, with the date blank, leaving it to him to fill the blank and act upon it, should I fail in my promise."[1] In April 1907, fed up with revelations in the press, Laurier dated the letter and effectively fired yet another minister of railways and canals from New Brunswick. "I can't go into my ministers' bedrooms and see whether they are sleeping with their own wives or not," Laurier reportedly said.[2] Emmerson had performed well in his role, but in Laurier's view, the performance of a minister was not purely measured by political or policy skills.[3] Emmerson's behaviour now reflected on the entire government, and good management required that Emmerson take his leave. It was the first publicly known case of a minister being dismissed on moral grounds in Canadian political history; it certainly would not be the last.

Laurier had been prime minister for over a decade at that point, long past the point where he needed to take lessons on how to manage a cabinet. He was the seventh prime minister of Canada but had as his role model just one of his predecessors, John A. Macdonald. (Alexander Mackenzie had the merit of showing Laurier how *not* to manage.) Laurier succeeded a turnstile of Conservative prime ministers (four in five years, 1891–6) who had little time to make much of a mark on either institutional or administrative practices. While not dramatically departing from Macdonald's approach, Laurier's tenure did feature several notable innovations in the areas of cabinet nominations, patronage practices, and regional representation. Laurier found greater success once he led the Liberal Party to follow Macdonald's model of patronage; once in power, Laurier and the Liberals used patronage as a tool just as the Conservatives had, and it became the "cement of [the] party."[4] Stewart wrote about the "remarkable similarity in how the [patronage] system worked under Macdonald and Laurier ... in a system that had the same structure in 1912 as it did in the 1880s."[5]

As the leader of cabinet, Laurier gave ministers responsibility and latitude but could pull decision-making to the centre when necessary. Some described Laurier as an "absolute monarch" with a style of "personal government."[6] Chubby Power, who eventually served in Mackenzie King's government, remembered that "one of the things that endeared him to the younger members of the party was his habit of meeting us in the corridors, inviting us into his office to smoke a cigarette ... inquiring about our own studies and our interests ... after ten minutes' talking we returned to the House ready and eager to do anything we possibly could for the leader."[7]

Journalist John W. Dafoe, a close observer of Laurier, described the prime minister's style as a "Personal Government" that relied on charm, diplomacy, and persuasion. This evolved over his tenure in the role: "In the government of 1896 Laurier was only primus inter pares; his associates were in the main contemporary with him in point of years and public service.... In the government of 1911 Laurier was the veteran commander of a company which he had himself recruited."[8] Oscar D. Skelton, who observed Laurier very sympathetically from an academic perch, wrote that "Sir Wilfrid was not a hard taskmaster. He did not intervene in the details of the administration of his colleagues. He believed in giving every minister wide latitude with large responsibility."[9]

Laurier's approach was rooted in the formation of his cabinet. In pursuing a national conciliation, Laurier's personal leadership qualities mattered. In his treatment of Laurier, journalist André Pratte concluded, "Everyone liked Laurier, even those who seriously disagreed with him. It is hard to say what made him so endearing. The man was certainly a model of politeness."[10] Possibly these personality traits made up for any lack of experience in leadership, especially when heading a cabinet that included so many former premiers. Later evaluations suggest that Laurier could quickly revert to an autocratic style of leadership, using his personal charm to present already-made decisions to his cabinet. According to political scientist W.A. Matheson, Laurier maintained harmony "partly through the somewhat contradictory practice of seeing that each minister had a great deal of independence while assuming a highly autocratic stance as master of the whole cabinet."[11]

Born in St-Lin, Quebec, in 1841, Laurier attended the law school at McGill University. He flirted with journalism, opposed Confederation, and opened a small law office in Arthabaska before launching himself in electoral politics on his thirtieth birthday. He was elected to the Quebec legislative assembly but opted to jump to the federal level and join the Alexander Mackenzie sweep in 1874. He would log twenty-two years in the House of Commons, including twelve months as Alexander Mackenzie's minister of inland revenue and nine years as leader of the opposition before becoming prime minister at age fifty-five in June 1896.

While Laurier may have brought a mix of leadership and governance strategies to his executive style, external factors also had an impact on his cabinet management. The external factors Laurier faced were no different from any other post-Confederation government as it had to address an issue that dominated the campaign that brought it to power (in Laurier's case, the Manitoba schools question) and ended up dealing with unexpected policy disputes (Boer War, Grand Trunk Railway, Canada-US trade, creation of the provinces of Alberta and Saskatchewan, foreign policy). The difference is found in Laurier's remarkable ability both to shape cabinet to fit the taste of Canadian voters and to maintain the trust and enduring energies of key individuals who loyally served him over the fifteen years he was in power. He led his party to four majorities, a feat equalled only by Sir John A. Macdonald, but he did so while managing a far more contentious set of issues that could have destroyed his ministry at any given moment. He lost in 1911 because the Liberal coalition fell apart over the notion that Canada should have its own navy and because the business-sector Liberals could not support his reciprocity agreement with the United States. This chapter examines how Laurier succeeded in keeping his cabinet intact for fifteen years and is divided into three sections that focus on cabinet construction, cabinet leadership, and ministerial resignations.

The First Cabinet: The "Ministry of the Talents"

Laurier was helped by facing few threats to his leadership in the beginning. His anointer as Liberal leader, Edward Blake, told supporters, "There is only one possible choice – Laurier."[12] Blake's other most likely successors were Richard

Cartwright and David Mills, and they respectively nominated and seconded Laurier as their new leader. Laurier did not deal with lingering bad political blood from this ascension to leadership. As with later prime ministers, Laurier faced challenges to his leadership from within. Yet, as historian John T. Saywell noted, "although racial and religious questions dominated Canadian politics from 1887 to 1896, he was able to consolidate his position and ... gather strength in all parts of the country."[13]

On 11 July 1896, Laurier unveiled his first cabinet, which has impressed observers and writers ever since. It was called both the "cabinet of all the talents"[14] and "ministry of the talents"[15] and was mythologized for Laurier's unprecedented and never-replicated approach of effecting regional representation in cabinet by cherry-picking multiple premiers from their provinces.[16] Oscar Skelton described the first cabinet as "an extraordinarily able one – none so strong before or since."[17] Almost a half century later, the writer George Bowering would joke in his book on prime ministers, "According to the stories the Liberal party tells itself, his first cabinet was the best ever seen."[18] The talent of the "ministry of the talents" (see image 5.1) is debatable, but its inclusion of former premiers has not been reproduced since.

Laurier's first ministry was composed of the following:

1   Prime Minister; President of the Privy Council – Wilfrid Laurier, 54, Quebec, Catholic
2   Agriculture – Sydney Fisher, 46, Quebec, Protestant
3   Customs – Mackenzie Bowell, 68, Ontario, Protestant
4   Finance and Receiver General – William S. Fielding, 47, Nova Scotia, Protestant*
5   Interior; Indian Affairs; Secretary of State of Canada – Richard W. Scott, 71, Ontario, Catholic (senator)
6   Inland Revenue – Henri Joly de Lotbinière, 66, Quebec, Protestant*
7   Justice and Attorney General – Oliver Mowat, 76, Ontario, Protestant* (senator)
8   Marine and Fisheries – Louis Davies, 51, Prince Edward Island, Protestant
9   Militia and Defence – Frederick Borden, 49, Nova Scotia, Protestant
10 Postmaster General – William Mulock, 53, Ontario, Protestant
11 Public Works – Israël Tarte, 48, Quebec, Catholic
12 Railways and Canals – Andrew Blair, 52, New Brunswick, Protestant*
13 Trade and Commerce – Richard Cartwright, 60, Ontario, Protestant
14 Without Portfolio – Richard Dobell, 60, Quebec, Protestant
15 Without Portfolio – Christophe-Alphonse Geoffrion, 52, Quebec, Catholic

*   denotes former premier

Image 5.1. Laurier's Cabinet of All the Talents, 1896

Source: Library and Archives Canada, item 3000508.

The average age of Laurier's new cabinet members came close to fifty-seven, older than the cabinet led by Tupper, but the key difference was that the prime minister was a full twenty years younger than Tupper had been. A third of them (five) came from Quebec, the same number as Ontario, for the first time in history. Remarkably, there was no representation west of Ontario, nor from Prince Edward Island. It featured former premiers of the country's founding provinces who were immediately admitted to Laurier's trusted inner circle of ministers. But it was not a closed circle. Laurier quickly set about making adjustments to resolve the Manitoba schools crisis. He needed the Manitoba Liberals on board to find a solution and worked hard to recruit Clifford Sifton, the attorney general of Manitoba. It worked, and Sifton was named minister of the interior and superintendent of Indian affairs in November 1896 (only thirty-five, Sifton also reduced the average age of ministers to 55.5, a full four years older than Macdonald's first cabinet). Laurier appointed Sir Oliver Mowat, the elderly premier of Ontario, who had dealt with the issue of French and Catholic education in his own province and was seen as someone who could manage the issue.[19] It took some cajoling, and a seat in the Senate, but Mowat accepted the challenge of finding a solution to the issue. It took a year to get representation in the cabinet for British Columbia, but it was accomplished in June 1897 when William Paterson joined as minister of customs, a post Laurier revived.[20]

Laurier's appointment philosophy stands out among other prime ministers. While there have been moments when prime ministers have reached outside of their caucus or to the provinces, no one else has pursued the approach so aggressively. Dafoe noted that "Laurier knew the kind of government he wanted and he provided himself with such a government by the direct method of getting the colleagues he desired wherever he could find them."[21] Nor was Laurier afraid of appointing ministers who had served in other parties. Cabinet included two former Conservatives, Israël Tarte and Richard Cartwright. David Mills noted that "[no former] first minister has cared so little for those who were his colleagues in opposition."[22] Laurier respected experience, but there were some limits. He did not reappoint Cartwright to the finance portfolio, where he had served under Alexander Mackenzie, because it would send a wrong signal. Instead, Cartwright was given trade and commerce, where he served loyally for the next fifteen years, performing remarkably well.[23]

To build a strong, governing coalition in a fractured country, Laurier felt the need to bring political, sectional and regional factions together, and this inevitably involved what may now appear to be unusual appointments. Part of this approach was related to party-building in the years following Confederation. Both the Conservatives and Liberals were loose political coalitions that mirrored the fractions of the country. Cabinet appointments were a method of reconciling the divisions in the country, and no one was more sensitive to these divisions than Laurier.

Laurier also diverted from precedent in the prime minister's formal role in particular departments. He did not follow Macdonald and Mackenzie's practice of assuming a portfolio, though he did maintain the presidency of the Privy Council and, of course, effectively served as minister of external affairs at a time when relations with London and Washington were particularly fragile.[24] Laurier knew that he could not be an effective prime minister and minister at the same time. He learned from his predecessors, according to Skelton, that leading a department would have meant that something would go undone, "either, as in Mackenzie's day, the work of policy shaping and party guiding or, as in Macdonald's day, the work of the department."[25]

In fact, Laurier's reluctance to take on a portfolio was connected to his appointment of experienced politicians. Laurier used his stars to cover the most important departments. The former premiers would fill major portfolios, including Fielding (finance), Mowat (justice), Joly (controller of inland revenue, though not in cabinet), Blair, and eventually Emmerson (railways). As well, the appointments were a continuation of the dynamics of the 1896 campaign victory, as Laurier had relied on provincial party organizations to help deliver his federal party victory.[26]

While the appointment of former premiers may have appeared to be a daring leadership risk for Laurier, the appointment of Israël Tarte was born of a different political calculation. In Quebec, Tarte had been a Conservative and ultramontane, a Catholic who believed the church should be the dominant institution in society. In the 1891 election, Tarte won a seat as a Liberal and easily became the flashiest MP from Quebec, especially in pinning contract scandals on Conservatives such as cabinet minister Hector-Louis Langevin and member of Parliament Thomas McGreevy. Tarte played the key role in orchestrating the transformative campaign in Quebec in 1896. In a biography of Laurier, Joseph Schull described Tarte as a "renegade Bleu" who had "beheaded his old party."[27] His reward was the public works portfolio. Tarte saw himself in a partnership with Laurier; he once wrote to the Liberal leader, "with your eloquence and your unblemished reputation, we can stir up many things."[28] Tarte envisioned an alliance with Oliver Mowat – "un parti appuyé sur le Bas Canada et sur le parti Mowat dans l'Ontario" – that could push the Conservatives out of power for years.[29] Tarte may have been the first minister to benefit from delivering projects to local communities on a grand scale – the government spent more than four times as much in 1900 than it had in 1867 ($55.5 million).[30] With powerful ministers such as Sifton and Tarte, Laurier's cabinet was the start of the golden age of regional ministers who also fuelled regional election campaigns with pork barrelling and patronage.

While Laurier's cabinet construction may have featured many innovations, its composition was similar to those that came before. Canada's first francophone prime minister did not increase Quebec representation, which may have been the consequence of having a prime minister from that province. (Ontarians often complained that they were underrepresented in cabinet in Sir John A. Macdonald's day.) The last two columns of Table 5.1 present the portfolio and ministerial turnover. In comparing the lengthy Macdonald and Laurier ministries it is clear that Laurier's ministers had longer staying power in both their portfolios and in cabinet. The net effect was an empowered ministerial environment where confidence in the prime minister's judgment reigned.

Five ministers served the entire ministry (or very nearly) in the same portfolio: Frederick Borden (militia and defence), Richard Cartwright (trade and commerce), William Fielding (finance), Sydney Fisher (agriculture), and William Paterson (customs). Richard Scott served as secretary of state for Canada for twelve years. Together, they constituted the veritable pillars of the Laurier ministry. Their endurance provided stability and predictability to policymaking as well as to the service delivery process. Others may not have been pillars but were certainly solid posts. William Mulock served as postmaster general for a full nine years. Rodolphe Lemieux and Louis-Philippe Brodeur served for seven years, and Frank Oliver for six years. Still others served for three to five years.

Laurier's cabinet also showed a few additional particularities, in comparison with his predecessors. It was older, more likely to include lawyers and more likely to include men who logged more years in the ministry than before.

Table 5.1. Cabinet Representation

Ministry	Average Age entering cabinet	Law Background (%)	Quebec Representation	Time in Portfolio	Time in Ministry
Macdonald (First)	50.8	50	0.34	0.34	0.46
Mackenzie	48.5	59	0.42	0.40	0.49
Macdonald (Second)	50.7	50	0.33	0.27 (3.37 years)	0.23
Abbott	53.0	60	0.24	0.57	0.76
Thompson	52.2	67	0.31	1.00	1.00
Bowell	52.5	55	0.24	0.88	0.79
Tupper	53.1	59	0.29	1.00	1.00
Laurier	55.5	65	0.30	0.32 (4.86 years)	0.42

Quebec Representation – average Quebec minister days divided by all cabinet days
Time in Portfolio – average portfolio days divided by ministry days
Time in Ministry – average ministry days per minister divided by ministry days
*Data drawn from Parlinfo, the Library of Parliament online database

Laurier's "Personal Government"

Laurier had a reputation for trusting ministers and commanding power. He was comfortable delegating major policy files to his ministers but would still pull in the reins when he desired a certain outcome. Laurier's cabinet has been depicted as part of a "golden age" of Canadian cabinets, when the phrase *first among equals* was close to a reality in practice. When Donald Savoie talked about the way cabinet "once was," he reached back to Clifford Sifton, most notably on the immigration file.[31] "Ottawa has had powerful ministers through the ages," Savoie observed. "They had their own brands and could point to major accomplishments that they had successfully promoted and that became part of their brand."[32] Practically speaking, Laurier's cabinet meetings were described to have a "senior management" type setting.[33] "In cabinet councils he never played the dictator," Skelton explained.

> Each minister in turn would state his point of view on this side and on that, while he himself sat silent or with only a guiding or inquiring word, until every opinion had been set out, when he would sum up the discussion, with rarely erring faculty for getting to the heart of the issue, and give his conclusions as to the course to follow.[34]

Every minister was also given to a different style. Some ministers could accumulate power through the means of their ministerial assignment. The

Department of the Interior was essentially viewed as a western portfolio. Political scientist Herman Bakvis described Sifton as "the figure who came closest to being a regional overlord." Using the so-called Sifton's Army of officials, Sifton used his department "to pursue his vision of the Canadian west." This was, in Bakvis's words, "a harbinger of the ministerial entrepreneurship that would arrive later under Mackenzie King."[35]

With these high-profile appointments came expectations of new political partnerships. Not only did these ministers receive important portfolios, but they were also responsible for patronage distribution in their respective regions.[36] Patronage in the West and in Quebec would be assumed by newcomers to federal office, Clifford Sifton and Israël Tarte, whose appointments received critical attention. The press presented Mowat's role as the equivalent to what George-Étienne Cartier had been to John A. Macdonald, with some even describing it as the "Laurier-Mowat administration."[37]

The role of patronage provided ministers with sources of power and influence. Clifford Sifton noted that everywhere he went, "the job-hunters descended upon him, singly, in droves and in battalions."[38] The Department of the Interior was a patronage machine, with the minister receiving hundreds of letters from job seekers.[39] "Laurier preferred men who thought as he did and who were less likely to rock the boat," D.J. Hall wrote in his biography of Clifford Sifton. "Sifton not only radiated power and authority, and inevitably appeared to be a rival, but he also had his own pronounced ideas and attracted controversy."[40] Sifton and Laurier's policy disagreement existed on the details of the separate schools issue and provincial versus federal control; in fact, when Laurier accepted Sifton's resignation, he acknowledged the "differences between us, were more of words than of substance."[41] Still, Sifton did not appreciate Laurier's appeal as much as others:

I was not Sir Wilfrid Laurier's colleague for eight years without finding out that he is, despite his courtesy and gracious charm, a masterful man set on having his own way, and equally resolute that his colleagues shall not have their way unless this is quite agreeable to him. I had a good many experiences of the difficulty in getting my policies accepted and acted upon where they did not make a special appeal to him; I should perhaps never have been successful in giving effect to some of the things upon which my heart was set if I had not had in the cabinet three or four associates who backed me up, and who I in turn backed up. At that, with a smile and a laugh that was in part a chuckle, the old chief was very frequently too much for all of us.[42]

In the stand-off between Sifton and Laurier on the use of French in the new provinces of Alberta and Saskatchewan, Sifton lost.

So, there is mixed evidence that Laurier was leading a truly "golden age" of cabinet. If a "golden age" of cabinet meant that ministers were equal to the prime minister, Laurier's actions do not entirely fit that classification. Laurier was more in control than Savoie imagines. A trusting leader, Laurier's diplomacy and collegial style masked his centralizing actions that would help solidify the strong prime ministerial role that John A. Macdonald had introduced in 1867. Laurier made sure his ministers knew he had the last word but allowed for some freedom for ministers on policymaking within their department, outside of major issues.[43] Every case was different. While Laurier deferred to ministers, he did impose his views. When Postmaster General Mulock attempted to dismiss the Montreal postmaster unilaterally he soon received word from the prime minister's office that it was either Mulock or the postmaster, an ultimatum from which he hastily retreated.[44]

The experienced cabinet caused headaches for Laurier. At times he was "so strained and wracked by the mere work of peacemaking that the issue itself was obscured for him" observed Joseph Schull in his still-commanding biography.[45] The issue of free trade divided major ministers, with Sifton in favour and Tarte opposed. When Laurier faced the decision of involvement in the Boer War, he found his cabinet divided along linguistic lines – English ministers supported involvement while French ministers were against, while Cartwright and Fielding tried to reconcile the two groups.[46] Day-long cabinet debates ensued, punctuated by Ontario minister William Mulock's storming out of the meeting.[47]

As with other long-serving prime ministers who would follow him, Laurier's grip on power appeared to tighten over time. With the exit of original ministerial colleagues and the growing tenure of the unelected inner circle, this evolution would become a common feature for most prime ministers. After the exit of Blair, Sifton, and Tarte, Laurier's dominance over his government gained attention. "The Premier is almost the absolute ruler of the country," the *Toronto News* noted on 28 November 1905. "Our Premier is really a species of absolute monarch of the medieval type."[48] Dutil argued that in "his fifteen years as prime minister, Laurier energized the centralizing forces of power … Laurier favoured trusted advisors and experts to join the team of deputy ministers … Laurier created a cult of personality."[49]

Breaking Faith: Laurier's Approach to Dissenting Ministers

Laurier subscribed to the notion that "practical politics mean that you must deal with men such as you find them and not such as you would like them to be."[50] Unlike Laurier's ministerial pillars who stayed in the government, some of cabinet's powerful regional ministers went a step too far in exercising their political and policy independence. Laurier's most lasting imprint on cabinet governance in Canada may have been his handling of ministerial responsibility, both individually and collectively. He did not face an event of the level of the Pacific Scandal or a coup to unseat him as Mackenzie Bowell had endured but did experience three policy disputes that were resolved with the departures of important ministers. The cases of Israël Tarte, Andrew Blair, and Clifford Sifton demonstrated the limits of Laurier's tolerance.

Tarte, already one of Laurier's riskiest cabinet appointments, was the first to cross the prime minister. From the moment he switched to the Liberals, Tarte's position in the party was tenuous, as many of his views ran against those of Ontario and Quebec Liberals – part of the intra-party coalition Laurier was attempting to maintain. When Laurier appointed Tarte to the public works portfolio, he said, "So long as I have Tarte and Sifton with me, I shall be master of Canada."[51] Often, the opposition pounced on Tarte's major role in the Laurier government, calling it the "Tarte government" and Tarte the "Master of the Administration," with some in media describing Tarte as "virtually the leader."[52] While Tarte may have threatened to resign over Canadian participation in the Boer War, it would be his views on free trade that would bring about his ministerial demise.[53]

In the summer of 1902, when the prime minister's health forced a European vacation, Tarte found space to publicly oppose the government's position on tariffs, launching a protectionist campaign in Ontario against Laurier's position on free trade with the United States. "Sweating, puffing, panting, he did not merely run, he flew, he whirled, from North Bay to Essex," in the words of one newspaper.[54] At a banquet for the Canadian Manufacturers' Association, he declared that if he were the head of government, he "would take the tariff item by item and adjust it so as to save to Canada the profit of the exportation of her resources and build up a nation here."[55] Tarte's actions were disavowed by his cabinet colleagues; Sifton told the *Globe* that Tarte spoke for himself, and Cartwright praised Sifton's defence of the ministry.[56] "Everyone who knows anything of the most elementary principles governing ministerial responsibility … must stand appalled at the apparently utter disregard by the Minister of Public Works," Andrew Blair, minister of railways and canals, wrote in a twelve-page memo to Laurier.[57] Returning in October, the prime minister demanded Tarte's resignation. Laurier's letters to Tarte were telling. The minister's actions were, Laurier wrote, "a self-evident violation of your duty towards the government of which you were a member." Tarte had been unable to convince his colleagues of his views, leaving him with two options: "either to accept their own views or to sever your connection with them, and then for the first time would you have been free to place your views before the public."[58] Within days Tarte resigned with a reminder from Laurier on collective cabinet responsibility: "The first thing for you to do as a member of the Government, before addressing your views to the public would have been to place them before your colleagues with the object of obtaining the unanimous action of the Cabinet which is the very foundation of responsible government."[59] Tarte left the government and returned to the Conservative Party and to his role as the director of *La patrie,* the Montreal daily newspaper long associated with Liberalism (the connection with the party was broken for good).[60]

Andrew Blair, who had taken a lead in criticizing Tarte's actions, would also find himself out of cabinet over a policy dispute. Blair was minister of railways when he could not support the government's position on the crucial issue of railway transportation and the Pacific Grand Trunk being built from Winnipeg to the west coast. Blair took issue not only with the policy option but also with the process, particularly Laurier's decision to consult with other ministers on the issue and begin negotiations long before telling Blair.[61] Blair quit cabinet two weeks before the legislation was introduced to Parliament. The loss of the minister of railways days before the government brought its railway policy to the House was certainly problematic. *Globe* reporter M.O. Hammond noted in his diary, "Blair never expected his resignation to be accepted, but in reality, Laurier was glad to get it."[62]

Laurier's other major cabinet confrontation came in 1905 over his disagreement with a compromise that guaranteed French-language education in the new provinces of Alberta and Saskatchewan. Cabinet was not consulted on legislation that provided for the creation of the provinces. As with Blair's resignation, this was not just a policy difference but also a question of Laurier's dominance in drafting the legislation. Sifton had been at odds with the government on the issue of provincial autonomy on education and did not see the bill until it was introduced in the House on 21 February 1905. Laurier's minister of justice, Charles Fitzpatrick, drafted the bill, and some suggest Sifton was left out because he hated Fitzpatrick. The feeling was mutual. "As long as Sifton is in the cabinet, we are sitting on a powderkeg," Fitzpatrick was overheard saying.[63]

William Fielding was concerned about the break. "It is being strongly urged upon me, and with apparent reason that any further break in the ranks of the Government would lead to the collapse of the Liberal party," he told Sifton.[64] Not only did Laurier lose his most powerful western minister, but he may have almost lost his finance minister. Laurier did change course, and no separate francophone Catholic schools were created in the new provinces of Saskatchewan and Alberta, though such services could be petitioned. When the legislation was introduced, Sifton was ill and recuperating outside of Ottawa. Six days later, Sifton wrote a brief resignation letter to Laurier: "I have arrived at the conclusion that it is impossible for me to continue in office under present circumstances and that it is better for all concerned that I should act at once."[65]

Taken together the trio of ministerial resignations could be evidence of the "golden age" of cabinet, but not in the sense Savoie envisioned it as cabinet government where the prime minister acts as first among powerful ministerial equals. Rather, the resignations could be seen as a "golden age" when ministers followed the idealized interpretation of collective cabinet responsibility and left the ministry when they could not agree with the government policy positions or actions.

Shuffles

Remarkably, there were no major shuffles in the fifteen years that Laurier was in power. Changes were numerous, but changes of portfolio were precise, typically carried out when a minister retired or was promoted to the bench. With the departure of Oliver Mowat, Laurier secured strong Ontario representation in University of Toronto vice chancellor William Mulock. After the death of Christophe-Alphonse Geoffrion in 1899, Laurier appointed Michel Bernier, another Quebecker. Between 1900 and 1904, Laurier lost influential ministers Blair and Tarte, but added long-serving Quebec MP Louis-Philippe Brodeur and former premier of New Brunswick Henry Emmerson as replacements. Laurier added lesser-known politicians Charles Murphy and Henri Béland before the 1908 and 1911 elections.

In the case of some ministerial departures, Laurier personally assumed the portfolio. He served as minister of the interior and superintendent general of Indian affairs for a few weeks in March–April 1905 after Clifford Sifton left and as minister of marine and fisheries in January 1906 after Raymond Préfontaine died. To put a Quebec-friendly face on the cabinet in anticipation of the election of September 1911, he moved Rodolphe Lemieux into the Naval Service Department and replaced Lemieux as postmaster general with Dr. Henri S. Béland.

Conclusion

According to Skelton, "The Laurier administration contained many men of strong will who had for years been autocrats in their own fields."[66] The durability of key ministers clearly set the tone of Laurier's government, while he succeeded in keeping Canada together and moving on major policy files. His cabinets may be remembered for his high-profile appointments, though some of those appointees challenged the prime minister on policy and soon found themselves out of cabinet.

Laurier had the confidence of a deeply loyal cabinet – men who enjoyed working with him and who respected him. They were the pillars and the posts that anchored the prime minister and allowed him to remain productive and innovative. He created a new Department of Mines in 1907, a Department of Labour in 1900 (the cabinet portfolio would come in 1909), and a Department of External Affairs in 1909. In 1910, a navy was founded. In 1910–11, he actively supported William Fielding in negotiating a reciprocity agreement with the United States, the culmination of many diplomatic breakthroughs with the emerging world power.[67] By 1911, Laurier had become indispensable to the

Liberal Party, and an error was likely made in that no new recruits were invited to bolster the now (misleadingly named) "one-man party."[68] The Liberal Party lost many seats in Quebec on the naval issue and in the rest of the country on apprehensions that Laurier's Reciprocity Treaty would spell the end of Canada's independence in economic policy.[69]

Through the fifteen years of his government, different individuals became influential and powerful ministers. Skelton, always in admiration, noted that "the new [Laurier] ministers at Ottawa ... were not content to the be 'merely flies on the wheel.'"[70] While most cabinets have included people who were deeply experienced in the ways of Ottawa, Laurier made his mark at first by attracting leaders from other jurisdictions, and did so repeatedly afterwards.

Laurier made cabinet management look easy, but his experience should be remembered as a crucial turning point in the history of statecraft in Canada. His leadership empowered ministers through strategic personal charm and diplomacy, which enhanced their competence and experience. The cabinets he constructed, starting with his first, would suggest that ministries can be built through strategic regional, provincial, sectional, and partisan appointments. Laurier emulated Macdonald while adapting the most powerful institution in the country to fit his leadership style and political needs. As Canada's fourth longest-serving prime minister, he played an essential role in how his successors would behave, regardless of whether they followed his precedents and process as first minister. It was a lesson absorbed by Mackenzie King, in particular, and to lasting effect. As Macdonald's approach to patronage influenced Laurier, so too did Laurier's approach influence Mackenzie King. The Laurier influence on King would be filtered through a more pragmatic lens but still contribute to the deployment of patronage after the public administration reforms of the Civil Service Act 1918.[71]

NOTES

1 Oscar Douglas Skelton, *Life and Letters of Sir Wilfrid Laurier* (London: Oxford University Press, 1922), 2:263.

2 Sandra Gwyn, *The Private Capital: Ambition and Love in the Age of Macdonald and Laurier* (Toronto: McClelland & Stewart, 1984), 418.

3 See Wendell E. Fulton, "Emmerson, Henry Robert," in *Dictionary of Canadian Biography*, vol. 14, accessed 30 August 2024, https://www.biographi.ca/en/bio/emmerson_henry_robert_14E.html.

4 Gordon Stewart, *The Origins of Canadian Politics: A Comparative Approach* (Vancouver: University of British Columbia Press, 1986), 74.

5 Gordon Stewart, "Political Patronage under Macdonald and Laurier, 1878–1911," *American Review of Canadian Studies* 10, no. 1 (1980): 3–26.

6 John W. Dafoe, *Laurier: A Study in Canadian Politics* (Toronto: Thomas Allen, 1922), 83–4.

7 *A Party Politician: The Memoirs of Chubby Power*, ed. Norman Ward (Toronto: Macmillan, 1966), 73.

8 Dafoe, *Laurier*, 83. Laurier is nicknamed the "Master of the Administration" in Skelton, *Life and Letters*, 2:88.

9 Skelton, *Life and Letters*, 2:70.

10 André Pratte, *Wilfrid Laurier* (Toronto: Penguin Books, 2011), 30.

11 W.A. Matheson, *The Prime Minister and the Cabinet* (Toronto: Methuen, 1976), 140. Patrice Dutil locates a turning point in Laurier's attitude at the turn of the century, when the cabinet issued a greater number of orders-in-council. See Dutil, *Prime Ministerial Power in Canada: Its Origins under Macdonald, Laurier, and Borden* (Vancouver: University of British Columbia Press, 2017), 271.

12 Skelton, *Life and Letters*, 1:341.

13 John T. Saywell, "The Cabinet of 1896," in *Cabinet Formation and Bicultural Relations: Seven Case Studies*, ed. Frederick W. Gibson (Ottawa: Queen's Printer, 1970), 37.

14 John Herd Thompson and Allen Seager, *Canada: Decades of Discord, 1922–1939* (Toronto: McClelland & Stewart, 1985).

15 D.J. Hall, *Clifford Sifton*, vol. 1, *The Young Napoleon, 1861–1900* (Vancouver: University of British Columbia Press, 1981), 133.

16 Robert Borden attempted to replicate Laurier's "cabinet of talents" by inviting four premiers into his first cabinet but managed to land only one, New Brunswick's John Hazen. See Herman Bakvis, *Regional Ministers: Power and Influence in the Canadian Cabinet* (Toronto: University of Toronto Press, 1991).

17 Skelton, *Life and Letters*, 2:5.

18 George Bowering, *Egotists and Autocrats: The Prime Ministers of Canada* (Toronto: Penguin Books, 1999), 134.

19 Joseph Schull, *Laurier: The First Canadian* (Toronto: Macmillan, 1966), 323. Laurier told Mowat's nephew, John S. Ewart, "It would be a pleasure for me to make any sacrifice in order to induce Sir Oliver to enter federal politics." See A. Margaret Evans, *Sir Oliver Mowat* (Toronto: University of Toronto Press, 1992), 328.

20 Customs was handled by a controller of customs, a position without cabinet rank, from 1892 to 1897.

21 Dafoe, *Laurier*, 67.

22 H. Blair Neatby, *Laurier and a Liberal Quebec: A Study in Political Management* (Toronto: McClelland & Stewart, 1973), 125.

23 Mary O. Hill, *Canada's Salesman to the World: The Department of Trade and Commerce, 1892–1939* (Montreal: McGill-Queen's University Press, 1977).

24 Dutil, *Prime Ministerial Power*.

25 Skelton, *Life and Letters*, 2:2.

26 Ken Carty, *Big Tent Politics: The Liberal Party's Long Mastery of Canada's Public Life* (Vancouver: University of British Columbia Press, 2015), 23–4.

27 Schull, *Laurier*, 323. Fred Schindeler wrote, "[With Laurier] there was no need for a French lieutenant since the Prime Minister was himself a French Canadian. But Sir Wilfrid Laurier did not need an English co-leader either and instead treated his English Canadian colleagues as spokesmen of their respective provinces and sections, reserving for himself the position of chief spokesman for 'La Belle Province'" (Fred Schindeler, "The Prime Minister and the Cabinet: History and Development," in *Apex of Power: The Prime Minister and Political Leadership in Canada*, 2nd ed., ed. Thomas A. Hockin [Scarborough: Prentice-Hall, 1977], 36).

28 Neatby, *Laurier and a Liberal Quebec*, 80.

29 Evans, *Sir Oliver Mowat*, 325.

30 Michael Bliss, *Right Honourable Men: The Descent of Canadian Politics from Macdonald to Chrétien* (Toronto: HarperCollins, 2004), 48.

31 Donald Savoie, *Democracy in Canada: The Disintegration of Our Institutions* (Montreal: McGill-Queen's University Press, 2019), 118.

32 Savoie, *Democracy in Canada*, 220.

33 Laurier's cabinet would meet daily except for Dominion Day, Christmas Eve, and New Year's Eve (Dutil, *Prime Ministerial Power*, 257).

34 Skelton, *Life and Letters*, 2:70.

35 Bakvis, *Regional Ministers*, 32, 38.

36 Laurier's willingness to delegate patronage to ministers was even codified in a 1904 order-in-council: "In the case of members of the Cabinet, while all have an equal degree of responsibility in a constitutional sense, yet in practical working out of responsible government in a country of such vast extent as Canada, it is found necessary to attach a special responsibility to each minister for the public affairs of the province or district with which he has close political connections." See Bakvis, *Regional Ministers*, 28.

37 Bakvis, *Regional Ministers*, 27.

38 Hall, *Clifford Sifton*, 1:124.

39 D.J. Hall, *Clifford Sifton*, vol. 2, *A Lonely Eminence, 1901–1929* (Vancouver: University of British Columbia Press, 1985).

40 Hall, *Clifford Sifton*, 1:161

41 Hall, *Clifford Sifton*, 1:176

42 Paul Stevens, "Wilfrid Laurier: Politician," in *Political Ideas of the Prime Ministers of Canada*, ed. Marcel Hamelin (Ottawa: Éditions de l'Université d'Ottawa, 1969), 73–4.

43 Laurier L. LaPierre, *Sir Wilfrid Laurier and the Romance of Canada* (Toronto: Stoddart, 1996), 226.

44 Schull, *Laurier*.

45 Schull, *Laurier*, 340.

46 LaPierre, *Sir Wilfrid Laurier*, 267.

47 C.P. Stacey, *Canada and the Age of Conflict: A History of Canadian External Policies*, vol. 1, *1867–1921* (Toronto: University of Toronto Press, 1977).

48 Dutil, *Prime Ministerial Power*, 118.
49 Dutil, *Prime Ministerial Power*, 99.
50 Stevens, "Wilfrid Laurier: Politician," 76.
51 Cited in Patrice Dutil and David MacKenzie, *Canada 1911: The Decisive Election That Shaped the Country* (Toronto: Dundurn, 2011), 24. Laurier's "right-hand man" in the West, Clifford Sifton played a central role on the federal government's expansion into the Prairies and Northwest. See Richard Clippingdale, *Laurier: His Life and World* (Toronto: McGraw-Hill Ryerson, 1979), 178.
52 Neatby, *Laurier and a Liberal Quebec*, 135.
53 At the peak of the debate, Tarte was reported to whisper to Laurier, "I may well have to resign." See LaPierre, *Sir Wilfrid Laurier*, 267.
54 Skelton, *Life and Letters*, 2:179.
55 Skelton, *Life and Letters*, 2:74.
56 Hall, *Clifford Sifton*, 2:92.
57 Dutil, *Prime Ministerial Power*, 232.
58 Skelton, *Life and Letters*, 2:76.
59 Dutil, *Prime Ministerial Power*, 232.
60 On the politics of Tarte and *La Patrie*, see Patrice Dutil, *Devil's Advocate: Godfroy Langlois and the Politics of Liberal Progressivism in Laurier's Quebec* (Montreal: Robert Davies, 1994).
61 Skelton, *Life and Letters*, 2:80.
62 Gwyn, *Private Capital*, 416–17.
63 Gwyn, *Private Capital*, 417.
64 Bruce Fergusson, *Rt. Hon. W.S. Fielding*, vol. 2, *Mr. Minister of Finance* (Windsor, NS: Lancelot Press, 1971), 38.
65 Quoted in J. Castell Hopkins, *The Canadian Annual Review of Public Affairs, 1905* (Toronto: Annual Review, 1906), 27.
66 Skelton, *Life and Letters*, 2:70.
67 See Patrice Dutil and David MacKenzie, "The Origins of Reciprocity Revisited: Canadian-American Rapprochement in the Era of Laurier and Taft," in *Trade-Offs: The History of Canada-US Trade Negotiations*, ed. Mark S. Bonham (Toronto: Canadian Business History Association, 2019), 61–82.
68 Skelton, *Life and Letters*, 2:89. After the 1911 election, a young minister in the Laurier cabinet, Mackenzie King, wrote, "We are nearing the close of the Laurier Administration" (Dutil and MacKenzie, *Canada 1911*, 289).
69 See Dutil and MacKenzie, *Canada, 1911*.
70 Oscar D. Skelton, *The Day of Sir Wilfrid Laurier: A Chronicle of Our Own Times* (Toronto: Glasgow, Brook, 1920), 220–1.
71 John Courtney, "Prime Ministerial Character: An Examination of Mackenzie King's Political Leadership," *Canadian Journal of Political Science* 9, no. 1 (1976): 77–100.

6 The Outsider: Robert Borden and His Cabinet

JOHN ENGLISH

Robert Borden served longer as leader of the Opposition in the Canadian House of Commons before he became prime minister than any other Canadian politician. A wealthy Halifax lawyer pushed into politics by his fellow Nova Scotian Charles Hibbert Tupper, he lost elections in 1904 and 1908. Unsurprisingly, diverse opponents challenged his leadership in 1910. His Conservative colleagues blamed him for ignoring caucus and announcing policies without proper consultation. They were correct. In his excellent biography of Borden, Craig Brown notes that his caucus found Borden in those Opposition days "distant, moody, imperious, sometimes almost scornful of their worth." He made policy with outsiders, businessmen, journalists, provincial potentates, men who understood little and cared less about the demands, the whims, and the welfare of the parliamentary party.[1] Borden almost lost the party leadership in 1910. He survived, but his tendency to reach outside the caucus endured. In 1911, "outsiders" including prominent Liberals, business leaders, provincial leaders, Quebec nationalists, and former Liberal minister Sir Clifford Sifton rallied behind Borden's attack on Sir Wilfrid Laurier's support for a reciprocal trade agreement with the United States. The coalition was a rickety structure but strong enough to gain victory in the general election on 21 September 1911.[2]

Borden has been described more recently as "deeply conservative," but the label does not fit well around his attitudes and actions as a political leader.[3] The description judges Borden by the wealthy ministers he chose, and the business leaders he favoured, but it fails to capture how much he stood apart from them and others. The "deeply conservative" Borden fought the 1911 election against reciprocity and Laurier's Canadian navy as opposed to a massive transfer to London to help the British build dreadnoughts. And yet he had considered reciprocity himself only three years earlier and had made an electoral pact with the Quebec nationalists, who opposed any contribution to the British navy. Among MPs in his first years, he was probably closest to his first cousin, Frederick Borden, Laurier's minister of militia, a *bon vivant* medical doctor and entrepreneur, but the relationship was not close.[4] He was extraordinarily tolerant when opinions were expressed that a Conservative normally did not share and could not express. When Sifton, angered by British incompetence and arrogance during the war years, told Borden that he thought that Canada should become independent, Borden noted it in his diary without comment.[5] The cluster of imperial and national ideas that surrounded Canadian conservatism in later Victorian and early Edwardian Canada did not fasten themselves tightly upon Borden as they did for many of his colleagues. In political scientist Philip Converse's terms describing political beliefs, Borden was at best a "near ideologue" who did not cling to a consistent set of beliefs or define himself by reference to a specific group. While his predecessor Laurier wrestled intellectually with the meaning of liberalism in the nineteenth century and Mackenzie King wrote a book expressing his vision of a new liberalism for the twentieth century, Borden did not muse about what conservativism meant in his times.[6]

Borden was the second prime minister born and raised outside Quebec and Ontario (John Thompson was the first, serving from 1892 to 1894) and that had a part in shaping his ideas of statecraft. Borden was born on 26 June 1854 in Grand Pré, Nova Scotia, to a family that had come from the United States to Nova Scotia before the Loyalists. He was deeply proud of his origins, but he was determined at an early age not to work the land as his ancestors had or to be the village stationmaster that his father, who shared his distaste for farm life, had become. He did well in school, but formal education ended when he was only fourteen when his favourite teacher left Grand Pré for a teaching position in the United States. So impressive was Borden's performance that the school appointed him as the teacher's replacement. Four years later in 1872, the teacher, Arthur Hamilton, persuaded Borden to join him as a teacher at Glenwood Institute in Matawan, New Jersey, as a professor of classics and mathematics. The title was impressive but his experience in the United States was not. He returned to Nova Scotia determined to be a lawyer.[7]

Borden became a highly intelligent lawyer, who acquired his skills entirely by articling rather than in a classroom. Although he was at the peak of the legal profession in Halifax and was president of the Nova Scotia Barristers' Society, Borden did not engage in or follow closely the debates about "science," law, and the legal profession that were occurring throughout North America in the late nineteenth century when he entered Canadian politics. He had an outstanding but not innovative mind, one that inclined towards the practical rather than the theoretical. After losing the 1904 election, he wrote to journalist John Willison, "My habit of mind is to dwell upon the past only so far as may be necessary to point the path for the future."[8] In that campaign,

Borden had advocated the building of a government-owned railway, which he expanded in 1907 to advocacy of a degree of public ownership in national franchises and eventual public ownership of telephones and telegraphs. The wealthy Harvard-educated Montreal MP Herbert Ames told Borden that Montreal "commercial and financial men condemn this plank as a step towards socialism." They regarded it as "a bit of [Theodore] Rooseveltism."[9] It was neither, but it was not conservative. It reflected a pragmatic approach to the compelling changes occurring in the way Canadians lived in the first decade of the twentieth century as automobiles began to shape cities, pilots took flight, telephones transformed communications, and thousands of immigrants landed weekly. And then came war.

The 1911 cabinet was composed of men with an average age of 55.5, the same as Laurier's first cabinet in 1896 and two years younger than the prime minister. There was no representation from Saskatchewan or Prince Edward Island. Ontario recovered its dominance with seven members, followed with five (including three francophones) from Quebec:

1 Prime Minister; External Affairs; President of the Privy Council – Robert Laird Borden, 57, Nova Scotia
2 Agriculture – Martin Burrell, 53, British Columbia
3 Customs – John D. Reid, 52, Ontario
4 Finance and Receiver General – William Thomas White, 44, Ontario
5 Indian Affairs; Interior – Robert Rogers, 47, Manitoba
6 Inland Revenue; Mines – Bruno Nantel, 53, Quebec
7 Justice and Attorney General – Charles Joseph Doherty, 56, Quebec
8 Labour – Thomas Wilson Crothers, 61, Ontario
9 Marine and Fisheries; Naval Service – Douglas Hazen, 51, New Brunswick
10 Militia and Defence – Sam Hughes, 58, Ontario
11 Postmaster General – Louis-Philippe Pelletier, 54, Quebec
12 Public Works – Frederick D. Monk, 55, Quebec
13 Railways and Canals – Francis Cochrane, 58, Ontario
14 Secretary of State of Canada – William J. Roche, 69, Manitoba
15 Trade and Commerce – George Eulas Foster, 64, Ontario
16 Without Portfolio – George H. Perley, 54, Quebec
17 Without Portfolio – Albert E. Kemp, 53, Ontario
18 Without Portfolio – James Alexander Lougheed, 57, Alberta (senator)

After his election, Borden chose Thomas White, an unelected but prominent Toronto Liberal business person, to be his finance minister, and in 1917 formed a coalition government where many of the leading Conservatives, notably Robert Rogers and R.B. Bennett were left out, and most prominent posts went to conscriptionist Liberals. His most influential adviser after 1911 may have been Sir Clifford Sifton, the owner of the Liberal *Manitoba Free Press*, and the western Conservatives' leading foe in the first decade of Laurier's government.

In his important study of prime ministerial power during the governments of John A. Macdonald, Wilfrid Laurier, and Robert Borden, Patrice Dutil describes Borden's pragmatism and flexible conservatism while emphasizing how the war upended his peacetime approach and created fundamental reforms in government administration and politics. In Dutil's view, Borden was an "inept reformer," one who promised and most likely wanted a reform of the patronage-riddled Canadian public service, but whose hesitation and clumsiness destroyed pre-war attempts at achieving the public service reform he had promised in Opposition and in the election campaigns.[10] Characteristically, Borden changed things cautiously but resisted fundamental restructuring. Dutil's careful analysis of Borden's approach to the office of prime minister points out that Borden did not dismiss senior public servants with Liberal credentials in 1911. He kept thirteen of the nineteen deputy ministers he inherited from the Liberal government, and he also appointed a record number of commissions of inquiry to deal with specific issues, including civil service reform.[11] To deal with his campaign promise of public service reform, he appointed Sir George Murray, a senior British public servant, to recommend changes to the Canadian service. Murray reported in 1913; Borden immediately rejected his report. In a harsh assessment of Murray's work in his memoirs, Borden complained that Murray's proposed reforms, which included "devolving more responsibility upon Minister and Deputy Ministers" and a reduction in the authority of the government to use orders-in-council, went far beyond Murray's mandate. It was, he wrote, "so formidable and far-reaching a programme that it would have been out of the question to carry it into full effect."[12] Borden rejected not only Murray's recommendations but also political scientist R. MacGregor Dawson's charge in his 1929 *The Civil Service of Canada* that Borden in the pre-war years had continued Macdonald's approach to patronage. An angry Borden pointed out the deputies he had retained and the many civil servants who kept their job. He even pointed out that he had saved the job of the Liberal East Block elevator operator.[13]

The pragmatic Borden understood that Murray's proposed reforms would spark a revolution. While he had earlier countenanced change, he believed that the turbulent times in which he came to power required a government that moved deliberately along familiar paths. Yet there is a paradox. Contemporary critics of Borden's pragmatism and caution, such as Conservative politicians Sir George Foster and Arthur Meighen and critical scholars such as Heaman and Dutil, also agree that Borden's prime ministerial period brought a fundamental change in the administration and character of the Canadian state and Canadian political parties.[14] War shattered the conservative carapace that covered pre-war politics and ended the patronage system put in place by Macdonald and accepted by Laurier while shattering the traditional Canadian two-party system. While war acted as the executioner, much of the scaffolding and surroundings had been put in place by the costive and cautious Borden. His fusty image conceals his impact on his times.

Borden was the last Nova Scotian to serve as Canadian prime minister. He knew that the political centre was moving rapidly away from the Maritime provinces. In his memoirs, he presents himself as a political leader who did not understand the intense passions that inflamed the politics of the central provinces and, later, the Canadian west. In writing about the controversy over separate schools in the new provinces of Alberta and Saskatchewan in 1905, Borden claimed that "the awakening of so intense a feeling was for me a novel experience."[15] He rightly believed that the "intense" issues of Canadian politics were not created in the Maritimes and were not felt so keenly by Maritimers like him. For Borden, "intense" feeling was politically dangerous and foolish, and he rightly points to his own efforts, with assistance from Laurier, to cool the fiery passions too often expressed in the House of Commons in the nineteenth century.

Both deserve credit for bringing greater dignity to parliamentary procedures and atmosphere in contrast to the wild, often drunken episodes that marked post-Confederation parliaments. Until the election of 1917, Borden thought that "politics" should avoid stirring debates about religious beliefs, values, and prejudices and should focus primarily upon the nation's interests and, in Harold Lasswell's realist definition: who gets what, when, and how. Unlike Macdonald, who revelled in the political maelstrom, and Laurier, a political artist of the highest rank, Borden made clear that he found little pleasure in the political arena. Just before he became Conservative leader, his doctor advised him that he "must lead a very quiet life and avoid anything that might tend to excitement."[16] He accepted his "duty" to be leader, but periodically he heeded the doctor's advice and temporarily stepped away from the political whirlwind. He had bouts of depression and exhaustion, retreated from political jousting, and spent seventy-eight of his last hundred weeks in office away from Ottawa, mainly in Europe.[17]

More than his predecessors and immediate successors, Borden stood away from his party and his cabinet. His diary is businesslike, crammed with events and names, but largely devoid of reflection. The historic debate in May 1917 on the two major issues of his prime ministerial tenure, conscription and the creation of a coalition to impose compulsory service, is described briefly although its current and historical importance is abundantly clear:

Sat in Council from 10.30 to six and debated on great length conscription and extension of Parl'y term. All agreed that conscription necessary. Patenaude and Blondin said they are prepared to stand by us but that it will kill them politically and the party for 25 years. Question of coalition Gov't came up in this connection and there was considerable divergence of opinion, majority favouring it. Foster and Meighen strongly in favour, Cochrane, White and Rogers against. Great division of opinion also as to putting through extension by majority vote. Foster and Cochrane strongly in favour and Meighen and Kemp very strongly against. Very weary with all this discussion and would gladly relinquish post.[18]

Borden kept his post, imposed conscription, created a coalition, and doomed his party in Quebec. The decisions were discussed, but they were his own.

Although later prime ministers are often criticized for turning away from elected representatives for guidance and advice, Borden may have been the prime minister who relied most on individuals formally unattached to his party. His own office was small, with A.E. Blount, who had served as his secretary since Opposition days, the central focus. Borden did find a place in his office for his brother Henry, but his influence was minimal. On 11 January 1918, he wrote in his diary, "Hal not in office and Blount does not know where he is." Prohibition was near, and it would be difficult for "Hal." George Yates, another secretary, kept Borden informed while abroad with "shrewd" and "often amusing" memoranda, but he merits only one brief mention in Borden's memoirs.[19] After 1913, Loring Christie, a brilliant young lawyer who had excelled at Harvard Law School, joined his staff. Christie grew close to Borden, admired his considerable strengths while aware of his weaknesses, and even considered joint business projects with Borden in an age when such possible conflicts of interest were possible for prime ministers. After his retirement, they remained close friends. The childless Borden developed an admiration and a fondness, moderated by Victorian reserve, in his relationship with his fellow Nova Scotian.

Unlike Borden, Christie was an intellectual, fully aware of contemporary debates about the nature of the law and the constitutional structure of the British Empire. As the war forced Canada and Borden to make fundamental decisions about the relationship with the Empire and character of democracy itself, the young Christie became the tutor to Borden. The prime minister was an eager and exceptional student whose intellectual ability matched that of his younger tutor.[20]

Although Borden had other ministers with him in London and Paris in the last year of the war and the many months in which the post-war world was shaped, their influence was less than that of Christie. There were, of course, other influences, not least Borden's colleagues in the Imperial War Cabinet such as Botha of South Africa, but the role of Canadian ministers, nearly all in distant Ottawa, was marginal in most decisions made in Europe. Arthur Sifton, Clifford's brother, was influential on labour questions. Borden also consulted often with Newton Rowell, who played an active role in London and Paris, but his comments suggest that Rowell's judgment was not always trusted. What is striking in his 1918–19 diary is how excited he was to be participating in what he regarded as the creation of a new international order and how little attention he paid to domestic affairs. The first volume of his two-volume memoirs ends in 1915 with the final five years of his government occupying an entire volume, which emphasized his work in Europe. After an intense parliamentary session following the election victory in 1917 in which the new Union government passed legislation that transformed the nation – votes for women, nationalization of major railways, prohibition, major tax reform, and civil service reform that ended most political patronage – Borden rapidly shifted his glance towards Europe. He left in May 1918 without giving his ministers instruction, "the usual haphazard leavetaking," Sir George Foster grumbled.[21] While abroad, Borden made it clear that the ministers in Ottawa should take responsibility for domestic decisions in his absence, and their pleas for his return or for his leadership increasingly irritated him. The times in Canada were troubled with labour unrest culminating in the Winnipeg General Strike, while angry farmers turned to direct political action against the Union government. Borden's minister of agriculture, Thomas Crerar of Manitoba, left the Union government to become the new Progressive Party's de facto leader. During this domestic political turbulence, the prime minister was largely absent. His cabinet, however, played a greater role than ever as it faced the challenges of extraordinary economic turmoil, national strikes, soldier re-establishment, and Spanish influenza.

The Union government was the only coalition government at the federal level in post-Confederation Canadian history, and its structure reflected its unique character. Borden's pre-war government had used commissions of inquiry frequently, as in the case of the vexing question of public service reform, and the tendency became stronger in wartime. In his study of the prime minister's office, Patrice Dutil concludes, "The war effort, that behemoth that now consumed almost all of Ottawa's finances ... was managed out of the Prime Minister's Office and a parallel bureaucracy that reported to him and a select few ministers." Borden's diary reflects how few the favoured ministers were. Prior to the creation of Union government, Robert Rogers was the major political organizer, and Borden respected his skills as unsavoury as they were.[22] Rogers, however, strongly opposed Union government and, understandably, civil service reform. He was pushed to the outside and did not run in 1917. Like Rogers, who had not been a candidate in the 1911 election, Thomas White became one of Borden's major cabinet advisers and would remain so until Borden's departure. As difficult as White could be, Borden trusted him more than any other minister and wanted him to be his successor. Borden favoured White over Arthur Meighen, whose energy and intellect he admired but whose judgment was not as much trusted.

Nevertheless, Meighen's outstanding ability brought him to the foreground after his appointment to the cabinet in 1913. Borden's disregard for the "old guard" was clear in 1911, when he initially tried to exclude Sir George Foster by appointing him to chair the Tariff Commission. Foster lobbied furiously, and Borden finally appointed him minister of trade and commerce but did not confide in him.[23] Although he distrusted J.D. Reid, a key leader in the revolt against his leadership the previous year, he appointed him to cabinet on the advice of Premier James Whitney of Ontario and others. Reid became one of his most competent and reliable ministers throughout his leadership. Sam Hughes had supported Borden during the 1910 rebellion and, despite a reputation for eccentricity, Borden gave him control of the Militia and Defence Department. It was a dreadful error, not least because Borden let his ministers exert a large degree of control over their own department and Hughes abused that privilege outrageously, forcing Borden to remove responsibilities from him before firing him in 1916.[24] Millionaires Edward Kemp, who replaced Hughes as minister, and Sir George Perley socialized with Borden, and played a greater role in wartime, particularly in London, but their personal relationships did not translate into significant political influence.[25]

The political influence of Conservative members and ministers decreased significantly when Borden formed his coalition in October 1917. Few Liberal MPs crossed the floor, and among them only F.B. Carvell and A.K. Maclean from the Maritimes became ministers. What was striking, not least because it was probably unnecessary, was the number of ministers appointed with no previous federal experience. Minister of Agriculture Thomas Crerar had been the head of the Manitoba Grain Growers' Association. Montreal millionaire Charles Ballantyne, who was president of the Canadian Manufacturers' Association, became minister of marine and fisheries. Sydney Mewburn was a serving major general when he became minister of militia and defence. Others had political experience in the provinces: Arthur Sifton was premier of Alberta, James Calder was a prominent and able member of Saskatchewan's Liberal government, and Newton Rowell was the Liberal leader of the Opposition in Ontario. Calder and Sifton were among the ablest of Borden's ministers and became increasingly influential in cabinet discussions. Although Rowell became the target of vitriolic attack from the Laurier Liberals and did not gain the full confidence of his colleagues, he was a highly articulate and intelligent lawyer whose skills and beliefs shaped the legislative achievements of the Union government.

Image 6.1. Poster of the Union cabinet, 1917

Source: Canadian War Museum, 20010106-001.

The cabinet on the first day of the Unionist ministry, 12 October 1917 (see image 6.1):

1 Prime Minister; External Affairs, Robert Laird Borden, Conservative
2 Agriculture – Thomas Alexander Crerar, Liberal
3 Customs – Arthur Lewis Sifton, Liberal

4 Finance and Receiver General – William Thomas White, Conservative
5 Immigration and Colonization – James Alexander Calder, Liberal
6 Inland Revenue – Albert Sévigny, Conservative
7 Interior – Arthur Meighen, Conservative
8 Justice and Attorney General – Charles Joseph Doherty, Conservative
9 Labour – Thomas Wilson Crothers, Conservative
10 Marine and Fisheries; Naval Service – Charles Colquhoun Ballantyne, Liberal [took office on 13 October]
11 Militia and Defence – Sydney Chilton Mewburn, Liberal
12 Mines; Secretary of State of Canada – Martin Burrell, Conservative
13 Overseas Military Forces – Albert Edward Kemp, Conservative
14 Postmaster General – Pierre-Édouard Blondin, Conservative
15 President of the Privy Council – Newton Wesley Rowell, Liberal
16 Public Works – Frank Broadstreet Carvell, Liberal [took office on 13 October]
17 Railways and Canals – John Dowsley Reid, Conservative
18 Trade and Commerce – George Eulas Foster, Conservative
19 Without Portfolio – Francis Cochrane, Conservative
20 Without Portfolio – James Alexander Lougheed, Conservative (senator)
21 Without Portfolio – Alexander Kenneth Maclean, Liberal
22 Without Portfolio – Gideon Robertson, Labour (senator)

With the guns finally silent and the soldiers returning, Rowell gave an address in December 1918, "One Year of Union Government." He concluded with a question: "In what year of Canadian history and under what administration whether Liberal or Conservative, can you point to a record of legislative and administrative work and achievement which will surpass that of the Union Government during the year which has just closed." Rowell makes clear that the major achievement was the reinforcement of the Canadian Corps, which was assured by the government's difficult but courageous decision to abolish the agricultural worker exemption.[26] "These reinforcements," the Canadian War Museum declares in summarizing recent scholarship, "allowed the Canadian Corps to continue fighting in a series of battles, delivering victory after victory, from August to the end of the war on 11 November 1918."[27] As Rowell strongly argued, the Union government did keep its greatest pledge, one that had bonded together Liberals and Conservatives and that had produced an overwhelming victory in the 1917 general election. Borden had kept his promise to the troops and his political supporters.

Despite the Canadian Corps' achievements in Europe and the government's legislative record in Ottawa, historians and other commentators consider the Union government a failure.[28] At the centre of Borden's failure was his management of cabinet, particularly his treatment and understanding of French Canadians. His problems preceded the war. The electoral agreement with the

Quebec nationalists in 1911 was negotiated by Frederick Monk, a Conservative MP since 1896 and Borden's Quebec "lieutenant" after he became leader. From the beginning, Borden disliked him, and his official biographer concludes that "neither man could work easily and continuously with the other."[29] They did agree in 1911 on the so-called "unholy alliance" of Quebec nationalists, who opposed naval assistance for Great Britain, with British imperialists, who wanted a direct contribution to the British navy. The alliance meant twenty-eight Conservative Quebec MPs in 1911 compared with twelve in 1908, and a promise by Borden that there would be a referendum on the naval question.

Despite the greater number, Borden chose only three francophones, Monk and two nationalists with Conservative backgrounds, Louis-Philippe Pelletier and W.B. Nantel, with Monk taking on the ministry of public works, which he did not want. Once they were chosen, Borden largely ignored them. When Manitoba's boundary expanded and the question of Catholic schools immediately became an issue, Borden accepted provincial jurisdiction as paramount, as he did in the case of Ontario's Regulation 17, which greatly limited the teaching of French. Moreover, Borden refused to allow a referendum on the naval contribution that nationalists believed he had promised to them before the election. Monk, the key to the nationalist alliance, resigned on 18 October 1912, and in a biographer's words, "Completely disillusioned, he went so far as to repudiate his party once and for all."[30] Pelletier and Nantel remained, but their influence was minimal and their mood sullen.

Things were much worse in 1917. Regulation 17 caused the Ontario Liberal leader Newton Rowell to attack Laurier in 1916 for allying with Henri Bourassa in opposing the Ontario government's forceful restrictions on bilingual schools.[31] In October 1917 Rowell became the leading Ontario member of the Union government. By that time, Borden's leading francophone minister, E.L. Patenaude, had resigned angrily on the issue of conscription. Albert Sévigny and Pierre Blondin remained, but both knew as did Borden that the Union government and the Conservative Party were doomed in Quebec. The Union government won only three of sixty-five Quebec seats in the 1917 general election. The campaign was disgraceful, the electoral system twisted by the War-Time Elections Act and the Military Voters Act into "a perversion of democracy."[32] Historian Elsbeth Heaman writes that "before 1917, Borden denounced gratuitous appeals to nationality but in 1917, he licensed them."[33] That licence freed his supporters among journalists, parliamentarians, and the general public to attack not only French Canadians but also others who did not share their views. Clifford Sifton's *Manitoba Free Press*, edited by the legendary J.W. Dafoe, ran a cartoon titled "Make every ballot a bullet for Bill."[34] Cruel, vicious, and unforgotten, the 1917 election, as his two Quebec ministers warned Borden, would end his party's hopes in Quebec for decades. And it did.

Borden's statecraft can only be defined as evolving. No Canadian prime minister has been so remote from his party, and probably none turned to outsiders so often for counsel. He despised patronage yet he turned away as Robert Rogers and Sam Hughes passed out contracts and favours to their party friends until their excesses became intolerable. Bill Waiser and Jennie Hansen convincingly argue that Borden's government even failed to punish Laurier government officials who profited from the sale of Indigenous reserve lands.[35] Borden's diary and his public orations do not reflect deeply held convictions on the major issues of the turbulent period, and the failure of his pre-war government and the Union government to convert a broad legislative record into lasting institutional and political achievement are a product of Borden's lack of interest in the broader economic and social issues of the time. Still, he survived many challenges to his leadership and left no doubt that the principal decisions of his government were his own. Indeed, his distance from his own colleagues probably facilitated that survival and his freedom to decide. Borden does not rank among the greatest Canadian prime ministers, but he is significant because his decisions deeply affected Canadians then and later. Elsbeth Heaman, a strong critic of Borden's political and economic leadership, captures well why Borden matters: "But Borden did something almost unprecedented in Canadian political history when he introduced conscription: he made a principled decision to back the troops. He consciously repudiated a decision-making steeped in brokerage of power and money."[36] In their introductory essay, the editors summarize British scholar James Bulpitt's views on statecraft: "To achieve successful statecraft, leaders had to demonstrate competence in office, of course, but also had to develop winning electoral strategies and carefully manage their colleagues in order to protect their place at the apex of power."

Given his belief that conscription and winning the war were Canada's greatest need and that creation of a coalition government that could win a wartime election was essential, Robert Borden's statecraft demonstrated in his management of colleagues and his controversial but effective electoral strategy was successful. Victorian in dress, ponderous in political style, distant from the modernism stirring beneath his times, the outsider Borden permanently damaged the Conservative Party and divided his country. The cost was high, but he never doubted the choices he made.

NOTES

1 Robert Craig Brown, *Robert Laird Borden: A Biography*, vol. 1, *1854–1914* (Toronto: Macmillan, 1975), 166.
2 The most authoritative account of the election is Patrice Dutil and David MacKenzie, *Canada 1911: The Decisive Election That Shaped the Country*

(Toronto: Dundurn, 2011). They have also written the fullest account of the 1917 election: Patrice Dutil and David MacKenzie, *Embattled Nation: Canada's Wartime Election of 1917* (Toronto: Dundurn, 2017). The 1917 book is harshly critical of Borden and, in particular, his treatment of French Canadians.

3 Elsbeth Heaman, *A History of the State in Canada* (Toronto: University of Toronto Press, 2015), 156. Heaman speculates that Borden probably had the most millionaires in the cabinet of any Canadian government. Heaman does credit Borden for undoing the "cronyism" of politics that had dominated since Macdonald, but the result was Liberal dominance in the twentieth century.

4 On Frederick Borden's death on 6 January 1917, Borden wrote in his diary, "Fred's death announced this morning. Sent tlgm of sympathy to Bessie.... His life was very successful in many ways but he had many difficulties of temperament and environment to contend with" (Library and Archives Canada [hereafter "LAC"], Borden Papers, MG 26 H, Borden diary). Carman Miller, Frederick's biographer, describes Borden as a *bon vivant* ("Sir Frederick William Borden," in *Dictionary of Canadian Biography*, vol. 14 [University of Toronto Press, 1998], 97–100).

5 Borden diary, 1 May 1917.

6 Philip E. Converse, "The Nature of Belief Systems in Mass Publics (1964)," *Critical Review* 18, nos. 1–3 (2006): 1–74.

7 Brown, *Borden*, vol. 1, chs. 1–3, gives an excellent account of his early years.

8 Borden to Willison, 11 February 1905, LAC, Willison Papers MG 30 D 29, box 7.

9 Ames to Borden, 28 August 1907, quoted in Brown, *Borden*, 1:134.

10 Patrice Dutil, *Prime Ministerial Power in Canada: Its Origins under Macdonald, Laurier, and Borden* (Vancouver: University of British Columbia Press), 125.

11 Dutil, *Prime Ministerial Power*, 131–4.

12 Robert Laird Borden, *Robert Laird Borden: His Memoirs*, ed. Henry Borden (London: Macmillan, 1938), 1:391–2.

13 R. MacGregor Dawson, *The Civil Service of Canada* (London: Oxford University Press, 1929). Dawson, surprisingly, sent Borden a copy, which he annotated with marks on offending passages. A copy is now with the University of Waterloo Archives. Borden attacked Dawson in his presidential address to the Canadian Historical Association in 1931; see Robert Borden, "The Problem of an Efficient Civil Service," in *Report of the Annual Meeting of the Canadian Historical Association* 10, no. 1 (1931): 14–16. On the elevator operator, see Borden, *Memoirs*, 1:333n.

14 Dutil quotes Foster and Meighen in supporting his criticisms while acknowledging the extraordinary changes that occurred during Borden's prime ministerial tenure (*Prime Ministerial Power*, 126, 139–46, 155). See also John English, *The Decline of Politics: The Conservatives and the Party System, 1901–1920* (Toronto: University of Toronto Press, 1977), 72–7.

15 Borden, *Memoirs*, 1:141.

16 Borden, *Memoirs*, 1:66.
17 English, *Decline of Politics*, 210–11.
18 Borden diary, 17 May 1917.
19 Borden, *Memoirs*, 2:1027.
20 The essential study of the relationship is Robert Bothwell, *Loring Christie: The Failure of Bureaucratic Imperialism* (New York: Garland Press, 1988).
21 Sir George Foster diary, 24 May 1918, LAC, MG 27 D 7.
22 A recent study of the Ferguson Commission established to investigate corruption in the administration of indigenous lands in western Canada is scathing in its treatment of Rogers, even though the commission's focus was upon the Laurier government (Bill Waiser and Jennie Hansen, *Cheated: The Laurier Liberals and the Theft of First Nations Reserve Land* [Toronto: ECW Press, 2023]).
23 In the 1930s, Borden reflected on politics and politicians in "letters to limbo" that he wrote for his personal papers. He claimed that Foster tried to extend "the jurisdiction of his department in every possible direction, although its original scope was quite sufficient to absorb his whole energies" (Robert Borden, *Letters to Limbo*, ed. Henry Borden [Toronto: University of Toronto Press, 1971], 69).
24 On Hughes's personality and wartime conflicts, see Tim Cook, *The Madman and the Butcher: The Sensational Wars of Sam Hughes and General Arthur Currie* (Toronto: Penguin Books, 2011).
25 The assessments generally reflect those in Brown, *Borden*, vol. 1, ch. 10. Dutil, *Prime Ministerial Power*, is more generous to Foster.
26 Newton Rowell, "One Year of Union Government," address of Hon. N.W. Rowell, Bowmanville, ON, 17 December 1918.
27 "Canada and the First World War – Conscription, 1917," Canadian War Museum, accessed 30 August 2024, https://www.warmuseum.ca/firstworldwar/history/life-at-home-during-the-war/recruitment-and-conscription/conscription-1917/.
28 In a perceptive essay, Jeff Keshen analyses the legislative record of the Union government and the failure of the government to make the imprint upon Canadian government that its promises and even its record suggested it would ("A Timid Transformation: The First World War's Legacy on Canada's Federal Government," in *Canada 1919: A Nation Shaped by War*, ed. Tim Cook and Jack Granatstein [Vancouver: University of British Columbia Press, 2019], 204–19).
29 Brown, *Borden*, 1:57.
30 François Béland, "Frederick Debartzch Monk," in *Dictionary of Canadian Biography*, 14:766. For a more extended discussion, see John English, "The 'French Lieutenant' in Ottawa," in *National Politics and Community in Canada*, ed. R. Kenneth Carty and W. Peter Ward (Vancouver: University of British Columbia Press), 184–200. In *Embattled Nation*, Dutil and MacKenzie are sharply critical of Borden's handling of his francophone Quebec ministers and language issues. The distinguished Quebec historian Réal Bélanger has written extensively on the Quebec Conservatives of this period. Bélanger's titles reveal the challenge

the Conservatives faced in Quebec: *L'impossible défi: Albert Sévigny et les conservateurs fédéraux (1902–1918)* (Quebec City: Presses de l'Université Laval, 1983); and *Paul-Émile Lamarche: Le pays avant le parti* (Quebec City: Presses de l'Université Laval, 1984).

31 Rowell to Laurier, 26 April 1916, LAC, Newton Wesley Rowell Papers, MG 27 II D 13, box 3.

32 Dutil and MacKenzie, *Embattled Nation*, 121.

33 E.A. Heaman, *Tax, Order, and Good Government: a New Political History of Canada, 1867–1917* (Montreal: McGill-Queen's University Press, 2017), 437.

34 *Manitoba Free Press*, 15 December 1917.

35 Waiser and Hansen, *The Laurier Liberals and the Theft of First Nations Reserve Land*.

36 Heaman, *Tax, Order, and Good Government*, 446. Jack Granatstein has analysed the impact on the party system in "Politics Undone: The End of the Two-Party System," in Cook and Granatstein, *Canada 1919*, 220–33.

7 Arthur Meighen: The Lost Opportunities of Leadership

MARY JANIGAN AND TOM KIERANS

Throughout the fall of 1921, as the approaching fourth anniversary of the Union government implied an imminent election, the lobbying for Senate seats became fierce and undignified. Former customs minister Rupert Wilson Wigmore, likely chafing at his exclusion from the new federal cabinet under Prime Minister Arthur Meighen, made a "very strong appeal" for an immediate appointment to the Senate before the upcoming election. He was "more entitled" to the vacant New Brunswick position than other candidates, he argued, because he had worked diligently for the Conservatives since he was eighteen. Once installed in the Senate, he promised Meighen, he "could go to St. John [*sic*] and start an active campaign" for his successor, J.B.M. Baxter, who was also the new customs minister.[1] Wigmore slyly added that he had already told his associates of Meighen's promise to take care of him.[2] Meighen's response was firm: "I do not think you should make any such condition [on your assistance].... The thing to do undoubtedly is to throw yourself into the contest without complaint, for there can be no just complaint."[3]

Wigmore was undeterred. He solicited support from the influential Royal Bank manager in Newcastle as well as five constituency officials who warned Meighen that their backing "absolutely depends upon Wigmore being given some appointment without further delay."[4] The campaign unnerved Baxter, who was running to succeed Wigmore. Mere days before the 6 December election, Baxter warned Meighen that the "Wigmore situation" was so disruptive that he could lose the election.[5] Wigmore again asked Meighen to confirm his Senate appointment privately by wire, and then announce it after the election.[6]

Meighen answered many of those appeals personally, often from the campaign trail. He complained to Baxter that Wigmore "keeps enlarging my words. The only difficulties are his own creation."[7] Three days later, the prime minister wired that the "conduct of several parties in St. John [*sic*] ... merit no consideration." Wigmore had lost all chance of an appointment. Meighen added a

Image 7.1. Arthur Meighen's visit to Toronto Harbour Commissioners, 13 August 1920
Source: Library and Archives Canada, PA-097014.

final defiant assertion: "I may be beaten but I will not be bullied."[8] Baxter won. Meighen lost his own seat, and his Unionist government was defeated.

The episode perfectly captures Meighen's domineering approach to cabinet government, as well as his tin ear for politics. As prime minister as well as secretary of state for external affairs, he was a workaholic and the clear first among no equals in his cabinet. Highly intelligent, enormously skilful in debate, he lacerated opponents (Quebec's anti-conscriptionists were favourite targets). He was generally polite in his correspondence with his cabinet members; only occasionally did his frustrations emerge as in his emphatic declaration to Baxter about Wigmore's fate.[9] He did react firmly when ministers were not paying enough attention to hot-button issues such as the "unnecessarily" alarming rumours that the Canadian National Railways (CNR) was moving its headquarters from Toronto to Montreal or Ottawa.[10] Even then he was well mannered, which perhaps ensured that he did not generate more political opposition.

As Meighen's devoted biographer Roger Graham explained, the prime minister "did the lion's share of the talking simply because he was a great deal better at it, and knew he was, than anyone else."[11] But Graham also quoted a Meighen friend in Victoria who noted, "It is a common, if exaggerated declaration that yours is a one-man government and that you do all the work."[12]

The result was an overwhelming workload – and a crucial failure to use his cabinet's talents as well as he should have. Meighen's two governments spanned times when economic and social conditions were changing more rapidly than many Canadians could grasp. Meighen contended with an immense range of hugely controversial issues, from tariff protection to early demands for social security to the management of the publicly owned CNR. But, as a politician who valued consistency, he rarely adjusted his positions as circumstances changed, and he largely dictated his government's views on those issues. Indeed, given his voluminous correspondence with his cabinet ministers and so many other Canadians, it appears that he often had little time to think deeply. There are no cabinet records from Meighen's two governments, but his letters and telegrams illuminate a prime ministerial life of dedication and near constant pressure. As he ruefully told British Columbia farmland developer J.M. Robinson on 21 April 1921, he had just played a round of golf, "practically the first recreation since the Fall, – and needless to say I enjoyed it."[13]

Throughout his first term in office (which lasted just over eighteen months, from 10 July 1920 to 28 December 1921), Meighen was beset with complaints about CNR service, shipbuilding contracts, federal resource control in the three prairie provinces, and Arctic exploration – to cite only a few topics. In the summer of 1921, he left Canada for seven weeks for a conference of prime ministers in Britain on the fate of the Anglo-Japanese Alliance. He shone at that conference, driving key diplomatic policy changes. But it was a politically difficult absence in an election year when he wanted to appoint a new cabinet and shuffle a few overlooked MPs into compensatory positions. As he wearily told H.S. Clements, the British Columbia MP who "insist[ed] upon" a Senate seat: "I sincerely wish the present responsibility as to these Senate seats were not mine.... I have not decided yet how they should be disposed of to get the best advantage or perhaps I should say how they may be disposed of with the least disadvantage."[14] The distractions seemed endless.

The Beginning

As a cabinet minister in the government of Sir Robert Borden, Meighen did recognize the need to work as part of a team. But his colleagues clearly regarded him as difficult. In 1920, when Borden consulted his caucus about a successor, he discovered that "a substantial majority" of MPs favoured Meighen, but "a considerable number" also backed former finance minister Sir Thomas White, who had resigned from cabinet in August 1919.[15]

On 5 July, Borden learned that *all* cabinet ministers, with the possible exception of Secretary of State Arthur Sifton, supported White. The cabinet members knew that Meighen's brilliance in Parliament was unlikely to translate into votes: His "icy image and incurable shyness hid a warm, sensitive nature ... [that] the public was never allowed to see."[16] Borden was taken aback. "It was apparent that Meighen would not receive the support of my immediate colleagues unless they were convinced that White would not accept."[17] White, in turn, flatly refused the honour, citing health concerns.[18]

Borden had suspected that there might be problems after a lengthy warning on 27 June 1920 from Immigration Minister James Calder: "Meighen is absolutely out of the question in so far as Quebec is concerned. In addition I know that several ministers will immediately retire should he be the choice." If it were decided to reconstruct the Conservative Party "in the hope of success at the second general election it might be advisable to select Meighen as leader at this time." But Calder doubted the wisdom of this approach: "I do not think Meighen possesses the necessary qualities to ensure his success as a leader at any time in the future."[19]

Calder did not expand on those oblique comments, but it is fair to speculate that he presumed Meighen's leadership would hasten the break-up of the Unionist government, driving away its more Liberal supporters. On 7 July, Borden learned that Justice Minister Charles Doherty and Marine Minister Charles Colquhoun Ballantyne would not support Meighen and would not remain in cabinet. Calder was "very doubtful."[20] Eventually, at the end of a very long day, Borden secured their agreement to stay.

The new prime minister's first task was to survive the initial wariness of many cabinet colleagues. He lost the esteemed health minister Newton Rowell, who had quietly told Borden in February 1920 that he believed the political life of the nation was "rapidly changing." Any evolution of the Unionist Party would attract "the most conservative elements of the population outside of Quebec, and probably there also."[21] Rowell identified with the nation's more progressive forces.[22] White was resolved to avoid the stress of another cabinet role, although he would remain as an MP. Customs Minister Martin Burrell, who was badly injured in the 1916 Parliament Hill fire, resigned to become parliamentary librarian. Sir George Foster was seventy-two, and still reeling from the death of his spouse in June 1919. He agreed to remain as minister of trade and commerce for another year, but he was exhausted.[23]

Meighen did keep the Borden cabinet almost intact. He brushed aside suggestions that the Union ideal had little appeal to an exhausted public that had survived a brutal war, a lethal flu pandemic, and the unsettling surge of revolutionary creeds. Instead, stubbornly cautious, he retained all but three of his former colleagues.[24] But he was uneasily aware that Rowell was right: the post-war political climate was changing rapidly. In 1919, Minister of Agriculture Thomas Crerar had resigned, forming the National Progressive Party to promote agrarian demands for more rapid tariff reduction. That same year, Mackenzie King won the leadership of the Liberal Party at a lively convention.

With such opposition, Meighen was anxious to retain the support of the remaining Liberal-Unionist MPs. Some left anyway. Former Liberals such as Nova Scotia MP William S. Fielding, former minister without portfolio Alexander K. Maclean and Ontario MP Frederick F. Pardee returned to their Liberal roots. That said, former Liberals James Calder; Arthur Sifton; future party leader Robert Manion; and Borden's solicitor general, Hugh Guthrie, remained with the Unionist government. The Unionist Party was even renamed the National Liberal-Conservative Party at the suggestion of Calder. (Caucus approved the clunky change despite Meighen's advice.)

Meighen's choice of only three new ministers in the summer of 1920 did not mark a break with the past. The trio included the contentious Wigmore from New Brunswick, along with Nova Scotians Edgar Keith Spinney and Fleming Blanchard McCurdy. The members of Meighen's first cabinet appointed on 13 July 1920 were:

1 Prime Minister; External Affairs – Arthur Meighen, 46, Manitoba
2 Immigration and Colonization; President of the Privy Council; acting
   Health – J.A. Calder, 51, Saskatchewan
3 Trade and Commerce – George Foster, 72, New Brunswick
4 Interior; Government Leader in the Senate; Superintendent General
   of Indian Affairs; acting Soldiers' Civil Re-establishment – James A.
   Lougheed, 65, Alberta (senator)
5 Finance and Receiver General – Henry L. Drayton, 51, Ontario
6 Secretary of State – Arthur L. Sifton, 61, Alberta
7 Railways and Canals – John Dowsley Reid, 61, Ontario
8 Labour – Gideon D. Robertson, 45, Ontario (senator)
9 Marine and Fisheries; Naval Service – C.C. Ballantyne, 52, Quebec
10 Public Works – Fleming B. McCurdy, 45, Nova Scotia
11 Justice – Charles J. Doherty, 65, Quebec
12 Postmaster General – Pierre-Édouard Blondin, 45, Quebec (senator)
13 Agriculture – Simon Fraser Tolmie, 53, British Columbia
14 Customs and Inland Revenue – Rupert W. Wigmore, 47, New Brunswick
15 Without Portfolio – Edgar K. Spinney, 69, Nova Scotia
16 Without Portfolio –Edward Kemp, 61, Ontario (senator)

Meighen appointed a cabinet that was much older than he was. The average age (56.2) was almost exactly the same as Borden's in 1911 and Laurier's in

1896, but Meighen was only forty-six, creating an unprecedented dynamic in the East Block. There were only three Quebeckers, and only four from Ontario. Five men came from the western provinces, and two came from each of Nova Scotia and New Brunswick (Prince Edward Island was shut out). Those ministers were a distinctly mixed lot. Agriculture Minister Simon Fraser Tolmie was "not an outstanding minister." As his biographer Ian D. Parker observes, "Generally he acted as a public relations man for the department."[25] Others such as Finance Minister Sir Henry Drayton could manage their portfolios but were not skilled politicians. (Drayton was blamed for not handling Mackenzie King's pointed questioning when he was House leader in 1926, which led to the fall of the second short-lived Meighen government.)[26]

There were few superstars. James Alexander Calder supervised the Health and Immigration departments as well as the presidency of the Privy Council until Meighen appointed him to the Senate in September 2021. Meighen's esteem was evident. In October 2020, Calder asked Meighen if he could mention in a speech that an election was inevitable.[27] Meighen replied that he had no objection but "I think a more positive forward-looking stand would probably be more effective." Then he added, in a concession that was rare for Meighen, "However, you can judge as well, or better, than I can."[28] Despite Meighen's trust, however, Calder knew better than to act on major files without consulting him. His interior minister, minister of mines, minister of soldiers' civil re-establishment, and superintendent general of Indian affairs was Senator Sir James Alexander Lougheed, who was also government leader in the Senate. Sir James was a shrewd politician, who had been in the Senate since December 1889, and he was a strong voice for western interests.

There were additions as the government approached its first anniversary; men who would eventually shape the Conservative Party in the next twenty years. In May 1921, Meighen reached out to the Calgary lawyer and wealthy businessman who would eventually replace him, R.B. Bennett, appointing him minister of justice and attorney general. As Bennett's biographer John Boyko notes, the new minister "soon learned that he had joined a cabinet that resembled a pick-up team … [most recent appointees] were of rather limited capabilities."[29] The two men were not close, and Meighen was always deferential in his dealings with Bennett.

Meighen's Managerial Approach

Perhaps there was no good time for Meighen to succeed Sir Robert Borden as prime minister, if only because he had undertaken so many controversial tasks during his five years in Borden's cabinet. Born into a farming family near the small town of St. Marys, Ontario, in 1874, Meighen was an exceptional student who attended the University of Toronto at the same time as his lifelong nemesis, William Lyon Mackenzie King. The two men were not close: King was outgoing, and he excelled in political science and extra-curricular activities; Meighen was bookish, and, in the words of biographer Roger Graham, "for the most part foregoing the frivolous social diversions of university life."[30] After graduation in 1896 with first-class honours in mathematics, English, and Latin, Meighen attended the Ontario College of Pedagogy to earn teaching qualifications and did a brief stint as a high school teacher, but quickly concluded he was not cut out for a career in education. By 1900, he was a student-at-law in Winnipeg and progressed quickly in his new career. Early in 1902, he took over the administration of a law practice in Portage La Prairie. By the spring of 1903, he was a qualified solicitor and barrister, but was restless in practising law. In 1908, he won election to Parliament, and within five years he was solicitor general, which was not then a cabinet post. In October 1915, he was sworn into the Privy Council. During the fall of 1917, Borden appointed him to the posts of secretary of state, minister of mines, and later minister of the interior.

It was a meteoric ascent. But it was during those years that Meighen accrued the reputation that many held against him when he became prime minister. His most provocative actions occurred during the First World War. In May and early June 1917, he prepared the Military Service Act authorizing conscription, which Borden presented to Parliament and Meighen fiercely defended. In a scathing attack during third reading, he blamed the dignified former prime minister Sir Wilfrid Laurier for "the shadow of disunion" across the nation, adding that there was "a backward and a forward portion of the population of every country."[31] Quebecers, who largely opposed conscription, resented and remembered his allusions. In September 1917, Meighen introduced the Wartime Elections Act, which denied the vote to those from so-called enemy alien nations who had become naturalized after March 1902. That same legislation bestowed the vote on women who were close relatives of soldiers serving overseas. Many Prairie farmers from Eastern Europe never forgave him.

When the Conservatives joined with pro-conscriptionist Liberals to form the Union government in October 1917, Meighen became minister of the interior and superintendent general of Indian affairs, later also taking on the post of minister of mines. But it was his role in the railway debates to create the publicly owned CNR that made new adversaries. In June 1919, he was the chief government spokesman for the bill to incorporate the CNR, which absorbed the struggling Canadian Northern Railway, the National Transcontinental Railway, and the Intercolonial Railway of Canada. Five months later, when Parliament debated legislation to nationalize the troubled Grand Trunk Railway, Meighen amazed his colleagues with lengthy detailed speeches without notes. "If mastery of the subject, skill in disputation and sheer physical endurance are valid criteria," notes biographer Graham, "his performance during the debate on this Bill was perhaps the most prodigious of his entire career in the House of Commons."[32]

His remarkable memory could not placate the Canadian Pacific Railway, which was appalled at the prospect of competing with a government-owned railroad. Many Quebec MPs along with a coterie of bipartisan supporters across the nation were opposed to public ownership on principle. The improbable charge of socialism was whispered against Meighen.

Meanwhile, many labour representatives remained unalterably opposed to Meighen after the Winnipeg General Strike of 1919. When more than 30,000 workers left their jobs in mid-May 1919, prominent business representatives, styling themselves as the Citizens' Committee of 1000, demanded a stern federal response. Acting Justice Minister Meighen and Labour Minister Senator Gideon Robertson arrived in Winnipeg on 22 May, consulted with business entrepreneurs, and refused to meet with labour representatives. In mid-June, Ottawa arrested eight labour leaders. Four days later, the Royal North-West Mounted Police charged into the strikers, killing two. A recent investigation has pinned much of the blame for the violence on Citizens' Committee member A.J. Andrews.[33] Still, Meighen "became identified ... as a big, bad anti-labour reactionary, the pliant creature of the business men [sic]."[34]

Perhaps most unsettling, Meighen made casual enemies with his cutting responses to political opponents. It was a performance that enchanted his fellow Unionist MPs but outraged many opposition members. Former Conservative leader John Diefenbaker recorded Meighen's response in 1926 to a "much beloved" senior citizen who asked why the prime minister opposed old-age pensions: "For ten minutes, Meighen took apart the old man as only he could. Support in that audience went down the drain."[35] It was a lifelong habit. As Mackenzie King wrote fearfully when Meighen once again became Conservative leader in November 1941: "He is the meanest & most contemptible of all political adversaries, bitter, unscrupulous, sarcastic.... He will detract from the Govt's record, & myself in particular.... Life day by day will be made intolerable by his attacks."[36]

King and Meighen disliked each other from their first days in Parliament. King was labour minister in 1909, when the two men first clashed over the adoption of an eight-hour day. (The bill was eventually shelved.) When Meighen pointed out inconsistencies in the Liberal approach, King warily equivocated in response. Meighen soon came to regard King "as an object worthy only of contempt."[37] Such disdain would eventually prove to be Meighen's undoing: He consistently underrated King's political skills, and King was a *very* resourceful if fearful enemy whose flexibility was far more suited to a nation evolving in the twentieth century.

As prime minister, it often seemed as though no issue was too small to attract Meighen's attention. When the administrative chairman of the Honorary

Advisory Council for Scientific and Industrial Research asked that his council be transferred from the authority of the trade ministry to the health ministry, the deputy minister of public health, Colonel J.A. Amyot, answered with one sentence: "You are not so smart as you think you are."[38] Council chairman A.B. Macallum brought the response to his boss, Trade Minister Sir George Foster, who wrote to Meighen about the incident. Foster added tartly: "It will be practically impossible for Government Departments to carry on their work if such a tone ... is allowed to be given to such correspondence."[39] Meighen, in turn, referred the incident to Health Minister Calder: "There would seem to me to be no justification for such a letter on the part of Doctor Amyot and steps should be taken to see that he is so advised."[40]

Only occasionally did Meighen take refuge in the collective power of the cabinet. In November 1920, Vancouver MP Harry Stevens sent an agitated dispatch to Meighen, defending Ottawa's shipbuilding contract with J. Coughlan & Sons Shipyard. Stevens alleged that Marine Minister Charles Colquhoun Ballantyne had unfairly concluded that the firm had violated its contract when it hired foreign subcontractors and was therefore ineligible for a loan. But the Vancouver-based firm was employing unemployed veterans who were arriving daily from other provinces; the loan would ensure it could "get going full force and help relieve situation."[41] On 11 December 1920, Meighen told Stevens that Ballantyne had reviewed the situation, and "feels he cannot possibly justify any other stand than that taken."[42] Three days later, Stevens appealed to Meighen to intervene personally because the shipyard was vital in stimulating the "critical industrial condition here."[43]

On 17 December, Meighen played his trump card, telling "Dear Harry" that "owing to the urgency of the representations made by you I have had the subject discussed in Council and can only say that Council agrees with the minister [Ballantyne]." He knew that Stevens would likely return to Ottawa after the New Year. "You can realize it is not possible for me to take very much time in the consideration of departmental matters, but I will assist you in any way in my power to get at the facts."[44] It was a generous offer to the MP that Meighen would elevate to the trade and commerce portfolio in September 1921. Instead, Stevens wired on 13 January that he was amazed to learn that the Justice Ministry had cancelled Coughlan's contract and demanded the repayment of deposits. He warned that "the arbitrary and unreasonable action of a Minister of the Crown ... will result in serious disaffection of government support."[45]

Meighen stayed firm. In a telegram to Stevens on 15 January, the prime minister declared, "Their difficulties are in our opinion entirely of their own making and they cannot be allowed to dictate government policy."[46] Ballantyne was sufficiently empowered to answer a threatening telegram from Vancouver mayor R.H. Gale with a warning: "Public opinion will fully sustain us when they are cognizant of the facts. Conditions as they now exist are due entirely to Coughlan attitude and the Government will stand by their rights [*sic*]."[47] He took care, however, to notify the prime minister of the exchange immediately. In late April, the firm's vice-president, J.J. Coughlan, visited Ballantyne in Ottawa, securing his "sympathetic" support for the use of British-built engines and equipment.[48] The shipyard was able to fulfil the orders and survived into the 1930s.

Meighen was seemingly involved in issues that touched every department. At the urging of Robert Borden, as external affairs minister, he became entangled in a lengthy negotiation with Canadian-born Arctic explorer Vilhjalmur Stefansson, who wanted to lead an expedition to claim Wrangel Island for Canada. External affairs legal adviser Loring Christie eventually concluded that Russia and Japan would resent the intrusion outside Canada's hemisphere: "The disadvantages far outweigh any possible advantages."[49] Meighen wisely took his advice.

When a Winnipeg acquaintance warned Meighen that German importers were pressing the wholesale hardware traders to ask Ottawa to treat German manufacturers more favourably, Meighen replied that he "quite agree[d] ... that every encouragement should be given to Canadian and British goods."[50] He copied Finance Minister Drayton on his opinion.

He was involved in the seemingly smallest issues. He asked Postmaster General Blondin to investigate the appalling mail delivery to an insurance company in the town of Wawanesa, Manitoba, that had 40,000 farmers as clients across the West. His repeated intercessions resulted in the establishment of a daily service to the town.[51] He was involved in the most difficult of issues. He responded to the parents of sons who died in World War I to explain why their remains could not be disinterred and brought to Canada. Although he was also careful to stipulate that Militia Minister Guthrie had "full charge" of the issue, he offered to meet one father from Saskatoon "and do the very best I can to satisfy him."[52]

The prime minister even had an appetite for the grittiest details. He answered a multi-point inquiry from Customs Minister Baxter about the conduct of the CNR in the Maritimes after a long discussion with the CNR's president of the board of directors David Blyth Hanna and Minister of Railways John Dowsley Reid. Then he answered each point in a detailed three-page letter to Baxter: "I have gone over one by one the various grievances ... [and] I have become absolutely convinced not only of the good faith of Mr. Hanna but that he has done everything that could reasonably be done to meet the situation fairly and in the general interest."[53] The railways and their freight rates were a perpetual issue for Meighen, as indeed for all federal politicians then, but it is worth noting that he undertook this meticulous research during an arduous election campaign.

His correspondence with his cabinet ministers indicates that he was an estimable man. He would tolerate no dishonesty: When informed that a Regina firm was producing illegal alcohol, he immediately demanded action, adding that "other than a local [customs] officer should handle [the] matter."[54] But, as historian John English points out, he "quietly lamented" the restrictions that the Unionist government had placed on patronage appointments, "not least because of their impact upon his political future."[55] He was not alone: As Garrett Tyrrell, organization secretary for the Central Liberal-Conservative Association of Toronto, told Meighen on 4 August 1920, "the boys want the old patronage system back."[56]

He had other blind spots. Although he had introduced legislation to grant the vote to women who were closely related to servicemen in 1917, he did not participate in Borden's post-war efforts to establish "a uniform federal suffrage law for enfranchised men and women across Canada."[57] As biographer Graham notes, Meighen was "less than enthusiastic about the theoretical merits of votes" for women.[58] In mid-November 1921, as the election campaign became more heated, Calder wired Meighen: "Am strongly of [the] view effort should be made from coast to coast to make strong appeal for women's votes during the last week of campaign. You should be prepared to give lead.... Appeal should centre around unity in war, unity in peace. The women are going over top. They will pull Canada through."[59]

All parties, of course, "sought to show how their own platforms contained the best policies to deal with the presumed interests of women voters: jobs for their husbands, concern for consumer prices, future opportunities for their children, and protection for society's unfortunates."[60] But Calder's wisdom did get through to the campaign organizers, who placed a large advertisement appealing to women in the *Globe* along with a personal message from Meighen on 30 November 1921: "I ask you to earnestly and thoroughly study the great issues that now confront the country, and to conscientiously seek a personal decision, refusing steadfastly to be moved by reckless appeals, or by the cry of prejudice or by class appeal."[61] But it was too late for Meighen to start paying special attention to those voters: Women divided their votes among the parties in almost the same proportion as men.

The 22 September 1921 Cabinet Shuffle

Three months away from an election, Meighen shuffled his cabinet, devoting days to the task of selecting colleagues by balancing regions, attitudes, and skills. He added another future successor, Northwestern Ontario MP R.J. Manion, as minister of soldiers' civil re-establishment. He also added the scrappy Vancouver businessman H.H. Stevens as trade and commerce minister, for whom he clearly had affectionate tolerance. (He usually addressed Stevens as "My dear Harry.")[62]

There was, however, a truly fatal flaw in every Meighen cabinet mix. The prime minister had created a subcommittee of cabinet in October 1920 that was nicknamed the Power Sub-com to discuss pivotal issues, and he had put Calder, Sir James Lougheed, Naval Service Minister Ballantyne from Montreal, Public Works Minister McCurdy from Nova Scotia, and Minister of Railways and Canals Reid, who was a physician from south-eastern Ontario, on the list of members. On paper, this powerful hub appeared to have adequate regional representation: The Maritimes, Montreal, Ontario, Manitoba (Meighen), Saskatchewan, and Alberta. But the problem with the sub-committee was the same as the problem with the cabinet as a whole: There was only one francophone minister in the entire cabinet, Postmaster General Pierre-Édouard Blondin from rural Quebec, and he was seated comfortably in the Senate. This group could not prepare the government's readiness for an upcoming election.

The problem haunted Meighen. He had two Montrealers in his cabinet – Justice Minister Charles Joseph Doherty and Naval Service Minister Ballantyne. He worked hard to woo back Esioff-Léon Patenaude, who had resigned from Borden's cabinet in 1917 to protest conscription. That effort failed. With the 22 September 1921 cabinet shuffle, Meighen added four Quebecers: Quebec City lawyer Louis de Gonzague Belley as postmaster general, Montreal lawyer Rodolphe Monty as secretary of state, Montreal lawyer Guillaume-André Fauteux as solicitor general, and physician Louis-Philippe Normand as Privy Council president.

He struggled to undo the damage that conscription and the creation of the CNR had done to his reputation in Quebec. In a speech in Trois Rivières in November 1921, Meighen assured the crowd that Quebec would "always find in me a sincere supporter.... I have given you an undeniable proof of this by calling to highest council of the nation four of your most distinguished compatriots." He added that there were rumours that "at some time of my career, I had said things derogatory to the French Canadians.... This is utterly false."[63]

It was a lost cause. All four francophone candidates from Quebec lost in the 6 December election. Seven other ministers including Ballantyne were defeated. Meighen lost his seat in this humiliation, but he would not give up. He returned to Parliament in an Ontario by-election in 1922. As Opposition leader, he attempted to teach himself French, reading and listening and spending time in Tadoussac, Quebec, in the summer of 1922. His biographer Graham says that he never learned to speak the language with genuine ease, but his pronunciation was acceptable, "and by 1923 he was delivering short addresses in French."[64]

Return to Power, 1926

The election held on 29 October 1925 kept the Liberals in power, but only by the thinnest of margins. King and eight ministers lost their seats. The Conservatives led by Arthur Meighen surprised many by taking more than 34 per cent of the vote in Quebec. Meighen had managed to make peace with Patenaude, who ran the provincial campaign. The Conservatives elected four Quebec MPs, but they were all anglophones, three from urban Montreal and one from the Montreal suburbs. Overall, the Meighen Tories won more than 46 per cent of the vote and increased their number of seats from 49 to 115, but it was not enough to dethrone the King Liberals. They had only 100 seats, but with the support of the Progressive Party, led by Manitoba MP Robert Forke, they could retain control of the government.[65]

It was after this election that Meighen's inability to make political concessions at the expense of his cherished virtue of consistency became glaringly apparent. The Progressives had usually supported the Liberals during King's 1921–5 government, and King appeared "more sympathetically disposed" to their western agrarian viewpoint.[66] But in the wake of the election, the Progressives were willing to strike a bargain in return for their support: they wanted "some understanding with regard to subjects like the tariff, [the completion of] the Hudson Bay Railway, rural credits and the transfer of control over their natural resources to the three prairie provinces from the Dominion."[67] To the astonishment of many followers, Meighen was insistent that he would not make any deal that would compromise Conservative policies. Indeed, in a letter to Forke, he was virtually unbending. In contrast, King was generous: he won a Saskatchewan seat in a by-election, and he itemized other concessions such as the completion of the railroad. The Progressives were divided but inclined to cooperate.

It could not last. In the spring of 1926, the government became publicly embroiled in a damaging customs scandal. When a special Parliamentary committee reported on that scandal in mid-June, the Conservatives proposed an amendment to the report's acceptance, demanding that it be sent back to committee with instructions to censure the government in general and King in particular. With Progressive support wavering and the prospect of near-certain censure looming, King asked the governor general to dissolve Parliament and call an election. When the governor general refused, King resigned. The governor general then asked Meighen to form a government on the chance that he could muster the support of at least some Progressives.

Meighen accepted. His approach to cabinet making in those early days of summer spoke eloquently of his stubborn and mistaken approach to politics. Once again, remarkably, he did not court the Progressives even though, with their support, his ministers could have complied with a law that required MPs who accepted ministerial appointments with salaries to resign and run again. He also concluded that the Liberals and the Progressives would not agree to an adjournment. He did not even deploy a statute that allowed ministers to keep their seats if they accepted no payments of any kind. Instead, he opted for a convoluted way to preserve his scant majority: He appointed six acting ministers including one Quebecer, industrialist Sir George H. Perley, as secretary of state, who would receive no salary except as MPs but who would purportedly be able to conduct business in Parliament and in their departments.

Justice department officials had insisted, that, as prime minister, Meighen had to surrender his seat. But his six acting ministers took their places in the House of Commons on 29 June. On 30 June, the Liberals proposed a motion that challenged the right of those acting ministers to control business in the House or to administer their departments. Their actions were a violation and an infringement of House of Commons privileges. After a gruelling sitting that stretched into the early morning hours of the next day, the Liberal motion won approval by one vote. The next day, Meighen asked Byng to dissolve Parliament. Meighen's government was defeated after only four days in the House of Commons.

With an election underway, Meighen was free to appoint a larger cabinet on 13 July 1926, with virtually every existing minister changing jobs. But Bennett, Guthrie, Drayton, Manion, Perley and Stevens remained the pivotal cabinet core with "the others being much more on the periphery."[68] Meighen did, however, appoint francophone ministers, including Patenaude as minister of justice, and then, five weeks later, Montreal lawyer Guillaume-André Fauteux as solicitor general, and physician Eugène Paquet in health and soldiers' civil re-establishment.[69] He also added a novelty, the first francophone from outside Quebec to be appointed to the federal cabinet: Dr. Raymond D. Morand, as minister without portfolio (who was sometimes known as the minister of francophone minorities).

The members of this cabinet included:

1 Prime Minister; Secretary of State for External Affairs; President of the Privy Council – Arthur Meighen, 52, Ontario (He would run to represent Manitoba in the upcoming election and lose.)
2 Secretary of State – Sir George Halsey Perley, 68, Quebec
3 Minister of Finance; Indian Affairs; Interior – R.B. Bennett, 56, Alberta
4 Justice and Attorney General; Marine and Fisheries – Esioff-Léon Patenaude, 51, Quebec
5 National Defence – Hugh Guthrie, 59, Ontario
6 Customs and Excise – Henry H. Stevens, 47, British Columbia
7 Agriculture – Simon Fraser Tolmie, 59, British Columbia
8 Railways and Canals – William Anderson Black, 78, Nova Scotia
9 Postmaster General – Robert James Manion, 44, Ontario
10 Trade and Commerce – James Dew Chaplin, 63, Ontario
11 Public Works – Edmond Baird Ryckman, 60, Ontario
12 Labour – George Burpee Jones, 60, New Brunswick

13 Immigration and Colonization; Without Portfolio – Sir Henry Lumley Drayton, 57, Ontario
14 Without Portfolio – Raymond Ducharme Morand, 39, Ontario
15 Without Portfolio – John Alexander Macdonald, 52, Prince Edward Island
16 Without Portfolio – Donald Sutherland, 63, Ontario
17 Health and Soldiers' Civil Re-establishment – Eugène Paquet, 58, Quebec (appointed on 23 August 1926)
18 Solicitor General – Guillaume-André Fauteux, 51, Quebec (appointed on 23 August 1926)

The members of Meighen's cabinet averaged 56.7 years of age, still four years older than he was. It was driven by central Canada: There were no less than eight men from Ontario among the eighteen and four Quebeckers. Only three were from the western provinces, the same as from the Maritime provinces.

After his 13 July appointments, most of Meighen's dealings with his cabinet ministers were focused on the coordination of their election campaigns. Such communications took arduous planning, often with the assistance of Arthur W. Merriam, his private secretary. But throughout the campaign, as he dashed across the nation, Meighen stubbornly upheld many traditional stances. Former Conservative leader John Diefenbaker, then an aspiring Tory candidate, recalled a conversation with the prime minister about the old-age pension. Meighen opposed the very idea: "It's wrong," he told Diefenbaker, who was backing the measure. "You must earn by the sweat of your brow, you cannot live off others."[70] Diefenbaker glumly added that Meighen "could not understand that social legislation and socialism were not synonymous terms."[71]

It is perhaps because Meighen was always in the spotlight, always answering questions, always addressing controversial issues, that his cabinet ministers were largely nonentities. A strong cabinet team might have improved his chances of winning elections. But no matter how many times Meighen shuffled his cabinets across his two governments, one thing was always clear: He was in charge. Meighen, for one, stubbornly defended relatively high tariffs. In 1921, he ignored warnings that the promise of continued protection was sending voters to the Progressives and the Liberals. Indeed, he defended the protective policy because "it makes possible an industrialization which is not the result of natural conditions but of the productive energy of its civilization."[72] In 1926, in response to a request for clarification on steel industry protection, he wired Cape Breton MP Finlay MacDonald that Maritime steel industries should be protected: "Conservative Party believes in protection adequate to enable industry workman and farmer [to] function and develop in Canada."[73]

Perhaps the most astonishing example of his approach to his caucus (and former cabinet ministers) occurred on 16 November 1925, in a speech at a banquet hall in Hamilton, Ontario. There, before his incredulous audience,

Meighen made an announcement "which he thought would appeal strongly to French Canadians."[74] Before troops were sent abroad in any future war, Canadians should express their will on the issue in a general election. Meighen had consulted Borden, Guthrie, Kemp, Reid, Drayton, and Major General Sydney Chilton Mewburn, the former militia minister in Borden's Union government. But the Conservative faithful, let alone the Conservative caucus, were stupefied: How could any government fight an election on that issue in wartime? How could Meighen grandly proclaim that this verdict would lead to national unity? As his long-time friend Grattan O'Leary gravely observed two years later, Meighen's decision appalled Conservative imperialists, who had to defend it in the 1926 election. "Some of them were cowed into it; others bludgeoned into it; and all of them cordially hated it."[75] Remarkably, to the consternation of many listeners, Meighen self-righteously defended the policy at the 1927 leadership convention. When Bennett won the leadership, he abandoned the policy.

After his few days in power in 1926, Meighen remained unwilling to change his appeal to the electorate. From the start, the constitution crisis attracted the headlines, "despite Meighen's scornful efforts at first to dismiss it as no issue at all."[76] That is, did Byng have the right to ignore King's request for a dissolution of Parliament? Constitutional scholars, then and now, remain divided on the issue. King exploited the issue from the beginning, deploring the so-called infringement on Canadian self-government. As Graham notes, "King went storming about the country proclaiming emotionally that the refusal had been unconstitutional and destructive of Canada's liberty and self-government."[77]

Meighen, for his part, was unmoved. He spoke about the tariff, the customs scandal that had prompted King to ask for a dissolution, freight rates, trade policy, the railways, and Maritime rights.[78] His supporters, however, saw the problem immediately. On 9 July 1926, Toronto barrister Frank Regan warned Meighen that the opposition "proclaims that the limited powers of the Crown in Canada should be limited to an even greater extent wiped out, in fact, and some form or another of autocracy substituted for it."[79] On 20 July, Justice Minister Patenaude told a Conservative mass meeting that he would deign to dignify "the 'alleged' constitutional issue" with comments: "Surely the action of the Governor General was right.... How could he have justified the gross affront to Parliament of which he would have been guilty had he granted Mr. King's request[?]"[80]

By the time Meighen paid attention, it was too late. As journalist Bruce Hutchison observed, Meighen was caught "between the deep cross-currents of Canadian life, between those who suspected him of surrendering Canada to an English governor and those who feared that his actions struck at the British constitution and damaged the British connection." Finally aware of his plight, the prime minister desperately tried to address the issue logically. But the voters' reactions "welled out of Canada's whole past," and even Meighen, "a poor judge of voters, saw the tide rising."[81]

Every one of his Quebec ministers except Perley lost. Meighen also lost his seat. His second government had lasted from 28 June to 24 September 1926.

After the Fall, Late 1926

There were many reasons why Meighen lost that election. Biographer Graham cites the popularity of the King government's budget along with the Liberal promise of further tax cuts, the King-Byng affair, and Meighen's feckless Hamilton speech about troop deployments, which offended many Conservatives. But it is also possible to see from his election correspondence with his private secretary and his cabinet ministers about his schedule that he was almost too busy to listen to the mood of the nation.[82] He fought valiantly, as did his cabinet ministers. But in the end, he did not create a sufficiently powerful cabinet team to offset his own liabilities.

In many ways, Meighen's political career was stunted by a character weakness that is often fatal for politicians: his conviction that he was the smartest person at the cabinet table. He could provide brilliance but not leadership. He would do what seemed logical with little consultation with most of his colleagues, convinced that consistency across time and Canadian space was the paramount virtue while the world changed around him. As the Rowell-Sirois Commission later detected, "the era of national growth based on western settlement, tariff protection, and east-west transportation links" had slipped away by the 1920s before Canadians grasped how much had changed.[83] Meighen was applying nineteenth-century remedies to twentieth-century problems – and he rarely altered his positions. When he did, as in the Hamilton speech, the results could be catastrophic.

To the extent that statecraft involves securing the assent of the majority to govern for the common good, it is clear that Meighen failed. Abroad in the United Kingdom in 1921, without the need for constant cabinet distractions, he dazzled his prime ministerial peers. At home, he rarely listened to good advice, politely treating most cabinet colleagues as underlings. Even the smartest person in the room – and Meighen was usually the smartest – needs to listen. Instead, Meighen disregarded too much advice on such issues as the tariff and made enemies too readily. Perhaps worse, he did too little to raise the stature of his cabinet members, or to bond them into a loyal team.

Confronted with controversial issues such as tariff rates, Mackenzie King would outline approaches of such ambiguity that no one was ever sure what he meant. As former Saskatchewan premier Tommy Douglas once noted, King "wrote his speeches with a back door in every sentence, so that he could back out of anything. Every sentence was qualified by another sentence, which gave him a perfect escape."[84] Meighen regarded that tactic as contemptible, and he made the mistake of seeing the calculating King as contemptible.

Meighen was self-confident to the point of arrogance. In private, with friends, he could be charming. In public, his austere demeanour and unsettling certitude could not inspire voter loyalty. At the cabinet table, he left little room for agency among its low-profile members. His approach to statecraft as a one-man band worked brilliantly. He was a superb parliamentarian, mastering intricate details and devising barbed ripostes, but he did not have the discipline of power. He could not muster the cabinet strength that might have helped him to succeed as prime minister and none of the wit and wisdom to survive a vote of confidence in the House of Commons. In short, Meighen was an estimable person who was likely in the wrong job at the wrong time. He was a natural Opposition leader. And many of his cabinet colleagues, although they respected him, recognized his flaws. His brief experiences in the prime minister's chair, nevertheless, are rich in lessons about cabinet government and what qualities are necessarily to make it a success.

Meighen returned to cabinet under R.B. Bennett in 1932 as leader of the government in the Senate and as minister without portfolio. In November 1941 he was again chosen to lead the Conservative Party, promising to put together a coalition of parties to lead the government in war. He resigned from the Upper Chamber to run for a seat in the House of Commons in a by-election but was defeated by the Co-operative Commonwealth Federation, the forerunner of the New Democratic Party. Meighen's career in cabinet had given him a chance to demonstrate his enormous abilities, but they alone were not enough to manage the myriad challenges of his treacherous post-war world.

NOTES

1 R.W. Wigmore to Prime Minister Arthur Meighen, 19 September 1921, Library and Archives Canada (hereafter "LAC"), Arthur Meighen Fonds, MG 26 I, series 2, Correspondence, 105115, C-3432, 652, https://heritage.canadiana.ca/view /oocihm.lac_reel_c3432/652. Wigmore addressed Meighen as "Dear Chief."

2 LAC, Arthur Meighen Fonds, MG 26 I, series 2, Correspondence, 105115, C-3432, 653.

3 Meighen to Wigmore, 19 September 1921, LAC, Arthur Meighen Fonds, MG 26 I, series 2, Correspondence, 105115, C-3432, 651, https://heritage.canadiana.ca /view/oocihm.lac_reel_c3432/651.

4 E.A. McCurdy to Meighen, 19 November 1921, 695, and M.E. Ager, Thos. Bell, F.T. Lewis, Wm. Swanton, J. Roy Campbell to Meighen, 2 December 1921, LAC, Arthur Meighen Fonds, MG 26 I, series 2, Correspondence, 105115, C-3432, 717.

5 J.B.M. Baxter to Meighen, 30 November 1921, LAC, Arthur Meighen Fonds, MG 26 I, series 2, Correspondence, 105115, C-3432, 711.

6 Wigmore to Meighen, 4 December 1921, LAC, Arthur Meighen Fonds, MG 26 I, series 2, Correspondence, 105115, C-3432, 724.

7 Meighen to Baxter, 1 December 2021, LAC, Arthur Meighen Fonds, MG 26 I, series 2, Correspondence, 105115, C-3432, 716.

8 Meighen to Baxter, 4 December 2021, LAC, Arthur Meighen Fonds, MG 26 I, series 2, Correspondence, 105115, C-3432, 722.

9 This assertion is based on an examination of all Meighen's correspondence with his cabinet members during his two terms.

10 Meighen to Minister without Portfolio Sir Edward Kemp, 20 August 1921, LAC, C-3220, 957. Ironically, the CNR did move its headquarters to Montreal in 1923, shortly after it finally absorbed the Grand Trunk Railway.

11 Roger Graham, *Arthur Meighen*, vol. 2, *And Fortune Fled* (Toronto: Clarke, Irwin, 1963), 23.

12 As quoted in F.D.L. Smith to Meighen, 7 February 1921, in Graham, *And Fortune Fled*, 22.

13 Meighen to J.M. Robinson, Summerland Development Company, Naramata, BC, 21 April 1921, LAC, C-3226, 1037.

14 H.S Clements to Meighen, September 12, 1921, C3432/302; Meighen to Clements, September 10, 1921, C3432/301. Clements did not get the Senate seat and he lost his riding in the 1921 election.

15 Robert Laird Borden, *Robert Laird Borden: His Memoirs*, ed. Henry Borden (Toronto: Macmillan, 1938), 2:1039.

16 Bruce Hutchison, *Mr. Prime Minister, 1867–1964* (Don Mills, On: Longmans Canada, 1964), 192. Hutchinson called his chapter on Meighen "The Heroic Failure."

17 Borden, *Memoirs*, 2:1039.

18 Borden, *Memoirs*, 2:1039.

19 Calder to Meighen, 27 June 1920, quoted in Roger Graham, *Arthur Meighen*, vol. 1, *The Door of Opportunity* (Toronto: Clarke, Irwin, 1960), 290. We are grateful to Patricia Finlay for her translation of Borden's French in his diaries.

20 Borden, *Memoirs*, 2:1040.

21 Newton Rowell to Borden, 15 February 1920, quoted in Margaret Prang, *N.W. Rowell: Ontario Nationalist* (Toronto: University of Toronto Press, 1975), 336.

22 Newton Rowell to Borden, 15 February 1920, quoted in Prang, *N.W. Rowell*, 336.

23 Robert Craig Brown, "Foster, Sir George Eulas," in *Dictionary of Canadian Biography*, vol. 16, accessed 30 August 2024, https://www.biographi.ca/en/bio/foster_george_eulas_16E.html.

24 Graham, *And Fortune Fled*, 114.

25 Ian D. Parker, "Simon Fraser Tolmie: The Last Conservative Premier of British Columbia," *BC Studies*, no. 11 (Fall 1971): 21.

26 John Boyko, *Bennett: The Rebel Who Challenged and Changed a Nation* (Toronto: Key Porter Books, 2010), 152.

27 James Alexander Calder to Meighen, 8 October 1920, LAC, Arthur Meighen Fonds, MG 26 I, series 2, Correspondence, 105988, C-3220, 387.

28 Meighen to Calder, 9 October 1920, LAC, Arthur Meighen Fonds, MG 26 I, series 2, Correspondence, 105988, C-3220, 388.

29 Boyko, *Bennett*, 119. Bennett and Lougheed were former law partners who had fallen out.

30 Graham, *Door of Opportunity*, 20.

31 Graham, *Door of Opportunity*, 142.

32 Graham, *Door of Opportunity*, 263–4.

33 Reinhold Kramer and Tom Mitchell, *When the State Trembled: How A.J. Andrews and the Citizens' Committee Broke the Winnipeg General Strike* (Toronto: University of Toronto Press, 2010), 5.

34 Graham, *Door of Opportunity*, 244.

35 John G. Diefenbaker, *One Canada: Memoirs of the Right Honourable John G. Diefenbaker, The Crusading Years, 1895 to 1956* (Toronto: Macmillan, 1975), 153.

36 William Lyon Mackenzie King, diary, 8 November 1941, LAC, item 23410, https://central.bac-lac.gc.ca/.redirect?app=diawlmking&id=11865&lang=eng.

37 Graham, *Door of Opportunity*, 55.

38 Col. J.A. Amyot to A.B. Macallum, 12 August 1920, LAC, Arthur Meighen Fonds, MG 26 I, series 2, Correspondence, 105988, C-3431, 1170. The Honorary Council would become the National Research Council of Canada in 1925.

39 Sir George Foster to Meighen, 21 August 1920, LAC, Arthur Meighen Fonds, MG 26 I, series 2, Correspondence, 105988, C-3431, 1173.

40 Meighen to Calder, 30 August 1920, LAC, Arthur Meighen Fonds, MG 26 I, series 2, Correspondence, 105988, C-3431, 1176.

41 Meighen, quoting telegram from Stevens to Ballantyne, 11 November 1920, LAC, Arthur Meighen Fonds, MG 26 I, series 2, Correspondence, 105988, C-3228, 1390.

42 Meighen to Stevens, 11 December 1920, LAC, Arthur Meighen Fonds, MG 26 I, series 2, Correspondence, 105988, C-3228, 1413.

43 Stevens to Meighen, 14 December 1920, LAC, Arthur Meighen Fonds, MG 26 I, series 2, Correspondence, 105988, C-3228, 1414.

44 Meighen to Stevens, 17 December 1920, LAC, Arthur Meighen Fonds, MG 26 I, series 2, Correspondence, 105988, C-3229, 8.

45 Stevens to Meighen, 13 January 1921, LAC, Arthur Meighen Fonds, MG 26 I, series 2, Correspondence, 105988, C-3229, 18.

46 Meighen to Stevens, 15 January 1921, LAC, Arthur Meighen Fonds, MG 26 I, series 2, Correspondence, 105988, C-3229, 27.

47 Marine Minister Ballantyne to Meighen, 19 January 1921, LAC, Arthur Meighen Fonds, MG 26 I, series 2, Correspondence, 105988, C-3229, 37.

48 "Coughlan Predicts Work for Shipping When Times Normal," *The Province*, 3 May 1921, 7.

49 Secret memo from Loring Christie to Meighen, 28 February 1921, LAC, Arthur Meighen Fonds, MG 26 I, series 2, Correspondence, 105988, C-3219, 313–14. Stefansson proceeded with the mission anyway, despite Canada's refusal to back him; his four recruits perished, and his attempt to take the island from Russia for Britain triggered an international incident.

50 L.T. Walls to Meighen, 1 June 1921, LAC, Arthur Meighen Fonds, MG 26 I, series 2, Correspondence, 105988, C-3225, 148.

51 Senator P.-E. Blondin to Meighen, 8 April 1921, LAC, Arthur Meighen Fonds, MG 26 I, series 2, Correspondence, 105988, C-3429, 1053.

52 Meighen to Minister without Portfolio James P. Wilson from Saskatoon, 19 August 1921. Wilson had told Meighen of the plight of former Saskatoon mayor William Hopkins, who had made two trips to Europe to find and bring home his only son's body.

53 Meighen to Baxter, 17 October 1921, LAC, Arthur Meighen Fonds, MG 26 I, series 2, Correspondence, 105988, C-3430, 963–5.

54 Meighen to Sir James Lougheed and Farrow, 15 November 1921, LAC, Arthur Meighen Fonds, MG 26 I, series 2, Correspondence, 105988, C-3221, 1394.

55 John English, *The Decline of Politics: The Conservatives and the Party System, 1901–1920* (Toronto: University of Toronto Press, 1977), 162. English emphasizes that the rather toothless Civil Service Commission, which was established in 1908, was strengthened when the Unionist program pledged to abolish patronage, making appointments based solely upon merit.

56 Garrett Tyrrell to Meighen, 4 August 1920, LAC, Arthur Meighen Fonds, MG 26 I, series 2, Correspondence, 105988, C-3434, 375.

57 Larry A. Glassford, "'The Presence of So Many Ladies': A Study of the Conservative Party's Response to Female Suffrage in Canada, 1918–1939," *Atlantis* 22, no. 1 (Fall/Winter 1997): 22.

58 Graham, *Door of Opportunity*, 196.

59 James Calder to Meighen, 17 November 1921, LAC, Arthur Meighen Fonds, MG 26 I, series 2, Correspondence, 105988, C-3323, 275.

60 Glassford, "'So Many Ladies,'" 22.

61 "The Fate of the Dominion rests in the hands of The Women of Canada," display advertisement, *Globe*, 30 November 1921, 5.

62 There are numerous examples of Meighen's unusual approach to Stevens, including Meighen to H.H. Stevens, 17 October 1921, LAC, Arthur Meighen Fonds, MG 26 I, series 2, Correspondence, 105988, C-3220, 1060.

63 Text of Meighen's remarks in Three Rivers, LAC, Arthur Meighen Fonds, MG 26 I, series 2, Correspondence, 105988, C-3230, 1355.

64 Graham, *And Fortune Fled*, 182.

65 After the 1926 election, Forke would accept an appointment in King's cabinet as immigration minister.

66 Graham, *And Fortune Fled*, 370.

67 Graham, *And Fortune Fled*, 373.

68 Graham, *And Fortune Fled*, 452.

69 In June 1926, a leading Quebec Conservative discreetly approached future Liberal prime minister Louis St-Laurent to see if he would accept a cabinet portfolio in Meighen's government. St-Laurent refused. We are grateful to Patrice Dutil for this reference to Dale C. Thomson, *Louis St. Laurent: Canadian* (Toronto: Macmillan, 1967), 85.

70 As recounted in Diefenbaker, *One Canada*, 152.

71 Diefenbaker, *One Canada*, 146. Diefenbaker lost that election.

72 Conclusion to Meighen speech, LAC, Arthur Meighen Fonds, MG 26 I, series 2, Correspondence, 105988, C-3230, 387, 1366 (n.d., n.p., but follows campaign speech in Maritimes).

73 Meighen to Finlay MacDonald, 10 September 1926, LAC, Arthur Meighen Fonds, MG 26 I, series 2, Correspondence, 125286, C-3551, 622.

74 Graham, *And Fortune Fled*, 355.

75 M. Grattan O'Leary, "Conservatism's New Prophet," *Maclean's*, 15 November 1927.

76 Graham, *And Fortune Fled*, 461.

77 Graham, *And Fortune Fled*, 461.

78 Graham, *And Fortune Fled*, 460–1.

79 Frank Regan to Meighen, 9 July 1926, LAC, Arthur Meighen Fonds, MG 26 I, series 4, C-3478, 685.

80 "Patenaude Tells Of Conservative Rapprochement; Makes Strong Plea for Government of Stability and Progress; Mackenzie King's Error," *Montreal Gazette*, 21 July 1926, 11.

81 Bruce Hutchison, *The Incredible Canadian: A Candid Portrait of Mackenzie King: His Works, His Times, and His Nation* (Toronto: Longmans, Green, 1952), 145.

82 See, for example, his correspondence with F.C. Cousins, secretary of the Prince Albert Conservative riding association: Cousins to Meighen, 13 July 1926, and Meighen to Cousins, 17 July 1926, LAC, Arthur Meighen Fonds, MG 26 I, series 4, C-3479, 319–20.

83 Robert Wardhaugh and Barry Ferguson, *The Rowell-Sirois Commission and the Remaking of Canadian Federalism* (Vancouver: University of British Columbia Press, 2021), 302.

84 T.C. Douglas, *The Making of a Socialist: The Recollections of T. C. Douglas*, ed. Lewis H. Thomas (Edmonton: University of Alberta Press, 1982), 347.

8 Cabinet Management after the Collapse of the Two-Party System: Mackenzie King in the 1920s

ROBERT WARDHAUGH

Mackenzie King has been recognized over the past few decades as one of the most successful prime ministers in Canadian history. The fact that he was the longest-serving prime minister (twenty-one years) positions him as an obvious contender for the title. In the years following his death, the explanation for King's success was that he was a bland, colourless leader who was blessed by good fortune and the ability to surround himself with capable ministers, while doing everything possible to maintain office at all costs. As time passes, however, King's remarkable longevity seems more impressive. His management of the war effort from 1939 to 1945, followed by his administration of post-war recovery, has led historians to rank Mackenzie King as Canada's "greatest" prime minister.[1]

This was not always the case. In the early governments of the 1920s, King's hold on federal office, not to mention the leadership of the Liberal Party, was tenuous. As the two-party system collapsed, King's approach to cabinet formation played a critical role in securing both. While remaining a powerful force, patronage gradually gave way to brokerage politics. The traditional canon of cabinet construction based on the three Rs – race, religion, and region – continued, but region became the most important factor.[2] Never a charismatic or commanding leader, King's statecraft, which included skills at conciliation and negotiation, made the brokerage-regional strategy a natural fit. The use of regional lieutenants was employed by both John A. Macdonald and Wilfrid Laurier, but it was Mackenzie King who brought it to an apotheosis. Laurier made effective use of the provincial Liberal parties, patronage, and premiers for organizational purposes as well as for potential cabinet ministers. King perfected the system.[3]

Mackenzie King became prime minister in 1921 in the long shadow cast by the Great War – a new modern era of protest, populism, consumerism, and technology. A pallor of scepticism and discontent hung over Canada, the economy was in tatters, nativism and racism lurked everywhere, class conflict flared up on the streets of Winnipeg, and, as if all this was not bad enough, a global pandemic arrived. Simultaneously, Canada experienced a generational shift in political leadership. Wilfrid Laurier died in 1919 and Robert Borden retired in 1920. Mackenzie King was selected leader of the Liberals, Arthur Meighen took over for the Conservatives, and Thomas A. Crerar emerged to lead a new third party, the Progressives. In the war's aftermath, however, with a generation lost on the battlefields of Europe, the shift was palpable. No longer would the nation speak of its political leaders as statesmen; now they were mere politicians. The nation was still bitterly divided over the conscription crisis of 1917.[4] But while many commentators in Canada feared the growth of radicalism, the real threat was regional. As bitter as Quebec was over the conscription crisis, the threat came from the Prairie West.[5] Defeating it and winning the West dominated the objectives of King's governments throughout the 1920s. Cabinet formation became the centrepiece in the prime minister's strategy.

The agrarian revolt was already underway in 1911, when the Prairie dream of reciprocity (free trade) with the United States championed by Laurier went down to defeat.[6] After waiting for fifteen years for the Laurier Liberals to fulfil their promises of lowering the tariff, the organized farmers' movement was at its wits' end. It seemed that neither traditional party was intent on defending the interests of the Prairie region or its main industry. The outbreak of war in 1914 put a lid on the simmering agrarian revolt, as it did on other reform movements. The formation of Borden's coalition government in 1917 bitterly divided the Liberal Party over the issue of conscription into two camps: the Laurier Loyalists mainly from Quebec and the Unionist Liberals mainly from English Canada. Prairie Liberals were overwhelmingly in the latter camp. When the war ended by 1919, however, this group, led by Manitoba's Crerar (who had served as minister of agriculture in the Union cabinet), found themselves in a quandary. While they found it impossible to remain in Borden's Union government as it returned to its Conservative roots and embraced its traditional protectionist stance, they also found it difficult to return to a Liberal Party that was dominated by Quebec and that had failed to advance agricultural interests in the past. The organized farmers' movement entered politics directly. The two-party system in Canada was broken, never to be restored.

The Liberals were searching for an answer. Laurier's death in February 1919 prompted the party decision to choose its next leader by a leadership convention, the first one held in Canadian history. The loyal heirs to Laurier were determined to maintain control of the party but were open to welcoming back those who had supported the Borden coalition. The result was a new party platform and the selection of Mackenzie King as leader. "I have not the slightest doubt," King recorded in his diary, "that it will be mine to link together Liberals, Farmers & Labour, and form a really progressive party in Canadian affairs."[7]

Mackenzie King, forty-four years old, saw an opportunity. Born and raised in Berlin (now Kitchener), Ontario, he was the maternal grandson of William Lyon Mackenzie (one of the leaders of the Rebellions of 1837–8). His educational achievements were impressive, first at the University of Toronto, then in graduate work at Harvard. He had served as deputy minister and then as minister of the newly created Department of Labour in the Laurier government. King was a progressive shaped by the social reform movement of the day. After his defeat in the 1911 election, he found work in the United States as a labour consultant with the Rockefeller family,[8] but his loyalties were always with Laurier, a man he idolized. King returned to Canada to contest and lose the seat of North York in the election of 1917.

The defeat did not diminish King's ambitions. In the race for the leadership, King appealed to Quebeckers, but he could not speak French and he had limited knowledge of Quebec politics.[9] A division existed within Quebec Liberals that went back to the Macdonald period between a group centred in Montreal and one based around Quebec City. The Montreal bloc was connected with commerce and industry (manufacturing, financial, and railway interests) while the Quebec City group was tied to rural, agricultural, and professional interests. King had trouble finding support. The most powerful of the Quebec members was former premier Lomer Gouin, who had powerful business connections in Montreal. Described as "amiably dispassionate as a bank manager," Gouin had an attitude towards King "not far removed from open contempt and defiance."[10] He supported W.S. Fielding at the 1919 convention for Liberal leader, despite the latter's support for conscription.[11] Fielding had once been premier of Nova Scotia and then federal minister of finance under Laurier before serving in the Union government. Both Gouin and Fielding were advanced in age, and both were high-tariff protectionists. King looked to the younger members from Quebec City, led by lawyer Ernest Lapointe, the architect of his leadership bid, to become his French-Canadian advisers. Lapointe had risen through the ranks of Quebec politics relatively slowly and he did not achieve minister status under Laurier. He was, however, "loyal, dependable, and above all, teachable."[12] By the time of the convention, Lapointe had attained prominence in his province and now represented Laurier's old seat of Quebec East.

Mackenzie King focused his efforts on wooing the West. Regional support could be a weapon to disarm the Montreal bloc but while King was prepared to be patient, the West was not. The United Farmers won the provincial election in Ontario in 1919, followed by victories in Alberta in 1921 and Manitoba in 1922. While the provincial government in Saskatchewan was Liberal in name, it broke from the federal party and was, in essence, a farmers' party. At the federal level, the farmers led by T.A. Crerar committed themselves to independent political action and became the National Progressive Party.

The Laurier years created the notion that Quebec controlled the party and the selection of King as leader only cemented this impression. King was seen as too weak to control these forces and "terrified lest the French-Canadian majority in his party may throw him overboard."[13] As the first post-war election approached, portents of danger were everywhere. During the campaign, King took seriously the rumours that Lomer Gouin and several others of the "Montreal Tycoons" were considering an alliance with the Conservatives to preserve a high tariff.[14]

The main issue in the federal election of 6 December 1921 was the tariff, with a wide range of parties contesting seats.[15] The government of Arthur Meighen went down to defeat, losing 104 seats and taking less than 30 per cent of the vote. The Liberals took over 41 per cent of the vote and won 118 seats, barely half of the 235 ridings in the House of Commons.[16] The electorate returned fifty-nine Progressives (including one Independent Progressive), fifty Conservatives (including one Independent Conservative), three Labourites, two representatives of the United Farmers of Alberta, and one representing the United Farmers of Ontario (UFO). In Ontario, the Liberals won only twenty-one of eighty-two seats. In the West, the Liberals elected three members in Manitoba, one in Saskatchewan, none in Alberta, and three in British Columbia. The Progressives swept the Prairies, winning thirty-nine out of a possible forty-three seats, but also taking twenty seats in Ontario, among them Agnes Macphail, the first woman ever elected to the House of Commons (representing Grey Southeast). For the first time since Confederation, the Liberals won all sixty-five seats in Quebec. If there was any doubt about Quebec's domination of the party before the election, there was none after. The Liberals also won thirty-five of forty seats in the Maritimes. The Conservatives, on the other hand, failed to win a seat in six of the provinces. But the most shocking aspect of the 1921 election was that the two-party system was shattered. There were 143 three-cornered contests for the 235 seats.

Canada was thus divided into a Liberal East, a Progressive West, and a divided Ontario, and "it was amidst this wreckage of the traditional two-party system that Mackenzie King set about constructing his cabinet."[17] King had to balance competing interests within his own party while attempting to heal the division of 1917 between Laurier and Unionist Liberals. He was well aware that his hold on the party leadership was tenuous. King's strategy was to invite Progressives to join the new cabinet to secure the government, but he realized the dangers this posed to holding the support of the central and eastern sections of his own party. At the same time, he was not willing to give all the choice positions in the cabinet to the older men, "the left-overs of the Laurier administration."[18] The problem was that these veterans constituted most of the talent and influence in the Liberal Party.

The new prime minister hoped to reduce the size of cabinet from twenty-one (under Meighen) to sixteen members by having fewer ministers without portfolio.[19] The plan was to give Ontario four ministers (in addition to King), Quebec four, and the other seven provinces one each. In every federal cabinet since 1867 except one, Nova Scotia was represented by two ministers. The initial decision to give the province only one, even though it returned all Liberals, reflected the beginning of King's neglect for the Maritimes in cabinet formation. A minister without portfolio would represent the government as its leader in the Senate. The top position was finance, and it went to W.S. Fielding, who had contested the leadership in 1919, though the elder sage from Nova Scotia was largely ignored in the cabinet consultations.[20] To diminish the influence of Lomer Gouin, and in keeping with practices established by Macdonald, Laurier, and Borden, King kept the positions of president of the Privy Council and the secretary of state for external affairs for himself.

The most important issue surrounding cabinet formation in 1921 was the role of the Progressives. King flirted with the notion of a coalition with the Progressives during the campaign, but he retreated as election day approached due to resistance from the Montreal group. He now set out to have the Progressive leaders enter the cabinet as Liberals but soon discovered that this strategy threatened the support of certain elements in the party. Ontario Liberals were engaged in both provincial and federal battles with the farmers' movement and were in no mood for generous treatment. The Liberal faction from Quebec City, led by Ernest Lapointe, Jacques Bureau, and Henri Béland, on the other hand, favoured accommodating the Progressives. The Montreal Liberals, led by Lomer Gouin, Walter Mitchell, Raoul Dandurand, and Rodolphe Lemieux, were unwilling to compromise.[21]

The preliminary cabinet list drawn up by Mackenzie King and Andrew Haydon (the main Liberal adviser and organizer throughout the 1920s) reflected an attempt to reach out westward and included T.A. Crerar, A.B. Hudson,[22] and W.R. Motherwell. It leaned heavily towards the agrarian interests and low-tariff Liberals. King wanted to convince the Progressives that their presence (and those of other westerners) would counterbalance that of the protectionists. Haydon was dispatched to Winnipeg to meet with Crerar. Meanwhile, Lapointe met with Liberal organizer and businessman Kirk Cameron in Montreal while travelling to Ottawa to consult with King.[23] According to Cameron (who then passed on the details to Crerar), Lapointe supported an arrangement with the Progressives as a means of reducing the influence of Gouin's group.[24] Upon meeting with King, however, Lapointe indicated that Gouin would be hostile to Progressives in the cabinet. The only way to succeed would be to provide the Montreal group with more influential posts than first intended. King wished to strike a deal with the agrarian leaders first in order to strengthen his position vis-à-vis the Gouin group. The new prime minister was already grooming

Lapointe to serve in the role of Quebec lieutenant and called on him first to come to Ottawa: "I told him I regarded him as nearest to me & wd. give him my confidence in full now & always. We would work out matters together. I regarded him as the real leader in Quebec, had sent for him first of all as promised. Asked which portfolio he wd. like and said he could have it."[25]

The cabinet negotiations in 1921 were relatively lengthy and occurred over a three-week period between the election on 6 December and Christmas. Meetings took place between Haydon and Crerar in Winnipeg on 12–16 December. The Liberal emissary made it clear that the Progressive leaders were needed in cabinet to "free" the government from the "domination by the Montreal interests and any reactionary influences." Cabinet positions, Crerar responded, would not be enough to placate the West. "Measures" were more important than "men." The discussion then turned to matters of policy with Crerar and Hudson putting forward a list of conditions that reflected western concerns. Crerar wanted four cabinet positions given to the Prairies, including one Progressive from Alberta, and he proposed that Hudson receive the influential justice portfolio. He also pronounced on the acceptability of King's preliminary cabinet list. Motherwell from Saskatchewan was unsatisfactory, and Charles Stewart (former premier) should represent Alberta. Before any deal was finalized, Crerar indicated that he would have to meet with a gathering of the western Progressives in Saskatoon.[26]

Mackenzie King responded favourably to the Progressive proposals that aligned with his own stance on Prairie issues, including tariffs, freight rates, and natural resources. He was not, however, prepared to make concrete promises. King was also not prepared to consider more than one cabinet minister for each of the Prairie provinces. Motherwell would have to represent Saskatchewan, and both Crerar and Hudson from Manitoba could enter the cabinet while Alberta would be left in the cold.[27] Pressure was increasing from the Montreal group and time was running out. King advised Crerar and Hudson to come to Ottawa immediately. While Crerar agreed, he indicated he first had to receive the support of the Saskatoon meeting. Premier Drury of Ontario would also come to Ottawa.

Mackenzie King was confident the cabinet negotiations were proceeding well but he was unaware of the strategy discussions going on behind the scenes with the Progressives. In Winnipeg, Crerar was advised by J.W. Dafoe, the influential editor of the *Manitoba Free Press*, and the newspaper's owner, Clifford Sifton. They took the position that unless King offered a formal coalition, there would be no chance of the Progressive leaders entering cabinet. The government would be left to "the Liberal antiques who are now congregating at Ottawa.... The Liberal party would in effect be a Quebec and Nova Scotia party with a Rump from the rest of the Provinces.... They should sit at the head table and the Farmers organization should take whatever crumbs that are offered to them."[28] Dafoe was consequently surprised to learn that the Progressive leaders were even contemplating entering King's cabinet without the guarantee of a coalition.[29] The situation became more complex when Drury indicated that he had come to the same conclusion and did not believe his Ontario following would support his entry into cabinet.[30]

A.B. Hudson arrived in Ottawa five days before Christmas. There was some confusion as to the results of Crerar's meeting with the western Progressives in Saskatoon. Whereas Crerar was given "tacit approval" to enter cabinet under satisfactory conditions, the Alberta Progressives were opposed.[31] King warned Hudson that the Progressive position was creating a "serious" situation in which the West could well end up with no representation.[32] The next day the negotiations were further threatened when Drury arrived from Toronto to inform King that his followers had refused to release him from provincial responsibilities until after the next election.[33] Crerar's position was weakened when he met with the Ontario Progressives in Toronto. The UFO group refused to support any cooperation of any kind, even on matters of legislation.[34]

King faced off against the Montreal bloc on 23–4 December. Gouin wanted six ministers from Quebec, including Rodolphe Lemieux (who was insulted at not being called first to Ottawa) and J.A. Robb (Quebec was traditionally represented by at least one English-speaking minister). Gouin's group preferred the Ontario Progressives to those from the West and favoured Drury over Crerar.[35] Despite King's earlier promises, Lapointe was persuaded to bide his time and take the department of marine and fisheries while Gouin was given the prestigious portfolio of justice. A tense exchange occurred between King and Gouin when the senior Quebec politician responded angrily to the decision that he would not also be given the presidency of the Privy Council, which the prime minister intended to keep for himself.[36] In addition to Gouin and Lapointe, Quebec was to be represented by Raoul Dandurand as government leader in the Senate, Jacques Bureau as minister of customs and excise, Henri Béland as minister of the new and small department of soldiers' civil re-establishment and health, and J.A. Robb as minister of trade and commerce. If Quebec was to have six ministers, Ontario would expect and demand the same.

The leaders of the Liberal and Progressive parties met on the same day. King was confident he deserved western support due to his refusal to bow to Montreal pressure. He presented Crerar with the offer to join the cabinet as a Liberal and made it clear that he would not discuss coalition or make policy promises. Crerar rejected the offer, based on the position of his members, but he indicated a desire to enter cabinet at a later date. Meanwhile, the two parties would work together in the House. Crerar told King that the Progressives did not intend to become the official opposition. They would maintain their identity as a party and support the government so long as legislation was progressive. King responded that the West would be left out of the councils of government, and he issued a veiled threat. With no Progressives in cabinet, it would be more difficult to offer incentives to the region. Nonetheless, he was confident that the Progressive cause would "suffer," and its followers would eventually be absorbed into the Liberal ranks.[37]

In the end, the cabinet of 1921 was a success in regional negotiation but a failure in quality recruitment. While Quebec provided a bounty of talent, "nowhere in that great expanse from the Ottawa River to the Pacific was there a goodly harvest awaiting a federal Liberal cabinet-maker."[38] As historians John Thompson and Allen Seager point out, "the new administration that was King's New Year's gift to Canada for 1922 was designed with an eye to regional symmetry; ministerial competence had been a consideration, but as usual in Canadian cabinet making it had placed a distant second."[39] Western representation was left to Motherwell (agriculture) and Stewart (mines and interior). Both were Laurier loyalists and "diehards" who refused to accommodate the Unionists or the Progressives, and neither was capable of filling the role of western lieutenant that Sifton had once served under Laurier. Stewart had lost in Alberta and a safe seat would have to be found in Quebec. King would have preferred a Manitoba representative, leaving Alberta isolated for its failure to elect any Liberals: "We were under no obligation to give Alberta representation. She must accept [the] situation as she had made it."[40] Crerar was not pleased to learn that since the Winnipeg negotiations, the cabinet slate had been altered considerably. Ontario was represented by an unimpressive group, all of whom were Laurier loyalists: W.C. Kennedy as minister of railways and canals, George Graham as minister of militia and defence (and naval service), James Murdock as minister of labour, Charles Murphy as postmaster general, and T.A. Low as minister without portfolio.[41] Maritime representation fell to W.S. Fielding as minister of finance, D.D. McKenzie as solicitor general, A.B. Copp as secretary of state, and John E. Sinclair as minister without portfolio.[42] While the Prairie West figured large in the cabinet formation of 1921, the Pacific West did not. Three Liberals were elected in British Columbia, but none was of cabinet quality. Mackenzie King pondered the war hero Arthur Currie as a possible representative but ended up finding a seat for J.H. King, a provincial Liberal cabinet minister who became minister of public works.[43]

The quality of its members may have been poor, but the 1921 cabinet negotiations proved crucial for Mackenzie King's leadership. The new prime minister faced two daunting challenges when he commenced the process: bringing the warring factions in the party together and returning the West to the Liberal fold. Although King failed to bring the Progressive leadership into the cabinet, he at least obtained their conditional support. The prime minister's overtures to the Progressives and the West would reap rewards in the future. And although King's rivals and critics emerged with influential positions in cabinet, as his biographer notes, "It was a diplomatic achievement to have formed a government at all out of the factions which made up the party in 1921."[44]

1   Prime Minister; External Affairs; President of the Privy Council – W.L. Mackenzie King, 47, Journalist, Ontario, Protestant
2   Agriculture – William R. Motherwell, 61, Farmer, Saskatchewan, Protestant
3   Customs and Excise – Jacques Bureau, 61, Lawyer, Quebec, Catholic
4   Finance – William S. Fielding, 73, Journalist, Nova Scotia, Protestant
5   Interior; Indian Affairs; Mines – Charles Stewart, 53, Farmer, Alberta, Protestant
6   Justice and Attorney General – Lomer Gouin, 60, Lawyer, Quebec, Catholic
7   Labour – James Murdock, 50, Union Leader, Ontario, Protestant
8   Marine and Fisheries – Ernest Lapointe, 45, Lawyer, Quebec, Catholic
9   Militia and Defence; Naval Service – George P. Graham, 62, Journalist, Ontario, Methodist
10 Postmaster General – Charles Murphy, 56, Ontario, Catholic (senator)
11 Public Works – Hewitt Bostock, 57, British Columbia, Protestant (senator)
12 Railways and Canals – William C. Kennedy, 53, Businessman, Ontario, Protestant
13 Secretary of State of Canada – Arthur B. Copp, 51, Lawyer, New Brunswick, Protestant
14 Soldiers' Civil Re-establishment; Health – Henri S. Béland, 52, Physician, Quebec, Catholic (senator)
15 Solicitor General – D.D. McKenzie, 62, Lawyer, Nova Scotia, Protestant
16 Trade and Commerce – James A. Robb, Businessman, 62, Quebec, Protestant
17 Without Portfolio – Raoul Dandurand, 60, Lawyer, Quebec, Catholic (senator)
18 Without Portfolio – J.E. Sinclair, 42, Farmer, Prince Edward Island, Protestant
19 Without Portfolio – Thomas A. Low, 50, Businessman, Ontario, Catholic

The average age was 55.6 years old. Like Meighen before him, King would be directing a team that was several years older than he was. Six came from Quebec, the same from Ontario (thus matching Laurier's cabinet composition of 1896). Only three came from the West (none from Manitoba) and three from the Maritimes (none from Prince Edward Island).

***

Mackenzie King's first term as prime minister was dominated by the struggle between the Montreal bloc in the Liberal Party and the Progressives over such issues as tariffs, railway policy and freight rates, and natural resource development. It challenged King's statecraft and in particular his abilities at collegial management. "The Party cannot live in the long future unless it can hold the West," Andrew Haydon advised King. "It will continue to hold the East.... I take the liberty of suggesting that you might show a bit of 'the big stick' in some of these things. Macdonald was Master of his Administration. Laurier was very much so. You have to be also."[45] Fortunately for the King government, the Progressives refused the mantle of official opposition. Instead they served as a pressure group to ensure progressive legislation. But keeping these groups (in addition to the Unionist and Laurier factions) together was no easy task and the first two years in office were the most vulnerable for King's leadership. The prime minister had to bide his time until the older members were gone, and he could place his own stamp on the party. Crerar believed that "Gouin is the boss of the administration.... The Government is divided and there are evidences of a cleavage behind it."[46] In truth, King realized that Gouin's influence was already declining. Lapointe was the de facto leader in Quebec.

The prime minister's patience was rewarded by the end of 1923, when the opposition of the "Old Guard" was removed suddenly with the retirement of both Gouin and Fielding, purportedly due to poor health.[47] "I think the time has come now to cut the Gordian knot to sever this [Montreal] connection and bring the Liberals and Farmers together," King recorded in his diary. "I do not want to lose Quebec support, much less incur active opposition of powerful financial & mffg. interests, they are against us anyway at heart & we might as well have the fight in the open."[48]

With Gouin and Fielding gone, King moved to shore up his position in the West. The prime minister had little confidence in his present ministers from Saskatchewan (Motherwell) or Alberta (Stewart). T.A. Crerar resigned the leadership of the Progressives in 1922 but King viewed him as more influential than Robert Forke, the Manitoban who became the new Progressive leader. Crerar and Charles Dunning (the Liberal premier of Saskatchewan) were invited to Ottawa early in 1924. Rather than offer cabinet positions, the discussions focused on changes to tariff and railway policy that would attract western support. Cabinet changes were made that reflected not so much a shift in influence from East to West as from Montreal to Quebec City. J.A. Robb replaced Fielding as acting minister of finance and Ernest Lapointe replaced Gouin as minister of justice. Despite the urging of the Montreal group, Rodolphe Lemieux was passed over and P.J.A. Cardin was appointed to marine and fisheries.

King obtained Progressive support for government legislation from Forke and felt confident. The Progressives "were ready to cooperate with the Govt. in an open manner.... I feel a greater freedom with Gouin & Fielding gone, will be able to take my own natural course."[49] The Throne Speech and budget of 1924 promised tariff reductions. King's confidence in his western strategy was bolstered by divisions within the Progressive ranks. The split between the more radical Alberta members (known as the Ginger Group) and the more moderate Manitoba group was becoming even more obvious. When Dunning's Liberals swept to office in an election in Saskatchewan, King was elated: "It seems to me that in the circumstances of Quebec and Saskatchewan being alike so largely Liberal, we have one great essential to national unity."[50] But King's focus on Quebec and the West as the two main bases of party support led him to ignore the other regions. The Conservatives defeated the United Farmers government in Ontario in 1923. Cabinet representation for the Maritimes was traditionally four positions but at times it was reduced to two, in order to provide more representation to the West. The Conservatives won provincial office in Prince Edward Island in 1923. The biggest shock, however, came in 1925, when the Liberals lost Nova Scotia for the first time in forty-three years. Six weeks later, New Brunswick also fell. The Conservatives took advantage of federal neglect, regional discontent, and the resulting Maritime Rights movement.

Despite being rid of the "Old Guard," King's pessimism about the upcoming federal election translated into criticism of the existing cabinet: "I felt that Cabinet was very weak, lamentably weak in fact – really nothing to grip to. Many like barnacles rather than fighters."[51] Particular criticism was aimed at the corruption and smuggling in the customs and excise department, as well as its minister, Jacques Bureau. The Quebec minister (who had mentored Ernest Lapointe) was seen as a pleasant person but a weak administrator.[52] He was in poor health and was rarely in his office. Mackenzie King was particularly critical of Bureau for his excessive drinking.[53]

The prime minister's focus as usual was on gaining support in the West. Manitoba was without a minister after E.J. McMurray (who became solicitor general in 1923) was asked to resign over the failed Home Bank.[54] Motherwell and Stewart were seen as ineffective because, like McMurray, they represented the Laurier Liberals and refused to accommodate the Unionists or Progressives. King wanted Dunning from Saskatchewan, but the premier was fresh from his provincial election victory and was not willing to take a chance on the doubtful upcoming federal contest.

Ontario was always the crucial electoral battleground, but the Liberals failed to recruit impressive talent in the province. Cabinet members and Laurier veterans such as George Graham and Charles Murphy were near retirement. T.A. Low and James Murdock were seen as ineffective ministers and could be discarded. As King's biographer, H. Blair Neatby notes, "Unfortunately, no back-benchers from Ontario had emerged as promising candidates for promotion."[55] Cabinet representation from the Maritimes was just as unimpressive. With Fielding gone, the region was left to individuals such as New Brunswick's A.B. Copp and Nova Scotia's E.M. Macdonald. King looked outside cabinet for new blood. Former premier of New Brunswick W.E. Foster replaced Copp as secretary of state. The prime minister offered positions to two wealthy businessmen and protectionists – Herbert Marler from Montreal and Vincent Massey from Toronto. Both entered the cabinet in September without portfolios. George Boivin was sworn in as minister of customs and excise, while Bureau was ushered away to the Senate.

The Liberals campaigned in the 1925 election on the idea that only Liberal policies were national policies and only the Liberal Party was a truly national party. Despite failing to advance any of the western issues, Mackenzie King believed his record was deserving of victory. At least he had thwarted the advancement of the protectionists and reduced their influence in the party and government. Cabinet representation, meanwhile, was the prime minister's stick with which to corral the western Progressives. If the West wanted policy action, the region should send a strong Liberal contingent to Ottawa, "men who will come into our caucus and fight for the needs of Western Canada." King would not again offer cabinet positions to those unwilling to fully support the government: "When the Progressives take the attitude that they will support us when we do what they want and we can go to blazes when we do not, you cannot get very far. You cannot get people to work together under that system."[56]

Mackenzie King left Quebec completely in the hands of his regional lieutenant, Ernest Lapointe. According to C.G. Power, "Lapointe became so completely the representative of the Liberal Party in Quebec that for many years King counted little in the political life of the province.... It was to Lapointe that we looked for leadership, for generalship, and for anything relating to either policy or tactics in Quebec political life."[57] But the legislative record of the King government was not impressive: "Both historians and contemporary observers have agreed that it is impossible to point to a single conspicuous legislative achievement between 1922 and 1925."[58]

Election Day was a disaster for the Liberals. King lost his seat in North York, along with eight cabinet ministers.[59] Five of the Ontario ministers were defeated as were four Maritime ministers (only E.M. Macdonald was returned). Herbert Marler lost his seat in Montreal. When the ballots were counted on 29 October 1925, no party won a majority of the seats, and the situation was even more uncertain than four years earlier. Liberal representation fell from 116 to 100 seats in the 245-seat House. The Conservatives under Meighen surged, earning over 46 per cent of the vote, doubling their representation and winning 115 seats, seven short of a majority. Only twenty-two Progressives were returned, compared to sixty-five in 1921. Two Independents and two Labour candidates completed the list. According to Neatby, "Eastern Canada had punished King for his preoccupation with the prairies."[60] In contrast to Quebec, which returned sixty of sixty-five Liberals, the Maritimes sent only six of twenty-nine, and Ontario elected an embarrassing twelve of eighty-two. The party did better in the West, winning one seat in Manitoba, fifteen in Saskatchewan, and four in Alberta, while maintaining its three seats in British Columbia.

While the Progressives had declined in numbers, their influence in the new House of Commons was increased. Since the Conservatives won the most seats and the popular vote, the governor general, Lord Byng, indicated that King should do the honourable thing and resign. The prime minister, aware that Meighen would have difficulty securing Progressive support, decided instead to maintain power and meet the new House. The uncertain situation renewed speculation about the Liberal leadership. King's popularity, even inside his own party, reached an all-time low at the end of 1925.

If cabinet reconstruction was important before the election, it was crucial after, and the prime minister informed the caucus that it would "depend" upon the West.[61] "The more I think of the Ministers I have had round me," King noted, "the less I find them worth aught as 'generals'"[62] The government needed every vote in the House, so no cabinet appointments were made before the session. A few days after the election, Dunning reversed his earlier decision to remain in Saskatchewan and decided to enter the federal government.[63] "Dunning would be the leader within the government for the west," King claimed, "as Lapointe was for Quebec."[64] Cabinet changes were delayed, however, until an adjournment could be obtained following the debates and votes of confidence on the Throne Speech. King needed to wait to allow time for the necessary resignations and by-elections without the government running the risk of defeat in the House. He decided to open one seat at a time. This allowed him to bring in Dunning as minister of railways and canals and J.C. Elliott as minister of labour to represent Ontario. Charles Murphy remained postmaster general, although King did not like the old practice of senators being in cabinet. A full cabinet shuffle would have to wait: "King was dissatisfied with the Cabinet representation from every province, with the exception of Quebec, but he would not take any risk of losing one of the precious seats in the House during the Session."[65]

In the early months of 1926, King worked assiduously to ensure Progressive support. After losing his Ontario seat in the election, the prime minister accepted the nomination for the seat of Prince Albert in the Liberal stronghold of Saskatchewan now under the command of the new premier, Jimmy Gardiner.[66] At the same time, he found himself mired in the customs scandal. Details of rampant smuggling were emerging, and the Progressives would soon have to decide whether to support the government or defeat the Liberals, thereby allowing the protectionist Tories into office. When the Special Committee on the Department of Customs and Excise issued its report, it became clear that the department was riddled with corruption. On 22 June an amendment to the report of the Special Committee on Customs that was highly critical of the Liberal administration of the Customs Department gained both Progressive and Conservative support and threatened to censure the government. Fearing defeat of the government on the vote, King requested that the governor general dissolve the House and call an election. To the prime minister's surprise, Lord Byng refused. He believed that Arthur Meighen deserved the chance, and had the constitutional right, to form a government.

King resigned on 28 June and Arthur Meighen was invited to form a government. The difficulty for the Conservatives was that if any members accepted a portfolio in the new government (which involved accepting a minister's salary), they would immediately have to vacate their seat and contest a by-election before returning to the House. As soon as he became prime minister, Meighen himself had to vacate his seat. If he named his other ministers, the new government would be deprived of its best debaters and, more importantly, the votes needed to maintain power. This problem was avoided by the unusual tactic of not assigning any portfolios. Meighen appointed seven ministers without portfolio to serve as acting heads of the major government departments. These men would not receive a minister's salary and therefore would not have to resign their seats to contest by-elections. Now leader of the opposition, King found unexpected success in attacking Meighen's "shadow cabinet." A vote of non-confidence proposed by J.A. Robb carried by one vote. When the Conservative government collapsed, Prime Minister Meighen, unlike King, was granted a dissolution and election, thereby setting the stage for the Liberals to campaign on the so-called constitutional issue.

Mackenzie King succeeded in making the constitutional issue the central issue in the 1926 election, held on 14 September, and in pushing the customs scandal into the background. The improving economic conditions certainly helped. But it was the fear of a Conservative victory that drove the majority of the Progressives back into the Liberal ranks. The Liberals, however, needed to improve their position in Ontario.

Mackenzie King emerged victorious from the 1926 election with his leadership secured. The Liberals gained fifteen seats to win a total of 116, still leaving them short of an official majority. But the party's position was bolstered by the election of twelve Progressives, ten Liberal-Progressives, two Independents, and three Labour members, many of whom would sit in caucus and all of whom could be relied upon for support. Even the eleven United Farmers of Alberta MPs were more likely to favour the Liberals over the Tories. The Conservatives lost twenty-four seats, holding on to ninety-one. "The angels are certainly on the side of Willie King," J.W. Dafoe, observed from Winnipeg.[67] In Ontario the Liberals gained eleven seats and the Liberal-Progressives two; in Manitoba the Liberals increased their seats by three and the Liberal-Progressives by seven. The Liberals gained three seats in the Maritimes, while Quebec remained unchanged, and sixty members were again elected. Saskatchewan returned one more Liberal and one Liberal-Progressive; Alberta elected only one Liberal; in British Columbia the Liberals lost two seats.

Despite the tumultuous political events, changes to the cabinet were less drastic. Of seventeen ministers to be sworn in, eight were rookies. With no alternative, Charles Stewart remained the representative from Alberta, as did J.H. King from British Columbia (demoted from public works to health and soldier's civil re-establishment). The only change in Prairie representation was the entry of Manitoba's Robert Forke as minister of immigration and colonization. King wanted Jimmy Gardiner but deferred due to the Saskatchewan premier's poor relationship with Charles Dunning.[68] The elderly Motherwell would again remain in cabinet as minister of agriculture.

With the West in a stronger position, King focused on Ontario. Charles Murphy was moved to the Senate, but King informed him that he would not be in cabinet. Anticipating Murphy's outcry, King appointed Peter Heenan to represent the Irish Catholics in Ontario as minister of labour, even though King did not think he would be strong or effective. The prime minister proposed bringing former Ontario Liberal leader N.W. Rowell into the government but such an appointment was bitterly resisted by the factions of Laurier Liberals, French Canadians, and Irish Catholics in Ontario who vividly remembered that Rowell had joined the Union government in 1917. King decided to bring W.D. Euler into cabinet to represent Ontario as minister of customs, James Malcolm as minister of trade and commerce, and J.C. Elliott as minister of public works.

The most impressive gain to cabinet came in the form of war hero Colonel J.L. Ralston to represent Nova Scotia. Ralston had been defeated but King moved a Nova Scotia member to the Senate so Ralston could enter the government as minister of national defence. Fernand Rinfret entered as a Quebec minister and secretary of state, while Lucien Cannon entered as solicitor general. Peter J. Veniot, the first Acadian premier of New Brunswick, became postmaster general (and the second francophone outside Quebec to be appointed to cabinet).[69] As in 1921, the Liberal cabinet was weak: "The other new members of the government did little more than fulfil the requirements of geography."[70]

1 Prime Minister; External Affairs; President of the Privy Council – W.L. Mackenzie King, 52, Journalist, Saskatchewan, Protestant
2 Agriculture – William R. Motherwell, 66, Farmer, Saskatchewan, Protestant
3 Customs and Excise – William D. Euler, 51, Teacher, Ontario, Protestant
4 Finance – James A. Robb, Businessman, 67, Quebec, Protestant
5 Immigration and Colonization – Robert Forke, 66, Farmer, Protestant
6 Interior; Indian Affairs; Mines – Charles Stewart, 58, Farmer, Alberta, Protestant

7 Justice and Attorney General – Ernest Lapointe, 50, Lawyer, Quebec, Catholic
8 Labour – Peter Heenan, 51, Union Leader, Ontario, Protestant
9 Marine and Fisheries – P.J. Arthur Cardin, 47, Lawyer, Quebec, Catholic
10 National Defence – James Ralston, 45, Military Officer, Nova Scotia, Protestant
11 Postmaster General – Peter Veniot, 63, Journalist, New Brunswick, Catholic
12 Public Works – John C. Elliott, 54, Lawyer, Ontario, Protestant
13 Railways and Canals – Charles A. Dunning, 41, Farmer, Saskatchewan, Protestant
14 Secretary of State of Canada – Fernand Rinfret, 43, Journalist, Quebec, Catholic
15 Pensions and National Health – James H. King, 53, Physician, British Columbia, Baptist
16 Solicitor General – Lucien Cannon, 39, Lawyer, Quebec, Catholic
17 Trade and Commerce – James Malcolm, 46, Businessman, Ontario, Protestant
18 Without Portfolio – Raoul Dandurand, 65, Lawyer, Quebec, Catholic (senator)

Canada enjoyed a few years of prosperity in the later 1920s. Finance Minister J.A. Robb was able to introduce so-called prosperity budgets due to accelerating economic activity and increased federal revenues. When Robb died in 1929, King moved Dunning into finance as planned. Robb's death also allowed the prime minister to remove Forke from the cabinet, because the Manitoban was ineffective as minister of immigration and had little influence on the Liberals' relationship with the Progressives. After many years of discussions, T.A. Crerar finally entered cabinet as minister of railways and canals. In King's mind, the entrance of Crerar not only secured the Liberal hold on the West, but also completed the long quest to absorb the Progressives.

As the election campaign of 1930 approached, Mackenzie King was confident of victory. The prime minister had survived the challenges to his leadership as well as the serious regional divisions both within his party and the nation. He turned a blind eye, however, to the portents of economic disaster. The party organization and financing had received no attention since King became leader in 1919, and the federal party continued to rely on its relationship with its provincial counterparts. The problem, however, was that throughout the decade these provincial organizations had been thrown into chaos by the factional divisions within the party over the handling of the Progressives.

The prime minister hoped that a cabinet shuffle would help Liberal electoral efforts (see image 8.1). Dunning and Crerar brought obvious strength, but more was needed. Ian Mackenzie was appointed to represent British Columbia as minister of immigration and J.H. King was moved to the Senate. Prince Edward

Image 8.1. The King cabinet, 1930

Source: Library and Archives Canada, C-009060.

Island was the only province left without representation, so Cyrus Macmillan (a PEI-born English professor at McGill University) was appointed minister of fisheries. While King remained unsatisfied with Ontario, he decided to wait until after the election. The situation in Quebec, meanwhile, was more urgent. Robb's death reduced representation from the Liberal stronghold. King wanted C.G. Power for the portfolio of pensions and national health but this move would also have to wait. In the meantime, Frederic Kay was appointed minister without portfolio as a pre-election gesture to Quebec.

The cabinet shuffle was in vain. In the election of 1930, R.B. Bennett's Conservatives took office with a majority government and 138 members. The Conservatives broke through in every province. Mackenzie King's Liberals were knocked from power, winning eighty-nine seats but losing twenty-seven overall. The Tories made inroads on the Prairies, where their numbers increased from one to twenty-three, while the Liberals and Liberal-Progressives fell from thirty-two to eighteen seats. Liberal constituencies went from four to one in Manitoba, sixteen to eleven in Saskatchewan, and remained at three in Alberta.

Most revealing, however, was the fact that both Dunning and Crerar lost their seats. The Liberals also suffered losses in Quebec, with the party winning only thirty-nine of sixty-five seats. In Ontario, the Liberals won twenty-two of eighty-one. The results in the Maritimes saw the Liberals win one of four in PEI, four of fourteen in Nova Scotia, and one of eleven in New Brunswick. In British Columbia, the Liberals won five of thirteen. The Liberal-Progressives, now leaderless, lost eight of their eleven. The United Farmers of Alberta would form the third party, with nine seats. Their leader, John E. Brownlee, had not even bothered to run for a seat. The picture was rounded out with the election of less than a handful of Labour and Independent candidates. The Liberals would spend the worst years of the Great Depression in opposition while the economic disaster destroyed the Conservative party. For Mackenzie King, who would return as prime minister in 1935, the defeat was providential.

***

The Prairie West has been sterile ground for the Liberal Party for decades. Indeed, it would be surprising for most Canadians today to learn that at one time, the unlikely bedfellows of Quebec and the West were the twin pillars of Liberal Party support. But in the 1920s this was the case for the governments of Prime Minister Mackenzie King. And while Quebec was firmly in Liberal control, the Prairie West was gradually slipping away. King used his cabinets as a means of satiating and controlling the West. While he still had over fifteen years to perfect the process, these lessons were learned in the 1920s.

An examination of Mackenzie King's cabinets and statecraft during the 1920s reveals several important points. First, this was not a period of structural cabinet innovation or change. The aftermath of the Great War and the so-called "Roaring Twenties" were tumultuous in many ways and signalled significant transformations in Canadian society and politics, but not when it came to the cabinet. The decade witnessed few changes in size or composition. Changes in the names of departments were minor and no new significant ones were created. There were no efforts to broaden representation beyond the three *R*s of race, religion, and region. And even these factors were narrower in scope than indications appear. Race and religion referred to the need to balance English and French, Protestant and Catholic. These two factors diminished in importance in the 1920s, but the cabinets did not become more diverse. As the "Persons Case" demonstrated at the end of the decade, the courts were still arguing over whether women could even sit in the Senate or were indeed "persons." It was the third factor – region – where King made his mark. The dominant influence in shaping his approach to cabinet formation was in the realm of collegial management and his reliance on regional lieutenants. While he may have inherited this strategy from his mentor Wilfrid Laurier, it was Mackenzie King who wielded it to full effect.

The second point to note is that the most challenging cabinet formation of Mackenzie King's long tenure as prime minister was his first. In the aftermath of the 1921 election, King's hold on both the leadership of his party and the government of the country was precarious. The cabinet negotiations thrust the new prime minister into the complex and bitter array of political factors that divided the nation and the Liberal Party at the end of the Great War. They forced him to demonstrate and sharpen his skills at brokerage politics that would come to characterize his career. They allowed him to secure his hold on the party leadership by elevating his preferred representatives in Quebec while commencing the process of wooing the West. As Thompson and Seager point out, "the creation of King's first government was thus to be characterized by the same sort of politically prudent compromise that became the hallmark of his twenty-three years as prime minister."[71]

But the King cabinets of the 1920s are also noteworthy for their weaknesses. The legacy of strong cabinets bequeathed by Macdonald and Laurier was not passed on. The aftermath of the Great War offered up a lacklustre pool of candidates. The disintegration of the two-party system and the weak Liberal showing at the polls throughout the decade, along with the party divisions and the necessity of balancing regional interests, diluted the pool. But while the confusing events of 1925–6 made King's hold on office even more uncertain, the pattern was set when it came to cabinet formation. Governing Canada was a balancing act of diverse interests. King was captain of the ship, but he relied on his regional lieutenants and made them masters of their own domains. By 1930 that ship had passed through several storms and Mackenzie King was confident that smooth waters lay ahead. This could not have been further from the truth.

NOTES

1   Stephen Azzi and Norman Hillmer, "Evaluating Prime-Ministerial Performance: The Canadian Experience," in *Understanding Prime-Ministerial Performance: Comparative Perspectives*, ed. Paul Strangio, Paul 't Hart, and James Walter (Oxford: Oxford University Press, 2013), 242–63; Stephen Azzi and Norman Hillmer, "Ranking Prime Ministers: Canada in a Commonwealth Context," *Journal of Imperial and Commonwealth History* 49, no. 1 (2021): 22–43; Norman Hillmer and J.L. Granatstein, "Historians Rank the Best and Worst Canadian Prime Ministers," *Maclean's*, 21 April 1997; Norman Hillmer and Stephen Azzi, "Canada's Best Prime Ministers," *Maclean's*, 10 June 2011; and Stephen Azzi and Norman Hillmer, "Ranking Canada's Best and Worst Prime Ministers," *Maclean's*, 7 October 2016.

2   "Since the concession of responsible government in the 1840s, both Liberal and Conservative cabinets had been delicately crafted to reflect a careful balance

of regional, religious, and linguistic groups" (John Herd Thompson, with Allen Seager, *Canada, 1922–1939: Decades of Discord* [Toronto: McClelland & Stewart, 1985], 20).

3 Herman Bakvis, *Regional Ministers: Power and Influence in the Canadian Cabinet* (Toronto: University of Toronto Press, 1991), 19, 17, 27, 39.

4 See Patrice Dutil and David Mackenzie, *Embattled Nation: Canada's Wartime Election of 1917* (Toronto: Dundurn, 2017).

5 See Robert Wardhaugh, *Mackenzie King and the Prairie West* (Toronto: University of Toronto Press, 2000).

6 See Patrice Dutil and David MacKenzie, *Canada 1911: The Decisive Election That Shaped the Country* (Toronto: Dundurn, 2011).

7 W.L. Mackenzie King, diary, 21 October 1919, Library and Archives Canada (hereafter "LAC").

8 King's position was head of the Industrial Relations Department of the Rockefeller Foundation.

9 H. Blair Neatby, "Mackenzie King and French Canada," *Journal of Canadian Studies* 11, no. 1 (1976): 5. On the party's factionalism between Quebec and Montreal in the Laurier era, see Patrice Dutil, *The Devil's Advocate: Godfroy Langlois and the Politics of Liberal Progressivism in Laurier's Era* (Montreal: Robert Davies, 1994).

10 J.W. Dafoe to Clifford Sifton, 10 November 1920, LAC, J.W. Dafoe Papers, box 4, file 4.

11 Quoted in Thompson and Seager, *Canada, 1922–1939*, 21.

12 Frederick W. Gibson, "The Cabinet of 1921," in *Cabinet Formation and Bicultural Relations*, ed. F.W. Gibson (Ottawa: Queen's Printer for Canada, 1970), 68.

13 *Grain Growers' Guide*, 21 July 1920, 8, 10–11.

14 "Rumours had already floated about an attempted coup d'état that would substitute Gouin for the 'Boy Leader' – the *Montreal Star*'s derisive nickname for King – at the head of the Liberal party and of the government." King demanded a public show of support from Gouin and Lemieux. The latter published a letter in the press, but Gouin sent only personal assurances of support. See Thompson and Seager, *Canada, 1922–1939*, 21.

15 The tariff dominated politics in Canada throughout the 1920s.

16 "The Liberals were thus one short of a majority of the House, although the Labour-Liberal and the Independent Liberal would give them the majority they needed.... The evidence is most confused on the political affiliation of several members. They have been classified here primarily on performance in the House and secondarily on their announced affiliation which is often obscure in the *Parliamentary Guide*" (R. MacGregor Dawson, *William Lyon Mackenzie King: A Political Biography, 1874–1923* [Toronto: University of Toronto Press, 1958], 356–9).

17 Bakvis, *Regional Ministers*, 44.

18 Dawson, *William Lyon Mackenzie King*, 359.

19 Dawson, *William Lyon Mackenzie King*, 361.

20 "King was inclined to be envious of Fielding's reputation, his general ability and experience, his superiority in debate, and he never entirely forgave the old rival who was still able, by contrast, to dim the lustre of King's leadership." Fielding had held finance in all Liberal cabinets going back to 1896. See Dawson, *William Lyon Mackenzie King*, 359.

21 Gibson, "Cabinet of 1921," 74.

22 A.B. Hudson was elected as an Independent Liberal in Winnipeg, but he was recognized as a Progressive. See J.E. Rea, *T.A. Crerar: A Political Life* (Montreal: McGill-Queen's University Press, 1997), 82.

23 Kirk Cameron was a Montreal businessman and Liberal organizer in the Laurier years. He was one of the main organizers of the 1919 leadership convention who supported Fielding. Cameron formed a close relationship with Crerar and his group in Winnipeg and became an intermediary for discussions with the Progressives. See Rea, *T.A. Crerar*; and Deborah Harflett, "The Public Career of Adam Kirk Cameron, 1874–1967" (MA thesis, McGill University, 1975).

24 Rea, *T.A. Crerar*, 82.

25 King, diary, 10 December 1921.

26 King to Andrew Haydon, 13 December 1921, LAC, W.L.M. King Papers, MG 26 J 1, reel 1947, vol. 61, 53105.

27 King to Andrew Haydon, 13 December 1921; Haydon to King, 14 December 1921, LAC, W.L.M. King Papers, MG 26 J 1, reel 1947, vol. 61, 53120; and Robert Wardhaugh, "'Awaiting the Return of Common Sense': Mackenzie King and Alberta," *National History*, Winter 1998, 262–71.

28 Clifford Sifton to Dafoe, 8 December 1921, LAC, J.W. Dafoe Papers, box 12, file 4.

29 Dafoe to Sifton, 19 December 1921, LAC, J.W. Dafoe Papers, box 4, file 4.

30 "Am of opinion that for sake of future progressives should guard against absorption by liberals. If alliance or coalition formed should be conditional on King professedly accepting fundamental parts of the progressive platform and leaving Gouin bloc out of Cabinet. This I think he is prepared to do – political continuity of progressive should also be assured. Fear I cannot accept invitation." Quoted in Gibson, "Cabinet of 1921," 86.

31 Rea, *T.A. Crerar*, 84.

32 King, diary, 20 December 1921.

33 King, diary, 21 December 1921.

34 Rea, *T.A. Crerar*, 85.

35 King, diary, 14 December 1921.

36 "The presidency of the Privy Council, traditionally a minor post, has taken on a greatly enlarged importance during the period of Union Government." See Gibson, "Cabinet of 1921," 89.

37 King, diary, 24 December 1921.

38 Gibson, "Cabinet of 1921," 69.

39 Thompson and Seager, *Canada, 1922–1939*, 21.

40 King, diary, 20 December 1921. This was the beginning of a long and poor relationship between King and Alberta. While King worked to win the West over his career, Alberta remained an anomaly.

41 "Choosing five others of cabinet quality to accompany himself as Ontario representatives proved more difficult for King. With only twenty members from whom to choose, the chosen were not particularly distinguished." King disliked George Graham and Charles Murphy even though they were very different characters. Murphy was important in representing the Irish Roman Catholic vote, but he was "an unforgiving and contumelious individual, a prey to ferocious animosities, and likely to prove an exceedingly difficult cabinet colleague." Graham, on the other hand, was "a shrewd and genial man of surpassing good humour," but he was a rival of King's in the 1919 leadership contest. Graham and Murphy were given departments with "good patronage potential for aging party hacks." W.C. Kennedy was a rookie MP and one of the only businessmen elected outside Quebec. T.A. Low was "assigned the important task of resurrecting the Liberal party electorally in that province." See Thompson and Seager, *Canada, 1922–1939*, 22; and Gibson, "Cabinet of 1921," 69–70.

42 Nova Scotia's D.D. McKenzie is described as unwaveringly loyal but a narrow-minded "cantankerous old warhorse," New Brunswick's A.B. Copp as a "lawyer who kept his convictions to himself to avoid making enemies and whose 'silence was rewarded' with a cabinet position," and PEI's John E. Sinclair as a "genial fox farmer who was not considered capable of managing a department." See Thompson and Seager, *Canada, 1922–1939*, 23; and Gibson, "Cabinet of 1921," 66.

43 Gibson, "Cabinet of 1921," 76.

44 H. Blair Neatby, *William Lyon Mackenzie King*, vol. 2, *The Lonely Heights, 1924–1932* (Toronto: University of Toronto Press, 1963), 5.

45 Andrew Haydon to King, 27 March 1922, LAC, W.L.M. King Papers, MG26 J 1, reel 2245, vol. 76, 63127.

46 Crerar to H.B. Mitchell, 10 June 1922, Queen's University Archives, T.A. Crerar Papers, 2117, series II, box 79.

47 Gouin threatened resignation on several occasions over the tariff direction of the government. He likely saw the writing on the wall and realized that he would be increasingly out of step with the younger members from Quebec.

48 King, diary, 3 January 1924.

49 King, diary, 6 January 1924.

50 N.T. Macmillan to King, 23 May 1925, LAC, W.L.M. King Papers, MG26 J 1, reel 2279, vol.136, 101344-7.

51 King, diary, 18 August 1925.

52 "A blithe and buoyant sprite of a man, Bureau had been for over 20 years one of the most popular members of the Commons, and although there had been

nothing remarkable about his tenure as Laurier's Solicitor General in succession to Lemieux, he had repeatedly, out of his inexhaustible wit and optimism, entertained the Liberals in office and lifted them in Opposition" (Gibson, "Cabinet of 1921," 67).

53 King, diary, 17 August 1925.

54 The Home Bank of Canada was incorporated in 1903 in Toronto. Its publicized failure in 1923 created a taint that followed certain politicians, such as T.A. Crerar, for the rest of their career. It was the subject of a Royal Commission in 1924.

55 Neatby, *Lonely Heights*, 66.

56 As quoted in Neatby, 70.

57 *A Party Politician: The Memoirs of Chubby Power*, ed. Norman Ward (Toronto: Macmillan, 1966), 377.

58 Thompson and Seager, *Canada, 1922–1939*, 112; "After four years in office, the government had no conspicuous achievement of which to boast" (Neatby, *Lonely Heights*, 59).

59 Only six of the cabinet ministers survived the term in office.

60 Neatby, *Lonely Heights*, 74.

61 Quoted in Neatby, *Lonely Heights*, 89.

62 King, diary, 16 November 1925.

63 King, diary, 4 November, 13 November 1925.

64 Neatby, *Lonely Heights*, 93.

65 Neatby, *Lonely Heights*, 121.

66 Robert Wardhaugh, "A Marriage of Convenience? Mackenzie King and Prince Albert Constituency," *Prairie Forum*, Fall 1996, 177–200.

67 Dafoe to John Willison, 17 September 1926, LAC, J.W. Dafoe Papers, box 5, file 5.

68 Robert Wardhaugh, "Cogs in the Machine: The Charles Dunning-Jimmy Gardiner Feud," *Saskatchewan History* 48, no. 1 (Spring 1996): 20–9.

69 Dr. Raymond Morand, a Franco-Ontarian, was the first, appointed by Arthur Meighen in his short-lived government in 1926.

70 Neatby, *Lonely Heights*, 174.

71 Thompson and Seager, *Canada, 1922–1939*, 21.

9 R.B. Bennett's "One-Man Government"

LARRY A. GLASSFORD

A story made the rounds of political circles in Ottawa, early in R.B. Bennett's time in office as prime minister. A tourist new to the city noticed a well-dressed gentleman marching up Wellington Street from the Chateau Laurier towards Parliament Hill, talking to himself. "Who could that be?" he wondered aloud. "Oh," said one of the local residents, "that's our new prime minister, holding a cabinet meeting."[1] In keeping with that theme, one of the lasting images of Bennett's term as prime minister is an editorial cartoon by the legendary Arch Dale of the *Winnipeg Free Press* called "My Government," which shows a likeness of the Calgary-based capitalist at the head of a boardroom table, and identical likenesses occupying every other chair in the room. Even the pictures on the wall, and the attending servant staff, bear a striking resemblance to the loquacious Westerner (see image 9.2). If ever in Canada there was a cabinet dominated by its prime minister, it was the one sworn into office on 7 August 1930, under the leadership of Richard Bedford Bennett.

In the vernacular of the day, R.B. Bennett was a self-made man. It was not literally true, of course – many people had helped him on his way to wealth, power, and fame. However, it is certainly true that he was born into a New Brunswick family of modest income in the Bay of Fundy village of Hopewell Cape in 1870. His father's wooden shipbuilding business was in decline, and in order to attend law school at Dalhousie University, Bennett first had to earn the money to pay for it by teaching elementary school for a time in rural New Brunswick (a path he shared with two other Conservative leaders, Robert Borden and Arthur Meighen). Upon graduation from Dalhousie, he practised law for a few years in the Miramichi region of that province before heading west in 1897 to seek his fortune in the small cowtown of Calgary, Alberta. There, he joined an established law firm headed by Conservative senator James Lougheed. Fortune smiled upon this migrant from the East, for before many years had passed, he was acting as solicitor for the mighty Canadian Pacific Railway, investing in thriving companies that prospered during the Laurier boom, and representing

Calgary as a Conservative in the territorial and provincial legislatures. It did not hurt his rise to power and wealth, of course, that he would eventually inherit majority control of the Hull, Quebec-based Eddy Paper company from a childhood friend, Jennie Shirreff Eddy, and her brother Harry Shirreff. Bennett's biographer, P.B. Waite, estimated that his income in the mid-1920s was roughly a quarter of a million dollars a year, and his share of the Eddy Company stock was worth about $2 million. Adding in his other investments would double that net worth. At a time when a manual labourer might earn a dollar a day, being a millionaire definitely separated Bennett from the vast majority of his fellow Canadians.[2]

At the time of his first election to the House of Commons as a protectionist Conservative in the Reciprocity election of 1911, the former Dick Bennett from small-town New Brunswick was already well on his way to becoming R.B. Bennett, prosperous spokesperson for the boom-and-bust settler society of southern Alberta. His constituents in Calgary knew him as "Bonfire" Bennett, a tribute to his bombastic speaking style and sure-fire command of the facts. But when he arrived in Ottawa, his career path was blocked by his own legal partner, Senator James Lougheed, whom Robert Borden had placed in his cabinet as government leader in the red chamber. An unrepentant workaholic, and a lifelong bachelor with time on his hands, Bennett chafed at the limitations placed on mere backbenchers. At this time in his career he was somewhat of a maverick in the House of Commons, and in one widely reported clash with another young westerner on the rise, he dismissed Arthur Meighen as "the gramophone of Mackenzie and Mann," the two swashbuckling speculators whose Canadian Northern rail line was in deep financial debt. Though he supported conscription, Bennett opposed the Union government, and did not run for re-election in 1917. He did accept a call from Meighen to serve as minister of justice in 1921, but he went down to defeat along with the "National Liberal and Conservative" government in the general election later that same year. Undeterred, Bennett successfully carried his Calgary riding for the Conservatives in 1925, served prominently on the Commons committee investigating the customs scandal that bedevilled the King government, and entered Meighen's short-lived cabinet of 1926 as minister of finance. He managed to hold onto his seat in the general election later that year, despite Meighen's defeat and the toppling of his administration at the polls.[3]

The national convention held in Winnipeg in 1927 marked the first time that the Conservative Party of Canada would choose its leader at a delegated convention, rather than from the parliamentary caucus. The victorious candidate would possess a mandate, not just from fellow MPs, but from the national party membership. R.B. Bennett won the leadership race over five opponents on the second ballot. His closest rival was Hugh Guthrie, a former Liberal who had joined Borden's Union government in 1917, then stayed on after the war's end, serving as the Conservative Party's parliamentary leader after Meighen's resignation in 1926. The second and third runners-up were, respectively, C.H. Cahan, a crusty spokesperson for Montreal's business class, and Robert J. Manion, another Unionist Liberal, who excelled in fiery stump speeches and the partisan cut and thrust of parliamentary debate. The final two candidates, Robert Rogers of Manitoba and Sir Henry Drayton of Toronto, received courtesy votes on the first ballot, then saw most of their supporters migrate to the frontrunner, R.B. Bennett. Of all the candidates, Bennett projected the strongest image as a potential winner on the hustings. On top of a successful career in both law and business, he had won re-election to Parliament in 1926, the only victorious Tory MP from the Prairies. A powerful speaker, he challenged the delegates to join his crusade towards victory in the next general election. "Promise here and now, as you walk out of yonder door," he thundered, "that you will be missionaries for the great party to which we belong, missionaries from the greatest political convention ever held in the Dominion of Canada, and if you are missionaries your efforts will be crowned with success, and you will have a government at Ottawa reflecting your principles."[4] With those stirring words ringing in their ears, the Conservative delegates left Winnipeg in buoyant spirits, prepared to follow where Bennett might lead their party.[5]

By the time of the next general election in 1930, the buoyant prosperity of the late 1920s had turned into the beginnings of the Great Depression. As Conservative Party leader, Bennett was able to convert Canadians' general discontent into a majority victory for his political team. Although he received some assistance from the five Conservative premiers, as well as a handful of frontbench caucus colleagues, the focus of the Tory campaign was on its leader. Travelling back and forth across the country in a private railcar, Bennett made major speeches in most of the large centres, and his remarks were broadcast far and wide over the new medium of communication, radio. For instance, an estimated two million Canadians heard his keynote Winnipeg address that kicked off the campaign. In contrast to Mackenzie King's cautious platform demeanour, Bennett boldly promised action to solve the unemployment crisis. "The Conservative party is going to find work for all who are willing to work," he pledged, "or perish in the attempt."[6] While Bennett's energetic campaign put the governing Liberals on the defensive, a stellar party organization put together over the previous two years ensured that the Conservative advantage on the hustings was realized at the polls. Behind the scenes, Bennett had contributed thousands upon thousands of dollars of his own money to ensure the viability of this organization. Not only as party leader, but also as party benefactor, it was clear that the incoming prime minister had contributed mightily to the Conservative victory on 28 July 1930.[7]

Bennett wasted little time in choosing his cabinet, though he faced the same constraints upon his selections as any other prime minister. Cabinet posts, then as now, were allocated not merely on the basis of native ability, nor even on political experience, though those two factors were certainly considered. Since Confederation, the Canadian cabinet has been viewed as a representative body whose makeup ought to reflect the composition of the country itself. Bennett was true to the conventions of his day, in that each province had at least one minister, while the more populous provinces, Quebec and Ontario, had five and seven members, respectively. French-speaking Quebec was represented by three of that province's five ministers. Religious balance in the two central provinces was maintained by having one Roman Catholic from Ontario, and two Protestants from Quebec. One characteristic that was not considered was gender. Though Canadian women had been granted the right to vote a decade previously, there were no elected female MPs in the Conservative caucus in 1930, and Bennett saw no need to appoint a woman from outside Parliament to his cabinet. And as for twenty-first-century preoccupations such as race, sexuality, and able-body status, these categories of diversity and inclusion were not even on his radar screen (see image 9.1).[8]

"Keep your friends close, and your enemies closer" is a bit of folk wisdom often heeded by prime ministerial cabinet makers. R.B. Bennett was no exception. His top three rivals for the party leadership in 1927 were all offered cabinet posts, though the second runner-up, C.H. Cahan, had coveted the justice portfolio that went instead to the former interim leader, Hugh Guthrie. The curmudgeonly Anglo-Montrealer had to be satisfied with the less exalted role of secretary of state. R.J. Manion, who represented the thriving grain lakeport of Fort William, became the minister of railways and canals. Most of the remaining Ontario representatives were less prominent. Representing the Bay Street business community was E.B. Ryckman, former president of Dunlop Tire and Rubber, and a generous financial donor to the party. He would head up the National Revenue Department. From south-western Ontario Bennett chose Dr. Donald Sutherland, a distinguished physician and First World War veteran, who was allocated national defence. He came recommended by Arthur Ford, editor of the Tory-leaning *London Free Press* and head of the regional party organization in that part of the province. From northern Ontario, a freshman MP, Wesley Gordon, was handed a double portfolio: immigration and colonization, and mines. And from eastern Ontario, a veteran backbencher, Hugh Stewart, was given the public works portfolio. Both of these appointments were pre-approved by the Ontario premier, Howard Ferguson, who had been a loyal Bennett supporter since the Winnipeg convention. Rounding out the Ontario contingent was a veteran senator, and former member of Robert Borden's Union cabinet, Gideon Robertson. The long-time trade unionist was tapped to be minister of labour and government leader in the Senate.

Picking ministers from Quebec proved to be a challenge. As the anointed "favourite son" of Quebec in the recent leadership race, Cahan was a shoo-in.

At the same time, Bennett wanted the benefit of the veteran but aging Sir George Perley's advice, so included him as minister without portfolio, from which position he was available to serve as acting prime minister whenever Bennett might be out of the country. With two spots allocated to the anglophone minority, that left only three positions available for the French-speaking majority. Given the longstanding regional rivalry between the Quebec City district and the Montreal district, dividing an odd number of spots evenly was bound to be tricky. Bennett resolved the issue by selecting the former provincial Conservative leader, Arthur Sauvé, and making him the postmaster general. Then from the Montreal district he chose a former Quebec MLA, Alfred Duranleau, and gave him the Marine Department. Sauvé recommended Armand Lavergne, the former *Nationaliste* firebrand, to represent the Quebec district, but Bennett chose instead a Laval- and Oxford-educated bilingual lawyer, Maurice Dupré, who, at forty-two years of age, might represent the future of the party. He accepted a minor position in the cabinet as solicitor general. Meanwhile, Lavergne was only somewhat mollified by becoming deputy speaker of the House of Commons, not a position ideally suited to his mercurial personality.

Turning to the Maritimes, Bennett followed the precedent of Arthur Meighen in appointing a minister without portfolio to represent Prince Edward Island in the cabinet, selecting John Macdonald for this role. From his native province of New Brunswick, Bennett passed over several higher-profile MPs by elevating Dr. Murray MacLaren to the cabinet. Like Dr. Sutherland a veteran of overseas service during the First World War, MacLaren became the minister of pensions and national health. To represent Nova Scotia, the prime minister went outside his parliamentary caucus by persuading the Conservative premier, Edgar Rhodes, to come to Ottawa, where he assumed the post of minister of fisheries. Tory MPs from the Prairies had been rare all through the 1920s, so Bennett was forced to look for cabinet potential from the rookie team elected in 1930. From Saskatchewan he chose Robert Weir, a prosperous farmer and rancher, to fill the agriculture portfolio, while from Manitoba he selected the low-profile Thomas Murphy to occupy the traditional western portfolio of interior and Indian affairs.

The province of British Columbia elected seven Conservative MPs in 1930 but Bennett's staunch supporter and able parliamentary lieutenant, H.H. Stevens, was not among them. Kept busy campaigning for other Conservative candidates across western Canada, Stevens was defeated in his own Vancouver riding. The prime minister was determined to have him as a cabinet colleague, however, and a new seat was quickly found for him in Kootenay East. Stevens was sworn in as the minister of trade and commerce. Finally, from Alberta Bennett designated himself as the provincial representative. In a stunning departure from precedent, he chose not only to serve as prime minister, president of the Privy Council, and secretary of state for external affairs, but also to take on the demanding post of minister of finance and receiver general. Overall, it was a workload that would test even someone as energetic and self-confident as R.B. Bennett.[9]

In the new Conservative cabinet that was sworn into office on 7 August 1930, seven ministers were from Ontario and five from Quebec. The West was hardly better represented than before, with four members (one for each province). The Maritime provinces each also had one member at the cabinet table. The cabinet was composed of men whose age averaged 55.8, five years younger than the prime minister:

1 Prime Minister; Secretary of State for External Affairs; President of the Privy Council; Minister of Finance and Receiver General – Richard Bedford Bennett, 60, Alberta
2 Agriculture – Robert Weir, 47, Saskatchewan
3 Fisheries – Edgar Nelson Rhodes, 53, Nova Scotia
4 Immigration and Colonization; Mines – Wesley Ashton Gordon, 46, Ontario
5 Interior; Indian Affairs – Thomas Gerow Murphy, 46, Manitoba
6 Justice and Attorney General – Hugh Guthrie, 63, Ontario
7 Labour –Gideon Robertson, 55, Ontario (senator)
8 Marine – Alfred Duranleau, 58, Quebec
9 National Defence – Donald Matheson Sutherland, 50, Ontario
10 National Revenue – Edmond Baird Ryckman, 64, Ontario
11 Pensions and National Health – Murray MacLaren, 69, New Brunswick
12 Postmaster General – Arthur Sauvé, 54, Quebec
13 Public Works – Hugh Alexander Stewart, 58, Ontario
14 Railways and Canals – Robert James Manion, 48, Ontario
15 Secretary of State of Canada – Charles Hazlitt Cahan, 68, Quebec
16 Solicitor General – Maurice Dupré, 42, Quebec
17 Trade and Commerce – Henry Herbert Stevens, 51, British Columbia
18 Without Portfolio – John Alexander Macdonald, 56, Prince Edward Island
19 Without Portfolio – George Halsey Perley, 72, Quebec

Immediately upon being sworn in as the new ministry, Bennett's cabinet approved a minute of council "regarding certain of the functions of the prime minister." Among these were the power to call meetings of cabinet; to recommend the dissolution and convocation of Parliament; to make recommendations in any government department; and to recommend a lengthy list of appointments, including cabinet ministers, lieutenant governors, senators, chief justices, and deputy heads of departments.[10] This council minute made clear that Prime Minister Bennett would far outrank any of his cabinet colleagues. Added to this list of legal prerogatives were two other factors that elevated his influence and power. For the first time in the history of the Conservative Party, its leader owed his position not to the parliamentary caucus, but to the national

Image 9.1. R.B. Bennett, surrounded by members of the cabinet, speaking by telephone to Sir George Perley at the British Empire Trade Fair at Buenos Aires, 13 March 1931

Source: Library and Archives Canada, c009076.

party membership as expressed at the Winnipeg convention. And in August 1930, Bennett had just led his party to a convincing majority victory, in a campaign that was focused upon him, both through his national tour with its nightly speeches, and via country-wide radio broadcasts. The cabinet and caucus owed their positions on the government benches to him, and both they and he knew it.

The charge of one-man government originated with the Liberal Opposition but was soon picked up by the press. Bennett's unprecedented decision to appoint himself as minister of finance made it an easy conclusion to draw. So too did his demeanour in the House of Commons, where he spoke often and at considerable length, not hesitating to interrupt his own cabinet colleagues, if he was dissatisfied with the content of their remarks. As a task-oriented perfectionist, he did not often stop to consider the emotional impact of his sharp and frank interventions. In fact, he seemed largely unbothered by the accusation of undue domination on his part. "It may be a one man government," he conceded at one point in Parliament, "but certainly it has more than one man's support."[11] Three years into his time in office, Bennett continued to be the self-driven workaholic. "He is still the Government," noted the *MacLean's* parliamentary reporter, "taking upon himself the work of his Ministers or of many of them, trying to be in a dozen places and

Image 9.2. In the view of cartoonist Arch Dale, Bennett ran a one-man government

Source: Arch Dale, "My Government," *Manitoba Free Press*, 19 January 1931, 11.

to do a dozen things at the same time."[12] Mackenzie King, who knew something of the demands placed upon a prime minister, privately predicted "I should not be surprised if his 'perish in the attempt' proved a prophecy."[13]

While generally considerate and supportive of his own office staff, Bennett could be prickly and arrogant in public, not just with his parliamentary opponents, but also with his own colleagues.[14] The Quebec Liberal Chubby Power best described the prime minister's public persona when he declared, "In this house, he often exhibits the manners of a Chicago policeman and the temperament of a Hollywood actor."[15] Naturally, the Opposition members delighted in provoking Bennett to these heights of scorn and indignation, for they wished to portray him at the next election as an ill-tempered would-be dictator out of touch with the norms of civilized discourse.

Bennett was perhaps at his most combative when dealing with members of the parliamentary press gallery. For instance, at the time of the Ottawa Imperial Conference in 1932, the prime minister openly accused both the Ottawa journalist Grant Dexter and his editor, J.W. Dafoe of the pro-Liberal *Winnipeg Free Press*, of deliberate distortion of the facts. "One of the saddest consequences of this conference for me," he publicly confronted Dexter in the dining room of the posh Rideau club, "is that throughout the entire proceedings some Canadian journalists – Dafoe at Winnipeg was one of them – and you, young man, were another, did everything in their power, stopped at nothing, to discredit your country's representatives, and your own Prime Minister. Is that fair journalism? Is it common decency?"[16] Bennett did not restrict his hostility to the Grit press. As the Tory newsman Grattan O'Leary recalled, "When the *Ottawa Journal* ran an editorial criticizing the government, Bennett failed to recognize me."[17] As Allan Levine, author of a longitudinal study of relations between Canadian prime ministers and the news media noted, "By the time Bennett was finished, he had alienated even the most ardent Tory journalists."[18] As early as September 1930 in a House of Commons debate, Bennett aired his grievances against newspapers for, in his view, wilfully misinterpreting politicians, and spoke approvingly of the power and potential of radio, which allowed the prime minister to communicate directly with Canadians.[19] Having used on-air broadcasts masterfully to get himself elected as prime minister, Bennett was well aware of how this new means of mass communication could be utilized to go around print journalists and connect directly with the voter.

Although no one knew it at the time, Prime Minister Bennett was at the height of his power in the autumn of 1930. Fresh off a convincing majority victory in the recent general election, he sensed that the Canadian voters had endorsed not just his party's traditional protectionist trade policy, but also his own self-confident pledge of immediate and decisive action to get the economy back on its feet. As his Quebec Liberal adversary, Chubby Power, noted in his memoirs, "There is no doubt that Bennett's high character, his great reputation, his forceful utterances, and his eloquence on the hustings had more to do with the victory achieved in 1930 than the allegiance of the electorate to the principles and policies of the Conservative Party."[20]

Quick work he had promised; quick work he would deliver. Parliament was summoned for a special fall session that took up just three weeks in September. The Throne Speech was held to a paltry twenty-one lines, and the traditionally long-winded Throne Speech debate was dispensed with. Bennett's recovery plan had two parts. First, an unprecedented sum of $20 million was approved for emergency economic relief. By comparison, the Union government's relief package to combat the post-war recession had amounted to only $2 million.

Even the Independent Farmer–Labour MP Agnes Macphail was impressed. "The Prime Minister," she noted approvingly, "has apparently the courage of his convictions, and I like people who ... act with despatch."[21] Bennett's main strategy for economic recovery was a muscular application of the "Canada First" tariffs he had promised from one end of Canada to the other in the recent election campaign. Additionally, Bennett would seek to persuade his Empire and Commonwealth partners at the October 1930 conference in London to erect similar trade barriers upon goods originating outside their group of nations.[22]

The Canadian delegation to the imperial conference numbered some two dozen and included three other cabinet ministers: H.H. Stevens, Hugh Guthrie, and Maurice Dupré. However, the dominant personality, as it had been during the special September session of Parliament, was the prime minister himself. Certainly, he had a supporting cast, but there was just one star in the show, and that was R.B. Bennett. This became even more evident as the Great Depression continued to worsen. Upon his return from Britain, Bennett received pleading messages from the three prairie premiers. The producer-owned wheat pools stood on the edge of bankruptcy. Bennett realized the devastating impact that would accompany the collapse of the Prairie wheat pools. Within days, he had issued a guarantee of their financial solvency. In return, he insisted on the appointment of John I. McFarland, former president of Alberta Pacific Grain, as general manager of the Central Selling Agency. McFarland continued as a kind of managing grain czar for the next five years. Looking back, Bennett credited McFarland with avoiding a "stark, complete, absolute disaster beyond the ability of any man to see."[23] Not for the first or last time, Bennett took decisive action to deal with a potential crisis, scarcely bothering to consult with his cabinet colleagues.

Bennett's central role in his government's decision-making again came through clearly in the next major challenge in the fall of 1931. He was enjoying his customary Sunday day of rest when he received shocking news by telephone: the United Kingdom was about to abandon the gold standard. Still minister of finance as well as prime minister, he had to decide quickly between two alternatives: let the Canadian dollar find its own (lower) level or defend the value of the Canadian buck. With little time for consultation he issued a defiant announcement: "Canada will pay her obligations in gold."[24] Bennett's reasoning was twofold: to preserve Canada's credit rating in international money markets, and to minimize the premium required for Canadian borrowers to repay borrowed funds and make interest payments. An order-in-council, adopted at Bennett's direction, prohibited the private export of gold from Canada. By the end of 1931 the Canadian dollar had stabilized at approximately 80 US cents. Bennett's bold action saved Canada's currency from further decline, but at a cost. The hard-money policy aggravated the problem of declining exports, thus contributing to rising levels of unemployment and business failures. But as Rhodes, by then minister of finance, explained months later in Parliament, "It was imperative that there would be no flight from the Canadian dollar."[25]

Along with sound money, Bennett and Rhodes believed in balanced budgets. Alas, as the economy plunged into a steep and prolonged decline so too did government revenues, whereas expenditures proved to be quite inelastic. Interest on the national debt and war pensions continued as ongoing claims on the public purse. On the campaign trail Bennett had blamed the recession of 1930 on Liberal mismanagement. After two years in office, his diagnosis of the economic collapse had changed quite profoundly. "What at that time seemed to be a local condition" he admitted in Parliament in the fall of 1932, "was a worldwide disease."[26] Despite its strenuous efforts to slash expenditures – including a 10 per cent rollback of civil servant salaries – and raise taxes, the federal deficit continued to balloon out of control. After three years of attempted cost-cutting the federal deficit for the 1933–4 fiscal year amounted to $134 million, with expenditures of $458 million. A modern observer might dub this a stimulative deficit, but for Bennett, Rhodes, and most of their cabinet colleagues, it was an embarrassment.[27]

Bennett did not shuffle his cabinet until 18 months after assuming office. Two causes precipitated this change in personnel. The first was the declining health of Gideon Robertson, the minister of labour and government leader in the Senate. As his replacement in the red chamber, the prime minister reached beyond Parliament to recruit his predecessor as party leader, Arthur Meighen. There had been unfounded rumours in 1930 that Meighen might be picked for the finance post, but he and Bennett had not spoken since the leadership convention in 1927. The cold shoulder aside, Bennett had a great respect for his fellow Westerner's ability, and particularly wanted the latter's parliamentary acumen in the upper chamber with a committee investigation of another Liberal scandal: the Beauharnois election-funding controversy. This became obvious when he shot back at Mackenzie King's gibe about the double-barrelled leadership of the Tory Party with the blunt rejoinder that, "it will mean two or three fewer senators at an early date."[28] As part of the arrangement between the two men, Bennett agreed that Meighen would attend cabinet meetings only when the Senate was in session.

The second part of the shuffle was to move Edgar Rhodes, one of the cabinet colleagues for whom he had genuine respect, from fisheries to finance. Bennett had been working twelve- to fourteen-hour days, six days a week, for eighteen months straight, and the strain on his health was beginning to show. Even the pro-Liberal *Winnipeg Free Press* was sympathetic: "The Prime Minister has taken the duties of his office with the utmost seriousness, and has sacrificed his time and strength to the task of carrying them out with an energy that totally disregarded the limits of his physical capacity.... The Prime Minister's load has been far too heavy."[29] What Bennett did not do at this time was promote any of his backbenchers, much to the chagrin of his fellow New Brunswick native, R.B. Hanson. "The Government needs a whole shaking up and Bennett has been told this by a multitude of people. He still apparently cannot find the time to do it or [if] he has the time he has not the inclination."[30] Robertson's Labour portfolio was handed to the rookie MP Wes Gordon, already burdened with two departments, while the fisheries portfolio was given to the minister of marine, Alfred Duranleau. It was a lost opportunity to bring in some fresh blood, but Bennett was too preoccupied to notice.

By this point, the Bennett government's hopes for economic recovery were tied to the imperial conference that Canada was hosting in Ottawa in the summer of 1932. The chief problem was that the British wished for a lowering of tariffs between Commonwealth countries, whereas the Canadians advocated holding the line on intra-empire tariffs, while jacking protective tariffs up even more against the rest of the world. Behind the scenes, the negotiations became increasingly acrimonious, particularly between Bennett and members of the British delegation. Neville Chamberlain, one of the key British delegates, laid much of the blame for the impasse at Bennett's feet. "Instead of guiding the Conference in his capacity as Chairman," he complained privately, "he has stretched our patience to the limit. He has insulted us personally and still more our officials. He has been threatening and bullying in his manner, shifty and cunning in his methods."[31] In the end, to avoid going home empty-handed, the British made the bulk of the concessions that permitted a partial trade agreement to be signed. Canadian natural products like wheat, fish, lumber, and minerals gained a preferential advantage in the British market, while U.K. manufacturers received preferred treatment for certain metal and textile products, mostly of the type not made in Canada. After three years, Canadian exports to Britain did increase quite markedly, from $175 million to $274 million, whereas British exports to Canada barely inched up, from $106 million to $111 million.[32] It was a gain for Canada, but in the midst of the severest economic collapse in decades it was woefully insufficient to turn things around.

As the hard times continued, social protests became more frequent. One of the more progressive cabinet members, Robert. J. Manion, felt sympathy for the protesters, noting that "hungry men can hardly be blamed for refusing to starve quietly."[33] Bennett, supported by his minister of justice, Hugh Guthrie, did not share this sentiment, blaming the social unrest chiefly on foreign agitators and communist sympathizers. In a public speech he invited his fellow Canadians to join the federal government in defending the established order: "We ask every man and woman to put the iron heel of ruthlessness against a thing of that kind."[34] Bennett's iron heel reference came to symbolize the Conservative government's hard-line approach to dissent. While civil libertarians and Opposition MPs took Bennett and the Tory government to task for trampling on individual freedom in their approach to civil dissent, a majority of the cabinet probably sympathized with their colleague, Hugh Guthrie, who stated in parliamentary debate, "Section 98 is not in any sense a hindrance to any right-thinking person."[35]

By this time, the prime minister himself had come to symbolize the futility of government policy to either cure the causes or even alleviate the symptoms of the Great Depression. He had won the election by guaranteeing a cure for hard times. After three years and counting, he had failed. His surname was widely and disrespectfully used around the country to describe horse-drawn cars (Bennett buggies), shanty towns (Bennett boroughs), and abandoned farms (Bennett barnyards). Oblivious to the self-destructive symbolism of it all, Bennett arranged with His Majesty the King of Canada to metaphorically turn the clock back on New Year's Day 1934. Amid the grim news of economic hardship and social ruin, one newspaper headline stood out: "Bennett Recommends Titles for Canadians."[36] This practice had been ended by a resolution passed in the Canadian House of Commons in 1919, but Bennett had never accepted this measure as binding. Consequently, forty Canadians received honours from the king at the beginning of 1934, all of them recommended by the Canadian prime minister. "The Honours List was prepared by me," he informed one correspondent, "and following the British custom, was not submitted to my colleagues."[37] To another he explained, "I desire to establish merit as worthy of honour by the State."[38] Among the recipients were prominent jurists, researchers, a poet, and a musician, as well as a number of accomplished women, including Charlotte Whitton, an influential social worker and future mayor of Ottawa. In terms of political imagery, the blatant re-introduction of privilege as represented by knighthoods and honours when so many ordinary Canadians were suffering real hardship just seemed wrong. R.B. Bennett did not care. He believed it was the right thing to do, and as prime minister, in possession of the power to recommend appointments, he was able to implement the change. The Opposition leader, Mackenzie King, denounced the departure as disrespectful to the elected House of Commons. Eventually, Canadian voters would decide which view prevailed.[39]

Although committed to balanced budgets and a sound currency, the Bennett-led government was not trapped in the status quo. Among its innovative accomplishments was the creation of the Canadian Radio Broadcasting Commission (CRBC), which lives on today as the Canadian Broadcasting Corporation. The prime minister's fingerprints were all over this major reform. When the Judicial Committee of the Privy Council granted exclusive jurisdiction over broadcasting to the federal government, Bennett moved quickly despite significant opposition from the private sector. Opponents of public broadcasting included the Canadian Manufacturers' Association, the Canadian Pacific Railway, the Canadian Association of Broadcasters, and several key advertising agencies. Bennett's stated motivations for a public system were twofold. The first reason was nationalistic, "This country must be assured of complete control of broadcasting from Canadian sources, free from foreign interference or influence," he explained. The second reason was egalitarian. "No other scheme than that of public ownership can ensure to the people of this country, without regard to class or place, equal enjoyment of the benefits and pleasures of radio broadcasting."[40] The vote in the House of Commons was nearly unanimous in favour of the CRBC, but there was little doubt that the real champion of public broadcasting was the prime minister. The new Radio Commission was up and running by October 1932.[41]

Bennett also championed the idea of a central bank for Canada, an idea strongly opposed by the chartered banks. Here, too, he was influenced by a nationalistic "Canada First" attitude. As he explained in the House of Commons, he became convinced of the need for such an institution when he realized "that this Dominion of Canada could not carry on direct exchange operations with London for any substantial amounts except through Wall Street."[42] A Royal Commission on Banking and Currency in Canada was duly established in 1933, and its commissioners recommended a central bank. Shortly after the release of its report, Bennett announced that legislation to establish a Bank of Canada would be introduced. When the chartered banks resisted, particularly over the price at which their reserves of gold would be transferred to the new institution, Bennett was adamant that there would be no windfall gain for the powerful banks. To one harried government official he offered this pledge: "It is just about time for us to find out whether the banks or this government is running the country."[43] So long as Bennett was prime minister, there was little ambiguity about who was in charge. And as usual, his cabinet colleagues deferred to his judgment.

Despite, or perhaps because of, the stressful times, Prime Minister Bennett did not often resort to a cabinet shuffle to revitalize his ministry. Thus, in late 1933, it was the ill health of a sitting minister that caused him to appoint the Toronto-area MP R.C. Matthews to replace the ailing E.B. Ryckman as minister of national revenue. The next shuffle, eleven months later, was different, however, occasioned as it was by the sudden resignation of the popular H.H. Stevens, minister of trade and commerce, after a heated row in cabinet over the latter's role in heading a parliamentary inquiry. In a public exchange of letters between cabinet minister and prime minister, words were used that would be hard to take back. "As much has been said about business ethics," the prime minister declared, "I cannot but think it is the duty of any member of a Government who is responsible for the publication and circulation of a pamphlet containing inaccurate statements, to take the earliest opportunity to correct or withdraw such statements, with an appropriate expression of regret."[44] Stevens's quick reply did not hold back his anger and bitterness. "When you refer in your closing words to 'British justice and fair play,' I cannot but bring to my mind the countless thousands of citizens of Canada who are patiently suffering while others whom you champion in such eloquent terms have been reaping rewards far beyond that which any citizen might reasonably expect to win."[45] Clearly each man felt a keen sense of betrayal by the other.

How did events reach this impasse? Both men had arrived in Ottawa from the West as freshman MPs in 1911, even sharing an office on Parliament Hill. In 1926 they had both served on the Commons committee that delved into the Liberals' customs scandal. At the Winnipeg leadership convention in 1927, Stevens had been one of Bennett's most prominent supporters. When Stevens briefly considered retirement from public life in 1929 to better support his family, Bennett would not hear of it, and went out of his way to reassure his frontbench colleague that he was still needed by his party and leader.[46] Then when Stevens lost his own Vancouver-area riding in the 1930 general election, Bennett brought him into the cabinet anyway, and a new riding was quickly found for him. Stevens had acquired a well-deserved reputation as a loyal and effective swordsman in Parliament, and given the large number of rookie MPs in the caucus, and even cabinet, Bennett could ill afford to do without him.

Still, though Stevens carried the title of minister of trade and commerce, it quickly became clear that the real trade minister was Bennett himself. Though Stevens sailed to England in the fall of 1930 as part of the Canadian delegation to the imperial conference, it was evident that Bennett was the man in charge, and further, that he was relying for advice on a few key civil servants, not cabinet colleagues. Again in 1932 at the Ottawa Conference Bennett hogged the limelight, relegating his trade minister to the sidelines. And in the spring of 1933, when the prime minister travelled to Washington to discuss trade and related matters with the newly elected American president, F.D. Roosevelt, he was accompanied by his executive assistant, R.K. Finlayson, and brother-in-law W.D. Herridge, the Canadian ambassador to the United States. Meanwhile Stevens was assigned to stay in Ottawa and deliver a speech defending the government's latest budget.[47] Evidently Bennett viewed Stevens as a valuable foot soldier in the trenches of Parliament, but just as clearly, did not value his judgment on trade or financial matters.

As the Depression wore on, Stevens became increasingly bothered by stories of small Canadian businesses being forced into bankruptcy by the market power of a few large corporations, whose profits seemed largely unaffected by hard times. Early in January 1934, he used a speaking engagement in Toronto to launch an aggressive attack on big businesses for abusing their financial power to the detriment of small business. In particular, he focused on the mass buying practices of large department stores. Bennett, who had asked Stevens to fulfil this speaking engagement in his place, was furious, and lectured his colleague for a breach of cabinet solidarity, by appearing to commit the Conservative government to a policy it had not discussed. Stevens responded by submitting a letter of resignation. Bennett had not expected that outcome, nor was he prepared for the widespread public support aroused by Stevens' sensational accusations. The resignation letter was set aside, and Stevens was placed in charge of a special parliamentary inquiry to investigate the alleged business abuses. Bennett even moved the Commons resolution to establish the multiparty committee, tasked with investigating the causes and effects of large price spreads and mass buying. The so-called Stevens Committee attracted nationwide publicity, as evidence of business collusion, manipulation, and exploitation mounted. With the end of the parliamentary session approaching, a 7 July 1934 order-in-council transformed the committee into a royal commission, again chaired by Stevens.[48]

On 26 June 1934 Stevens addressed sixty-five backbench Conservative MPs, providing a lively and informal summary of the price spread inquiry's findings to date. It was an impassioned speech that quickly turned into a blistering attack on many of Canada's leading corporations and business leaders. A transcribed copy of his remarks was printed and circulated widely within Conservative ranks. Inevitably, a copy was leaked to the Liberal press, and on 7 August, the *Winnipeg Free Press* published the entire pamphlet. While many ordinary Canadians, and more than a few Tory backbenchers, applauded Stevens for taking on big business, several of his cabinet colleagues were appalled at Stevens's behaviour. For one thing, some of the specific points he had cited from memory turned out to be factually inaccurate. Worse in their view, the tone of his speech revealed clearly that he was not an impartial chairman. When the full cabinet next met on 25 October 1934, a number of his colleagues insisted that Stevens must express regret for this breach of propriety. The trade minister refused, and subsequently informed Bennett that he would resign from cabinet. Perhaps he felt the shock of his resignation would cause the prime minister to reconsider. Instead, Stevens's resignation was publicly accepted, leading to an acrimonious exchange of letters between the prime minister and his former colleague.[49]

The loss of Stevens necessitated a cabinet shuffle, only the third in over four years in office. The new minister of trade and commerce was R.B. Hanson, a likeable but not distinguished MP from New Brunswick. To replace Stevens as British Columbia's minister, the low-profile Grote Stirling was made minister of national defence. He took the place of Donald Sutherland, who was moved over to pensions and national health, replacing Murray MacLaren, who would soon be appointed lieutenant governor of New Brunswick. Necessary though these changes were, they did nothing to rejuvenate the Conservative government's image, with an election less than a year away. Bennett's closet political advisers, Finlayson and Herridge, agreed with that assessment. They persuaded the prime minister that he should launch a Canadian version of Franklin Roosevelt's New Deal. Accordingly, Bennett took to the Canadian airwaves in a series of five dramatic broadcasts that he personally paid for early in 1935. In the very first address he sought to establish a progressive image of himself, in contrast to the Opposition Liberals. "I am for reform," he declared. "And, in my mind, reform means Government intervention. It means Government control and regulation. It means the end of *laissez faire*."[50] In the addresses that followed, Bennett proceeded to itemize the reform measures he intended to introduce in the final year of his government's mandate. There was nothing even vaguely revolutionary in the proposed program, but taken as a whole, it did seem to represent a radical departure for a Conservative government.

It was characteristic of R.B. Bennett that he did not consult his cabinet about the content of his New Deal broadcasts prior to their delivery. Some of the ministers were encouraged by them; others were dismayed. The Liberal Opposition shrewdly opted to avoid an ideological debate, and instead invited the government to bring in the promised reforms. One piece of legislation that was ready to go was the unemployment insurance bill, which Bennett had promised back in 1931. Beyond that, however, most of the other promised measures existed only in draft form. When the prime minister suffered a serious health breakdown in February that kept him on the sidelines for the next three months, the Conservative government was caught flat-footed. "As was his custom," Edgar Rhodes explained to Sir Robert Borden, "he had kept both the contents of the Bills and the material to be used with them entirely to himself, with the result that we are now in the position of having different Ministers coached by his Secretary."[51] Nothing more clearly revealed the prime ministerial dominance of Bennett than the three-month period when he was ill, and unable to carry his normal load.

As part of his recovery, Bennett had sailed to England in April to attend the king's Silver Jubilee celebration, and to consult London doctors about the state of his health. Their advice echoed that of his Canadian physician: more rest and less stress, or expect even graver heart problems. Accordingly, Bennett returned to Canada prepared to search out a capable successor. However, neither of his preferred choices, Edgar Rhodes and Arthur Meighen, was prepared to take on the job. The one person who clearly wanted the job, and felt himself to be the logical successor, was the one person that Bennett simply would not countenance as his replacement: Harry Stevens.[52] When a mutual friend had dared to raise the former trade minister's name in his presence, the prime minister had snapped back, "That man has done me irreparable harm."[53]

Bennett was aware of Stevens's continuing popularity with the public, and doubtless realized the validity of R.J. Manion's reading of the Conservative caucus. "If R.B. dropped out," he predicted, "there would be a majority demand that Stevens be put in as leader."[54] Accordingly, Bennett determined that if someone must take on the increasingly brazen former trade minister in debate, it might as well be himself. The head-to-head showdown came on 19 June 1935 in the House of Commons. Stevens spoke first, belittling the government's hesitant and almost apologetic legislation to implement the recommendations of his beloved Price Spreads Commission. He sat down to scattered applause, largely from the Opposition benches. Bennett followed with a full-scale denunciation of anyone who might raise false hopes among Canadians by advocating measures that were clearly prohibited by the constitution. He was rewarded with an enthusiastic, desk-thumping salute from the government benches. That evening at a banquet organized in his honour, the prime minister confirmed he would lead the Conservatives into the next election. Harry Stevens would play no role in that campaign. Bennett's reasoning was crystal clear, as he wrote privately to a party loyalist: "Ignorance can be forgiven. Stubbornness one understands, but treachery can neither be forgotten nor forgiven."[55]

Stevens was now out of the Conservative Party, but he was not out of options. Four months earlier he had previewed what might come next, in a final letter sent to the prime minister. "I express my views and beliefs to you as though I were writing them to a close and fast friend," he explained, "and for that reason I know that you will consider them in the light of staunch amity. Otherwise, you and I shall fight on the hustings of our Country against each other, John L. Sullivan style."[56] On 7 July 1935, Stevens announced to the press that he would be heading a new party with the intent of contesting the next general election, from coast to coast. Initially known as the Stevens party it soon adopted the name Reconstruction Party. The field would be crowded though, as in addition to the Bennett-led Conservatives and Mackenzie King-led Liberals, two other new parties would launch their campaigns: the socialist Co-operative Commonwealth Federation and populist Social Credit.

Bennett made one final cabinet shuffle late in the summer of 1935. Vacancies were created by appointing two ministers – Sauvé and Macdonald – to the Senate, while Duranleau received a judicial appointment, and Guthrie went to the Railway Board. A fifth minister, Matthews, retired to private life. In their places, Bennett promoted seven Conservative backbenchers: W.G. Ernst from Nova Scotia; Samuel Gobeil, L.H. Gendron, and Onésime Gagnon from Quebec; and G.R. Geary, J.E. Lawson, and Earl Rowe from Ontario.[57] However, the appointments came so late in the life of the government, and the new ministers had such low profiles that there was no appreciable impact on the electoral fate of the government. Just as they had in the last campaign, Conservative hopes for victory rested with R.B. Bennett. Times had changed, however. The economic recession of 1930 had turned into the Great Depression. Five years earlier, Bennett could attack the Liberal record. Now he had to defend his own. In 1935 a former cabinet colleague, H.H. Stevens, was leading a new protest party that was sure to drain away some traditional Conservative support. Although Bennett campaigned valiantly, he could not overcome the disadvantages of incumbency. When the votes were counted, only forty Conservatives were elected out of a total of 245 seats. It was the worst defeat the Conservative Party had suffered since Confederation in 1867.[58]

Bennett had saved his own seat in the election debacle of 1935, although many in his cabinet did not. He continued to serve diligently as leader of the Opposition until 1938. In that year, the Conservatives held a leadership convention in Ottawa, and his former cabinet colleague, Robert J. Manion, was the choice of the party to replace him. Bennett resigned his seat, and soon moved to England, where he lived his final decade as a member of the British House of Lords.[59] He is the only former prime minister not buried in Canada. The bitterness of rejection that he felt at that time was starkly revealed in this candid rejoinder to Charlotte Whitton, who had inquired in 1939 about whether he might ever return to public life in Canada.

> Don't you think I was given a furlough by the Canadian people in 1935? They rejected me and all my plans and ideas and hopes. Hadn't I right to accept the views of doctors? I think I had. And for one with your intellect do you not think that you are already wrong in even suggesting that I will ever be missed to the extent of being thought of a few months from now? As for wanting me back that is sheer nonsense, Charlotte, and you must know it. They gave me a great "send off" for many reasons. Some for "conscience sake"; some for real regard; some glad to be rid of me. But it just became a bit of mob manifestation; Hosanna in the highest and "Crucify Him Crucify Him" a week later.[60]

It is telling that the religious metaphor used by Bennett, a churchgoer all his life, cast himself in the role of sacrificial saviour.

As this account makes clear, the Conservative government that held office from 1930 to 1935 was dominated by one man, and that man was the prime minister, R.B. Bennett. He was chosen party leader at a national convention, the first time that the Conservative Party had used this method to pick their leader. When the general election of 1930 resulted in a Conservative-majority government, all agreed that Bennett's vigorous campaign had contributed mightily to that outcome. His cabinet consisted of eighteen members in addition to himself, but they never collectively challenged his position of dominance. When the demands of his multiple responsibilities began to pile up, he relinquished the finance portfolio but his central role in government policy-making remained. Even after the bitter resignation of H.H. Stevens, Bennett was still fully in charge. A serious health breakdown in the fifth year of office came the closest to threatening his command of the government, but once he made it clear he was back, and intended to lead the party into the next election, any thoughts of replacing him with Stevens melted away. Ultimately, it was the electorate who ended Bennett's period of prime ministerial dominance, when they voted in the Opposition Liberals with a strong parliamentary majority.

If the concept of statecraft is understood to be the degree of astuteness by which prime ministers manage their cabinet colleagues, and through them the vast state bureaucracy, in order to govern efficiently and effectively, then R.B. Bennett's five-year tenure in office stands as a spectacular failure. Leading up to his entry into office, the confident Calgarian exuded astute political management. Elected leader by the first delegated convention in Conservative Party history in 1927, he spent the next three years modernizing, energizing, and personally financing a rejuvenated party organization. In the election campaign of 1930 Bennett outshone his Liberal rival, Mackenzie King, on the hustings and made far more effective use of the new medium of mass communication, the radio, to connect with the Canadian electorate. Ironically, winning a parliamentary majority marked the beginning of his decline. Bennett overloaded himself with work, taking on the finance portfolio on top of a prime minister's usual crushing burden of responsibilities. When the recession of 1929–30 turned into the Great Depression, Bennett had no answers. Under his direction, the Conservative government initiated needed reforms like Unemployment Insurance and the Prairie Farm Rehabilitation Act, and created lasting new institutions like the Bank of Canada, the Wheat Board, and the CBC. Despite this evidence of innovative state management, the twin dragons of worker unemployment and business failures were not slain. In 1935, economic conditions were far worse than in 1930, not better as he had promised from coast to coast. Policy failure was greatly exacerbated by inept collegial management. R.B. Bennett was by nature a commander, not a consensus builder. His overbearing manner and lone-wolf style alienated the press, his own party, and eventually, the general public. The dramatic split with his long-time political friend and ally H.H. Stevens symbolized Bennett's failure to manage and motivate his cabinet team. Finally, the innovative and robust party organization he himself had nurtured in the years leading up to 1930 had been allowed to wither and die. The new structure that was cobbled together in the months prior to the decisive 1935 campaign was but a shadow of its former self. Failures of policy implementation, political management, and people skills ensured that Bennett would be a one-term prime minister. Ultimately, the voters graded his statecraft skills as an "F," for failure.

NOTES

1 One version of this oft-repeated tale, which may or may not be literally true, is included in Grattan O'Leary, *Recollections of People, Press, and Politics* (Toronto: Macmillan, 1977), 70. See also Ernest Watkins, *R.B. Bennett: A Biography* (London: Becker & Warburg, 1963), 167; and Lord Beaverbrook, *Friends: Sixty Years of Intimate Personal Relations with Richard Bedford Bennett* (London: Heinemann, 1959), 82.

2 P.B. Waite, *The Loner: Three Sketches of the Personal Life and Ideas of R.B. Bennett, 1870–1947* (Toronto: University of Toronto Press, 1992), 59–60.

3 Bennett's pre-1927 political career is capably summarized in P.B. Waite, "Richard Bedford Bennett, 1st Viscount Bennett," in *Canada's Prime Ministers, Macdonald to Trudeau: Portraits from the Dictionary of Canadian Biography*, ed. Ramsay Cook and Real Belanger (Toronto: University of Toronto Press, 2007), 302–8.

4 Verbatim report: National Liberal-Conservative Association Convention, 10–12 October 1927, Library and Archives Canada (hereafter "LAC"), Progressive Conservative Party Papers, vol. 239, 271.

5 For a detailed account of the 1927 Conservative convention, see Larry A. Glassford, "Choosing a New Chieftain," ch. 2 in *Reaction and Reform: The Politics of the Conservative Party under R.B. Bennett, 1927–1938* (Toronto: University of Toronto Press, 1992).

6 R.B. Bennett's speech in Moncton, New Brunswick, 10 July 1930, read by W.L. Mackenzie King, in *Debates of the House of Commons of the Dominion of Canada*, 17th parl., 1st sess., 9 September 1930, 25.

7 J.M. Beck, "'Blasting a Way' to National Prosperity," ch. 17 in *Pendulum of Power: Canada's Federal Elections* (Scarborough: Prentice-Hall, 1968), is still valuable. See also Larry A. Glassford, "The 1930 Election," ch. 4 in *Reaction and Reform*.

8 Bennett's cabinet-making is covered in P.B. Waite, *In Search of R.B. Bennett* (Montreal: McGill-Queen's University Press, 2012), 86–91.

9 For further detail on Bennett's cabinet choices, see Glassford, *Reaction and Reform*, 102–5.

10 Privy Council minute, 7 August 1930, LAC, H.H. Stevens Papers, vol. 29.

11 *Debates of the House of Commons of the Dominion of Canada*, 17th parl., 2nd sess., vol. 1, 17 March 1931, 57.

12 A Politician with a Notebook, "Backstage at Ottawa," *Maclean's*, 15 April 1933, 50.

13 W.L. Mackenzie King, diary, 16 September 1930, LAC.

14 See Andrew D. MacLean, *R.B. Bennett: Prime Minister of Canada* (Toronto: Excelsior, 1935), 38, for an insider's account of Bennett's relationship with his staff. "He can be cruel to a Cabinet Minister who is dull and argumentative, but very generous to a minor employee who has made a mistake." Maclean worked inside Bennett's Ottawa office from 1931 to 1935.

15 *House of Commons Debates*, 1932, cited in Waite, *In Search of R.B. Bennett*, 129.

16 Grant Dexter to J.W. Dafoe, 16 October 1932, LAC, J.W. Dafoe Papers.

17 O'Leary, *Recollections*, 74.

18 Allan Levine, *Scrum Wars: The Prime Ministers and the Media* (Toronto: Dundurn, 1993), 151.

19 Levine, *Scrum Wars*, 159.

20 *A Party Politician: The Memoirs of Chubby Power*, ed. Norman Ward (Toronto: Macmillan, 1966), 265.

21 *House of Commons Debates*, 16 September 1930, 295, cited in Waite, *In Search of R.B. Bennett*, 93.

22 C.P. Stacey, ed., *Historical Documents of Canada*, vol. 5, *The Arts of War and Peace, 1914–1945* (Toronto: Macmillan, 1972), 482–4.

23 *House of Commons Debates*, 14 June 1935, 3608, cited in Waite, *In Search of R.B. Bennett*, 235. See also Glassford, *Reaction and Reform*, 112–13.

24 Cited in Waite, *In Search of R.B. Bennett*, 121.

25 *Debates of the House of Commons of the Dominion of Canada*, 26 April 1932, cited in Glassford, *Reaction and Reform*, 121.

26 *Debates of the House of Commons of the Dominion of Canada*, 17th parl., 4th sess., vol. 1, 10 October 1932, 49.

27 For a more detailed account of the Bennett government's ardent efforts to hold the line on budgetary deficits in hard times, see Glassford, *Reaction and Reform*, 113–14.

28 *House of Commons Debates*, 1932, vol. 1, 7, cited in Roger Graham, *Arthur Meighen*, vol. 3, *No Surrender* (Toronto: Clarke Irwin, 1965), 34.

29 Repr. in *Ottawa Journal*, 21 November 1937, and cited in Waite, *In Search of R.B. Bennett*, 124.

30 Hanson to R.C. Matthews, 2 December 1933, Public Archives of New Brunswick, R.B. Hanson Papers.

31 Cited in Waite, *In Search of R.B. Bennett*, 143.

32 *The Economist*, 18 January 1936, in Stacey, *Historical Documents*, 5:212–13.

33 Manion to Bennett, 1 July 1931, LAC, R.J. Manion Papers, vol. 4.

34 *Debates of the House of Commons of the Dominion of Canada*, 17th parl., 4th sess., vol. 2, 1 February 1933, 1688. J.S. Woodsworth read Bennett's iron heel statement into Hansard from an article in the *Toronto Mail and Empire*, 10 November 1932.

35 *Debates of the House of Commons of the Dominion of Canada*, 17th parl., 4th sess., vol. 2, 14 February 1933, 2102.

36 *Toronto Globe*, 30 December 1933.

37 Bennett to Bruce, 25 July 1938, Queen's University Archives, Herbert A. Bruce Papers, vol. 1.

38 Bennett to Rev. R.G. Hardy, 2 January 1934, University of New Brunswick Archives (hereafter "UNB Archives"), R.B. Bennett Papers, reel M-1069.

39 For more on Bennett's decision to re-institute honours, see Waite, *In Search of R.B. Bennett*, 180–2; Waite, *The Loner*, 65–6; and Glassford, *Reaction and Reform*, 99, 123.

40 *Debates of the House of Commons of the Dominion of Canada*, 17th parl., 3rd sess., vol. 3, 18 May 1932, 3035–6.

41 See Waite, *In Search of R.B. Bennett*, 133–5; and Glassford, *Reaction and Reform*, 124–5.

42 *Debates of the House of Commons of the Dominion of Canada*, 17th parl., 5th sess., vol. 1, 30 January 1934.

43 Cited in Waite, *The Loner*, 84. See also Waite, *In Search of R.B. Bennett*, 172–4;
    and Glassford, *Reaction and Reform*, 125–6, 143–4.
44 Bennett to Stevens, 26 October 1934, LAC, H.H. Stevens Papers, vol. 71.
45 Stevens to Bennett, 30 October 1934, UNB Archives, Bennett Papers, vol. 436.
46 Richard Wilbur, *H.H. Stevens, 1878–1973* (Toronto: University of Toronto Press,
    1977), 75–82.
47 Wilbur, *H.H. Stevens*, 102–3.
48 Glassford, *Reaction and Reform*, 148–50.
49 Wilbur, *H.H. Stevens*, 131–43.
50 "The First Address, January 2nd, 1935," in J.R.H. Wilbur, *The Bennett New Deal:
    Fraud or Portent?* (Toronto: Copp Clark, 1968), 80–3.
51 Rhodes to Borden, 12 March 1935, Public Archives of Nova Scotia, E.N. Rhodes
    Papers, vol. 1199.
52 Bennett confirmed his intention to retire in a letter to his friend, Lord
    Beaverbrook: "In 1935 I had intended, as you know, to retire and had hoped
    to take up residence in England. But Stevens's action made that impossible"
    (Beaverbrook, *Friends*, 89).
53 Leon Ladner to Ernest Watkins, cited in Watkins, *R.B. Bennett*, 209–13.
54 Cited in Wilbur, *H.H. Stevens*, 156.
55 Bennett to William H. Price, 17 July 1935, UNB Archives, Bennett Papers, vol. 435.
56 Stevens to Bennett, 25 February 1935, LAC, H.H. Stevens Papers, vol. 125.
57 Glassford, *Reaction and Reform*, 184–5.
58 Beck, *Pendulum of Power*, 206–22.
59 Waite, "Richard Bedford Bennett," 323–7.
60 Bennett to Whitton, 15 February 1939, LAC, Charlotte Whitton Papers, vol. 4.

10 Mackenzie King's Upgrading of Prime Ministerial Power: Cabinet Management, Luck, and Circumstance

ROBERT BOTHWELL

On 16 October 1935,[1] Canada's two most senior politicians met to discuss the results of the dominion election the day before. Conservative prime minister R.B. Bennett, the loser, was anxious to be out office as soon as possible; Liberal William Lyon Mackenzie King, the winner, was just as anxious to move in. The decencies had to be observed, and the practicalities agreed. The two men opined that the election result had been foreordained, singling out H.H. Stevens as a principal cause. Bennett growled about his treacherous rogue minister, and King agreed. Stevens was a man of low character, an impossible colleague, a destructive force. But King knew well that the actual author of the Conservative defeat was sitting before him. Stevens was merely the most obvious manifestation of Bennett's inability to get along with his cabinet and his caucus, and to organize decision-making beyond himself. His failure to govern had been punished by the people. Bennett and King eventually agreed that the new government would take office in a week's time, on 23 October.

Stevens's electoral escapade was a sharp reminder to King of what damage a dissatisfied, ambitious minister could do. A party leader, a prime minister, had the power to hire and fire; but a minister had the power to resign. Under the right circumstances, a ministerial resignation could be fatal to a prime minister or to a party, and it was an axiom that King never forgot. More problematic were decision processes that led to confusion and stagnation. As King settled into his chair at the cabinet table, he slowly but surely developed two new, but still vague, ambitions to bring a new sophistication to managing the government executive so that its decisions could be transmitted to the bureaucracy and to the public. The first was a solid conviction that the *country had to be governed* while preserving national unity. The second was to use a new mastery of facts and figures to wear down any potential cabinet recalcitrant. King's new approach was built on a recognition that his 1920s management style was no longer applicable to the dogged problems of economic depression and, then, war. He proved equal to the task, though not without difficulty or consequence.

King engineered what political scientist J. Stefan Dupré called the introduction of an "institutionalized cabinet."[2]

If we define statecraft as the *art* of directing and managing government, King had had plenty of examples from Sir Wilfrid Laurier to guide and define his practice. It was not a science. There were no hard and fast rules: "scientific management" as a field of study had existed since the turn of the century. King undoubtedly knew the term and how the theory was applied in industry, but he would have considered it absurd to apply it to the exercise of statecraft. Like his predecessors, King saw the management of a state as intensely personal.[3] He endlessly dwelt in his diary on the merits and foibles of the men and women with whom he came into contact – and as we shall see, King was not indifferent to the role women could play in managing their politician husbands. It is also true that King preferred to work with known quantities, especially in his later cabinets where he had experience with individuals to guide him.[4]

Nor were King's cabinets a shapeless mass, cast up by chance and circumstance, representatives of region or religion.[5] The ministers had to accept direction: they had to accept that they were "Mackenzie King Liberals," which meant not only accepting King as leader, but accepting his guidance on policy. The fundamental policy was "national unity," which no minister ever defied – in public at least, but also in practice. Disagreement might have lurked in the background, but no minister, even during the conscription crises of 1942 and 1944, emerged to contradict or undermine it. Nor was King devoid of ideology, though he spooned it out carefully over time. He believed in the primacy of government, of the state, and saw it as potentially a beneficent force. This principle emerged time and again in his actions and those of his ministers, even those who consciously clung to a less interventionist and less melioristic philosophy of politics. He could also be innovative. In May 1943, he appointed four parliamentary assistants (secretaries) to senior ministers. A notable example was the appointment of Douglas Abbott as parliamentary assistant to the minister of finance.

King had been party leader for sixteen years by the time he was asked to form a government again in 1935. He was now sixty years old, and his political life stretched back over thirty years. The politicians who had made their mark in his youth were almost all gone, with the sole exception of Raoul Dandurand, the government leader in the Senate: personally prominent and greatly respected, Dandurand was not a major political figure by virtue of his status as a senator.[6] King's electoral success in the 1920s and his ability to survive and recover from the Beauharnois scandal of 1932 enhanced his legend within the party as someone who could always figure his way out of any political fix – a skill mixed with that essential political ingredient, luck.

In 1934 King set down his conception of a cabinet in a letter to the new Ontario Liberal premier, Mitchell Hepburn. It shed valuable insight into King's view of cabinet government, distilled from eight years as prime minister in the 1920s.

> My own experience has disclosed to me the wisdom of the collective mind and the collective will in public affairs. It is, I think, of the very essence of our British system of government. You will be wise to win as completely as you can the confidence of all your colleagues and this can be done most effectively by giving them, to the exclusion of others, your own confidence, though, with respect to many things, there will be much which you will find inadvisable to share even with them, but best to keep wholly to yourself. Don't forget what I said to you about having it understood that you would expect all major decisions to be discussed in advance with respect to appointments as well as policies. Adoption of this course will save you many pitfalls.[7]

King put his anxieties on full display in his diary: his anticipations of opposition, his fears of cabinet splits, of disunity, and of his sense of mission, as the one who would or should triumph over all these forces. King's management of the various conscription events among other "events" (some of which are better called "crises") is well known and need not be repeated here.[8]

King worked hard and long hours, like all his predecessors. He was also lucky, but luck is hard work, even for someone as fortunate as Mackenzie King. Unmarried and childless,[9] King had few interests to compete with politics and governments.[10] His acquaintances in his spiritual life served to confirm his instincts or his judgments, and his successive dogs may well have been more comfort than an actual human family would have given. They did not at any rate interfere with King's relations with his cabinet, a field in which he excelled and which defined his statecraft. Already informed by his experience in the 1920s, when he had very few ministers of talent, and reminded of the impact of the Stevens affair, he vowed to do better. Mackenzie King was acutely conscious that his political survival, and thus his ability to direct the government, depended not only on the coherence and political unity of his cabinet, but also on his skill in inspiring trust or if not trust, at least obligation, among his ministers – creating and feeding that unity. It depended, in the much-used phrase, on character and circumstance. Competence was also a factor, though perhaps not as important as imagined because Mackenzie King was very successful in attracting exceptional talent to join the public service. His massive reforms of the Privy Council Office and of the Prime Minister's Office were also highly effective in promoting the legitimacy of his office and in ensuring a sustainable level of unity at the cabinet table.[11]

Mackenzie King's First Cabinet

The sixteenth government of Canada would last from October 1935 to November 1948 (thirteen years and twenty-three days, or 4,772 days, second only to Wilfrid Laurier's fifteen years and eighty-six days). Thirty-four ministers served in the cabinet, two (apart from King) for its entire duration, and several almost so. Four ministers died in office. Two had been provincial premiers – both from Saskatchewan: Charles Dunning and Jimmy Gardiner, the minister of agriculture. Thomas A. Crerar had led the Progressives and had been a minister in Borden's Union government and was appointed minister of the interior as well as superintendent of Indian affairs and minister of immigration and colonization until November 1936 (he would serve as minister of mines and resources after that, and until war's end). Several had been at least part-time professors, and some held post-graduate degrees, though Mackenzie King was the only PhD among them.

It was a post-Great-War group: veterans were a major component. One, a full general, recently unwillingly retired, had previously served in the Great War as a brigadier general; there was also a recent major general, another Great War veteran; and then a lieutenant colonel, a major, and a brace of lieutenants, plus a private and a sergeant major, all veterans of the Great War. One minister had served in the Royal Navy before coming to Canada. Only the generals could be called professional military men: the rest had been volunteers for the duration of the war. If any profession predominated in the King cabinet, it was lawyers, as in most Canadian cabinets, and they included most of the veterans described above.[12] There were three immigrants, but two like their local colleagues were by birth British subjects, which was the same thing legally as being Canadian-born. Only C.D. Howe, a Massachusetts native, had had to change citizenship: as he more than once told his colleagues, he was the only minister who chose to be Canadian. Between 1935 and 1948, four ministers were translated to the Senate, a dignified fate that eased their departure from cabinet: William Euler, James A. MacKinnon, Thomas A. Crerar, and Ian Mackenzie.

The most important category in the cabinet, the one to which King paid most attention, was Quebec, or more broadly, francophones. Twelve of the thirty-four ministers between 1935 and 1948 were French-speaking; of those, two, Charles Gavan (Chubby) Power and Louis St-Laurent, had English as their mother tongue. (In St-Laurent's case this ranks merely as a "curious historical fact," since in every other respect he should be considered as a francophone, though a perfectly bilingual one. The same was true of Power.) Two others came from outside Quebec. One, Paul Martin, was unclassifiable: though he was half-French, it was the other, Irish, half that predominated. In a practical sense, one's linguistic origins did not figure: Cabinets functioned in English, and in King's time all francophone ministers were expected to have at least a competence in that language.

To detail these characteristics is almost to list party-political construction materials. Some had been ordered, some had been bought, some were inherited, and some were political flotsam and jetsam, cast onto Mackenzie King's shore by the political tides: not accidental, exactly, but unknown quantities.

King, like his predecessors, named himself president of the Privy Council and *ex officio* the secretary of state for external affairs. He would combine the prime ministership and external affairs positions until 1946, when he named Louis St-Laurent to external affairs. It was a radical departure, but one that reflected the increasing complexity of Canada's relations with the international community. His second step was to summon Ernest Lapointe. Lapointe certainly had no problem getting down to business with King when the two men met on 17 October 1935, to discuss the ministry that King was about to form. Lapointe acted in two capacities: as a senior and trusted colleague – the longest-serving cabinet member after King himself; and as the senior minister from Quebec, reprising a role he had had in King's previous government.

Lapointe arrived at one o'clock. "The sun was shining brightly," King wrote in his diary, adding that Pat, his Irish terrier, gave Lapointe "a great welcome also." The signs were thus propitious. King began the conversation by enunciating his first principle, "that I would not have men in the cabinet who drank," to which Lapointe soberly replied, "You will have a pretty difficult time." This was demonstrated by the first name King and Lapointe considered, Lucien Cannon. King observed that "not only were his habits bad," but he was "disloyal." King conjured up a vision where Cannon and his wife were both *hors de combat* because they were overcome by drink. Lapointe agreed, but added that another hard drinker from Quebec, Charles Gavan (henceforth Chubby) Power, was strongly favoured by the young Liberals of Quebec. Power had another advantage: he would represent Irish Catholics in the cabinet, meaning that he would symbolize that they were welcome and important at the cabinet table. Power had been the provincial Liberals' chief organizer in the 1931 provincial election, knew all regions of the province, was practical and not ideological, and valued by all sections of what was a badly factionalized provincial party.[13] He was an anglophone, obviously, but so close to French Canadian Liberals that he acted in effect as one of them. Not all these considerations emerged between Lapointe and King, but they were in the background. There was trouble ahead for the Liberals in Quebec and Power was the most effective tool the federal party had to deal with the approaching storm. It was at this point that King's first principle of cabinet-making was discarded. Lapointe promised to have a serious talk with Power and his wife and lay down the law of sobriety.

One unusual aspect of King's cabinet-making was the role of wives in his considerations. In preliminary discussions with Lapointe about appointing Chubby Power to the cabinet, and then with Power himself, Mrs. Power's role was emphasized. Undoubtedly King and Lapointe counted on her to keep Power (and possibly also herself) sober, but the discussions indicate that her role was larger, and that King counted on her character. It may well be that without his wife, Power would not have been appointed to the ministry.[14] Pierre Casgrain, a senior Quebec Liberal, was not appointed to the cabinet but consoled with the prestigious post of speaker of the House of Commons; he was plainly told that his wife, Thérèse, had been a major factor in his appointment. It was clear that King expected more from Thérèse than from Pierre, and her subsequent career more than confirmed his judgment.[15] When it came to Norman Rogers, King remarked on his and his wife's "spiritual quality," which enhanced his standing with the prime minister.[16]

Lapointe did have a request for himself. Could he be minister of external affairs instead of the prestigious but unchallenging post of minister of justice? The request made some sense. He took a strong interest in foreign affairs, and he had represented Canada at various foreign functions, including heading the Canadian delegation at the League of Nations. King asked Lapointe to consider the implications of his request, which he, King, must refuse. It might revive the recently buried animosities between English and French Canadians on questions of war and peace. There was the possibility of war – neither man was naive enough to ignore it. Baldly, the question was: would English Canadians trust a French Canadian to manage a world where Canada might once again be called to stand at Britain's side in its hour of peril? As King's diary makes plain, he himself wondered whether Lapointe could be relied on to put forward an interventionist, and not an isolationist, policy. He knew that he could appeal to and rely on Lapointe's loyalty to the party, and to national unity, and the matter was dropped.

It was an indication of close personal as well as close political relations between the two men. Though slightly younger than King, Lapointe was a member of the same political generation, formed by the experience of the Laurier government, and shocked by the national unity crisis around conscription in 1917. Both saw the necessity of a link between the majority-English-speaking national party, and its Quebec wing, and through it to the Quebec francophone electorate. And both were accommodating and compromising, if not on all subjects, then at least on those that had political salience. Lapointe understood, and it seems shared King's view of a cabinet and how it should function. He is said to have been the only one of the ministers who could address the prime minister as something other than Mister King. There was certainly trust, perhaps a kind of affection, and what must be called political intimacy. There was also a distance, even a discomfort on Lapointe's part. Lapointe's son long afterwards remembered and repeated his father's description of an evening at King's residence, when after dinner the prime minister entertained the Lapointes by posing with Pat, at the piano, manoeuvring the animal's paws on the keyboard, and singing or howling in unison. In telling his son of the incident, Lapointe commented that it was definitely odd if not incomprehensible behaviour.

The two men then talked of other people and other principles. Over the next few days, with Lapointe's frequent advice, the cabinet was secured. All provinces but Alberta and Prince Edward Island were represented. Ian Mackenzie, a

Scot, a war veteran, and a university-trained classicist, who had performed very effectively on the opposition benches, was rewarded with the Department of National Defence. King's anti-drink rule was punctured again: Mackenzie had a strong affection for the spirits of his birthplace, and it was not to be displaced. James L. Ilsley of Nova Scotia provided an antidote. His sentiments on alcohol are unknown, but he was an overwhelmingly serious personage.[17]

Almost all the individuals cited above had been members of Parliament. Jimmy Gardiner, premier of Saskatchewan, had never been a federal member of Parliament, but he was such a familiar figure nationally that he had no political ground to make up. Then there were the newcomers. The most important, the closest to King, was Norman Rogers, a professor of political science from Queen's University, who had attracted King's notice and affection by assembling and publishing a highly flattering biography of the Liberal leader. Rogers proved to be much more than a sycophant as a minister and was regarded as one of King's most effective appointments.[18] From the other end of Ontario was C.D. Howe, a prominent engineer with an international reputation for building grain elevators. King gave him not one but two departments, Railways (which Crerar had wanted) and Marine, with the mission to merge them into a single Department of Transport.[19]

Ontario in some respects was the greatest problem. It was King's native province, but it had rejected him thrice, defeating him personally in the elections of 1911, 1917, and 1925.[20] From 1926 until he was defeated there in 1945, King held the seat of Prince Albert in Saskatchewan, though he was seldom if ever thought of as a representative of the province. Ontario had elected a majority of Liberal MPs, but the provincial capital, Toronto, remained a bastion of Toryism. The fact that there was a Liberal provincial government had helped during in the federal election, in which Premier Hepburn had campaigned for the federal cousins, but King neither liked nor trusted Hepburn, either his personality or his associations inside the Toronto speculative mining community. Among those elected was Arthur Slaght, a Toronto lawyer of outstanding forensic ability as Mackenzie King certainly realized.[21] But Slaght lived high, and he was close to Hepburn and to some notorious speculators.[22] These attributes were fatal to his chances. Association with Premier Hepburn was far worse than drink as far as Mackenzie King was concerned, though Hepburn and drink were far from incompatible in real life.

Instead, King preferred C.D. Howe, the engineer. He owed nothing to Hepburn, he was not tainted by mining speculation, and he did not come from Toronto. "We owe Toronto very little," the prime minister told his diary, "as she has given us only two members." That clinched it: Howe was in, and Slaght was out.[23]

There were details to be ironed out: the government leader in the Senate (Senator Dandurand, appointed to that body in 1896), the speakers, a few odds and ends, making a cabinet of sixteen, comfortably down from the number under Bennett.

1 Prime Minister; External Affairs; President of the Privy Council – William Lyon Mackenzie King, 60, Ontario
2 Agriculture – Jimmy Gardiner, 51, Saskatchewan
3 Finance – C.A. Dunning, 50, Saskatchewan
4 Fisheries – Joseph-Enoil Michaud, 47, New Brunswick
5 Indian Affairs; Interior; Immigration and Colonization; Mines – T.A. Crerar, 59, Manitoba
6 Justice and Attorney General – Ernest Lapointe, 59, Quebec
7 Labour – Norman Rogers, 41, Ontario
8 Marine; Railways and Canals – C.D. Howe, 49, Ontario
9 National Defence – Ian Mackenzie, 45, British Columbia
10 National Revenue – J.L. Ilsley, 41, Nova Scotia
11 Pensions and National Health – Charles Gavan Power, 47, Quebec
12 Postmaster General – John Campbell Elliott, 63, Ontario
13 Public Works – Arthur Cardin, 56, Quebec
14 Secretary of State of Canada – Fernand Rinfret, 52, Quebec
15 Trade and Commerce – William Daum Euler, 60, Ontario
16 Without Portfolio; Government Leader in the Senate – Raoul Dandurand, 73, Quebec (senator)

In retrospect, the cabinet appointed in 1935 has come to be seen as a ministry of all the talents, but it did not seem that way at the time. The average age of cabinet was 53; King was noticeably seven years older, one of the most important differences in age ever recorded: he was the senior man, with the exception of John Elliott and Raoul Dandurand, the political warhorse from Montreal who had worked so closely with his hero Wilfrid Laurier.

There were five members from Quebec, a third of the cabinet, all of whom were French-speaking. They were matched with five representatives from Ontario. There was no representation from Alberta, nor Prince Edward Island. Most of its members were appointed on very familiar lines: political effectiveness; regional political; leadership; loyalty; and, finally, talent. The anticipated talents, Howe, Ilsley, and Rogers, actually lived up to their promise. Others were loyal, and in most cases inoffensive. From Quebec, Arthur Cardin, a very reluctant appointment by King and Lapointe, was as much trouble as they anticipated. Cardin expected to get the Department of Marine and was told he could not have it. (Lapointe and King knew that Cardin had enriched himself from dredging contracts, an obvious danger sign.) Cardin promptly caught the train back to Montreal and had to be coaxed to return by King over the long-distance phone. The inducement was to appoint Cardin to the patronage-rich

Department of Public Works. And Chubby Power proved to be what they both had expected: a very effective organizer, with very serious political talent and insight, essential to the party in the Quebec political crisis that unfolded after the defeat of the provincial Liberals in 1936.

King's relations with Lapointe proved to be crucial over the next four years of worsening international crises, and in justifying and then managing the politics of wartime Canada. Lapointe's death in November 1941 deeply moved King, as many pages of his diary that month attest. Lapointe's function survived him. Of course, King needed a senior adviser on Quebec and the role was transferred to Louis St-Laurent, who soon became irreplaceable in the government. Nevertheless, the link to old times was gone, and with it the personal affection.

King was at the height of his powers in 1935. He had held the Liberal party together through five elections, winning two outright, managing one evenly divided Parliament, while turning a constitutional crisis into a political triumph. Even his most serious defeat, in 1930, eventually turned out to have a silver lining, in the inability of the victorious Conservatives to master the Great Depression and the repellent qualities of their leader, Bennett.

Institutionalizing Cabinet

Cabinet government worked remarkably informally until the mid-1930s. The agenda-setting process was left entirely to the prime minister and though cabinet met several times a week, if not daily, no minutes were taken and decisions were recorded only on occasion. Returning to power in the depths of the Depression, King grew convinced that the approach was insufficient and that the government was running risks it could avoid. A subcommittee had been created to deal with increased spending in the military, but better coordination was needed across government. He talked to various advisers on the hunch that he needed a principal secretary of sorts, though was impressed by what had been taking place at 10 Downing Street, particularly as a result of Maurice Hankey's transformations of cabinet processes during the Great War. (Hankey had been secretary of the Imperial War Cabinet – which included Canada – during the First World War, and subsequently clerk of the British Privy Council.) The problem was finding the right sort of person to lead the government down this path. His idea was that this individual would report to him personally and be a Liberal partisan.

As J.L. Granatstein described it, Arnold Heeney, a Montreal lawyer, came to the prime minister's attention informally in the mid-1930s and was hired in the fall of 1938 as a new principal secretary to King. Within a year, war was declared, and cabinet was forced to make better decisions with more accuracy and far more quickly. A cabinet War Committee was established. Heeney's *savoir faire* was immediately tested and won the confidence of the prime minister. He appropriated the title of clerk of the Privy Council in the winter of 1940, earning the highest pay in the Canadian bureaucracy.[24]

What is remarkable was that Heeney, age thirty-six, had no experience in government or public administration whatsoever. Affable, very smart and good-looking, somewhat bilingual, he specialized in commercial law. It seems that the only real qualification was that he had heard Hankey speak while he was studying in England in 1925. Regardless, he convinced King and his peers that he was equal to the task, and the cabinet was organized into subcommittees that would allow individual ministers to focus on particular tasks. The idea of sitting around the cabinet table for hours on end during the week eventually lost out to pressing administrative matters that crowded the desks of most ministers. More staff were hired to work around the prime minister to corral evidence, consult various departments, and write briefings and speeches.

Cabinet government thus became far more professional and polished. It took some years before minutes were recorded, but already in the mid-1930s ministers could see priorities more clearly and accountabilities were more evident. At the same time, it was not lost on ministers that the information was mostly flowing to the prime minister. The tension created by the new realities seemed easily manageable, but one minister in particular, Chubby Power, took notice. In the 1948 leadership convention, he denounced the intrusion of public service advice on the political machinery of the Liberal party.[25]

The Wartime Shuffles

King's allocation of portfolios hardly constituted a departure, but there were aspects that left him with the conviction that government priorities were not well reflected by the departments on which it relied. In 1936, the offices of minister of marine and minister of railways and canals were abolished and replace by the office of minister of transport.

As the government prepared for its fourth anniversary in September 1939 and was now officially at war with Nazi Germany, King made many changes (see image 10.1). Charles A. Dunning became ill and could no longer perform his functions, and carrying on in wartime was unthinkable. Dunning's departure was a relief on the personal as well as the administrative and political level as he had troubled relations with Jimmy Gardiner, his fellow Saskatchewanian. He was replaced by J.L. Ralston.

The 1939 shuffle affected other departments. Ian Mackenzie was hastily moved out of the portfolio of minister of national defence after a report to cabinet that King judged "pathetic." He was replaced by Norman Rogers. Norman Rogers's post as minister of labour was assumed by Norman McLarty from Windsor, Ontario. Power was removed from pensions and national health to

Image 10.1. The King Cabinet on the outbreak of war, 1939.

Source: Library and Archives Canada, C-090191.

postmaster general and replaced by Ian Mackenzie. The portfolio of secretary of state for Canada passed from the deceased Fernand Rinfret to Ernest Lapointe.

Nine months of war were instructive regarding the machinery of government and by late spring King effected the largest switch. The first was the creation of a new cabinet seat: minister of munitions and supply, a post given to C.D. Howe. The portfolio of national war services was also created and given to Jimmy Gardiner. Ralston, who had just been appointed to finance in September 1939, would serve to deliver only one budget, and instead was given the all-important portfolio of national defence, replacing Norman Rogers, who had died in a plane crash. James Ilsley assumed finance in July 1940 and would serve until 1946. Power was named associate minister of national defence and minister of national defence for air while Angus Macdonald was given the responsibility as minister of national defence for naval services. Colin Gibson was named minister of national revenue. William Pate Mulock was named postmaster general. Pierre Casgrain was named secretary of state for Canada, replacing Ernest Lapointe. The Department of Trade and Commerce was given to James MacKinnon and the Department of Transport went to Arthur Cardin. The only substantive additions until the war's end were Louis St-Laurent, who joined cabinet as minister of justice to replace Ernest Lapointe, who had died in November 1941, and General Andrew McNaughton, who joined the cabinet as minister of national defence in the midst of the conscription crisis of 1944.

King had to make changes in November 1944, when Ralston was dismissed, and then Power resigned as minister of national defence for air to protest the implementation of conscription. King assigned a new portfolio, minister of veterans affairs, to Ian Mackenzie. At the end of 1945 the two judged most worthy were appointed to the imperial Privy Council: Ilsley and St-Laurent. There was an immediate storm. C.D. Howe had one of his periodic fits of stress, and sulked. King was informed, and in June 1946 Howe was awarded "that degree." Then it was agriculture minister Jimmy Gardiner's turn: more sulking. Finally, there was Ian Mackenzie, who could claim seniority as well as faithful service. His sentiments are recorded in the King diary – frequently. King cut his losses, dipped one more time into the well of rewards, and Mackenzie became Right Honourable too.

The end of the war saw a renovation of the cabinet, and a changing of the guard among the ministers. The 1940 election had brought in a younger cohort of MPs, five men (all men), a generation down from King, Howe, and Gardiner. (The exception was Ilsley, born in 1894, who had been appointed to the cabinet in 1935 at the age of forty-one, and who would retire, prematurely worn out, at fifty-four.) These were, first, Brooke Claxton, and later Douglas Abbott, Paul Martin, and Lionel Chevrier. At the very end was Lester Pearson, who had still to be elected, but whose political qualifications were fully the equal of the first four. Pearson was also the exception in his profession. While the other four were lawyers, he was a civil servant, and a professional diplomat. Abbott and Claxton were both Anglo-Quebeckers, a species that was usually restricted to a single cabinet post, but since their appointments were balanced by Chevrier and Martin, francophone (more or less) Catholic Ontarians, King could afford to make this one exception.[26]

King, with his usual perception, saw them as intelligent, ambitious, and young enough to provide the Liberal party with a future, beyond his immediate successor, Louis St-Laurent. Their qualities varied. Claxton had unusual political talent as an organizer and manager and would go on to play a major role as Canada's first minister of health and welfare and in the elections of 1945, 1949, and 1953.[27] In King's opinion, Martin might have been too ambitious, but that of course was a quality that could be put to use. By the second half of 1944 Mackenzie King was thinking actively of the next election. And he thought of Martin.

If there was to be an election, King liked to prepare the ground with a puff piece that would laud his policies and praise himself. One such had been prepared, and King found it satisfactory. The only question was, Who would sign it? Finally, King had an inspiration. "What about that lugubrious fellow Martin?" When Martin, still an ordinary MP, got the call to report to the prime minister's office, he thought his hour, and a cabinet appointment, had come. Full of hope and ambition, Martin arrived in front of King's desk. "Sign this," said the prime minister, shoving the puffery across the desk. His spirits drooping, Martin managed, "Can I read it first?" Happily for Martin, it was a case of hope deferred, not dashed: the appointment came early in 1945.

The last major shuffle took place on 9 December 1946. Ilsley was exhausted by tense disputes with the provinces, and King removed him from finance and sent the Nova Scotia lawyer to justice to replace Louis St-Laurent. The latter was moved to external affairs, King's own treasured portfolio, a signal that the prime minister might have designated a successor (Ilsley, it must be remembered, was very popular in the country, a remarkable accomplishment for anyone occupying the finance portfolio). Douglas Abbott was given finance, and Brooke Claxton replaced Abbott in national defence. Paul Martin succeeded Claxton at national health and welfare.

King's Management of Cabinet

King's attitude to his ministers varied, as we might expect, with their personality, competence, and salience. And, most of all, what counted was their loyalty, the sine qua non for Mackenzie King. Judged by historical standards, King's ministers were more loyal than most.[28] The record shows that King was unusually retentive of his ministers, which opens the door to another observation: King was endowed with a very healthy ego, but he was not a narcissist, and engaged with his ministers' foibles, their families, and their tragedies. He was of course censorious – second nature to someone raised in the bosom of Presbyterian piety.

An example is Chubby Power. Over the nine years Power served in the King cabinet, he appears frequently as an essential component of the Liberal party's fortunes in Quebec. He did not cause embarrassment to the government in the administration of his departments, Pensions and National Health or the air component of National Defence, unlike some other ministers. A discreet press did not report Power's occasional binges, and despite clucking in the diary, Mackenzie King never came close to firing him.

Objectively the temptation ought to have been strong. Over the years, Power lapsed and relapsed. His lapses were very noticeable since he was a binge drinker and during the binges could not even simulate sobriety. That at least spared him (and the country) from decisions that might have seemed rational but were not. He was simply hors de combat. The binges would be followed by sermonizing from King, threats implicit and explicit, and repentance, in which Power would promise not to do it again, until next time.

Power's most spectacular next time occurred on 12 August 1943. That day Mackenzie King and select ministers were in Quebec City to host a conference between Winston Churchill and Franklin D. Roosevelt. King was the anxious host and maître d' of the conference, concerned that arrangements should work smoothly and comfortably for his important guests. While Churchill and Roosevelt and their staffs debated in private, King escorted Mrs. Churchill, while keeping an eye on his own entourage to make sure they did not get out of line. Power, however, did. King directed General Kenneth Stuart, the Canadian army chief of staff, to make sure that Power did not return to the conference.

Power may be considered an extreme case because his drinking bouts were well known. The drink did not, however, become a public scandal, an essential consideration for a man as politically sensitive as Mackenzie King. Political sensitivity also dictated a certain caution. Power had been and was still a political asset. Finally, the accumulation of years during which King fulminated but tolerated points to the probability that he genuinely liked Power.[29]

It may even be that King had a weakness for alcoholics, and that the frequent sermons recorded in his diary on the matter were directed as much to himself as to the object of his attention. It was a question of charity, perhaps: Christian charity, resembling his attempts as a youth to turn prostitutes from the path of sin. In any case, drink was the social norm in politics, journalism, and business in the 1940s. Power might be extreme, but he was not exceptional.

Even at a lower level of competence and political functionality King did not usually put his reproaches into practice. Ian Mackenzie, from 1935 to 1948 British Columbia's principal representative in the cabinet, was also a notable drinker, but unlike Power he was a daily drinker with a constant blood alcohol level. Like Power, he had rendered notable political service to the Liberal party, and like Power he was indefatigable and effective on the hustings. It was the kind of effort that impressed King and stimulated his gratitude.

Appointed minister of national defence in 1935, Mackenzie failed to grasp the rudiments of the job. Observers considered that that was a result of laziness rather than a lack of intelligence. Laziness progressed to ignorance, ignorance to negligence, and negligence to scandal, when the Defence Department became enmeshed in the Bren Gun affair, a scandal that in 1938 rivalled Hitler's European aggressions for newsworthiness. When Hitler proceeded to actual war against Poland in September 1939, and Canada joined the British Empire in war against Germany, Mackenzie King felt the need to remove Mackenzie lest his mere presence undermined the credibility of the Liberal government in directing the war effort. In the view of his biographers, Mackenzie did much better as minister of pensions and national health and subsequently as minister of veterans affairs. A veteran himself, he had some feeling for the task; the policies that originated under his authority suggest that at the very least he did not get in the way and may indeed have made a positive contribution.[30]

Other ministers enjoyed King's trust, without having to evoke the same level of tolerance that the prime minister displayed to his drunks. An example was C.D. Howe, the MP from Port Arthur, and a poster recruit for the 1935 election. Howe had no political experience, and thus none of the ties that bound

King to Lapointe, Power, or Mackenzie. Howe became in effect the regional minister for Northern Ontario, with a vague mandate for the west generally, where Howe was well known for his construction of grain elevators to move the west's principal crop, wheat – including through Howe-built grain elevators in Vancouver, where he also had connections.

Howe was the architect of one of the government's major achievements between 1935 and the outbreak of war, the merger of two departments, Railways and Canals and Marine, into one. Marine in particular had an overripe reputation, and Howe was emplaced there for good reason, as someone who had experience in railways, canals, and tidewater, and who abhorred scandal. Throughout, King defended Howe. Howe for his part joined with Norman Rogers, another Ontario minister, in carrying on a defensive campaign against an embittered and hostile Mitch Hepburn.[31]

Another trusted minister was Jimmy Gardiner, the minister of agriculture. Gardiner was a Laurier Liberal – like King. Conscription in 1917 and conscription in 1944 were linked in his mind. King stood where Sir Wilfrid had stood, and beside him stood Jimmy Gardiner. Gardiner took the issue so seriously that he took time out from his wife's funeral – at the height of the 1944 conscription crisis – to assure King of his steadfastness over conscription.

The war with Premier Mitch Hepburn merged into the larger Second World War. Hepburn was by then all too ready to believe that the Mackenzie King Liberals were unable to provide the competent and decisive direction that the Canadian war effort required. There should instead be a National Government, like the one in the Great War (on its way to being renamed as the First World War). King spotted a political opening and seized it, dissolving Parliament in January 1940 and calling an election for the end of March, over the misgivings of the few ministers he let in on the secret. The days of dual loyalties to the King government in Ottawa and the Hepburn government in Toronto were over, the prime minister told the Liberal caucus. "There could be no other than Mackenzie King Liberals as candidates, who would be recognized as such." The result was twofold: a reinforcement of King's position in the country, with over 50 per cent of the popular vote and a crushing majority in the House of Commons, and the enhancement of King's position as party leader, because the election call validated his political instincts – and demonstrated that he had the essential qualification for leadership: luck.

King's negative instincts were at work as much as the positive ones. He had a horror of the experience of 1917, including its version of the National Government. When later in the year the National Government tag was used against C.D. Howe, King sprang to his support. Howe, by then minister of munitions and supply and thus in charge of Canada's industrial war effort, had stretched and even broken the rules that bound governments' financial responsibility. At first chaotically but more and more effectively, the economy moved to a war footing, and munitions and supplies began to flow to the Canadian and British war machines.

King appreciated that Howe, like Power or Mackenzie, had his weaknesses. When it came to work, Howe had no appetite control, and as a result he became exhausted trying to do too many things, and when exhausted he became fractious. In August 1941 he proposed to use force to break a strike in the aluminum plant at Arvida, Quebec. Lapointe, with far better connections and understanding of the situation, intervened. The strikers were neither malingering nor deliberately obstructing the war effort: they wanted some respect for local customs, including blueberry picking in August. Lapointe with King's support calmed Howe down: the strike was settled, and the minister went on to other things – positive things politically as well as economically, as King understood.[32]

Howe was not always reliable in cabinet. He was one of those who was prepared to back J.L. Ralston in the struggle to impose conscription in October–November 1944, and later, with Ralston gone, to insist that conscription be immediately applied, despite the risks that that posed for national unity. Howe left his office for the crucial cabinet meeting, believing it was his last. His staff was waiting apprehensively, but when the minister returned, he was smiling and shaking his head. "The old man pulled it off," he said wonderingly.

As with the election of 1940, the resolution of the conscription crisis affirmed and consolidated King's position with most of his ministers. There were exceptions, notably Nova Scotia's Angus L. Macdonald, who would leave Ottawa in disgust a few months later, denouncing King (in private) and despising his works. Even King's legislative achievements such as family allowances, Macdonald commented, were "more a product of opportunity and political expediency than the fulfilment of any fixed ideal."[33] But his fellow Nova Scotian J.L. Ilsley, arguably as minister of finance much more essential to the war effort than Macdonald, and better known to the public, stayed on. Ilsley's departure would have shaken the government, but he remained in his seat and his post – like Howe. Ilsley, Howe, and St-Laurent, would be the foundation of King's post-war government, politically and administratively.

When it came to positive inducements for his ministers, King had fewer tools than his predecessors. Borden and Bennett distributed knighthoods to worthy politicians, generals, and businessmen. King had ended the practice, though a few lower-level honours were still on offer. In point of prestige only an appointment to the imperial Privy Council in London yielded a noticeable distinction, because with it came the title "Right Honourable" instead of the mere "Honourable" that marked members of Canadian cabinets. As Bruce Hutchison put it, King "seldom erred in judging men."[34] If pandering was required, King was not too proud to indulge.

Most of the cases and personalities mentioned up to this point illustrate a relationship of mutual support, but it could hardly be taken for granted. First,

King was well aware of the unpredictability as well as the malleability of "events," as the British prime minister Harold Macmillan once described the phenomenon.[35] He needed to be, for the signposts of the world order that he knew from his youth or young manhood changed out of recognition, with most of the changes occurring during the mandate of the 1935–48 government.

King's relations with most of his colleagues most of the time were respectful and indulgent. King's political pre-eminence, his legend, predisposed the ministers to believe in his star, and to accept that their leader's record, especially in the 1935 and 1940 elections, justified their trust. As Howe said, "The old man did it." There was a corollary that illustrates King's view of his minister, or any minister who ventured into territory that was not his own, which was never put into words between prime minister and minister, but which survives in King's diary. Describing Howe's contacts with the Americans about a possible free-trade agreement, and justifying his cancellation of the agreement, King illuminated his sense of superiority. *"In matters of this kind,"* meaning free-trade negotiations with the United States, "Howe is almost an innocent abroad."[36] Even the contemplation of such an arrangement meant touching the third rail of Canadian politics, and King knew this even if Howe did not. Howe may have swallowed hard, but he accepted King's decision, knowing at the back of his mind that the prime minister had been right so many times before – and might be right again.

King imposed himself on cabinet less through displays of raw power than by employing his extraordinary patience and stamina. He husbanded his forces, and sometimes he treated the cabinet almost as a mini-parliament, allowing contrary opinions to be ventilated, sometimes fashioning compromises to avoid any existential confrontation, as in the conscription debates in cabinet in the spring and summer of 1942 and the fall of 1944. Conscription is the best-known contention from the war years, but there were others that posed issues of principle, and thus disturbed the ideologies of more traditional ministers. An excellent example is the question of family allowances in 1943–4.

Family allowances had a complicated background, but essentially, they were a cash transfer to poorer families that would at one and the same time address real poverty, augment family incomes, and avoid compromising Canada's strict wage controls. King attached high importance to the measure, but he faced problems. Ilsley, the sponsoring minister, was half-hearted in support. Crerar, perhaps the most conservative of the ministers, could be counted on to oppose. Others were doubtful. As so often, luck was with King. Crerar had to leave for Winnipeg to attend a funeral. Ilsley departed the meeting to meet a commitment in Toronto, leaving his deputy minister, Clifford Clark, to defend family allowances and to anticipate and answer likely criticisms. King was thrilled. As he later told his diary, he knew that most ministers would not dare to stand against Clark. So it proved, and coupled with King's strong support family allowances carried the day. There was no doubt where King stood, and when he polled the ministers, only one stood out against it: C.D. Howe. Howe took the view that family allowances were only a means of rewarding the shiftless out of the hard-earned incomes of the middle class. The new measure harvested the support of almost all ministers and left the one who opposed family allowances gasping on an antediluvian sandbar. King was so pleased that he later took the very unusual step of telephoning Clark and effusively congratulating him.[37]

The manner in which the cabinet accepted family allowances is noteworthy in itself, as is the way Mackenzie King achieved consensus. Unable to eliminate opposition entirely, he circumvented it, bided his time, and chose the right moment: and so in January 1944 he isolated Howe, gave him rope to figuratively hang his arguments if not himself, and let the case against family allowances disintegrate in Howe's own speech.

Conclusion

The cabinet of 1935–48 is regarded as one of Canada's best. It contained outstanding innovators, administrators, and first-rate politicians and it drew on the energies of a keen public service. It presided over one of the greatest crises in Canada's history, the Second World War, and it did so under the leadership of an odd little man who commanded deference, certainly, but also obedience. Wily, indirect, opaque in his leadership style, King escaped from one potential disaster after another. His attention to detail – and the time and thought that he gave to the effort by advancing reforms to the cabinet decision process – helped make him cabinet's best strategist.

King also improved the level of bureaucratic support for cabinet. Until this point, the cabinet operated without a written agenda, meaning that ministers were often unprepared for the discussions that took place. Officials were not allowed in cabinet meetings, so there was no systematic written record of decisions. The pressures of war demanded a more efficient system. In 1940, King created a cabinet secretariat in the Privy Council Office to see that government decisions were communicated and carried out, bringing order to a haphazard decision-making process. In short notice, the secretary to the cabinet also assumed the role of clerk of the Privy Council, the country's senior public servant.[38] King allowed a written agenda to be prepared for each meeting, first of the War Committee, then of full cabinet, and eventually allowed the document to be distributed in advance, along with background materials on key agenda items. Minutes of the meetings, known as "Cabinet Conclusions," were circulated, though King insisted they be returned to the cabinet secretariat, where all but the original were destroyed.

King implemented several changes to the workings of cabinet, some reluctantly, with many forced upon him by the exigencies of war. Previously, cabinet committees had tended to be ad hoc and informal in nature, places to which the prime minister could refer complicated issues for more detailed discussion. (The notable exception was the Treasury Board, a committee created by statute.) In December 1939, King created a cabinet War Committee, which increasingly made the government's key decisions. The Government Business Committee followed, established to handle regulations and other routine matters that need not take up the time of the full cabinet.

The success also spoke to King's personal management methods. Unlike Ralston, he was never the prisoner of detail. Where Ralston despaired, as he did in the fall of 1944, King saw beyond, and if one expedient failed, he tried another. Ralston failed because he was chained to the rock of principle. King had no such encumbrance. The sheer improbability of so many narrow escapes created a legend – that the old man would pull it off again. A cabinet of formidables never became a collection of rivals. The discontented, like Angus L. Macdonald and Chubby Power, seethed and departed. King assured his own survival, and chose his successor, a privilege not always granted to retiring leaders. What he bequeathed to Louis St-Laurent was a transformed cabinet structure, one that exists to this day.

NOTES

1 I am indebted to my friend J.L. Granatstein for a careful reading of this chapter, and some timely corrections.
2 Stefan J. Dupré, "The Workability of Executive Federalism in Canada," in *Federalism and the Role of the State*, ed. Herman Bakvis and William M. Chandler (Toronto: University of Toronto Press, 1987), 236–58. Dupré's father had been in the Bennett cabinet.
3 See Patrice Dutil, *Prime Ministerial Power in Canada: Its Origins under Macdonald, Laurier and Borden* (Vancouver: University of British Columbia Press, 2017).
4 Scientific management was devised by engineers and is sometimes associated with an engineering point of view. It is worth noting that the only engineer in Mackenzie King's cabinets, C.D. Howe, never applied the theory; his form of management was highly personal and individual. Like King's, in fact.
5 I note J.L. Granatstein's path-breaking study on this topic, "King and His Cabinet: The War Years," in *Mackenzie King: Widening the Debate*, ed. John English and J.O. Stubbs (Toronto: Macmillan, 1978), 173–90. My conclusions are certainly cousin to his, though we each present different evidence.
6 Dandurand was thirteen years older than King and had been a senator since 1898. He had served as speaker of the Senate from 1905 to 1909. As government leader in the Senate after 1921, he took on the title of minister without portfolio, which entitled him to sit in the cabinet.

7 King to Hepburn, 12 July 1934, quoted in H. Blair Neatby, *William Lyon Mackenzie King*, vol. 3, *The Prism of Unity, 1932–1939* (Toronto: University of Toronto Press, 1976), 127.

8 The analysis begins with Bruce Hutchison, *The Incredible Canadian: A Candid Portrait of Mackenzie King: His Works, His Times, His Nation* (Toronto: Longmans, Green, 1952), and continues through MacGregor Dawson, *The Conscription Crisis of 1944* (Toronto: University of Toronto Press, 1961); J.W. Pickersgill, *The Mackenzie King Record*, 4 vols. (Toronto: University of Toronto Press, 1961–70); C.P. Stacey, *A Very Double Life: The Private World of Mackenzie King* (Toronto: Macmillan, 1976); and Christopher Dummitt, *Unbuttoned: A History of Mackenzie King's Secret Life* (Montreal: McGill-Queen's University Press, 2017).

9 "Childless" may once have seemed an exceedingly obvious corollary of "unmarried," at least in public life, but there are plenty of examples in Canadian, British, and American public life that prove the contrary.

10 On this point, see Norman Ward's essay on bachelor prime ministers, "The Fewer the Higher: A Field Note on Fecundity among Politicians," in *Mice in the Beer* (Toronto: Longmans, Green, 1960), 81–3.

11 On this topic, see J.L. Granatstein, *The Ottawa Men: The Civil Service Mandarins, 1935–57* (Toronto: Oxford University Press, 1982), as well as his *Canada's War: The Politics of the Mackenzie King Government, 1939–1945* (Toronto: Oxford University Press, 1975).

12 It is a question of which experience shaped them the most. The answer is almost certainly not uniform: each would have experienced the war directly and been influenced by it in different ways, and whether this predominated over their experiences of their civilian lives we cannot now say. Some of this observation derives from a conversation with Lieutenant Governor Hugues Lapointe, a veteran of the Second World War, in June 1977.

13 See the account in *A Party Politician: The Memoirs of Chubby Power*, ed. Norman Ward (Toronto: Macmillan, 1966).

14 When I interviewed Senator Power in February 1966, his wife was present, and illuminated the conversation: it was an interview with both, and not just himself: an indicative but hardly conclusive experience.

15 W.L. Mackenzie King, diary, 23 October 1935, LAC, William Lyon Mackenzie King fonds, MG 26 J 13.

16 King, quoted in Robert Bothwell and William Kilbourn, *C.D. Howe: A Biography* (Toronto: McClelland & Stewart, 1979), 67.

17 Austin Cross, *The People's Mouths* (Toronto: Macmillan, 1943), 68. There was also the very obvious fact that Mackenzie was a racist of the "anti-oriental" variety, as it would have been put at the time. That fact enhanced his political appeal in British Columbia, where probably a majority of the voters agreed with him.

18 Mark Moher, "The 'Biography' in Politics: Mackenzie King in 1935," *Canadian Historical Review* 55, no. 4 (December 1974): 239–48.

19 The detailed conversation with Howe came on 23 October. King emphasized the scandalous past of the Department of Marine, and that part of Howe's task – we would now say "mandate" – was to clean it up.

20 King would, however, end up representing an Ontario riding, after being personally defeated in Saskatchewan in the election of 1945.

21 King, diary, 19 October 1935.

22 "Mitch and Arthur Slaght lived on the edge of scandal," Hepburn's biographer wrote. The two were drinking companions and notorious womanizers. So notorious was their conduct that forty years later stories still circulated about them. Whether the individual stories were true is moot; the point is that they were believable. See J.T. Saywell, *Just Call Me Mitch: The Life of Mitchell Hepburn* (Toronto: University of Toronto Press, 1991), 139.

23 King, diary, 19 October 1935.

24 Granatstein, *Ottawa Men*, 187–207. See also A.D.P. Heeney, "Cabinet Government in Canada: Some Recent Developments in the Machinery of the Central Executive," *Canadian Journal of Economics and Political Science* 12, no. 3 (August 1946): 282–301; and A.D.P. Heeney, "Mackenzie King and the Cabinet Secretariat," *Canadian Public Administration* 10, no. 3 (September 1967): 366–75.

25 Warren Baldwin, "Return to Liberalism Power's Cry in Joining Party Leadership Race," *Globe and Mail*, 2 August 1948, 1.

26 They could be seen as Franco-Ontarians as well, but Martin was half-Irish, and, in the opinion of his contemporaries, more Irish than French in character. His French was not as fluent as his English.

27 See Reginald Whitaker, *The Government Party: Organizing and Financing the Liberal Party of Canada, 1930–58* (Toronto: University of Toronto Press, 1977); and David Jay Bercuson, *True Patriot: The Life of Brooke Claxton, 1898–1960* (Toronto: University of Toronto Press, 1993).

28 Some of Bennett's ministers were so distressed by their bullying leader that they took their problems to Mackenzie King. There were rivalries inside the St-Laurent cabinet, though these never broke out in public, and St-Laurent's mental state in his last years as prime minister was the subject of worry to ministers, who discussed it frequently among themselves. A couple of Diefenbaker's ministers let their distress with their leader be known, and Pearson harvested their complaints. Some of Pearson's ministers were outraged at their chief's treatment of the minister of justice, Guy Favreau, and vented their rage at private social functions. In one case, the minister's wife snapped that if he really felt that way about the prime minister, the only proper path was to resign.

29 King's principal secretary, Jack Pickersgill, liked to tell the story of an incident during the 1945 election campaign in Quebec. King was taking a nap in his suite at the Chateau Frontenac, with instructions not to be disturbed. While he was napping in his bedroom, Power arrived. The secretaries were putting him off when

the bedroom door opened and Mackenzie King emerged in long underwear, hand outstretched. "Why, Chubby," he began.

30 I am indebted to the excellent *Dictionary of Canadian Biography* analysis of Ian Mackenzie by Patricia Roy and Peter Neary. A story told about Mackenzie at the time involved a practical joke by his drinking companion Donald Gordon, who headed the Wartime Prices and Trade Board and reputedly drank a bottle of whisky a day, using ration coupons collected from his staff. Gordon persuaded Mackenzie that King had dissolved Parliament and called a snap election. Mackenzie, three sheets to the wind, phoned King, though it was one in the morning. "Chief," he is reported to have said, "why'd you do it?" "Do what, Mackenzie?" "Dissolved the House." "You're drunk, Mackenzie. Go to bed." The story may have been apocryphal – obviously we cannot now say. Nevertheless, the story catches the spirit(s) of the King-Mackenzie relationship.

31 Bothwell and Kilbourn, *Howe*, 117–19.

32 Bothwell and Kilbourn, *Howe*, 162–4.

33 Macdonald quoted in T. Stephen Henderson, *Angus L. Macdonald, a Provincial Liberal* (Toronto: University of Toronto Press, 2007), 125. It has been argued, by the historian Ernie Forbes among others, that Howe favoured an Ontario steel plant in the award of government contracts over a Nova Scotian one. The author disagrees with this assessment. Canadian war production was stretched to the limit. Moreover, the Nova Scotians in Howe's entourage, like Ralph Bell, the powerful director general of aircraft production, would have had something to say on the matter.

34 Bruce Hutchison, *The Far Side of the Street* (Toronto: Macmillan, 1976), 220.

35 In the standard form of the anecdote, Macmillan was asked what worried him most, and replied, "Events, my dear boy, events." Whether Macmillan ever uttered the phrase, or when, is a matter for debate. That it was apropos in describing the rhythms of politics is beyond question. The first use of the quote was by the journalist Adam Raphael in 1984. It has since become a classic.

36 Bothwell and Kilbourn, *Howe*, 220, 381n51 (emphasis added).

37 King, diary, 13 January 1944. In his diary King underlined how important the cabinet meeting was, and how notable. It was a subject that the prime minister had studied for almost fifty years, knew well, and cared about.

38 The description of the clerk's role should be carefully nuanced. It was far less comprehensive than it later became, and in the King period other senior deputy ministers and civil servants would not have tolerated direction by the clerk, nor would their ministers.

11 Louis St-Laurent: The Cabinet's Centre of Gravity

STEPHEN AZZI*

C.D. Howe was used to getting his way. By 1951, Canada's minister of trade and commerce had served in cabinet and Parliament for sixteen years. He was such an essential part of the government that the prime minister, Louis St-Laurent, had accepted the Liberal leadership only upon receiving a commitment that Howe would remain in cabinet. St-Laurent later described Howe as "the most effective general director of all our economy that Canada has had since Confederation."[1] The two men worked together in harmony for many years, until they finally clashed in 1951. The issue was a proposal to provide $65 million in relief to farmers as partial compensation for losses incurred after Canada had agreed to sell wheat to Britain at below market price. St-Laurent strongly favoured the idea; Howe staunchly opposed it. The stakes were high, as Dale Thomson, an aide in St-Laurent's office, remembered: "The other ministers observed the confrontation with tense interest, realizing that the outcome might well determine the government's future." St-Laurent "had imposed his will on lesser colleagues, and even scolded them on occasion, but he had not previously asserted his authority over the strong-minded 'general manager' of the Canadian economy."[2] It seemed clear that either Howe would resign or St-Laurent would back down, his stature diminished.

But St-Laurent refused to pull back, announcing the subsidy in the House of Commons on 2 May. When the media and members of the opposition commented on a split in the cabinet, and after Liberal MPs criticized the government's decision in their weekly caucus meeting, the prime minister made his position clear in the Commons.[3] "Our system is Cabinet government," he said, "and Cabinet government involves Cabinet responsibility and Cabinet solidarity." In case anyone missed his point, St-Laurent emphasized that "all members of the government" agreed on the contribution to the wheat farmers. "On the facts, we in the government are agreed. On the policy, we are agreed. On the recommendations we make to Parliament, we are agreed."[4] With that, the crisis ended. Although no doubt displeased with the outcome, Howe accepted the pre-eminence of the prime minister, as he would on the rare occasions when the two men would again find themselves at odds.

Louis St-Laurent was neither the first among equals in his cabinet nor the mere chair of the board, as has often been said.[5] He was the dominant figure in his government. His position was the product not of rewards and threats but rather of the respect he earned from ministers for his intellect and integrity. Although he allowed ministers a free hand in running their departments, he was the central figure in the cabinet room, making decisions with cold efficiency, while many ministers sat in intimidated silence. He controlled the agenda, set the brisk pace for meetings, and made the key decisions. No proposal went forward without the prime minister's approval, and he sometimes voiced his own view without waiting for others to speak first, effectively pre-empting cabinet discussion.

Hierarchies reflect the strengths and weaknesses of the individual at the top. St-Laurent's ministry was, at its outset, a talented and energetic group of capable administrators who ran the Canadian government with an unmatched level of effectiveness. But over time, as the prime minister experienced long bouts of low spirits and little energy, the government lost its edge. Accomplished ministers moved on, and St-Laurent, like so many of his predecessors and successors, did little to recruit high-quality replacements. The prime minister knew and cared little about partisan politics and, as a result, his government failed to pay sufficient attention to the state of the Liberal party and to innovations in campaign techniques. This neglect led directly to the Liberal defeats of 1957 and 1958.

Shaping Cabinet

For Louis St-Laurent, building a cabinet was not a difficult task. From William Lyon Mackenzie King, St-Laurent inherited an experienced and capable ministry, in which he himself had served for almost seven years. He saw no need to make changes to reward supporters or placate rivals. The new prime minister had not needed to convince others to support him for the job; it had been up to others to persuade him to accept it. This left him with no debts to pay. And St-Laurent had no scores to settle, his personality being such that he was incapable of holding a grudge.[6]

Upon assuming office, St-Laurent kept seventeen of King's ministers in the same portfolio. The incoming prime minister enlisted two newcomers: Manitoba premier Stuart Garson as minister of justice and Robert Winters, a confident and competent engineer from Nova Scotia, as minister of reconstruction and supply. Only one cabinet in Canadian history more closely mirrored its predecessor.[7] St-Laurent had played a part in determining King's final ministry. He wanted to sideline Ian Mackenzie, the minister of veterans affairs, whose judgment and administrative ability were clouded by alcoholism. King appointed Mackenzie to the Senate in January 1948.[8] Also on St-Laurent's request, King brought Lester Pearson, the deputy minister of external affairs, into cabinet to serve as foreign minister, the portfolio St-Laurent was relinquishing.

When the St-Laurent cabinet took office on 15 November 1948, the ministers had an average age of 55.6, with the prime minister a full decade older. It was one of the oldest first cabinets in Canada's history. There was a near parity of members from the two largest provinces (six from Quebec, seven from Ontario). The four western provinces had one representative each, as did New Brunswick. Nova Scotia had two representatives; PEI had none. The cabinet consisted of these ministers (see image 11.1):

1 Prime Minister; President of the Privy Council: Louis St-Laurent, Quebec, 66
2 Agriculture: James Gardiner, Saskatchewan, 64
3 External Affairs: Lester B. Pearson, Ontario, 51
4 Finance and Receiver General: Douglas Abbott, Quebec, 49
5 Fisheries: Robert Mayhew, British Columbia, 68
6 Justice and Attorney General: Stuart Garson, Manitoba, 49
7 Labour: Humphrey Mitchell, Ontario, 54
8 Mines and Resources: James MacKinnon, Alberta, 67
9 National Defence: Brooke Claxton, Quebec, 50
10 National Health and Welfare: Paul Martin, Ontario, 45
11 National Revenue: J.J. McCann, Ontario, 62
12 Postmaster General: Ernest Bertrand, Quebec, 59
13 Public Works: Alphonse Fournier, Quebec, 55
14 Reconstruction and Supply: Robert Winters, Nova Scotia, 38
15 Secretary of State of Canada: Colin Gibson, Ontario, 57
16 Solicitor General: Joseph Jean, Quebec, 58
17 Trade and Commerce: C.D. Howe, Ontario, 62
18 Transport: Lionel Chevrier, Ontario, 45
19 Veterans Affairs: Milton Gregg, New Brunswick, 56
20 Government Leader in the Senate; Minister without Portfolio: Wishart Robertson, Nova Scotia, 57 (senator)

If King had built an imposing cabinet, St-Laurent's changes improved it. It was perhaps as impressive a group of ministers as had been seen since Laurier's Cabinet of All the Talents of 1896, with most ministers bringing energy, intelligence, and managerial competence to their departments. Howe had been one of the stalwarts of King's cabinet, an innovative minister with a rare gift for administration. As the senior minister, Howe was de facto deputy prime minister, acting for St-Laurent in the prime minister's absence from Ottawa. Like so many other members of the cabinet, Finance Minister Doug Abbott was able and clear-minded, but to these traits he added charm and skill in handling the House of Commons. Jimmy Gardiner was a formidable organizer and administrator, though St-Laurent disapproved of the agriculture minister's ambition and lack of focus in cabinet meetings. External Affairs Minister Lester Pearson was a gifted negotiator and Canada's pre-eminent diplomat. Paul Martin was a hard worker and a capable politician who served as the government's social conscience. Defence Minister Brooke Claxton combined drive with intellect, imagination, and strong political judgment. Justice Minister Stuart Garson was known for his skill in managing public affairs, though he was never as imposing in Ottawa as he had been as premier of Manitoba. Transport Minister Lionel Chevrier was a superb orator and skilled parliamentarian. Several other strong ministers later joined the cabinet, including Walter Harris, whom St-Laurent considered a possible successor in later years; Jean Lesage, who later became a consequential premier of Quebec; and Jack Pickersgill, a former senior bureaucrat who understood the machinery of Canadian government better than anyone else. The new prime minister himself was, in Mackenzie King's view, the ablest person ever to sit in a Canadian cabinet.[9] In all likelihood, St-Laurent was the prime minister who came to office with the greatest preparation for the role. King, in his final years in office, had come to rely increasingly on St-Laurent, who served as acting prime minister several times when the prime minister was out of town.[10]

Cabinet Changes

The St-Laurent cabinet was striking for its consistent membership. The prime minister rarely shuffled his ministers, and, when he did so, few of them changed portfolios. The adjustments were almost always reactive. St-Laurent undertook his first shuffle because Newfoundland had joined Confederation and needed a representative in cabinet. The later death of two ministers required further modifications.[11] Other changes, the vast majority, took place because ministers wished to leave politics. Eleven of them received federal appointments, six to the judiciary, two to the Senate, one as speaker of the Senate, one as president of the St. Lawrence Seaway Authority, and one as an ambassador.[12] One left to go into the private sector.[13]

St-Laurent did not push ministers from cabinet. He was reluctant even to suggest that it might be time for a minister to retire.[14] The case of George Prudham illustrates the larger problem.[15] The minister of mines and technical surveys and Alberta's representative in cabinet from December 1950, Prudham proved to be a weak minister, an excessively stubborn and opinionated cabinet colleague, and a poor political organizer. He was at the centre of a scandal in 1953 after news broke that his company, Prudham Supplies Limited, continued to do business with the government while Prudham was minister. Liberals in Alberta wanted him replaced with Bill Hawrelak, the popular mayor of Edmonton.[16] St-Laurent liked the idea, in part because it would, for the first time, give cabinet representation to Ukrainian Canadians, one of the largest immigrant groups in Canada. Yet the prime minister absolutely refused to force Prudham out. The minister eventually decided himself that he would not run again and suggested Hawrelak as Alberta's representative in cabinet. As the 1957 election approached, Hawrelak was nominated as the Liberal candidate in Edmonton East and was about to be appointed to cabinet when Prudham came to resent the suggestion in Ottawa that he was being ousted. He insisted that St-Laurent delay the naming of Hawrelak to cabinet until after the election. St-Laurent agreed, taking the unusual step of writing to assure Hawrelak that he would be appointed to cabinet after voting day.[17] Hawrelak ended up losing his seat by three hundred votes. He might well have won had he campaigned with the prestige of a cabinet post.

At the same time, St-Laurent did little to convince talented ministers to stay, beyond the notable exception of C.D. Howe. Doug Abbott, Lionel Chevrier, and Brooke Claxton all left cabinet on the same day in 1954. St-Laurent may well have seen Abbott as his successor but did nothing to dissuade the finance minister from leaving for a seat on the Supreme Court.[18] Chevrier suggested that he might have remained in cabinet, had only the prime minister made the request: "Although the lustre of my political career had waned somewhat over time, I had no desire to leave it."[19] The same was true of Claxton: had St-Laurent pressed him to stay, Claxton later wrote, "I would hardly refuse."[20] The departure of three key ministers on one day was a blow to St-Laurent, but he would not tell them that he needed them.[21]

St-Laurent pursued three priorities when choosing ministers, according to Dale Thomson, who worked in the prime minister's office and later wrote his biography.[22] The first was administrative ability. Above all, ministers had to be competent stewards of public institutions. Yet they need not be experts in the area of their portfolio. When labour minister Humphrey Mitchell died in 1950, the prime minister replaced him with Milton Gregg, who worried that his lack of expertise in labour relations left him unqualified for the position. St-Laurent was not concerned, believing that "human qualities were more important than active knowledge," in Pickersgill's words.[23] St-Laurent's second criterion was an ability to work well as part of a team. The St-Laurent cabinet was unusually harmonious, and the prime minister wished to avoid adding any ministers who might upset that esprit de corps. The third consideration was representation. In religion, region, ethnicity, and vocation – but not gender – cabinet should look like the country, to the greatest extent possible. Like all his predecessors, St-Laurent did not include any women in his cabinet. Nor does the thought ever seem to have occurred to him. He is the last Canadian prime minister never to have appointed a woman as minister.

Image 11.1. The St-Laurent cabinet in the Privy Council Chamber, 1953

Credit: Library and Archives Canada, PA-196460.

In short, St-Laurent chose ministers with one consideration above all others – to govern Canada effectively. Winning elections was not a direct concern, and cabinet posts were not doled out as rewards for service to the party. "It is not what a man has done in the past but what it was felt he might do in the future that was looked upon as important," St-Laurent later explained.[24] He sought Pearson because of his expertise in foreign affairs, not for his allegiance to the Liberal party, which Pearson joined only on the day he entered cabinet. The same applied to J.W. Pickersgill, who was recruited from the public service directly into cabinet, leapfrogging dozens of backbench MPs who had faithfully served the Liberal cause for years. But Pearson and Pickersgill were exceptions. Most new ministers came from the Liberal backbench after first serving an apprenticeship as parliamentary assistant to a senior minister. Of the thirteen ministers who joined after the original St-Laurent cabinet had taken office, ten had been backbenchers and eight had apprenticed to a senior minister.

Thomson suggested that competence was more important than collegiality, but sometimes those priorities were reversed. The case of Paul-Émile Côté illustrates the point. St-Laurent had his eye on Côté, a hardworking backbencher who had served as parliamentary assistant to the minister of labour.

When the prime minister mentioned that he planned to appoint Côté to cabinet, St-Laurent's wife asked why he had not considered the other Côté, Alcide, who was a popular member of Parliament with an easy smile and strong interpersonal skills. "St-Laurent saw the point at once," according to Pickersgill, and appointed Alcide, whose promotion was welcomed by Liberal backbenchers.[25] Many were surprised to see the post go to that Côté instead of his namesake. Quebec Liberal MPs joked that the prime minister had "trompé de Côté," a play on words that meant both that St-Laurent had taken the wrong side and that he had chosen the wrong Côté. In the end, Alcide Côté proved ill-equipped for a cabinet post and died of a heart attack after three years in office.

Representation

Mackenzie King had tried to convince St-Laurent of the value of a strong second in command from the other linguistic group. King's leadership had been strengthened by his two lieutenants from francophone Quebec, Ernest Lapointe and St-Laurent. As prime minister, St-Laurent could benefit from an anglophone lieutenant from Ontario, or so King suggested. St-Laurent disagreed. After all, Laurier functioned well without a lieutenant from the other language community, as had Macdonald after George-Étienne Cartier's death in 1873. King responded that those cabinets contained so many strong ministers from across the country that a designated deputy was unnecessary. According to Thomson, the new prime minister "drew the obvious conclusion that in a cabinet built of strong timber from all parts of Canada, the debate over dual leadership would become an academic one."[26] The key was to maintain a strong cabinet of impressive ministers.

In some ways, St-Laurent succeeded in creating a representative cabinet. He worked to ensure that each of Canada's two main linguistic groups was well represented in cabinet.[27] This he accomplished. In 1948, cabinet included six francophones (30 per cent) and fourteen anglophones (70 per cent), almost perfectly mirroring the proportion of the two language groups in the Canadian population.[28] Ontario had seven ministers, Quebec six (including the prime minister), and the remaining provinces one each, with two exceptions. Prince Edward Island was too small to merit a minister, while Nova Scotia had two ministers, one of whom was Wishart Robertson, the government leader in the Senate, who held no portfolio. British Columbians pushed for a second representative, recognition of their province's growing population.[29] In 1952, Robert Mayhew was replaced with two ministers, Ralph Campney and James Sinclair, doubling British Columbia's representation. Nova Scotia dropped from two ministers to one in 1953, when Robertson resigned as government leader of the Senate to become the speaker of that chamber. Half the ministers were lawyers, including the prime minister himself, but several other professions were represented. Cabinet included a teacher, a farmer, an electrical worker, a physician, a diplomat, a soldier, two engineers, and two businesspeople.

Yet St-Laurent did not always ensure adequate representation from the different regions or from ethnic or religious groups in Canada. Cabinet had no representative from Toronto, the country's second-largest city. There was one credible candidate, David Croll, who was a former minister in Ontario and one of very few Jews in the Commons. According to Croll's biographer, St-Laurent told the MP that antisemitism in both Quebec and the Liberal Party made his appointment to cabinet impossible. The prime minister disapproved of this prejudice but also thought that he could not, for political reasons, ignore it. As a consolation, St-Laurent offered Croll a Senate seat.[30] A Torontonian was finally appointed in 1957, on the eve of the election, when Paul Hellyer became the St-Laurent government's first minister from that city. For the voters of Toronto, this was too late, and Hellyer lost his seat.

St-Laurent worked to recruit new ministers to replace those who were leaving, particularly in his early years in office. He enlisted a few accomplished individuals from outside Parliament. In addition to Pearson and Pickersgill, St-Laurent brought in George Marler from the Quebec legislature and the Manitoba premier, Stuart Garson. Some turned down positions because of health or other personal reasons.[31] Toronto businessperson Walter Gordon was offered a junior portfolio in 1954, but declined, believing that he had more freedom and a more interesting position as senior partner of Clarkson Gordon, the country's largest accounting firm; president of Woods Gordon, a management consultancy; and president of Canadian Corporate Management, a corporate conglomerate.[32] Brigadier General Jean Allard was invited to join cabinet in 1955. But then St-Laurent appeared distraught to discover local opposition to parachuting Allard in as a Liberal candidate in one of the available ridings. Sensing St-Laurent's ambivalence, Allard declined the offer and remained in the army.[33] These recruitment efforts dwindled over time, one measure of St-Laurent's waning energy.

Frequently the prime minister plugged vacancies by assigning double duty to ministers. J.J. McCann served concurrently as minister of national revenue and minister of mines and technical surveys for eleven months, Stuart Garson as solicitor general and minister of justice for more than two years, and Ralph Campney as solicitor general and associate minister of national defence for eleven months. Howe served in two portfolios (defence production and trade and commerce) for more than six years. After Postmaster General Alcide Côté died in August 1955, St-Laurent first chose Roch Pinard to fill the position while he continued as secretary of state and then asked Hugues Lapointe to serve in the role while carrying on as minister of veterans affairs. For the last two years of the government, the prime minister appointed no permanent replacement for Côté. All of these were missed opportunities to reinvigorate cabinet. The situation was particularly bad during the four years from 1 July 1953 until the eve of the 1957 election, when St-Laurent recruited no new ministers.

Structural Changes

St-Laurent introduced few structural changes to cabinet. The biggest adjustment came in 1950, when two departments (Mines and Resources, and Reconstruction and Supply) were replaced by three (Mines and Technical Surveys, Resources and Development, and Citizenship and Immigration). The government no longer needed a department dedicated to post-war renewal, so Reconstruction and Supply was shuttered, and responsibility for housing, the Trans-Canada Highway, and employment were moved to Resources and Development. The government did require a department dedicated to citizenship and immigration, at a time when immigration numbers were dropping as fewer people were settling in Canada from the British Isles, then Canada's main source of new arrivals. A new department was cobbled together from the Citizenship Branch of the Department of the Secretary of State and the Immigration Branch of the Department of Mines and Resources. By adding another department, the government created a portfolio that could be given to an Alberta minister. Previously, Alberta had been represented by Senator James MacKinnon, who was a minister without portfolio. Now, George Prudham joined cabinet and became minister of mines and technical surveys.

Another new portfolio, defence production, was created in 1951. Canada was rearming for the Korean War, which had started in June 1950. The department was similar to the old Department of Munitions and Supply, the government's procurement agent for defence materiel, which Howe had led in the Mackenzie King cabinet. Before the new department was created, St-Laurent announced that Howe would be the minister. The legislation granted the minister wide powers to review the books of any company engaged in a defence contract, to order a company to take and fulfil a defence contract, to appoint a controller to seize control of a plant to make it work more efficiently, and to requisition and reallocate supplies from any source to fill a defence contract, including diverting materials from civilian to defence production. During the debate over the legislation, the opposition argued that the bill gave the minister dictatorial powers.[34] The hubris that later came to characterize St-Laurent's government was already on display. "Nobody cares much what you think," Howe told opposition leader George Drew. "Do not take yourself too seriously."[35]

St-Laurent appointed an associate minister of national defence, a post that had not existed since Chubby Power's resignation in the midst of the 1944 conscription crisis. The National Defence Act provided for the appointment of an associate minister only during an emergency, but the legislation was amended in 1953 to allow for such a position at any time. Ralph Campney, a capable administrator, was appointed associate minister on 12 February, while serving concurrently as solicitor general. In the face of a looming scandal in the Department of National Defence, which ultimately included the sensational but false accusation that horses were on the payroll, Campney stepped in to handle the day-to-day administration of the department, leaving the minister, Brooke Claxton, to focus on policy and planning.[36]

Cabinet Meetings

Cabinet held a formal decision-making meeting in the Privy Council Chamber in Parliament Hill's East Block at 10:30 a.m. each Thursday. On the remaining weekdays, when the Commons was sitting, the ministers frequently gathered at 2:00 p.m. in Centre Block to discuss what would now be called issues management.[37]

As chair of the cabinet, St-Laurent displayed a curious mix of traits. He ran a collegial government, trusting his ministers and allowing them to handle details within their own portfolios.[38] He was happy for ministers to take credit for the government's successes.[39] Traditionally, the prime minister selected deputy ministers, the public service heads of each department. In a noticeable break with his predecessors, particularly Mackenzie King, St-Laurent consulted his ministers on their preferences before appointing their deputies.[40] Yet the situation was quite different inside the cabinet chamber. There, St-Laurent was dominant.

The prime minister hated time wasting. Cabinet meetings began and ended punctually. He moved efficiently through the cabinet agenda, like a sawmill processing lumber, not allowing any small talk or other unnecessary discussions. Ministers would present each item of business, and St-Laurent would ask the others to comment. Once he believed there had been a fair opportunity for the expression of different views, he would sum up the discussion, propose a solution, and ask, "Are we in agreement?" Cabinet would almost always accept the prime minister's proposal without further discussion.[41] Issues that would take hours to solve were referred to a committee, so as not to take up the time of the whole cabinet.[42] When Doug Abbott left politics in 1954, Paul Martin suggested that Garson, who was known to be longwinded, replace the departing finance minister. "But we'll have to listen to him all the time," St-Laurent groaned.[43]

St-Laurent ruled the cabinet room not by threatening to fire ministers who disagreed with him but by virtue of the respect he engendered for his personal qualities, particularly his honesty, civility, and sense of fairness. Ministers were reluctant to challenge a prime minister who held what Pickersgill called "moral ascendancy" over cabinet.[44] Young members of cabinet saw St-Laurent as a father figure and were loath to appear critical of him.[45] "In fact, the close personal relationship between St. Laurent and me made my job more difficult," recalled Paul Martin. "Not willing to go the whole hog on every contentious issue, I would often defer or back off, to avoid hurting his feelings."[46]

St-Laurent also held, in Pickersgill's words, "intellectual primacy" over his cabinet.[47] The prime minister arrived at meetings well prepared, often knowing issues better than the responsible minister.[48] His mind grasped issues quickly, faster than most other members of cabinet. "I've never known anybody who had such a rapid power of comprehension as he did," remembered transport minister George Marler.[49] This intellectual prowess inhibited discussion in two ways. First, some ministers would not speak up in St-Laurent's presence for fear of appearing foolish.[50] "He had a way of stating a case so reasonably and so convincingly that there just did not seem to be any other position a sensible person could take," according to Pickersgill.[51] Second, issues became clear to St-Laurent before they did to others. Sometimes St-Laurent would voice his views before most ministers had a chance to speak, essentially shutting off all further discussion. "He would recite the facts and give his judgement right away," Paul Martin remembered. "I resented St-Laurent's technique. I went to him several times and said that this was not the Cabinet system." In Martin's view, a minister's recommendation should become "a subject for Cabinet decision, not for prime ministerial decision."[52]

Every member of cabinet, including C.D. Howe, deferred to St-Laurent. Donald Fleming, a prominent Conservative MP, referred to Howe as "the strong man, the one-man ruler of Canada."[53] Howe was undoubtedly the most influential member of cabinet after the prime minister, but the trade minister did not always get his way. The first conflict was over the payment to wheat farmers in 1951. Another came in April 1955, with the appointment of the Royal Commission on Canada's Economic Prospects, chaired by Walter Gordon. It has been said frequently that the commission could have been appointed only when Howe was out of town, because otherwise he would have blocked it.[54] Actually, Howe was present in the cabinet room when the commission was discussed, argued against it, and lost.[55] He lost again in July 1955 over the proposal to extend his wide-ranging powers under the Defence Production Act. Howe insisted that the government stand its ground when the bill faced complaints from Liberal backbenchers and a Conservative filibuster in the Commons. Instead, St-Laurent offered a concession, placing a three-year limit on the minister's defence procurement powers, which ended the parliamentary standoff. Howe was livid but accepted the prime minister's decision.[56] "St. Laurent had the greatest respect for Howe's knowledge of the economy and for his judgment of business prospects," according to Pickersgill, "but he gave

Howe's recommendations to Cabinet the same careful scrutiny that he gave to those of the most junior minister."[57]

Cabinet Committees

Most matters went to cabinet first and were then referred to committee if the issue merited more extensive discussion and special consideration. Cabinet had few standing committees, the most important being the Treasury Board, which was established by statute. St-Laurent continued the Special Committee of Council, which Mackenzie King had created under the name Government Business Committee to handle routine business, such as government regulations, which did not require consideration by the full cabinet.

St-Laurent's government implemented two significant changes to the cabinet committee system. When he became prime minister, cabinet handled a wide range of issues, including contracts. This changed in 1952, when the Financial Administration Act came into force, replacing the Consolidated Revenue and Audit Act. The new legislation increased the power of the Treasury Board to approve contracts and to deal with other routine administrative matters delegated by cabinet. As a result, the Treasury Board grew substantially in authority and importance as a central agency of government. Political scientist Donald Savoie claims that the St-Laurent and Pearson cabinets made decisions "even on questions of detail, such as awarding relatively minor government contracts."[58] This was true only for the first three years of St-Laurent's government, and not at all true for Pearson's. In 1952, St-Laurent introduced a second innovation by creating a cabinet Legislation Committee, responsible for managing the government's legislative agenda, reviewing draft bills, and recommending them for cabinet approval.[59]

Exhaustion and Mental Illness

The government's quiet efficiency depended on a prime minister who was working at his highest level. But over time, St-Laurent's leadership skills became less consistent. He was exhausted by the pressures of the job and by family difficulties, including deep concern about the mental health of his daughter, who suffered from bipolar disorder. St-Laurent himself suffered from an ulcer and likely from depression, perhaps cyclothymia, a rare mood disorder that is less extreme than bipolar disorder. The problem existed as early as 1952, when he was seventy, but was noticed only by those who worked closely with the prime minister. It became pronounced and apparent to everyone in Ottawa, including politicians, political staff, public servants, and the media, after the prime minister returned from his world tour in 1954.[60] St-Laurent was often ineffective in his final two years in office. After meeting with the prime minister in March 1956, Canada's ambassador to the United States, Arnold Heeney, described in his diary what many in Ottawa saw but were reluctant to voice:

> None of the accustomed sparkle of reaction in his [St-Laurent's] black eyes – any response an effort. My own judgement is that he is bone tired and worried deeply about the present and the future. It is almost a pathetic spectacle. In long intervals he says nothing and is completely withdrawn. … Surely the P.M. will have to give up…. It seems to me we are approaching a crisis.[61]

According to Brooke Claxton, when St-Laurent was in high spirits during the period from 1955 to 1957, he would pursue initiatives even if others were advising against them. "If he was in low spirits, he did nothing at all."[62]

St-Laurent's mental state affected his performance in cabinet, where he was a much less effective chair, and in the Commons.[63] His condition certainly explains his inactivity during the raucous 1956 parliamentary debate over the government's proposal for a natural gas pipeline from Alberta to Quebec. Several ministers urged the prime minister not to leave the matter in Howe's hands, but rather to introduce closure and manage the bill's progress through the Commons himself or delegate those tasks to House leader Walter Harris.[64] Instead, St-Laurent remained passive, and Howe, who had little expertise in parliamentary procedure, rammed the bill through the Commons, in the process irreparably damaging the government's reputation.

Party Management

St-Laurent's great weakness as prime minister was his ineffectiveness as party leader, which long predated his emotional decline. At his best, the prime minister was a superb head of government and chair of cabinet, but he never excelled as party chief. He was not a creature of the Liberal Party and never understood partisan politics. When King first considered appointing St-Laurent to cabinet, Senator Raoul Dandurand, cabinet's longest-serving minister, objected on political grounds. According to King, Dandurand believed that "St-Laurent lacked a certain political sense," that he was "too much a lawyer," observations that proved prophetic.[65] Quebec premier Adélard Godbout also balked, at least at first. "His feeling," King wrote, "was that St-Laurent had never done much to assist the party in any way."[66] "I don't think Mr. St. Laurent was a politician at all," Jimmy Gardiner later said. "He was a lawyer's lawyer – but that isn't politics!"[67]

As prime minister, partisan advantage rarely entered St-Laurent's calculations. He held the naive belief that, in Pickersgill's words, "if policy was clearly explained, it would command public support."[68] St-Laurent's duty, as he saw it, was to run an effective government. Electoral success would follow naturally. He disapproved of Gardiner and those other colleagues whom he found excessively partisan, and he discouraged ministers from taking political considerations into account when making policy decisions. At one point, Mayhew considered abolishing a subsidy to the fishing industry but hesitated, because such an action might carry a substantial political cost. "Do you really think that this is the right thing to do?" St-Laurent asked the fisheries minister. Mayhew answered in the affirmative. "I think it is right too," St-Laurent responded, "and I think we should do what we feel is right, and then face the political consequences afterward."[69]

St-Laurent had no experience or touch for political organization.[70] He delegated his duties as party leader to his ministers.[71] In those days, the Liberal party was a top-down organization, what political scientists call a *cadre party*, with the cabinet in charge. Ministers oversaw the National Liberal Federation, the party's extra-parliamentary wing. C.D. Howe was responsible for party fundraising. Brooke Claxton served as liaison between cabinet and the party office, the de facto party leader behind closed doors. When Claxton found himself bogged down in the defence portfolio, St-Laurent appointed, on Pickersgill's recommendation, a liaison committee of ministers, chaired by Claxton, to oversee party affairs. When Claxton retired from political life in 1954, the chair became Pickersgill, who had only one year's experience in the Liberal party.

The senior minister for each province was responsible for party organization. Howe was at the helm in Ontario but delegated some of his authority to Martin, Harris, and Chevrier. Francophone Quebec was handled by two ministers, Ernest Bertrand and Alphonse Fournier, who were eventually replaced by Alcide Côté and Roch Pinard. Brooke Claxton and then George Marler managed Montreal's English-speaking ridings.

St-Laurent did not concern himself with election campaigns, beyond his own tour.[72] It was clear from his first national election in 1949 that he disliked campaigning. "He found it an ordeal," according to journalist Peter Dempson. "He was testy with newsmen most of the time."[73] Eventually, though, he grew more comfortable on the campaign trail. Despite the Liberal party's unpopularity in 1949, St-Laurent emphasized continuity from Mackenzie King's government, not promising any innovations in policy or program, a move that proved wise. As John Turner, Kim Campbell, and Paul Martin all later discovered, the public distrusts an incumbent party that, under a new leader, tries to distance itself from its own record. St-Laurent avoided this trap.

The cabinet came to neglect party organization. The National Liberal Federation was made up of provincial wings that were allowed to wither. Ministers spent less time on their political responsibilities. Those with expertise as party organizers, Brooke Claxton foremost among them, were allowed to leave. As Gardiner pointed out, "There weren't many in the Cabinet who were politicians."[74] Ministers became increasingly out of touch with public opinion in their provinces – and increasingly arrogant.

Several ministers should have been replaced before the 1957 election. By that time, agriculture minister Jimmy Gardiner was seventy-three and had, in the view of Dale Thomson, outlived his usefulness. He had lost his influence in cabinet and was out of step with his constituents.[75] Howe was seventy-one, secretive, and contemptuous of the House of Commons. When the opposition proposed that Parliament review his extraordinary powers under the Defence Production Act every three years, Howe responded, "I've more to do than spend my time amusing Parliament."[76] He had also become more irascible than ever. "You go to hell!" was his succinct response to a reporter's question in Winnipeg.[77] The prime minister himself was now seventy-five and was ineffective for long periods. After the government's defeat, Howe told a friend that he and St-Laurent had agreed that they would both retire in 1954 or 1955, but then St-Laurent changed his mind, "which was a mistake, both for him and the party."[78] The cabinet was so old that those ministers whom Howe dismissed as "junior leaguers," Pickersgill and Harris, were both in their fifties.[79]

The 1957 election was clear evidence of the problem. The Liberals expected to win easily. They were so sure of themselves that they did not bother to fill sixteen Senate vacancies. The party was unworried about the impact St-Laurent's age might have on voters, publicly celebrating the prime minister's seventy-fifth birthday a few months before the campaign began. By this point, St-Laurent's cognitive decline was clearly visible to voters. He often stumbled through his speeches, looking and sounding like he had never seen the text before.[80]

Television had suddenly become part of politics, and the Liberals had done nothing to adapt to it. St-Laurent was not at ease with the medium, finding it excessively staged and believing, therefore, that it was dishonest. He refused to use a teleprompter or wear make-up when making television appearances. "I will be more interested in seeing people than in talking to cameras," he snapped at a television reporter at the beginning of the campaign.[81] During the 1957 campaign, he made three planned television appearances, each time reading a text and looking older than he was. While the Conservatives were exploiting television, Liberal strategists decided to limit the prime minister's time in front of the cameras.[82] "The elections of 1957 and 1958 made it clear that the public had gone far beyond their leaders in terms of political sophistication," Liberal organizer Richard Stanbury later wrote. "The technical advances in communications had exposed to the public view the patronizing nature of the old cadre system."[83] Under Stanbury and others, the party would undergo a substantial and much-needed overhaul after St-Laurent stepped down as party leader.

St-Laurent had excelled at administering public affairs and managing his cabinet colleagues, but he neglected other key aspects of statecraft, namely managing his party and winning elections.

Conclusion

Louis St-Laurent was the centre of gravity in Ottawa. The cabinet consisted of ministers he had chosen, whether for their competence, their collegiality, or the perspective they would bring to the government's deliberations. No major decision went forward without St-Laurent's approval. Ministers often hesitated to contradict a prime minister who was more intelligent, better briefed, and quicker on his feet than most of them. Even the most powerful of ministers, C.D. Howe, had to back down in any conflict with the prime minister. Yet St-Laurent was not a micromanager. Ministers were given a free hand to run their departments and did not have to worry that they might be fired by an unhappy prime minister. This system worked – and it worked well – because of St-Laurent's extraordinary personal traits.

But the system could not work forever. A structure built around one highly capable individual will inevitably break down when that person's capacity becomes impaired. In the last two years of St-Laurent's tenure, the prime minister was still in charge, but he was often passive or despondent. For long periods of time, the government seemed to have lost its way. It says much about the conceit of senior Liberals that they could not see that their time was coming to an end. The debacles of 1957 and 1958 were the result of a government led by a man who was both a prime minister no longer fit for the job and a party leader who had never cared to lead his party.

NOTES

* The author is grateful to Norman Hillmer and Adriana Gouvêa, who provided insightful comments on an earlier draft of this chapter, and to Samantha Blais and Marielle Rochefort, who assisted with the research.

1 St-Laurent, interview with Dale Thomson, 1962, quoted in Dale C. Thomson, "The Cabinet of 1948," in *Cabinet Formation and Bicultural Relations: Seven Case Studies*, ed. Frederick W. Gibson (Ottawa: Queen's Printer, 1970), 145.

2 Dale Thomson, *Louis St. Laurent: Canadian* (Toronto: Macmillan, 1967), 311.

3 On the criticism in caucus, see "Eastern Liberals Ask Farm Subsidy Extended," *Globe and Mail*, 15 March 1951, 3.

4 *House of Commons Debates: Official Report*, 21st parl., 4th sess., vol. 2, 15 March 1951, 1282, 1284.

5 See, e.g., Donald Creighton, *The Forked Road: Canada, 1939–1957* (Toronto: McClelland & Stewart, 1976), 159–60; W.A. Matheson, *The Prime Minister and the Cabinet* (Toronto: Methuen, 1976), 158–9; Christina McCall-Newman, *Grits: An Intimate Portrait of the Liberal Party* (Toronto: Macmillan, 1982), 201; Philip

Resnick, *The Masks of Proteus: Canadian Reflections on the State* (Montreal: McGill-Queen's University Press, 1990), 49; Ian Urquhart, "Ten Who Led the Country," *Toronto Star*, 4 April 1999, F1, F4; Robert Fulford, "When I Was Very Young," *Queen's Quarterly* 111, no. 2 (2004): 173; Desmond Morton, *A Military History of Canada*, 5th ed. (Toronto: McClelland & Stewart, 2007), 231; Raymond Blake et al., *Narrating a Nation: Canadian History, Post-Confederation* (Toronto: McGraw-Hill Ryerson, 2011), 297; and Paul Litt, *Elusive Destiny: The Political Vocation of John Napier Turner* (Vancouver: University of British Columbia Press, 2011), 398.

6 Charles Ritchie, *Diplomatic Passport: More Undiplomatic Diaries, 1946–1962* (Toronto: Macmillan, 1981), 70.

7 John Abbott, who replaced John A. Macdonald upon his death in June 1891, kept all of Macdonald's ministers.

8 J.W. Pickersgill, *My Years with Louis St. Laurent: A Political Memoir* (Toronto: University of Toronto Press, 1975), 46; and J.W. Pickersgill, *Seeing Canada Whole: A Memoir* (Markham, ON: Fitzhenry & Whiteside, 1994), 301.

9 J.W. Pickersgill, "The Greatest Canadian of Our Time," address to the Canadian Club of Fort William, 27 November 1959, Library and Archives Canada (hereafter "LAC"), Clarence Decatur Howe fonds, MG 27 III B20, vol. 108, file 75(6).

10 Bruce Hutchison, *The Incredible Canadian: A Candid Portrait of Mackenzie King, His Works, His Times, and His Nation* (New York: Longmans, Green, 1953), 425; Arnold Heeney, *The Things That Are Caesar's: The Memoirs of a Canadian Public Servant*, ed. Brian D. Heeney (Toronto: University of Toronto Press, 1972), 85; Thomson, *Louis St. Laurent*, 205; Pickersgill, *My Years*, 38; and notes of J.W. Pickersgill interview with Howard Lentner, 3 August 1974, p. 3, LAC, Howard Lentner fonds, R11232, vol. 2, file 24.

11 They were Alcide Côté and Humphrey Mitchell.

12 To the bench: Douglas Abbott (Supreme Court of Canada), Ernest Bertrand (Court of the King's Bench Court, Quebec), Alphonse Fournier (Exchequer Court of Canada), Colin Gibson (Supreme Court of Ontario), Joseph Jean (Superior Court of Quebec), Édouard Rinfret (Court of the Queen's Bench, Quebec). To the Senate: Gordon Bradley and James MacKinnon (who remained in cabinet as minister without portfolio for another year and a half). To become speaker of the Senate: Wishart Robertson (who had previously served in cabinet as government leader in the Senate). To become president of the St. Lawrence Seaway Authority: Lionel Chevrier. To become ambassador to Japan: Robert Mayhew.

13 Brooke Claxton, who became vice-president of the Metropolitan Life Insurance Company.

14 Pickersgill, *My Years*, 105.

15 This account is based on Diane King Stuemer, *Hawrelak: The Story* (Calgary: Script, 1992), 109–16; and Thomson, *Louis St. Laurent*, 344–5, 503. Hawrelak would likely have turned out to have been an even bigger liability than Prudham. In 1959, a provincial royal commission found that Hawrelak had committed

"gross misconduct" as mayor over the zoning of land he owned, forcing his resignation. He was elected again as mayor in 1964, this time defeating Prudham, but was removed from office in 1965 on new charges of conflict of interest.

16 J. Harper Prowse, leader of the Alberta Liberal Association, to St-Laurent, 20 December 1956, LAC, Louis St-Laurent fonds, MG 26 L, vol. 193, file O-20-9-P; Senator J.W. Stambaugh to St-Laurent, 20 December 1956, LAC, Louis St-Laurent fonds, MG 26 L, vol. 193, file O-20-9-P; Prowse to Duncan MacTavish, 2 January 1957, LAC, Louis St-Laurent fonds, MG 26 L, vol. 193, file O-20-9-P; and J.M. Dechene to St-Laurent, 11 April 1957, City of Edmonton Archives, William Hawrelak collection, MS327, class 2, box 5, file 55.

17 St-Laurent to Hawrelak, 12 April 1957, City of Edmonton Archives, William Hawrelak collection, MS327, class 2, box 5, file 55.

18 Tom Kent, *A Public Purpose: An Experience of Liberal Opposition and Canadian Government* (Montreal: McGill-Queen's University Press, 1988), 10.

19 In the original French, the quotation reads, "J'avais fait partie du cabinet neuf ans et, bien que l'éclat de ma carrière politique se fût quelque peu atténué avec le temps, je n'avais nulle envie de la quitter" (Lionel Chevrier, *La voie maritime du Saint-Laurent* [Ottawa: Le Cercle du Livre de France, 1959], 58).

20 David Jay Bercuson, *True Patriot: The Life of Brooke Claxton, 1898–1960* (Toronto: University of Toronto Press, 1993), 265.

21 Dale Thomson, interview with Robert Bothwell, 14 August 1975, p. 2, LAC, Robert Bothwell fonds, MG 32 G 4, vol. 1, Thomson file.

22 Thomson, "Cabinet of 1948," 145.

23 Pickersgill, *My Years*, 123.

24 St-Laurent, interview with Dale Thomson, 1962, quoted in Thomson, "Cabinet of 1948," 145.

25 Pickersgill, *My Years*, 106.

26 Thomson, "Cabinet of 1948," 145.

27 Thomson, "Cabinet of 1948," 152.

28 I have placed Paul Martin on the list of francophones, though he is not easy to categorize. English and French were both spoken in Martin's childhood home, but his parents, Philippe and Lumina, claimed French as their first language. Martin attended a French high school, Collège St-Alexandre, which "would sharpen Martin's identity as a French Canadian," in the words of his biographer (Greg Donaghy, *Grit: The Life and Politics of Paul Martin Sr.* [Vancouver: University of British Columbia Press, 2015], 7). The 1951 census showed that 5.91 million Canadians identified English as a first language, while 2.83 million listed French, a ratio of 68:32 (Canada, Dominion Bureau of Statistics, *Ninth Census of Canada, 1951*, vol. 1, *Population, General Characteristics* [Ottawa: Dominion Bureau of Statistics, 1953], table 53).

29 By 1951, British Columbia's population was 8.3 per cent of Canada's (Dominion Bureau of Statistics, *Ninth Census of Canada*, vol. 1, table 1).

30 "A Strange Appointment," *Globe and Mail*, 15 June 1953, 6; "Why Mr. Croll Was Passed Over," *Globe and Mail*, 20 June 1953, 6; George Bain, "The Forgotten Man of Parliament Hill," *Maclean's*, 1 November 1954, 20–1, 51–4; George Bain, "There Are Two Louis: One on the Hustings, One in the East Block," *Globe and Mail*, 1 June 1957, 7; and R. Warren James, *The People's Senator: The Life and Times of David A. Croll* (Vancouver: Douglas & McIntyre, 1990), 151. The same prejudice and the same unwillingness to confront it likely prevented Louis Rasminsky from becoming governor of the Bank of Canada in the St-Laurent years. See Bruce Muirhead, *Against the Odds: The Public Life and Times of Louis Rasminsky* (Toronto: University of Toronto Press, 1999), 147–8.

31 Thomson, "Cabinet of 1948," 151. Thomson does not specify who these distinguished Canadians were.

32 Stephen Azzi, *Walter Gordon and the Rise of Canadian Nationalism* (Montreal: McGill-Queen's University Press, 1999), 28.

33 Pickersgill, *My Years*, 269; and Jean V. Allard, *Mémoires du Général Jean V. Allard* (Ottawa: Éditions de Mortagne, 1985), 289–92.

34 The words "dictator," "dictatorship," or "dictatorial" were used by three Progressive Conservative MPs: party leader George Drew (Carleton, Ontario), Arthur Ross (Souris, Manitoba), and Gordon Higgins (St. John's East, Newfoundland). Social Credit leader Solon Low pleaded with Howe, "For goodness' sake, do not give these fellows [the Conservatives] ammunition to throw back at you and to claim that you are a dictator." "They could not throw anything," Howe responded. See *House of Commons Debates: Official Report*, 21st parl., 4th sess., vol. 1, 2 March 1951, 854, 869–70, 875–6, 880–1.

35 *House of Commons Debates: Official Report*, 21st parl., 4th sess., vol. 1, 2 March 1951, 853.

36 Bercuson, *True Patriot*, 246; and Robert Bothwell, *C.D. Howe: A Biography* (Toronto: McClelland & Stewart, 1979), 279.

37 Norman Robertson to St-Laurent, 13 October 1951, LAC, Records of the Privy Council Office, RG2, vol. 136, file C-20-1/1950–51; "Meetings of Ministers during Parliamentary Session: Procedure," memorandum, cabinet document 291/53, LAC, George Carlyle Marler fonds, MG 32 B 21, vol. 87, file 98-1-2; and "Meetings of Ministers: Procedures," memorandum from Secretary to the Cabinet R.B. Bryce, cabinet document 54/57, 13 March 1957, LAC, Marler fonds, MG 32 B 21, vol. 119, file 14. Donald Savoie has misunderstood this as "several Cabinet meetings weekly." See Donald J. Savoie, *Governing from the Centre: The Concentration of Power in Canadian Politics* (Toronto: University of Toronto Press, 1999), 43.

38 Notes of J.W. Pickersgill interview with Howard Lentner, 3 August 1974, p. 8, LAC, Howard Lentner fonds, R11232, vol. 2, file 24; and Paul Martin, *A Very Public Life*, vol. 2, *So Many Worlds* (Toronto: Deneau, 1985), 23.

39 Pickersgill, *My Years*, 327–8; and notes of Pickersgill interview with Howard Lentner, 3 August 1974, p. 4, LAC, Howard Lentner fonds, R11232, vol. 2, file 24.

40 R.B. Bryce to John Diefenbaker, 16 April 1968, LAC, Robert B. Bryce fonds, MG 31 E59, vol. 10, file 2.

41 Lentner, interview with Dale Thomson, 12 September 1975, p. 9, LAC, Howard Lentner fonds, R11232, vol. 2, Thomson file; and Thomson, *Louis St. Laurent*, 262–3.

42 Lionel Chevrier, interview with Peter Stursberg, 17 August 1976, p. 59, LAC, Peter Stursberg fonds, MG 31 D 78, vol. 28, file 9.

43 Martin, *Very Public Life*, 2:20.

44 Notes of Pickersgill interview with Lentner, 28 August 1974, p. 4, LAC, Howard Lentner fonds, R11232, vol. 2, file 24. See also Pickersgill, *My Years*, 174–5; and Gordon Robertson, *Memoirs of a Very Civil Servant: Mackenzie King to Pierre Trudeau* (Toronto: University of Toronto Press, 2000), 100.

45 According to Dale Thomson, "St-Laurent's relations with Jean Lesage and Hugues Lapointe were almost on a father-son basis." Martin uses the phrase "in loco parentis" to describe reprimands from the prime minister. See Thomson, "Cabinet of 1948," 148; and Martin, *Very Public Life*, 2:24.

46 Martin, *Very Public Life*, 2:25.

47 Notes of Pickersgill interview with Lentner, 28 August 1974, p. 3, LAC, Howard Lentner fonds, R11232, vol. 2, file 24.

48 Martin, *Very Public Life*, 2:17; Pickersgill, *My Years*, 174–5; Pickersgill, *Seeing Canada Whole*, 379; Robertson, *Memoirs*, 100–1; Thomson, *Louis St. Laurent*, 262–3; untitled typewritten notes for Claxton's memoirs, pp. 1–2, LAC, Brooke Claxton fonds, MG 32 B5, vol. 224, Memoir Notes Politics file; Pickersgill, interview with Lentner, 28 August 1974, LAC, Howard Lentner fonds, R11232, vol. 2, file 24; and George Marler, interview with Peter Stursberg, 13 September 1978, p. 63, LAC, Peter Stursberg fonds, MG 31 D 78, vol. 36, file 12.

49 Marler, interview with Stursberg, 13 September 1978, pp. 63–4, LAC, Peter Stursberg fonds, MG 31 D 78, vol. 36, file 12.

50 Pickersgill, interview with Lentner, 3 August 1974, p. 4, LAC, Howard Lentner fonds, R11232, vol. 2, file 24.

51 J.W. Pickersgill, "The Greatest Canadian of Our Time," address to the Canadian Club of Fort William, 27 November 1959, p. 5, LAC, Clarence Decatur Howe fonds, MG 27 III B20, vol. 108, file 75(6). See also Jack Pickersgill, interview with Peter Stursberg, 14 October 1976, pp. 13–14, LAC, Stursberg fonds, MG 31 D 78, vol. 31, file 11.

52 Paul Martin, interview with Norah Story and Josephine Phelan, 1969–70, tape 5, side 1, pp. 13–14, University of Windsor Archives, Paul Martin Papers, subseries B, box 25, file 9. See also Paul Martin, interview with Richard Alway, 1972, in "Canadian Public Figures on Tape: J.R. Smallwood and J.W. Pickersgill," audio

tape collection, Ontario Institute for Studies in Education, 1972; and Martin, *Very Public Life*, 1:381, 2:17.

53 *House of Commons Debates*, 22nd parl., 3rd sess., 5 June 1956, 4692.

54 Walter Gordon appears to have been the source of this tale, which has been repeated by journalists and scholars. See Walter Gordon, *A Political Memoir* (Toronto: McClelland & Stewart, 1977), 64; Kent, *Public Purpose*, 30; McCall-Newman, *Grits*, 27–8; Denis Smith, *Gentle Patriot: A Political Biography of Walter Gordon* (Edmonton: Hurtig, 1973), 33; and Creighton, *Forked Road*, 258.

55 Azzi, *Walter Gordon*, 38.

56 Thomson, *Louis St. Laurent*, 402–3.

57 Pickersgill, *My Years*, 66. See also C.D. Howe's comments to journalist Grattan O'Leary: "King never interfered. He let me have my head. He didn't know a damn thing about business or industry. Didn't really give a damn. But St. Laurent, with his experience as a corporation lawyer, is always one jump ahead. He knows exactly what's going on. You never have to spell things out. This is good in some ways. But you can't put anything over on the bugger." See Grattan O'Leary, *Recollections of People, Press, and Politics* (Toronto: Macmillan, 1977), 108.

58 Savoie, *Governing from the Centre*, 127. It is not clear why Savoie focused on St-Laurent and Pearson, omitting John Diefenbaker's government from his generalization.

59 Cabinet Conclusions, 30 June 1952, p. 8, LAC, Records of the Privy Council Office, RG2, series A-5-a, vol. 2650.

60 Stephen Azzi, "The Predominant Prime Minister: St-Laurent and His Cabinet," in *The Unexpected Louis St-Laurent: Politics and Policies for a Modern Canada*, ed. Patrice Dutil (Vancouver: University of British Columbia Press, 2020), 81–3.

61 Arnold Heeney, diary, 28 March 1956, LAC, Arnold Danford Patrick Heeney fonds, MG 30 E 144, vol. 2, file 25.

62 Brooke Claxton, untitled typescript beginning, "Further appointments appear likely," section beginning, "What should the Liberals do," summer or early fall 1957, LAC, Brooke Claxton fonds, MG 32 B 5, vol. 79, Liberal Assn. file.

63 Lentner, interview with Thomson, 12 September 1975, p. 9, Howard Lentner fonds, R11232, vol. 2, Thomson file.

64 Norah Story, interview with Paul Martin, transcript of tape 15, side 1, track 1, pp. 37–8, LAC, Paul Joseph Martin fonds, MG 32 B 12, vol. 352; Renault St. Laurent, interview with Dale Thomson, 9 August 1965, McGill University Archives, Dale Cairns Thomson fonds, MG 2040, container 10, file 211.

65 W.L. Mackenzie King, diary, 29 November 1941, 3, LAC, William Lyon Mackenzie King fonds, MG 26 J 13.

66 King, diary, 29 November 1941, 4.

67 James Gardiner, interview with Peter Regenstreif, 8 January 1961, quoted in Samuel Peter Regenstreif, "The Liberal Party of Canada: A Political Analysis" (PhD thesis, Cornell University, 1963), 387.

68 Pickersgill, *My Years*, 71.

69 Thomson, *Louis St. Laurent*, 263.

70 "He has never had any genius for organization," Claxton wrote (Claxton, untitled typescript beginning, "Further appointments appear likely"; see n. 62).

71 "I trusted others to attend to that part of the duties that I suppose would normally be those of the leader," he later said (St-Laurent, interview with Peter Regenstreif, 6 December 1960, quoted in Regenstreif, "Liberal Party," 185). Paul Lafond, second in command at National Liberal Federation headquarters, remembered, "On party matters, he [St-Laurent] never was one to make decisions. He would make very constructive suggestions" (Paul Lafond, interview with Tom Earle, April 1988, p. 26, LAC, Library of Parliament fonds, R1026, vol. 2567, file 13).

72 Pickersgill, *My Years*, 92.

73 Peter Dempson, *Assignment Ottawa: Seventeen Years in the Press Gallery* (Toronto: General Publishing, 1968), 60.

74 James Gardiner, interview with Peter Regenstreif, 8 January 1961, quoted in Regenstreif, "Liberal Party," 387.

75 Dale Thomson, interview with Robert Bothwell, 14 August 1975, LAC, Robert Bothwell fonds, MG 32 G 4, vol. 1, Thomson file.

76 Blair Fraser, "Backstage at Ottawa," *Maclean's*, 20 August 1955, 6.

77 Eric Hutton, "What You Don't Know about Howe," *Maclean's*, 21 July 1956, 58.

78 C.D. Howe to Irvin Studer, 23 May 1958, LAC, Clarence Decatur Howe fonds, MG 27 III B20, vol. 107, file 75(2).

79 Tom Kent, "Mr. Howe Hot, Civil Servants Cold," *Winnipeg Free Press*, 21 April 1958, 21.

80 Victor Mackie, "Careful, Confident, Colorless," *Winnipeg Free Press*, 16 May 1957, 33.

81 Peter C. Newman, "The Powerful Gifts and Glaring Flaws of John Diefenbaker," *Maclean's*, 23 March 1963, 46.

82 Thomson, *Louis St. Laurent*, 512.

83 Richard J. Stanbury, "The Liberal Party of Canada: An Interpretation," 15 June 1969, pp. 3–5, LAC, Richard J. Stanbury fonds, MG 32 C 5, vol. 13, file 5.

12 John Diefenbaker: The Chief Stands Alone

PATRICIA I. MCMAHON

John G. Diefenbaker once observed, "I've got all of my enemies here in the Cabinet where I can keep an eye on them." That strategy may have brought comfort to Canada's thirteenth prime minister, but it did not, ultimately, serve him well in the practice of statecraft. Few cabinet disagreements have been displayed so publicly or with so much drama as the crisis that brought down his government in 1963. But the schism and resulting political meltdown were not inevitable. They were a crisis of Diefenbaker's own making, brought on by his political experience and personal temperament. That temperament is something highlighted in the critiques of many historians who study the period and tend to characterize Diefenbaker as a gifted orator but otherwise indecisive Prairie populist with a penchant for anti-Americanism.[1] As with most caricatures, there is a grain of truth in the characterization, but it is also incomplete. There was much more to Diefenbaker than irrational paranoia. Experience, especially his legal training, shaped Diefenbaker's approach to governing and cabinet.

John George Diefenbaker – the "Chief" – was an unlikely prime minister. Although few expected the Conservative Party to defeat the Liberals in 1957, there were signs the Liberal government's days were numbered. Louis St-Laurent had accomplished much but the Liberal Party had been in power for twenty-two years. His government was vulnerable to accusations of arrogance and looked out of touch.

Diefenbaker offered something new, if not fresh. Canadians in a sufficient number of ridings were interested enough to give him a minority government and the Conservative Party's first federal victory in twenty-seven years. Tepid support turned into genuine enthusiasm, and when Diefenbaker called a snap election in 1958, Canadians rewarded him with the largest majority in Canadian history: 78 per cent of the seats (208 of 265) in the House of Commons.[2]

Yet Diefenbaker's was a government of missed opportunity. A creature of small-town Saskatchewan, Diefenbaker genuinely wanted to bring about a different approach to northern Canada and Indigenous peoples. His experience in the law fuelled his campaign to adopt a Canadian Bill of Rights and his opposition to capital punishment and to apartheid in South Africa.[3] There were glimmers of greatness, more apparent in historical perspective than to contemporary eyes, but they were overshadowed by Diefenbaker's failures in his approach to statecraft.

His cabinet proved to be a "team of rivals," but unlike John A. Macdonald or even Robert Borden, Diefenbaker never learned to harness strength through difference.[4] Where conflict and disagreement could have been an asset, helping to compensate for weaknesses and improve decision-making, it destroyed Diefenbaker's government. He became notorious for treating people poorly. There were grumblings about his methods throughout the ministry, but it was the prime minister's management of Canada's nuclear policy that ultimately caused his downfall. It is a stark contrast to his success in establishing the Bill of Rights and tarnishes his legacy.

An entire book could be dedicated to the shortcomings of Diefenbaker's approach to statecraft. From his shabby treatment of francophone ministers, relegated to relatively minor positions in cabinet despite helping to secure his historic victory, to his ugly public – and personal – confrontation with James Coyne, the governor of the Bank of Canada, the examples are abundant. Instead, this chapter focuses on Diefenbaker's handling of Canada's nuclear policy. An issue he dealt with for his entire time as prime minister, nuclear policy required Diefenbaker to draw upon the expertise of others and to manage relations with foreign leaders and within his own cabinet. When faced with a crisis, Diefenbaker's approach failed him. In many ways, the handling of nuclear policy shows the prime minister at his worst. It is thus perhaps the best example of how Diefenbaker's approach to statecraft served him so poorly.

Diefenbaker's Quest for Political Leadership

Born in 1895 in southern Ontario, Diefenbaker and his family moved to what was then the Northwest Territories when he was eight years old, as the area was on the cusp of becoming the province of Saskatchewan. His small-town Prairie roots shaped Diefenbaker and his approach to politics. He understood western alienation because he lived it. He mistrusted what he saw as the central Canadian elites, who, in turn, regarded him as a bit of a buffoon. He was also sensitive about his German heritage and instinctively felt the discrimination that many immigrants faced if their names were not British in origin, especially during and after the First World War.

Diefenbaker attended high school in Saskatoon and then university at the newly built University of Saskatchewan. He was in university when the war broke out, but finished his BA, earned a master's degree, and started to study law before enlisting in 1916. Although he went overseas, he never saw combat, developing a heart condition within a few months of his arrival in England, a mysterious ailment that led to his medical discharge.[5] Interested in politics and history from a young age, Diefenbaker returned to the university to resume his legal studies in the spring of 1918.

The process of becoming a lawyer in Saskatchewan at that time required university graduates to article for three years in a solicitor's office, while high school graduates took five years to complete the requirements. During their articles, students wrote three annual exams set by the Law Society. The College of Law at the University of Saskatchewan was new, created in 1913. Diefenbaker joined the following year, taking jurisprudence and contracts during the second year of his BA. He also took courses in municipal, company, and sales law, while receiving credit for some of his political science courses.

Diefenbaker, who articled with three different lawyers, began the process in June 1916 before resigning in August to report for military duty. He resumed his articles in the spring of 1918, switching offices before re-enrolling in the college that fall. Even for the era, Diefenbaker spent very little time on his formal legal studies. He received one full year of law credit for his undergraduate course work, and the university – closed by the Spanish flu until the end of 1918 – gave him another year of credit in recognition of his military service. By then, he was in his third year of law school, and his officemate was Emmett Hall, a future Supreme Court of Canada justice.[6]

By the spring of 1919, Diefenbaker had finished the nine remaining courses, and benefited from the Law Society's decision to let university students skip the first two required professional exams. He passed his final exam, finishing seventh out of thirty-nine. As one author noted, "Even at a time when legal education was just becoming formalized, Diefenbaker seems to have received an unusually small amount of legal training ... less than five months at law school, and about eleven months of sporadic articling."[7] With the rest of the required articling time waived, Diefenbaker was called to the bar at the end of June. He hung out his shingle in Wakaw the day after.

It was the perfect location. Wakaw had one lawyer, a district court, and stood (as it does today) between the King's Bench circuit venues of Saskatoon, Prince Albert, and Humboldt. But the town was unwelcoming; no one would even rent him office space. Undaunted, Diefenbaker built his own, a small shack on a vacant lot.[8] He worked tirelessly and got results. Those results – he claimed to have won about half the sixty-two jury trials he had in his first year of practice – swayed locals.[9] Soon, he was so busy that he took on a partner. Together, they dominated the local courts.[10]

Many politicians in Diefenbaker's time had legal training, but few had Diefenbaker's courtroom prowess, especially before juries. It was a career that allowed him to hone the oratorical skills that made him such a force in the

House of Commons and on the hustings. Objectively, Diefenbaker was a persuasive speaker; compared to Lester B. Pearson, the Opposition leader, it was no contest. Diefenbaker's life in the law left its mark in other ways, however. He came to be sceptical about the death penalty, certain that a client had been wrongfully convicted and hanged. Experience with this and his other criminal work influenced his promotion of a Bill of Rights to protect various fair trial rights.[11]

But Diefenbaker's true love was politics, combined with an ardent passion for Conservatism. He coveted public office in a way that bred perseverance in the face of repeated failure. Whether it was running for Parliament or the party's leadership, Diefenbaker ran for it and lost – a lot. Part of the problem was his party affiliation; he was a Conservative in a province dominated by the Liberals.[12] In the 1925 federal election, he ran in the Liberal stronghold of Prince Albert. Like the previous Tory candidate, the twenty-eight-year-old Diefenbaker won so little of the vote that he lost his deposit. It was considered such a safe seat that the victorious Liberal made way for Mackenzie King to run in a by-election after his defeat in Ontario. King won that by-election, and stayed, running again in September 1926 after Meighen's government fell. Diefenbaker was up for the fight, but the prime minister decimated him. Diefenbaker lost provincially in 1929 when the Conservatives formed their first government in Saskatchewan. He lost again in 1933 – this time by just a handful of votes – when he ran for mayor of Prince Albert.[13] Dogged determination finally paid off in 1936 when Diefenbaker, now in his forties, became leader of the provincial party, but the Conservatives did not elect a single member to the Assembly. Despite the electoral thrashing, Diefenbaker stayed on as leader while continuing to practice law, now from Prince Albert. Finally, in the general election of 1940, Diefenbaker won the federal riding of Lake Centre, defeating the incumbent Liberal in what was an otherwise horrible showing for the Conservatives, who won just 39 seats (out of 245), as Canadians gave Mackenzie King a bigger majority than in 1935.

With that, Diefenbaker was off to Ottawa to sit across from King, who continued to represent Prince Albert. The Conservatives were in a shambles because their leader, Robert Manion, had lost his seat. The party turned to Arthur Meighen, by then a senator, to return. He agreed and resigned from the Senate to run in a by-election, which he lost. Diefenbaker took a shot at the leadership, but the party preferred the Liberal-Progressive premier of Manitoba, John Bracken. But Bracken did not secure a seat in the House until the 1945 election, when Diefenbaker won his own riding handily and no doubt took great delight in seeing King finally defeated in Prince Albert.

Bracken was unimpressive. When King announced his retirement in 1948, the Progressive Conservative leader was pushed to do the same. Diefenbaker once more entered the fray. Dominated by Toronto financiers, party leaders wanted George Drew, the Ontario premier, who had won three consecutive victories in the province. Supporters believed he could do the same federally. The contest was not even close; Diefenbaker lost to Drew on the first ballot.

As expected, Prime Minister Louis St-Laurent saw an opportunity and called an election. The Liberals thumped the Tories in the June 1949 contest, the latter winning only forty-one seats. Diefenbaker was re-elected, although he did not get to represent Prince Albert until 1953.

Without success at the polls, calls for Drew's resignation grew. Diefenbaker was not among the agitators, though he did not enjoy a warm relationship with the leader. Nevertheless, the Liberals had been in power a long time, and they acted like it. Drew and the Tories seemed to be making headway in 1956, when they took the Liberals to task during the Trans-Canada Pipeline debate. Then, in August, Drew got sick. One month later, he resigned.

Diefenbaker pounced. He was among the first to announce his candidacy, but Drew's supporters wanted an alternative. First, there was Sidney Smith, the president of the University of Toronto. He was not interested. However, another Torontonian was Don Fleming, a fifty-year-old lawyer who had run against Drew in 1948. Davie Fulton, the forty-one-year-old MP from Kamloops, British Columbia, rounded out the candidates. Others considered but declined to run. Dief won easily on the first ballot with the support of the western delegates. Organizers were disappointed but pragmatic: the new leader was sixty-one and unlikely to win the next election. Another shot at the leadership was around the corner.

They were wrong, but when St-Laurent dissolved Parliament in April 1957, there was no reason to think so. Nor was there much on the campaign trail to suggest otherwise. The final Gallup poll showed the Liberals leading with 48 per cent and the Tories at 34 per cent.[14] Yet the Conservatives won 112 seats, while the Liberals won only 105.[15] St-Laurent resigned, and Diefenbaker became prime minister.

The First Cabinet

Diefenbaker excluded from his first cabinet the one person in his caucus with government experience. Earl Rowe from Dufferin-Simcoe was the only Progressive Conservative MP who had previously served in government. But Rowe had also served as interim leader and had flirted with running for the leadership. He and the new prime minister were not friendly, so it was easy to leave him out of cabinet. But the pickings were slim, and Diefenbaker had to make do with many who had not supported him. "I have to form a cabinet, and it begins to look as though I shall have to form it largely of my enemies," he groused.[16]

Diefenbaker's first cabinet included seventeen people (including himself) holding twenty briefs around the table. Two were without portfolio, while several people held two ministries. Cabinet was balanced regionally. Five ministers hailed from the west (six, if you included the prime minister, who held external affairs until the fall), with the same number from Ontario, four from Atlantic Canada, and just two from Quebec. Western ministers held defence and justice, while Ontario had the powerful finance portfolio. No senators sat in the initial cabinet.[17] The average age in cabinet was 55.5 years – the median a touch older at 56. Diefenbaker was nearing 62.

1 Agriculture; Northern Affairs and National Resources – Douglas Scott Harkness, 54, Alberta
2 Defence Production; and Public Works – Howard Charles Green, 51, British Columbia
3 External Affairs – John George Diefenbaker, 61, Saskatchewan
4 Finance and Receiver General – Donald Methuen Fleming, 52, Ontario
5 Fisheries – John Angus MacLean, 43, Prince Edward Island
6 Justice and Attorney General; Citizenship and Immigration – Edmund Davie Fulton, 41, British Columbia
7 Labour – Michael Starr, 46, Ontario
8 Mines and Technical Surveys; Solicitor General – Léon Balcer, 39, Quebec
9 National Defence – George R. Pearkes, 69, Alberta
10 National Health and Welfare – Alfred Johnson Brooks, 66, New Brunswick
11 National Revenue – George Clyde Nowlan, 58, Nova Scotia
12 Postmaster General – William McLean Hamilton, 38, Quebec
13 Secretary of State of Canada – Ellen Louks Fairclough, 52, Ontario
14 Trade and Commerce – Gordon Churchill, 58, Manitoba
15 Transport – George Harris Hees, 47, Ontario
16 Veterans Affairs – Alfred Johnson Brooks, 66, New Brunswick
17 Minister without Portfolio – William Joseph Browne, 60, Newfoundland
18 Minister without Portfolio – James MacKerras Macdonnell, 72, Ontario

Diefenbaker had few friends in Parliament, but one exception was George Pearkes, who was about as close as a cabinet colleague got to Diefenbaker, having introduced him at the 1956 leadership convention. Major General Pearkes was a career military officer and a genuine war hero. Born in England in 1888, Pearkes and his family moved to Alberta in 1906, settling near Red Deer. He worked briefly for the North-West Mounted Police before the war but enlisted in 1915, winning the Distinguished Service Order and the Victoria Cross. After the war, he served in various posts across Canada and England, including on staff at the Royal Military College in Kingston and the Imperial Defence College in London. When war broke out in 1939, Pearkes was a brigadier serving as the district commanding officer in Calgary. Over the course of the war, he held various leadership positions with the Canadian forces at home and in Europe, including Canada's defences in the Pacific. He retired in February 1945 and then ran for the Tories in Nanaimo, British Columbia. He won that election and each through 1958. He was a natural choice for defence minister.

Diefenbaker's first cabinet included firsts like Ellen Fairclough (the first woman) and Michael Starr (born in Canada but the first minister of Ukrainian heritage), but also the seeds of his discontent. Fairclough, who served first as secretary of state and then as minister of citizenship and immigration, had not supported Diefenbaker for leader in 1956. Other ministers were equally suspicious, if not hostile, including Léon Balcer (solicitor general), George Nowlan (national revenue), and J.M. Macdonnell (minister without portfolio). In a category of their own were leadership rivals Fleming in Finance and Fulton in Justice.

After serving several months as his own secretary of state for external affairs, Diefenbaker named Sidney Smith to the post in September 1957. Although the former university administrator had not entered the leadership fray, Drew's supporters wanted him to run and win. But Drew made Diefenbaker leery, and he appointed Smith in deference to that faction. Nova Scotian by birth, Smith taught law at Dalhousie and Osgoode Hall before turning to university administration, first as dean of law at Dalhousie then as president of the University of Manitoba and the University of Toronto. With his appointment to cabinet, the sixty-year-old Smith needed a seat; a by-election followed in the reliable riding of Hastings-Frontenac, which the new minister won easily.

Smith was smart and popular but inexperienced. He struggled in the role, especially given the comparison to his predecessor, Pearson, who now had a Nobel Peace Prize. There were also the mandarins at External Affairs whom Diefenbaker dubbed the "Pearsonalities" because of their perceived loyalty to their previous minister and the Liberal Party.[18] Smith was not much of a voice in cabinet, and certainly could not allay Diefenbaker's concerns about the department. After eighteen months on the job, Smith was just starting to find his voice when he died suddenly. It was then that the prime minister chose Howard Green from Vancouver to fill the role.

Two years older than Smith, Green had a limited sense of the world beyond Canada's borders. Like Diefenbaker and others in cabinet,[19] Green had served in the First World War, but travelled little afterward and had a limited world view. First elected in 1935, Green served twenty-two years in Opposition before joining the cabinet. Like so many others, he had aspired to be leader, running for the position in 1942. Having placed fourth, he never tried again. That almost certainly won him points with the Chief. A dedicated anglophile, Green was a harsh critic of the Liberal government's approach to the Suez crisis. He joined the cabinet in 1957 as public works minister, though there was nothing about his performance that made him a natural choice to replace Smith. Nor was he a known proponent of disarmament. No one could have anticipated that

Image 12.1. Elizabeth II, Prince Phillip, and Governor General Vincent Massey with the Diefenbaker cabinet, 13 October 1957

Source: Library and Archives Canada, item 4301722.

Green would cause conflict with anyone, let alone Pearkes or his replacement, Douglas Harkness.

Eight years younger than Green, Harkness was born in Toronto but raised in Alberta. A schoolteacher and farmer in Red Deer, his was the Second World War, not the first. He enlisted in 1939 and won Britain's George Medal for bravery for his service during the Sicilian Campaign. Elected in 1945, Harkness was the party's critic for northern affairs and natural resources, and his experience as a farmer made him a natural choice to serve as Dief's first agriculture minister. When Pearkes left cabinet to return to BC as lieutenant governor in October 1960, Harkness was a solid choice to replace him as minister.

In 1957, Diefenbaker's cabinet appeared stable and united, and the prime minister looked for opportunities to convert his minority win into a majority (see image 12.1). Just days after securing the Liberal Party's leadership, Pearson obliged. During debate on 20 January 1958, Pearson moved an amendment to supply calling not for a snap election, but for Diefenbaker to resign and hand over the government to the Liberals. Blaming the economic downturn on the Tories, Pearson argued that only the Liberals knew how to handle the economy. It was an arrogant thing to do and gave Diefenbaker the opening he needed. He responded by reading from a report, prepared for the former Liberal government, that predicted the current economic difficulties. It allowed Dief to accuse the Liberals of hiding the downturn from Canadians. The rebuttal was devastating. Pearson knew immediately that he had made a mistake, recalling later that the prime minister "tore me to shreds." Gleeful, Diefenbaker revelled in his attack. "I operated on him without anaesthetic," he recalled.[20] Within days, the governor general dissolved Parliament with an election set for the end of March.

Historic Majority

Diefenbaker campaigned like a winner in the ensuing campaign, while Pearson stumbled. On election day, the Progressive Conservatives won the largest number of seats in Canadian history to that time with 208. It still holds the record for the largest percentage of seats in the House of Commons. Pearson, who had hoped to minimize the losses and retain at least one hundred seats, took only forty-nine. It was as crushing a defeat for the Liberals as it was an earth-shattering victory for the Tories. Diefenbaker's victory – and it was his, not the party's – was truly historic. With voter turnout at a record-high 79.4 per cent, the Chief held 78.5 per cent of the seats in the House of Commons and a 151-seat majority. He had the world, or at least the country, in the palm of his hand. He had the luxury of representation from every part of the country, with MPs elected from every province and territory except for the Northwest Territories. With an historic majority, Diefenbaker could have governed accordingly. Yet he did not.

Over the next four years, Diefenbaker governed with caution, as if he had a minority that was perpetually on the verge of defeat. Nowhere was this more apparent than in his approach to nuclear policy. Diefenbaker had the freedom to do what he wanted without fear of immediate political consequence. But the office of prime minister, finally attained, meant everything. Now that Diefenbaker had tasted victory, he worried more than ever about possible defeat. That Diefenbaker, who had experienced more than his share of defeat, would savour his triumph is not surprising. What is puzzling is that he did so little to try to persuade Canadians to support him on potentially controversial policies. He was, after all, a skilled advocate and talented orator. Comments about the impact of his legal training from those who knew him best may explain the crisis that grew up around his government's nuclear policy.

Despite his ability to digest a brief and defend a position, Diefenbaker tended to focus on the big picture and not details. He was not concerned with technicalities associated with implementing an idea. Fulton attributed this in part to his legal training, and his work specifically in criminal law. "One of the things that stands out in my mind about John Diefenbaker is that, while he had great concepts, he was not strong on an actual program by which they would be implemented," he said. "Perhaps this was the result of his training as a defence counsel. It was not his responsibility to build a positive case, it was his responsibility to destroy the Crown's case. I think maybe that this training, this whole background and attitude, made it difficult for [him] to sit down and plan out step by step the positive program."[21] It many respects, it made him better suited to leading the Opposition than the government.

But Diefenbaker's practice, according to one study, dealt with criminal matters only about 5 per cent of the time.[22] It seems unlikely, then, that Diefenbaker was stuck perpetually in the stereotypical role of criminal defence counsel. As a small-town lawyer, Diefenbaker would have done all kinds of legal work – criminal and civil, barrister and solicitor – to make ends meet.[23]

Jack Pickersgill, the clerk of the Privy Council turned Liberal minister and member of Parliament in 1953, was more cynical but possibly more accurate in his assessment: "Mr. Diefenbaker is one of those people who is a merchant of words and when he says something he thinks he has done something. Now, I attribute this to his long period in Opposition, to the fact that he was a courtroom lawyer where when you say something and it is effective you have done something. I also attribute it to another thing: that he was a loner. He never learned how to work cooperatively."[24]

True though the observation may have been, the inability to work cooperatively had little to do with Diefenbaker's legal training, especially not in a small town, where everyone knew everyone else. Courtroom victories would not have been enough to make Diefenbaker a success. Roy Fabish, a speechwriter to the prime minister who had served as the executive assistant to Northern Affairs Minister Alvin Hamilton, may have captured the problem best when he talked about Diefenbaker's reluctance to resolve conflict that occurred during cabinet discussions:

> If there wasn't a consensus and he didn't think the person holding out was a fool, to the exasperation of those of us who knew we were on the right course and wanted to get on with it, he'd roll it over, bring it up another time, try to bring him around, almost like a lawyer trying to bring a jury around so you've got all the twelve heads nodding.[25]

It was this willingness to defer decisions rather than work towards consensus that led Diefenbaker into trouble with his nuclear policy. Time and again, when given the chance, the prime minister refused to resolve conflict on the issue. Not only did he miss an opportunity to lead on what should have been a straightforward issue in cabinet, but his delay exacerbated the growing division.

Division on Canada's Nuclear Diplomacy

Canada's involvement in nuclear matters predated Diefenbaker's government by more than a decade. Having provided the uranium used by the Manhattan Project in the first atomic bombs, Canada had refused to acquire nuclear weapons for use by Canada's armed forces until the 1950s.

When Diefenbaker came to power, he did not know the Liberals had already decided to join the United States in a continental defence pact called the North American Air Defense Command (NORAD). The two nations agreed to integrate their air defence forces under a single, joint command. Well into the Cold War between Western democracies and the communist bloc, both Canada and the United States feared an air attack from the Soviet Union. Integrated continental defence seemed like the best protection from bombers carrying conventional bombs. The Liberals assumed, as did everyone else, that their re-election was a foregone conclusion, so the NORAD announcement was deferred until after the election.

Diefenbaker was not sold on the idea, but US president Dwight Eisenhower made all the difference. Diefenbaker had confidence in the American president and his team. Despite their obvious differences, the two had a lot in common. They were of the same generation. Both had grown up in small towns, served in the Great War, and felt the sting of prejudice that accompanied surnames of Germanic origin. And Eisenhower was respectful. By all accounts, he genuinely liked Diefenbaker, and the feeling was mutual. Together, the two developed a bond that went beyond what we might now see as a party-based natural affinity.

Diefenbaker was no isolationist, and he supported Canada's involvement in NATO. But NATO was a multilateral organization where many voices could counterbalance the American juggernaut. NORAD was different. There, it would just be Canada and the United States. Diefenbaker worried that, as the junior partner, Canada would not be treated as an equal partner. He needed assurances, and Eisenhower gave them. Satisfied, Diefenbaker announced that Canada was joining the continental alliance in August 1957.

The implications of joining NORAD were not necessarily clear to the Canadian public or even Diefenbaker when the announcement was made. At the time, Eisenhower asked Diefenbaker to consider allowing the Americans to store nuclear warheads on US bases in Canada, bases that had been leased during the Second World War. The Canadian prime minister was willing to consider it.

Two months later, the stakes changed. On 4 October 1957, the Soviets launched a satellite: Sputnik. It was more than a satellite; it was the opening salvo for the battle to control space. The west was now the technological underdog. It was a psychological blow, but there were tangible implications for continental defence, too. With the ability to launch a satellite into orbit, the Soviets could also launch something more threatening: a missile. Immune from armed conflict during the Second World War, North America was now suddenly vulnerable. A new approach was necessary. Missiles, launched from silos hundreds if not thousands of kilometres away, not bombers, were the future. Suddenly, NORAD did not look like a precaution but a necessity.

The Avro Arrow and Bomarc Missiles

The creation of an integrated continental defence pact meant that Canadian and American defence systems were now inextricably connected. In 1958, Eisenhower asked Diefenbaker to accept American warheads for storage on Canadian soil. It made the cancellation of Canada's prized but expensive Avro Arrow jet interceptor aircraft almost inevitable, and with it, the acquisition of nuclear weapons. When cabinet agreed to cancel the Arrow in 1958 (as the Liberals had seemingly decided in 1957), everyone agreed to accept Bomarc missiles. Waiting until after he had a majority, Diefenbaker made the announcement in February 1959. As he cancelled the Arrow, the prime minister also stated that Canada would accept Bomarc missiles. The Bomarc cost about half of what it cost to produce the Arrow and were designed to be armed with nuclear warheads.

There was no reason to think that the decision to accept Bomarcs in 1958 would also lead to Diefenbaker's demise. No minister questioned the decision. The decision was a non-issue. By joining NORAD, Canada could be nothing less than part of that nuclear umbrella. Deep into the Cold War, Canadians expected nothing less. There was certainly little opposition to nuclear weapons among the public. That, however, was about to change. Diefenbaker's public hesitation combined with changes in cabinet gave opposition the chance to grow.

The move to shuffle Howard Green, then serving as public works minister, to External Affairs in the spring of 1959 changed the consensus. For Green, landing in External Affairs was a huge promotion. What he lacked in expertise he made up for with political experience and his close relationship to the prime minister. Green had easy access to Diefenbaker in a way that Smith had not, and relations between the prime minister and the department improved.[26] Green was no peacenik,[27] but he was almost entirely dependent on the department, which was led by Norman Robertson, the deputy minister, who was increasingly devoted to promoting disarmament. Over time, Robertson (and anti-nuclear activists[28]) persuaded Green that Canada should play a greater role in promoting global disarmament. In principle, it was a terrific idea. In practice, having just joined NORAD and as a founding member of NATO, Canada was in a bit of a bind.[29]

As Green's enthusiasm for disarmament grew, another change in cabinet brought the issue to a head. Diefenbaker named Douglas Harkness as defence minister in October 1960 to replace Pearkes, who left Ottawa to become lieutenant governor of British Columbia. Harkness, like his predecessor, believed Canada should acquire nuclear weapons from the Americans. Cabinet had already decided to pursue negotiations with the US, and Harkness saw no reason to change course. Green, however, disagreed. Although all signs pointed to the Canadian acceptance of nuclear weapons in 1958–9, no formal agreement with the Americans had been concluded. The US presidential elections forced negotiations to be put on hold in the spring of 1960, but no one expected a change of Canada's attitude.

At the same time, Green became more strident in his opposition to Canada's acquisition of nuclear weapons. He argued in cabinet that an agreement was premature and that there was no pressure to act until late 1961 or early 1962 (when the missile systems were expected to arrive in Canada). He wanted time to promote disarmament internationally and convinced Diefenbaker that concluding a nuclear agreement would undermine that position. Harkness disagreed, saying that Canada should be ready to accept the warheads if – and when – disarmament talks broke down.

Diefenbaker's approach threaded the needle in a way that may have been too nuanced to persuade doubters. He thought that a disarmament agreement was unlikely but allowing time for even failed negotiations would show Canadians that nuclear weapons were necessary. Waiting until talks broke down would show that their leaders had done everything to forego nuclear weapons. Others encouraged this approach, but there was a divide between Defence and External Affairs.

The true sticking point was the Diefenbaker government's demand for "joint control" of the warheads on Canadian soil. The Eisenhower administration said the approach might violate the US Atomic Energy Act. However, the provision was part of Great Britain's agreement with the United States, and there was no reason it was impossible to do the same in Canada. In December 1960, cabinet agreed to resume talks with the Americans as "soon as they can usefully be undertaken" to secure what was described as a "package agreement" covering warheads under NORAD, NATO, and the Bomarc missile systems.[30]

The John F. Kennedy Factor

The growing rift in Diefenbaker's cabinet was exacerbated by the election of John F. Kennedy less than a month after Harkness became defence minister. Diefenbaker and Kennedy met twice in 1961. The first meeting, held in Washington, DC, on 20 February 1961, went far better than anticipated. The young president, barely sworn in, was impressive, despite what Basil Robinson of External Affairs described as Diefenbaker's "irrational prejudice" against Kennedy and his foreign policy team.[31] Kennedy's visit to Ottawa in May 1961 was a public relations success, but it was a disaster behind the scenes. Diefenbaker's views of Kennedy changed. The Bay of Pigs fiasco of April 1961, when the US government's attempt to land soldiers in Cuba failed spectacularly, had hurt Kennedy's reputation in Ottawa, giving Howard Green saw it as an opportunity to press his view.

Green was increasingly keen to push Canada's role in promoting global disarmament, a position that found favour with the anti-nuclear movement, which was increasingly vocal. During their talks, the president asked Diefenbaker, repeatedly, about finalizing agreement on several issues related to nuclear weapons. The prime minister refused, saying he still needed more time, now more than ever, due to growing anti-nuclear sentiment in Canada.[32] He promised, however, to persuade the Canadian public that the country ought to join the nuclear club. The president was keen to have Canada honour its commitment to take the nuclear warheads that would make the Bomarc missiles effective. Without the warheads, the missiles were useless. Kennedy had every right to be frustrated. But when Diefenbaker asked for time to educate the Canadian public about the need for weapons to help protect the continent from a Soviet attack, the president acquiesced.

Cabinet tension grew in the summer of 1961. Harkness was adamant in his support for Canada's acquisition of nuclear warheads. Green trumpeted disarmament, even refusing to support renewed talks on allowing nuclear weapons at US bases in Newfoundland. Diefenbaker knew that only a minority of Canadians opposed the acquisition of nuclear weapons, but the conflict within cabinet made him pause. Diefenbaker sided with Harkness, notwithstanding his disinclination towards Kennedy. Green reluctantly acquiesced, accepting that the Americans should be allowed to store nuclear warheads on US bases in Newfoundland, though he continued to oppose Canadian forces going nuclear.[33]

In August, Diefenbaker gave a speech in Halifax saying that Canada needed to acquire nuclear weapons from the Americans. The speech seemed to be his long-promised effort to educate the public about the need for nuclear weapons. Alas, almost no one noticed.[34] Diefenbaker may have been frustrated by the lack of attention, but he did not use his considerable talents of advocacy to try to change it. Given his general tenacity, the prime minister's willingness to shy away from an opportunity to pontificate and rail against the Opposition was surprising. Maybe he thought he would avoid creating a controversy where none yet existed. Perhaps he thought there really was something to the potential volatility of the electorate on the subject and the rise of the anti-nuclear movement. What is beyond doubt is that Diefenbaker did not forcefully persuade Canadians that the country should acquire nuclear weapons. What voters perceived was indecision.

With serious nuclear talks underway, Diefenbaker was horrified when news of those secret talks leaked to the newspapers with surprising accuracy. A headline in the *Montreal Gazette* announced that "JFK Presses Canada on Nuclear Warheads." The source was an article to appear in *Newsweek* that speculated Kennedy had pushed to resume the talks. The White House confirmed that talks were underway instead of offering the traditional "no comment."[35]

Diefenbaker had warned the president he would suspend the talks if there were any leaks. Sensitive about any perception that Canada was kowtowing to the Americans, he feared Canadians would think his government was weak in the face of US pressure, a concern surely exacerbated by the knowledge that Pearson would try to do just that. With a headline that practically screamed American pressure, how could he possibly accept nuclear warheads without looking like he had caved?[36] He could not. When asked about it in the House of Commons, Diefenbaker said there was no agreement but did not deny the existence of negotiations, nor would he commit to presenting the agreement to Parliament for its review or consideration. He said something similar to CBC. Underscoring the current state of international affairs, Canada's role in disarmament and test ban talks, he never denied the existence of talks, focusing instead on the absence of a formal agreement.[37]

Diefenbaker had decided there was no urgency to deciding the issue, and so he waited. By the end of 1961, global tensions were waning. The situation in Berlin – the city's famous wall had been erected in August – had stabilized. Yet the Cold War intensified. Harkness continued to push for a resolution because Bomarcs were scheduled to arrive at North Bay, Ontario, and La Macaza, Quebec, and Canadian forces were supposed to receive Honest John missiles in Europe. The defence minister wanted an agreement, and he appealed to Diefenbaker's electoral ambitions to get it. He pointed to Gallup polls that showed 61 per cent of Canadians supporting nuclear weapons for Canadian forces.[38] What the defence minister failed to appreciate was the extent to which the prime minister feared looking weak in the face of American pressure.[39]

Indeed, relations between Canada and the US went from bad to worse during the 1962 election campaign. Diefenbaker asked that Parliament be dissolved on 18 April, allowing two months for the campaign. When the votes were tallied on 18 June 1962, the results were almost worse than Diefenbaker had feared. Rather than a decisive outcome – win or lose – what Diefenbaker won was more political insecurity: a minority government. If he had been reluctant to make a potentially unpopular statement before the election, he was less so now that he had a thin minority. The Conservatives went from a historic 208-seat majority to just 116 seats in the House of Commons. Pearson increased the party's take by fifty seats, but despite Diefenbaker's increasingly weak public profile, still won only ninety-nine seats.[40]

Diefenbaker stewed. He could have seen the election as an opportunity to re-group, form a new cabinet, and eliminate conflict. Instead, he kept Harkness and Green in place, though Fulton moved to Public Works and Fleming moved from Finance to Justice. A more deliberate cabinet shuffle could have resolved the division between Harkness and Green, and this was a lost opportunity. But the prime minister had other problems: there were calls for his resignation as leader, and a monetary crisis led the government to announce an austerity program at the end of June.[41]

As summer turned to fall, Harkness continued, as before, to push the nuclear issue in cabinet. He seemed to be making progress by the beginning of October, when there were renewed discussions in cabinet. But now Green had the upper hand. Diefenbaker caved and agreed with his proposal to pursue an agreement only insofar as they could negotiate the type of "standby arrangement" that Green wanted in which nuclear warheads would be stored outside Canada but ready for immediate shipment to the missile sites within Canada in the event of an emergency.[42] It was an impractical solution.

Theory turned to reality very quickly when the Americans discovered Soviet nuclear missiles being installed Cuba in October 1962. Diefenbaker's cabinet was divided throughout the crisis. While Green wanted to use the emergency to promote disarmament, Harkness was focused on Canada's military response. He wanted to move the armed forces to DEFCON-3, just as the Americans had done, but lacked the authority to do so on his own.[43] Instead, he needed cabinet's approval, but Dief refused to act. Meeting on 23 October, cabinet agreed to discuss the issue but nothing else. Harkness was livid and decided to take matters into his own hands.[44] Undeterred by the lack of cabinet authorization, Harkness met with defence staff anyway and told them to do everything that was included with DEFCON-3. He did so without issuing the formal alert.[45] Cabinet talked about it again the next day. Once more, the prime minister refused to put forces on alert. It was only after the meeting, when Harkness told the prime minister that the Americans had now moved to DEFCON-2 that the prime minister was willing to act.[46] On 25 October, he announced Canada's support for Kennedy's proposed naval blockade of Cuba. Three days later, the Soviets backed down.

Diefenbaker's continued concern about maintaining political support fuelled continued divisions in cabinet. He contemplated calling a snap election on nuclear policy,[47] while Green tried to persuade him that the missile crisis had left Canadians opposed to the acquisition of nuclear weapons. Public opinion polls showed otherwise.[48] Harkness, having finally lost all semblance of patience, refused to cajole the prime minister anymore about concerns of this nature.[49]

The cabinet crisis came to a head in January 1963 when Pearson announced to a crowd in Scarborough, Ontario, that his party would "honour Canada's commitments" and accept nuclear warheads. That pledge sparked the implosion that destroyed Diefenbaker's cabinet.

Cabinet Crumbles

Many of Diefenbaker's advisers and ministers were pleased that Pearson had agreed to accept nuclear weapons, thinking Diefenbaker would finally move forward unequivocally. The Conservative Party's annual general meeting was held shortly after the Scarborough speech, and organizers thought it was the perfect moment for Diefenbaker to debut a decisive nuclear policy.

Eddie Goodman, a party organizer and chair of the policy resolution committee at the upcoming annual general meeting, met with the prime minister after the Scarborough speech. He found Diefenbaker in a buoyant mood. To his surprise, the prime minister responded with joy to the Liberal leader's speech. "We've got him now!" Goodman disagreed, pointing out that Pearson was only doing what the Conservative government had already said it would do. He urged Dief to make a clear, concise statement in support of acquiring the warheads.[50]

Advisers failed to understand that Pearson's very acceptance of nuclear weapons made Diefenbaker believe that he could no longer do the same. Where Dief had once worried that supporting the acquisition of nuclear weapons would lead the Liberals to attack, now he feared looking weak for appearing to follow the Liberal Party's example. No matter that Canada was engaged in negotiations with the Americans for nuclear weapons or that Diefenbaker had contemplated making nuclear weapons a central issue in the coming election. Diefenbaker was behaving like an Opposition leader, not a prime minister.

When Parliament reconvened, nothing was any clearer now than in the preceding months. Cabinet met on 20 January 1963, just before Parliament returned, and Diefenbaker suggested deferring a decision on nuclear policy until after the next election.[51] But increasingly, ministers sided with Harkness over the prime minister. As cabinet discussed the issue several times over the next few days, the division between the prime minister and his cabinet grew. On 22 January, Dief created a subcommittee comprising Harkness, Green, Churchill, and Donald Fleming to examine the question. Fleming aside, these were the men already involved with drafting the nuclear agreements with the Americans, so it is not surprising they agreed – after much wrangling between Green and Harkness – to continue negotiations. To their collective dismay, Diefenbaker rejected the recommendation. The men persevered, bringing their recommendation to the full cabinet on 24 January. Everyone agreed. Except Diefenbaker. At long last, Harkness decided to resign.[52]

The defence minister gave the prime minister one last chance to state clearly that Canada would accept nuclear weapons and decided to hold his resignation until after Diefenbaker spoke to Parliament on 25 January. The statement was so confusing that it was not immediately clear what Diefenbaker meant. He rambled, talking about joint authority and fears of nuclear proliferation but also the subcommittee's recommendations. Having already rejected the recommendations, Harkness thought Dief now seemed to accept them. He was pleased, believing the prime minister had finally agreed to accept nuclear weapons for Canada's armed forces.[53]

This delight was short-lived. The interpretation of the press was different, and, ultimately, more accurate. They heard the prime minister support Green's position. Outraged, Harkness responded by issuing his own "clarification" on 28 January.[54] Two days later, the US State Department weighed in with a press release on the subject.[55] The State Department denied the prime minister's assertion that nuclear negotiations were underway and blamed the Canadian government for the current stalemate. Basically, the State Department called Diefenbaker a liar.

Again, Diefenbaker proposed to call a snap election on nuclear policy when he convened cabinet on 31 January. Harkness and other ministers were appalled. They rejected the call and agreed to issue a formal protest to the US instead.[56]

Harkness finally made good on his promise and resigned on 3 February. Two days later, the government was defeated on a non-confidence motion and Parliament was dissolved a day later. In the days that followed, various cabinet ministers also departed. George Hees and Pierre Sévigny resigned on 9 February. Davie Fulton had already decided to leave federal politics to run for the leadership of the Conservative Party in British Columbia and had left Justice for Public Works in the summer of 1962. Donald Fleming, who took over the justice portfolio, had decided to leave politics altogether and did not stand for re-election either. Hees hardly campaigned at all, spending much of the campaign in Europe skiing.[57]

Diefenbaker was forced to make a few adjustments to cabinet in response, as Gordon Churchill took over from Harkness at Defence while Wallace McCutcheon took over Trade and Commerce.

The 1963 campaign ended not with a bang, but a whimper. The Progressive Conservatives were reduced to ninety-five seats, and Diefenbaker's cabinet was devastated: Richard Bell, Ellen Fairclough, and Raymond O'Hurley were all defeated, as was Howard Green. Doug Harkness, however, survived, as did John Diefenbaker.

The Liberals had not campaigned particularly well, and Canadians were not sold on Pearson either.[58] They fell four seats short of the coveted majority. Diefenbaker, eager to stage a return to power, managed to stay on as leader until 1967, but never served as prime minister again. He did, however, keep Pearson from ever securing a majority. Diefenbaker refused to retire from Parliament, even after being turfed as party leader. He remained an MP until his death in August 1979.

Conclusion

Diefenbaker's handling of nuclear policy was revealing of his approach to cabinet governance more generally. On numerous occasions during his nearly six years in power, he publicly displayed an obstinacy and a desire to confront that did nothing to convince Canadians that he was in command of the facts. Whether it was in his confrontations with James Coyne, the governor of the Bank of Canada, or with British leaders over the UK's joining of the European Community, Diefenbaker appeared distracted and aimless. Moreover, as Jack Pickersgill suggested, Diefenbaker never learned to collaborate. He never took advantage of the advisory role cabinet can play despite his ability to engage with and digest large amounts of material. His legal training and trial experience stood him in good stead in this regard, especially when he needed to marshal material for use in the House. Yet the inability (or unwillingness) to collaborate is only part of the explanation.

Diefenbaker erred in appointing Howard Green to External Affairs and was not moved to eliminate divisions in cabinet. Perhaps he simply enjoyed the cut and thrust of a good debate. He may have thought that enemies in cabinet could cancel each other out, allowing him a freer hand. That approach might be laudable in a university seminar, but it is no way to govern. What Diefenbaker failed to appreciate is that governing, unlike a debating society, required leaders to resolve conflicts, not just discuss them. Leaders must lead.

The more Diefenbaker deferred, the worse the division became. He was a skilled communicator and a zealous advocate for his passions, like the Bill of Rights. But, after trying to make the case for nuclear weapons in Halifax, he seemed to give up and did little else. His efforts to promote nuclear weapons likely reflected his ambivalence towards the subject. The same could be said about his response to the deteriorating economy in 1962.

Perhaps Diefenbaker wanted to win more than he wanted to govern. Whether it was the economy and the Bank of Canada, his emotional attachment to romantic ideas of the British Empire, or his apparent dithering on nuclear policy, his only calculation seemed to be his personal electoral fortunes. Most likely, Diefenbaker did not worry about the divisions in cabinet because he thought he had time. Delay and ambiguity had served Mackenzie King well in the Second World War. Lawyers will recognize his tendency to defer completing a task until the last minute, in part to make sure something is necessary before doing it. Diefenbaker's talents as a trial lawyer never left him, and trial lawyers know that many disputes are settled on the courthouse steps. Why put out an ember when a flame exists elsewhere that threatens to become an inferno? The Cuban missile crisis was that tomorrow, and by then, it was too late.

Diefenbaker's lack of attention to the implications of his policy choices, his tendency to pick fights he could not win, and his acceptance of division in cabinet all sapped his support. Time and again, he showed he was not in command, cabinet members abandoned him one by one or chose to remain silent. The remarkable thing is that few of them came to his defence. The Ontarians in cabinet never liked him, the Quebeckers did not trust him, the Westerners did not know what to make of him. He lost their confidence.

During the 1962 election, the Liberals issued an *Election Colouring Book* designed to appeal to the parents of the baby boom generation. One of them featured a cartoon of Diefenbaker at the head of a poorly attended cabinet meeting. "This is a Conservative cabinet meeting," the subheading read, "Oops.... Some of the ministers are missing. I wonder where they went? Colour them quick ... before they all disappear." If a picture is worth a thousand words, this cartoon said so much more. It captured at once Diefenbaker's inability or unwillingness to manage his cabinet, a flaw that led to the demise of his government less than one year later. The outcome reflected Diefenbaker's approach to statecraft that proved deficient when tested by crisis.

NOTES

1 Peter C. Newman, *Renegade in Power: The Diefenbaker Years* (Toronto: McClelland & Stewart, 1963); J.L. Granatstein, *Canada, 1957–1967: Years of Uncertainty and Innovation* (Toronto: McClelland & Stewart, 1986); Robert Bothwell, Ian Drummond, and John English, *Canada since 1945: Power, Politics, Provincialism* (Toronto: University of Toronto Press, 1989); and Denis Smith, *Rogue Tory: The Life and Legend of John G. Diefenbaker* (Toronto: Macfarlane Walter & Ross, 1995). More recent work is more sympathetic: D.C. Story and R.B. Shepard, eds., *The Diefenbaker Legacy: Politics, Law and Society since 1957* (Regina: Canadian Plains Research Centre, 1998); Patricia I. McMahon, *Essence of Indecision: Diefenbaker's Nuclear Policy, 1957–1963* (Montreal: McGill-Queen's University Press, 2009); and Janice Cavell and Ryan M. Touhey, eds., *Reassessing the Rogue Tory: Canadian Foreign Relations in the Diefenbaker Era* (Vancouver: University of British Columbia Press, 2018).
2 John C. Courtney, *Revival and Change: The 1957 and 1958 Diefenbaker Elections* (Vancouver: University of British Columbia Press, 2022).
3 These topics are outside the scope of this chapter, but see Christopher MacLennan, *Toward the Charter: Canadians and the Demand for a National Bill of Rights, 1929–1960* (Montreal: McGill-Queen's University Press, 2003); Asa McKercher, "Sound and Fury: Diefenbaker, Human Rights, and Canadian Foreign Policy," *Canadian Historical Review* 97, no. 2 (2016): 165–94; and Francine McKenzie, "A New Vision for the Commonwealth" and Kevin A. Spooner, "The Diefenbaker Government and Foreign Policy in Africa," both in Cavell and Touhey, *Reassessing the Rogue Tory*, 25–44, 186–208.
4 The concept is brilliantly described in Doris Kearns Goodwin, *Team of Rivals: The Political Genius of Abraham Lincoln* (New York: Simon & Schuster, 2006). For the Canadian equivalent, see Patrice Dutil, "Macdonald, His 'Ottawa Men' and the Consolidation of Prime Ministerial Power, 1867–1873," in *Macdonald at*

200: New Perspectives and Legacies, ed. Patrice Dutil and Roger Hall (Toronto: Dundurn, 2014), 282–319.

5 Library and Archives Canada (hereafter "LAC"), Canadian Expeditionary Force, RG150, accession 1992–93/166, box 2514–75.

6 Hall owed his judicial career to Diefenbaker, who appointed him to Saskatchewan's Court of Queen's Bench in 1957, the Court of Appeal in 1961, and the Supreme Court of Canada in 1963.

7 Ken Whiteway, "The Legal Career of John G. Diefenbaker," *Saskatchewan History*, no. 53 (2001): 30.

8 Garrett Wilson and Kevin Wilson, *Diefenbaker for the Defence* (Toronto: James Lorimer, 1988), 32–4.

9 Peter C. Newman, *Renegade in Power* (Toronto: McClelland & Stewart, 1963).

10 Denis Smith, *Rogue Tory: The Life and Legend of John G. Diefenbaker* (Toronto: Macfarlane Walter & Ross, 1995), 34–5.

11 Whiteway, "Legal Career," 26–38.

12 Newman, *Renegade in Power*, 19–20.

13 He skipped the 1930 federal election, thus missing an opportunity to be part of Bennett's majority, and the provincial election in 1934.

14 Gallup poll, February 1957, LAC, Progressive Conservative Party Papers, vol. 415, file: The Canadian Liberal, 1957–1961; and Dick Spencer, *Trumpets and Drums: John G. Diefenbaker on the Campaign Trail* (Vancouver: Greystone Books, 1994), 28.

15 The Tories won 39 per cent of the vote, while the Liberals won 42 per cent. See "Canadian Election Results by Party, 1867 to 2021," Canadian Elections, Simon Fraser University, accessed 31 August 2024, https://www.sfu.ca/~aheard/elections/1867-present.html.

16 J.L. Granatstein, *Canada, 1956–1967: The Years of Uncertainty and Innovation* (Toronto: McClelland & Stewart, 1986), 28.

17 Senator John T. Haig served as minister without portfolio and leader of the government in the Senate from 9 October 1957 to 11 May 1958. A.J. Brooks was appointed to the Senate on 12 September 1960, and remained minister of veterans affairs until 10 October 1960. Senator Wallace McCutcheon served as minister without portfolio from 9 August 1962 to 11 February 1963 and minister of trade and commerce from 12 February to 22 April 1963.

18 John Hilliker, "The Politicians and the 'Pearsonalities': The Diefenbaker Government and the Conduct of Canadian External Relations," in *Canadian Foreign Policy: Historical Readings*, ed. J.L. Granatstein (Toronto: Copp Clark Pitman, 1993), 152–67.

19 Over the course of Diefenbaker's tenure, there were sixteen veterans in cabinet, including seven who had served in the Great War: Alfred Brooks, Gordon Churchill, Howard Green, James Macdonnell, George Nowlan, George Pearkes, and Sidney Smith.

20 Spencer, *Trumpets and Drums*, 49.

21 Davie Fulton, quoted in Peter Stursberg, *Diefenbaker: Leadership Gained, 1956–62* (Toronto: University of Toronto Press, 1975), 178.

22 Whiteway, "Legal Career," 27.

23 Wilson and Wilson, *Diefenbaker for the Defence*, 34–5.

24 J.W. Pickersgill, quoted in Stursberg, *Leadership Gained*, 224–5.

25 Stursberg, *Leadership Gained*, 177–8.

26 H. Basil Robinson, *Diefenbaker's World: A Populist in Foreign Affairs* (Toronto: University of Toronto Press, 1988), 98.

27 Daniel Heidt, "From Bayonets to Stilettos to UN Resolutions: The Development of Howard Green's Views Regarding War" (MA thesis, University of Waterloo, 2008).

28 On the role of anti-nuclear activists, see Patricia I. McMahon, *Essence of Indecision: Diefenbaker's Nuclear Policy, 1957–1963* (Montreal: McGill-Queen's University Press, 2009).

29 McMahon, *Essence of Indecision*, 54–5.

30 Cabinet Conclusions, 6 December 1960, LAC, Privy Council Office, RG 2.

31 Robinson, *Diefenbaker's World*, 168.

32 Diefenbaker explained that it was not just communists and radicals, but increasingly mothers and wives – people with real credibility. See Department of State, "Memoranda of Conversation, Trip to Ottawa, May 17, 1961, Subject: Disarmament," John F. Kennedy Papers (JFK Papers), NSF, vol. 18, file: Canada – General – Ottawa Trip 5/17/61, John F. Kennedy Library, Boston, Massachusetts (Kennedy Library); and "Memoranda of Conversation, Trip to Ottawa, May 17, 1961, Subject: NATO and Nuclear Weapons," File: Canada – General – Ottawa Trip 5/17/61, JFK Papers, Kennedy Library. See also "Memorandum of Conversation," 423, *Foreign Relations of the United States [FRUS], 1961–1963*, 13: 1157–58.

33 Cabinet Conclusions, 24 July 1961, LAC, Privy Council Office, RG 2.

34 McMahon, *Essence of Indecision*, 117–18.

35 Armstrong (Ottawa) to secretary of state, no. 316, 20 September 1961, Kennedy Papers, NSF, vol. 20, file: Canada – Subjects: Diefenbaker Correspondence, 01/20/61–8/10/61, JFK Library.

36 McMahon, *Essence of Indecision*, 122–4.

37 John Diefenbaker, Notes for speech "The Nation's Business," 20 September 1961, Diefenbaker Canada Centre, Saskatoon, John G. Diefenbaker Papers, vol. 17, MG 01/XIV/E/222: Defence (Haslam), part 2 (1961–1963).

38 Although 31 per cent of Canadians opposed the acquisition of nuclear warheads, only 8 per cent were undecided (Cabinet Conclusions, 30 November 1961, LAC, Privy Council Office, RG 2).

39 Diefenbaker Canada Centre, John G. Diefenbaker Papers, vol. 176, MG 01/VII/A/1646.2: Nuclear Weapons, 1961–1962.

40 Social Credit won thirty seats and the New Democratic Party won nineteen in its first election since rebranding from the CCF.

41 Smith, *Rogue Tory*, 430; and Spencer, *Trumpets and Drums*, 66.

42 H.B. Robinson, "Nuclear Weapons Policy," 16 October 1962, LAC, H.B. Robinson Papers, vol. 9, file 9.4: Nuclear Weapons Policy, 1962.

43 DEFCON, short for Defence Readiness Condition, is a five-level military alert system introduced by the United States during the Cold War and used in NORAD. On this five-level scale, DEFCON-5 is the normal state of readiness during peacetime, while DEFCON-1 represents imminent war. Declaring DEFCON-3 represented a serious state of heightened alert and readiness for war.

44 Douglas Harkness, "The Nuclear Arms Question," LAC, Douglas S. Harkness Papers, vol. 57, 9–11; and Cabinet Conclusions, 23 October 1962, LAC, Privy Council Office, RG 2.

45 No personnel were permitted to go on leave, although no one was recalled from leave either.

46 Harkness, "Nuclear Arms Question," 13.

47 Harkness, "Nuclear Arms Question," 16–17.

48 Bryce, "Lessons of the Cuban Crisis," 20 November 1962, LAC, H.B. Robinson Papers, vol. 9, file 9.4: Nuclear Weapons Policy, 1962.

49 Harkness, "Nuclear Arms Question," 17.

50 Eddie Goodman, *Life of the Party: The Memoirs of Eddie Goodman* (Toronto: Key Porter Books, 1988), 95–9; and Eddie Goodman, interview with author, 8 April 1999.

51 Harkness, "Nuclear Arms Question," 23–4.

52 Harkness, "Nuclear Arms Question," 23–4, 32.

53 *House of Commons Debates*, 25th parl., 1st sess., vol. 3, 25 January 1963, 3125–39.

54 Harkness, "Statement in the House of Commons," 28 January 1963, LAC, Douglas S. Harkness Papers, vol. 57, file: The Nuclear Arms Question – Background Correspondence, 1963.

55 Department of State, "Press Release no. 59 – United States and Canadian Negotiations Regarding Nuclear Weapons," 30 January 1963, no. 444, *FRUS*, 1961–1963, 13:1195–96.

56 Harkness, "Nuclear Arms Question," 46.

57 Spencer, *Trumpets and Drums*, 81.

58 The various Liberal campaign gimmicks failed: homing pigeons got lost, the Election Colouring Book was nasty, and the Truth Squad looked silly. See John English, *The Worldly Years: The life of Lester Pearson* (Toronto: Alfred A. Knopf Canada, 1992), 262; Alex Mogelon to NLF, 16 August 1960, LAC, National Liberal Federation Papers, vol. 702, file: Comics, 1960; *Marketing*, 2 October 1959; Keith Davey, "Press Release," 12 March 1963, LAC, National Liberal Federation Papers, vol. 694, file: Memos from Keith Davey to Provincial Campaign Chairmen & Communications Chairmen, 1963; vol. 696, file: Truth Squad 1963.

13 Lester Pearson and Cabinet Government: The Diplomat in Charge

P.E. BRYDEN

Few prime ministers had had as much, and as varied, experience with cabinet before taking office as Lester "Mike" Pearson. He had witnessed the Mackenzie King governments from afar, in external affairs postings in Washington and London, working most closely with the diplomats and civil servants that populated the increasingly important department. In 1948, he shifted from the outside looking in to a seat at the cabinet table in Louis St-Laurent's administration, gaining eight years of experience as secretary of state for external affairs; six years in Opposition gave him yet another perspective – an intimate outsider's view of another man's cabinet. By 1963, now sixty-six years old, he settled in to craft his own first cabinet, bringing more than thirty years of observation to the task.

If lessons had been learned from his predecessors, however, they were hard to detect. Nor was it possible to discern any clear plan of cabinet management under Pearson. He made and remade his cabinet in the face of scandal, hurt feelings, and shifting priorities. Pearson himself offered little direction, frequently appeared indecisive, and managed in a way that gave every impression of being designed to produce the maximum amount of chaos. This disorder would be easy enough to assess were it not for one glaring incongruity: the accomplishments of the Pearson government were extraordinary. In the midst of crisis and calamity, the Pearson government built a welfare state, installed a national medicare program, confronted Quebec separatism, adopted a new flag as a national symbol, and navigated the Cold War, all with only a minority Parliament. Sixty years later, the questions still endure: How could this be? How could a cabinet that functioned without a plan ultimately be so successful at the one thing it is supposed to do – govern?

Much has been written about all the many purposes of cabinet, from securing regional representation at the centre to wresting power from the democratically elected Parliament and protecting it at the apex.[1] But really, it has one job: "By constitutional convention ... [it] sets the federal government's policies and priorities for the country."[2] To view the way that the Pearson cabinet set those policies and priorities is a bit like viewing how a sausage gets made, but there is no underestimating the results. Pearson led an extremely successful pair of minority governments; whether they functioned according to any kind of logic whatsoever is another matter.

The secret to the success of cabinet governance in the mid-1960s in Canada, I will suggest here, is Mike Pearson himself. The very fact that he was not quite as he seemed – brighter than people gave him credit for, more decisive than he appeared, ambitious rather than just lucky – resulted in the unexpected successes in the midst of what seemed to be absolute mayhem. Pearson epitomized contradictions, and in many ways, his government did too. To understand how these paradoxes worked in practice, and how they came to shape the Pearson cabinet, the prelude to government is instructive. A great deal of Pearson's approach to cabinet governance, and to the executive branch more generally, was shaped during the one period in his life that he did *not* have access to cabinet, either through departmental channels, as was the case during his diplomatic career, or at the table itself, as was the case during the St-Laurent years. The years between 1958 and 1963, when Pearson was leader of the Opposition, were formative, although perhaps unintentionally so. Decisions made then, out of necessity and by choice, shaped the government that Pearson ultimately led in the five years after 1963. Not only did the party establish a policy agenda that guided much of the work of government, but it also fell into a management structure that determined the way that cabinet would function. While the policy work was done intentionally, the structural realignments that occurred during the course of six long years in Opposition were more unexpected in their significance.

There is ample evidence that Mike Pearson initially expected that his stint in Opposition would be brief. After the Liberals were ousted from office by the Diefenbaker Conservatives in 1957, the party faithful devoted much attention to assessing why and how and what to do about it. The election loss had initially been a shock to many, but on reflection seemed strangely inevitable. Some put the blame on the indolence of twenty-two years in government; as former cabinet minister Brooke Claxton wrote later, "the Liberal Party failed to renew its outworn skin, to recharge its batteries, to overhaul its organization, to take fresh stock of the country it has helped so much to create, to revise and expand the whole corpus of political philosophy and administrative principle on which it was based."[3] Others pointed to policy failures – either too much "creeping Socialism," according to the right, or too few tangible proposals, according to the outsiders.[4] Regardless, the quick fix offered by St-Laurent's decision to retire, and the opportunity presented by a leadership convention, should solve the problem.

Mike Pearson's victory at the Liberal leadership convention in January 1958 looked easy: the candidate seemed not to have campaigned, the vote wasn't close.[5] The strategy of forcing an early election by demanding Diefenbaker's resignation, however, which Pearson followed at the first parliamentary opportunity, smacked of misplaced confidence. It also suggested that Pearson had little expectation of remaining in Opposition for long. Fate, with a good dose of Diefenbaker-mania added in, handed Pearson a rude return to reality with a crushing defeat in the 1958 election, ensuring that the Liberals would languish in Opposition for another several years.

Pearson's Leadership

To later generations, Pearson is often depicted as the prime minister in the bow tie with the lisp, a caricature that seems to telegraph an unlikely rise to power. Nothing could be further from the truth: few men have seemed so fated for power than Lester Pearson. The middle son of a Methodist minister in small-town Ontario, his childhood at the turn of the nineteenth century was idyllic. Popular and athletic, he joined the Canadian war effort in 1915, returned to the home front and an abbreviated degree in history from the University of Toronto in 1919, and then on to Oxford for a graduate degree. His academic performance was middling – he earned a high second – but his wit and athleticism were memorable. When a permanent position in the University of Toronto's History Department seemed unlikely, he jumped at the offer of a job in External Affairs, where O.D. Skelton was building a department of extraordinary talent. As his biographer has noted, his "intelligence, artfully concealed ambition, good looks and health, and exceptional personal charm" served him well then and later.[6]

Pearson's rise through the ranks of External was legendary, but not surprising: people liked him and were generally happy to see him succeed. He began as a junior officer in Washington in 1927, headed to Ottawa the following year, spent the early Depression participating in League of Nations conferences, and then was posted to London as first secretary, where he remained through the start of the Second World War. The attack on Pearl Harbor sent him to Washington where his reputation soared thanks to an attentive American media. He chaired a variety of committees that became part of the United Nations, was touted as a potential candidate for its first secretary general, and eventually was appointed Canadian ambassador to the United States in 1945. He was, by then, Canada's top and most famous diplomat.

Shifting to the political side of diplomacy, with the strong encouragement of retiring Prime Minister King, who had tapped him as a potential future successor, and incoming prime minister Louis St-Laurent, who had been Pearson's minister of external affairs, Pearson ran successfully for a seat in the 1948 election. A win in the Algoma riding in Northern Ontario sent Pearson to Ottawa, where he served as minister of external affairs until the Liberal defeat in 1957, guiding the department through what historians have called the "golden age" of Canadian foreign policy. Along the way, he crafted a solution to an international crisis over the nationalization of the Suez Canal by proposing the creation of a United Nations peace force and collected a Nobel Peace Prize for his efforts. There was little, it seemed, that was not within Pearson's reach.

Until, that is, his rise to the top of the Liberal Party left him languishing in Opposition for considerably longer than anticipated. This detour on the road back to government detached Pearson from the two sources of advice that had shaped his experience to date– cabinet and the bureaucracy. He had been part of both in his own day, but now as the leader of the Opposition, had access to neither. Everything he knew about policy design and development, not to mention implementation, he had experienced from the winning side of the bench. Opposition required a whole new set of rules. Key to crafting the new advisory environment were two people who would become central to cabinet governance, on the one hand, and to the Prime Minister's Office, on the other, in the later Pearson administrations.

The first was Walter Gordon, Pearson's friend since the two had crossed paths in the 1930s and the financier of his successful leadership bid; the second was Tom Kent, former editor of the *Winnipeg Free Press* and a more recent associate of Pearson's who had been tapped to write his Nobel Peace Prize acceptance speech in 1957. In the absence of a cabinet to "set policies and priorities" and a bureaucracy to put ideas into action, Pearson chiefly relied on Gordon and Kent as well as a handful of others. Gordon, for example, was instrumental in planning the Liberal Rally, an enormous (by the standards of the day) gathering of the faithful to vote on policy directions. While the thousand or so Liberals who attended may have felt like they were determining the direction of the party, it was really Gordon who had decided which proposals would be voted on and which issues would be highlighted. He couldn't control everything: a proposal from the floor ensured that old age pensions had a place in the Liberal platform, but for the most part, Gordon was something of a puppet-master.

Kent had moved into Pearson's entourage as a speechwriter, but the process of putting words in the mouth of the man quickly evolved into something closer to putting ideas in the head of the politician. Or at least that was the way Kent saw his role. As he explained later in his memoirs, he and Pearson "had many viewpoints in common, but our temperaments were very different. From 1958 to 1961 Mike's relationship with me was probably not much different from that with other close friends, except that spasmodically he asked me to do more work for him." In 1961, however, following the two successes of the 1960 Kingston Conference, a thinkers' meeting designed to produce a new pot of ideas from which the Liberals could build a platform, and its more political twin, the Liberal Rally in January 1961,[7] Kent became something more akin to "the employed assistant."

> That did not cause much change of attitude, on either side, but it made our contacts so frequent that most of them had to be strictly business. Under pressure, we grew to need each other greatly, and to use each other without mercy. Mike's demands on my time and energy often seemed to be without limit. I reciprocated by pressuring him to be definite and firm on many occasions when his disposition was to evade and to waver, by pressing him to make decisions however much he wanted to put them off and watch a hockey or ball game on television instead.[8]

Pearson had an extraordinary ability to make people believe he needed their help, and the result was a remarkable gravitational pull towards Ottawa that left a lasting impact on both government and the Liberal Party. They came to provide advice and time, talent and direction; they came to stiffen the leader's backbone. They all "exhibit[ed] a curious habit of assuming he shares their own views," in the words of journalist Robert Fulford, a perspective destined to end in disappointment.[9] According to Gordon, even the leader's "most ardent supporters" feared that he might lack "the necessary toughness to be a successful Prime Minister,"[10] so they came to offer support. "'Help me, I need you' was a sentiment Pearson expressed countless times in countless ways," a subsequent PMO insider noted, "confident of the effect of his charm."[11] Those who believed their help was instrumental, however, did not last forever in Pearson's inner circle, only as long as their usefulness was apparent. But that "team" in Opposition, as ephemeral as it proved to be, nevertheless profoundly shaped the way Pearson approached government when the elusive electoral victory was finally his in 1963.

Like those who preceded him, Pearson understood cabinet's role as both a representative body, reflecting regional interests as well as, increasingly, the generational, religious, ethnic and gendered complexion of the nation, but also as an advisory body. Cabinet needed to be *seen* to be something, as well as to actually *do* something. Determining the right balance of personnel was "agonizing," although some choices were more obvious than others.[12] Where Pearson's cabinet differed from earlier iterations was in its relationship to the unelected advisers in the Prime Minister's Office. While the PMO under Pearson did not grow in size, a fact that he bemoaned later, it did certainly expand in influence, and that ended up having implications for the way cabinet functioned.[13] With the advantage of hindsight, all of this was apparent immediately after the election of 1963, although no one was aware of it at the time.

In crafting that first cabinet, Pearson actually interviewed thirty-five potential ministers, consulted with Kent and Gordon, and narrowed his selection to twenty-five individuals. While he maintained that the decisions were his alone, those consultations were important: "No one," Pearson admitted, "had greater influence in the party than Walter [Gordon],"[14] and no one was as quick to offer his opinion on anything bearing on policy as Tom Kent. Gordon got a bit of a sense of the rift that would develop between him and the prime minister in the years to come when Pearson offered him the cabinet post of minister of industry, a clear step down from the Finance Department he had been promised. After the initial offer, though, Gordon "was appointed to Finance without further question," admitting that he "would not have joined Cabinet otherwise."[15] In Kent's case, cabinet positions were not on the table, but Pearson did seek his opinion on the health, finance and defence appointments to cabinet (also floating the idea of putting Gordon in Industry), and he asked him to privately contact senior civil servants to start them working on the Liberal agenda, all before officially inviting him to join the Prime Minister's Office as "Co-ordinator of Programming."[16] It was billed as a "special assignment for one year," established to allow Kent to "work with committees of cabinet in the development of legislation" and serve as a liaison between Pearson and his ministers.[17] The early months of the Pearson Liberal government were the apex of Kent's powers and authority; Gordon's fall from grace began in those same months.

Pearson established ten standing committees and insisted that any decision going to the full cabinet be vetted by one of them. The cabinet that emerged from these consultations, but perhaps more directly from Pearson's own mind (a prospect that so few of his colleagues and advisers seemed to acknowledge), had "few surprises" with representatives from all provinces but Saskatchewan, both men and women – or, more accurately, woman (Judy LaMarsh) – folks with experience and to whom the Liberal Party owed much, like Jack Pickersgill and Paul Martin, as well as nine newcomers who had served in Parliament no more than a year, including Mitchell Sharp and Walter Gordon.[18] It was a diverse group, carefully representative not only of region and identity but also, as it turned out, of "political philosophy. Among them are theorists and dreamers, practical vote-getters, fighters and compromisers, conservatives, liberals and socialists."[19] It made for the potential for feisty cabinet meetings, but the fact that there seemed to be a hierarchy apparent in that first cabinet suggested that the left-leaning dreamers might have the upper hand.

The first Pearson cabinet:

1   Prime Minister – Lester Bowles Pearson, 65, Ontario
2   Agriculture – Harry William Hays, 53, Alberta
3   Citizenship and Immigration – Guy Favreau, 45, Quebec
4   Defence Production – Charles Mills Drury, 50, Quebec
5   External Affairs – Paul Joseph James Martin, 59, Ontario
6   Finance and Receiver General – Walter Lockhart Gordon, 57, Ontario
7   Fisheries – Hédard Robichaud, 51, New Brunswick

8 Forestry – John Robert Nicholson, 61, British Columbia
9 Justice and Attorney General – Lionel Chevrier, 60, Quebec
10 Labour – Allan Joseph MacEachen, 46, Nova Scotia
11 Mines and Technical Surveys – William Moore Benidickson, 52, Ontario
12 National Defence – Paul Theodore Hellyer, 39, Ontario
13 Associate Minister of National Defence – Louis Joseph Lucien Cardin, 44, Quebec
14 National Health and Welfare – Julia Verlyn LaMarsh, 38, Ontario
15 National Revenue – John Richard Garland, 45, Ontario
16 Northern Affairs and National Resources – Arthur Laing, 58, British Columbia
17 Postmaster General – Azellus Denis, 56, Quebec
18 President of the Privy Council – Maurice Lamontagne, 45, Quebec
19 Public Works – Jean-Paul Deschatelets, 50, Quebec
20 Secretary of State of Canada – John Whitney Pickersgill, 57, Newfoundland
21 Solicitor General – John Watson MacNaught, 58, Prince Edward Island
22 Trade and Commerce – Mitchell William Sharp, 51, Ontario
23 Transport – George James McIlraith, 54, Ontario
24 Veterans Affairs – Roger Joseph Teillet, 50, Manitoba
25 Without Portfolio – William Ross Macdonald, 71, Ontario (senator)
26 Without Portfolio – John Watson MacNaught, 58, Prince Edward Island
27 Without Portfolio – René Tremblay, 40, Quebec

The average age was 52.3, more than a decade younger than the prime minister himself. Ontario held ten of the cabinet seats, while Quebec had eight, the Atlantic provinces five, and the West four.

Gordon was clearly the senior member of cabinet, not because of his experience in government, which was virtually non-existent, but because of his proximity to the leader and his role in the campaign that got the Liberals back into power. Other ministers seemed to accept this informal ranking, and Gordon played the role enthusiastically, despite having his confidence somewhat shaken by Pearson's initial offer of industry rather than finance. Therein lay the origins of the first cabinet restructuring under Pearson – not a formal rearrangement of offices, but a more insidious realignment of reputations. With "all the public indications" pointing to Gordon as Pearson's "chief lieutenant and source of initiative," Gordon stepped into his position as finance minister assuredly. He announced to reporters following his swearing-in that the campaign promise of "sixty days of decision" had begun, and a budget would be delivered within that time frame.[20] He then took a broom to the civil servants in Finance, requesting the appointment of R.B. Bryce as deputy minister. That required removing Kenneth Taylor, who was caught off-guard and "naturally was unhappy and upset,"[21] so his move was delayed until after the budget was presented to Parliament. That delay meant the bad feelings in Finance would simmer, leading Gordon to seek outside assistance in preparing the federal budget, a decision that, in turn, had calamitous effects. The knock-on effects of the Pearson government's insistence on speed were felt for years.

The biggest blow to the cabinet structure that emerged from the electoral victory of 1963, however, was the response to the first budget. For fifty-two days, Pearson appeared to preside over a cabinet that both leaned left, thanks to the prominent position occupied by Walter Gordon, and rested on experience, thanks to the high percentage of more "traditional" Liberals, all the while emphasizing action on the legislative front. And then on the fifty-third day of the ill-conceived yet promised "60 days of decision," Gordon delivered his first budget as finance minister. First, he was attacked in Parliament for having used outside advisers – David Stanley, a financial consultant with Wood Gundy, investment dealer Martin O'Connell, and Harvard PhD student Geoff Conway. Each had separate assignments, but given his doctoral research, it was Conway who was responsible for focussing on issues of taxation. Gordon had already been warned of Conway's "inability to know when to let go."[22] Gordon hired Conway anyway.

The second line of attack on the budget was more substantive. In keeping with his long-term concerns over foreign ownership of Canadian companies, Gordon introduced a 30 per cent tax on foreign takeovers, a decision that similarly reflected Conway's interests. In a long letter to Gordon, Conway had outlined the constraints to action on curtailing foreign ownership, but also underlined the assumption that the goal was "to walk softly but carry a big stick."[23] Gordon discussed the resulting budget with Pearson, who thought it "would put the Liberal Party on the map" but was largely "indifferent to financial matters" so may not have been particularly well-placed to comment. While Gordon had consulted outsiders and the prime minister, he hadn't adequately convinced either his fellow cabinet ministers, or the rest of the country, of the threat of foreign capital or the need to solve the problem of American investment.[24] The ensuing debate in the House was acrimonious: attacked for his use of advisers, as well as for the draconian takeover tax, Gordon was on the defensive for the next three days, "trying to keep my head out of the way of the sledge hammers as best I can."[25] In the end, he withdrew the takeover tax and offered his resignation; the former was accepted and the latter was not, but the damage to Gordon's reputation in Parliament, in the business community, and in Pearson's eyes had been catastrophic.[26]

Within three months, the leadership within cabinet had begun to shift, and the hands-off administrative style that Pearson had used so successfully in the past had begun to crack. It was clear that it was not enough to let smart, thoughtful people discuss difficult issues and reach an agreement; there had to be strong leadership from the prime minister. As Tom Kent reminded him, "you have a heavier responsibility for the initiation and coordination of policy than any Prime Minister has ever had before."[27] Pearson balked at taking some of the decisions he probably knew he should: he did not, for example, force Gordon out of cabinet over the budget debacle, despite clear indications that that would have been his preference.[28] He was somewhat more decisive in securing a French lieutenant, but not much. Having first named Lionel Chevrier to cabinet – a nod to the old guard, and a comment on his indispensability during Opposition – Pearson soon realized that the Franco-Ontarian was ill-suited to serve as a leader of the Quebec caucus. Maurice Sauvé desperately wanted the job, although he too failed to win respect in Quebec, and so Pearson ultimately tapped Guy Favreau for the job, replacing Chevrier not only as minister of justice but also as the all-important Quebec lieutenant.

The senior Quebec cabinet minister in an English-speaking prime minister's cabinet has always been an important position.[29] In the mid-1960s, it was absolutely central to the success of Pearson's ambitious program, which included acting on the report of the Bilingualism and Biculturalism Commission, named during the first flurry of activity in June 1963, and managing national unity during a period of rising separatism in Quebec. Unfortunately, for a variety of reasons, Pearson was ill-served by his French counterpart. Chevrier had proven to be too old and too distant from the events of a modernizing Quebec, but no one would call him naive. The same could not be said of Guy Favreau who "stumbled on from one blunder to another, dragging his government into a quagmire of scandal."[30]

Despite having been warned of a potential crisis brewing, Favreau had done little to prepare for the accusations that came to be known as the "Rivard affair" – a case of a Montreal man wanted in the US on drug-smuggling charges, the lawyer who handled the extradition proceedings for the US government, and a $10,000 bribe to have the charges dropped. The minister of justice handled the unfolding situation poorly as he was certain that the RCMP had dealt with the case and dispensed of it, offering first vague and then panicked answers to questions in the House.[31] But the suggestion that "persons in high positions in Ottawa have sought to bring influence to bear by calling on Mr. Pierre Lamontagne, who is a lawyer acting for the United States government"[32] had the rumour mills working overtime. Indeed, there were quite a few well-placed Liberals who were involved in attempting to bribe the lawyer, including Raymond Denis, the executive assistant to the minister of citizenship and immigration and, more damning, Guy Rouleau, parliamentary secretary to the prime minister. Both resigned. So too did Favreau, once the ensuing commission criticized the justice minister for not laying charges against the two who had offered bribes.[33]

Pearson tried as much as possible to stay above the fray. On the one hand, Favreau was a vital link to the Quebec caucus and to the Liberal voters in the province, as well as having already achieved a key agreement on a constitutional amending formula with the provincial premiers. On the other, though, he was increasingly a liability in Parliament, where a hungry Conservative Opposition circled. Pearson's approach, in this case as always, was to let his ministers fend for themselves. One of his great strengths as leader was his capacity to delegate and not interfere; those moments when Pearson himself had to step in suggested that the trust had been misplaced. In the Rivard affair, Pearson largely left Favreau to manage the crisis, which eventually meant that Favreau had little option but to resign his position in Justice.[34] The prime minister convinced him to stay in cabinet as president of the Privy Council and continued to rely on him as his Quebec lieutenant, but Favreau was broken – politically and physically. He died two years after the release of the Dorion report on the Rivard Affair, barely fifty.

Other scandals rocked the Pearson cabinet in the winter of 1964–5 as well: Yvon Dupuis, minister of state, was accused of accepting a bribe during his previous political incarnation in the Quebec assembly and faced criminal charges. Favreau was tasked with securing his resignation, a vastly more onerous process than had been anticipated. At the same time, two other scandals were developing, one involving Maurice Lamontagne's "purchase" on credit of expensive furniture from a Montreal store that declared bankruptcy in 1964, the other a case of administrative favouritism in a deportation case. Pearson's press secretary, Dick O'Hagan, warned that the government could not "afford to allow another tempest to develop into a major storm" and as a result, the deportation case of Onofrio Minaudo largely evaded scrutiny.[35] Lamontagne's furniture-on-credit problem, however, erupted into a parliamentary circus. The Liberal scandals of the "winter of discontent" all eventually subsided from view, as scandals are wont to do, when the Gerda Munsinger affair – concerning Conservative behaviour in the Diefenbaker years rather than current Liberal malfeasance – turned attention elsewhere. The damage had already been done to the Quebec representation in Pearson's cabinet, however, where he largely continued with a program heavy on legislation relating to Quebec but lacking a strong voice around the cabinet table.

Pearson was able to manage a legislative agenda that included several important social policy initiatives, all of which represented threats to provincial autonomy, by building alliances with the Lesage Liberal regime in Quebec City, and by relying on English-speaking cabinet ministers and advisers who were sympathetic to the increasingly disgraced French contingent in cabinet. The result was an important decentralization of constitutional power in Canada, and the completion of an enviable national social security net. Neither was achieved exactly to plan.

Among the many promises of the sixty days of decision was preliminary work on the achievement of a national contributory pension scheme, a job that fell to the inexperienced but highly regarded new minister of national health and welfare, Judy LaMarsh. She was Pearson's one nod to gender in a cabinet otherwise dominated by men: when Pauline Jewett asked about a cabinet position, she was informed there was already a woman in cabinet.[36] LaMarsh had seventeen years of devoted service to the Liberal Party under her belt, a thriving law practice, and energy and determination in equal measure; what she lacked in moderation she made up for in enthusiasm. But energy and enthusiasm were not alone enough to manoeuvre a national pension plan into being, and the early missteps that characterized LaMarsh's time in office diminished her star considerably.

Negotiations around a portable pension scheme began badly with an awkward confrontation between Ontario Conservative premier John Robarts and LaMarsh at a ministerial meeting, followed by the increasing opposition of the insurance industry to any sort of public pension scheme, and finally capped off with a Dominion-Provincial conference in Quebec City over Easter 1964. There, Jean Lesage announced, to great fanfare, a provincial pension scheme. Quebec would not be joining any federal pension plan, nor, it would seem, were many of the other provinces. LaMarsh and Gordon, two lions of the left in the Pearson cabinet, "left the conference in low spirits," believing that "all the work had been in vain, and the pension plan was dead."[37]

As it turned out, the pension plan was revived, but the left wing of the Pearson cabinet had been fatally wounded. The social policy saviours came from the backrooms, not the cabinet room, in the spring of 1964. Progressive cabinet ministers, including Guy Favreau, Maurice Lamontagne, Walter Gordon, Allan MacEachen, Judy LaMarsh, and Harry Hays "were adamant: no concessions, no retreat."[38] The federal government had devised a plan that would provide portable retirement pensions to Canadians from coast to coast, and they were not about to have that derailed by a premier who had a similar and, frankly, better plan up his sleeve. Knowing that any solution to the logjam would have to be both political and worked out behind the scenes, both Tom Kent in the Prime Minister's Office and Gordon Robertson in the Privy Council Office set to work – independently – convincing Pearson to let them try to salvage the deal. Kent urged Pearson to get some control over the issue and make "a deal with Quebec," the absence of which had been "our great failure." He then pondered, "What can we offer Quebec which is enough for Lesage to triumph over his wild men[?]" and ended up concluding that that would entail meeting "Quebec's pride by, in several other respects, adopting its plan, ... [with] the extra fund [being] under provincial control for investment."[39]

A hurried trip to Quebec City followed, which, due to its success, received considerable attention in the press once it was made public.[40] The other negotiation was within the cabinet, where Pearson had to convince a table full of colleagues who had resisted retreat of any kind that this particular deal was worth supporting, and was considerably better than nothing at all. LaMarsh was livid that she had not been part of the negotiations, and offered her resignation; others, in particular Gordon, moved together in solidarity and supported the deal.[41] But at the end of the day, the agreement over what would become known as the Canada Pension Plan and the Quebec Pension Plan was a political agreement reached by non-elected advisers. It was hardly a power-grab, as it was clearly a solution cobbled together in the face of near total failure, but the result was a siphoning of power away from the Pearson cabinet. Nowhere was this truer than for the left-leaning ministers who had arranged themselves around Pearson in the previous decade.

With more failures than successes to his credit, Walter Gordon's "disenchantment with politics was running deep," and he had no real intention of running again in the next election. But Pearson's power of persuasion worked its magic, and with the understanding that he would retain his position as finance minister, Gordon agreed once again to take on the task of running the next campaign.[42] He leapt into the role enthusiastically, encouraging the prime minister to run on his social policy successes. Gordon agreed, for example, that it would be impossible to jump right into a fight with the provinces over national health insurance but urged that "some mention or reference to medicare should be included in the Speech [from the Throne]. Its complete omission would be unwise." He also pressed Pearson to emphasize "what we have done and are doing in the field of old age pensions, [and] unemployment assistance."[43] There was little in Gordon's behaviour in the spring of 1965 that suggested the early missteps around the budget or the pension plan had left him chastened. Instead, he pressed the prime minister constantly to call an election, and to do so on the grounds that the government he led was building an important social security net and needed a majority mandate to do so more effectively. Pearson vacillated. The Liberals prospects, according to pollster Oliver Quayle, fluctuated as well. By the time Pearson did call an election in the fall of 1965, the path to a majority was uncertain and the Liberals proved unable to navigate towards one, falling two seats short of the elusive goal.

The election of 1965 was a turning point in the organization of the Pearson cabinet. While the first administration was led by a group of mostly men who could rightly claim to lean to the left, the second administration shifted in the opposite direction. Gordon's leadership disappeared: in the wake of the disappointing election results, he offered his resignation. "I gave you bad advice, both as a minister and as a campaign chairman," he wrote. "I accept full responsibility for this and therefore submit my resignation from the Cabinet."[44] In accepting this, Pearson decapitated the left; in appointing Mitchell Sharp as finance minister, and Robert Winters as minister of trade and commerce, he empowered the right wing of the Liberal Party and tipped the whole balance of cabinet.[45] Gone were Gordon, Lamontagne, and René Tremblay; LaMarsh was demoted to secretary of state; there was still a reformist section, but it was now younger, less experienced, and considerably less powerful. The social policy agenda that had been set in 1963 was in jeopardy.

And yet, despite a more cautious finance minister, despite a change in leadership at the Department of National Health and Welfare, and despite, more importantly, the shift in who had the prime minister's ear, the new Pearson administration moved in remarkably similar directions to the previous one. Sharp's tenure in Finance was marked by some concessions to chartered banks in amendments to the Bank Act and the tabling of a motion on economic nationalism that essentially silenced the issue that had been so central to Walter Gordon; it also, however, saw an agreement reached over the implementation of an extraordinarily costly national health insurance system.

One of the reasons that the change in the ideological orientation of cabinet did not seriously subvert the social policy agenda of the Pearson government was that other, less ideologically divisive, issues began to dominate the landscape. Quebec was the most pressing. While Lesage had been something of a thorn in the pension discussions, he had actually proved to be amenable to working with Ottawa. The same could not be said either of the Front de Libération du Québec, which was beginning to make itself known through its bombing campaign, or of the rejuvenated Union Nationale under Daniel Johnson. Separatist forces were gaining strength in Quebec, and that became a matter that preoccupied the federal cabinet in the years after 1965. The work of the Bilingualism and Biculturalism Commission, the concessions over pensions, and the introduction of a Canadian flag in 1965 were all part of a commitment to linguistic accommodation, but they were not enough. With the arrival in 1965 of the "three wise men"– Pierre Trudeau, Jean Marchand, and Gérard Pelletier – the cabinet commitment to solving the Quebec problem was complete, and increasingly focused on the constitution and therefore on the Department of Justice. Old divisions of left and right no longer seemed quite as relevant in the new environment.

The new cabinet:

1 Prime Minister – Lester Bowles Pearson, 68, Ontario
2 Agriculture – John James Greene, 45, Ontario
3 Citizenship and Immigration – Jean Marchand, Quebec
4 Defence Production – Charles Mills Drury, 52, Quebec
5 External Affairs – Paul Joseph James Martin, 61, Ontario
6 Finance and Receiver General – Mitchell Sharp, 53, Ontario
7 Fisheries – Hédard Robichaud, 54, New Brunswick
8 Forestry – Maurice Sauvé, 42, Quebec
9 Justice and Attorney General – Lucien Cardin, 46, Quebec
10 Labour – Robert Nicholson, 64, British Columbia

11 Mines and Technical Surveys – Jean-Luc Pépin, 41, Quebec
12 National Defence – Paul Theodore Hellyer, 42, Ontario
13 Associate Minister of National Defence – Léo Cadieux, 57, Quebec
14 National Health and Welfare – Allan MacEachen, 48, Nova Scotia
15 National Revenue – Edgar J. Benson, 42, Ontario
16 Northern Affairs and National Resources – Arthur Laing, 61, British
     Columbia
17 Postmaster General – Jean-Pierre Côté, 39, Quebec
18 President of the Privy Council – Guy Favreau, 48, Quebec
19 Public Works – James McIlraith, 57, Ontario
20 Secretary of State of Canada – Julia Verlyn LaMarsh, 40, Ontario
21 Solicitor General – Lawrence Pennell, 51, Ontario
22 Trade and Commerce – Robert H. Winters, 55, Ontario
23 Transport – John W. Pickersgill, 60, Newfoundland
24 Veterans Affairs – Roger Joseph Teillet, 53, Manitoba
25 Without Portfolio – John Turner, 36, Quebec
26 Without Portfolio – René Tremblay, 42, Quebec
27 Without Portfolio – John Connolly, 59, Ontario (senator)

For the most part, Pearson left Quebec to others. Indeed, that was his approach to each of the departments – even to External Affairs, with which he had been so long intimately involved. He rarely intervened in the broad-ranging cabinet discussions he moderated. One exception, however, was over medicare, and then only at the end of his tenure in office. Owing much to the way that the pension negotiations with the provinces had unfolded, civil servants in the Department of Finance first proposed a strategy for reaching agreement over health insurance. While the politicians fretted over when to call an election, Al Johnson, a new assistant deputy minister of finance recruited from the CCF government of Saskatchewan, was thinking about health insurance. To avoid confrontations with the provinces over jurisdiction, Johnson argued, why not simply make federal funding contingent upon provinces "enact[ing] legislation which established a plan in conformity with the principles enunciated by the Federal Government after, and as a consequence of, consultation with the provinces."[46] The plan was, as Tom Kent recalled, "the kind of solution that, once you have heard it, you kick yourself for having failed to think of."[47]

With a strategy in place, all that remained was to put it into action. Provincial premiers were unsurprisingly irritated by the federal government's perceived blackmail: money for health insurance would come only if provinces introduced plans that conformed to Ottawa's criteria, but the amount of money (50 per cent sharing of costs) was ultimately too good to turn down. Cabinet, now without Gordon's leadership or Kent's management from the PMO, was more resistant – not, as Sharp recalled, because of the policy itself, but because of "the timing

Image 13.1. Pearson with his three successors as Liberal leader, Pierre Trudeau, John Turner, and Jean Chrétien, April 1967

Source: Duncan Cameron, Library and Archives Canada, PA-117107.

of the introduction of medicare," which might create "administrative problems" and "adverse effects upon international confidence in the financial position of the government."[48] Others were equally reluctant to push ahead towards implementation on 1 July 1967, and health insurance was postponed until the following year. Even that later date was too early for some, and as the cabinet spiralled towards crisis, cash-strapped premiers reluctant to privilege health care over other pressing provincial issues became more voluble in their criticism.[49]

Eventually, Pearson himself had to step in. This was a rare occurrence in his handling of cabinet, where he was known more for his "pragmatism and diplomacy" and his reluctance "to take a clear position when there was dissent."[50] Indeed, it was that very capacity to let the debate rage, combined with his building of a cabinet team with many strong and diverse voices, that frequently irritated colleagues most about Pearson. Often accused of indecision, which was probably more likely a failure to take the side of the commentator, Pearson's successful management of cabinet depended on his charm. As his administration wound to a close in 1968 – he had already announced his retirement, and cabinet was roiling as much because of competing leadership campaigns as about disagreements over medicare[51] – Pearson dropped the charm and put his foot down. Cabinet needed to decide to either proceed or delay, and it needed to decide immediately. The forces in favour of proceeding with the 1 July deadline carried the day, but not without necessitating a warning from the prime minister that "all members of the government would be expected to support the government's position unequivocally."[52]

The leadership race that had interfered with the functioning of cabinet in the waning days of the Pearson government was eventually won by Pierre Trudeau, the minister of justice. He took immediate steps to distance himself from the Pearson approach to cabinet government by introducing a new system that empowered committees "to take decisions in a wide area of activity" and thereby share the burden formerly carried by the cabinet as a whole.[53] The goal was to streamline decision-making; the implication was that decisions in the Pearson period had been taken haphazardly or at least inefficiently. Perhaps that was true. Perhaps Trudeau's principal secretary, Marc Lalonde, was insightful in describing Pearson's office as akin to a train station, with only one person sure where the trains were heading.[54] Regardless of the appearance of chaos, regardless of the commitment to debate around the cabinet table, regardless of consistently naming to cabinet strong, experienced, and voluble people with widely divergent ideas, Pearson's cabinet worked. Its legislative legacy is a lasting one, with pensions and health insurance, a national flag and a tentative truce with Quebec, an Auto Pact that pointed the direction towards the North American Free Trade Agreement and so much more. If there is a lesson in Pearson's statecraft, it is that there are benefits to a light hand and a thick skin, to using quiet diplomacy over administrative management strategies, and to taking the long view rather than the short, even in a minority parliamentary position. And also, perhaps, that the key to a cabinet that works is to create alliances that will lead to actual governing.

NOTES

1 Herman Bakvis, *Regional Ministers: Power and Influence in the Canadian Cabinet* (Toronto: University of Toronto Press, 1991); Herman Bakvis, "Prime Minister and Cabinet in Canada: An Autocracy in Need of Reform?," *Journal of Canadian Studies* 35, no. 1 (2001): 60–79; Donald Savoie, *Governing from the Centre: The Concentration of Power in Canadian Politics* (Toronto: University of Toronto Press, 1999); Donald Savoie, *Breaking the Bargain: Public Servants, Ministers, and Parliament* (Toronto: University of Toronto Press, 2003); and Graham White, *Cabinets and First Ministers* (Vancouver: University of British Columbia Press, 2005).
2 "About Cabinet," Government of Canada (website), last modified 26 June 2023, https://www.canada.ca/en/privy-council/services/about-cabinet.html.

3 Quoted in David Bercuson, *True Patriot: The Life of Brooke Claxton, 1898–1960* (Toronto: University of Toronto Press, 1993), 281. For a review of the St-Laurent government, see Patrice Dutil, ed., *The Unexpected Louis St-Laurent: Politics and Policies for a Modern Canada* (Vancouver: University of British Columbia Press, 2020).

4 Charles Dunning to Connolly, 13 November 1957, Library and Archives Canada (hereafter "LAC"), National Liberal Federation Papers, vol. 876, J.J. Connolly file; and P.E. Bryden, *Planners and Politicians: Liberal Politics and Social Policy, 1957–1968* (Montreal: McGill-Queen's University Press, 1997), 34–5.

5 See John English, *The Worldly Years: The Life of Lester Pearson, 1949–1972* (Toronto: Alfred A. Knopf, 1992), 195–8. Pearson received 1,084 votes to Paul Martin Sr.'s 305.

6 John English, "Pearson, Lester Bowles," in *Dictionary of Canadian Biography*, vol. 20, accessed 5 September 2024, https://www.biographi.ca/en/bio/pearson_lester_bowles_20E.html.

7 See Bryden, *Planners and Politicians*, 55–64.

8 Tom Kent, *A Public Purpose: An Experience of Liberal Opposition and Canadian Government* (Kingston: McGill-Queen's University Press, 1988), 63–4.

9 Robert Fulford, "The Puzzling – to Almost Everyone – Personality of Lester B. Pearson," *Maclean's*, 6 April 1963, 7.

10 Gordon to Pearson, 5 November 1959, J.L. Granatstein Archives (hereafter "JLGA"), Walter Gordon Papers.

11 Christina McCall-Newman, *Grits: An Intimate Portrait of the Liberal Party* (Toronto: Macmillan, 1982), 165.

12 *Mike: The Memoirs of the Rt. Hon. Lester B. Pearson*, vol. 3, ed. John A. Munro and Alex I. Inglis (Toronto: University of Toronto Press, 1975), 85.

13 *Mike*, 3:93.

14 *Mike*, 3:89.

15 Quoted in Denis Smith, *Gentle Patriot: A Political Biography of Walter Gordon* (Edmonton: Hurtig, 1973), 134.

16 Kent, *Public Purpose*, 202–26.

17 Press release, 15 May 1963, LAC, James Coutts Papers, R13437, vol. 18, file 29, Office of the PM, 1964–66.

18 Stanley Westall, "Mr. Pearson's Cabinet: A Deep Bow toward Confederation," *Globe and Mail*, 23 April 1963.

19 Stanley Westall, "Evolution of the Cabinet," *Globe and Mail*, 11 July 1964, SM10.

20 Smith, *Gentle Patriot*, 136–7.

21 Smith, *Gentle Patriot*, 137.

22 David Stanley to Walter Gordon, 16 April 1963, JLGA, Walter Gordon Papers.

23 Conway to Gordon, 13 April 1963, JLGA, Walter Gordon Papers.

24 Stephen Azzi, "'It Was Walter's View': Lester Pearson, the Liberal Party and Economic Nationalism," in *Pearson: The Unlikely Gladiator*, ed. Norman Hillmer (Montreal: McGill-Queen's University Press, 1999), 120.

25 Quoted in Stephen Azzi, *Walter Gordon and the Rise of Canadian Nationalism* (Montreal: McGill-Queen's University Press, 1999), 106–7.

26 See Azzi, *Walter Gordon*, 102–10; Stephen Azzi, "Minority Governments and Canada's Confused Foreign Investment Policy," *International Journal* 75 no. 4 (December 2020): 505–6; John N. McDougall, *The Politics and Economics of Eric Kierans: A Man for All Canada* (Montreal: McGill-Queen's University Press, 1993), 43–7; and Peter C. Newman, "What Really Happened to Walter Gordon," *Maclean's*, 19 October 1963. Eric Kierans, president of the Montreal Stock Exchange, wrote Gordon a scathing letter that was instrumental in the withdrawal of the takeover tax; it began, "The financial capitals of the world have just about had enough of Canada...." See Kierans to Gordon, 18 June 1963, LAC, L.B. Pearson fonds, MG 26 N 3, vol. 51, file 251-1963.

27 Kent to L.B.P., 4 August 1963, Queen's University Archives (hereafter "QUA"), Thomas Worrall Kent fonds, vol. 2, Correspondence, 1 August 1963–19 August 1963.

28 English, *Worldly Years*, 275.

29 See Frederick W. Gibson, ed., *Cabinet Formation and Bicultural Relations: Seven Case Studies*, Studies of the Royal Commission on Bilingualism and Biculturalism (Ottawa: Queen's Printer, 1970).

30 Richard J. Gwyn, *The Shape of Scandal: A Study of Government in Crisis* (Toronto: Clarke, Irwin, 1965), 13.

31 Gwyn, *Shape of Scandal*, 11–26; and Kent, *Public Purpose*, 324–30.

32 Tommy Douglas, in *House of Commons Debates*, 26th parl., 2nd sess., vol. 10, 23 November 1964, 10367.

33 *Special Public Inquiry 1964: Report of the Commissioner, the Honourable Frédéric Dorion* (Ottawa: Queen's Printer, 1965).

34 Pearson wriggled out of being implicated in the Rivard affair himself by corresponding directly with Dorion about the details of the testimony that had been given – clarifying, elaborating, and creating a parliamentary maelstrom in December 1964, but a clearer statement of his own innocence when the report was finally released the following July. See Kent, *Public Purpose*, 328; and LBP to Dorion, 29 June 1965, LAC, Pearson Papers, MG 26 N 3, vol. 210, file 574, Rivard Case – correspondence with Justice Dorion.

35 Richard O'Hagan to LBP, 22 December 1964, LAC, Pearson Papers, MG 26 N 3, vol. 209, file 574-Minaudo.

36 English, *Worldly Years*, 266–7.

37 Judy LaMarsh, *Memoirs of a Bird in a Gilded Cage* (Toronto: McClelland & Stewart, 1967), 90. The most thorough analysis of the negotiations around pensions remains Richard Simeon's *Federal-Provincial Diplomacy: The Making of Recent Policy in Canada* (Toronto: University of Toronto Press, 1972; repr., 2006).

38 Kent, *Public Purpose*, 275.

39 Kent to Pearson, 7 April 1964, QUA, Tom Kent fonds, box 3, file 10, Correspondence, April 1964.

40 See, e.g., Bruce Macdonald, "PM Promises to Boost Provinces' Tax Share: Adopt Lesage View on Pensions Level," *Globe and Mail,* 20 April 1964, 1.

41 Gordon to LBP, "Re: Tom's Note on Timing," 15 April 1964, LAC, Walter Gordon Papers, vol. 16, file Pearson, Rt. Hon. L.B. – Correspondence and Memos; and LaMarsh, *Gilded Cage*, 89–92.

42 Smith, *Gentle Patriot*, 211–12.

43 Gordon to LBP, 27 January 1965, LAC, Walter Gordon Papers, vol. 16, file 11.

44 Gordon to Pearson, 9 November 1965, LAC, Walter Gordon Papers, vol. 16, file 11.

45 See Smith, *Gentle Patriot*, 242–68, for a complete discussion of the Gordon resignation. Smith maintains that it did not have to unfold in this way: cabinet as a whole had agreed on the timing of the election, and cabinet as a whole had accepted responsibility for failing to win enough seats to form a majority. Gordon acted on a point of honour – that he would resign if the Liberals failed to secure a majority – but also manoeuvred (through the entreaties of others) to retain his finance portfolio. Pearson wasn't amenable to this and seems to have seen the election results as a useful opportunity to rearrange cabinet.

46 Al Johnson to Robert Bryce, 16 July 1965, LAC, RG19, Department of Finance Papers, vol. 4854, file 5508-02, pt. 1.

47 Kent, *Public Purpose*, 366.

48 Mitchell Sharp, *Which Reminds Me ... : A Memoir* (Toronto: University of Toronto Press, 1994), 149.

49 Walter Gordon, who had returned to cabinet in 1967, provides a useful timeline of the brewing crisis. See "Summary of Views Expressed by Provincial Ministers of Finance on the Subject of Medicare at the November 16–17 Meeting of Finance Ministers," cabinet document no. 761/67, LAC, Walter Gordon Papers, vol. 16, file 13; "Note of Matters to Discuss with Mike on 29 December 1966," confidential memo to file, 4 January 1967, LAC, Walter Gordon Papers, vol. 16, LBP file; and "The Position of the Government at the Present Time," 3 October 1967, LAC, Walter Gordon Papers, vol. 16, file 13.

50 Sharp, *Which Reminds Me*, 109.

51 See F. Burns Roth, "Health," in *Canadian Annual Review of Public Affairs, 1968*, ed. J.T. Saywell (Toronto: University of Toronto Press, 1969), 380.

52 Cabinet Conclusions, 1 February 1968, LAC, Privy Council Office, Series A-5-a, vol. 6338.

53 Pierre Trudeau, letter to all ministers, 10 July 1968, LAC, P.E. Trudeau fonds, MG 26 O 11, vol. 60, file *312, Government – Federal Executive – The Cabinet – Personal and Confidential 1968–Sept. 1969.

54 Marc Lalonde, in Robert Bothwell and J.L. Granatstein, *Trudeau's World: Insiders Reflect on Foreign Policy, Trade and Defence, 1968–84* (Vancouver: University of British Columbia Press, 2017), 16.

14 Pierre *inter pares*: Cabinet under Pierre Elliott Trudeau, 1968–1979

ASA MCKERCHER

Upon becoming prime minister in April 1968 amid great hoopla, Pierre Trudeau declared a break from the past: "new guys with new ideas" were now in office and cabinet procedures would be overhauled accordingly.[1] As Trudeau later noted, he had hoped to reinforce ministerial solidarity and reassert ministers' role in decision-making over that of the civil service.[2] However, other commentators, led principally by political scientist Donald Savoie, traced an alternate result of Trudeau's cabinet reforms: instead of bolstering ministers, they reinforced the prime minister's authority at their expense. In Savoie's view, Trudeau consolidated his control by strengthening the Prime Minister's Office (PMO) and the Privy Council Office (PCO).[3]

It is difficult to contradict this claim. Trudeau was motivated to avoid the seeming tumult of Lester B. Pearson's ministry and by a sense that, with the growth of government, a more centralized power was needed to steer the ship of state. Moreover, there was, I argue, a particular set of circumstances that accelerated the age-old drive to centralize, namely a magnetic, intelligent, highly capable individual serving as first minister who eroded the confidence of the more independent ministers. They gradually left the government, yielding their portfolios to a more malleable bunch. This mix of factors produced a situation in which it was indeed possible to govern from the centre. However, judged from this volume's focus on statecraft, Trudeau, for all his gifts, proved a lacklustre figure. When it came to political management, collegial management, and state management, his centralization of power over the course of his first ministry made the task of statecraft an unwieldly one.

Cabinet-making for Trudeaumanic Times

Trudeaumania swept through Canada in early 1968, seemingly promising a new dawn. Delegates to the Liberal leadership convention, enthused the *Ottawa Citizen*'s editors, had "made a decision to embark on an adventurous and challenging approach to the future of the nation," while the *Toronto Star* dubbed the new Liberal leader and prime minister Pierre Elliott Trudeau, "A Modern Man for Canada."[4] Yet when Trudeau unveiled his first cabinet on 20 April, Canadians discovered it was very much a carryover from that of Lester B. Pearson.

Of the twenty-five members of the cabinet, there were only three new faces, all ministers without portfolio: Donald S. Macdonald from Toronto, John Munro from Hamilton, and Gérard Pelletier, the former editor of *La Presse* in Montreal. He, Trudeau, and Jean Marchand, were the "Three Wise Men" from Quebec, recruited by Pearson to fight the budding Quebec separatism. Of the remaining cabinet portfolios all but a few were filled by their previous occupants, including Trudeau as minister of justice and president of the Privy Council (a combination Sir John A. Macdonald had devised in 1867). The exceptions were: Mitchell Sharp taking over External Affairs, paving the way for Edgar (Ben) Benson to serve at Finance; Bud Drury replacing Jean-Luc Pepin at Trade and Commerce; Pepin becoming labour minister; and John Turner becoming solicitor general in addition to retaining his prior post at Consumer and Corporate Affairs. Jean Marchand held his existing position at Manpower and Immigration to take on the role of secretary of state. Paul Martin Sr., formerly at External Affairs, was now one of six ministers without portfolio while also serving as government leader in the Senate. As Pearson had done since 1967, Trudeau left the position of associate minister of national defence empty and would continue to do so throughout his premiership. Reflecting the cabinet's transitory nature, several ministers did double duty – triple in Drury's case.

1 Prime Minister; Justice and Attorney General; President of the Privy Council – Pierre Trudeau, 48, Quebec
2 Agriculture – John James (Joe) Greene, 48, Ontario
3 Consumer and Corporate Affairs; Solicitor General – John Turner, 38, Ontario
4 Energy, Mines and Resources; Labour – Jean-Luc Pepin, 43, Quebec
5 External Affairs – Mitchell Sharp, 56, Ontario
6 Finance and Treasury Board – Edgar J. (Ben) Benson, 44, Ontario
7 Fisheries – Hédard Robichaud, 56, New Brunswick
8 Forestry and Rural Development – Maurice Sauvé, 44, Quebec
9 Indian Affairs and Northern Development – Arthur Laing, 63, British Columbia
10 Industry; Defence Production; Trade and Commerce – Charles M. (Bud) Drury, 55, Quebec
11 Manpower and Immigration; Secretary of State – Jean Marchand, 49, Quebec

12 National Defence – Léo Cadieux, 59, Quebec
13 National Health and Welfare – Allan MacEachen, 46, Nova Scotia
14 National Revenue – Jean Chrétien, 34, Quebec
15 Postmaster General – Jean-Pierre Côté, 42, Quebec
16 Public Works – George McIlraith, 59, Ontario
17 Transport – Paul Hellyer, 44, Ontario (on 1 May, Hellyer was also named "Senior Minister," a designation that he could act as prime minister if Trudeau was absent.)
18 Veterans Affairs – Roger Teillet, 55, Manitoba
19 Without Portfolio – Charles Granger, 55, Newfoundland
20 Without Portfolio – Paul Martin, 64, Ontario (senator)
21 Without Portfolio – Donald Macdonald, 36, Ontario
22 Without Portfolio – Bryce Mackasey, 46, Quebec
23 Without Portfolio – John Munro, 37, Ontario
24 Without Portfolio – Gérard Pelletier, 48, Quebec

Overall, this minor housekeeping had stemmed from a handful of retirements (John Robert Nicholson at Labour and Lawrence Pennell as solicitor general), as well as two notable resignations by members of Pearson's cabinet: Judy LaMarsh, Pearson's secretary of state and a fierce critic of Trudeau at the Liberal leadership convention, and Minister of Trade and Commerce Robert Winters, Trudeau's chief leadership rival and the standard-bearer of the party's conservative wing. Even though the cabinet remained largely unchanged from Pearson's ministry, press coverage stressed a more youthful look: the members' average age was 48.7, more than two years younger than under Pearson, and the cabinet included Jean Chrétien (34), Macdonald (36), Munro (37), and Turner (38).[5] This was the cabinet Trudeau brought into the 25 June 1968 federal election.

The Liberals' decisive victory – the first majority government elected through four elections – put Trudeau on firm ground to bring about his goals of implementing his promise of a "Just Society" with participatory democracy for all. Columnist Peter C. Newman urged him to fulfil his "duty to represent all the long repressed aspirations of his generation."[6] Doing so meant, first, increasing government's capacity for rational planning and, then, implementing policies to reach these goals, which in turn necessitated a series of reforms to cabinet, PCO, and PMO. These structural concerns were necessary to fight the habits of the Pearson government's chaotic decision-making process. What they accomplished was to transform federal governance in Canada, chiefly by centralizing power under the prime minister and creating, in the critical judgment of one of his ministers, government "run by the PMO and PCO."[7] Trudeau's initial popularity among Canadians ensured that as these reforms unfolded, ministers largely followed along. As Mitchell Sharp commented at the time, "In Pearson's cabinet we looked at Mike and said to ourselves he is

Image 14.1. Trudeau and ministers arrive for their swearing-in ceremony, 6 July 1968. From left to right: James Richardson, Don Jamieson, Trudeau, John Turner, Jean Marchand, Gérard Pelletier.

Source: Doug Ball, Canadian Press, CP2873172.

here because we're here. In Trudeau's cabinet, we looked at Pierre and said we're here because he's here."[8]

Trudeau shuffled his cabinet right after the election. Most members of the pre-election cabinet carried on, but in new roles. More than half were deeply experienced: Of the twenty-nine ministers, seventeen had served under Pearson. Two (Martin and Hellyer) had even served under Louis St-Laurent. Clearly, Trudeau sought to retain talent but did not abandon his promise to bring in some fresh blood, given that he himself was a relative novice in federal politics. Marc Lalonde, Trudeau's principal secretary, acknowledged that the new prime minister and many of his key advisers were "a whole bunch of amateurs who were given the Liberal Party by its members."[9] In a show of party unity, Trudeau took the step of appointing to cabinet six of his challengers at the leadership convention: Joe Greene, Eric Kierans, Paul Hellyer, Allan MacEachen, Paul Martin, and John Turner. Later commenting on this team of rivals, one cabinet member marvelled that Trudeau was able "to keep so many egos in line and working full tilt."[10] That observation proved true, at least for a time. Unlike with the caretaker cabinet, no ministers did double duty except for

Jean-Luc Pepin, who served as minister of industry and minister of trade and commerce, foreshadowing the imminent merging of these two departments. Trudeau, for his part, abandoned the justice portfolio, handing it to Turner.

Appointments reflected the favourable electoral results in that Liberal MPs had been returned in every province save Prince Edward Island. The West had greater representation than under Pearson. Appointed minister of agriculture, Bud Olson was one of four Alberta Liberals elected (from a rural riding no less), while Otto Lang, as minister without portfolio, was one of two Liberals elected in Saskatchewan. British Columbia's representation jumped from a single minister to three, with Ron Basford (consumer and corporate affairs) and Jack Davis (fisheries) joining Arthur Laing (public works). Roger Teillet, the first self-identifying Métis member of the federal cabinet, had lost his nomination in June 1968, and so James Richardson represented Manitoba as a minister without portfolio. Electoral fortunes also played out in regard to Newfoundland, where Charles Granger had been defeated, leaving Don Jamieson to represent the province while sitting as minister of defence production. Hédard Robichaud had not run in 1968, and so Jean-Eudes Dubé (veterans affairs) stood in for New Brunswick, while Allan J. MacEachen (manpower and immigration) remained chieftain of Nova Scotia. As would be expected from a Liberal government by this time, the bulk of cabinet ministers hailed from Ontario and Quebec.

Some commentators have stressed that Trudeau's first true cabinet was "thoroughly engrossed in Quebec politics" or otherwise very Quebec-centric.[11] That may have been true in terms of outlook, but not raw numbers. Trudeau's caretaker cabinet had had nine individuals from Ontario holding eleven portfolios and ten individuals from Quebec holding fifteen positions, while his post-election cabinet had ten Ontario ministers with ten portfolios and nine Quebec ministers with ten portfolios. These numbers are equivalent to the cabinet assembled in the waning days of Pearson's government, which had nine Ontario ministers with ten portfolios and nine Quebec ministers with twelve portfolios. Throughout Trudeau's ministry, Ontario and Quebec would have a rough parity in representation around the cabinet table.

Of the Quebec contingent, Trudeau had his fellow Wise Men, Marchand and Pelletier, other francophone ministers from across the province, as well as anglophone Montrealers Bud Drury, Bryce Mackasey, and Eric Kierans. As for Ontario ministers, cabinet members hailed from all the major cities, including Windsor (Paul Martin), Hamilton (John Munro), and Kingston (Ben Benson). Having won back legendary Liberal warhorse C.D. Howe's old seat at Port Arthur from the NDP, Robert Andras entered cabinet as a minister without portfolio. Notably, there were no female members of Trudeau's cabinet:

1 Prime Minister – Pierre Trudeau, Quebec
2 Agriculture – Horace (Bud) Olson, Alberta

3 Consumer and Corporate Affairs – Stanley Ronald Basford, British Columbia
4 Defence Production – Donald Jamieson, Newfoundland
5 Energy, Mines, and Resources – John James (Joe) Greene, Ontario
6 External Affairs – Mitchell Sharp, Ontario
7 Finance and Receiver General – Edgar (Ben) Benson, Ontario
8 Fisheries – Jack Davis, British Columbia
9 Forestry and Rural Development – Jean Marchand, Quebec
10 Indian Affairs and Northern Development – Jean Chrétien, Quebec
11 Industry; Trade, and Commerce – Jean-Luc Pepin, Quebec
12 Justice and Attorney General – John Turner, Ontario
13 Labour – Bryce Mackasey, Quebec
14 Leader of the Government in the Senate – Paul Martin, Ontario (senator)
15 Manpower and Immigration – Allan MacEachen, Nova Scotia
16 National Defence – Léo Cadieux, Quebec
17 National Health and Welfare – John Munro, Ontario
18 National Revenue – Jean-Pierre Côté, Quebec
19 Postmaster General – Eric Kierans, Quebec
20 President of the Privy Council – Donald Macdonald, Ontario
21 Public Works – Arthur Laing, British Columbia
22 Secretary of State of Canada – Gérard Pelletier, Quebec
23 Solicitor General – George McIlraith, Ontario
24 Transport – Paul Hellyer, Ontario
25 Treasury Board – Charles M. (Bud) Drury, Quebec
26 Veterans Affairs – Jean-Eudes Dubé, New Brunswick
27 Without Portfolio – Robert Andras, Ontario
28 Without Portfolio – James Richardson, Manitoba
29 Without Portfolio – Otto Lang, Saskatchewan

Given the veteran ministers and new talent, it was a strong cabinet, one that, in the view of Trudeau's biographer, "reflected hope for the future, with little reference to Ottawa's past." One minister, disagreed, offering instead that it was a cabinet that "honoured the past."[12] Certainly the general appearance was that of a more youthful ministry.

One year after assuming office, Trudeau made several additions, either through consolidating portfolios or creating new ministerial positions to meet the demands of the prime minister's structural changes to government departments. On 1 April 1969, Jean-Luc Pepin saw his two portfolios merge, making him minister of industry, trade, and commerce. Similarly, the offices of minister of fisheries and minister of forestry and rural development were replaced by a minister of fisheries and forestry, with Jack Davis at the helm. Rural Development was hived off into a new Department of Regional Economic Expansion, headed by Jean Marchand. Don Jamieson became the minister of supply and services, a position incorporating his position of minister of defence production. Finally, Eric Kierans was put in charge of a new Department of Communications.

Cabinet Reform to Ensure "Reason over Passion"

When Trudeau's first real cabinet convened three days after the swearing-in ceremony at Government House in July 1968, the prime minister declared his expectations for his ministers. His first point was to emphasize "Cabinet solidarity," the principle that decisions taken by the cabinet were backed by all ministers. "If a Minister did not agree with a decision," he stated, then they "had a right, and indeed a duty, to resign." Adding that ministerial appointments "were not forever," Trudeau mused about the possibilities of "movement out of Cabinet as well as into it," and he promised "merciless" action against anyone who leaked Cabinet confidences or documents, a reaction to the frequent leaks in the Pearson years. Next, he turned to the issue of committees, which would play a big role in the way in which his cabinet system functioned. If the committee system did not work as intended, he vowed to "move to an inner cabinet system," meaning that only a handful of ministers would wield decision-making power, leaving others with little influence.[13] With this blunt language, Trudeau asserted his authority as first minister. Behind the scenes, he had already put in motion processes to ensure that cabinet functioned more efficiently than in the past.

Cabinet unity was shaken within a year when Paul Hellyer, the "senior minister" (essentially the deputy prime minister), resigned over a dispute with the prime minister on housing policy. Trudeau buried the issue quickly and Hellyer's withdrawal seemed to be forgotten as James Richardson replaced him. Hellyer had quickly grown disillusioned with the new prime minister and his governing style. "He seemed to allow ministers total freedom to talk," Hellyer later complained, "but no decision would be taken until one by one they learned what he wanted and shifted their positions toward his."[14] Other ministers recalled that, around the cabinet table, Trudeau was less imperious than Hellyer would have it. Even so, the new prime minister's reform agenda caused some friction with ministers. In particular, the structural reforms to cabinet reinforced their awareness that their ministerial autonomy was going to be challenged by the PMO and PCO.

As Trudeau later reflected, one of his primary goals was to "review the way government itself was run."[15] Partly, this desire sprang from practical observation. When he had been appointed to Pearson's cabinet in 1967, Trudeau had been "struck by the amateurism that reigned in the upper echelons of the federal government." Notable deficiencies included lengthy and unproductive cabinet meetings and a disorganized decision-making process that bordered on the "frivolous." "I decided," he recalled, "to introduce a measure of order and rationality."[16] Rational planning was a guiding ethos for Trudeau – his slogan was "reason over passion" – a view shared by close advisers, all of whom were influenced by systems analysis. At the time, a trendy means of improving process and procedures to guide business and government, systems analysis emphasized breaking systems down into component parts to understand how they worked together, and then building guiding structures to ensure that the components worked better together to meet overarching goals. As Trudeau had explained several years before becoming prime minister, creating "political instruments which are sharper, tougher and more firmly controlled" and implementing "rational standards" were necessary steps given the growth of the modern state.[17]

In this thinking and in this task, Trudeau was joined by two key advisers, his principal secretary, Marc Lalonde, a close associate for some time, and Gordon Robertson, who had served as clerk of the Privy Council and secretary to the cabinet since 1963. Trudeau had worked for Robertson in PCO from 1949 to 1950, dealing largely with constitutional issues, and the two men had resumed contact when Trudeau returned to Ottawa as a MP in 1965. As prime minister, Trudeau met with Lalonde and Robertson at the start of each workday, and the three men would often lunch together at 24 Sussex when there was pressing business. Given Robertson's extensive experience at the top of the public service, he had become convinced, like Trudeau, that the huge growth of the state necessitated reform of government processes. "It seems to me," Robertson wrote in 1968, "that without changes from present methods there is a real risk of a steady reduction in the efficiency of government in coping with growing needs together with a shift of effective decision-making from the ministers, where it ought to be, into the hands of civil servants."[18] Likewise, Lalonde believed that, "Big government [had] overtaken both Cabinet and Parliament," with "negligible" means of controlling the "leviathan."[19] Together, they supported Trudeau's efforts to increase the power of the PMO and PCO in order to leash government, while also altering the way that cabinet functioned.

Efforts to reform cabinet focused first on improving the committee system that Pearson had introduced and second, through a formalization of decision-making. When Parliament was sitting, Trudeau's cabinet met on Thursday mornings. Cabinet committee meetings were held on Tuesday mornings and on Tuesday and Wednesday afternoons following Question Period, but also sometimes on Thursday afternoons. Clearly, ministers spent more time in committees than in full cabinet.

Cabinet committees had emerged during Pearson's premiership partly at Gordon Robertson's insistence, and Trudeau retained them as an effective means of streamlining deliberation and decision-making. A full cabinet of around thirty ministers was too large to permit effective review or debate. Smaller, more focused committees, where membership tended to average ten ministers, were more likely to develop expertise and better recommendations. Trudeau began his reform within a month of assuming office by creating eight committees: four functional committees to develop policy and four coordinating committees. The functional committees were Economic Policy, External Affairs and Defence, Social Policy, and Government Operations. The four coordinating committees, dealing with the larger direction and management of the government, were the all-important Priorities and Planning (P&P), Legislation and Planning for the House, Treasury Board, and Federal-Provincial Relations. The latter committee would eventually be merged with P&P. From time to time, Trudeau also created ad hoc committees to deal with specific issues. Ministers were assigned, on average, to two committees broadly relevant to their positions. Senior civil servants – mainly, but not exclusively deputy ministers – attended committee meetings, though only rarely in the case of P&P.

In a continuation of the practice begun under Pearson, the prime minister chaired P&P (Trudeau also chaired the Federal-Provincial Relations Committee), whose members were the chairs of the other committees as well as select ministers. P&P was the premier committee because it set government plans, which were top of mind for Trudeau and his advisers, who were committed to building policy to meet an overall plan rather than building it incrementally and in a hodgepodge fashion. Here, matters of broad and long-term scope were debated, and goals were set for ministers, whose policy proposals then had to relate to these overall plans. P&P was also where big disputes over planning were settled, rather than in the full cabinet.[20] Given its influence over the government's direction, there were accusations that P&P was an inner cabinet. However, both ministers and Gordon Robertson denied the charge, principally because the full cabinet still had to approve P&P's decisions.[21] Even so, P&P had significant influence, as did the prime minister as its chair. In this role, Lalonde noted, Trudeau "directs the setting of government priorities, the orderly development of policies and the evaluation of on-going programs."[22] Trudeau's control of P&P proved one of the markers of his central dominance.

Beyond the committee system, other cabinet processes underwent formalization. In contrast to Pearson, Trudeau brought a new rigour to cabinet discussions, cracking down on crosstalk. He demanded that agenda items be evaluated through written submissions. "I began making it clear to ministers," Trudeau later wrote, "that the cabinet could not consider a single question without having before it a formal memorandum drawn up on the authority of the minister responsible."[23] These memoranda had to follow a prescribed formula, chiefly a clear statement of the question and a listing of all possible solutions to it. Only in emergencies were oral briefings permitted.[24] The process naturally created a deluge of paper that kept gathering strength. As one veteran of the Pearson and

Trudeau governments observed, cabinet memoranda increased from an average of two pages under the former, to over a dozen under the latter, while attached supporting documents could be "a foot thick."[25] Similarly, Donald Macdonald recalled that when he first entered cabinet in 1968, he could fit cabinet memoranda into a slim ring binder; when he departed as a minister in 1977, cabinet memos required a binder three inches thick.[26] The value of this documentation flood was questioned. "Sometimes," speculated Eric Kierans, "I had a feeling that some policy wonks were more interested in writing stuff which wouldn't involve them in any sort of responsibility for the written word."[27]

All submissions to the full cabinet were first dealt with at a lower level in the committees, where debate over the nitty gritty occurred. To inform discussion, public servants – mainly deputy ministers – were invited into the committees. In Robertson's opinion, the interaction between ministers and senior officials in committee was beneficial in that it exposed civil servants "to the thinking and policy concerns of ministers" in order "to explain to their departments the logic of decisions that might otherwise seem wrong, incomprehensible or 'petty politics.'" Likewise, officials were able to brief ministers on the "functional and operations aspects" of policy questions.[28] Although civil servants were meant to provide functional advice, sometimes their briefings could get out of hand. In his memoirs, Mitchell Sharp recalled interrupting a briefing in the P&P committee by Simon Reisman, the pugnacious deputy minister of finance, by ironically observing that it was "wonderful to listen to a civil servant who knows his place." After laughs from all those present, Reisman, undeterred, continued unabated.[29] Eric Kierans noted a different phenomenon, that of officials, again from the Department of Finance, who would only distribute documents supporting cabinet memoranda at the last minute, thereby giving ministers little time to review them. In this manner, he theorized, public servants sought to have their positions "bulldozed and bamboozled" through committee.[30] While influence is always difficult to measure, a vague consensus existed that the committee system served to limit the impact of the civil service over decision-making. This was a goal for Trudeau, who viewed mandarin power as undemocratic.

If the committees reached a provisional decision, a report would then be referred to the full cabinet. If no decision on a submission was reached, the committee could send the issue to P&P or to the full cabinet in what was called a recommendation. The full cabinet tended to approve committee decisions automatically, provided there were no objections raised. And objections were seldom voiced at this stage. As Kierans noted, "when you spoke about somebody else's portfolio it was resented," with the exception that ministers could address how an issue would play locally in their constituency.[31] One commentator dubbed the resulting process by which full cabinet approval was given as "a managed consensuality."[32]

Trudeau, of course, was the central director of the process, and he was largely pleased with his overhaul to cabinet decision-making. In his memoirs he boasted that the reforms "made the practice of ministerial solidarity much easier," ensuring "coherence" across the government. Further, the committee system "vastly improved the quality of the decisions taken."[33] Certainly, much of the tough work was done in committee, meaning that by the time reports reached all ministers, they were ready to be approved. As a result, cabinet meetings were shorter and less frequent than in the past. "During my several mandates," Trudeau observed, "the Cabinet never met more than once a week ... and, except on very rare occasions, never sat longer than four hours."[34] Yet, the pace of ministerial work remained high. In 1971, Robertson reflected on the previous two and half years of the committee system, observing that as opposed to the Pearson years, under Trudeau, cabinet was "dealing with a larger volume of business but taking only half as many cabinet meetings to do it," with "minister hours" remaining the same.[35] For Trudeau and his close advisers, streamlining decision-making seemed to be a success.

Among ministers, however, there was disagreement about the utility and effectiveness of these reforms. Applauding Trudeau's efforts to reinforce cabinet solidarity, Mitchell Sharp conceded that ministers did have to spend more time in Ottawa and in committee "than they would prefer."[36] Alastair Gillespie, who first joined the cabinet in 1971, was of the latter view. Committees, he reflected, were "robbing Ministers of too much of their discretionary time." As Gillespie added, the nature of the committee work, with its meetings and lengthy memoranda, was often a distraction, leaving ministers without "sufficient time" to devote to the actual implementation of policy.[37] In effect, there was more of an emphasis on process than on performance.

Certainly, the committee system slowed down decision-making because of the steps that proposals had to go through in order to receive the full cabinet's approval. From drafting memoranda and supporting documents, to submitting proposals to committee, debating them, and then forwarding a successful report on to cabinet, decision-making was a drawn-out process. On one occasion, Gordon Robertson freely admitted that "speed of action is certainly less" than in the past, with ministers having "less chance to appear in roles of clear and firm decision."[38] On another, he mused "that C.D. Howe would have gone mad."[39] Moreover, under this system, committee members who might lack a full understanding of a file nonetheless could overrule a minister presenting their department's preferred course of action. As John Turner once groused, it was difficult to make a budget "with twenty-three God damned ministers of Finance!" In his view, the committee system "reinforced the weak and frustrated the strong."[40] Along similar lines, Marcel Cadieux, undersecretary of state for external affairs from 1964 to 1970, complained of the difficulty in getting approval for proposals put forward by his minister, Mitchell Sharp, who was forced to "submit to the vote of a majority of his colleagues who [were] concerned with their own special interests" rather than the national interests of Canada.[41]

Having a check on individual ministers and blunting the power of deputy ministers was part of Trudeau's motivation for the reforms.[42] In this respect, then, they were a success. However, even Trudeau admitted that he had "gone a bit overboard" at least in planning aspects.[43] Jim Coutts, Trudeau's principal secretary from 1975 to 1981, agreed. "While the government assembled elaborate study groups instead of action teams," he wrote, "those who simply wanted to get on with the old way of governing by solving problems were frustrated."[44] Paul Martin, who had first entered cabinet in 1946 under William Lyon Mackenzie King, likened Trudeau-era cabinet discussions to university seminars.[45] It was not a compliment.

Trudeau, erudite to a fault, excelled in this system. A voracious reader, he devoured the memoranda churned up by PCO and PMO on items coming before cabinet. What that meant, in the view of Michael Pitfield, who served as clerk of the Privy Council and cabinet secretary from 1975 to 1979, was that Trudeau "had the great advantage of knowing every minister's brief, so he knew how they would react."[46] He was, recalled Ivan Head, Trudeau's personal adviser on foreign affairs, the "best prepared at any cabinet."[47] With his intellect and with the preparation afforded him by his staff, the prime minister enjoyed a broad awareness of policies being worked out across the various departments, giving him a sense of where they could fit into the government's overall plans. Hence, the importance of P&P, and the prime minister's direction of that committee. In an interview in 1977, Trudeau remarked that he had little interest in serving as a mere "chairman of the board … waiting for a consensus to develop, and … calling out that consensus." Rather, he wanted to be in the position of being "able to challenge the minister and say, look this may be good to your particular department but have you thought of the effects of it on agriculture, on transport, or on the Treasury."[48] A large staff in the PMO gave him the ability to comment widely, enhancing his authority.

What, then, of Trudeau's conduct around the cabinet table? Observers have offered conflicting accounts. To Mitchell Sharp, he was "a remarkably effective chairman of cabinet – firm yet fair," with a penchant for asking probing questions over giving his own opinion and "genuinely" seeking consensus on issues.[49] He was not a dictatorial leader, agreed Donald Macdonald, adding that "if anything, several of us considered that he was too patient" in permitting debate.[50] For instance, Macdonald recalled that on the issue of whether Canada should pull its military forces out of Western Europe, ending its NATO commitment, Trudeau allowed debate to go on for weeks in P&P and the full cabinet. A slim majority of ministers, particularly powerful ones such as Sharp and Turner, favoured the status quo, while Macdonald and Eric Kierans were among the vocal but small minority advocating withdrawal. "Pierre never revealed his own position," Macdonald recalled, "letting the arguments play out around him," before delivering a compromise solution: Canada's military forces in Europe would be halved.[51] The middle path was perhaps typical of Trudeau. In cabinet, Chrétien revealed, the prime minister "listened more and compromised more than most Canadians imagine."[52] Indeed, as H.D. Munroe has documented, during the October Crisis, Trudeau consulted extensively with his colleagues – in committees and in the full cabinet – over the government's reaction and the invocation of the War Measures Act. This deliberative response stands in contrast to the swashbuckling prime minister of "Just watch me" fame.[53]

There was an edge to Trudeau, too. "Occasionally," Chrétien admitted, "I saw him get his way simply by interjecting a turn of phrase that indicated his position."[54] On legal or constitutional matters or questions pertaining to federalism and Quebec, Trudeau was more open about expressing his own views and debating dissenters. And so, as Macdonald acknowledged, when it came to this suite of issues of personal importance to the prime minister, "ministers learned to tread with caution."[55] Trudeau also had little patience for ill-prepared ministers. Coutts noted that the prime minister "almost always sided with the sponsoring minister's proposal as long as it was well developed," but that he could be "bitingly impatient with sloppy presentations or illogical proposals." In this regard, when a minister once made an emotional outburst and stood up to storm out of cabinet, Trudeau stated flatly, "You can stay and make your case again, or you can leave. If you leave, don't come back."[56] His rigour was a clear advantage, as was the flow of information given to him by his staff. Along these same lines, Chrétien recalled that when the prime minister's "ideas were challenged or when he wanted to get to the heart of a matter in cabinet Trudeau could be ruthless in debate, asking probing questions that demolished the logic underlying the counterarguments."[57] The prime minister himself once revealed his own method of dealing with dissent:

> If I know that I am going to have a confrontation in cabinet, if a minister is recommending something and I think it's dead wrong, I won't let him put the thing to Cabinet. I'll see him in my office, I'll set up an interdepartmental committee, I'll meet him privately ... And if I think it's going in a way that I approve, fine, I'm happy to let the consensus develop. If I think it's not going in the right direction, I ask them [the PMO and PCO] to arm me with the arguments and facts and figures.[58]

Trudeau was neither the first nor the last prime minister to use these sorts of tactics to manage ministers and bend cabinet to his will. Even so, he was no micromanager of the day-to-day functions of government departments. Rather,

Trudeau was "happy to have a minister who ran a good shop and didn't create any problems."[59] Setting the tone from the apex of power was enough. The prerogatives that come with being first minister are considerable, and Trudeau had expanded the machinery allowing him to control his putative ministerial colleagues.

"The Land Is Strong," the Cabinet, Not So Much

Donald Macdonald judged the cabinet Trudeau formed after the 1968 election as "by far the best ... in the modern era" because "each minister represented the interests of his portfolio with vigour and vision. Camaraderie and co-operation were our watchwords."[60] Whatever the relative quality of that initial cabinet, it was not stable. While any long-serving government can be expected to face change among its makeup, the twentieth ministry was notable for the sheer number of cabinet shuffles, the most to that point in Canadian history. Resignations over policy differences and the vicissitudes of electoral politics took a heavy toll. Older ministers steadily disappeared, replaced by ministers eager to follow the cabinet procedures. Several former PMO staffers (Lalonde, Roméo LeBlanc, Martin O'Connell) all became ministers. From 1971 to 1979, there were eight major cabinet shuffles – five of them between the 1974 and 1979 elections. This churn of ministers explains some of the weaknesses of the cabinet vis-à-vis the PMO and PCO, with many independently minded ministers departing. The shuffles and Trudeau's cabinet-making efforts reveal the political priorities of the era and the government efforts to address them, while showcasing the difficult task of statecraft during this era.

Paul Hellyer was only the first cabinet heavyweight to leave. Léo Cadieux stepped down as minister of national defence in September 1970 after winning the bruising fight in cabinet to keep Canada in the NATO alliance. His departure triggered a minor shuffle. Four ministers took on new portfolios:

Manpower and Immigration – Otto Lang (replacing Allan J. MacEachen)
National Defence – Donald Macdonald (replacing Léo Cadieux)
National Revenue – Herbert Gray (replacing Jean-Pierre Côté)
President of the Privy Council – Allan J. MacEachen (replacing Donald
    Macdonald)

Paul Martin Sr.'s protégé from Windsor, Herb Gray, became the first Jewish cabinet minister at the federal level. A few months later, Eric Kierans, a deeply experienced former minister in the Jean Lesage government, departed after clashing over management of government finances.

The government's Ministries and Ministers of State Act of 1971 established a new title, minister of state, which encompassed two categories: a minister of state overseeing a ministry of state, meant to function as a temporary department; and a minister of state without portfolio, who could assist another minister or ministers. The move allowed the government to quickly address pressing issues. On 30 June 1971, Robert Andras, minister without portfolio, became the first minister of state, overseeing a new Ministry of State for Urban Affairs. In August, he was joined by Scarborough MP Martin O'Connell, who became minister of state without portfolio, and Etobicoke MP Alastair Gillespie, who became minister of state for science and technology.

Collectively, these appointments showcase two issues. First, Trudeau's willingness to promote talented individuals, either from the Liberal caucus in the cases of Gillespie and O'Connell, or, as the other appointments attest, from among his ministers without portfolio. Second, these appointments demonstrate both the growth of the state and the Trudeau government's interventionist instincts. Indeed, 1971 also saw the creation of the Office of the Minister of the Environment, the first department of its kind among Western governments and a response to growing environmentalism. The new office incorporated the Department of Fisheries and Forestry, with the position of minister of fisheries held concurrently by the minister of the environment, in this case Jack Davis (Capilano, British Columbia).

Trudeau shuffled his cabinet in January 1972, in anticipation of an election. The portfolios and individuals affected in the shuffle were:

Consumer and Corporate Affairs – Robert Andras (replacing Stanley Basford)
Energy, Mines and Resources – Donald Macdonald (replacing John James (Joe) Greene)
Finance – John Turner (replacing Edgar (Ben) Benson)
Justice – Otto Lang (replacing John Turner)
Labour – Martin O'Connell (replacing Bryce Mackasey)
Manpower and Immigration – Bryce Mackasey (replacing Otto Lang)
National Defence – Edgar (Ben) Benson (replacing Donald Macdonald)
Public Works – Jean-Eudes Dubé (replacing Arthur Laing)
Urban Affairs – Stanley Ronald Basford (replacing Robert Andras)
Veterans Affairs – Arthur Laing (replacing Jean-Eudes Dubé)

The only addition was Patrick Mahoney, from Calgary, one of the four Alberta MPs elected in 1968, who became a minister of state without portfolio. Trudeau brought this revamped cabinet into the 30 October 1972 election.

The Liberals' campaign slogan was "The Land is Strong" but voters disagreed. The government's popularity was buffeted by a sagging economy and declining enthusiasm among progressives. The Liberals lost thirty-eight seats, beating the Progressive Conservatives led by Robert L. Stanfield by just two seats. Trudeau's cabinet was rocked. Ben Benson, Arthur Laing, and Jean-Pierre

Côté – three veteran ministers – had chosen not to run. Several ministers were then defeated: Jean-Luc Pepin, Martin O'Connell, Patrick Mahoney, and Bud Olson – the latter two ousted in a Progressive Conservative sweep of Alberta, part of a larger Liberal rout in Western Canada.

Trudeau was able to form a minority government, with the NDP holding the balance of power. Otto Lang remained a minister as the sole Saskatchewan Liberal elected; James Richardson, as one of two Liberal Manitoba MPs, also retained a post. In BC, four Liberals had been elected, and two of them, Jack Davis and Ron Basford, remained in cabinet. In the East, slim pickings also determined cabinet appointments: Allan J. MacEachen, the sole Nova Scotia Liberal; the lone Liberal from Newfoundland, Don Jamieson; and PEI's Daniel MacDonald. One of five New Brunswick Liberals, Jean-Eudes Dubé remained a minister. Due to these electoral fortunes, the cabinet was dominated by central Canadians, twelve ministers from Ontario and nine from Quebec, or twenty-one of twenty-nine portfolios.

Trudeau turned to people he knew well. Marc Lalonde won in Montreal and was named minister of national health and welfare. Jeanne Sauvé, also from Montreal, became the first woman to join a Trudeau cabinet as minister of state for science and technology. Roméo LeBlanc, who had served as press secretary to both Pearson and Trudeau and who had won in New Brunswick, was named minister of state for fisheries in 1974. There were also several promotions for long-time Liberals MPs: Eugene Whelan from south-western Ontario became the agriculture minister; Toronto's Stanley Haidasz was named the first minister of state for multiculturalism; Hugh Faulkner, from Peterborough, served as secretary of state; and, from Montreal, Warren Allmand (solicitor general) and André Ouellet (postmaster general). A notable development was Jean Marchand's demotion from the Department of Regional Economic Expansion to Transport, a blow for the former labour leader and a marker of declining political fortunes. Finally, as a measure of reassurance regarding the new cabinet's abilities, the senior-most portfolios, finance and external affairs, remained the purview of John Turner and Mitchell Sharp, respectively. There were no ministers without portfolio and Haidasz was the sole minister of state, giving the cabinet a slimmed down appearance:

1 Prime Minister – Pierre Trudeau, Quebec
2 Agriculture – Eugene Whelan, Ontario
3 Communications – Gérard Pelletier, Quebec
4 Consumer and Corporate Affairs – Herb Gray, Ontario
5 Energy, Mines, and Resources – Donald Macdonald, Ontario
6 Environment – Jack Davis, British Columbia
7 External Affairs – Mitchell Sharp, Ontario
8 Finance – John Turner, Ontario

 9 Indian Affairs and Northern Development – Jean Chrétien, Quebec
10 Industry, Trade, and Commerce – Alastair Gillespie, Ontario
11 Justice and Attorney General – Otto Lang, Saskatchewan
12 Labour – John Munro, Ontario
13 Leader of the Government in the Senate – Paul Martin, Ontario (senator)
14 Manpower and Immigration – Robert Andras, Ontario
15 Minister of State for Multiculturalism – Stanley Haidasz, Ontario
16 National Defence – James Richardson, Manitoba
17 National Health and Welfare – Marc Lalonde, Quebec
18 National Revenue – Robert Stanbury, Ontario
19 Postmaster General – André Ouellet, Quebec
20 President of the Privy Council – Allan MacEachen, Nova Scotia
21 Public Works – Jean-Eudes Dubé, New Brunswick
22 Regional Economic Expansion – Don Jamieson, Newfoundland
23 Science and Technology – Jeanne Sauvé, Quebec
24 Secretary of State of Canada – Hugh Faulkner, Ontario
25 Solicitor General – Warren Allmand, Quebec
26 Supply and Services – Jean-Pierre Goyer, Quebec
27 Transport – Jean Marchand, Quebec
28 Treasury Board – Charles M. (Bud) Drury, Quebec
29 Urban Affairs – Stanley Ronald Basford, British Columbia
30 Veterans Affairs – Daniel MacDonald, Prince Edward Island

The Liberal minority government lasted less than two years, during which the economy staggered as inflation mounted. In addition to his cabinet post, Allan J. MacEachen served as government House leader, deftly managing the minority situation until May 1974, when the Liberals engineered their own defeat over the budget. When the NDP withdrew backing, an election was set for 8 July. Despite the poor economic situation, stumbles by the Progressive Conservative leader and a collapse of NDP support led to a jump in Liberal fortunes and a majority government.

   Much of the cabinet remained unchanged, with regional electoral realities – few MPs from Western Canada, and none from Alberta – dictating appointments. However, there were several notable exceptions. Jack Davis's defeat necessitated two changes. First, Jeanne Sauvé replaced him as environment minister, making her the first woman to head a full-fledged department in a Trudeau government. Second, was the need to appoint someone to represent British Columbia. Here, Trudeau named Senator Ray Perrault as government leader in the Senate, bumping Paul Martin Sr. out of the position and out of cabinet, a move that was far from amicable.[61] Another Liberal stalwart, Mitchell Sharp, moved from External Affairs to become president of the Privy Council, with MacEachen taking over as foreign minister. Unlike Martin, Sharp had asked for a change, though he was displeased with this new portfolio.[62] There were other forced departures: Stanley Haidasz, Jean Dubé, Robert Stanbury, and Herb Gray were all dropped. One right-wing commentator hostile to Trudeau in the extreme dubbed it the "Tuesday Night Massacre."[63]

This characterization overstates the severity of the firings given the handful of ministers involved. Liberal tactician Keith Davey, who had advised the prime minister on forming this post-election cabinet, cited in particular Gray's "perceived inability to communicate" as the reason for being shuffled out, adding that as Trudeau "had often said, when dispatching ministers, that there was no reason why they could not return."[64] Gray was a case in point, returning to the cabinet table in 1980.[65] Beyond Perrault, the only new faces in cabinet were Barney Danson and Judd Buchanan, both promoted from the ranks of parliamentary secretaries.

1 Prime Minister – Pierre Trudeau, Quebec
2 Agriculture – Eugene Whelan, Ontario
3 Communications – Gérard Pelletier, Quebec
4 Consumer and Corporate Affairs – André Ouellet, Quebec
5 Energy, Mines, and Resources – Donald Macdonald, Ontario
6 Environment – Jeanne Sauvé, Quebec
7 External – Allan MacEachen, Nova Scotia
8 Finance – John Turner, Ontario
9 Indian Affairs and Northern Development – Judd Buchanan, Ontario
10 Industry, Trade, and Commerce – Alastair Gillespie, Ontario
11 Justice and Attorney General – Otto Lang, Saskatchewan
12 Labour – John Munro, Ontario
13 Leader of the Government in the Senate – Raymond Perrault, British Columbia (senator)
14 Manpower and Immigration – Robert Andras, Ontario
15 Minister of State – Roméo LeBlanc, New Brunswick
16 National Defence – James Richardson, Manitoba
17 National Health and Welfare – Marc Lalonde, Quebec
18 National Revenue – Stanley Ronald Basford, British Columbia
19 Postmaster General – Bryce Mackasey, Quebec
20 President of the Privy Council – Mitchell Sharp, Ontario
21 Public Works – Charles M. (Bud) Drury, Quebec
22 Regional Economic Expansion – Don Jamieson, Newfoundland
23 Science and Technology – Charles M. (Bud) Drury, Quebec
24 Secretary of State of Canada – James Hugh Faulkner, Ontario
25 Solicitor General – Warren Allmand, Quebec
26 Supply and Services – Jean-Pierre Goyer, Quebec
27 Transport – Jean Marchand, Quebec

28 Treasury Board – Jean Chrétien, Quebec
29 Urban Affairs – Barney Danson, Ontario
30 Veterans Affairs – Daniel MacDonald, Prince Edward Island

Despite the majority victory in 1974, significant cracks began to show in the Trudeau government. In August 1975, Gérard Pelletier, tired of politics, resigned; the following month, after squabbling with fellow ministers and the prime minister over economic matters, John Turner departed, a blow to the government but also to the Liberal Party's business-friendly constituency. Turner's resignation necessitated a small shuffle on 26 September that saw two new faces join cabinet – Quebec MP Marcel Lessard and Ontario MP Bud Cullen – while Jean Marchand was further demoted to a minister without portfolio:

Energy, Mines, and Resources – Alastair Gillespie (replacing Donald Macdonald)
Finance – Donald Macdonald (replacing John Turner)
Industry, Trade, and Commerce – Don Jamieson (replacing Alastair Gillespie)
Justice and Attorney General – Stanley Ronald Basford (replacing Otto Lang)
National Revenue – Jack Sydney (Bud) Cullen (replacing Stanley Basford)
Regional Economic Expansion – Marcel Lessard (replacing Don Jamieson)
Transport – Otto Lang (replacing Jean Marchand)

As for Pelletier's portfolio as minister of communications, Trudeau appointed a technocrat, former Canadian Radio and Television Commission chairperson Pierre Juneau, to the role. When Juneau failed to win a by-election in October, he was replaced by Jeanne Sauvé, with Roméo LeBlanc becoming environment minister. Meanwhile, Marchand was soon caught up in scandal as were André Ouellet and Liberal warhorse Bud Drury, all of whom resigned their cabinet positions in early 1976. Then, Mitchell Sharp announced that he did not intend to run in the next federal election, while the popular Bryce Mackasey resigned to run provincially in Quebec, winning his seat in the November 1976 election that returned a Parti Québécois government (Marchand had run too, but lost). These were heavy losses of key Liberals and veteran ministers. In an attempt to give the sagging government a facelift, on 14 September, Trudeau made a major shuffle:

Consumer and Corporate Affairs – Anthony Abbott (replacing Bryce Mackasey)
External Affairs – Don Jamieson (replacing Allan J. MacEachen)
Indian Affairs and Northern Development – Warren Allmand (replacing Judd Buchanan)
Industry, Trade, and Commerce – Jean Chrétien (replacing Don Jamieson)
Manpower and Immigration – Bud Cullen (replacing Robert Andras)
Minister of State for Small Business – Leonard Marchand

Minister of State for Sport – Iona Campagnolo
National Revenue – Monique Bégin (replacing Bud Cullen)
Postmaster General – Jean-Jacques Blais (replacing Bryce Mackasey)
President of the Privy Council – Allan MacEachen (replacing Mitchell Sharp)
Public Works – Judd Buchanan (replacing Charles (Bud) Drury)
Science and Technology – James Hugh Faulkner (replacing Charles (Bud) Drury)
Secretary of State – John Roberts (replacing James Hugh Faulkner)
Solicitor General – Francis Fox (replacing Warren Allmand)
Treasury Board – Robert Andras (replacing Jean Chrétien)

The shuffle was marked by promotions rather than demotions. First, Jean Chrétien continued his rise as an influential minister. Next, there were new members appointed from the ranks of parliamentary secretaries: John Roberts, Anthony Abbott, and Francis Fox. Also joining the cabinet were two women, Monique Bégin, first elected in 1972, and Iona Campagnolo, elected in 1974. They brought the complement of female ministers to three. From British Columbia, Campagnolo became minister of state for sport. Not least, Leonard Marchand became the first First Nations federal cabinet minister. His newly created position as minister of state for small business was a marker of the importance of economic issues for the government's fortunes. In forming this cabinet, Trudeau had apparently considered creating a Ministry of State for Women's Affairs, but ultimately had rejected the notion as "tokenism." Overall, the losses over the past year, and the lack of standout ministers led one observer to note that the shuffle "confirmed that [Trudeau] alone is the government and the government is him alone."[66] Less than a month later, the government was rocked by another crisis, when James Richardson resigned in protest over bilingualism policy, his departure leaving no cabinet representative for Manitoba. Barney Danson replaced Richardson, with André Ouellet taking over at Urban Affairs. Despite the taint of scandal, Ouellet was needed amid rising Quebec separatism, signified by the PQ election victory just weeks after the shuffle.

The Quebec election served to improve the Trudeau government's standing, reinforcing the Liberal brand as the party of federalism. In April 1977, Alberta PC MP Jack Horner crossed the floor of the House of Commons, joining the Liberal caucus and becoming a minister without portfolio; Jacques Lavoie, another Tory, followed suit in June. In by-elections in May, meanwhile, 5 of 6 Liberal candidates were elected, all of them in Quebec. Despite the obvious bump in popularity, Trudeau ruled out calling an early general election. "Tonight's victory," Trudeau stated following the announcement of the by-election results, "doesn't show that we're in great need of a new mandate."[67] It was, in his biographer's judgment, the "worst political decision" of Trudeau's career.[68] Instead, the government was left to stagger through an increasingly poor economic situation, as inflation continued to mount amid rising unemployment.

A week after the PQ's 1976 election win in Quebec, J.J. Macdonell, Canada's auditor-general, had warned of out-of-control government spending and budgetary mismanagement. "I am deeply concerned," he stated in his annual report, "that Parliament – and indeed the government – has lost, or is close to losing, effective control of the public purse."[69] At a loss for a solution, the government appointed a Royal Commission to examine the issues. To be seen to be addressing stagflation – the terrible mix of high inflation, high unemployment, and low demand – on 15 August 1977, Trudeau transformed the Department of Manpower and Immigration into the Department of Employment and Immigration. This window dressing was typical of a government that, in the view of Finance Minister Donald Macdonald, was "stale and out of ideas."[70]

Macdonald's departure from cabinet necessitated a major shuffle on 16 September 1977:

Consumer and Corporate Affairs – Warren Allmand (replacing Anthony Abbott)

Finance – Jean Chrétien (replacing Donald Macdonald)

Indian Affairs and Northern Development – Hugh Faulkner (replacing Warren Allmand)

Industry, Trade and Commerce – Jack Horner (replacing Jean Chrétien)

Minister of State for the Environment – Leonard Marchand

Minister of State for Federal-Provincial Relations – Marc Lalonde

Minister of State for Multiculturalism – Norman Cafik

Minister of State for Small Business – Anthony Abbott (replacing Leonard Marchand)

National Health and Welfare – Monique Bégin (replacing Marc Lalonde)

National Revenue – Joseph-Philippe Guay (replacing Monique Bégin)

Science and Technology – Judd Buchanan (replacing Hugh Faulkner)

Noteworthy changes included Jack Horner's appointment to Industry, Trade, and Commerce, a reward for his floor-crossing and a sop to Alberta since he had become that province's sole Liberal MP. Further, to deal with Quebec separatism Marc Lalonde was appointed to a new Ministry of State for Federal-Provincial Relations. Finally, Trudeau named Allan J. MacEachen to the new post of deputy prime minister, a largely ceremonial role.

The shuffle did little to raise the government's plunging popularity. In 1978, there were several high-profile departures, with Bud Drury, Ron Basford, and Jean-Pierre Goyer all retiring. Worse, in fifteen by-elections held across the country on 16 October, the Liberals won only two seats, both in Quebec, with the Tories making big gains. A final cabinet shuffle followed on 24 November, necessitated by the creation of a new Ministry of State for Economic

Development, another effort to show that the government was trying to tackle the issue foremost in many voters' minds.

Justice: Marc Lalonde (replacing Otto Lang)
Labour: Martin O'Connell (replacing André Ouellet)
Minister of State for Economic Development: Robert Andras
Minister of State for Federal-Provincial Relations: John Reid (replacing Marc Lalonde)
National Revenue: Anthony Abbott (replacing Joseph-Philippe Guay)
Public Works: André Ouellet (replacing Judd Buchanan)
Science and Technology: Alastair Gillespie (replacing Judd Buchanan)
Supply and Services: Pierre De Bané (replacing Jean-Pierre Goyer)
Treasury Board: Judd Buchanan (replacing Robert Andras)

The Trudeau government was defeated in the general election held on 22 May 1979. Over the previous decade, the cabinet had lost most of its stars: Turner, Pelletier, Marchand, Macdonald, Mackasey, Sharp, and Drury. Instead, it was a government dominated by Trudeau. Just as he had been the star attraction in 1968, he had become the focus of voters' ire in 1979. The Liberals won 114 seats, 19 fewer than in 1974, but still managed over 40 per cent of the vote. The Progressive Conservatives under Joe Clark took 136 seats, 38 more than in 1974, and would form a minority government.

Conclusion

The Royal Commission on Financial Management and Accountability, or Lambert Commission, released its report ahead of the 1979 election. Among its findings the commission was careful to emphasize the "need to maintain that pre-eminent position of the first minister," but it was also clear that "the Prime Minister alone cannot exercise the collective responsibilities of the cabinet for the governing of the nation."[71] When it came to government management, the commission recommended that the prime minister share authority with several key ministers empowered to act collectively on cabinet's behalf. A gentle rebuke of Trudeau, the suggestion was a non-starter. Nonetheless, it reflected doubts about the extent to which it was possible to govern from the centre.

What, then, to make of Trudeau's cabinet reforms? Certainly, they were a legitimate response to the growing disfunction of cabinet processes as witnessed in the Pearson years, which itself was a symptom, as Trudeau readily admitted, of the growth of government "in a modern and complex society."[72] But judged on that basis, his reforms did little to arrest the situation.

As for Trudeau's wider reforms to cabinet, some analysts – including former ministers – cited the committee system and the work and commitment it required, as having "dangerously eroded" ministers' and deputy ministers' time to actually manage their departments.[73] The committees were a part of the wider effort by Trudeau and his staff to streamline collective decision-making while also wresting away independent decision-making on the part of ministers and the civil service. In this respect, the system worked. The diminution of ministers' autonomy had other causes too. Constant shuffles and portfolio changes made ministers less effective, while departures of high-profile ministers – many of whom were veterans of prior governments where independence was encouraged or at least tolerated – sapped the cabinet's overall strength. At the same time, though, Trudeau was no micromanager of his ministers' day-to-day affairs. He was a singularly intelligent individual who, around the cabinet table, was often more than *primus inter pares*. Overall and despite his many attributes, when it came to political management, collegial management, and state management Trudeau was a poor practitioner of statecraft.

By the spring of 1979, few people could make the claim that the Trudeau government had been a success. Government had grown dramatically during his decade in power, but the country was beset by grave regional tensions – pressures against which cabinet was unresponsive. The economy was torn by both inflation and high unemployment, Canada's foreign policy was often aimless and self-contradictory, and the prime minister was held in contempt in many parts of the land. For all its sophistications, the Trudeau cabinet had produced few grand policies and had instead allowed itself to be diminished.

NOTES

1 Quoted in Richard Gwyn, *Northern Magus: Pierre Trudeau and Canadians* (Toronto: McClelland & Stewart, 1980), 72.
2 Pierre Elliott Trudeau, *Memoirs* (Toronto: McClelland & Stewart, 1993), 110.
3 Donald J. Savoie, *Governing from the Centre: The Concentration of Power and Canadian Politics* (Toronto: University of Toronto Press, 1999), 84, 8.
4 "On to Trudeau's 'Just Society,'" *Ottawa Citizen*, 8 April 1968; and "A Modern Man for Canada," *Toronto Star*, 8 April 1968.
5 "First Trudeau Cabinet Lists Average Age 49," *Montreal Gazette*, 22 April 1968.
6 Peter C. Newman, "Trudeau for Unity," *Regina Leader-Post*, 27 June 1968.
7 Eric Kierans, with Walter Stewart, *Remembering: A Political Life* (Toronto: Stoddart, 2001), 199.
8 Mitchell Sharp, *Which Reminds Me ...: A Memoir* (Toronto: University of Toronto Press, 1994), 168.
9 Quoted in Robert Bothwell and J.L. Granatstein, *Trudeau's World: Insiders Reflect on Foreign Policy, Trade, and Defence, 1968–84* (Vancouver: University of British Columbia Press, 2017), 16.

10 Donald S. Macdonald, *Thumper: The Memoirs of the Honourable Donald S. Macdonald* (Montreal: McGill-Queen's University Press, 2014), 93.

11 John English, *Just Watch Me: The Life and Times of Pierre Elliott Trudeau, 1968–2000* (Toronto: Alfred A. Knopf, 2009), 39; and "Trudeau Cabinet Leans Heavily towards Quebec," *Montreal Gazette*, 22 April 1968.

12 English, *Just Watch Me*, 39; and Macdonald, *Thumper*, 92.

13 Cabinet Conclusions, 8 July 1968, Library and Archives Canada, RG 2, series A-5-a, vol. 6338.

14 Quoted in Bothwell and Granatstein, *Trudeau's World*, 134.

15 Trudeau, *Memoirs*, 109–10.

16 Trudeau, *Memoirs*, 107–8.

17 Pierre Elliott Trudeau, "Federalism, Nationalism and Reason," in *Federalism and the French Canadians* (Toronto: Macmillan, 1968), 203.

18 Gordon Robertson, "The Canadian Parliament and Cabinet in the Face of Modern Demands," *Canadian Public Administration* 11, no. 3 (1968): 276.

19 Smith, quoted in Marc Lalonde, "The Changing Role of the Prime Minister's Office," *Canadian Public Administration* 14, no. 4 (1971): 511.

20 George Radwanski, *Trudeau* (Toronto: Macmillan, 1978), 174.

21 Gordon Robertson, "The Changing Role of the Privy Council Office," *Canadian Public Administration* 14, no. 4 (1971): 495; and Sharp, *Which Reminds Me*, 165.

22 Lalonde, "Prime Minister's Office," 514.

23 Trudeau, *Memoirs*, 109–10.

24 Donald S. Macdonald, "The Trudeau Cabinet: A Memoir," in *Trudeau's Shadow: The Life and Legacy of Pierre Elliott Trudeau*, ed. Andrew Cohen and J.L. Granatstein (Toronto: Random House, 1998), 164.

25 Sharp, *Which Reminds Me*, 166.

26 Macdonald, "Trudeau Cabinet," 165.

27 Alastair W. Gillespie, with Irene Sage, *Made in Canada: A Businessman's Adventure in Politics* (Montreal: Robin Brass Studio, 2009), 119.

28 Robertson, "Privy Council Office," 500–1.

29 Sharp, *Which Reminds Me*, 166.

30 Kierans, *Remembering*, 188.

31 Kierans, *Remembering*, 151.

32 Radwanski, *Trudeau*, 170.

33 Trudeau, *Memoirs*, 112, 110.

34 Trudeau, *Memoirs*, 109–13, 113.

35 Robertson, "Privy Council Office," 493.

36 Mitchell Sharp, "Decision-Making in the Federal Cabinet," *Canadian Public Administration* 19, no. 1 (1976): 1–7.

37 Gillespie, *Made in Canada*, 133.

38 Robertson, "Privy Council Office," 500.

39 Radwanski, *Trudeau*, 165.

40 Gordon Robertson, *Memoirs of a Very Civil Servant: Mackenzie King to Pierre Trudeau* (Toronto: University of Toronto Press, 2000), 256.

41 Brendan Kelly, *The Good Fight: Marcel Cadieux and Canadian Diplomacy* (Vancouver: University of British Columbia Press, 2019), 314.

42 Trudeau, *Memoirs*, 110.

43 Trudeau, *Memoirs*, 113.

44 Jim Coutts, "Trudeau in Power: A View from Inside the Prime Minister's Office," in Cohen and Granatstein, *Trudeau's Shadow*, 155.

45 Paul Martin, *A Very Public Life*, vol. 2 (Toronto: Deneau, 1985), 648. Trudeau made the same comparison (Gwyn, *Northern Magus*, 87).

46 Quoted in Bothwell and Granatstein, *Trudeau's World*, 35.

47 Quoted in Bothwell and Granatstein, *Trudeau's World*, 24.

48 Thomas Hockin, "Three Canadian Prime Ministers Discuss the Office," in *Apex of Power: The Prime Minister and Political Leadership in Canada*, 2nd ed. (Scarborough: Prentice-Hall, 1977), 263.

49 Sharp, *Which Reminds Me*, 167.

50 Macdonald, "Trudeau Cabinet," 168.

51 Macdonald, *Thumper*, 98.

52 Jean Chrétien, *Straight from the Heart* (Toronto: Key Porter Books, 1985), 75.

53 H.D. Munroe, "Style within the Centre: Pierre Trudeau, the War Measures Act, and the Nature of Prime Ministerial Power," *Canadian Public Administration* 54, no. 4 (2011): 537.

54 Chrétien, *Straight from the Heart*, 75.

55 Macdonald, "Trudeau Cabinet," 170.

56 Jim Coutts, "Trudeau in Power: A View from inside the Prime Minister's Office," in Cohen and Granatstein, *Trudeau's Shadow*, 156.

57 Chrétien, *Straight from the Heart*, 75.

58 Quoted in Savoie, *Governing from the Centre*, 85.

59 Chrétien, *Straight from the Heart*, 73.

60 Macdonald, *Thumper*, 103.

61 Greg Donaghy, *Grit: The Life and Politics of Paul Martin Sr.* (Vancouver: University of British Columbia Press, 2015), 335.

62 Sharp, *Which Reminds Me*, 225.

63 Lubor Zink, "Trudeau's Cabinet Shuffle," *Toronto Sun*, 9 August 1974.

64 Keith Davey, *The Rainmaker: A Passion for Politics* (Toronto: Stoddart, 1986), 192.

65 Jennifer Levin Bonder, "Herb Gray and the Founding of the Foreign Investment Review Agency," in *People, Politics, and Purpose: Biography and Canadian Political History*, ed. Greg Donaghy and P. Whitney Lackenbauer (Vancouver: University of British Columbia Press, 2022).

66 Richard Gwyn, "Trudeau's on His Own as the Gap Yawns Wider with Shuffled Cabinet," *Toronto Star*, 15 September 1976.

67 "Liberals Win 5 of 6 Byelections," *Montreal Gazette*, 25 May 1977.
68 English, *Just Watch Me*, 353.
69 "Says Government Spending Is Going out of Control," *Sherbrooke Record*, 23 November 1977.
70 Macdonald, *Thumper*, 176.
71 Royal Commission on Financial Management and Accountability, *Final Report* (Hull: Minister of Supply and Services, 1979), 63.
72 Pierre Elliott Trudeau, *The Essential Trudeau*, ed. Ron Graham (Toronto: McClelland & Stewart, 1998), 74.
73 J.R. Mallory, "The Lambert Report: Central Roles and Responsibilities," *Canadian Public Administration* 22, no. 4 (1979): 517.

15 "Welcome to the 1980s": Pierre Elliott Trudeau's Quasi-Gaullist Style*

FRÉDÉRIC BOILY

The Liberal Party of Canada's victory in February 1980 was without a doubt the most important mandate of Pierre Elliott Trudeau's career. Few prime ministers are given a second chance after losing their incumbency. Unlike John A. Macdonald, Arthur Meighen, or Mackenzie King, Pierre Elliott Trudeau only had to wait a few months before returning to power. This brief interlude, carefully managed by the advisers and ministers who urged him to return, allowed Trudeau to establish himself among those prime ministers remembered as transformational, as his government faced challenging circumstances both at home and abroad. Notably, this second mandate was marked, as final mandates typically are, by both the urgency of getting things done, and freedom from the pressure to build popularity toward re-election.[1]

This chapter will examine the question of presidentialization in section 1 and the composition of the cabinet that was created on 3 March 1980, as well as its mid-mandate shuffle (section 2). The third section will cover the cabinet's involvement in the Quebec referendum of 1980 and the patriation of the Constitution in 1982. Trudeau's rebirth provides a unique opportunity to observe the dynamics of cabinet relations and the assignment of priorities among those ministers who played a major role in the referendum battle. The fourth section will analyse the regional challenges of cabinet representation, as significant tensions undermined Canadian unity in the early 1980s, followed by a brief review of the steps taken by John Turner to distance himself from Trudeau (section 5).

Trudeau as Leader: Presidential?

There have been countless descriptions of Trudeau's prime-ministerial style, most of them tending in the same direction: that of a strong leader who, while placing a premium on ministerial solidarity,[2] stood fast toward the provinces[3] with a so-called "indetermined inflexibility."[4]

In October 1969, Denis Smith, in a paper for the Tory Thinkers' Conference in Niagara Falls, mentioned Trudeau's "unerring presidential instincts," an appraisal reiterated by Walter Stewart in 1971.[5] According to Donald J. Savoie, it was Trudeau who accelerated the trend of concentrating power in the hands of the prime minister and put himself firmly in charge of decision making.[6] This gave rise to the thesis of "presidentialization" to characterize a profound change in both campaigning style – as with Trudeaumania – and of governance, with the prime minister uncontestably at the controls.

Following John Turner's cabinet announcement in June 1984, a Québécois columnist observed that the new prime minister wanted to break from Trudeau's "French" approach to governance.[7]

"French" or "Latin" likely refers here to the paramount role played by a French president, not only in decision-making, but also in determining political priorities.[8] This approach – itself a specific nuance of presidentialism – may be described as one where the leader is not merely one who contemplates but rather governs and steers a nation on the path to emancipation. In Trudeau's case, this meant combatting Québécois nationalism as well as patriating the Constitution to free Canada from its British overlord. In Trudeau's estimation, it was his mandate to speak for Canada. Even those who would criticize his interventionist policies found much to admire in the breadth of his national vision and his determination to combat "the separatists." In sum, the presidentialist shoe fits, not without a touch of French-style presidentialism – as an observer once quipped, "the de Gaulle fist in the Kennedy glove."[9] This was especially evident during constitutional debates and the project to "Canadianize" the energy sector, moments when the prime minister resolutely took centre stage.

Observers often refer to the profoundly rationalist aspect of Trudeau's political thought, his so-called "functional rationalism," to describe his approach to management.[10] In *Governing from the Centre*, political scientist Donald J. Savoie explains how, under Trudeau's first government, the decision-making system was meant to allow for a thorough examination of policies and shifted the weight of deliberations away from deputy ministers toward the cabinet. According to Savoie, "Trudeau, wanted ... to wrestle policy influence away from departments and to give Cabinet the ability to make policy based on competing advice. Indeed, Trudeau decided to overhaul the Cabinet process precisely to break the stranglehold ministers and long-serving deputy ministers had on departments."[11] To implement this functionalist approach, the prime minister had set up a new structure of cabinet committees, supported by secretaries, allowing an initial deliberation between ministers. "Pierre Trudeau had a fraught relationship," write Bothwell and Granatstein, "with civil servants and with diplomats in particular."[12] This distrust caused the prime minister to want to return power to cabinet members, but without giving them the freedom to act independently.

While some characterized this as Trudeau's "Socratic style,"[13] building the consensus he desired through persuasion and debate, others used the more assertive "presidential style" to describe his manner of governance.[14] It would seem that Trudeau himself did not object to the characterization, remarking instead that his style of governance was required by the circumstances: the reality of a "modern and complex society" as well as the threat of Quebec nationalism. In other words, the Quebec referendum forced him, so to speak, to adopt a presidential posture. Arguing in favour of his prime minister, Michael Pitfield defended against suggestions that Trudeau had an imperial bent. In Pitfield's own words, "he was the least imperial."[15]

On some issues, it would appear that Trudeau did step back and give free rein to the minister responsible for the file, all the while allowing collective deliberation to work its course in establishing policy. For example, regarding the US-led boycott of the 1980 Olympic Games in Moscow, the prime minister allowed Secretary of State Mark MacGuigan (External Affairs) to follow the US lead and support the boycott, despite his own scepticism on the issue. When asked by the press about his own position, Trudeau replied, "in any case, my personal opinion matters little."[16] MacGuigan later confirmed that it took some work to convince the prime minister to support the boycott.[17] Henceforth, the relationship between the two became tense, a likely cause of MacGuigan's later removal from External Affairs. On the foreign relations front, there were two issues where the prime minister acted singly, independently of his external affairs ministers: the North-South Initiative (1980–81) and the so-called Peace Initiative (1983–84).

There were some areas where Trudeau manifested little interest, letting his ministers manage the issues without getting involved. This was notably the case with John Roberts, minister of the environment.[18] Monique Bégin, minister of health and welfare from 1980 to 1984, claims to have had only a few thirty-minute meetings with the prime minister, and not a single question regarding her portfolio.[19] It should be said, however, that the prime minister was regularly informed by the Privy Council Office of Bégin's endeavours, and kept abreast of the deliberations regarding penalties to be imposed on the provinces that permitted the direct billing of user fees for some health services.[20] Ultimately, there is testimony to the fact that, with some ministers and in some areas, Trudeau showed little inclination to get involved. On constitutional issues, meanwhile, the prime minister was clearly and firmly in command; there was little room for improvisation, despite promises of collegiality. Thus, Monique Bégin affirmed that the cabinet was tightly organized and the clerk of the Privy Council, Michael Pitfield, gave the documents to the ministers only the day before cabinet meetings. Additionally (also according to Bégin), the ministers could not intervene on another file unless they notified the Privy Council Office one day in advance.[21]

Throughout this mandate, it seems Trudeau maintained a fairly good relationship with his caucus. According to Jerry Grafstein, politician and senator from 1984 to 2010, Trudeau listened to his caucus: "In early Liberal caucus under Pierre Trudeau that I attended as Senator, a stunning lesson was learned.... Trudeau, unlike his successors, never took steps to manipulate the disorganized and disparate views of caucus. He never pre-empted caucus discussion and waited until the very end of each caucus to knit together a stirring consensus."[22] But other observers recall a different leader, one who cared little about his party or his caucus, who seemed to owe nothing to party politics–"un politicien sans fibre partisane," to use the words of an editor at *La Presse*.[23]

This haughty attitude toward his caucus seems to have deepened in the final two years of his mandate. To wit, a working paper on the reform of the federal Liberal party was published in February 1984 by Iona Campagnolo, the president of the party. Without naming the prime minister, the paper nevertheless decried his high-handed management of the party, which had become little more than an empty shell.[24] It appears that, by the winter of 1984, recriminations against his leadership forced the prime minister to reckon that he had lost the confidence of both his caucus and the nation.

The Cabinet: Old Guard, New Program

By the time ballots were counted on 18 February 1980, ideology in Canadian governance had begun to shift away from Keynesian liberalism, but Trudeau's government, buoyed by its massive victory, stubbornly resisted this trend. As two close observers put it, "They [Liberals] were bringing a new enthusiasm, a new vision, and a new ruthlessness to the exercise of power."[25]

The Speech from the Throne, where ministerial responsibilities and mandates were detailed, emphasized the new government's economic objectives, and included a warning against "the siren song of regional isolationism," at that time rumbling in all parts of Canada.[26] Consequently, cabinet ministers received a mandate to breathe life into the struggling Canadian economy.[27] As one commentator noted, the challenge facing the new cabinet was to put in place an economic program carrying an economic nationalism to match that of the past.[28]

The leading question for the prime minister was to translate this "new enthusiasm" into a government project and, above all, to identify those within the new cabinet who would be responsible for making this impulse a reality. In the context of deepening fractures along national and regional tensions, the "desirable criteria"[29] to select the 32 cabinet members (3 more than Joe Clark's) were threefold. Experience came first, as it was crucial to act quickly and effectively within this singular mandate. Secondly, coast-to-coast representation was key to the cabinet's nationwide legitimacy, and finally, univocal ideological support for the advocacy of left-leaning Keynesian liberalism. The government's aim was to implement an industrial policy to direct Canada's economic development. To this end, the Liberal government bet on the natural resources sector to spearhead economic renewal.[30]

The prime minister built on known values to navigate the *terra incognita* of a Quebec referendum, in tandem with his ambitious project to "federalize" or "Canadianize" the energy sector through the National Energy Program. The value of experience is prized by prime ministers[31]; and this was not a time for experimenting with unknown actors. This was the composition of the cabinet:

1   Prime Minister – Pierre Elliott Trudeau, 60, Quebec
2   Agriculture – Eugene Francis Whelan, 55, Ontario
3   Communications; Secretary of State of Canada – Francis Fox, 40, Québec
4   Consumer and Corporate Affairs; Postmaster General – André Ouellet, 40, Québec
5   Minister of State for Economic Development – Horace Andrew (Bud) Olson, 54, Alberta (senator)
6   Employment and Immigration – Lloyd Axworthy, 40, Manitoba
7   Minister of Energy, Mines and Resources – Marc Lalonde, 51, Quebec
8   Environment; Minister of State for Science and Technology – John Roberts, 46, Ontario
9   External Affairs – Mark McGuigan, 49, Ontario
10 Finance – Allan MacEachen, 58, Nova Scotia
11 Fisheries and Oceans – Roméo LeBlanc, 51, New Brunswick
12 Indian Affairs and Northern Development – John Munro, 48, Ontario
13 Industry, Trade and Commerce – Herbert Gray, 48, Ontario
14 Justice and Attorney General; Minister of State for Social Development – Jean Chrétien, 46, Quebec
15 Labour – Gerald Regan, 52, Nova Scotia
16 Leader of the Government in the Senate – Raymond Perrault, 54, British Columbia (senator)
17 National Defence – Gilles Lamontagne, 60, Québec
18 National Health and Welfare – Monique Bégin, 44, Quebec
19 National Revenue – William Rompkey, 43, Newfoundland
20 President of Privy Council – Yvon Pinard, 39, Québec
21 Public Works – Paul Cosgrove, 45, Ontario
22 Regional Economic Expansion – Pierre de Bané, 41, Québec
23 Solicitor General – Robert Kaplan, 43, Ontario
24 Supply and Services – Jean-Jacques Blais, 39, Ontario
25 Transport; External Relations – Jean-Luc Pepin, 55, Québec
26 Treasury Board – Donald Johnston, 43, Quebec

27 Veterans Affairs – Daniel Joseph MacDonald, 61, Prince Edward Island
28 Minister of State (Canadian Wheat Board) – Hazen Argue, 58, Saskatchewan (senator)
29 Minister of State (Mines) – Judy Erola, 46, Ontario
30 Minister of State (Small Business and Tourism) – Charles Lapointe, 35, Québec
31 Minister of State (Multiculturalism) – James Fleming, 40, Ontario
32 Minister of State (Finance) – Pierre Bussières, 40, Québec.
33 Minister of State (Trade) – Edward Lumley, 40, Ontario

The average age was 47, thirteen years younger than the prime minister. Fourteen of the 32 ministers were under 45 years of age. The ministers entrusted to realize Trudeau's social and economic project had proven themselves in Trudeau's previous cabinets, and had a long history with him (Marc Lalonde, notably). Indeed, some major dailies dubbed the new cabinet "the old guard."[32] This moniker was fairly accurate, given that a majority of 18 former ministers were joined by 14 new ones, including 3 senators. More significantly, key posts were given to three stalwarts (Marc Lalonde, Allan MacEachen, Jean Chrétien), while 6 ministers were returned to former offices (Eugene Whelan, agriculture; Daniel MacDonald, veterans affairs; Raymond Perrault, government leader in the Senate; Roméo LeBlanc, fisheries; Monique Bégin, health and welfare; Andre Ouellet, consumer and corporate affairs and postmaster-general). Francis Fox (Secretary of State and communications minister) and John Munro (Indian affairs and northern development) also reintegrated cabinet.

The linchpin of the cabinet was Marc Lalonde (minister of energy, mines and resources), deemed at the time the prime minister's quasi *alter ego*. "Lalonde is a good deal like Trudeau," wrote journalist Walter Stewart, "cool, quick, humorous, highly intelligent and complex. Like Trudeau, he is a Quebecker, a lawyer, an intellectual, a strong federalist and an intensely pragmatic politician."[33] Principal secretary to Trudeau from 1968 to 1972, Lalonde won his seat in 1972 (Outremont, Québec) and was immediately appointed minister of national health and welfare; during his tenure, he published a significant opus (*A New Perspective on the Health of Canadians*, 1974) that drew international attention to the social determinants of health. For Trudeau, Lalonde represented a trusted minister, a pillar who had accompanied him since the beginning (1968) and who shared the same political objectives.[34] Monique Bégin reportedly claimed that Lalonde would even, on occasion, take over the leadership of cabinet meetings and bring the ministers back to the items of the agenda.[35] The prime minister could also count on Jean Chrétien (minister of justice and attorney general) to lead partisan battles in the political trenches, as he famously did during the referendum and the negotiations leading to patriation. Finally, the prime minister relied on Allan MacEachen, "Celtic Sphinx"[36] and baron of the Atlantic, whom Trudeau had named deputy prime minister in 1977. MacEachen inaugurated the role, most likely for his effectiveness as House leader. He belonged to a narrow circle of ministers (including Lalonde) to whom the prime minister listened with genuine respect.[37] According to de Montigny Marchand (a prime minister's personal representative for G7 summits in the eighties), MacEachen had the prime minister's ear, communicating with him directly rather than through committees.[38]

Lalonde, Chrétien, and MacEachen were the most influential in the cabinet, those on whom Pierre Elliott Trudeau relied to establish the government's broad political orientations: "Trudeau always began with these three, and then built on that base," remembered Tom Axworthy. "When I became principal secretary to the prime minister in 1981, one of my jobs was to brief these three ministers on the latest public opinion surveys so that they could help Trudeau chart the political water."[39] To this trio one must also add Axworthy's brother Lloyd, who, as minister of employment and immigration, played an important role as a representative of the liberal left.

In terms of regional representation, the composition of the cabinet gave a large place to Québécois ministers, including Marc Lalonde and Jean Chrétien, as well as Pierre de Bané (regional economic expansion), André Ouellet (consumer and corporate affairs and postmaster-general), Francis Fox (secretary of state and communications minister), Gilles Lamontagne (minister of defence) and Monique Bégin (health). In addition, Mr. Trudeau named four new Quebec ministers to his cabinet. Donald Johnston became president of the Treasury Board and the new spokesman for Quebec's English community in cabinet. Yvon Pinard was appointed House leader, Charles Lapointe, minister of state for small business and tourism, and Pierre Bussières, minister of state in the Department of Finance. In total, the cabinet included 15 French-speaking MPs, including 12 from Quebec.[40] Given the upcoming referendum, a strong Quebec presence in cabinet could not be eschewed.

For the most part, newcomers were given less important positions, excepting Mark MacGuigan (secretary of state for external affairs) and Lloyd Axworthy (minister of employment and immigration). Ontario was well represented with MacGuigan, Eugene Whelan (Agriculture), Jean-Luc Pépin, the Quebec-born, francophone MP for Ottawa-Carleton (Transport), and Jean-Jacques Blais (Supply and Services). If we are to believe MacGuigan, several MPs had hoped for the external affairs portfolio, especially Jean Chrétien. Trudeau chose instead MacGuigan in part to avoid ruffling the feathers of other, competing Francophones, and for MacGuigan's reputation as someone who "would be cool under fire."[41] With MacEachen as minister of finance and Roméo LeBlanc, an Acadian from New Brunswick, minister of fisheries and oceans, the Atlantic region was also well represented. The West, however, was left underrepresented. With only two Liberal MPs among the 77 from the region, Trudeau had to call on senators to provide the West with more representation, as will be further discussed below.

When it came to establishing the ideological and programmatic orientation of the cabinet, Trudeau deliberately assembled a team that signaled, per the *Toronto Star*, "a return toward genuine liberalism."[42] Bégin and Axworthy represented the left in a role described by Donald J. Savoie as that of "mission participants": ministers working first and foremost for a cause.[43] Along the same lines, Herb Gray's appointment as minister of industry, trade, and commerce gave pride of place to the prime minister's strategy of economic nationalism. Eugene Whelan, for his part, seemed more of a "process politician," those skilled at leading projects and making announcements.[44] The colourful, cowboy-hat-wearing populist was one of the few Easterners who could be dispatched to the West and there receive a warm welcome.[45]

Outside cabinet, trusted staffers from the 1970s were likewise still on board and exerted a considerable influence, among them Jim Coutts (principal secretary, 1976–81), a staunch advocate of doctrinal left liberalism,[46] as was Tom Axworthy (principal secretary, 1981–4). Jim Coutts's influence, inescapable at the time of Trudeau's return to power, could not help but wane when Coutts ran for and lost a by-election in Toronto, in 1981. On the other side, long-time staffer André Burelle complained of the disproportionate influence exercised by these advisers, believing that they would lead Pierre Elliott Trudeau towards a liberalism unconcerned with the aspirations of Quebec.[47] Moreover, relations between Trudeau's advisers and his most influential ministers could also be strained. For example, MacEachen reportedly flew into a "holy rage" when he learned that Tom Axworthy intended to invite peaceful protesters to a cabinet meeting in Val Morin, Quebec, held in the summer of 1983, to discuss the issue of cruise missile testing. MacEachen appealed to the prime minister to invite representatives from both sides, and ultimately prevailed.[48] Such tensions also manifested between Chrétien and Trudeau's advisers regarding the process of constitutional patriation.

In terms of cabinet structure, Trudeau abandoned the 11-member "inner cabinet" as well as the four ministerial committees, both designed by Joe Clark in 1979.[49] Instead, Trudeau revived the Priorities and Planning Committee that functioned as cabinet's central decision-making entity.[50] This centralized design as well as the cabinet membership that favoured long-time loyalists signaled Trudeau's intention to maintain a firm grip on critical operations, especially over constitutional matters. It also lends credence to the presidentialist viewpoint.

Image 15.1. Prime Minister Pierre Trudeau (centre), Deputy Prime Minister Allan MacEachen (left), and Indian Affairs Minister John Munro (right), during voting on amendments to the Constitution, House of Commons, 23 April 1981

Source: Andy Clark, Canadian Press, CP2773453.

The Shuffle

During the first two years of his term, the prime minister did not make any major personnel changes to the cabinet. Rumours of an upcoming shuffle began to stir in late summer 1982, as the Liberal government was preoccupied with an economy now mired in recession. The tax reform proposed in the 1981 budget, targeting the affluent individuals and large corporations to increase revenue, had been ill received, while the 1982 budget, forecasting a dramatically growing deficit, came across as out of control. The government had retained the Clark government's Expenditure Management System, designed to give ministers an opportunity to decide among them how moneys would be allocated in certain policy areas. It was renamed the Policy and Expenditure Management System (PEMS), but it did not work. Trudeau used a classic instrument – shuffling ministers – to breathe new life into a government that had just, after tough negotiations, patriated the Canadian Constitution. Changes were not made to placate a rival threat, as if often the case, but rather to accelerate the implementation of Trudeau's program, as well as to signal a recalibration of its economic policy with a distinctly rightist bent.

The shuffle took place in two stages, the first and most important in early September 1982. First, the prime minister removed MacEachen from Finance and entrusted the office to Lalonde, while Chrétien – believed to have the personal qualities to appease both the West and Newfoundland, the other oil producer – replaced him at the Department of Energy, Mines, and Resources. Chrétien, himself disappointed with his new assignment, was coldly received in Alberta.[51] Lalonde, for his part, had received another critical portfolio, as inflation and unemployment roiled at the time. Another significant change was to grant MacEachen the Foreign Office, whose mandate had been enlarged in January 1982 by the merger of External Affairs with the Trade Commissioner Service. His predecessor, MacGuigan, had been removed due to differences with the prime minister, and this former Dean of the University of Windsor Law School was handed the Department of Justice.[52] Generally speaking, the shuffle was deemed to favour continuity.[53]

The second stage occurred later in the same month. Herb Gray, minister of industry, trade, and commerce, had been given the additional mandate of regional economic expansion the previous January. The September shuffle saw the left-leaning minister lose both appointments as he was shifted to president of the Treasury Board, while the more conservative Ed Lumley replaced him at Trade, Industry, and Commerce. This signaled an ideological shift within the party, as did the appointment of Donald Johnston as minister of state for economic development. Pierre de Bané became minister of fisheries and oceans.[54] At the same time, to refresh the cabinet, the prime minister promoted some junior ministers, most notably Serge Joyal (secretary of state) and Charles Lapointe (minister of state for external relations); Public Works went to Roméo LeBlanc, of New Brunswick. These changes were the result of compromise between two ideological tendencies within the party, the so-called Business Liberals, led by Don Johnston and Ed Lumley, and the Welfare Liberals – Axworthy, Gray, LeBlanc, and Bégin – who championed an interventionist State.[55] Finally, in October 1982, Michael Pitfield, clerk of the Privy Council in the 1970s and again in 1980, was replaced by Gordon Osbaldeston. This was interpreted as the end of an era given the close personal relationship between the outgoing clerk and the prime minister.[56]

The changes were intended to revive a government dealing with severe challenges due to a faltering economy (especially inflation), as well as hostility from the Ronald Reagan administration in Washington. The American administration was especially irritated by Trudeau's peace initiative, launched in 1983. Trudeau was seen as a socialist, one who placed the USSR and the United States on an equal footing.[57] The shuffle made known that the original team was still in charge, for the most part, albeit with new responsibilities. Remarkably, only a handful of ministers held a single portfolio throughout their tenure. These include Monique Bégin (health), Eugene Whelan (agriculture), John Munro (Indian affairs and northern development), and Francis Fox (communications, with a brief mandate as secretary of state in 1980–81). The shuffle was also meant to indicate that the government was turning its attention to pressing economic matters, which had taken a back seat to the intense constitutional negotiations of the previous two years.

Girding for the Referendum Battle

The referendum battle was a critical juncture in Pierre Trudeau's career. Having entered politics specifically to oppose Quebec's nationalist movement, he addressed the challenge with urgency.[58] Indeed, the question was debated in the Quebec National Assembly on 4 March 1980, one day after Trudeau unveiled his new cabinet. Moreover, the date of the referendum was announced just as the Liberal government began its session, on 15 April, after the Speech from the Throne,[59] in which the Liberal government committed to "renew federalism" and to "revive the process of constitutional reform."[60]

With a sovereignty referendum on the horizon, Trudeau intensified his Canadian-nationalist rhetoric. Above all, the Trudeau government promised a renewal of the federation if the referendum failed: "Because my Government wants to strengthen the spirit of Canadian unity and nurture the seeds of renewal, it promises to interpret a vote of 'no' to sovereignty-association as a vote for the rebuilding of the Canadian federation. My Government also promises to give effect to a 'no' vote by mobilizing all the forces at its command in order to ensure the renewal of the Federation in a spirit of respect and justice for all."[61]

Indeed, when forming the cabinet, "[t]he Prime Minister took personal command of a third potentially stormy area, abolishing the Ministry of State for Federal-Provincial Relations," to quote journalist Jeffrey Simpson.[62] The message was clear: Trudeau would be personally involved, to a high degree, in the referendum contest. To be fair, his ministers also played a crucial role, though Jean Chrétien claims to have only reluctantly agreed to lead federalist troops in the campaign.[63]

On that front, Quebec Premier René Lévesque understood Jean Chrétien to be the actual leader of the "No" campaign, rather than Claude Ryan, then leader of the Liberal Party of Quebec.[64] Towards the end of March 1980, polls favouring a "yes" result worried members of the Liberal Party of Canada in Québec. Claude Ryan was criticized for having poorly prepared for the debate, and for having published the "Beige Book," a document revealing the Quebec Liberals' constitutional policy, at an inopportune time. A feeling of dread ("angoisse sourde") began to spread among federal party members, urging them to develop a "positive" strategy, according to Liberal Senator Jean Marchand.[65] Thus, pressure increased on Chrétien to take a more important role beginning in April 1980.[66]

Very present from the start of the campaign, Chrétien distinguished himself with his trademark colourful style, and with speeches denouncing what he described as "hate" present in the discourse. Another minister with an important role was Pierre de Bané (minister of regional economic expansion), who was equally fierce in his criticisms of the sovereigntist project.[67] Other members of the cabinet also participated in the referendum campaign, including Jean-Luc Pépin (minister of transport) who not only praised the Beige Book in a speech at the Richelieu Club in Vanier, but had actually inspired its contents through his own report (Pépin-Robarts) in 1978.[68]

Of course, pressure was equally felt at the prime ministerial level.[69] Trudeau's speech at the Paul-Sauvé Arena (14 May 1980) constitutes the strongest moment of his involvement in the referendum campaign, repeating the promise of the Speech from the Throne to renew federalism in Canada,[70] a moment where he truly stepped up to centre stage. Soon after, on the heels of the No victory, the prime minister quickly began the patriation process by inviting the ten provincial premiers to a meeting on 9 June 1980, at his official residence.[71] Jean Chrétien was handed the mandate of patriating the Constitution, with an amendment formula and a Charter of Rights and Liberties.[72] It was understood that the process should be set in motion posthaste.

According to Barry L. Strayer, a telling sign of what he calls a "new aggressive attitude" in patriating the Constitution was the appointment of Michael Kirby as secretary of cabinet for federal-provincial relations, replacing Gordon Robertson, who had retired during the Joe Clark interlude.[73] Kirby, who had previously served as Pierre Trudeau's assistant principal secretary in 1974–6,[74] enjoyed repeating "When the going gets tough, the tough get going," and was known for his combative style. He was considered an architect of the policy leading to patriation and would play an important role in signing the Kirby Memorandum (30 August 1982), to which 15 authors had collaborated, and which reviewed the negotiations and proposed a number of strategies toward a successful conclusion.[75]

This memorandum was of critical importance because the Liberal government had the obligation to establish its constitutional positions in anticipation of the 1980 First Ministers' Conference on the Constitution. The conference was slated for September, only a few months after the Quebec Referendum campaign, during which Trudeau had firmly committed to constitutional renewal. A central element of patriation was the inclusion of the Charter of Rights and Freedoms, because, as Chrétien put it, "The boss wants this Charter."[76] Negotiations between premiers and the federal government were complex, to be sure, but equally those within the federal team. Chrétien had to battle with Trudeau's close advisers (Michael Pitfield and Michael Kirby) who, like some in the Liberal caucus, preferred to submit the amending formula and the Charter to a referendum, a strategy Chrétien personally opposed.[77]

The key moment in the patriation process occurred during the "interminable" federal-provincial conference from 2 to 5 November 1981. The agreement was ultimately made without the consent of Quebec and is referred to as the "nuit des longs couteaux," or night of long knives.[78] The patriation officially took place on 17 April 1982, completing an important project for Trudeau. However, Trudeau's challenges were not over. The Liberal government had also embarked on a project to Canadianize the energy sector, fanning the fires of Western alienation in a region where the prime minister found few kindred souls.[79]

The Regionalist Challenge

The issue of regional equalization was one of the Liberal team's five campaign themes.[80] In the Speech from the Throne, the government announced significant changes to energy policy with the National Energy Program: "Canada's resource base will be used as the basic building block of a vigorous industrial policy."[81] When the composition of his cabinet was announced, some observers were already noting that the government's "major test" would be in oil country.[82] In November 1980, the program was announced in MacEachen's budget. The challenge, for the prime minister, was that he had only two MPs in the West.

Unlike Quebec, Western Canada was largely absent from the cabinet given the few elected Liberals from the region. Alongside Manitoba's Lloyd Axworthy (employment and immigration), nicknamed the "regional minister in a hurry,"[83] were three senators from the West, each representing a particular province, whom the prime minister had appointed ministers of state (Hazen Argue, Horace "Bud" Olson, and Ray Perrault, also leader of the government in the Senate). This meagre representation made it difficult to advance nationwide, transformative projects. Indeed, in an attempt to increase the legitimacy of the Liberal government for the patriation process, Trudeau had turned to the New Democrats, offering Ed Broadbent and his party "five or six Cabinet portfolios" in a coalition offer refused by the NDP.[84] As such, the Liberal party's poor regional representation complicated the goal of revitalizing Canada's economy and unity.

Lalonde established himself firmly in control of the entire program. He was seconded by a "small group of Liberal party campaign strategists"[85] who handled the fraught relations with Western provinces regarding the National Energy Program. Because there were few interceders within cabinet to champion the project, it encountered resistance and, according to Pitfield, discussions were tense on the subject.[86]

Meanwhile, the Liberal government wanted to act quickly on both the referendum and the major overhaul of the energy policy. According to Trudeau biographers Christina McCall and Stephen Clarkson, Lalonde, Trudeau, and Pitfield "no longer wanted to play philosopher-kings but to achieve constitutional reform and restructure the energy sector."[87] It was under the impetus of Michael Pitfield, the "Metternich of the Canadian public service,"[88] that a new system was implemented in 1980 which gave ministers (Lalonde specifically) greater leeway, especially to pilot the energy-sector reform. Dubbed "EnFin," a group of high-level bureaucrats had their own budget and reported directly to the Priorities and Planning Committee, and not to the Cabinet Committee on Economic Development, as had been prior practice. As a result, this group acted as a committee of the prime minister, allowing him to maintain greater control. "Even the inner cabinet was largely excluded from EnFin's deliberations."[89] In the high-stakes context of this second mandate, decision-making could no longer take the tortuous paths of deliberation put in place during the 70s.

The regionalist dimension was not limited to Western Canada, and some ministers gave it particular importance, for example Pierre de Bané, MP for Matane (Gaspésie, Québec). The first MP of Arab origin, de Bané explicitly asked to be appointed minister of regional economic expansion. In an interview with political scientist Herman Bakvis, de Bané complained that the federal nature of Canada prevented the central government from implementing specifically regional policies.[90] At the time of his appointment, de Bané asked the prime minister for a review of his ministerial mandate, as he felt that he could not perform the duties assigned to him.[91] His request was partially successful; a reform was carried out, but by the Privy Council Office. Indeed when, in January 1982, the prime minister made changes to the three economic and regional ministries, de Bané was demoted to the office of minister of state for external affairs under the aegis of MacGuigan.[92] In September 1982, de Bané was transferred again, this time to Fisheries and Oceans to replace Roméo LeBlanc. An apparently minor shuffle, this reform significantly brought trade-related activities back to the Department of External Affairs, while the Department of Economic and Regional Expansion disappeared. Most notably, a new central body was created, the Department of State for Economic and Regional Development, to support the regional development objectives while ensuring that the federal government received all due credit[93] for its policies.

These regionalist concerns meshed with an age-old, deeply-rooted political patronage system, which the Liberals continued to nurture, especially in the fight against Québécois sovereigntists. If Trudeau was not involved directly, he nonetheless approved of its use: "Trudeau took little, if any, interest in the routine patronage: the awarding of contracts for services, the appointments of a local or regional nature. He remained, of course, fully supportive of the massive federal spending in Quebec which he believed formed an indispensable part of convincing Quebeckers that the federal government could serve their interests."[94] This responsibility was entrusted to regional ministers who made sure to redistribute and favour the Liberal ridings, the objective being to obtain high visibility for the federal government. "[Trudeau] introduced reforms that gave MPs offices in their ridings, increased office and research staff. In Quebec, it remained an abiding practice to credit the local MP with any federal spending or good deed."[95]

In Quebec, it was Lalonde who took care of such ministrations: "Lalonde's dominance of the Quebec caucus had been supreme since he took over from Jean Marchand as the province's party boss in 1975."[96] Patronage, appointments, and the allocation of funds all passed through him. For example, it was apparently Lalonde who pushed for Davie, a shipbuilding company on the south shore of Quebec, to be granted frigate contracts.[97] To this end, Lalonde established a system of delegation where designated "subregional" ministers were charged with redistribution. For example, André Ouellet (minister of consumer and corporate affairs, 1980–3, postmaster general, 1980–1, minister of labour, 1983–4) handled the Montreal region, while Pierre Bussières (minister of national revenue, 1982–4), Pierre de Bané, and Lloyd Axworthy were responsible for Quebec City, Gaspésie, and Manitoba respectively.[98] This strategy of regional diffusion maintained a sort of balance of favours across the country, supported by a complicated web of alliances, and subjected to all the expected accusations of favouritism.

The Legacy

John Turner, Trudeau's successor, was prime minister for only a few months, long enough nonetheless to announce a new cabinet on 30 June 1984. Turner took the reins of the Liberal party at a difficult juncture, when his predecessor's policy directions had fostered controversy in many regions of the country.[99] His most pressing challenge, beyond forming a government, was implementing policies before the upcoming election, expected within the year.

To prepare for this election, Turner brought fresh faces to the Prime Minister's Office, demarcating his team from his predecessor's to the point where it looked almost like the arrival of an opposition party.[100] With regard to the cabinet, however, Turner mixed old blood with new, retaining part of Trudeau's team, dismissing 13 members, and reducing the number of ministers from 37 to 29. Chrétien, his leadership rival, was given a key role in Quebec, along with André Ouellet, who had organized Turner's campaign in the province. Lalonde lost his position as lieutenant in Quebec but was rewarded with a continuing mandate at the Department of Finance.[101]

Above all, Turner asserted that the model put in place by his predecessor was inadequate, in particular because it diminished ministerial responsibility.[102] He criticized the system for being too elaborate and complex.[103] In fact, Turner asserted that his predecessor's government had become "too heavy, too complex, too slow, and too expensive."[104] He thus abolished three cabinet committees and two ministries of state, and reshaped the decision-making hierarchy, notably by creating a Bureau of Regional Development.[105] Turner also reduced the number of regional ministers by dismissing the three Western senators from cabinet. In the eyes of some observers, the system put in place followed a more entrepreneurial model, breaking with Trudeau's Latin American or French approach to government management discussed earlier in this chapter,[106] and it stands to reason that Turner, closer to the business community, would choose this model to shape his government. For example, with the approaching election and the attendant loosening purse strings, Lloyd Axworthy could announce projects endorsed by the prime minister without going through the cabinet or Treasury Board approval procedures.[107] In the end, however, John Turner did not have enough time to leave a significant mark. The partisan appointments inherited from his predecessor as well as his own poor campaigning ultimately sunk his party and ended his short tenure as prime minister.[108] We will therefore never quite know how cabinet might have functioned under his leadership. The party suffered one of its worst defeats, electing only 40 MPs and losing 25 cabinet members.

The eminent place of Pierre Elliott Trudeau in Canadian political history was consolidated during this particularly intense four-year term, especially at the start of his mandate. But it was not quite a one-man show. Faced with daunting challenges, the prime minister composed his cabinet with experienced ministers in key government positions. These well-known figures, notably Marc Lalonde, Allan MacEachen, and Jean Chrétien, managed and often steered the most difficult dossiers. Only a few new recruits entered the cabinet, and in this regard, the prime minister favoured continuity in a fairly conservative way. In terms of regional representation, the cabinet suffered from a significant imbalance with a meagre roster in the four provinces west of Ontario. Therefore, the figureheads of the cabinet were largely from the eastern and Atlantic provinces.

The cabinet consultation process was modified to give more control to the prime minister and his closest associates than had been the case in the seventies, in large part because the political environment demanded a less cumbersome and faster decision-making structure than in the past. In particular, Minister Lalonde was given much leeway to carry out the National Energy Program, while Chrétien led the federal efforts in the referendum fight. A few years on, the mid-term shuffle in September 1982 signaled that the Liberal government was moving in a different ideological direction. The challenging economic context exerted greater pressure; the interventionist approach was losing its appeal such that the small-government right wing of the party took over from the more statist left. Changes in the cabinet reflected this new orientation.

To be sure, by 1982, the high points of Trudeau's career were already behind him. The presidential style of governance he had adopted in the 1970s gave him control of the political agenda that would cement his legacy, most strikingly during the first two years of his 1980 mandate, a time when Trudeau wholly spoke for Canada during the constitutional negotiations and patriation process.

Even as persistent economic challenges and disappointing budgets created a wave of discontent among electors that eventually shook his party's hold on power, Trudeau never quite shook his presidential mantle, as evidenced by his personal engagement on the international stage toward the end of his final mandate. "Statecraft is about maintaining popularity with the electorate," write Patrice Dutil and Stephen Azzi in the first chapter of this book. However, in the beginning of the Eighties, statecraft was more about maintaining Canada's national integrity than maintaining popularity with the electorate. Sometimes, history provides the opportunity for a prime minister to rise above partisan politics in favour of national statesmanship. Trudeau most certainly seized his.

NOTES

* I would like to thank Natalie Boisvert for her inestimable help with the English version.

1 Ron Graham, *The Last Act: Pierre Trudeau, the Gang of Eight, and the Fight for Canada* (Toronto: Allen Lane, 2011), 37.

2 John English, *Just Watch Me: The Life of Pierre Elliott Trudeau, 1968–2000* (Toronto: Vintage Books, 2010), 40.

3 Donald S. Macdonald, "The Trudeau Cabinet: A Memoir," in *Trudeau's Shadow: The Life and the Legacy of Pierre Elliott Trudeau*, ed. Andrew Cohen and J.L. Granatstein (Toronto: Vintage Books, 1999), 168.

4 Christina McCall and Stephen Clarkson, *Trudeau and Our Times*, vol. 2, *The Heroic Delusion* (Toronto: McClelland & Stewart, 1994), 431.

5 Denis Smith, "President and Parliament: The Transformation of Parliamentary Government," in *Apex of Power: The Prime Minister and Political Leadership in Canada*, ed. Thomas A. Hockin (Scarborough: Prentice–Hall, 1977), 322; and Walter Stewart, *Shrug: Trudeau in Power* (Toronto: New Press, 1971), 190.

6 Donald J. Savoie, *Governing from the Centre: The Concentration of Power and Canadian Politics* (Toronto: University of Toronto Press, 1999).

7 "M. Trudeau avait de la gestion gouvernementale une conception plus française, plus latine: tout, en définitive, devait aboutir sur la table du conseil des ministres et le chef du gouvernement pouvait en tout temps intervenir dans les affaires des autres ministères" (Michel Roy, "L'ère John Turner," *La presse*, 2 July 1984, A6).

8 Jean Massot, "Le Président de la République et le Premier ministre," in *La vie politique en France*, ed. Dominique Chagnollaud (Paris: Éditions du Seuil, 1993), 55–66.

9 Steward, *Shrug*, 188.

10 Peter Aucoin, "Organizational Change in the Machinery of Canadian Government: From Rational Management to Brokerage Politics," *Canadian Journal of Political Science* 19, no. 1 (March 1986): 6–7.

11 Savoie, *Governing from the Centre*, 84.

12 Robert Bothwell and J.L. Granatstein, *Trudeau's World: Insiders Reflect on Foreign Policy, Trade, and Defence, 1968–84* (Vancouver: University of British Columbia Press, 2017), 85.

13 McCall and Clarkson, *Heroic Delusion*, 253.

14 Graham White, *Cabinets and First Ministers* (Vancouver: University of British Columbia Press, 2005), 68–9.

15 Bothwell and Granatstein, *Trudeau's World*, 35.

16 Michel Vastel, "Le boycott des Jeux: Trudeau est sceptique," *Le Devoir*, 19 April 1980, 1.

17 Bothwell and Granatstein, *Trudeau's World*, 76.

18 English, *Just Watch Me*, 464.

19 Nancy Southam, ed., *Trudeau tel que nous l'avons connu*, trans. Geneviève Roquet et al. (Montreal: Fides, 2005), 76.

20 Paul Barker, "The Canada Health Act and the Cabinet Decision-Making System of Pierre Elliott Trudeau," *Canadian Public Administration* 32, no 1 (1989): 97.

21 Daniel Raunet, *Monique Bégin: Entretiens* (Montreal: Boréal, 2016), 128–9.

22 Jerry S. Grafstein, *A Leader Must Be a Leader: Encounters with Eleven Prime Ministers* (Oakville, ON: Mosaic Press, 2019), 132–3.

23 Marcel Adam, "Un parti en désarroi, un gouvernement aux abois," *La Presse*, 11 February 1984, A6.

24 "Le PLC en plein désarroi," *La Presse*, 4 February 1984, A12.

25 McCall and Clarkson, *Heroic Delusion*, 157.

26 *Throne Speech*, 14 April 1980, 10. The text used comes from the collection of political texts made available on the Poltext platform (Poltext, accessed 28 November 2024, http://www.poltext.org) by the Center for Public Policy Analysis at Laval University, with the financial support of the Fonds de recherche du Québec – Société et culture.

27 *Throne Speech*, 14 April 1980, 9.

28 Ivan Guay, "Le grand défi du Cabinet Trudeau," *La Presse*, 6 March 1980, A4.

29 Matthew Kerby and Feodor Snagovsky, "Not All Experience Is Created Equal: MP Career Typologies and Ministerial Appointments in the Canadian House of Commons, 1968–2015," *Government and Opposition* 56, no. 2 (2021): 330.

30 Christian Deblock, "La politique économique canadienne 1970–1988," in *La politique canadienne à l'épreuve du continentalisme*, ed. Christian Deblock and Richard Arteau (Montreal: ACFAS, 1988), 30–1.

31 Matthew Kerby, "Worth the Wait: Determinants of Ministerial Appointment in Canada, 1935–2008," *Canadian Journal of Political Science* 42, no. 3 (September 2009): 607–8.

32 Gilles Paquin, "La vieille garde," *La Presse*, 4 March 1980, A1, A8.

33 Walter Stewart, "The 30 Men Trudeau Trusts," *Maclean's*, 1 October 1969.

34 Christina McCall-Newman, *Grits: An Intimate Portrait of the Liberal Party* (Toronto: Macmillan, 1982), 279.

35 Raunet, *Monique Bégin*, 129.

36 Xavier Gélinas, "Allan MacEachen, the 'Celtic Sphinx' (1921–2017)," Canadian Museum of History, 30 November 2021, https://www.historymuseum.ca/blog /allan-maceachen/.

37 McCall and Clarkson, *Heroic Delusion*, 293.

38 Bothwell and Granatstein, *Trudeau's World*, 117.

39 Thomas S. Axworthy, "Old-Timers' Day: What Grits Can Learn from Hall-of-Famer Allan J. MacEachen," *Policy Options*, 1 March 2012, https:// policyoptions.irpp.org/fr/magazines/the-liberal-renewal/old-timers-day-what -grits-can-learn-from-hall-of-famer-allan-j-maceachen/.

40 Jeffrey Simpson, "Lalonde, MacEachen in Key Jobs: Cabinet List Shows Trudeau's Tight Rein," *Globe and Mail*, 4 March 1980, 1.

41 Bothwell and Granatstein, *Trudeau's World*, 75.

42 "Promising Trudeau Cabinet," *Toronto Star*, 4 March 1980, A8.

43 Savoie, *Governing from the Centre*, 244.

44 Savoie, *Governing from the Centre*, 245.

45 Canadian Press, "Former Agriculture Minister Eugene Whelan Dead at 88," *CBC News*, 19 February 2013, https://www.cbc.ca/news/canada/windsor/former -agriculture-minister-eugene-whelan-dead-at-88-1.1365656.

46 McCall-Newman, *Grits*, 138.

47 André Burelle, *Pierre Elliott Trudeau: L'intellectuel et le politique. Témoignage et archives personnelles d'un conseiller du premier ministre Trudeau* (Montreal: Fides, 2005).

48 Gilbert Lavoie, "Trudeau encore premier ministre le 30 mars …," *La Presse*, 8 February 1984, A4.

49 Michel Vastel, "Trudeau confie à des vétérans les ministères importants," *Le Devoir*, 4 March 1980, 1.

50 Savoie, *Governing from the Centre*, 44.

51 Gilles Paquin, "Chrétien déçu, MacEachen soulagé," *La Presse*, 11 September 1982, A7.

52 Kim Richard Nossal, "The PM and the SSEA in Canada's Foreign Policy: Dividing the Territory, 1968–1994," *International Journal* 50, no. 1 (Winter 1994/5): 198.

53 Michel Roy, "Le remaniement de la continuité," *La Presse*, 11 September 1982, A6.

54 McCall and Clarkson, *Heroic Delusion*, 263–4.

55 McCall and Clarkson, *Heroic Delusion*, 250.

56 Gilbert Lavoie, "Pitfield quitte Trudeau," *La Presse*, 27 October 1982, A5.

57 J.L. Granatstein, "Gouzenko to Gorbachev: Canada's Cold War," *Canadian Military Journal* 12, no. 1 (Winter 2011): 50.

58 Donald J. Savoie, "The Federal Government: Revisiting Court Government in Canada," in *Executive Styles in Canada: Cabinet Structures and Leadership Practices in Canadian Government*, ed. Luc Bernier, Keith Brownsey, and Michael Howlett (Toronto: University of Toronto Press, 2005), 18

59 English, *Just Watch Me*, 449.

60 *Throne Speech*, 14 April 1980, 16.

61 *Throne Speech*, 14 April 1980, 10–11.

62 Simpson, "Lalonde, MacEachen in Key Jobs."

63 Jean Chrétien, *Dans la fosse aux lions* (Montreal: Éditions de l'homme, 1994), 130–1.

64 "Le refus de Trudeau ne vise qu'à effrayer le Québec, estime Lévesque," *Le Devoir*, 17 April 1980, 1.

65 Paul Longpré, "Les libéraux fédéraux dans les douleurs référendaires," *La Presse*, 29 March 1980, A10.

66 English, *Just Watch Me*, 449.

67 "Chrétien et De Bané tentent de faire vibrer les cordes sensibles des Québécois," *Le Devoir*, 19 April 1980, 5

68 Presse Canadienne, "Pépin n'entend pas se croiser les bras," *La presse*, 7 March 1980, A7; and English, *Just Watch Me*, 445.

69 Pierre Bellemare, "La réplique du camp du 'non' viendra d'Ottawa," *La Presse*, 31 March 1980, A11.

70 François Barbeau, "Trudeau s'engage à renouveler immédiatement le fédéralisme," *Le Devoir*, 15 May 1980, 1.

71 Graham, *Last Act*, 39.

72 Jean-François Lisée, "Constitution 1982 et 1992 aux sources de l'échec," in *Le nouvel ordre constitutionnel canadien du rapatriement de 1982 à nos jours*, ed. François Rocher and Benoît Pelletier (Quebec: Presses de l'Université du Québec, 2013), 86.

73 Barry L. Strayer, *Canada's Constitutional Revolution* (Edmonton: University of Alberta Press, 2013), 120.

74 J.L. Granatstein, "Michael J.L. Kirby," *The Canadian Encyclopedia*, last modified 16 December 2013, https://www.thecanadianencyclopedia.ca/en/article/michael-jl-kirby.

75 Strayer, *Canada's Constitutional Revolution*, 132

76 Strayer, *Canada's Constitutional Revolution*, 121.

77 Graham, *Last Act*, 174.

78 Robert Dutrisac, "Il y a 25 ans, la nuit des longs couteaux – Une Constitution inachevée," *Le Devoir*, 4 November 2006, https://www.ledevoir.com/politique/canada/122165/il-y-a-25-ans-la-nuit-des-longs-couteaux-une-constitution-inachevee.

79 Frédéric Boily, "Le libéralisme de Pierre Elliott Trudeau à l'épreuve du nationalisme et du régionalisme: 1968–1980," in *The Political and Constitutional*

Legacy of Pierre Elliott Trudeau / L'héritage politique et constitutionnel de Pierre Elliott Trudeau, ed. Noura Karazivan and Jean Leclair (Toronto: LexisNexis, 2020), 193–211.

80 Stephen Clarkson, *The Big Red Machine: How the Liberal Party Dominates Canadian Politics* (Vancouver: University of British Columbia Press, 2005), 98.

81 *Throne Speech*, 14 April 1980, 14.

82 Ivan Guay, "Le grand défi du Cabinet Trudeau," *La Presse*, 6 March 1980, A4.

83 Herman Bakvis, *Regional Ministers: Power and Influence in the Canadian Cabinet* (Toronto: University of Toronto Press, 1991), ch. 8.

84 English, *Just Watch Me*, 447.

85 Bakvis, *Regional Ministers*, 120

86 Bothwell and Granatstein, *Trudeau's World*, 42.

87 McCall and Clarkson, *Heroic Delusion*, 172.

88 Bothwell and Granatstein, *Trudeau's World*, 96.

89 McCall and Clarkson, *Heroic Delusion*, 174.

90 Bakvis, *Regional Ministers*, 124.

91 Donald J. Savoie, "Implantation d'une nouvelle organisation en matière de développement économique," *Canadian Public Administration* 28, no 4 (Winter 1985): 607.

92 Gilbert Lavoie, "Le ministère de l'Expansion économique et régionale disparaît," *La Presse*, 13 January 1982, C1.

93 Savoie, "Implantation d'une nouvelle organisation," 608–10.

94 Jeffrey Simpson, "The Two Trudeaus: Federal Patronage in Quebec, 1968–84," *Journal of Canadian Studies* 22, no. 2 (Summer 1987): 107.

95 Simpson, "Two Trudeaus," 106.

96 McCall and Clarkson, *Heroic Delusion*, 300.

97 Donald J. Savoie, *Democracy in Canada: The Disintegration of Our Institutions* (Montreal: McGill-Queen's University Press, 2019), 143.

98 Bakvis, *Regional Ministers*, 135–6.

99 Clarkson, *Big Red Machine*, 110–11.

100 Clarkson, *Big Red Machine*, 116.

101 "Chrétien et Ouellet: les plus influents du Québec," *La Presse*, 2 July 1984, A9.

102 Aucoin, "Organizational Change," 3–27.

103 Barker, "Canada Health Act," 91.

104 "Trudeau-Pitfield Bureaucracy First Item on Turner's Overhaul," *Globe and Mail*, 2 July 1984, 5, quoted in Savoie, "Implantation d'une nouvelle organisation," 611.

105 "Réorganisation majeure du processus de décision," *La Presse*, 2 July 1984, A9.

106 Roy, "L'ère John Turner."

107 Bakvis, *Regional Ministers*, 234.

108 Hugh Winsor, "Former PM John Turner Was Old Liberalism's Darling and Its Final, Flawed Champion," *Globe and Mail*, 19 September 2020, https://www.theglobeandmail.com/canada/article-obituary-john-turner-pm-for-79-days-was-old-liberalisms-darling/.

16 Brian Mulroney: Statecraft for Radical Change

RAYMOND B. BLAKE*

Brian Mulroney formally met his full cabinet for the first time on 17 September 1984, immediately after it was sworn in. He had a portrait of John A. Macdonald hung in the cabinet room in the Langevin Block to remind ministers that Conservatives had played an important role in nation-building, even if the Liberal party had governed for most of the time since "Old Tomorrow's" death in 1891. Mulroney had effectively been elected Canada's eighteenth prime minister on 4 September 1984, with 211 seats and 50.3 per cent of the vote, a crushing victory by all standards. Four years later, he won a second consecutive majority, becoming the first prime minister since 1953 to do so.

This latter campaign, in 1988, would be his last, as he grew immensely unpopular afterwards. Although he retired before the 1993 general election, Canadians overwhelming rejected his party. Still, Mulroney and his cabinet had an enormous impact: they reshaped Canada. Mulroney's cabinet charted a new course by negotiating free trade, first with the United States and then Mexico to create the North American Free Trade Agreement; pursued an aggressive foreign policy; participated in the Gulf War to remove Saddam Hussein from Kuwait; invested heavily to end South African apartheid; elevated the environment and climate change as new priorities, including an Acid Rain Treaty with the US and several international protocols; changed the relationship between state and citizen by reforming many aspects of Canada's much vaunted social security system; introduced a value-added tax and embarked on a policy of deregulation and privatization; and, not least, twice negotiated constitutional accords to address Quebec's frustrations with the 1982 constitution. The Mulroney government also heightened the rhetoric around the dangers of deficit spending and a burgeoning national debt and, even if both grew during their term, brought spending in line with revenues for the first time in years. The government also attempted to address Indigenous issues, especially around self-government and land claims and laid the groundwork for the creation of Nunavut.[1] It might well have been too much too quickly. Mulroney's senior policy adviser, Charles McMillan, had warned him that while the public wanted change, "too much will scare people."[2]

Such a record of policy change in less than nine years necessitates an examination of how the prime minister managed. Any attempt to assess Mulroney and his cabinet must give some credence to his claim "I always tried to do what I thought would be right for Canada in the long term, not what would be politically popular in the short term."[3] It was a strange maxim for any politician, but especially for Mulroney who, by most accounts, had a great desire to be accepted, respected, and even loved. He and his cabinet understood fully that many of their initiatives were risky politically and unlikely to be popular with voters. Yet, as Mulroney reminded Michael Wilson in a conversation at 24 Sussex Drive shortly after their 1984 victory, "Mike, you and I are here to make a difference ... we are in government to change things for the better."[4] They paid a heavy price for the changes they wrought.

Although much has been written about the Mulroney ministry, an assessment of its significance and impact may still be premature more than thirty years after it was voted out of office. Access to the personal records of those who served in the Mulroney's cabinet, including Mulroney himself, is not yet available to researchers, and cabinet records remained closed. Any attempt to understand the mindset, philosophy, and functioning of Mulroney and his cabinet must rely on media accounts from the period and on biographies and memoirs, including Mulroney's own. Even the published materials on the period are often based on interviews with unidentified sources, largely civil servants and party insiders who were mindful of cabinet confidentiality.[5] Mulroney had come to the prime minister's office as an outsider and in the 1983 Progressive Conservative leadership race he had vowed to hand out "pink slips and running shoes" to bureaucrats that he believed were too cozy with the Liberal party.[6] He wanted to simplify the central executive machinery of government and initially depended upon the partisans and friends who had helped him win the party leadership and the 1984 general election to do so. When that failed to deliver the results he wanted, he sought change, especially to those around him. Within two years of becoming prime minister, he turned to the bureaucracy and experienced Conservative insiders – even having the former take over the Prime Minister's Office – to help him and his cabinet achieve their objectives.

In fact, Mulroney struggled throughout his mandates to find a workable managerial style and system of cabinet governance. On those items that were a priority for Mulroney, he usually got his way, but when decisions were made by the Prime Minister's Office that upset a particular cabinet minister, Mulroney generally supported his minister. His cabinet seems to be one where cabinet ministers and the prime minister shared a similar vision and worked with remarkable unity but there was a constant struggle to find the best way to manage the government, and he embarked on a number of changes when his agenda for Canada was derailed. Throughout his years in Ottawa, he introduced several changes to the machinery of government. He reduced the number of cabinet committees upon assuming office but established a powerful Operations Committee to control both spending and ministerial autonomy. Despite his efforts, he never delivered the changes he promised to the machinery of government after the 1988 election to make the system more manageable and efficient. There were no fewer than fifteen committees on the books by 1993.

Mulroney's Approach to Management

Brian Mulroney was 45 years old when he became prime minister. Remarkably, he had never served in public office, making him unique in the annals of Canadian politics. Born in a very modest family in Baie-Comeau, he left Quebec in 1957 to attend St. Thomas College in Chatham, New Brunswick, and then St. Francis Xavier University in Nova Scotia where he became active in the Conservative Party before completing law school at Université Laval. A successful labour lawyer in Montreal and then president of Iron Ore Company of Canada, Mulroney had learned the art of compromise and negotiation and of moving people with divergent interests and objectives towards common goals. It was a skill at brokerage he used avidly when he became leader of the Conservative party on 11 June 1983 and would continue to use as prime minister. The party had been gravely divided for years over the leadership issue to the point where a "Tory Syndrome" had been diagnosed by scholars,[7] but Mulroney knew the importance of "the small kindness that motivates caucus members and inspires their families," such as personal notes and flowers on special occasions, or an invitation to join him for a drink after work.[8]

Mulroney began that practice in Ottawa the day after his leadership victory, when he reached out to the defeated candidates, their advisors and campaign teams, and notable MPs.[9] The divisions in the party extended beyond leadership, however, as Red Tories insisted that to win Conservatives had to compete for moderate centrist voters while Blue Tories wanted a compelling conservative alternative based on minimal interference by government in the economy, private ownership, controlled public spending, and unfettered trade. Not least were the western Conservatives, often socially and fiscally conservative and suspicious of the economic elites in Central Canada. Mulroney's party also included Quebec Liberals disillusioned with Trudeau and sovereigntists angry over the patriation of the constitution in 1982. Mulroney believed Conservatives had to be a party of moderation, accept bilingualism, for instance, and stay clear of "hot-button" issues, which often made the party out-of-touch with voters.[10] Mulroney knew he had created a witch's brew, but he performed his magic and held the coalition together for nearly a decade, sometimes through the sheer force of his personality.

Part of his strategy was to mobilize a group of senior party members he dubbed the 'Special Consultants' for advice that he kept secret from his advisors and the Cabinet. Not considered part of the government structure, the group of Red Tories included former leader Robert Stanfield, Senator Lowell Murray, who Mulroney met at St Francis Xavier University, Hugh Segal, long-time Conservative strategist, and David Macdonald and Douglas Roche, both former Conservative MPs.[11] He also talked constantly with friends across Canada, many of whom were members of the St. F.X. Progressive Conservative Club. This would have included Murray, Fred and Gerry Doucet, Pat MacAdam, and Sam Wakim, also a former Conservative MP. Charles McMillan was also a key adviser to Mulroney and had led a small group in the Conservative party's Research Office that eventfully became the Policy Unit in the Prime Minister's Office to develop policy. McMillan recalls that the prime minister demanded of those around him "frank and candid memos for his nightly reading" that would be discussed widely before a decision was made.[12]

Mulroney more formally relied on the Prime Minister's Office (PMO) whose staff complement increased by one-third and budget by half over Trudeau's last year in office.[13] From the beginning, it was staffed by partisans and friends Mulroney appointed, but it soon became clear that it was not up to the task of managing the machinery of government. Within 18 months, his government was in trouble. As he admits in his *Memoirs*, the government's message "wasn't getting out" and the PMO "was under bitter attack." Caucus was not happy, and ministers were "grumbling." One senior Conservative reportedly described the prime minister's staff to *Maclean's* as "knuckleheads who had a complete inability to run the machinery of government." There was considerable criticism of Fred Doucet, senior adviser to the prime minister, and Bernard Roy, the principal secretary, both long-time Mulroney friends.[14] John Crosbie claims there was "great tension between the staff of the PMO and ministers and their staffs." The PMO staff treated ministers as "servants," he suggests, adding it was "arrogant, heavy-handed, seldom thoughtful, and not particularly insightful." Of course, the PMO had to protect the prime minister, Crosbie acknowledges, but "ministers were regarded as likely not to be competent, to be continually getting themselves into trouble." It "believed that all power flowed from the centre" and it "could and should be directly involved in all activities of the government, with or without reference to the minister responsible. They regarded cabinet ministers as impotent appendages." Yet, Crosbie notes that when he and other ministers reached out directly to Mulroney, he supported them in their quarrels with the PMO.[15]

With Conservative approval at 28 percent, behind both the Liberals and the NDP, by mid-1986, MPs were worried about their political prospects. Mulroney reached out to Bill Davis, former premier of Ontario, and to Joe Clark for advice, searching for a chief of staff as one important step in better managing the government and his Cabinet, and implementing a more effective communications plan.[16] Derek Burney, a long-time External Affairs officer, was recruited. As Mulroney put it, he told Burney, "I want to focus my time on major issues like free trade and tax reform, not tainted tuna," a reference to a minister's 1985 interference with the work of food inspectors, leading to the sale of canned tuna previously deemed unfit for human consumption.[17] Burney recalls telling Mulroney that the PMO was "a bit like a wagon wheel without a rim," there was a hub but nothing holding it all together. Mulroney wanted better organization in his office, realizing that it had to be led by someone who knew how the bureaucracy functioned, was familiar with the major policy issues, and could bring the various parts of government together. Burney focused "the prime minister's time and his message on key issues and ensured consistency between the message and the delivery of action." He imposed order on those around Mulroney, running the PMO as a government department, building a coherent team from a collection of individuals while preventing disputes from getting out of hand and managing crises as they invariably arose.[18]

Other changes included the appointment of two veteran Conservative strategists, Marjory LeBreton as deputy chief of staff in the PMO, and Dalton Camp in the Privy Council Office as special adviser to the Cabinet, although placing Camp in PCO rather than PMO blurred the line between what Mulroney saw as partisans and civil servants. Mulroney later brought other officials from government departments into the PMO.[19] Stanley Hartt, the Deputy Minister of Finance, replaced Burney when the latter was appointed Ambassador to the US, and in January 1992, Segal replaced Norman Spector who had been appointed chief of staff in September 1990. They essentially followed the template that Burney had created, as the chief of staff became, as Segal recalls, "the single funnel of view and decisions to and from the prime minister and the regular controller and coordinator of his ever-changing agenda" so that the prime minister could stay on message and manage his agenda successfully.[20] It is noteworthy too that Mulroney's chiefs of staff were knowledgeable and proficient in the major policy issue of the day as Burney was on trade, Hartt on taxation, and Spector on federal-provincial relations.

A creative tension existed between the PMO, the ministers, caucus and Mulroney himself. One episode reveals both the extent of PMO control but also how Mulroney managed in moments of conflict and discord within his administration. It involved a dispute between France and Canada over the boundary with St. Pierre and Miquelon, two French islands off the coast of Newfoundland. When Canada declared a 200-miles exclusive economic zone in 1977, France took similar action around the two islands resulting in a boundary dispute that lasted for a decade. Then, in January 1987, without consulting Newfoundland MP John Crosbie and External Affairs minister Joe Clark, Mulroney allowed an agreement to be negotiated that gave France access to cod stocks while the boundary dispute was being arbitrated, even though there was growing concern over chronic overfishing in the area. Crosbie was outraged, criticized Mulroney publicly for being insensitive to Newfoundland while indulging in his desire to promote La Francophonie as a counterweight to Quebec.[21] Mulroney backed down and wrote an apology to Crosbie read by the deputy prime minister in the House of Commons assuring Crosbie that in further negotiations, "Canadian interests, not relations with France, are the paramount consideration."[22] As Crosbie notes, Mulroney quickly understood when a blunder had been made and took immediate steps to smooth things over.[23]

Choosing a Cabinet

The leading of a successful government requires not only crafting an effective and able cabinet but also instilling in ministers – and caucus – an appreciation of the demands of governing. As Mulroney relates in his *Memoirs*, he saw Conservatives as content with Opposition, but the prize for him was not Stornoway but 24 Sussex Drive.[24] Discipline and cabinet solidarity were important, and he broadcast that message when he instructed appointees to cabinet to gather in the Centre Block of the Parliament Buildings. His idea was that they would leave together for Rideau Hall rather than each straggling up separately. All male nominees had been instructed to wear dark blue business suits; all complied except Joe Clark who chose light brown.[25] One party insider told the *Globe and Mail*, "We want to be able to go to sleep at night knowing that all loose cannons have been lashed to the deck."[26]

Brian Mulroney's ministry on the day it took office, 17 September 1984:

1 Prime Minister – Brian Mulroney, 45, Quebec
2 Agriculture – John Wise, 48, Ontario
3 Communications – Marcel Masse, 48, Quebec
4 Consumer and Corporate Affairs – Michel Côté, 41, Quebec
5 Employment and Immigration – Flora MacDonald, 58, Ontario
6 Energy, Mines, and Resources – Pat Carney, 49, British Columbia
7 Environment – Suzanne Blais-Grenier, 48, Quebec
8 External Affairs – Joe Clark, 45, Alberta
9 External Relations – Monique Vézina, 49, Quebec
10 Finance – Michael Wilson, 46, Ontario
11 Fisheries and Oceans – John Fraser, 52, British Columbia
12 Government House Leader – Ramon Hnatyshyn, 50, Saskatchewan
13 Indian Affairs and Northern Development – David Crombie, 48, Ontario
14 International Trade – James Kelleher, 53, Ontario
15 Justice and Attorney General – John Crosbie, 53, Newfoundland
16 Labour – Bill McKnight, 44, Saskatchewan
17 Leader of the Government in the Senate – Duff Roblin, 67, Manitoba
   (senator)

18 Minister of State (Canadian Wheat Board) (Grains and Oilseeds) – Pierre Blais, 35, Quebec
19 Minister of State (Finance) – Barbara McDougall, 47, Ontario
20 Minister of State (Fitness and Amateur Sport) – Otto Jelinek, 44, Ontario
21 Minister of State (Forestry and Mines) – Gerald Merrithew, 53, New Brunswick
22 Minister of State (Mines) – Robert Layton, 59, Quebec
23 Minister of State (Multiculturalism) – Jack Murta, 50, Manitoba
24 Minister of State (Science and Technology) – Thomas Siddon, 41, British Columbia
25 Minister of State (Small Business) – André Bissonnette, 39, Quebec
26 Minister of State (Tourism) – Thomas McMillan, 39, Prince Edward Island
27 Minister of State (Transport) – Benoît Bouchard, 44, Quebec
28 Minister of State (Youth) – Andrée Champagne, 45, Quebec
29 National Defence – Robert Coates, 56, Nova Scotia
30 National Health and Welfare – Jake Epp, 45, Manitoba
31 National Revenue – Perrin Beatty, 34, Ontario
32 President of the Privy Council and Deputy Prime Minister – Erik Nielsen, 60, Yukon
33 Public Works – Roch LaSalle, 56, Quebec
34 Regional Industrial Expansion – Sinclair Stevens, 57, Ontario
35 Secretary of State of Canada – Walter McLean, 48, Ontario
36 Solicitor General – Elmer MacKay, 48, Nova Scotia
37 Supply and Services – Harvie Andre, 44, Alberta
38 Transport – Don Mazankowski, 49, Alberta
39 Treasury Board – Robert de Cotret, 40, Quebec
40 Veterans Affairs – George Hees, 74, Ontario

Mulroney's difficulties were amplified in choosing a cabinet with 211 members from which to select. Like his predecessors, he weighed provincial and regional representation, ethnicity and gender, and ideological differences as well as considering individual competence, experience and probity. A 40-member ministry was chosen (28 ministers, 11 ministers of state, and Prime Minister Mulroney), the largest in Canadian history (see image 16.1). Mulroney essentially kept the ministerial portfolios that Trudeau and John Turner had created but he more than doubled the number of ministers of state in Turner's cabinet.[27] Many of his shadow cabinet and contenders for the leadership were selected. Clark was given External Affairs for the sake of party unity and because they shared a certain view of Canada's place in the world, although Mulroney claims that some of his advisors had recommended leaving Clark out.[28] Ray Hnatyshyn, a loyal Clark supporter, became Government House Leader. Six women, including Flora MacDonald at

Image 16.1. Canada's largest ministry takes office: the forty members of the
Mulroney ministry with Governor General Jeanne Sauvé, 17 September 1984

Source: Doug Griffin, Getty Images, 502808787.

Employment and Immigration, joined the Cabinet, a new record. Geographically, thirteen members were from the West and North, and held important portfolios: deputy prime minister, external affairs, energy, and health and welfare;
eleven each were appointed from Ontario and Quebec, and one each from the
Atlantic provinces. The cabinet was more representative of the entire country
than any since Pierre Trudeau's first term in office.[29] The average age was 49.

Fifteen members had some cabinet experience but 23, including Mulroney,
had none. The 11 ministries of state (with junior ministers) reflected the government's commitment to particular issues (e.g., youth unemployment and
multiculturalism) but the appointment of ministers of state – as well as more
than 20 parliamentary secretaries – was a political rather than a managerial
choice. It was a means of grooming younger, inexperienced MPs for senior
roles, responding to the strong Quebec representation in Parliament, and keeping a large caucus happy.[30] Even though the role of ministers of state and ministers without portfolio had evolved since the positions were first established,
Mulroney claims in his *Memoirs* that they were all members of his cabinet and,
in 1985, he introduced a bill to provide for the establishment of ministries of
state and the appointment of ministers of state.[31]

Cabinet ministers were told to avoid speaking to the press, which often
received information only through press releases. The media complained as
early as September 1984 that Mulroney was avoiding them. He did not, for
instance, meet the press about his cabinet selections. Erik Nielsen, who soon

earned the nickname "Velcro Lips," had been tasked by Mulroney to oversee "the maintenance of the health of the cabinet" which Nielsen took to mean health in a political sense, managing the government's message and ensuring ministers behaved ethically.[32] One new minister told the *Globe and Mail*, "Erik said we'd be out on our ear if anybody was caught talking to you [the press]."[33]

Mulroney had a wide-ranging view of what Progressive Conservatism stood for, but certainly, believed that its overarching principle was to fight the deficit and debt for the well-being of the nation and begin a process of national reconciliation. Wilson and Robert de Cotret at Finance and Treasury Board, respectively, signaled that fiscal conservatives were in decision-making chairs: both came from the finance sector. The same signal was broadcast by putting Sinclair Stevens, a wealthy Toronto lawyer, developer, and banker who had run for the leadership of the party in 1976, in charge of the Department of Regional Industrial Expansion, usually a spendthrift portfolio. As president of the Treasury Board in the Clark government, he was nicknamed "The Slasher" for his plan to reduce the civil service by 60,000 employees. Several others, including Robert Coates (defence), Perrin Beatty (national revenue), Barbara McDougall (secretary of state for finance and another Bay Street executive), Nielsen (deputy prime minister), and Don Mazankowski (transport) also identified with the right-wing of the party.[34] Mulroney himself was no right-wing ideologue in the tradition of Margaret Thatcher and Ronald Reagan, however, and he, along with Flora MacDonald, Clark, David Crombie, and Jake Epp, represented the moderate wing of the party. When, for instance, Mulroney ran into considerable opposition from seniors opposed to plans to partially de-index old-age pensions, it was he and not Finance Minister Wilson who decided to abandon the measure.[35]

Mulroney arrived in Ottawa worried about how he might manage the bureaucracy to achieve his vision of Canada. With the Conservatives out of office for all but nine months over the previous two decades, he was sceptical of a bureaucracy that had long embraced a liberal interventionist view of Canada and of the press that he saw as too cozy with a succession of Liberal administrations. He promised to reform the civil service, but despite his threats of issuing pink slips, Mulroney did not fire deputy ministers when he assumed his office in the Langevin Block. He even re-assigned and appointed deputy ministers (DM) with the assistance of the Gordon Osbaldeston, the clerk of the Privy Council, and through the DMs he hoped to monitor what was happening in each department. Most days, Mulroney had lunch with either the clerk, his chief of staff and several close parliamentary colleagues to discuss policy questions, political problems, and the prime minister's agenda.[36] He appointed new senior-level chief-of-staff positions in all ministries that would work as a counterweight to the role of the civil servants in policy formation.[37] Policy, Mulroney saw, was the primary responsibility of him and his ministers.

The day after he took power, Mulroney established a ministerial Task Force on Program Review headed by Nielsen. It became an unwieldy committee, involving both public and private sector members that established study teams on specific files to identify inefficiencies and waste, often without the input of ministers and their deputies. Although its final reports were published, the perception arose that the task force was merely looking for cuts to balance the budget but by most accounts its impact was minimal.[38] By November 1984, just three months after taking office and long before Nielsen's Task Force reported, the cabinet had agreed upon its direction and priorities, outlined by Wilson in *A New Direction for Canada: Agenda for Economic Renewal*. It described Canada's economic legacy as "one of high unemployment, inadequate investment, eroded confidence and personal hardship," with "troublesome" deficits and an accumulated debt, and announced $4.2 billion in expenditure cuts, tax increases, a review of several programs (including Unemployment Insurance and transfers to provinces and individuals), changes to the Foreign Investment Review Agency, and the elimination of Trudeau's National Energy Program (NEP), while at the same time increasing the Spouse's Allowance Program for widows and widowers between 60 and 64 and veterans pensions. It also promised to direct social programs to those most in need, as he outlined four broad objectives: put the nation's fiscal house in order to deal with the massive debt; redefine the role of government; foster an environment for innovation, investment, and improved competitiveness; and proceed in a fair, open and compassionate manner as the government implemented its policies. The way forward, Wilson proclaimed, was a market-oriented approach with less government involvement to create a more productive and efficient economy with a focus on technology, trade, investment, and training.[39]

Cabinet Structure

Trying to determine how Mulroney's cabinet worked without access to cabinet records remains, at best, a work in progress, but a few of Mulroney's outspoken ministers have provided some indication of what transpired at that time. Michael Wilson claims that Mulroney found "the perfect knife-edge balance between managing his team to help him achieve his own aspirations and leaving room for others to set their own strategies." Wilson claims that he and the prime minister discussed strategy on important matters such as the budget, but Mulroney never got into the "technical details."[40] Pat Carney shares that view. When she was negotiating the Atlantic Accord, an agreement with Newfoundland and Labrador on offshore petroleum resource management and revenue sharing, she led on the file, meeting regularly with Mulroney and deciding on a negotiating position "with little input beyond that of Wilson, who controlled the energy taxing powers." On that file, the normal cabinet process of committees, discussion and consensus did not happen because Mulroney was fulfilling a promise made while the party was in opposition. Such procedural shortcuts were "rare," she asserts, but others have described the approach on the Atlantic Accord as common.[41] John Crosbie observed that ministers not on the Priorities and Planning Committee of cabinet (P&P) had "little opportunity to influence anything outside their own departments," but he, too, notes that ministers often went to Mulroney with their favourite projects, often with considerable success.[42]

In 1984, Mulroney largely adopted the decision-making system that he inherited from the Liberals, and it evolved over the life of his government to meet changing circumstances, but he was never able to reform the machinery of government as he would have liked or promised. Cabinet committees and subcommittees were an essential element of the Mulroney government even as the machinery of government evolved. Arthur Kroeger, a former deputy minister, claims that Mulroney once said that "he favoured any decision-making system that minimized the time he had to spend in cabinet."[43] From the beginning, Mulroney chaired the Priorities and Planning Committee of cabinet and saw it as critical to his government's success. Consisting of the fifteen or so most influential ministers, it met on Tuesdays. Attendance was mandatory, with Mulroney telling ministers they could miss the meetings only if they were "dying or dead: this is the most exclusive club in town, so be here."[44] Mulroney began P&P meetings by updating members on his activities and his view on current issues. Each member followed, identifying issues of importance to their own province or region and offering their assessment of the state of the nation. The agenda then turned to new policies and planning with P&P subcommittees providing reports.

It was in the cabinet committee meetings that decisions were made, and recommendations forwarded to P&P. A Record of Decision was agreed upon in the committees that would be prepared by officials in the Privy Council Office and submitted to P&P and then, if found acceptable, to the full cabinet for final approval. Few policies moved forward without the endorsement of Treasury Board, however.[45] Gordon Osbaldeston, Mulroney's first clerk of the Privy Council, met with all deputy ministers one day before P&P and prepared a briefing book for the Prime Minister, outlining what each of the ministers was to propose, noting which ministers supported particular proposals and those who had reservations or objections. The clerk also made a recommendation to the prime minister to either support, deny, or defer each agenda item. It was in P&P that "proposed legislation and policies were scrutinized, attacked, defended, and eventually rejected or accepted by committee members drawn from the full cabinet."[46] The final item of business, before P&P wrapped up by noon, was a review of pending appointments. During the meeting, Mulroney moved ministers through the agenda efficiently and "usually without extensive debate." After all, most issues would have been discussed and debated earlier, and some consensus had already been reached. When there was debate, "the prime minister's position inevitably carried the day."[47]

The full cabinet, perhaps because of its size, met on average every two weeks. Carney claims that few of the major decisions were made by the full cabinet: "Decisions are typically reached in private with the PM, or in private meetings with cabinet colleagues, or in committee." Any cabinet member could attend any of the cabinet committee meetings except for Treasury Board and P&P. Treasury Board had its own bureaucracy, the Treasury Board Secretariat, and it provided cabinet with advice on the financial implications of all proposals that came before it.[48] When matters did come to the full cabinet, several ministers, notably Crosbie, Wilson, Clark, Murray, and MacDonald, were "active contributors," but other ministers generally kept their interventions to matters concerning their departments.[49] There was a formal hierarchy among ministers: those sitting on P&P (and later the Operations Committee) were clearly at the top.[50]

From time to time, Mulroney appointed ad hoc committees to deal with particular issues such as sales tax reform in 1989, chaired by Michael Wilson, and constitutional affairs that examined the conditions laid out by Premier Robert Bourassa for Quebec to rejoin the discussion on constitutional renewal. In 1991 Don Mazankowski chaired an ad hoc cabinet committee on energy mega-projects, which also offers some insight into how Mulroney's cabinet system worked. The decision on further investment in Hibernia offshore oil development, for example, came after many in the caucus, including Mulroney, blamed Newfoundland Premier Clyde Wells for the failure of the Meech Lake constitutional accord. Several Quebec MPs wanted to punish Wells for his role in the failure of Meech, but Mazankowski had his committee consider all the issues involved in the matter, including having oil executives in for questioning, and then he made a recommendation. As was usually the case, especially if the prime minister supported the project, the full cabinet would concur with the recommendations of the committee. In this instance, it did, and it shows how Mulroney was able to balance the demands of competing interests in his cabinet – a form of brokerage politics.[51] Mulroney chaired only one ad hoc committee, on the Gulf War after Iraq invaded Kuwait in 1990. Kim Campbell recalls how he brought "together the military and political sides of the government to consider Canada's position."[52] However, it has been suggested that Mulroney agreed to participate in the Gulf War in a conversation with President George Bush and only raised the matter in cabinet to be able to report that cabinet had indeed approved the decision. In any event, cabinet did approve Canada's participation and the motion to participate was debated vigorously in the House of Commons.[53]

At times, Mulroney had little patience with cabinet when there were issues he considered urgent. In August 1987, at the height of the free trade negotiations,

Mulroney created an executive cabinet committee on trade with himself as chair. In his *Memoirs* he claims the new committee effectively removed Minister of International Trade Pat Carney "from a position of influence or control in the free trade negotiations," even though she was the chair of the P&P Sub-Committee on Trade which was responsible "for forging a consensus within the cabinet on the complex issues involved in the negotiations." Burney became Mulroney's "personal representative" on the file as Carney had become a distraction, insisting continually that Simon Reisman, a career civil servant and former deputy minister of finance who Mulroney appointed as chief negotiator, be fired.[54] The negotiations proceeded slowly and by early September 1987, the cabinet committee and indeed the whole cabinet were worried about the fate of negotiations as the US Congress became more protectionist.[55] Wilson, Crosbie, Mazankowski and others were determined to push ahead, as Carney and others wavered on the issue. Mulroney claims that in the four weeks from 2 September 1987, the Trade Executive Committee, P&P, and the full cabinet met at least twenty-two times on the matter. The main concern was how to protect many of the features of Canada that had become part of the national fabric, such as social programs, regional development strategies, supply management, and cultural institutions. Flora MacDonald, as minister of communications responsible for culture, worried that the US saw culture (films and magazines, particularly) as business concerns.[56] The final stumbling block was a binding dispute resolution settlement that would arbitrate trade disputes between the two nations. Mulroney never lost hope, but as the deadline approached to fast-track a deal through Congress, Canadian Ambassador Allan Gotlieb recorded, Mulroney "had been let down by the Americans and to a large extent by his own cabinet."[57] When the negotiations were in danger of collapsing, Mulroney despatched, without Carney's knowledge, Wilson and Burney to Washington to meet with James Baker, US Secretary of the Treasury.[58] Burney confirms much of this and claims that Mulroney had instructed him to lead the team that reached a deal with the Americans at the 11th hour.[59]

After the collapse of the Meech Lake Accord, which had seen the departure of Mulroney's long-time friend, Lucien Bouchard, from the cabinet, Mulroney appointed Clark minister of constitutional affairs and chair of the cabinet Committee on Canadian Unity which included several other senior ministers. At times, Mulroney joined the committee, an indication of the importance he attached to its work.[60] As a bilingual westerner and with the prestige of being a former prime minister, Clark was the "best person for the job," Mulroney wrote in his personal journal.[61] Mulroney claims that his team responsible for constitutional affairs was divided. In December 1991, his chief of staff, Norman Spector warned Mulroney that Clark "is mismanaging Canada towards disaster ... and PMO exacerbates and does not mitigate the resulting dysfunctions."[62] Although the cabinet committee had a very public role, the group of officials and advisors close to the prime minister played a critical role in preparing the federal proposals. This group included Paul Tellier, the clerk of the Privy Council; Spector; Jocelyne Bourgon, assistant secretary to the cabinet; Dan Gagnier, deputy-secretary to the cabinet for communication and consultations; Hugh Segal, special adviser to the prime minister; and James Judd, Clark's chief of staff.[63] There were also disagreements and confusion, especially between Quebec and non-Quebec ministers.[64] Mulroney took charge, worked closely with Clark and reached out "privately and quietly with recalcitrant Quebec and Ontario ministers." Only Mulroney commanded the loyalty of Quebec ministers in the cabinet to reach a consensus. Cabinet subsequently agreed to a set of proposals, and, after months of negotiations, new constitutional proposals, known as the Charlottetown Accord, were agreed to.[65] It was rejected in a national referendum in October 1992.

Firings and Resignations

Mulroney's first firing came in February 1985, just five months after becoming prime minister, when he asked Defence Minister Bob Coates to resign for visiting a strip club near a Canadian military base in West Germany. Mulroney said Coates "was a man of honour" who believed that resigning in such circumstances was in the parliamentary tradition. It was an approach to ministerial responsibility that Mulroney later admitted was "costly" to his administration. As a new and inexperienced prime minister, he wrote that he "believed that any variance from the strict interpretation of ministerial responsibility and of proper personal conduct should be dealt with by a resignation."[66]

Other resignations and firings followed, all of which attracted crushing media attention and criticism in the House of Commons; most came as a result of misdeeds rather than disagreement over policy and government direction.[67] Among those generating the most controversy was the allegation in September 1985 that John Fraser, the minister of fisheries, had ignored problems at the StarKist tuna-canning plant in New Brunswick and allowed what the media described as "tainted tuna" to be released for sale. Also in September, the minister of communications, Marcel Masse, was fired when the RCMP launched an investigation into his campaign spending in the 1984 election.[68] Masse was cleared of any wrong-doing and re-joined the Cabinet on 30 November 1985. On 12 May 1986, Mulroney fired Sinclair Stevens after it was revealed that Stevens's wife had negotiated a $2.6 million loan for their holding company, York Centre Corporation, from Magna International Inc., the car parts manufacturer, which had received grants from Stevens's department. Mulroney refused to sign Stevens's nomination papers in the 1988 election. Mulroney called a public inquiry, which found Stevens to be in a conflict of interest. Stevens protested vehemently and was later vindicated by the Federal Court of Canada.[69] On 19 January 1987, Mulroney fired André Bissonnette, the minister of state for transport, for the allegation he was involved in a land speculation deal in St-Jean-sur-Richelieu in 1985.[70] The week that Bissonnette was fired, *Maclean's* ran a photo of the Prime Minister on its cover with the lead story, "Days of Scandal."[71] There was a widespread fear that the government was in no shape to face the electorate again.

Shuffling the Cabinet

Mulroney first shuffled his Cabinet on 30 June 1986, a few days after a nationally televised address announcing he was pursuing free trade with the US. Selling free trade required a unified caucus and a cabinet able to communicate to Canadians the benefits of a trade pact. Mulroney also had to turn the page on the scandals, resignations, and firings that marked the early years of his government. Communications had not been a particularly strong feature of his administration, and Mulroney recounts how, on one occasion in spring 1986, 21 ministers missed the daily question period strategy meeting, which he described as a "dereliction of responsibility." He scolded his ministers that his government "has been driven by crisis and events. It must become," he insisted, "more strategic and better coordinated." As he prepared to shuffle his Cabinet he asked the caucus – as he did each year and as a way to keep it onside – to send him confidential letters on issues of concern.[72] Mulroney also told reporters "We do the big things well; we do some of the small things poorly. I want better communication, I want better management, and we want to carry the message more effectively." To the new Cabinet, he said, "We are strongest when we act as a team. We succeed when we have a game plan. We communicate best when we do our homework ... We need to tighten up our planning, to have all ministers working on the game plan."[73]

Four ministers were replaced, and eight new ones were added. The Quebec presence was strengthened, with Quebec MPs given major economic portfolios of energy, employment, and immigration, and regional industrial development as well as supply and services, through which much of the federal spending flowed. Nielsen, often accused of being domineering, had alienated caucus and was dropped as deputy prime minister. Alberta MP and transport minister Don Mazankowski, who had a reputation for being effective in handling people and had managed his department well, became the new deputy prime minister. Mulroney brought two young MPs into cabinet: Jean Charest as minister of state for youth and Bernard Valcourt as minister of state for small business and tourism. Senator Lowell Murray became minister for federal-provincial relations and government leader in the Senate. Norman Spector, a civil servant in British Columbia, was appointed cabinet secretary for federal-provincial relations.[74]

At the same time, Mulroney streamlined the decision-making process for cabinet, appointing an Operations Committee to ensure the smooth functioning of the executive and to exert greater control over the decision-making process, achieve rapid results, and allow him to focus on the larger picture.[75] Mazankowski was chair, who Mulroney described as chief operating officer of the government.[76] Membership on the Operations Committee was limited to six ministers, including the minister of finance, the president of the Treasury Board, and the chair of several key cabinet committees. Mulroney's chief of staff and the clerk of the Privy Council and secretary to the Cabinet (the redoubtable Paul Tellier, who assumed the post in 1985 from being deputy minister of energy, mines, and resources) and the deputy minister of finance also attended to ensure that the ministers and the bureaucracy were working together to achieve the government's priorities. The Operations Committee was described as an executive committee for P&P as it "prepares decisions for P&P, including spending decisions." Crosbie termed it a "facilitating body" that reviewed issues and prepared proposals for P&P or the full cabinet, noting that once the Operations Committee vetted a proposal and gave its approval, "the minister in charge of that issue was home free." The Operations Committee and P&P were the major power brokers in Ottawa, making the 40-member cabinet a "cabinet" in name only. Mazankowski, it should be noted, was more powerful than any previous deputy prime minister, but he and Mulroney were not ideologues, they operated on a pragmatic basis in the making of decisions. The Operations Committee made the Mulroney government run more efficiently.[77] It might be noted, too, that Mazankowski's position, not only as chair of the Operations Committee but also as a kind of C.D. Howe-type "minister of everything," made him one of the most important individuals in Mulroney's cabinet. Because Mulroney had made confronting the deficit a priority, he personally chaired an Expenditure Review Committee to ensure that monies were directed to matters of greatest importance while ensuring the government remained committed to deficit reduction.[78]

At the same time, Mulroney realized the importance of regional ministers. For much of the time since Confederation, prime ministers had appointed regional ministers responsible for patronage within their region while also acting as liaisons with the provinces. In 1984, Mulroney dispensed with the practice, believing that the PMO was able to deal with provincial governments and federal activities in each province rather than giving particular ministers that responsibility. Nielsen had created provincial action committees to recommend who should receive governor-in-council positions. It was also a way, they hoped, to manage ethical concerns and conflicts of interest. Mulroney soon discovered the PMO had neither the time nor the knowledge to deal effectively with local matters across Canada, and in the June 1986 cabinet shuffle, he appointed regional ministers.[79] Mulroney later established regional development agencies across Canada, including the Atlantic Canada Opportunities Agency (ACOA), Northern Ontario Development Board (FED-NOR), and Western Diversification Strategy Office (WDO) to enhance the position of ministers and the government's visibility in the various regions of the country.[80]

Prior to the 1988 election Mulroney shuffled his cabinet again. Most of the changes were made for political rather than policy considerations. The major change was the appointment of Lucien Bouchard, a 49-year-old lawyer and classmate of Mulroney's and one of his most trusted Quebec advisors, as secretary of state. Bouchard had been Canada's ambassador to France and a strong proponent of sovereignty in the 1980 Quebec referendum. The *Globe and Mail* reported that Bouchard had been given the task of improving the image of Mulroney's Quebec caucus, which had been blackened with the image of scandal and corruption, and implementing new rules regarding political fund-raising. The appointment also encouraged nationalist voters in Quebec to vote Conservative as they had in 1984. Moving Carney out of the trade portfolio to Treasury Board made way for John Crosbie to shepherd the US-Canada trade deal through Parliament and to sell the idea to Canadians. At the swearing-in ceremony, Crosbie told reporters he wanted to live down his reputation "for being a loose cannon on the deck."[81]

On 21 November 1988 Mulroney became the first party leader to win consecutive majorities in 35 years. The Conservatives captured 43 percent of the vote and 169 seats but lost six cabinet ministers. Among those defeated were Communication Minister Flora MacDonald, Justice Minister Ray Hnatyshyn, and Public Works Minister Stewart McInnes.[82] Two ministers did not seek re-election. When he announced his new cabinet on 30 January, Mulroney shuffled 19 ministers to new roles and reduced the size of cabinet by one. Most senior ministers retained their portfolios and two ministers each from British Columbia, Ontario and Quebec were added. Two women, Mary Collins as associate minister of defence and Kim Campbell as minister of state (Indian affairs and northern development), were both from British Columbia. Lucien Bouchard, the new minister of the environment, was added to P&P and the Operations Committee of cabinet. Mulroney promised within two years to undertake a longer-range departmental reorganization to eliminate some departments and consolidate others as part of a process to cut federal expenditures and improve the machinery of government.[83] As a first step in that direction, he kept the Expenditure Review Committee of cabinet, noting, however, it would be subordinate to the 19-member Planning and Priorities Committee through which the other 15 committees of cabinet would report. All policy proposals were to be analyzed first by those committees and then by P&P and the Treasury Board to ensure they met the government's priorities, as Mulroney promised "prudent fiscal management."[84]

He was putting in place a two-tiered system to bring more effective management to the operations of government. In his first term, he largely followed the system he inherited from the Liberals, but the committee system was too large to be effective. The government had initially planned its operations on a series of spending envelopes for several policy areas and departments, and the committees of cabinet overseeing those envelopes authorized spending. Going forward, any spending authorized by the new committees had to be approved by P&P. Although P&P had already become the central committee in the cabinet system of government, it had not worked effectively because cabinet ministers often ignored the system and lobbied Mulroney directly for their pet projects. Making P&P the "supreme" committee would eliminate that problem, he hoped.[85] The Operations Committee of cabinet which had operated informally for about 18 months with Mazankowski as chair was given an institutional role to control the weekly agenda of cabinet and help P&P effectively manage the government's work. With eight of the most powerful and senior ministers of cabinet – nine including Mulroney – it held the most power in Ottawa.[86]

The second term was not an easy one for Mulroney and his Cabinet. Opposition grew to the Meech Lake Accord, and the economy tipped into a two-year recession in 1990. Mulroney claims in his *Memoirs* that Canada had become a "nation of discontent." There was dissension within the cabinet, too. Clark was among the most disaffected and contemplated retirement, as he believed that the financial situation was driving the government's agenda. He warned Mulroney that many ministers no longer believed in the policies being pursued and that the "government had lost its legitimacy."[87] To add to Mulroney's problems, two of the young French-speaking ministers were forced to resign. First, Bernard Valcourt, after crashing his motorcycle in 1989 while intoxicated, and then in early 1990, Jean Charest, for telephoning a judge in the hope of influencing a decision on an athlete's eligibility for the upcoming Commonwealth Games.[88] Both Valcourt and Charest later returned to cabinet. In April 1991, Mulroney made a number of significant changes to his cabinet, with a view to strengthening the party in the West. In addition to Clark's appointment as constitutional affairs minister, Mazankowski assumed the finance portfolio giving the West several key portfolios, including House leader, agriculture and justice. After seven years in finance, Wilson moved to industry, science, and technology.[89]

Towards the end of his mandate, Mulroney received a report from Secretary of State Robert de Cotret on how best to manage the machinery of government promised after the 1988 election. De Cotret had worked with three former deputy ministers to consider a drastic realignment of 32 government departments and 408 agencies to produce a cabinet with a maximum of 24 members and a simplified decision-making process. While the report allowed Mulroney to reboot the party for the upcoming election, its stated goal was to improve the delivery of services and better organize government operations. The Mulroney government had already closed nearly 50 agencies and boards, including the

Economic Council of Canada and the Science Council of Canada, and it wanted further streamlining to ensure that government was better organized. The task force asked, for instance, why was there one department setting tax policy (Finance) and another department (National Revenue) collecting the taxes. It suggested that a small core group could make decisions more quickly and more efficiently without the layering of several committees that then dominated the Canadian cabinet system.[90] Gordon Osbaldeston, a member of de Cotret's task force and a former clerk of the Privy Council, was later quoted as saying "No other country in the world has so many cabinet ministers. It is time to take the ship of state into drydock to scrape off all the barnacles."[91]

On 4 January 1993, Mulroney shuffled his cabinet for the final time, replacing five long-term ministers who had announced they would not be seeking re-election, reassigning nine ministers, adding one backbencher, and reducing the number of ministers to 35, but he avoided the reforms that the de Cotret task force recommended. Ministers and ministers of state remained in transport, environment, agriculture, finance, employment and immigration, and Indian and northern affairs. Among the most noteworthy appointments was naming Kim Campbell Canada's first woman defence minister in addition to veteran's affairs and elevating her to the Operations Committee of cabinet. Among those dropped were Energy Minister Jake Epp, de Cotret, Defence Minister Marcel Masse, and Science Minister William Winegard. As part of the reorganization of cabinet, Mulroney abolished the expenditure review committee claiming that its goals had been accomplished, as program expenditure had been reduced significantly since he took office.[92]

Conclusion

Unlike his three immediate predecessors in the prime minister's office, Mulroney never had to manage a minority parliament, but his statecraft and leadership have been undervalued and under-estimated by some observers. In some ways, Mulroney's approach – not unlike Pearson's – was at times marked by chaos and disorganization but in the end, he had a solid list of accomplishments. Brian Mulroney's management of cabinet showed that he learned the importance of an effective administrative structure both in and around his Cabinet, and he came to understand that professionalism was more important than partisanship. The first two years of his mandate were noteworthy for mistakes in the PMO and cabinet, marked best by the number of ministers who were forced to resign and a muddled policy agenda, which portrayed the government with both incompetence and poor judgement. By 1986, Mulroney removed many of his political friends in the PMO, having learned an important lesson in governance and management, and brought into his inner circle an experienced administrator in Derek Burney and several other people from the civil service. From then on, Mulroney realized the importance of having the PMO work effectively with Cabinet and the importance of regional ministers. The appointment of Mazankowski as deputy prime minister was another important change as was the creation of the Operations Committee of Cabinet to streamline and manage the government's agenda. Without him, Mulroney's government may have been far less effective. With effective organizers in key roles it allowed Mulroney to focus, as he wrote in his *Memoirs*, not on "tainted tuna" but matters of state. He had in his Cabinet many capable, innovative but strong-willed leaders who, like Mulroney himself, had a deep desire to bring much-needed change to the nation. Mulroney's statecraft and leadership worked most effectively when Mulroney reached out to career civil servants to reorganize and manage the internal operations of his government so that vital information and procedures could be channeled smoothly from the bureaucracy to the political centre and back to the civil service. Mulroney learned the importance of balancing administrative and political demands in decision-making, but he failed to achieve the reconciliation that he sought with Quebec, either through the Meech Lake or Charlottetown Accords, and sustain for the Progressive Conservatives party the political gains he had made in the West in 1984 and 1988. Canada had changed much since the days of Mackenzie King, and Mulroney discovered that an approach to statecraft and leadership that embraced a brokerage style politics and coalition building no longer worked for a prime minster and his party. Even so, Mulroney launched a new agenda for Canada and succeeded in setting a policy agenda, especially in trade, economics, the environment, and special recognition for Quebec and Indigenous peoples, that prime ministers who followed would not be able to ignore.

NOTES

* The author wishes to thank Steve McLellan for comments on an earlier draft of this chapter.

1 For an overview of the major policy initiatives, see Raymond B. Blake, ed., *Transforming the Nation: Canada and Brian Mulroney* (Montreal: McGill-Queen's University Press, 2007).

2 Brian Mulroney, *Memoirs, 1939–1993* (Toronto: McClelland & Stewart, 2007), 323.

3 Quoted in *Montreal Gazette*, 25 February 1993. See Konrad Yakabuski, "Mulroney at 80: Where Are the Great Leaders?," *Globe and Mail*, 15 March 2019.

4 Quoted in Michael Wilson, *Something within Me: A Personal and Political Memoir* (Toronto: University of Toronto Press, 2022), 179–80.

5 On the government structures in Ottawa, see Donald J. Savoie, *Governing from the Centre: The Concentration of Power in Canadian Politics* (Toronto:

University of Toronto Press, 1999); Donald Savoie, *Thatcher, Reagan, Mulroney: In Search of a Bureaucracy* (Toronto: University of Toronto Press, 1994); Peter Aucoin, "Organizational Change in the Machinery of Canadian Government: From Rational Management to Brokerage Politics," *Canadian Journal of Political Science* 19, no. 1 (March 1986): 3–28; Herman Bakvis, "Prime Minister and Cabinet in Canada: An Autocracy in Need of Reform?," *Journal of Canadian Studies* 35, no. 4 (Winter 2001): 60–80; and James C. Simeon, "Prime Minister's Office and White House Office: Political Administration in Canada and the United States," *Presidential Studies Quarterly* 21, no. 3 (1991): 559–80.

6 Konrad Yakabuski, "The Grits Are Back in Charge, All's Right in Ottawa," *Globe and Mail*, 5 November 2015, A6.

7 See George C. Perlin, *The Tory Syndrome: Leadership Politics in the Progressive Conservative Party* (Montreal: McGill-Queen's University Press, 1980).

8 John C. Crosbie, *No Holds Barred: My Life in Politics* (Toronto: McClelland & Stewart, 1997), 234–5; and Mulroney, *Memoirs*, 78–9.

9 Wilson, *Something within Me*, 92; Crosbie, *No Holds Barred*, 240–1; and Mulroney, *Memoirs*, 252.

10 Paul Gessell, "Political Minefield," *Maclean's*, 2 February 1987, 9–12; and Mulroney, *Memoirs*, 270–2.

11 Gessell, "Political Minefield."

12 Charles McMillan, *The Age of Consequence: The Ordeals of Public Policy in Canada* (Montreal: McGill-Queen's University Press, 2022), xvii, 25, 35.

13 Aucoin, "Organizational Change," 22.

14 Aucoin, "Organizational Change," 22.

15 Crosbie, *No Holds Barred*, 248–9, 257–9.

16 "Can Mulroney Win Again?," *Report on Business*, October 1996, 71–6.

17 Mulroney, *Memoirs*, 503–6; and Crosbie, *No Holds Barred*, 414–15.

18 Derek H. Burney, *Getting It Done: A Memoir* (Montreal: McGill-Queen's University Press, 2005), 83–6.

19 "Plans for a New Start," *Maclean's*, 15 September 1986, 12.

20 Hugh Segal, *No Surrender: Reflections of a Happy Warrior in the Tory Crusade* (Toronto: HarperCollins, 1996), esp. ch. 8.

21 On Mulroney's promotion of La Francophonie and giving Quebec and New Brunswick an international role, see Mulroney, *Memoirs*, 412–15.

22 "Heating Up the Cod War," *Maclean's*, 23 February 1987, 12–13; R.B. Byers, ed., *Canadian Annual Review of Politics and Public Affairs, 1987* (Toronto: University of Toronto Press, 1992), 127–9; Bakvis, "Prime Minister and Cabinet in Canada," 65; Donat Pharand, "The Cod War Between Canada and France," *Revue générale de droit* 18, no. 3 (1987): 627–40; and Crosbie, *No Holds Barred*, 261–6.

23 Savoie, "Governing from the Centre," 412–13.

24 Mulroney, *Memoirs*, 265; and Jeffrey Simpson, *Discipline of Power* (Toronto: University of Toronto Press, 1996).

25 James Rusk, "Mulroney Appoints Record Cabinet of 40," *Globe and Mail*, 18 September 1984, 1; and Mulroney, *Memoirs*, 315–19.

26 Hugh Winsor, "Mulroney Backers Reap Rewards for Loyalty: Analysis," *Globe and Mail*, 18 September 1984, 4.

27 See "Guide to Canadian Ministries since Confederation: Twenty-Fourth Ministry," Government of Canada, last modified 25 September 2023, https://guide-ministries .canada.ca/dtail.php?lang=en&min=24&id=1.

28 See Mathew Hayday, "Brian Mulroney and Joe Clark: A New Constructive Internationalism," in *Statesmen, Strategists and Diplomats: Prime Ministers of Canada and Their Foreign Policy*, ed. Patrice Dutil (Vancouver: University of British Columbia Press, 2023), 262. It should be noted, however, that on most major foreign policy issues, including the Ethiopian famine, apartheid in South Africa, and Canada-US free trade, Clark played a secondary role to Mulroney.

29 James Rusk, "Mulroney Appoints Record Cabinet of 40," *Globe and Mail*, 18 September 1984, 1; Jeffrey Simpson, "It Takes All Kinds," *Globe and Mail*, 18 September 1984, 6; "Life Begins with 40," *Globe and Mail*, 18 September 1984, 6; Mulroney, *Memoirs*, 315–19; and Crosbie, *No Holds Barred*, 245–7.

30 Jean Charest, *My Road to Québec* (Saint-Laurent, Quebec: Éditions Pierre Tisseyre, 1988), 43–4.

31 Mulroney, *Memoirs*, 316. On this subject, see Ministries and Ministers of State Act, R.S.C. 1985, c. M-8, https://laws-lois.justice.gc.ca/eng/acts/M-8/page-1.html.

32 Erik Nielsen, *The House Is Not a Home: An Autobiography* (Toronto: Macmillan, 1989), 247.

33 Hugh Winsor, "Mulroney Restricts News on Changeover Plans," *Globe and Mail*, 20 September 1984, 1.

34 "40-Member Cabinet Includes 23 First-Time Ministers: Ontario, Quebec Provide 22 Members, the West and North 13, and Atlantic Canada 5," *Globe and Mail*, 18 September 1984, 4; and Bruce Little and David Stewart Patterson, "Wilson, de Cotret Responsible for Holding Spending in Line," *Globe and Mail*, 18 September 1984, B1.

35 Wilson, *Something within Me*, 110–11.

36 Mulroney, *Memoirs*, 998–9. See also Patrice Dutil, "Prime Ministers and Public Administration," *Canadian Public Administration* 51, no. 2 (2008): 335–54.

37 Donald J. Savoie, *Court Government and the Collapse of Accountability in Canada and the United Kingdom* (Toronto: University of Toronto Press, 2008), 79; and Aucoin, "Organizational Change," 10.

38 Kirsti Nilsen, *The Impact of Information Policy* (Westport, CT: ABLEX, 2001), 60; Donald J. Savoie, *The Politics of Public Spending in Canada* (Toronto: University of Toronto Press, 1990), 131–42; Crosbie, *No Holds Barred*, 250–2; and Canada, Privy Council Office, Task Force on Program Review (Ottawa: Supply and Services Canada, 1986).

39 Michael Wilson, *A New Direction for Canada: Agenda for Economic Renewal*, (Ottawa: Department of Finance, 1984), https://publications.gc.ca/collections /collection_2016/fin/F2-62-1984-eng.pdf; Wilson, *Something within Me*, 83, 103–7; and Mulroney, *Memoirs*, 335–6.

40 Wilson, *Something within Me*, 182–3.

41 Pat Carney, *Trade Secrets: A Memoir* (Toronto: Key Porter Books, 2000), 217–18; and McMillan, *Age of Consequence*, 65.

42 Crosbie, *No Holds Barred*, 248–9.

43 Arthur Kroeger, "A Retrospective on Policy Development in Ottawa," *Canadian Public Administration* 39, no. 4 (Winter 1996): 465.

44 Carney, *Trade Secrets*, 249, 259–62.

45 Savoie, *Politics of Public Spending*, 40; and Charest, *My Road to Québec*, 56–8.

46 Savoie, *Politics of Public Spending*, 39–40; and Carney, *Trade Secrets*, 259–62, 249.

47 Burney, *Getting It Done*, 91; and John C. Crosbie, "Governing from the Centre: Reflections on the Mulroney Cabinet," in Blake, *Transforming the Nation*, 394–5.

48 Carney, *Trade Secrets*, 263–5; Mulroney, *Memoirs*, 481–2; Charest, *My Road to Québec*, 105; and Kim Campbell, *Time and Chance: The Political Memoirs of Canada's First Woman Prime Minister* (Toronto: Doubleday, 1996), 117.

49 Burney, *Getting It Done*, 92.

50 Charest, *My Road to Québec*, 106.

51 Crosbie, *No Holds Barred*, 441–7. Donald J. Savoie, "The Rise of Court Government in Canada," *Canadian Journal of Political Science* 32, no. 4 (December 1999): 640, suggests that Crosbie was the only minister in favour of federal investment in Hibernia, but he convinced Mulroney to support the project. Similarly, Savoie argues that Saskatchewan premier Grant Devine convinced Mulroney to provide a $1 billion aid package to prairie farmers.

52 Campbell, *Time and Chance*, 117–19, 153; and "Cabinet Committee to Deal with Crisis: Group Prime Decision-Maker on Gulf," *Globe and Mail*, 8 January 1991, A8.

53 Luc Bernier, Keith Brownsey, and Michael Howlett, eds., *Executive Styles in Canada: Cabinet Structures and Leadership Practices in Canadian Government* (Toronto: University of Toronto Press, 2005), 27; and Mulroney, *Memoirs*, 829–35.

54 Mulroney, *Memoirs*, 266–7, 574–5; Burney, *Getting It Done*, 109–32; and Crosbie, *No Holds Barred*, 309–10.

55 Flora MacDonald and Geoffrey Stevens, *Flora: A Woman in a Man's World* (Montreal: McGill-Queen's University Press, 2021).

56 Mulroney, *Memoirs*, 563–5.

57 Gordon Ritchie, *Wrestling with the Elephant: The Inside Story of the Canada-US Trade Wars* (Toronto: Macfarlane Walter & Ross, 1997), 102–4; and Mulroney, *Memoirs*, 571. See also Allan Gotlieb, *The Washington Diaries, 1981–1989* (Toronto: McClelland & Stewart, 2006), 490.

58 Carney, *Trade Secrets*, 228–9, 234, 236, 243.

59 Burney, *Getting It Done*, 113, 116.

60 Burney, *Getting It Done*, 137–8.

61 Mulroney, *Memoirs*, 212–13, 596, 846–8.

62 Quoted in Mulroney, *Memoirs*, 879–80.

63 Graham Fraser, "The Constitutional Backroom Gang," *Globe and Mail*, 5 October 1991, D2.

64 Arthur Kroeger claims Mulroney was not a member of the cabinet committee on national unity, but he was very active on the file, nonetheless (Kroeger, "Policy Development in Ottawa," 465).

65 Graham Fraser, "Lingering Problems Lead Cabinet to Ask Mulroney to Resolve Differences," *Globe and Mail*, 14 September 1991, A1; Mulroney, *Memoirs*, 865, 889–90; and Jeffrey Simpson, "Package Filled with Last Minute Compromises," *Globe and Mail*, 28 September 1991, A1.

66 Charlotte Montgomery, "Coates Judgment Poor: PM: Choice of Bar Was 'an Error,'" *Globe and Mail*, 14 February 1985, 1; Mulroney, *Memoirs*, 355; and Nielsen, *House Is Not a Home*, 247–51. In his autobiography, Nielsen is critical of patronage and the lack of ethics in government, but he was appointed chair of the National Transportation Agency by Mulroney.

67 See Sharon Sutherland, "Responsible Government and Ministerial Responsibility: Every Reform Is Its Own Problem," *Canadian Journal of Political Science* 24, no. 1 (March 1991): 101.

68 Mulroney, *Memoirs*, 390–2; and Nielsen, *House Is Not a Home*, 252–5.

69 Mulroney, *Memoirs*, 446–7; and Nielsen, *House Is Not a Home*, 261–8.

70 "Diary of a Scandal," *Maclean's*, 2 February 1987, 9; and Bruce Wallace, "A Property in Question," *Maclean's*, 2 February 1987, 14–16.

71 Gessell, "Political Minefield," 9–12.

72 Mulroney, *Memoirs*, 454–5.

73 Mulroney, *Memoirs*, 457.

74 Crosbie, *No Holds Barred*, 286.

75 Kroeger, "Policy Development in Ottawa," 465; and Mulroney, *Memoirs*, 457.

76 Burney, *Getting It Done*, 91–2; and Charest, *My Road to Québec*, 106.

77 Jeffrey Simpson, "Operations Unlimited," *Globe and Mail*, 19 May 1988, A6; Ross Howard, "Cabinet Shifts May Begin Restructuring for Ottawa," *Globe and Mail*, 19 January 1989, A1; Crosbie, "Governing from the Centre," 394–5; and Peter Aucoin, "The Mulroney Government, 1984–1988: Priorities, Positional Policy and Power," in *Canada under Mulroney: An End-of-Term Report*, ed. Andrew B. Gollner and Daniel Salée (Montreal: Véhicule Press, 1988), 346–7.

78 Crosbie, "Governing from the Centre," 395.

79 Crosbie, *No Holds Barred*, 253–5.

80 Herman Bakvis, *Regional Ministers: Power and Influence in the Canadian Cabinet* (Toronto: University of Toronto Press, 1991), esp. ch. 10; and Savoie, *Politics of Public Spending*, 199–200.

81 Hugh Winsor, "Mulroney Fine-Tunes His Cabinet: Last Shuffle before Election," *Globe and Mail*, 1 April 1988, A1.

82 For extensive coverage of the election results, see *Globe and Mail*, 22 and 23 November 1988.

83 Christopher Waddell, "Cabinet Shuffle Signals Spending Cuts: 19 Ministers Change Jobs; Six Added," *Globe and Mail*, 31 January 1989, A1.

84 Waddell, "Cabinet Shuffle," A1.

85 Ross Howard, "Inner Cabinet Will Have Spending Control," *Globe and Mail*, 31 January 1989, A3.

86 Jeffrey Simpson, "Where the Real Power Is," *Globe and Mail*, 31 January 1989, A6.

87 Mulroney, *Memoirs*, 713–15.

88 Mulroney, *Memoirs*, 648–9, 726; and Ross Howard, "Shuffle of Cabinet Signals PM's Return to Fighting Trim," *Globe and Mail*, 24 February 1990, A8.

89 Hugh Winsor, "New Cabinet Sends Message to English Canada," *Globe and Mail*, 22 April 1991, A1.

90 Hugh Winsor, "Report Offers Mulroney Chance at Fresh Start: Drastic Realignment of Departments, Agencies Recommended," *Globe and Mail*, 30 October 1992, A7.

91 Quoted in Terrance Corcoran, "No Hope for Major Cabinet Reform," *Globe and Mail*, 5 January 1993, B5.

92 Graham Fraser, "PM Rearranges Cabinet: Minor Changes Leave Mulroney's Options Open," *Globe and Mail*, 5 January 1993, A1.

17 Jean Chrétien: The "Friendly Dictator"

LORI TURNBULL

There probably is no greater irony in the history of Canadian political literature than this: the prime minister who occasioned two important books on the centralization of power in Ottawa was removed from office as a result of his caucus's loss of confidence in him. Donald Savoie's influential *Governing from the Centre: The Concentration of Power in Canadian Politics* appeared in 1999 and was followed by Jeffrey Simpson's *The Friendly Dictatorship* in 2001. Scholar and eminent columnist both insisted that the power exercised in the Prime Minister's Office (PMO) and the Privy Council Office (PCO) in Chrétien's day was unprecedented, making the prime minister almost unassailable. Nine months after Simpson's book appeared, a majority of Liberal MPs signed a letter demanding that Chrétien submit to a leadership review. The prime minister reluctantly concluded that he could no longer command his party and announced in August 2002 that he would resign, finally stepping down on 12 December 2003. To twist a now famous formula, the Chrétien experience showed that Canada's political culture might tolerate "friendly" dictatorships if necessary, but not necessarily "dictatorships."

Chrétien's legacy is not entirely clear. There were certainly indications that both the Prime Minister's Office, under the direction of Jean Pelletier, his old friend and a former mayor of Quebec City, and the Privy Council Office assumed more authority, particularly in shaping the government's fiscal policy and in conducting the Program Review that slashed departmental budgets as never before in Canadian history. The decision not to get involved in the American attack on Iraq seems to have been made by the prime minister, largely alone. Chrétien also made use of three-and-a-half-year terms, calling elections early to take advantage of events, to keep the many parties in Parliament in check and to maintain his own party on a permanent war footing. At the same time, there is ample evidence to show that Chrétien, shaped by his long experience as a cabinet minister, allowed his ministers remarkable leeway, carefully striking a balance between the social-liberal wing of the party and its more conservative, business-friendly faction. That compromise held for a decade, not a day more.[1]

Like all prime ministers, Chrétien's decade in office (1993–2003) was defined by a series of events beyond his immediate control. There were many: The rapidly deteriorating fiscal situation, the Quebec secession referendum in 1995; NATO's response to Serbian aggression in 1999; the 9/11 terrorist attacks; and the war in Iraq beginning in 2003. In 2000, the media reported on shoddy accounting practices at Human Resources Development Canada, which the opposition misleadingly dubbed the "billion-dollar boondoggle." The most ruinous of them was the Sponsorship Scandal: more than $100 million was directed to Quebec advertising firms with federalist leanings and Liberal ties to promote Canada in Quebec the wake of the 1995 referendum, with practically no accountability attached. In addition, there were scandals, eruptions, and unforced errors that were very much within the prime minister's control, such as the 2000–01 debacle known as "Shawinigate," which involved allegations that Chrétien pressured the Business Development Bank of Canada to grant a loan to the owner of a Shawinigan business who owed him money.

The Chrétien government was effective in several policy areas as it set the agenda and made the choices to advance platform goals and objectives. The government introduced the long-gun registry in 1995, created the *Clarity Act* in 1999 to set rules for future referenda, and made investments in the research capacity of universities through the creation of Canada Research Chairs and the Canadian Foundation for Innovation. The Chrétien government also brought about a fiscal revolution in balancing the federal budget within five years by slashing intergovernmental transfers and by exacting unprecedented cuts to all areas of federal government spending, except Indian Affairs. These actions limited the government's ability to respond to critical challenges like social housing, defence, environmental protection and climate policy which, some argue, set the stage for the pressure that Canada faces today.[2]

The Chrétien Leadership Style

Known colloquially as the "little guy from Shawinigan," Jean Chrétien described himself as a "street fighter" on the political scene, a man who fought to win and was not afraid of hitting back. In the biography *Iron Man: The Defiant Reign of Jean Chrétien*, journalist Lawrence Martin described the erudite and classical-music-loving Chrétien as a savvy, scrappy underdog who made a career of surprising those who underestimated him.[3] Bob Plamondon painted him as an "optimist" and a "populist" who based his political appeal on personality and pragmatism rather than ideology or partisanship. Chrétien's authenticity was his trademark and not-so-secret political weapon. Plamondon portrayed Chrétien's approach to governance and his presence in cabinet as more similar to a chair of the board than to a manager.

Jean Chrétien was born in the humblest of circumstances in Shawinigan Falls, Quebec, on 11 January 1934 (same day as Sir John A. Macdonald), the 18th of 19 children for Marie and Wellie Chrétien. Money was short, but ambition was not, and Jean was encouraged to pursue his studies. He was educated at Université Laval and worked as a lawyer in Shawinigan before being elected as the Member of Parliament for Saint-Maurice–Laflèche in 1963. He continued as the representative for Saint-Maurice for a total of 34 years (the riding was renamed in 1966).

Chrétien's time as prime minister was shaped by his long political career and years of experience in a range of ministerial portfolios. He attended his first cabinet meeting on 6 April 1967, as a minister without portfolio in Prime Minister Lester Pearson's government. He and Pierre Elliott Trudeau had been sworn into cabinet just two days earlier. During Chrétien's time as a minister, which spanned the governments of Prime Ministers Pearson, Trudeau, Turner, and then his own, Chrétien held ten separate portfolios – more than any other minister of the Crown since Confederation. He was a key minister in the Trudeau government, where he held the following portfolios: national revenue; Indian affairs and northern development; Treasury Board; industry, trade, and commerce; finance; justice and attorney general; social development; energy, mines and resources. Chrétien seemed at ease in all his portfolios, working with the knowledge that Trudeau had every confidence in him. There was one exception, when in the late summer of 1978, when Trudeau returned from a G7 Summit in Bonn and announced that the government's budget would immediately be slashed by $2 billion. "I was made to look like a fool," Chrétien wrote in his memoir, noting that most ministers would have resigned under such a circumstance. He stayed on, concerned "about the effect of a French-Canadian senior minister resigning when a separatist government was in power in Quebec."[4]

Chrétien and John Turner squared off in the leadership competition to replace Prime Minister Pierre Trudeau in 1984. Though Turner was ultimately successful, Chrétien had a strong second-place finish on the final ballot. Trudeau supporters largely backed Chrétien, whose pragmatic, no-nonsense way of practising politics was appealing to them. Chrétien served as deputy prime minister and minister of external affairs in Turner's short-lived cabinet. Chrétien's career as a member of Parliament and minister of the Crown was interrupted by his resignation from formal politics in February 1986, after he and Turner clashed publicly over who would serve as the president of the Liberal Party's Quebec wing.[5]

Chrétien became leader of the Liberal Party of Canada in 1990, after an infamously divisive leadership race that strained the party for years. He won a seat in Parliament for Beauséjour, New Brunswick, later that year. He returned as the member of Parliament for Saint Maurice in the general election of 1993, when he formed his government. It took little time for experts and practitioners to observe a palpable shift in the centre of gravity in Canadian politics. Gordon Robertson, who had served as Clerk of the Privy Council for Prime Ministers Pearson and Trudeau, noted during the Chrétien years that "the concentration of power in the hands of this prime minister is as great as I have ever seen it."[6] Previous chapters have documented how prime ministers concentrated power in their own ways, and Chrétien was not exceptional in this regard.

Inevitably, Chrétien's approach to decision making was shaped by his deep experience. Jean Pelletier, his chief of staff, noted that Chrétien knew the issues in practically every department: "he had a fantastic political nose" that gave him a rare ability to predict reactions.[7] However, it is equally important to consider the ways in which Chrétien's approach differed from Mulroney's, as this contrast can help to explain why Chrétien has often been cited, by Donald Savoie and others, as having made the concentration of power phenomenon considerably worse. While Prime Minister Brian Mulroney had relied on the advice, authority, and political instincts of key cabinet ministers whom he trusted to act autonomously and on their own judgment, Chrétien is said to have centralized decision-making power inside the PMO among non-elected political appointees who were loyal to him personally and did not, as political staffers, have any responsibility to account to the public (as, for example, a cabinet minister would). Journalist John Geddes observed that Chrétien's PMO had a tendency toward "obsessively tight control over both the government and the Liberal caucus" that resulted in "fewer and fewer real decision-makers" in Ottawa.[8] Jean Pelletier described his boss as "a bulldozer."[9]

Savoie blamed Chrétien for contributing to the growing concentration of power in the PMO and, in particular, in the hands of a select few courtiers – some of them political staff, others public officials – who provided direct advice and support to the prime minister. That said, other prime ministers have been described in similar ways – including Prime Minister Harper, who came after Chrétien. While the power of non-elected political appointees as strategic decision-makers was a hallmark of Chrétien's time in office, there were many matters for which Chrétien was happy to let ministers be ministers and run their files without interference. At the department level, Chrétien ministers were expected to manage as much as possible using their own statutory authority, rather than bringing items to full cabinet as a default. "Prime Minister Chrétien's style for the most part was to give his ministers a fair degree of latitude," according to Lloyd Axworthy. "He certainly gave me a good deal of space."[10] Indeed, Don Boudria wished he had received more direction from the prime minister: "He would never tell you anything. You were craving some feedback."[11]

This might give the appearance that Chrétien was generally keen to delegate or share power, but this impression would be misleading if too broadly applied. Savoie's work demonstrated how Chrétien differentiated between strategic decisions and priority-making on the one hand, and the tasks and the routines involved in managing issues and running departments on the other.[12] Decisions about key strategic priorities or matters of political importance were taken by the prime minister, while issues that were less politically explosive or more squarely within the purview of ministers' mandates were left to ministers to solve on their own. In 1998, a senior cabinet minister described Chrétien's attitude towards ministers: "The PM is often willing to let us do things, even when he himself is not convinced we're right. ... Chrétien can be forceful. If he has an opinion he lets you hear it. But his ministers don't live in fear of him."[13]

Increasingly over time, Chrétien trusted his own instincts more than anyone else's and was not shy to take decisions into his own hands and solve problems as he saw fit, often to the frustration of colleagues who were hoping to be drawn in. For example, in January 2003, Chrétien faced a fiery Liberal caucus when MPs returned from their winter break. Caucus members were upset over having not been consulted on a newly introduced political financing bill that would make it illegal for unions, corporations, and associations to make political contributions. Chrétien retorted with a threat to call a snap election if Liberal MPs did not back the legislation. Caucus chairman John McKay described Chrétien's approach in the following terms: "either do it my way or hit the road."[14] By this point, Chrétien seems to have lost interest in consultations and consensus-building, making it more difficult for him to maintain unity within caucus and cabinet. To further complicate matters, those who were irritated with Chrétien's style could find a home in Paul Martin's omnipresent leadership campaign.

The Chrétien Cabinet: Who made the cut?

When it came to cabinet appointments and governance, Prime Minister Chrétien emphasized simplicity, pragmatism, and ministerial autonomy on matters within their departments. His cabinet included representatives from the country's various regions as well as from both the left and the right of the Liberal Party. He was focused on getting things done, keeping the country together (which could not be taken for granted at the time), and resetting the economy. His cabinet reflected those goals, both in design and composition (see image 17.1).

In an interview with the CBC in October 2021, almost twenty years after he had left political office, Chrétien described the singular accountability and responsibility that a prime minister has with respect to appointing a cabinet. Invoking Canadian conventional wisdom, he said that the overall composition of a ministry had to be balanced, inclusive of a representative from every province (if possible) and reflective of the diversity within the country with respect to sex, language, and religion. It also had to be a team of the best and brightest. "It is very difficult because you have all sorts of constraints," he observed. "You know that for one person who is pleased there are ten that are very unhappy. ... This is a very difficult task, and you are alone."[15] Eddie Goldenberg devoted thirteen pages to the formation of Chrétien's cabinet in his insightful *The Way it Works: Inside Ottawa.* The guiding principles were not new: ensuring party solidarity, positioning "roman guards" who would support the prime minister in all circumstances, rewarding party loyalists who had shown an ability to defend the government in the House of Commons, achieving a mix of cabinet veterans as well as newcomers, and of course achieving a balance of ethnic, gender, and regional representation. Fitness for portfolios mattered a great deal and, not least, a concern for ethics.[16]

Chrétien's first ministry featured the following portfolios:

1 Prime Minister – Jean Chrétien, 59, Quebec
2 Agriculture – Ralph Goodale, 44, Saskatchewan
3 Communications; Multiculturalism and Citizenship – Michel Dupuy, 63, Quebec
4 Consumer and Corporate Affairs; Industry, Science, and Technology – John Manley, 43, Ontario
5 Employment and Immigration; Labour; Western Economic Diversification – Lloyd Axworthy, 53, Manitoba
6 Energy, Mines and Resources; Forestry – Anne McLellan, 43, Alberta
7 Environment; Deputy Prime Minister – Sheila Copps, 40, Ontario
8 External Affairs – André Ouellet, 54, Quebec
9 Finance – Paul Martin, 55, Quebec
10 Fisheries and Oceans – Brian Tobin, 39, Newfoundland
11 Indian Affairs and Northern Development – Ron Irwin, 57, Ontario
12 International Trade – Roy MacLaren, 59, Ontario
13 Justice and Attorney General – Allan Rock, 46, Ontario
14 Leader of the Government in the House of Commons; Solicitor General – Herb Gray, 62, Ontario
15 Leader of the Government in the Senate – Joyce Fairbairn, 53, Alberta (senator)
16 National Defence; Veterans Affairs – David Collenette, 47, Ontario
17 National Health and Welfare – Diane Marleau, 50, Ontario
18 National Revenue – David Anderson, 56, British Columbia
19 President of the Privy Council – Marcel Massé, 53, Quebec
20 Public Works; Supply and Services; the Atlantic Canada Opportunities Agency – David Dingwall, 41, Nova Scotia
21 Secretary of State of Canada – Sergio Marchi, 37, Ontario
22 Transport – Douglas Young, 53, New Brunswick
23 Treasury Board – Arthur Eggleton, 50, Ontario

Averaging 50.3 years old, it was a relatively young cabinet. Few of the ministers had federal cabinet experience. After Chrétien took office, a separate Department of Citizenship and Immigration was created to integrate and coordinate activities, policies, and programs that had been dispersed across the several portfolios. The budget and employee allocation were pulled from existing entities so that the new department was created without the need for new expenditure.

Chrétien's balancing act was impaired by the lack of representation from Western Canada, as the Liberal caucus was heavily drawn from Ontario and Quebec. The party system shifted significantly during the 1990s to further align with and reinforce regional cleavages. The failure of the Meech Lake Accord in 1990 had caused a split in the conservative coalition that Prime Minister Mulroney had formed between Quebec and the West. Voters in both regions were alienated, frustrated, and disenfranchised after the years of constitutional negotiations that ended in collapse. Many in Quebec felt isolated from the constitutional fold, while many in the West resented the hyper-focus on Quebec's demands that had captivated Canadian politics to the exclusion of Western concerns. Two new parties emerged and drew strength from the ruins of Meech Lake, each with a strong base that stifled Liberal growth in its respective region. A group of disgruntled former Progressive Conservative and Liberal MPs in Quebec came together in 1991 to form the Bloc Québécois, a Quebec sovereigntist party that quickly became the most popular party in the province. The Reform Party, a populist, right-wing party committed to a better deal for the West, had already been picking up steam west of Ontario and had elected its first MP, Deborah Grey, in a 1989 by-election.

Of the 177 Liberal MPs elected in 1993, two-thirds came from the two largest provinces: 98 were from Ontario and 19 were from Quebec. In the general election of 1997, the Liberals were reduced to 155 seats, nearly losing their majority, and 82 per cent of caucus members came from either Ontario or Quebec. In 2000, the Liberals managed to increase their caucus size to 172 members, with 100 from Ontario and 36 from Quebec (79 per cent overall). Given these results, it is no surprise that MPs from Canada's two largest provinces were strongly represented around the cabinet table. They also held many of the most prominent positions. For example, all three of Chrétien's deputy prime ministers were from Ontario (Sheila Copps, Herb Gray, and John Manley). Long-time Minister of Finance Paul Martin represented the Montreal riding of LaSalle-Émard. All ministers of foreign affairs during Chrétien's tenure were either from Quebec or Ontario, except for Lloyd Axworthy from Manitoba. Both ministers of intergovernmental affairs, Marcel Massé and Stéphane Dion, came from Quebec – which was no surprise, given the need to respond to and contain the growing sovereignty movement in Quebec at the time.

Though the presence and influence of ministers from Quebec and Ontario was undeniable, Chrétien demonstrated a deep commitment to regional representation around the cabinet table and made special efforts to ensure that each province had a voice. One particularly shocking outcome of the 1997 election was that the Liberals did not elect any MPs in Nova Scotia, a traditional Liberal stronghold. Chrétien appointed Senator Alasdair Graham from Nova Scotia as the leader of the government in the Senate to make sure the province had a point person in the ministry. In 1997, Chrétien appointed both Liberal MPs from Alberta to cabinet and four of the six Liberal MPs from British Columbia. So, even when more than 80 percent of caucus members were from Quebec and Ontario, the cabinet was far more regionally balanced than the caucus was. Also, though the most prominent and influential portfolios were often held by Quebec and Ontario ministers, it is fair to say that some of Chrétien's key ministers came from other parts of the country. For example, Anne McLellan (Alberta), Ralph Goodale (Saskatchewan), and Lloyd Axworthy (Manitoba) held prominent files, including health, natural resources, and foreign affairs at times when these issues were dominating Canadian politics.

Regional balance is a must-have in any federal cabinet; ideological balance is also essential for the various constituencies and perspectives within the party to feel represented. The Liberal Party is a big-tent party, and Chrétien's caucus included both left- and right-wing Liberals. Having both perspectives around the cabinet table was especially important considering the fiscal situation at the time. Prime Minister Chrétien and Finance Minister Paul Martin were making the kinds of budgetary cuts that left-leaning Liberals found hard to accept.[17] Caucus was not happy after the 1995 budget, many pointing out that they did not seek election so that they could scale back the size and scope of government. To provide further legitimacy to program cuts, Chrétien appointed left-wingers like Herb Gray, Sheila Copps, Brian Tobin, and Sergio Marchi to cabinet and gave them the majority on the important Program Review Committee, which made the bulk of the difficult choices that led to a balanced budget.[18] At the same time, fiscally conservative Liberals like Paul Martin and John Manley held important decision-making portfolios, so that the policy direction of the government stayed focused on rebuilding the economy.

Chrétien was typically unruffled when ministers found themselves in political hot water. He was unmoved by opposition pressure to shuffle or fire ministers for alleged corruption or incompetence. For example, during the "billion-dollar boondoggle," the opposition calls for the resignation of Human Resources Development Minister Jane Stewart grew louder by the day. But Chrétien would not budge. He stepped in to take questions on her behalf during heated Question Periods, insisting that he would not accept her resignation even if it were offered.[19] That said, Chrétien preferred that ministers keep a low profile, particularly when it came to personal matters.[20] He would not let ministerial scandals drag the government down if they became too distracting. For example, in 2002, Art Eggleton left cabinet after media reports that he had awarded a government contract to a former girlfriend. The Liberal government's popularity was already plummeting at the time, as both the Sponsorship Scandal and the Chrétien/Martin tension made headlines, and it is possible that Chrétien wanted Eggleton to resign because he did not want to see things get worse.[21] Eggleton had been having a difficult year already. In January, both he and Chrétien were accused of misleading the House over whether Canadian troops in Afghanistan had given captured Taliban and al-Qaeda members over to the Americans, whose behaviour at Guantanamo Bay had given rise to concerns over abusive treatment of prisoners.[22]

Chrétien was not prone to routine cabinet shuffles, but in January 2002, there was a significant shake-up on the government's front benches. This was triggered at least in part by the unanticipated departure of Fisheries Minister Brian Tobin, who, until he left cabinet, was considered a serious contender to succeed Chrétien. Rather than simply replace his Newfoundland and Labrador minister, the Prime Minister used the moment as an opportunity to reset cabinet and assert his own authority as leader and prime minister amid rumours that he was thinking of leaving. Eight ministers did not continue, ten new ones were brought in, and 13 ministers were moved to new positions. The newly-appointed cabinet was heavily populated by Chrétien loyalists. The left-right balance that had been present in the earlier days of the Chrétien government was now weighted more heavily towards the right. Lloyd Axworthy, regarded as one of the last left-leaning Liberals in the ministry, was moved to foreign affairs. This suggested that a greater emphasis on human rights issues was coming. One of the departing individuals was Public Works Minister Alfonso Gagliano, who was increasingly under suspicion for being a key player in the Sponsorship Scandal as well as other ethical quagmires.

In addition to being an opportunity to assert his leadership, the shuffle also allowed Chrétien to reorganize cabinet in accordance with new and urgent priorities. In the aftermath of the terrorist attacks in the U.S., there was a need for greater focus on security and military preparedness. John Manley was moved from the foreign affairs portfolio, where he had received much praise from both within Canada and in Washington, to the position of deputy prime minister with responsibility for security issues as well as all major national public works projects. Upon accepting his new post, Manley explained that he would be taking on many of the hands-on issues that Chrétien himself had been dealing with in connection with the security file.[23]

Overall, there was continuity in cabinet over the course of Chrétien's time in office. It was not uncommon for ministers to hold portfolios for three years or more, which gave them time to grow in their files, build trust and familiarity with relevant stakeholders and the public, and become more comfortable and confident

Image 17.1. Governor General Adrienne Clarkson with Jean Chrétien and his cabinet at Rideau Hall, 14 October 1999

Source: Fred Chartrand, Canadian Press, CP2770884.

around the cabinet table. There was a robust cadre of veteran Chrétien ministers whose time in the ministry spanned all three Parliaments during the Chrétien era.

The Structure and Design of the Chrétien Cabinet

The ministry that took office in November of 1993 had 30 members in addition to the prime minister himself, which was relatively compact compared to Prime Minister Brian Mulroney's cabinet of 40. Chrétien introduced a new two-level structure: Twenty-two were full members of cabinet while the remaining eight were secretaries of state, junior ministers sworn into the Privy Council and therefore part of the ministry but not members of cabinet. Secretaries of state were assigned to specific cabinet ministers to assist with their portfolios. They earned a reduced salary at a rate of 75 percent of that of full ministers, had smaller offices with fewer staff, and, for most of Chrétien's tenure, did not have dedicated cars and drivers.[24] Much of the work of the secretaries of state focused on job creation and economic growth, which were key priorities for the government at a time of fiscal and economic strain.

This distinction between ministers, who were in cabinet, and secretaries of state, who were not, was a significant innovation in cabinet design during the Chrétien era. He justified the hierarchy between ministers, which was commonplace in the United Kingdom and Australia, as an austerity measure that would help to contain the costs associated with designing a new government. Also in keeping with efficiency, the Chrétien government eliminated the position of chief of staff in ministers' offices and reduced the size of these offices overall. Chrétien promised that a trimmed-down political staff complement, as compared to the largesse of the Mulroney government, would lead to a savings of $10 million per year.[25] Over the course of Chrétien's time in office, budgets for exempt staff for ministers and secretaries of state increased. Secretaries of state were given significantly more support including a dedicated car and driver, the designation of an assistant deputy minister, and the allocation of a departmental assistant.

In keeping with his platform commitment to smaller, more efficient government, Chrétien created a simplified system of only four cabinet committees in 1993:

- Economic Union Committee;
- Social Union Committee;
- Special Committee of Council, which handled regulatory issues; and
- Treasury Board, which managed the government's financial, personnel, and administrative matters.

The absence of a Priorities and Planning Committee was striking in contrast to governments dating back to Pearson's day. At Chrétien's first cabinet meeting as prime minister in 1993, he told ministers that he eliminated this committee out of desire for a leaner cabinet than Mulroney's.[26] This streamlined roster of standing committees was maintained throughout the Chrétien government and ad hoc committees and reference groups were appointed when matters arose that required dedicated attention. Critically, the issue of environmental protection fell to the Economic Union Committee, a decision that would smooth the way for massive cuts to Environment Canada (1400 employees and $235 million). The prime minister wanted the standing committees to focused on the issues that fell within their jurisdictions, ostensibly so that the full cabinet could devote itself to the most important and urgent political and policy matters. Reference groups were struck to consider matters of policy such as official languages, climate change, Indigenous policy, and the voluntary sector. Chrétien also appointed ad hoc committees to deal with specific opportunities and challenges that were weighing heavily on the minds of Canadians. To supply the briefings to cabinet and to ensure coordination of policy decisions, the number of PCO employees had grown from 350 in 1993 to over 1100 by 1995.[27]

Marcel Massé chaired the Program Review Committee, which made the necessary cuts to balance the federal budget. In April 2001, Chrétien appointed a new cabinet committee on energy to coordinate federal efforts to take advantage of opportunities to develop natural gas resources in the North.[28] After the terrorist attacks in the United States on 11 September 2001, Prime Minister Chrétien appointed a Security and Intelligence Committee.

Cabinet was not a decision-making body in itself during the Chrétien era, which made some ministers come to resent the lack of value placed on cabinet discussions. Most decisions were made in cabinet committee and were ratified in full cabinet. In a small number of areas, those of particular concern to Chrétien, the decisions were made in conversation with the responsible minister. For example, in a 1997 pre-budget exercise, the Privy Council Office asked ministers to submit ideas for how to spend a modest budget surplus. Chrétien and Martin thought this a waste of time, but the prime minister allowed the exercise to continue, only to ignore its results. Allan Rock, the minister of health, is reported to have blown up over the situation. Ministers learned their lesson: if you want something, go to Chrétien directly.[29]

The size of the Chrétien ministry swelled over time. Following the general election in 1997, a total of 36 cabinet ministers and junior ministers were sworn in – 28 of whom had been part of the ministry prior to the election. The larger ministry reflected Chrétien's desire for regional balance at a time when his caucus was disproportionately drawn from the country's two most populous provinces. He wanted to keep the strength he had from Quebec and Ontario but also add ministers from regions where the party was less popular and where other parties had grown in strength by appealing specifically to regional concerns (namely, the Reform Party in the West and the Bloc Québécois in Quebec). Nine ministers came from west of Ontario and four from Atlantic Canada.[30]

Prime Minister Chrétien's relationships with ministers

When Jean Chrétien formed his government in 1993, he knew that part of the task ahead was to build fences with leadership rivals Paul Martin and Sheila Copps, whom he had defeated on the first ballot in a 1990 leadership convention. To heal wounds and keep them close, he appointed Martin to the finance portfolio, a position he held for almost a decade, and Copps as minister of the environment and the first woman deputy prime minister. She had first been elected as the MP for Hamilton East in 1984, a role she occupied for twenty years and for almost the entire duration of Chrétien's time as prime minister. She had proven herself a force to be reckoned with while on the opposition benches during the Mulroney years. Copps was a member of the "rat pack" – a group of young Liberal MPs who took on the task of making life particularly miserable for the Mulroney government. The group's pointed criticisms have been credited for ending the political careers of several Mulroney ministers. Other rat pack members – Brian Tobin and Don Boudria – ended up with cabinet positions too, which speaks to Chrétien's affinity for rewarding loyalty. At times, Chrétien was seen to be showing favouritism to certain ministers, but frustrations over this matter never seemed to become so problematic as to disrupt the peace. For example, Jane Stewart's appointment as minister of Indian affairs was not warmly accepted by all. There was a sense that her family connections were responsible for her promotion; her father, Robert Nixon, was a friend of the prime minister's and a former leader of the Ontario Liberals.[31] Another example was Stéphane Dion. "I became closer to him than any other minister," Chrétien wrote in his memoirs.[32]

The relationship between Chrétien and Paul Martin was the most impactful and defining of the Chrétien cabinet, not only because of their solidarity in managing the fiscal crisis and his willingness to trust Martin on matters of fiscal and economic policy, but also because of the deep and lasting rivalry between the two individuals that came to define and divide the Liberal Party for years to come.[33] The feud began in earnest in 1990, when Chrétien won the leadership of the Liberal Party over Martin and Copps. The Meech Lake Accord was going down to defeat at the time and Chrétien and Martin, both Quebec politicians, were on different sides of it. The wounds from these exchanges never fully healed. However, Martin did well enough in the leadership contest that he could not be ignored and was appointed co-chair of the committee that crafted the Liberal platform for the 1993 campaign. He served as finance minister and Chrétien's key partner in balancing the federal books. Once the government was in surplus territory, Martin's itch to become leader flared up again and he began to mobilize. Many caucus members aligned with Martin, feeling that it would be prudent for the party to solidify Martin's leadership in time for the next federal election. This only caused Chrétien to double down and hold onto the leadership even more fiercely. He won a majority government in 2000 but the party was more internally divided than perhaps ever before.

The tension between the two camps continued into Chrétien's third term. In January 2002, as he announced a significant cabinet shuffle, he made it clear that the Martin camp's organization would not affect his personal timeline: "I will go when I decide I will go. But as long as I'm prime minister, I am prime minister."[34]

In June of that year, Martin left cabinet, which gave him the time and opportunity to tour the country and drum up support for his leadership. Chrétien announced in the fall of 2002 that he would resign in February 2004, a date later changed to 12 December 2003, paving the way for Martin's coronation.

The dynamic between Chrétien and Martin did not prevent them from working together to turn the economy around. This relationship was unique and the most important in cabinet. Despite their intense rivalry and interpersonal tension, Chrétien trusted Martin and deferred to his judgement on the all-important matter of economic stability. But once that major objective was reached, the relationship soured to the point where it was untenable. Martin grew tired of waiting and positioned himself to challenge Chrétien's leadership. Meanwhile,

Chrétien, who always insisted that he would go on his own terms, ended up leaving only when he could not convince the majority of caucus members to support his sticking around. In the end, Chrétien spent a decade in PMO and achieved what he wanted to achieve, but the rivalry with Martin was a dark cloud over his exit from formal politics. Further, the drama of the Sponsorship Scandal did not hit in earnest until Martin had become prime minister. The public reaction to this, combined with a growing sense of voter fatigue with the Liberals and a successful campaign to "unite the right" in Canada, meant that Martin was prime minister only for two years.

How did cabinet manage issues?

Chrétien's three main areas of focus were national unity; economic stability and growth; and Canada's relationship with the United States. To keep cabinet on a similar footing, retreats were organized two or three times a year, usually a day or a day-and-a-half.[35] For each of these files, Chrétien tended to deal directly with the relevant minister rather than to bring the full discussion to cabinet for a decision. Therefore, when we speak of how the Chrétien cabinet "managed" his pet issues, it should be understood that issues were not managed by full cabinet or even by cabinet committee. Instead, the management strategy was largely a bilateral one between the prime minister and the minister in question. Chrétien was goal-oriented and trusted key ministers to work through whatever steps were necessary to achieve the desired result. So, ministers might have some autonomy along the journey, but Chrétien determined the end game on these issues.

National Unity

Constitutional negotiations designed to bring Quebec into the constitutional fold had been dominating Canadian politics for decades by the time Chrétien became prime minister. He had long been opposed to the sovereignty movement in Quebec and was also suspicious of constitutional talks as a way of solving political problems, including the national unity crisis and the question of Quebec's place in Confederation.[36]

Chrétien was particularly active on issues surrounding national unity. His doubts about the utility of formal constitutional negotiations do not in any way diminish the sense of personal responsibility he felt to keep the country together. Cabinet ministers from outside Quebec were not brought into the decision-making fold. Instead, Chrétien, PMO, and some key Quebec ministers determined strategy. In the final days leading up to the historic 1995 Quebec referendum, Chrétien took a lead role for the federalist side, appealing directly to Quebec voters at public rallies and through media campaigns. He tried to dissuade Quebecers from voting yes strategically to empower the Quebec government to get a better deal from Canada. He explained in plain terms that a yes vote was a vote for separation.[37]

Once the referendum was over, with the federalist side winning with just 50.6 per cent of the vote, the Chrétien government established a pro-Canada advertising campaign within Quebec to nurture positive attitudes toward federalism. This program became the nucleus of the Sponsorship Scandal when Auditor General Sheila Fraser reported in 2003 that significant sums of money had been mismanaged. He also appointed a new minister of intergovernmental affairs in 1996. Stéphane Dion was a professor at the Université de Montréal who came into Parliament in a by-election following his appointment to cabinet. His key role was to shepherd the federal government's response to the national unity question following the referendum. In 1996, the federal government posed a reference question to the Supreme Court of Canada on the legal and constitutional rules, both domestically and internationally, pertaining to the unilateral secession of a province from Canada. In 1998, the Supreme Court responded that under the Canadian constitution, unilateral secession was not legal. However, Canada would have no right to obstruct efforts of a province to secede if the results of a referendum indicated that this was the will of the public. Both the federalist and sovereigntist sides claimed to be satisfied with the court's approach. Immediately following the release of the decision, Dion began work on what came to be known as the *Clarity Act*. The legislation, which passed in the House of Commons in 2000, established the conditions under which the federal government would negotiate with a province following a vote on secession. The legislation stipulates that a 50%+1 result in favour of secession would not be enough to satisfy the threshold for a clear majority on a clear question. Support for sovereignty-association in the province of Quebec dropped to 24% in 1999, which suggests that the Supreme Court reference and Dion's attempts to take the oxygen out of the sovereignty movement had been successful.[38] There were serious doubts about this approach within Cabinet, but Chrétien and Dion ploughed ahead.

Deficit, Debt Reduction, and Economic Growth

Managing the deficit and debt, and getting the country's fiscal house in order, was a key objective for Chrétien. The economic picture at the time was bleak. The deficit for 1993–94 stood at $45.7 billion. Though their relationship was filled with tension that later boiled over to the point that Martin left cabinet, Chrétien and Martin were united in their approach to fiscal balance and responsibility. The 1994 budget pulled $400 million from the operating budgets of government departments for the 1994–95 fiscal year, to be increased to $620 the following year. Public sector salaries were frozen and pay increments eliminated. But it was the 1995 budget that sent massive shock waves in the form of deep program cuts and slashes to provincial transfer payments. The deficit that the Chrétien government inherited was eliminated in five budgets, but not without significant costs at the polls, as well as strain in the caucus room and around the cabinet table. Chrétien's senior adviser Eddie Goldenberg recalls how ministers would beg Chrétien to spare them and their departments from the drastic cuts, but he held his ground, always supporting the finance minister. To blunt the criticism from the left wing of the party, Chrétien appointed a Program Review Committee whose members would decide on which programs to cut. Membership included Sheila Copps, Brian Tobin, Herb Gray, and Sergio Marchi – ministers who were not inclined to support cuts to programs and therefore had the trust of the party's left. This measure was intended to communicate the urgency and necessity of deep spending cuts.[39] No doubt, the fiscal prudence of the 1990s contributed to the decline in support for the Liberals in the 1997 election. Though they held onto their majority, they lost seats and ministers – including Dave Dingwall in Cape Breton – as voters punished the government for what they experienced as its ongoing frigid austerity. For many Liberals, the approach was off brand, lacking in compassion, and tone deaf.[40]

Throughout this period, it was the Chrétien-Martin relationship that provided the foundation for the government's fiscal policy. They agreed on the gravity of the fiscal situation and their unity provided a protective armour for Prime Minister Chrétien against the protestations from ministers who wanted to take a more relaxed approach. In an interview in 2011, the former prime minister compared Canada's situation in the mid-1990s to that of Greece at the time. The *Wall Street Journal* had described the Canada of 1994 as an "honorary member of the Third World." Drastic measures were necessary to shock Canada's economy to life. Chrétien recalls saying to himself: "I will do it. I might be prime minister for only one term, but I will do it."[41] Canada's deficit was eliminated and transformed to a surplus by the late 1990s, and Canada's economy went from the second worst in the G7 to one of the strongest.

Canada–US Relations

Chrétien always told the public that the Canada-U.S. relationship was "healthy and strong," but that he was taking more distance from the White House than Prime Minister Mulroney had before him. Some, including journalist and Chrétien biographer Lawrence Martin, have pointed out that, despite this rhetoric around wanting to end Canada's junior partner status in its relationship with the United States, not much really changed under Chrétien's administration.[42] Chrétien had come to office promising changes to the North American Free Trade Agreement, but not a word in the agreement was altered. When terrorist attacks hit the United States on 11 September 2001, he pledged Canada's full support in the form of military strength to defend North America from terrorist threats. In the weeks that followed, Foreign Affairs Minister John Manley stressed that, though Canada was committed to a strong partnership with the United States, it would not succumb to pressure to "curb immigration policies" or increasing controls along the countries' undefended border.[43]

While Canada participated in the subsequent war in Afghanistan, one of Chrétien's most impactful legacies was the decision not to join American and British allies in the war in Iraq. Reflecting on the decision years later, he maintains that it was the right thing not to go to war without a resolution from the United Nations.[44] The decision was informed in part by a memo from the clerk of the Privy Council, Alex Himelfarb, which argued that the U.S. decision to invade Iraq was motivated by regime change. Chrétien did not take the final decision to full cabinet, though the issue was discussed several times in the weeks leading up to the war. Chrétien consulted with Defence Minister John McCallum and Foreign Affairs Minister Bill Graham, but relied primarily on advice from Claude Laverdure, the prime minister's foreign and defence policy adviser, and political advisers, including Eddie Goldenberg. Caucus was firmly against Canadian involvement in the Iraq war, which made the decision an easier one. Perhaps even more importantly, there was no United Nations resolution to justify action.

Conclusion

During the Chrétien era in the late 1990s, Savoie wrote that cabinet government was a thing of the past. Instead of being a decision-making body, cabinet had "joined Parliament as an institution being bypassed." Real power had become concentrated in the hands of the prime minister and a "small group of carefully selected courtiers," among them key ministers, senior public servants, lobbyists, pollsters, and friends.[45]

Yet the situation cannot be so easily summarized. The government's decision-making style depended on the specific issue. On the issues that mattered most to him, Prime Minister Chrétien used cabinet neither as a decision-making chamber nor a focus group. He listened to the advice of the people he trusted and forged policy in bilateral discussions with the key minister, whether Stéphane Dion for national unity or Paul Martin for economic recovery. That said, on most issues, Chrétien provided the government's overall objective, but it was up to ministers, individually in their departments or collectively in Cabinet committees, to make the key decisions, often with no input from the prime minister.

Chrétien's feeling of being alone as leader of the party and the country had a definitive effect on his attitude toward the role of cabinet. In an interview with veteran CBC journalist Don Newman as he left politics, Chrétien said: "The leader is the one who calls the shots at the end of the day. It's why you have a leader ... There is a moment in our system where the problem is in front of the leader. And he has to decide ... Everything goes on his desk. No piece of legislation, no budget, no Speech from the Throne is not approved by the prime minister ... The buck stops here. And that's life."[46]

He spoke of the achievements of which he was most proud, including having balanced the budget following years of crippling debt, standing up to the United States, and stabilizing national unity following the Quebec referendum on sovereignty. Although at times he spoke of the accomplishments of the government as a collective, he often referred to himself in the first person as being responsible for the government's agenda and results, whether good or bad. In the conversation with Newman, he said, "When I started, we were a bankrupt nation. Now we are in a good situation." He also spoke of having more problems with the United States before "I took the government." He took the national unity crisis as a personal challenge, both as leader of the country and as a Quebecer. Chrétien dominated his cabinet, until he no longer could, however. Paul Martin's departure glowingly showed the limits of this approach.[47]

Even the sharpest critic could not cast reasonable doubt on Prime Minister Chrétien's lasting impact on governance in Canada and on the most critical policy challenges that the country faces.

NOTES

1 Chrétien later declared Pelletier "the best chief of staff ever in Ottawa." See Gilbert Lavoie, *Jean Pelletier: Entretiens et témoignages* (Quebec: Septentrion, 2009), 145.

2 Paris Marx, "Jean Chrétien's Austerity Made Canada Less Prepared for COVID-19," *Canadian Dimension*, 7 July 2020, https://canadiandimension.com /articles/view/jean-Chrétiens-austerity-made-canada-less-prepared-for-covid-19.

3 Lawrence Martin, *Iron Man: The Defiant Reign of Jean Chrétien* (Toronto: Viking, 2003).

4 Jean Chrétien, *Straight from the Heart* (Toronto: Key Porter Books, 1985), 117–18.

5 Reuters, "Around the World; Canadian Politician Resigns after 23 Years," *New York Times*, 28 February 1986, https://www.nytimes.com/1986/02/28/world /around-the-world-canadian-politician-resigns-after-23-years.html.

6 Bruce Wallace, "Chrétien, a Closet Autocrat?," *Maclean's*, 19 October 1998, https://www.thecanadianencyclopedia.ca/en/article/chretien-a-closet-autocrat.

7 Lavoie, *Jean Pelletier*, 133.

8 John Geddes, "Remembering the Chrétien PMO: Will That Be Donolo's Way?," *Maclean's*, 28 October 2009, https://macleans.ca/politics/ottawa/remembering-the -chretien-pmo-will-that-be-donolos-way/.

9 Lavoie, *Jean Pelletier*, 137.

10 Lloyd Axworthy, *Navigating a New World: Canada's Global Future* (Toronto: Alfred A. Knopf, 2003), 57.

11 Lawrence Martin, *Harperland: The Politics of Control* (Toronto: Viking, 2010), 63. See also Anne McLellan's comments quoted in Martin, *Iron Man*, 100.

12 Donald J. Savoie, "The Rise of Court Government in Canada," *Canadian Journal of Political Science* 32, no. 4 (1999): 635–64.

13 Wallace, "Closet Autocrat?"

14 Jane Taber, "Fundraising Bill Upsets PM's Caucus," *Globe and Mail*, 30 January 2003, https://www.theglobeandmail.com/news/national/fundraising-bill-upsets -pms-caucus/article4126375/.

15 "Former PM Chrétien Reflects on Difficulties of Forming a Cabinet," interview with Jean Chrétien by Rosemary Barton, *Rosemary Barton Live*, 24 October 2021, posted by CBC News, YouTube video, 11:18, https://www.youtube.com /watch?v=QiOisghe_gI.

16 Eddie Goldenberg, *The Way It Works: Inside Ottawa* (Toronto: McClelland & Stewart, 2006), 57–69.

17 The complicated relationship between the Prime Minister's Office and the Department of Finance is discussed in Goldenberg, *Way It Works*, 113–30.

18 Martin, *Iron Man*.

19 "PM Stands by Stewart, Refuses Calls for her Resignation," *CBC News*, 7 February 2000, https://www.cbc.ca/news/canada/pm-stands-by-stewart-refuses -calls-for-her-resignation-1.244862.

20 E. Kaye Fulton, Mary Janigan, and Anthony Wilson-Smith, "Chrétien Shuffles Cabinet," *Maclean's*, 5 February 1996, https://www.thecanadianencyclopedia.ca /en/article/Chrétien-shuffles-cabinet.

21 Anne McIlroy, "Chrétien in Crisis," *Guardian*, 3 June 2002, https://www .theguardian.com/world/2002/jun/03/worlddispatch.annemcilroy.

22 "Eggleton Confirms JTF2 Has Taken Prisoners in Afghanistan," *CBC News*, 30 January 2002, https://www.cbc.ca/news/canada/eggleton-confirms-jtf2-has-taken -prisoners-in-afghanistan-1.313599.

23 William Orme, "Chretien Shuffles Canadian Cabinet," *Los Angeles Times*, 16 January 2002, https://www.latimes.com/archives/la-xpm-2002-jan-16-mn-22979 -story.html.

24 "Guide to Canadian Ministries since Confederation: Twenty-Sixth Ministry," Government of Canada, archived 5 March 2012, https://web.archive.org /web/20120305011838/http://www.pco-bcp.gc.ca/mgm/dtail.asp?lang=eng&mstyi d=26&mbtpid=1.

25 Office of the Prime Minister, "Release," 4 November 1993.

26 Canadian Press, "Chrétien's First Cabinet Meeting Focused on Ministers' Office Spending," *CBC News*, 3 February 2014, https://www.cbc.ca/news/politics /chrétien-s-first-cabinet-meeting-focused-on-ministers-office-spending-1.2520982.

27 Paul Wells, *Right Side Up: The Fall of Paul Marin and the Rise of Stephen Harper's New Conservatism* (Toronto: McClelland & Stewart, 2006), 286.

28 "Chrétien Urges Development of Resources," *CBC News*, 6 April 2001, https://www.cbc.ca/news/canada/Chrétien-urges-development-of-resources-1.288233.

29 Wallace, "Closet Autocrat?"

30 John Demont, Dale Eisler, and Luke Fisher, "Chrétien's New Cabinet," *Maclean's*, 23 June 1997, https://www.thecanadianencyclopedia.ca/en/article/Chrétiens-new-cabinet.

31 Fulton, Janigan, and Wilson-Smith, "Chrétien Shuffles Cabinet."

32 Jean Chrétien, *My Years as Prime Minister* (Toronto: Alfred A. Knopf, 2007), 156.

33 Edward Greenspon and Anthony Wilson-Smith, *Double Vision: The Inside Story of the Liberals in Power* (Toronto: Doubleday, 1996).

34 DeNeen L. Brown, "Chrétien's Hand Strengthened in Cabinet Shuffle," *Washington Post*, 16 January 2002, https://www.washingtonpost.com/archive/politics/2002/01/16/chretiens-hand-strengthened-in-cabinet-shuffle/94e6b9a8-af9f-4f35-8744-42fc8f7881a0/.

35 Goldenberg, *Way It Works*, 105.

36 Canadian Press, "Meech Lake Was a Waste of Time: Chrétien," *CBC News*, 22 June 2010, https://www.cbc.ca/news/canada/montreal/meech-lake-was-waste-of-time-chrétien-1.870441.

37 Bob Plamondon, "Excerpt: Now We Know Jean Chrétien's Secret Plan Had He Lost the Quebec Referendum," *National Post*, 31 October 2017, https://nationalpost.com/opinion/excerpt-now-we-know-jean-chretiens-secret-plan-had-he-lost-the-quebec-referendum.

38 "Canada's Clarity Bill," *CBC News*, 1999, https://www.cbc.ca/player/play/video/1.3334896.

39 Brooke Jeffrey, *Divided Loyalties* (Toronto: University of Toronto Press, 2010).

40 See David A. Good, *Politics of Public Money: Spenders, Guardians, Priority Setters, and Financial Watchdogs inside the Canadian Government* (Toronto: University of Toronto Press, 2007); Gilles Paquet and Robert Shepherd, "The Program Review Process: A Deconstruction," in *How Ottawa Spends 1996–97: Life under the Knife*, ed. Gene Swimmer (Ottawa: Carleton University Press, 1996), 39–72; and Evert A. Lindquist, "On the Cutting Edge: Program Review, Government Restructuring and the Treasury Board of Canada," in Swimmer, *How Ottawa Spends 1996–97*, 205–52.

41 Reuters, "Lessons from Canada's 'Basket Case' Moment," *Financial Post*, 21 November 2011, https://financialpost.com/uncategorized/lessons-from-canadas-basket-case-moment.

42 "Chrétien and Clinton: A Cross-Border Friendship," 1997, CBC Archives, https://www.cbc.ca/player/play/637114435615.

43 "Response to Attacks on Bush-Chrétien Agenda," *CNN*, 24 September 2001, https://www.cnn.com/2001/US/09/24/ret.bush.canada.index.html.

44 "Ten Years Later, Chrétien Remembers 9-11," *CTV News*, 6 September 2011, https://www.ctvnews.ca/ten-years-later-chretien-remembers-9-11-1.693180.

45 Savoie, "Court Government in Canada," 635.

46 "Life after Politics for Chrétien," interview with Jean Chrétien, *CBC News*, 2003, CBC Archives, https://www.cbc.ca/player/play/1735308849.

47 Jean Pelletier describes it as "la guerre ouverte." See Lavoie, *Jean Pelletier*, 167–72.

18 Paul Martin's Cabinet: The Unforgiving Consequences of Flawed Statecraft

PATRICE DUTIL AND STEPHEN AZZI

Barely out of government, Paul Martin promptly set to work on his memoirs, *Hell or High Water: My Life in and out of Politics*, which appeared in less than two years. Although his twenty-six-month tenure as prime minister constituted only about 40 per cent of the book, Martin felt an urgency to address the criticism that had stung the most: that he was often indecisive and torn between numerous priorities. He acknowledged that he had many objectives as prime minister but insisted that he had no regrets: "I do not ... accept that my agenda was too large for the country." Still, he did offer that perhaps he had tried to accomplish too much in a minority parliament: "I might even accept that my agenda was too large for the political circumstances in which I found myself."[1]

That diagnosis has not lost its validity almost twenty years later. Martin and his Liberal Party were in power from 12 December 2003 to 6 February 2006, a tumultuous period that saw two election campaigns, an intensification of the war effort in Afghanistan, raucous debates on a wide range of issues from Indigenous governance to the fallout from revelations of corruption in government sponsorship activities in Quebec, a national child care initiative, a New Deal for Cities and Communities, and the Kelowna Accord, in which Ottawa and the provinces agreed to provide billions of dollars to improve the lives of Indigenous peoples.

Martin had assumed office with three broad priorities for improving governance: he wanted to show that Ottawa was capable of ethical conduct, able to clearly account for its expenses, and in tune with newly emerging demands for democratic reform. In anticipation of an election, the government proposed a laundry list of reforms (over 230 measures, new rules, and procedures) to strengthen the audit process within departments and agencies. These measures included re-establishing of the Office of the Comptroller General within the Treasury Board Secretariat and hiring of hundreds of internal auditors across the government's departments and agencies. Some have considered the Martin reforms, though deeply rooted in Canadian precedents, to be the most substantial to the centre of government since the late 1970s.[2] Regardless, for all its ambitions and the considerable strengths of its leader, the Martin government had great difficulty in promoting its program of reforms and it ultimately failed. It was a hard lesson to learn, for successful statecraft depends on democratic validation. The political landscape was changing rapidly as Martin's government evolved. Most notably, conservative voters were given something Martin and his colleagues had not faced since 1993: a united front that had a fighting chance to overturn the Liberals. In Quebec, Martin's politics did not register well. It was clear he and his team were unable to communicate their visions and values to important segments of that population.

Paul Martin had so long wanted to be prime minister of Canada that he could hardly contain himself when he was chosen by members of the Liberal Party to become their leader on 14 November 2003. He was sixty-five, a few months younger than Lester Pearson when the latter had assumed the central chair of the cabinet in 1963 (only John Abbott, Mackenzie Bowell, Charles Tupper, and Louis St-Laurent were older on their first day as prime minister), but Martin took hold of the office with the energy and the ambitions of a man half his age. The new prime minister planned to put his ideas to work immediately, careful to follow but one rule: not to do things the way his predecessor might have done them. This extended to the manner in which he engaged the members of his cabinet. In his eagerness to hear the views of his ministers and to give them an opportunity to participate in decision-making, Martin opted to multiply their involvement in a series of committees, even allowing parliamentary secretaries to provide input. This approach reflected Martin's personal preference and his democratic values, but it also contributed to slowing the government's ability to make decisions. Martin adopted a system of constant consultations, but as with Pierre Elliott Trudeau in the 1970s, his process helped solidify his reputation as a hesitant decider.

Martin's ambitions meant that he always found himself pressed for time. Given a longer spell in office, he may well have had a chance to multiply successes. But his government was defeated on a motion of no confidence on 28 November 2005, when the opposition parties (Conservatives, New Democrats, and Bloc Québécois) expressed their wish to go to the polls. Had the New Democratic Party, led by Jack Layton, supported the government, the Liberals would have survived. Regardless, it was only a matter of time before the government would be defeated: the Opposition sensed that the prime minister would have enormous difficulty in defending his confusing record, especially now that the political air was saturated with the revelations of the first report of the Commission of Inquiry into the Sponsorship Program and Advertising Activities led by Justice John Gomery.

Paul Martin's Administrative Style

Paul Martin was born in Windsor in 1938, the son of Paul Martin Sr., the Member of Parliament for Essex East. The boy was six years old when the father entered Mackenzie King's post-war cabinet as minister of national health and welfare. He would serve in cabinet for the remainder of King's time in office and throughout the entire tenure of King's successor, Louis St-Laurent. The elder Martin lost the Liberal leadership to Lester Pearson in 1958 but later became a member of Pearson's cabinet. He then lost the Liberal leadership to Pierre Trudeau in 1968 but served in Trudeau's cabinet for six years. From his earliest political awareness, the son was a devoted fan of his father's politics and inherited his ambition. The younger Martin, who always ran in Liberal political circles, played an important role in his father's 1968 run for leadership. It seemed as if it was just a matter of time before he himself would jump in.

But Martin could wait. The Trudeau cabinet held no special appeal, and Martin was making too much money directing the fortunes of Canada Steamship Lines (CSL), a subsidiary of Power Corporation, the place where he learned his management skills. He had started studies at the University of Ottawa in 1956 and transferred a year later to the University of Toronto, where he studied history and philosophy. Not surprisingly, he joined the campus Liberal club. He was admitted to the university's law school, graduating in 1965. By 1966, he was married, a homeowner, and the executive assistant to Maurice Strong, the president of Power Corporation, headquartered in downtown Montreal. Children followed, and Martin took his place in the reaches of Montreal's business elite.

As he learned the ins and outs of business at Power Corp, his trajectory was set. The company purchased CSL in 1969 and named the thirty-five-year-old Martin as president in late 1973. Martin performed well in his functions. In 1981, as a grave recession paralysed many sectors of the Canadian economy, Power Corp decided to sell CSL. Paul Desmarais offered it to Martin, who (with Laurence Pathy, the president of Fednav, Canada's largest maritime shipping company) promptly raised the capital necessary to make the purchase. Desmarais signed the loan guarantee required by the Royal Bank, and Martin became a business owner (Pathy would be mostly a silent partner and was eventually bought out). Martin proceeded to strip CSL to its core business, a move that assured the firm's survival. In the process, he learned a great deal about the strengths and weaknesses of enterprises. Within seven years, he had sufficiently reinvented CSL and made enough money to consider, at age fifty, a new career in politics.

Martin's career as president and then owner at CSL shaped his approach to management. CSL's executive team was small, and the issues it faced required an acute risk-management sensitivity. The recession of 1981–3 buffeted the most conservative financial expectations, and interest rates were high. CSL was always on the lookout for opportunities to raise cash, yet at the same time had to invest in its structures to be in a position to quickly exploit global economic upturns. Success depended on a clever selection of targets and a constant demand for the best intelligence on commercial and economic outlooks.

According to biographer John Gray, Martin revealed himself as "not a man to shrink from harsh measures. Sentimentality did not intrude."[3] It was this willingness to take chances, combined with careful attention to detail, that made him a successful businessperson.

Those qualities were brought to bear when he entered politics, running for the new seat of Lasalle-Émard, a multicultural riding at the south-western tip of the city of Montreal. Martin ran for the leadership of the Liberal Party to succeed John Turner two years later but was easily defeated by Jean Chrétien. He stayed in politics, won re-election in 1993, and was asked by Chrétien to join the cabinet as minister of finance. Martin had asked for the industry portfolio, imagining it as it was in the halcyon days of Louis St-Laurent and C.D. Howe. But Chrétien could not imagine Martin's talents being spent elsewhere, as he had the rare-among-Liberals credibility required in the business sector and was ideologically flexible. At the last minute, Martin changed his mind and accepted the finance portfolio.[4]

Though intelligent and hardworking, Martin was not much of a political animal, and the habits he had witnessed in his father did not rub off on him. He was uncomfortable in the political light, uneasy with the grip and grin, and unable to make small talk. He had an open mind, keen on the concerns of the business community but equally mindful of social needs; he was not blinkered by ideology. Martin's approach was marked by a tendency to challenge settled opinions, to return to first principles, and to decide only when he felt he had considered an issue in depth, at length, and from all angles. He had to deal with the Liberal promises of the campaign of 1993, notably the commitment to replace the unpopular Goods and Services Tax (GST), which was increasingly proving to be a significant revenue stream for a government that believed that the deficit and the debt had to be reined in urgently. He also felt uncomfortable in dealing with Quebec's nationalist aspirations, and his role in the 1995 referendum was limited to the backrooms.

Because he often felt between arguments, concern with clear communication became an obsession, causing speeches to be constantly rewritten.[5] Frustrations often mounted, and Martin's explosive temper quickly became notorious inside the department. "Friends, relatives, government officials, political advisers and cabinet colleagues will all testify that Paul Martin may not be unbearable all the time, but that he is certainly unbearable part of the time," observed Martin's biographer. Martin was "unpredictable and unsettling most of the time. In fact, by the measure of your average politician, a quite unusual man."[6]

Martin drove a demanding process, one that focussed on oral arguments to clarify issues. He would gather many people in a room, political advisers and public servants, and would provoke a wide-ranging debate in which everyone's views were treated equally, regardless of position. As David Dodge, his deputy minister, recalled, "His idea of a good time is to sit up at a table at a seven-hour meeting in front of 20 people and the 20 people fight with each other. Joining in the fight himself, sometimes provocatively." Dodge added, "If enough people worry a bone long enough, in his view, you will expose all of the options and all of the vulnerabilities and all of the strengths." The deputy minister was careful in pointing out that Martin confronted others and was willing to be confronted himself, never holding a grudge afterward. "That takes a lot of getting used to because everybody gets really challenged, quite directly."[7]

Martin put in brutal days. An early riser, he worked until as late as 10:00 p.m.[8] Seven-day weeks were his norm. He was notorious for calling public servants for clarifications, even on weekends.[9] He ignored time zone differences, once calling Finance Minister Ralph Goodale at 7:00 a.m. in Ottawa, 5:00 a.m. in Regina, Goodale's home.[10] The prime minister telephoned John Godfrey, minister of state for infrastructure and communities, on Christmas Day to chase down further details on a policy issue.[11] It seemed he could never get enough information and was reluctant to end any discussion by announcing a decision.[12]

With these strengths and foibles, Martin was always eager to collect the few political staffers who could work under those conditions: individuals who were affable and willing to compromise, but thick skinned and agile in the cut and thrust of debate. Martin's staff, much like the prime minister himself, enjoyed the collegiality of being with each other and working in a horizontal structure. To allay his fears of being trapped in an echo chamber of advisers, Martin called on key members of Earnscliffe Strategies, an Ottawa-based consulting firm, to massage his message. Three of its executives were at the core of his kitchen cabinet: Elly Alboim, David Herle, and Scott Reid.

Martin was equally demanding of the Finance bureaucracy, because he was often unhappy with the options presented to him.[13] A department insider seemed to speak for many in describing a "lengthy deliberative process" where arguments for various options were sought and heard, and then reconsidered. "It takes him longer than it takes most people to be comfortable that he's found the right answer because he's so restless that 'there must be something better out there; there must be an idea that we have not yet stumbled across.' He changes his mind all the time. He changes his mind more than anybody at this level that I've ever seen in my life."[14] Martin was always eager to get to the root of things. He was described by a political ally as "sufficiently self-confident intellectually" to take on debate, willing to challenge the doxa of the bureaucracy and even of his own party.[15] Curious and an insatiable reader, he was always open to ideas from the outside, and from the inside too: "Whether in the business world or at Finance, I had never been one to respect rigid hierarchies," Martin wrote of himself. "I didn't have much taste for the pablum that makes it up through two or three levels of bureaucratic editing to the desks of many ministers. If something was on my mind, I went to the expert, not his or her boss."[16]

It was this approach that Martin brought to the office of the minister of finance and then as prime minister. In Opposition, Martin chided the Conservative government for its relentless cutting. "When this government came to power, it had one goal: deficit reduction. It has failed miserably. Why? Because of its failure to understand that deficit reduction does not come only from cutting; it comes from growth, and growth comes from investment."[17] Now he was poised to exactly carry out what he had harshly criticized. After consultations with officials at Finance and in the Bank of Canada, the International Monetary Fund prescribed in the fall of 1994 that Canada had to cut government spending.

The tortuous decision-making process notwithstanding, Martin delivered decisive policy. John Gray described Martin as simultaneously "the most cautious and deliberative of creatures and at other times an apparently reckless gambler who revels in the adrenaline of the game."[18] The government of Canada's program spending in 1996 fell to 12.6 per cent of GDP, a level last achieved in 1949–50 during the Louis St-Laurent government.[19] Martin was known to be thorough in his identification of risk. This was shown repeatedly in his time as president of CSL as well as during his nine years as minister of finance in Jean Chrétien's government. That said, he did make many decisions, large and small.

Martin led the drive to cut Established Program Financing for provincial healthcare and post-secondary education and to eliminate the Canada Assistance Plan, which paid about 50 per cent of the costs of provincial programs such as Medicare. Instead, he created the Canada Health and Social Transfer, a block funding mechanism that reduced funding but allowed the provinces a much greater latitude to spend it as they saw fit. "From his earliest days at Finance Martin insisted constantly on the need for national consensus and he fretted about 'the feeling of disconnection Canadians have from their governments,'" according to Gray.[20]

The relationship between Martin and Chrétien was always tense, but carefully mediated by their respective staffs, through to the turn of the millennium. Yet, as the regime aged, Martin's patience eroded.[21] Regardless of whether he was dismissed or whether he resigned, Martin was no longer minister of finance on 3 June 2002. Replaced by John Manley, a staunch Chrétien loyalist, Martin threw himself into organizing support for a review of the Liberal leader's leadership. It took little time for Chrétien to realize that he could no longer command his party, and he stepped down, allowing the Liberals to organize a leadership vote for November 2003. Martin won handily, a remarkable feat for a man who in his early years at Finance, had said "no" to practically every request for new funding.

The First Cabinet, December 2003

Martin's cabinet consisted of thirty-one ministers, including the prime minister. Martin had two objectives in mind. The first was that the new ministerial team would be transitional. Martin believed that an election would necessarily bring in new talent, so no assignment was to be seen as anything more than temporary. The second objective was to give the Liberal government a new face, one that would include more women and more westerners (see image 18.1). Martin rewarded the people who had supported him in his quest for the leadership.

1 Prime Minister: Paul Martin, 65, Quebec
2 Agriculture and Agri-Food: Robert Speller, 47, Ontario*
3 Atlantic Canada Opportunities Agency Act: Joe McGuire, 56, Prince Edward Island*
4 Canadian Heritage: Hélène Chalifour Scherrer, 53, Quebec*
5 Citizenship and Immigration: Judy Sgro, 59, Ontario*
6 Leader of the Government in the House of Commons and Economic Development Agency of Canada for the Regions of Quebec: Jacques Saada, 56, Quebec*
7 Deputy Leader of the Government in the House of Commons: Mauril Bélanger, 48, Ontario*
8 Leader of the Government in the Senate: Jacob (Jack) Austin, 71, Alberta (senator)
9 Deputy Prime Minister and Solicitor General: Anne McLellan, 53, Alberta
10 Environment: David Anderson, 46, British Columbia
11 Finance: Ralph Goodale, 54, Saskatchewan
12 Fisheries and Oceans, Geoff Regan, 44, Nova Scotia*
13 Foreign Affairs: Bill Graham, 63, Ontario
14 Health and Intergovernmental Affairs: Pierre Pettigrew, 52, Quebec
15 Human Resources Development: Liza Frulla, 54, Quebec*
16 Indian Affairs and Northern Development: Andrew Mitchell, 50, Ontario*
17 Industry, Lucienne Robillard, 58, Quebec
18 International Cooperation: Aileen Carroll, 59, Ontario*
19 International Trade: Jim Peterson, 62, Ontario*
20 Justice and Attorney General: Irwin Cotler, 62, Quebec*
21 Labour: Claudette Bradshaw, 53, New Brunswick
22 National Defence: David Pratt, 58, Ontario*
23 Associate Minister of National Defence: Albina Guarnieri, 50, Ontario*
24 National Revenue: Stan Keyes, 50, Ontario*
25 Natural Resources: John Efford, 58, Newfoundland and Labrador*
26 President of the Privy Council: Denis Coderre, 40, Quebec

Image 18.1. The Martin cabinet at its swearing-in, 12 December 2003

Source: Shaun Best, Reuters, Bridgeman Images, 7823901.

27 Public Works and Government Services: Stephen Owen, 55, British Columbia*
28 Transport: Tony Valeri, 56, Ontario*
29 Treasury Board: Reg Alcock, 55, Manitoba*
30 Veterans Affairs: John McCallum, 52, Ontario
31 Western Economic Diversification: Rey Pagtakhan, 68, Manitoba

The cabinet was broadly representative of the provinces, but not of the territories. The average age was fifty-five, but the prime minister was a full ten years older, the largest gap since Tupper briefly assumed office in 1896. It was, ironically, inexperienced, as nineteen individuals (identified with an asterisk) entered the cabinet for the first time. Twelve portfolios went to Ontarians; seven were occupied by Quebeckers. Anne McLellan, who had always been supportive of Martin's ambitions, was made both deputy prime minister (an honorific, mostly) and solicitor general (a government department that would be replaced by the Department of Public Safety and Emergency Preparedness). McLellan was one of eight women in cabinet. Although three of the most important portfolios (finance, public safety and emergency preparedness, environment) went to westerners, only six westerners sat in cabinet (seven if Senator Jack Austin is included, though he held no portfolio), hardly an improvement on the Chrétien record. Ontario had a lock on anything to do with foreign relations (foreign affairs, international cooperation, international trade). Quebeckers were notably in charge of the important portfolios of health and justice.

This was not a cabinet of rivals: Twenty-two people who had been appointed to cabinet by Chrétien were relegated to the backbenches. Among the most prominent were Sheila Copps, a former deputy prime minister, whom Martin had soundly defeated for the leadership. Other leading lights, such as Allan Rock, Martin Cauchon, Sharon Carstairs, Elinor Caplan, Herb Dhaliwal, Stéphane Dion (to Martin's later regret), Wayne Easter, David Collenette, Bob Nault, Maurizio Bevilacqua (who declined an offer from Martin for a below-cabinet posting on cities), Don Boudria, Jane Stewart, were set aside for a new team. John Manley, who had succeeded Martin as the minister of finance, had enjoyed high visibility through most of the Chrétien years, and had been critical of Martin, was left empty-handed. Martin retained a few figures from the Chrétien government: Ralph Goodale, Denis Coderre, Anne McLellan, David Anderson, Bill Graham, Pierre Pettigrew, Claudette Bradshaw, John McCallum, Rey Pagtakhan, and Lucienne Robillard.

Martin split Human Resources Development Canada into two departments: a new Department of Human Resources and Skills Development and a new Department of Social Development. The Department of the Solicitor General would become the Department of Public Safety and Emergency Preparedness.

As had Chrétien, Martin appointed several ministers of state, who were not members of cabinet. They would assist cabinet ministers on specific files. The twelve ministers of state included Carolyn Bennett (public health), Gar Knutson (new and emerging markets), and Raymond Chan (multiculturalism). In a confusing twist, four ministers of state also held cabinet posts. Stan Keyes, for instance, was both minister of state (sport) and minister of national revenue. Albina Guarnieri was both minister of state (civil preparedness) and associate minister of national defence.

Martin also appointed twenty-eight parliamentary secretaries and gave them unprecedented privileges. He had them sworn into the Privy Council and allowed them to attend cabinet meetings if their issues were on the agenda. Martin's idea was to give them the profile of junior ministers as is the practice in the United Kingdom. Three of them were designated to assist Martin: Scott Brison was to focus on Canadian-American relations, Joe Fontana was to look after science and small business (two files not usually linked in policy), and John Godfrey's priority was the urban sector. Other parliamentary secretaries with very specific mandates were John McKay, parliamentary secretary to the minister of finance for public-private partnerships; Dan McTeague on Canadians abroad; Paul Bonwick on student loans; Joe Jordan on regulatory reform; David Price on the role of military reserves; and Roger Gallaway on democratic reform.

Martin could count on a handful of colleagues who remained in their roles during the entirety of the ministry. For the duration of the government, Ralph Goodale served at Finance, Anne McLellan at public safety, Geoff Regan at Fisheries and Oceans, Aileen Carroll at International Cooperation, Jim Peterson at International Trade, Irwin Cotler at Justice, John Efford at Natural Resources, Reg Alcock as president of the Treasury Board, and Joe McGuire as the minister responsible for the Atlantic Canada Opportunities Agency Act.

Martin broke new ground by creating an assortment of new cabinet committees. This was not an entirely novel practice, as Brian Mulroney had created an Operations Committee and an Expenditure Review Committee, as well as a variety of ad hoc committees and sub-committees. The difference was that Martin's new committees were formalized and staffed with a range of experts. Priorities and Planning (first created by Lester Pearson but abandoned by Chrétien) was the most important, of course, as it was chaired by the prime minister. It included three westerners (David Anderson, Ralph Goodale, Reg Alcock), five Quebeckers (Pierre Pettigrew, Jacques Saada, Irwin Cotler, Hélène Scherrer, and the prime minister himself), six Ontarians (Andy Mitchell, Bill Graham, Joe Volpe, Judy Sgro, Tony Valeri, Andy Scott), and one Atlantic Canadian (Geoff Regan).

Martin also chose to chair three other committees: Global Affairs, Canada-US affairs, and Aboriginal Affairs. Each committee triggered the formation of special teams inside the Privy Council Office (PCO) to supply briefs and ensure follow-through. Because each committee was cross-departmental, focusing on horizontal issues requiring high levels of collaboration, the consultations were heavy. Not happy with the capacity inside either Foreign Affairs or PCO to manage Canadian-American relations, Martin created a new Canada-US Secretariat within PCO, as well as an Aboriginal Secretariat and a Cities Secretariat. To help make sense of the deluge of briefs and reactions coming from all parts, Martin set on a path to hire more personal advisers. In addition to the adviser on foreign policy (which had been a fixture since the early days of Pierre Trudeau's tenure), he appointed specialists on national security, science, and Indigenous affairs.

The Operations Committee was chaired by Anne McLellan, the deputy prime minister, who also presided over the Security, Public Health, and Emergencies Committee. Rounding out the assortment were the Domestic Affairs Committee, chaired by Pierre Pettigrew; the Treasury Board; and, in another novelty, the Committee on Expenditure Review, which would be chaired by the president of the Treasury Board, Reg Alcock.

Cabinet meetings tended to drag on without focus, a radical departure from the practice of Jean Chrétien. Martin seemed reluctant to cut people off, to compel ministers to focus, to force discussions to move towards decisions. "You could be in the Cabinet meeting from nine till noon," remembered David

Emerson, "and really nothing would happen other than people would download their views."[22]

Canadian prime ministers have traditionally allowed themselves to become personally active on a handful of subjects. For Martin, the list of prime ministerial issues was long. He decided that he would focus on international affairs (particularly Canada-US relations), federal-provincial relations, the economy, Indigenous issues, health care, childcare, and urban renewal.

The involvement of the Prime Minister's Office was hotly contested during the Chrétien years and continued to be a concern. As one participant in the Martin entourage vividly painted it: "This was Mr. Fix-up, Mr. Change, Mr. Clean-Up, Mr. Go Across the Country and Shoulder the Responsibility for Fixing This Up," and his staff carried with them that urgency.[23] Martin had famously declared derisively that, under Jean Chrétien, "it's who you know in the PMO" that mattered, and the new prime minister had committed himself to addressing what he called "this democratic deficit."[24] Yet the tight-knit group around Martin, with him since his days at Finance, seemed to wield the same power as had Chrétien's PMO, if not more so. Martin's group has been described at times as a "loose association" and yet as "tight knit" as a "Spartan army" and as a "guerilla group." Some were reminded of an "Irish family" that "defended its prerogatives and didn't let anyone have too much autonomy. Including Martin."[25]

The group was nicknamed "the Board" and its composition changed to accommodate his needs. Some Board members worked in Martin's office, but others worked elsewhere, several of them for the government relations firm Earnscliffe Strategies. At the core of the group were David Herle, who had once worked for Martin at Canada Steamship Lines; his common-law partner, Terrie O'Leary, who was Martin's chief of staff at Finance; and Elly Alboim, a former CBC journalist, Carleton University professor, and a principal at Earnscliffe. None of the three worked in the Prime Minister's Office. The Board also included Michele Cadario (director of Martin's 2003 leadership campaign), Véronique de Passillé (president of the Young Liberals of Canada), Ruth Thorkelson (O'Leary's replacement as Martin's chief of staff at Finance), Brian Guest (Martin's director of communications at Finance), Dennis Dawson (a former Quebec MP who worked with Martin at CSL and later served as one of Martin's key Quebec advisers), Mike Robinson (a partner at Earnscliffe), Scott Reid (Martin's communications director at Finance and a former employee of Earnscliffe), Tim Murphy (Martin's chief of staff), Francis Fox (a cabinet minister under Pierre Trudeau), Hélène Scherrer (an MP from Quebec), and many others.[26] The group was overwhelmingly anglophone, with a few struggling to express themselves in French to the Liberal caucus.

The Board's size reflected Martin's preference to have many voices in the decision-making process. He was suspicious of the bureaucracy that answered to him, fearing that he was not informed of the whole truth. He needed other sources of advice, and the Board's personal assistance, attuned to his concerns, served him at will. This could create problems with internal communications. Staff members could deal directly with Martin, not having to go through his chief of staff. As one insider put it, "I would meet with him and we'd agree on several things and then, the next thing I knew, this was all up in the air again because one of the Board had spoken with him afterwards and expressed doubts, or talked about poll results. They were heavily conditioned by polling, and very parochial."[27]

In Finance, Martin had needed a dedicated staff to manage relations with the strongly impressive Prime Minister's Office and Privy Council Office under Jean Chrétien. Many of those staff members followed Martin into the Langevin Block, and under constant electoral and then minority status, they exercised a strong presence that occasionally offended Liberal backbenchers. One of them told journalist Paul Wells that the group became arrogant, "not nice to caucus members, not nice to a bunch of people."[28] Some ministers saw PMO staff as a praetorian guard, shielding Martin from his ministers. "It's an open secret in Ottawa that PMO dictates when and where and how ministers make announcements," wrote *Toronto Star* columnist Susan Delacourt, perhaps the best-connected journalist in Martin's Ottawa. "Few members of the Cabinet are free even to hire aides without first getting the PMO seal of approval."[29]

Within months of assuming his desk in the Langevin Block, Martin was facing the most serious challenge of his time in office. He had to manage expectations after the auditor general released a report on the sponsorship issue on 10 February 2004. "I personally believe that government whose ethics are doubted – rightly or wrongly – is a government paralyzed," Martin said.[30] By his reading, most Liberal MPs, though notably not members of the party's Quebec caucus, were in favour of commissioning a deeper study of what happened. The Martin government, with its support in the polls plummeting (fifteen percentage points in two days), felt obliged to respond.[31] Martin created an Office of the Ethics Commissioner, answerable to Parliament to replace the Office of the Ethics Counsellor, which had reported to the prime minister. More importantly, he asked John Gomery, a nearly retired Montreal judge who specialized in family law, to conduct investigations into the practices of the Chrétien government. Martin had known little of the government's sponsorship activities. "I was mad at Jean Chrétien for having left me this time bomb," he remembered. "It drove me crazy that I had to deal with this leftover mess when there were so many more important issues I had come into government to confront."[32] Martin had two cards to play to protect his reputation: First, although he was from Quebec, he was totally outside the circles where government money had been handled fraudulently. The second was that he was obsessed with doing things differently, more openly, and with nothing to hide.

Martin's determination to act soon defined his government's reputation. He wanted to do everything quickly in order to cast the Gomery Commission into the shadow of great accomplishments, but he also wished to win the approval of major stakeholders. *Moving Canada Forward: The Paul Martin Plan for Getting Things Done*, issued in June 2004, was an impressive election manifesto that was at once comprehensively ambitious and detailed in its provisions. The concern with re-election created an aversion to risk that inevitably led to delays, eroding the government's reputation with each month in power.

The Martin government's first budget promised "sound financial management" – reassuring Canadians that the spending ways of the Chrétien government were over. Total expenditures amounted to $183 billion, 14.5 per cent of Canada's GDP. The government created the Canada Public Health Agency to monitor epidemic trends after the SARS crisis of 2003, which claimed forty-four lives, and provided $2 billion in additional funding for Medicare programs administered by the provinces and territories. The government also provided $7 billion in relief for municipalities on their GST payments. Despite the new spending, this was the seventh consecutive federal budget to be balanced. It targeted $1 billion in reallocations and was committed over the next four years to saving $3 billion, which would be reallocated.[33] Martin was confident that his government represented a real change and asked that Parliament be dissolved, calling for an election for 28 June 2004.

The Liberals lost their majority, dropping thirty-three seats and more than four percentage points in the popular vote (to 36.7 per cent). The gains had been made by the Bloc Québécois, which picked up twenty-one ridings and now occupied fifty-four seats, and by the NDP, which won five more seats for a total of nineteen. The Conservatives also increased their tally by twenty-seven seats, for a total of ninety-nine seats in the House of Commons, but the party's share of the vote had dropped to below 30 per cent, eight percentage points lower than in 2000. Leading in a minority situation is always difficult, but for Paul Martin it was especially challenging given his personal agenda for change. It would test his administrative style as never before.

The July 2004 Shuffle

Martin decided on an important cabinet shuffle in July 2004. Replacements were needed for several ministers who had been defeated in the election. Andy Mitchell took over from Bob Speller in Agriculture, John McCallum from Stan Keyes at National Revenue, Bill Graham from David Pratt at National Defence, and Liza Frulla from Hélène Scherrer at Canadian Heritage. (Scherrer was named Martin's principal secretary, replacing Francis Fox.) Pierre Pettigrew replaced Bill Graham at Foreign Affairs. Andy Scott replaced Andy Mitchell at

Indian Affairs and Northern Development. Tony Valeri became government House leader, in place of Jacques Saada, who was given responsibility for democratic reform and the Francophonie. Mauril Bélanger was appointed associate minister of national defence, replacing Albina Guarnieri who moved to Veterans Affairs.

Eight newcomers joined the cabinet, including a few highly visible Martin supporters. From British Columbia, David Emerson, a corporate executive and former senior provincial bureaucrat, became minister of industry, and Ujjal Dosanjh, the province's former New Democratic premier, took on the health portfolio. Ken Dryden, a lawyer, writer, sports executive, and former hockey superstar, took on the human resources development portfolio. Scott Brison had crossed the floor from the Conservative Party in 2003 and now became minister of public works, replacing Stephen Owen, who became minister of western economic diversification. Joe Fontana and Tony Ianno, two experienced Ontario MPs, were brought in. Fontana went to Labour, replacing Claudette Bradshaw, who was demoted to minister of state, and Ianno became minister of families and caregivers. Stéphane Dion returned to cabinet, this time as minister for the environment, replacing David Anderson, who had decided not to run again. Jean Lapierre, who had abandoned the Liberal Party in 1990 to help form the Bloc Québécois, was named minister of transport and was named Martin's Quebec lieutenant. What was striking was the degree to which Martin had cancelled out most of the ministers who had been close to Jean Chrétien. The only one remaining was Dion.[34]

On balance, Martin's cabinet had been improved. Although the position of women had not been enhanced and there were no changes in the prairie west, there were valuable additions elsewhere. New blood revitalized the cabinet presence in British Columbia. Quebec's place in the cabinet was somewhat strengthened with the addition of strong (though differing) tenors such as Lapierre and Dion. The addition of Ken Dryden could also help. Nevertheless, it seemed to add to the impression that Martin was too busy experimenting to actually govern on clear principles and to demonstrate competence when the Gomery Commission was undertaking its public hearings. It was patently unfair to be tainted by the revelations of the commission, but that turn of events had the effect of feeding the narrative of Liberal arrogance. In hindsight, appointing such a high-profile investigation was clearly a mistake.

Confusion in and around the PMO

Martin's indecision was probably most evident in the area of Canadian-American relations, a policy field that few Canadian voters engaged with, but one that was a high priority for him. When Martin was forming his cabinet in late

November 2003, John Manley expressed an interest in the foreign affairs portfolio, presenting, in the prime minister's own words, "a challenge." Martin writes in his memoirs that he was "determined to play much of that role myself" and could only see conflicts if Manley became foreign minister.[35] Martin, who was comfortable in international relations as a result of both his experience in the private sector and as minister of finance, aimed to play an active role. By chairing two cabinet committees on aspects of foreign policy and boosting the capacity of PCO in dealing with this area because many important departments conducted their own foreign policy, Martin to some extent sidelined the Department of Foreign Affairs. Martin also noted that he was hardly an innovator in that regard, as "policy making in most areas has gradually been centralized in the Privy Council office – a process that began in earnest under Pierre Trudeau."[36]

The first confusion was initiated early in the ministry, when the idea of dividing the Department of Foreign Affairs and International Trade into two separate entities emerged. Martin is careful to say in his memoirs that officials in PCO had spawned the idea, and he blames the controversy on the resistance coming from senior public servants who produced a "spectacular bureaucratic turf war" over the issue. The fact that the public servants all reported to him seems too embarrassing to point to, perhaps, but it is undeniable that it was the prime minister who defended an idea that was ultimately rejected by Parliament.

In the same area, Martin wanted an international policy statement and asked the various departments to conceive of one. Clearly, neither the Privy Council Office nor the Liberal Party were of much help in this critical policy area. In Martin's words, the challenge "quickly bogged down in internal bureaucratic rivalries. The Department of Foreign Affairs was not able to seize the lead and integrate the work to the degree I would have reached." Ministers seemingly were little involved, nor were they of a capacity to bring insight to the matter. The PMO was unable to provide a steadying influence. Instead, a young academic outsider based at Oxford University was sought to integrate the work.[37]

Finally, on Ballistic Missile Defence, the government also equivocated.[38] The issue was that the Bush administration was contemplating a new generation of continental defence systems. As a NORAD partner, Canada was naturally invited to participate. At first, Martin signalled that Canada would join the project, but then he hesitated. He was concerned its costs would spiral out of control and that if Canada were to have a stake in it, it would have to pay some of the cost. "I wanted a commitment stating plainly that Canada would not be asked to fund the system now or at any later point."[39] Secondly, Martin wanted "to make sure that the system was designed with as much concern for Canadian lives and territory as American." As he put it, "I wanted Canada to be involved in the design of the BMD system and its technical parameters to ensure our interests, and I made it clear if I was not prepared to proceed without this undertaking."[40]

And yet the prime minister was frustrated. "I could not get the answer to my questions" and people "were stalling" on his requests for information.[41] The Americans, meanwhile, were pushing for a decision. President Bush raised the subject privately during a state visit in Ottawa in 2004, but Martin pleaded for more time. At a public speech the next day, Bush publicly urged Canada to join the BMD arrangement. In December 2004, Martin again raised the issues with his ministers and with officials. "I was still not getting clear answers," he remembered.[42] What finally motivated Martin to act was the anti-American sentiments being expressed in the House of Commons and the "increasingly shrill" rhetoric "across the land."[43] Martin decided not to pursue the deal and concluded his discussion of the episode by saying that "We could, and should, have done a better job of managing public expectations and communicating our decision-making process," but the confused process of policy making clearly was far more evident.[44] Martin's final decision revealed a government that had trouble articulating priorities and positions. At the same time, Martin lectured the US on greenhouse gas emissions and on softwood lumber negotiations. David Wilkins, the US ambassador to Canada, did not take lightly to the prime minister's remarks, and delivered a tart speech on 13 December 2005, cautioning the government against constantly criticizing the US.[45]

The issue of interdepartmental disagreement and the utter failure of the Department of Foreign Affairs and International Trade (DFAIT) in articulating a policy that would satisfy Martin emerged again when it came to deciding the scale of Canada's military effort in Afghanistan. Martin's memoirs again express the view that his decision was clear. While acknowledging the policy failure shared by DFAIT and the Department of National Defence, he writes that when the issue landed on his desk in the late winter of 2005, "the decision was a straightforward one and was made within a few weeks."[46] Martin insists he agreed only to a one-year commitment (with perhaps a supplemental year as optional) but acknowledges again that "I don't think anyone, including me, expected the Taliban resurgence that Canadian troops encountered when they moved to Kandahar."[47] The reality was that Canada was to stay in Kandahar, perhaps the most unwelcoming and dangerous part of the troubled country. Fifty soldiers died within months of the deployment, and Canada would remain in that province until 2009.[48]

The Martin government did register several successes, mostly on the domestic front. In just over two years, the government developed a national childcare program, reached a ten-year agreement with the provinces to increase funding for health care, and negotiated the Kelowna Accord to improve education, employment, and living conditions for Indigenous peoples. Yet the government's defeat in 2006 meant that most of its accomplishments were short-lived, fated to be undone by Martin's successor, Stephen Harper.

***

The Martin government had barely celebrated its first anniversary when the prime minister gave a televised speech on 21 April 2005. In it, he assumed part of the blame for the misspent moneys on government sponsorship in Quebec, and apologized for being insufficiently vigilant when he was minister of finance. He also promised to call an election one month after the Gomery Commission submitted its report in the fall of 2005. From that point onwards, the Opposition knew exactly what to prepare for, and when.

The first report was issued in October 2005 and uncovered little that was new, but more Canadians grew tired of hearing about the Sponsorship Scandal. The House of Commons gave the government a vote of no confidence, and an election was scheduled for 23 January 2006. The campaign was embittered as the RCMP announced that it was launching an investigation of whether the government had leaked news of a tax change that would benefit income trusts, feeding the suspicion that the Liberals had grown arrogant in power. In Toronto, the shooting death of a teenage shopper on Yonge Street on Boxing Day made crime a key election issue and suggested to many voters that the Liberals, in office since 1993, were spent.

In the end, the Liberal Party lost thirty seats, winning barely 30 per cent of the vote. The Conservative Party under Stephen Harper won twenty-six more seats and increased its take of votes by 6.6 percentage points to 36 per cent. With 124 seats, the Conservatives would form a minority government. The NDP under Jack Layton, in his second election as leader, showed that it had also learned lessons from the 2004 campaign. The party gained two percentage points of the vote (17.5 per cent), which translated into eleven more seats in the House of Commons. The Bloc Québécois surged following the Martin speech in April 2005 but lost some of its altitude as the campaign got underway. The Bloc lost two seats and two percentage points of the popular vote (down to 10.5 per cent).

Does the Paul Martin interlude constitute a case of failed statecraft? It certainly shows the salient importance of a few key ingredients in the recipe for successful statecraft. Martin's cabinet management was undoubtedly partly responsible for the defeat. Eager to distance the party from the Chrétien legacy, he appointed a vast army of inexperienced people to cabinet. Eager to make progress and to show that he could make a minority government succeed, he involved his staff in a multitude of files, often achieving success. But the narrative was not compelling, and neither was Martin's personal style. In 2004 the Liberals collected 36.7 per cent of the vote, a four-percentage-point drop, as two opposition parties, the Bloc Québécois and the NDP, increased their vote and seats. In 2006, the voters rejected the Martin government, giving it only 30 per cent of the vote, another drop of 6.5 percentage points. The Conservatives picked up the votes and seats lost by the Liberals and formed a minority government.

Martin's style certainly played a role, but there were other factors. For one thing, the Conservatives had learned important lessons from the 2004 experience. As the 2005–6 campaign progressed, Harper was more confident and became more acceptable in Canada's suburbs. For the more conservative-minded electors, Martin's policies were seen as rationales to spend money unwisely and to be involved in more areas of public policy where Ottawa was viewed with suspicion.

In hindsight, Martin assumed power as if a majority was assured. To use a baseball metaphor, he adopted a difficult hit-for-the-fences strategy that promised a reinvention of government, when perhaps an easier sequence of targeted singles and doubles might have led to a better outcome. As ministers swung unsuccessfully at hard pitches, wondering why their swats were failing, the reputation quickly spread that the cabinet was thinking itself into an analysis paralysis. "I have no regrets about my desire to shake things up as prime minister. That's why I wanted the job," Martin later wrote, but he was unable to translate his energy and vision to the Canadian public.[49] His best intentions were defeated by a grave underestimation of how a large number of massive changes complemented by massive consultations, would tie up government. Martin, decisive as he could be in finance and affable as he usually was with his colleagues, was reduced to an appearance of dithering, showing how errors in managing the state led to defeat. Bold programs and policies did do not necessarily lead to success, according to the rules of statecraft. What mattered was delivering on core promises, appearing to work honestly and keeping an ear to the ground to sense the changes in the electorate's mood, matters more. Paul Martin learned quickly the hard and unforgiving consequences of flawed statecraft.

NOTES

1 Paul Martin, *Hell or High Water: My Life in and out of Politics* (Toronto: McClelland & Stewart, 2008), 259.

2 Evert Lindquist, Ian Clark, and James Mitchell, "Reshaping Ottawa's Centre of Government: Martin's Reforms in Historical Perspective," in *How Ottawa Spends, 2004–2005: Mandate Change in the Paul Martin Era*, ed. G. Bruce Doern (Montreal: McGill-Queens University Press, 2004), 338.

3 John Gray, *Paul Martin: The Power of Ambition* (Toronto: Key Porter Books, 2003), 56.

4 Martin, *Hell or High Water*, 111; Eddie Goldenberg, *The Way It Works: Inside Ottawa* (Toronto: McClelland & Stewart, 2006), 66–7; and Jean Chrétien, *My Years as Prime Minister* (Toronto: Alfred A. Knopf, 2007), 28.

5 Gray, *Paul Martin*, 95.

6 Gray, *Paul Martin*, 129. On Martin's temper, see Gray, *Paul Martin*, 137–9; David Olive, "Paul Martin Takes the Watch," *Canadian Business*, April 1984, 33; and Martin, *Hell or High Water*, 21, 120.

7 Gray, *Paul Martin*, 121.

8 Donna Jacobs, "No Morning Blues for Martin, Just Lots of Coffee," *Ottawa Citizen*, 2 April 2005, A9.

9 Gray, *Paul Martin*, 120, 127.

10 Jacobs, "No Morning Blues," A9.

11 Douglas Gibson, *Stories about Storytellers: Publishing Alice Munro, Robertson Davies, Alistair MacLeod, Pierre Trudeau, and Others* (Toronto: ECW Press, 2010), 313–14.

12 Paul Wells, *Right Side Up: The Fall of Paul Martin and the Rise of Stephen Harper's New Conservatism* (Toronto: McClelland & Stewart, 2006), 283.

13 Gray, *Paul Martin*, 118.

14 Gray, *Paul Martin*, 120.

15 Gray, *Paul Martin*, 132.

16 Martin, *Hell or High Water*, 260.

17 *House of Commons Debates*, 34th parl., 2nd sess., vol. 13, 1 March 1991, 17860.

18 Gray, *Paul Martin*, 55.

19 David A. Good, *The Politics of Public Money*, 2nd ed. (Toronto: University of Toronto Press, 2014), 25.

20 Gray, *Paul Martin*, 125.

21 That erosion is described in detail in Susan Delacourt, *Juggernaut: Paul Martin's Campaign for Chrétien's Crown* (Toronto: McClelland & Stewart, 2003).

22 David Emerson, quoted in Lawrence Martin, *Harperland: The Politics of Control* (Toronto: Viking, 2010), 54.

23 Wells, *Right Side Up*, 102.

24 Paul Martin, "Proposals for Reform of the House of Commons," speech to Osgoode Hall, York University, 21 October 2002, cited in Good, *Politics of Public Money*, 93.

25 Wells, *Right Side Up*, 103.

26 Martin, *Hell or High Water*, 241–2.

27 Cited in Brooke Jeffrey, *Divided Loyalties: The Liberal Party of Canada, 1984–2008* (Toronto: University of Toronto Press, 2010), 533. Jeffrey describes at length the growing liability of Martin's personal advisers (pp. 531–6).

28 Wells, *Right Side Up*, 105. See also Jeffrey, *Divided Loyalties*, 536–40.

29 Susan Delacourt, "Shaking Off the Chrétien Effect," *Toronto Star*, 11 December 2004, H1, H3.

30 Martin, *Hell or High Water*, 279.

31 Mark Kennedy, "The Man: He Must Make His Ideas Match His Mantra," *Ottawa Citizen*, 24 May 2004, A3.

32 Martin, *Hell or High Water*, 281.

33 Good, *Politics of Public Money*, 18.
34 See Jeffrey, *Divided Loyalties*, 527–8.
35 Martin, *Hell or High Water*, 251.
36 Martin, *Hell or High Water*, 354
37 See Stephen Azzi, "Thwarted Ambitions: The Foreign Policy of Paul Martin," in *Statesmen, Strategists and Diplomats: Canada's Prime Ministers and the Making of Foreign Policy*, ed. Patrice Dutil (Vancouver: University of British Columbia Press, 2023), 304–30.
38 See Stephen Azzi and Norman Hillmer, "Intolerant Allies: Canada and the George W. Bush Administration, 2001–2005," *Diplomacy and Statecraft* 27, no. 4 (2016): 738–41.
39 Martin, *Hell or High Water*, 386.
40 Martin, *Hell or High Water*, 387. The policy confusion is well described in James G. Fergusson, *Canada and Ballistic Missile Defence, 1954–2009: Déjà vu All Over Again* (Vancouver: University of British Columbia Press, 2010), 243–55. See also Janice Gross Stein and Eugene Lang, *The Unexpected War: Canada in Kandahar* (Toronto: Viking, 2007), 152–77.
41 Martin, *Hell or High Water*, 387.
42 Martin, *Hell or High Water*, 388.
43 Martin, *Hell or High Water*, 388.
44 Martin, *Hell or High Water*, 389.
45 Daniel Leblanc and Gloria Galloway, "US Tired of Canadian Attacks on Environment, Trade Policies," *Globe and Mail*, 14 December 2005, A1.
46 Martin, *Hell or High Water*, 394
47 Martin, *Hell or High Water*, 395.
48 Janice Gross Stein and Eugene Lang make the point that many in the Department of National Defence "needed to do something significant for Washington – something the Pentagon really wanted – to compensate for the refusal to participate in Ballistic Missile Defence" (*Unexpected War*, 181).
49 Martin, *Hell or High Water*, 260.

19 Stephen Harper: Alone at the Top

R. PAUL WILSON*

Before leaving office on 4 November 2015, Prime Minister Stephen Harper held a final meeting with Wayne Wouters, the Clerk of the Privy Council. According to Howard Anglin, Deputy Chief of Staff in the Prime Minister's Office (PMO), "The Clerk asked Harper what he would miss most about the job. 'Being prime minister,' he replied and, gesturing at the stacks of paperwork on his desk, added, 'Doing this.'"[1]

This was how PMO often chose to depict Harper to Canadians. From January 2013 until the government's defeat, the prime minister's website highlighted a photo of Prime Minister Harper alone at his desk, ploughing through piles of memoranda and briefing notes, doing the business of government (see image 19.1).[2]

It was an image of solitary reflection, hard work, and dedication to serving the country. These are desirable traits in a national leader, but Harper's style often meant prioritizing efficiency over collegiality and reaching decisions over exchanging ideas. A former senior staffer in PMO summarized Harper's approach to politics and government as "I am the CEO." It was a business, not a family.[3] This approach had implications for the prime minister's approach to structuring cabinet and working with other ministers.

Harper's governing style closely reflected his personal style: in particular, his tendency towards aloofness and preference for written briefings, his high level of preparation and high expectations for others, and his no-nonsense efficiency. This chapter will examine Prime Minister Harper's statecraft in structuring his cabinet and relating to ministers, and will discuss four important process or structural choices that flowed from or reinforced his style: the use of a Priorities and Planning Committee (P&P) for policy deliberation instead of full cabinet; the innovation of daily Question Period (QP) practice meetings with the full cabinet; the briefing notes process within PMO; and the prohibition on unfunded memoranda to cabinet (MCs). These machinery of government choices reflected his personality and fit his preferred working style. Yet as a consequence (unintended but not unwelcome) they all ended up reinforcing his position as the dominant decision-maker.

Image 19.1. Stephen Harper, 2012

Source: Jason Ransom, Library and Archives Canada, R16093-43504-8-E.

Gauging a prime minister's management methods without access to the full documentary record of government decisions requires caution. Given the strictures of cabinet confidentiality, interactions between ministers in cabinet and in cabinet committees happen behind closed doors. Journalists may establish an initial narrative based on the day's headlines, but these impressions are bound to change significantly when original documentary sources become available. The Harper PMO prided itself on its "culture of documentation,"[4] and Library and Archives Canada has described the digital records for Prime Minister Harper and his office as "unprecedented."[5] When these are released, researchers will have a stronger foundation for drawing conclusions. Until then, students of government should hold their views loosely.

A public narrative of the Harper era has been established by journalists[6] and former political staffers in the PMO.[7] Stephen Harper, born in 1959 and raised in Toronto, moved to Edmonton and then to Calgary to study, eventually obtaining a master's degree in economics. Volunteering for the Progressive Conservative Party in the 1985 election, he worked for a year as parliamentary assistant for MP Jim Hawkes, but, disillusioned with the Mulroney government and with politics in Ottawa, he returned to Calgary. After being introduced to Preston Manning, he became chief policy officer for the fledgling Reform Party and served as executive assistant to the first Reform MP, Deborah Grey. Harper was himself elected to the House of Commons in 1993 but retired in 1997 before serving a complete term. He was elected leader of the Canadian Alliance in March 2002 and, after negotiating a merger between the Alliance and the Progressive Conservative party under Peter MacKay, Harper won the leadership of the new Conservative Party of Canada (CPC) in March 2004. In June 2004 in his first election as leader, the CPC lost to Paul Martin's Liberals, although they reduced the government to a parliamentary minority. Two years later in the January 2006 general election, the CPC obtained a plurality of seats, and consequently on 6 February 2006 Stephen Harper was sworn in as Canada's twenty-second prime minister. He remained in office for almost ten years, becoming the longest serving Conservative prime minister since Sir John A. Macdonald.

Harper's Cabinet Appointments

The Conservative Party elected 124 MPs in the 2006 election, and out of these Prime Minister Harper opted to appoint a cabinet of 27 ministers (including himself),[8] a ministry about thirty percent smaller than Paul Martin's had been (32 cabinet ministers and 6 ministers of state)[9] at its conclusion. The first Harper ministry was composed as follows (with each minister's age at time of appointment):

1 Stephen Harper, Prime Minister, 46, Alberta
2 Rob Nicholson, Leader of the Government in the House of Commons / Democratic Reform, 53, Ontario
3 David Emerson, International Trade / Pacific Gateway and the Vancouver-Whistler Olympics, 60, British Columbia
4 Jean-Pierre Blackburn, Labour / Economic Development Agency of Canada for the Regions of Quebec, 57, Quebec
5 Greg Thompson, Veterans Affairs, 58, New Brunswick
6 Marjory LeBreton, Leader of the Government in the Senate, 65, Ontario (senator),
7 Monte Solberg, Citizenship and Immigration, 47, Alberta
8 Chuck Strahl, Agriculture and Agri-Food / Canadian Wheat Board, 48, British Columbia
9 Gary Lunn, Natural Resources, 48, British Columbia
10 Peter MacKay, Foreign Affairs / Atlantic Canada Opportunities Agency, 40, Nova Scotia
11 Loyola Hearn, Fisheries and Oceans, 62, Newfoundland
12 Stockwell Day, Public Safety, 55, British Columbia
13 Carol Skelton, National Revenue / Western Economic Diversification, 60, Saskatchewan
14 Vic Toews, Justice, 53, Manitoba
15 Rona Ambrose, Environment, 36, Alberta
16 Michael Chong, President of the Queen's Privy Council / Intergovernmental Affairs / Sport, 34, Ontario
17 Diane Finley, Human Resources and Social Development, 48, Ontario
18 Gordon O'Connor, National Defence, 66, Ontario
19 Beverley Oda, Canadian Heritage and Status of Women, 61, Ontario
20 Jim Prentice, Indian Affairs and Northern Development, 49, Alberta

21 John Baird, President of the Treasury Board, 36, Ontario
22 Maxime Bernier, Industry, 43, Quebec
23 Lawrence Cannon, Transport, Infrastructure and Communities, 58, Quebec
24 Tony Clement, Health / Federal Economic Development Initiative for
     Northern Ontario, 45, Ontario
25 Jim Flaherty, Finance, 56, Ontario
26 Josée Verner, International Cooperation / La Francophonie and Official
     Languages, 46, Quebec
27 Michael Fortier, Public Works and Government Services, 44, Quebec
     (senator)

The cabinet as first appointed in 2006 was relatively young. On average ministers were 50.1 years of age, with the prime minister four years younger. Altogether, nine ministers were appointed to cabinet from Ontario and four from British Columbia, which was proportionate with those provinces' representation within the Conservative Party caucus. Alberta, with 28 Conservative MPs, received only three ministers in addition to the prime minister; but Quebec, having elected 11 Conservative MPs, received five cabinet posts (including the unelected Senator Michael Fortier), more than double its share of Conservative MPs. Manitoba, Saskatchewan, Nova Scotia, New Brunswick and Newfoundland and Labrador received one cabinet position each, while Prince Edward Island, electing no Conservative MPs, received none.

According to Ian Brodie, Harper found this number "too restrictive,[10] and so in January 2007, he expanded the ministry (but not the cabinet) by adding five ministers of state (styled secretaries of state).[11] After winning 166 seats and a majority government in the May 2011 election, Harper increased the size of the ministry to 28 cabinet ministers and 11 ministers of state. The ministry reached its zenith in January 2015 with 27 ministers and 13 ministers of state.

Brodie provides a detailed account of Harper's initial cabinet appointments, arguing that, given the constraints of political expectations, he had "little discretion" over many of his original cabinet choices in 2006.[12] Former party leaders such as Peter MacKay and Stockwell Day; experienced former provincial ministers such as Ontario Progressive Conservatives Jim Flaherty, John Baird, and Tony Clement, former Quebec Liberal Lawrence Cannon, and former Manitoba Attorney General Vic Toews: these are examples of MPs who, in Brodie's view, were pretty much guaranteed a position in cabinet. Harper also strove to respect expectations for regional representation. For example, when Gail Shea was elected in 2008 as the CPC's first and only MP from the tiny province of Prince Edward Island, Harper immediately appointed her to cabinet as minister of fisheries.

Harper's boldest stroke in 2006 was appointing two ministers who had not won seats in the House of Commons as Conservatives in order to give cabinet representation to Montreal and Vancouver, metropolitan centres which, like Prince Edward Island, had elected no CPC MPs. If Paris was worth a mass to King Henri IV, then, Harper must have thought, Montreal was worth a Senate seat, and he appointed Michael Fortier, a banking executive from Montreal, to the upper house and then to cabinet. At the same time, he appointed David Emerson, Liberal minister of industry under Paul Martin, to his cabinet as minister of international trade, inducing him to cross the floor and join the Conservative caucus. These appointments caused significant controversy and represented political risk for Harper, especially with old Reformers who opposed the Senate in principle and considered crossing the floor a breach of an MP's duty to their constituents. Nevertheless, for political but also nation-building reasons, Harper was committed to seeing Montreal and Vancouver represented in cabinet regardless of the controversy.

Overall, a total of 52 individuals (in addition to the prime minister himself) held cabinet positions at some point during the Harper ministry. The prime minister also appointed 29 individuals as ministers of state, ten of whom were later promoted to cabinet.[13] Brodie argues that "Harper was remarkable for keeping ministers rather than cycling through them."[14] Five ministers held office for the entire period, from 6 February 2006 to 3 November 2015: Rona Ambrose, Tony Clement, Diane Finley, Peter MacKay, and Rob Nicholson. On average, each minister spent five years in cabinet, and an average of about two and a half years in each portfolio. Of those ministers who left before the Trudeau government was sworn in, only four resigned under obvious political pressure,[15] although press and opposition will always speculate about the genuine motive for departure.

Looking at the ministry from a departmental perspective, every portfolio changed hands at least three times except for Agriculture and Agri-Food and Finance (two ministers each). Further, Marjory LeBreton was the only minister to serve as leader of the government in the Senate. The most tumultuous area was the broad International portfolio: six people served as minister of foreign affairs, four as minister for international cooperation, and five for international trade.

Brodie argues that ensuring loyalty in cabinet was not a problem for Harper since he had support among all the prominent factions within the party, especially after the defection of Belinda Stronach, an outspoken advocate of progressive social policies who had opposed Harper for the CPC leadership, to the Liberals in May 2005.[16] Notably, Harper managed to overcome the old Reform–PC division that had split the conservative movement since the late 1980s. Harper, as a former Reform MP himself, naturally appointed former Reformers whom he knew and respected, such as Chuck Strahl, Jay Hill, Gerry Ritz, Monte Solberg, and Jason Kenney. However, he also leaned heavily on former PCs. He appointed Senator Marjory LeBreton, an established fixture in the PC party going back to Diefenbaker, as government leader in the Senate and to the Priorities and Planning Committee (including as vice-chair of P&P beginning in June 2011). And he appointed Jim Prentice, who had run for the PC leadership in 2003, as chair of the cabinet Operations (Ops) Committee. Since during the Mulroney government the chair of Ops (Don Mazankowski) had also served as deputy prime minister, this gave Prentice very high standing in cabinet. Rob Nicholson, whom Harper initially appointed as government House Leader, was a former Mulroney era PC MP who had served briefly in Kim Campbell's cabinet. Significant credit for the lack of Reform versus PC factionalism goes to former PC leader Peter MacKay, whom Harper appointed to senior portfolios at Foreign Affairs, National Defence and Justice, and who in turn gave strong support to the prime minister.

Harper's Cabinet Structure

Harper adopted the same cabinet structure that Brian Mulroney had used: a Priorities and Planning committee chaired by the Prime Minister; an Operations committee chaired by a senior minister who held the prime minister's confidence; Treasury Board; and three to five policy committees.[17] This was intentionally more streamlined than Paul Martin's elaborate cabinet structure since, in a minority parliament, the Conservatives needed strict discipline and focus and "couldn't afford the risk of failure."[18] Compared to Martin, Harper had a smaller number of policy committees with fewer ministers, and larger coordinating committees. At certain times, up to 70 per cent of Harper ministers sat on either P&P or Ops, with some ministers sitting on both committees.[19]

Full cabinet, supported by PCO, met regularly, usually every third week. The meeting gave the prime minister an opportunity to address all ministers and both update them and hear from them on matters of broad strategic concern for the government. Full Cabinet also considered most Governor-in-Council appointments. Ministers recommending appointments were expected to have done their homework and to have consulted with relevant regional ministers. If another minister raised an objection, the PM often deferred a decision so that ministers could resolve their concerns. Yet, while full Cabinet may be useful to "create a sense of exclusivity and fellowship" among ministers,[20] due to its size it is inefficient and unsatisfactory as a deliberative, decision-making body. Prime Minister Harper chose efficiency over collegiality, using P&P instead of full cabinet for most policy discussions.

The prime minister himself chaired Priorities and Planning, which met every Tuesday morning when the House was sitting. Membership varied over time, from 11 ministers (including the prime minister) in March 2006 to 16 ministers in January 2015. Typically, this included the chairs of other committees, key regional ministers, and other senior ministers in the government whose judgement the prime minister respected. Sometimes P&P decided strategic direction on important issues, which ministers would then incorporate into a memorandum to cabinet (MC) for consideration by a cabinet policy committee. Sometimes P&P might consider an MC in the first instance, for example, if the matter were urgent or "so significant, so core to the government agenda" that the prime minister wanted the discussion to take place with ministers at Priorities and Planning without beginning with a policy committee.[21] Sean Speer, a senior economic adviser in Harper's PMO, recalls that after 2011 two first-run MCs were usually included on each week's P&P agenda. This, he said, created a challenge for identifying two suitably substantive submissions each week, and "the work of the policy committees often became even less substantive because we often had to cannibalize the best content for P&P."[22]

A key responsibility for P&P was ratifying MCs that had been previously discussed and endorsed either at one of the cabinet policy committees or at the Operations committee. On a heavy day the list of these annex items might consist of 30 or more MCs gathered into multiple binders. Under previous governments, annex items would be routinely approved in short order and almost never challenged.[23] This was not the case under Harper, who invited ministers to comment on each item and often made comments himself. If he and other ministers were satisfied, he would declare the item approved. If not, he would send it back to the committee or else hold the item *"ad referendum"* for his own consideration and approval.

As chair, the prime minister imposed several iron rules. First, ministers were limited to 20-minute presentations. "He didn't suffer fools. He didn't allow long soliloquies," said Chuck Strahl, or else items were in danger of being yanked from the agenda.[24] Second, presentation decks were limited to 12 slides, with no exceptions. And third, no "for information updates" were permitted; rather, all presentations had to lead to a decision. This helped to keep the agenda focused but also meant that sometimes ministers were not given early warning on emerging issues. In the view of a senior deputy minister, the "information asymmetry" between the prime minister and other ministers was a problem because "if they don't attend the right cabinet committee meeting or it [a given policy topic] doesn't come up in caucus, they're relying on CBC news or something. And that's not a great place to be on some issues."[25] Nevertheless, Prime Minister Harper's chief objective was making efficient decisions and not necessarily sharing information or building consensus.

Harper's Personal Style and Relations with Ministers

By nature, Stephen Harper was quiet, pensive, and somewhat aloof. In contrast to Prime Minister Brian Mulroney who liked to broker deals through personal meetings,[26] Harper "was very interior" and "worked things through by reading and thinking" rather than conversations.[27] Rachel Curran, director of policy in PMO from 2011 to 2015, explained that he was not a "touchy-feely guy, didn't like the one-on-one discussions in a more intimate setting." Because of this he "very much gravitated towards a more formal structured setting and discussion."[28] A senior PCO official observed that "he wasn't one for storytelling and jokes and small talk, you know, the way Martin was ... I remember a couple of exceptions where he ended up sort of teasing ministers and telling a funny story and so on. And that was so out of the norm that people noticed it."[29]

As prime minister, Stephen Harper met with ministers frequently: as a group in full cabinet or P&P; in one-on-one or bilateral meetings on the margins of cabinet or caucus; in scheduled meetings in his office; on the telephone; sometimes on the plane while travelling. Yet his preferred way of receiving and digesting information was in writing. A senior official observed that Harper was "very much a written person."[30] Chuck Strahl said the same thing: Harper "likes it in writing and he's more thoughtful in writing." If Strahl needed something addressed, he would write a letter rather than seek a meeting since "that was the better way to get him to put some thoughtful effort into it."[31] As will be explained below, this had implications for how PMO and PCO provided information and for how the prime minister interacted with ministers.

Harper did not go out of his way to talk with ministers one on one, tending to be "standoffish with his cabinet, which didn't promote collegiality, but it did promote professionalism."[32] Generally, he expected to interact with ministers in formal settings, usually full cabinet or Priorities and Planning. But some ministers report that he was responsive when they asked for time with him, though it was prudent not to ask too often or for small matters. Monte Solberg, who served in cabinet from 2006 to 2008, observed that "if I ever needed to go see him about an issue, the door was open. He never said no. It was just a question of when."[33] Another minister said "I rarely saw the PM. I knew what I had to do. It wasn't necessary." But he added, "if I ever did need to speak with him, in person or on the phone, he was available within hours."[34] Some ministers were not so restrained. Strahl said some ministers sought regular meetings with the prime minister. "I never understood that. Given his nature, why would you want to poke the bear?" But Strahl thought most ministers were more circumspect. "He always had an open door. He always said that, and I think any minister who wanted to come to see him could ... But they were a little nervous about getting in front of the prime minister and what was going to come out of that. So, I don't think ministers took up his offer necessarily on a regular basis."[35]

The combination of Harper's native intelligence, his voracious appetite for written briefing notes, and his "spooky memory"[36] meant that he was usually the best prepared minister in any meeting. Tony Clement, who served in cabinet for the entirety of the Harper government, was impressed that the prime minister "read everything, *every thing.* And he was incredibly detail oriented." So ministers "had to know their MC backwards and frontwards just to survive the process, because if you didn't know something, I guarantee you he knew it."[37] In this he set a high standard. "If you were a minister in the Harper government you would know that there's just no way you could half-ass your way through any interaction with the prime minister," recalled Andrew MacDougall, a former director of communication in PMO.[38] Another former PMO staffer observed that Harper "did his homework and most people didn't. Most ministers read the précis and that was it and hoped to get away with it because they didn't want to engage."[39] This was a risky strategy. "Woe betide them if they were not prepared," remarked Darrel Reid, a former PMO deputy chief of staff. "He never abused them. But the silence or the way that he played with ministers and their lack of knowledge was something fearsome to behold.... He would raise questions that he knew they didn't have the answers for."[40]

While Harper valued the advice of ministers, he listened to some more than others. Sometimes it was because he was familiar with them from opposition days and respected them, or because they had previous government experience, including at the provincial level, that he lacked (such as Flaherty, Clement, Baird, and Nicholson).[41] Clement perceived that the prime minister counted on him, and some other ministers, to provide a "challenge function" in order "to keep the whole system accountable." But he recognized that Harper's tolerance for "contrarians" had limits, and so ministers needed to ensure they were raising objections on issues that were central to the government's agenda.[42] Mostly, "Harper evaluated people on their judgement," said Chuck Strahl. "Do you tilt at windmills or get whatever needs to be done, done?"[43] The nature of the portfolio mattered too. "If he had ministers that he trusted in portfolios that he wasn't worried about, he gave them lots of latitude," said Reid. But with departments that he didn't trust, then "no matter how much he trusted the integrity of the ministers, he watched that much more closely."[44]

Like most first ministers, Harper could have his way in cabinet when he wanted it, and often he did. But sometimes he deferred to ministers. Speer recalled an occasion where he "let his instinct to be more collaborative" persuade him to agree with ministers on a policy direction that he found unconvincing.[45] And sometimes reasoned arguments persuaded him to change his view. "I think Harper actually respected a good scrap up to a point, if he felt the person on the other side knew their brief," said Scott Streiner, a former PCO assistant secretary.[46] One minister remembered an occasion when he had spoken out in cabinet to suggest that another minister had been "bamboozled" on a file by the public service. The PM disagreed "and got that huffy look about him," but a week later he came back and agreed with the concern. "He was amenable to change," if it was well argued and thought out.[47]

The 2008 coalition crisis is perhaps the best-known example of ministers changing Harper's mind. When the opposition leaders announced that they had signed a coalition agreement and intended to bring down the Conservative government, Harper was reportedly despondent and resigned to giving up power, but, spurred on by the combative consensus in caucus and in an Operations committee meeting, Ministers Jim Prentice, Jay Hill and James Moore talked Harper into fighting.[48] As Reid summed it up, the ministers "read him the riot act and just said, put some starch in your shorts. And by the end of that meeting, he was full on."[49]

The most consistently influential minister was Finance Minister Jim Flaherty. Of course, the relationship between finance minister and prime minister is always of paramount importance to any government and, working closely together, the incumbents develop a unique relationship.[50] Solberg recalled that Flaherty "was one guy who argued vociferously with the prime minister and would completely disagree with him, and they were at loggerheads sometimes."[51] Harper did not take pushback from many people,[52] but he did from his finance minister, as he himself described in a eulogy at Flaherty's funeral in 2014:

> As we talked through budget planning meetings, our divergences always narrowed and usually vanished. When they didn't, occasionally I imposed a final decision. Occasionally, I decided he was probably right. And occasionally, I decided he was wrong but let him have his way, just because I got so tired of arguing with him.[53]

Rachel Curran confirmed that "very frequently" the prime minister would defer to Flaherty, even when the PMO's policy staff had expressed "concerns on something or we didn't think it was necessary or maybe it looked like a bit of a pet project of the finance minister's."[54] According to Brodie, Harper insisted on following through with the second phase of the GST cut (from 6 to 5 per cent) as promised in the 2006 election despite the Finance Minister's concerns. But Flaherty won his share of policy debates, including what Brodie calls "the big one" on income trusts in October 2006. He thought this demonstrated an important lesson:

> It is possible to walk in and tell the prime minister, 'Here's this high-profile election promise you've made, which you're kind of personally attached to because it was also part of your leadership campaign, and you know all the stakeholders on this side. But we have to screw them over and break this promise. And here's why.' And Jim managed.[55]

Harper was willing to listen to reasoned arguments, but they were more likely to succeed when he had confidence in the judgement of the minister making them.

Structural and Process Choices with Cabinet Implications

Choosing ministers and structuring cabinet are some of the most important decisions a prime minister can make. However, prime ministers control many less obvious mechanisms for managing government processes and relationships. Three important but little-known structures during the Harper era – the daily Question Period practice, the daily notes process within PMO and the prohibition on unfunded memoranda to cabinet – had significant though often hidden implications for the prime minister's relationship with ministers.

Daily Question Period Practice

PMO's preoccupation with message control and issues management led to one of the defining innovations of the Harper ministry: the daily Question Period Practice. In effect, the full cabinet gathered each day, not in a formal way supported by the public service but as partisan warriors preparing for the fight.

Soon after taking office in 2006, the prime minister directed that ministers and parliamentary secretaries attend a practice session for about 45 minutes prior to Question Period each day when the House of Commons was sitting.[56] The Government House Leader chaired the meeting, but the prime minister always attended if he was going to be in QP.

During the meeting ministers rehearsed their answers to questions which they anticipated the opposition would ask in QP. This was a risk for ministers since these daily sessions gave the prime minister regular insight into how well they understood their files. Showing shallow comprehension or relying on talking points prepared by one's officials risked the loss of standing with the boss. On the other hand, the meeting instilled collective message discipline and gave ministers insight into issues outside their own portfolios.[57] Further, it also allowed ministers to hear the prime minister express his own views on key issues, and permitted direct, personal interaction with him, unfiltered by the usual staff gatekeepers. Effectively the QP practice acted as a meeting of the full cabinet where "every issue the government faced was hashed out."[58] But Question Period remained the vital context. These were rough and ready, politically motivated discussions as part of preparation for the day's most publicized political theatre.

It is instructive to note who attended and who did not. In addition to ministers and parliamentary secretaries, the QP practice sessions were the domain of PMO issues management and communications advisors. PMO policy advisors did not attend,[59] nor, since it was a partisan political forum, did officials from PCO who normally supported cabinet and its committees. Ministers would be armed with QP briefing binders which had been drafted by departmental officials but massaged by their political staff. They were also armed with specific lines of response on current issues prepared by PMO Issues Management and often pre-approved by the prime minister. These ad hoc materials were designed for the partisan cut and thrust of Question Period, not for careful policy deliberation. To this extent, no matter how many ministers participated, QP practice was not a substitute for regular cabinet meetings. Further, the meetings provided an avenue for the prime minister to direct in real time what ministers were saying on issues, sometimes relatively minor ones, within their own portfolios.

PMO Briefing Notes Process

The institutionalized daily written briefing notes process which evolved in PMO over the course of Harper's time in office had significant implications for the prime minister's relationship with ministers.[60]

Following the 2006 election, PMO's initial process for briefing the prime minister was "chaotic, informal, and primarily oral."[61] Briefings typically involved long daily meetings of the prime minister with the clerk of the Privy Council and PMO chief of staff, sometimes supported by another senior PMO staffer.[62] The Privy Council Office also sent memoranda to the prime minister each day. But those memos were not distributed systematically to PMO policy advisors who, according to Darrel Reid, deputy director for policy and research and then deputy chief of staff at PMO from 2007 to 2010, were never sure what information or analysis was passed on to the prime minister.[63]

After becoming chief of staff in 2008, Guy Giorno introduced a systematic PMO briefing notes process similar, though on a larger scale, to the practice in Ontario Premier Mike Harris's office (where he had also served as chief of staff). As Giorno explained, "verbal advice is not professional, thorough, accurate, or precise," whereas the act of writing forces advisers to be better prepared and enhances accountability.[64]

According to long established practice, each evening the clerk of the Privy Council sent public service memos for information and for decision directly to the prime minister. Beginning in March 2009, PMO policy advisers each day received copies of these PCO Clerk notes relevant to their areas of responsibility and prepared a political memo corresponding to most PCO memos. A tracking sheet informed the prime minister whether PMO intended to respond to the PCO note and when he could expect to receive the response.

While Harper was often impatient to provide his opinion or decision to PCO, he made a point to wait until he had received written advice from the political side. This discipline worked in reverse too. On one occasion, PMO sent a memo to the prime minister on their own initiative – that is, without being in response to a PCO note – recommending funding for a policy direction supported by some Conservative MPs. As usual, Prime Minister Harper handwrote his response at the top, but this time he was critical of his political staff for attempting to circumvent the public service. "I will not agree to anything without a PCO note and, so far, I have none,"[65] he wrote, pointedly instructing that this not happen again, at least with respect to spending asks.

Although this political briefing-note process was internal to PMO, it had significant implications for the prime minister's relationship with ministers. In particular, the notes process served as a magnet that drew decision-making away from ministers into the prime minister's hands.

Harper had an insatiable appetite for information. While he might sometimes complain about the number and length of daily briefing notes – and both PMO and PCO at times took efforts to reduce the volume – if he learned about an issue that he had not been briefed on, he would ask why. This motivated both PCO and PMO to provide to the prime minister detailed information about issues that might previously have been left at the ministerial level. This allowed the prime minister to get involved, but, as a senior official said, it also encouraged the system to "delegate up"[66] to him decisions that normally would have been resolved elsewhere.

Ministers realized that they could use the notes system to raise issues directly with the prime minister and sometimes circumvent normal channels of decision making. Perhaps collaborating with PMO staff, a minister might write directly to the prime minister and the system would kick in: PCO would write a memo in response to the letter with their advice; PMO would write a memo with their advice; and the prime minister would decide. In Rachel Curran's view, this "bypassed" departmental gatekeepers and permitted ministers to obtain the prime minister's direction in order to advance their issues.[67] But a senior PCO official recalled that these letters created "problems vis à vis the machinery of government" since there might be no MC, no cabinet committee discussion and no cabinet ratification, just the prime minister's written direction in response to the minister. This "reinforced the relationship between minister and the prime minister and decision making outside the cabinet committee or cabinet process," and, according to the official, PCO would sometimes put the issue onto a cabinet agenda anyway in order to secure ratification.[68]

However, if ministers could use the PMO notes system to their advantage, PMO advisers could also attempt to use it to constrain ministers. Internal PMO documents obtained and released by the RCMP as part of the investigation into Senator Mike Duffy in 2013 reveal how PMO Issues Management staff had pressured Senator Marjory LeBreton, the government leader in the Senate, to write a letter to the prime minister explaining her position.[69] PMO then used Senator LeBreton's letter as a justification for sending their own memo to the prime minister explaining their perspective and including a draft letter for the prime minister to sign and return in response.[70] Piggy-backing PMO advice on top of a minister's letter (just as they did on top of PCO notes) was standard practice. While the process gave ministers access to the prime minister, it also gave PMO staff a means to weigh in. Of course, the prime minister always had the last word.

Unfunded MCs

Over decades, reforms to budgeting and expenditure management practices have oscillated between more central control and more responsibility for ministers.[71] In 1994, the Chrétien government introduced a new expenditure management system which, in the context of deficit reduction, stipulated that funding decisions on policy proposals would be done through the budget process, that is, by the prime minister and minister of finance, and not cabinet committees, which previously had been responsible for determining priorities and allocating funding out of predetermined envelopes.[72] The result, as a senior Treasury Board official explained in 2005, was that "cabinet committees are engorged with memoranda to cabinet."[73] Ministers were free to rubber-stamp proposals, knowing that the difficult decisions about funding competing proposals would be taken elsewhere.

The Harper government inherited this practice, but in November 2006 the auditor general highlighted it as a problem, pointing out that since the Chrétien-Martin changes "departments can now submit spending proposals without identifying the source of funds.[74] This policy was problematic for four reasons. First, as the auditor general pointed out, departments were encouraged to seek money from the budget and discouraged from reallocating funds from their existing, perhaps lower-priority and lower-performing programs.[75] Second, ministers were being asked to make decisions at cabinet committees without full information about what trade-offs might be involved in funding the proposal.[76] Third, a long list of cabinet approved but unfunded MCs created pressure to spend and was therefore unhelpful to the government's desire to maintain fiscal discipline. Fourth, MCs that might never receive funding nevertheless consumed significant departmental and ministerial energy to develop, and gummed up the cabinet committee agenda to boot.

None of this was likely to sit well with either Prime Minister Harper or Finance Minister Flaherty. In the wake of the AG's report, PMO made it clear to ministerial staffers that ministers were to be very wary of bringing forward any unfunded MCs and that these were unlikely to receive budget funding. And soon this became established practice. By the time the government announced a new Expenditure Management System in Budget 2007,[77] it was understood internally that unfunded MCs would not be scheduled on a cabinet committee agenda. A senior ministerial staffer recalls that "it became part of our process, for sure," and that the Finance Minister's office "worked quite closely with officials on policing that [restriction] and being quite strong on that."[78]

A salutary lesson from the 1980s, however, is that restrictions in an expenditure management system incentivize minsters to find ways of "working the system" to secure funding for their proposals.[79] In the Harper government, the obvious work around, in light of the prime minister's willingness to respond to letters, was for ministers to write to him directly to seek funding for their MC proposals outside the budget cycle, or at least to seek permission to bring an MC to cabinet, especially if it was not included in their mandate letter.[80] This had two implications. First, a former deputy minister expressed concern that it sometimes led to reduced analysis at the front end: "Without putting people through the due diligence of running an MC through the obstacle course," decisions were made in the budget context based on Finance two-pagers which, while useful to the minister of finance and prime minister for considering budget proposals, were "pretty skimpy" next to a fully developed MC.[81] Second, the restriction on unfunded MCs, adopted in part to protect ministers' time and prevent cabinet committees from drowning in proposals that may have no political viability, resulted in delegating more decision making up to the prime minister and away from ministers deliberating together in cabinet.

Conclusion

As the leader who brought the newly united Conservative party into government after years of factionalism and opposition, Stephen Harper enjoyed undisputed primacy within caucus and cabinet. His ministry was relatively stable under his leadership and, although with its share of resignations and media controversy, saw no significant in-fighting and notably no significant division between former Reformers and PCs, as might have been anticipated. Harper's approach to statecraft reinforced this dominant position in that he used the levers of government to establish structures and processes that drew decision-making to him. Often this was an unintended consequence. His choice to rely heavily on a Priorities and Planning Committee rather than full cabinet was consistent with practice under the Mulroney government. The briefing notes system and the Question Period practice sessions were instigated by PMO respectively to improve their service to the prime minister and, vitally in the initial years of minority government, to mitigate significant communications risk. Prohibiting unfunded MCs represented another oscillation in the expenditure management system, prompted by the auditor general. Yet the prime minister's choices in structuring government and interacting with ministers tended to reflect his personal style which emphasized efficiency in decision-making over team building, and written communication over intimate relationships. Ultimately, the prime minister interacted with his cabinet in a way that worked for him and fit his personal style yet ended up enhancing his pre-eminence: the solitary CEO at his desk processing the business of government.

NOTES

* The author served as director of policy in Prime Minister Harper's office from February 2009 to June 2011.

1 Howard Anglin, review of *Backrooms and Beyond: Partisan Advisers and the Politics of Policy Work in Canada*, by Jonathan Craft, *Policy Options*, 15 August 2016, https://policyoptions.irpp.org/fr/magazines/aout-2016/backrooms-and -beyond-partisan-advisers-and-the-politics-of-policy-work-in-canada-book-review/.

2 Prime Minister of Canada (website), archived 4 November 2015, https://web .archive.org/web/20151104013335/https://pm.gc.ca/.

3 Interview with PMO 1, 11 June 2021. This chapter uses interviews with anonymous PMO staffers, ministers, and deputy ministers. They are identified as PMO 1, Minister 1, DM 1, DM 2, etc.

4 Prime Minister's Office, "Response of the Prime Minister's Office to 'Who Is Getting the Message? Communications at the Centre of Government,' Submission to the Commission of Inquiry into Certain Allegations respecting Business and Financial Dealings between Karlheinz Schreiber and the Right Honourable Brian Mulroney in Response to the Draft Research Report (March 2009), Prepared by Dr. Paul G. Thomas," 11 June 2009, https://www.atlas101.ca/pm/wp-content /uploads/2016/08/PMO-response-to-Thomas-Report-2009.pdf.

5 "Prime Minister Harper Project," Library and Archives Canada, archived 15 July 2022, https://webarchiveweb.wayback.bac-lac.canada.ca/web/20220715094113 /https:/www.bac-lac.gc.ca/eng/transparency/briefing/2019-transition-material /Pages/prime-minister-harper-project.aspx.

6 See, e.g., Paul Wells, *Right Side Up: The Fall of Paul Martin and the Rise of Stephen Harper's New Conservatism* (Toronto: McClelland & Stewart, 2006); Lawrence Martin, *Harperland: The Politics of Control* (Toronto: Viking, 2010); Paul Wells, *The Longer I'm Prime Minister: Stephen Harper and Canada, 2006–* (Toronto: Random House, 2013); and John Ibbitson, *Stephen Harper* (Toronto: McClelland & Stewart, 2015).

7 Ian Brodie, *At the Centre of Government: The Prime Minister and the Limits on Political Power* (Montreal: McGill-Queen's University Press, 2018); and Bruce Carson, *14 Days: Making the Conservative Movement in Canada* (Montreal: McGill-Queen's University Press, 2014).

8 Privy Council Office, "The Canadian Ministry," 6 February 2006, archived 8 February 2006, https://web.archive.org/web/20060208025138/http://www .pm.gc.ca/grfx/docs/cabinet.pdf. Lists of cabinet ministers and cabinet committee membership used throughout this chapter derive from versions of the same document as posted on various dates on the site www.pm.gc.ca, usually obtained through the Internet Archive.

9 "The Ministry," Office of the Prime Minister (website), archived 3 February 2006, https:// web.archive.org/web/20060203015411/http://www.pm.gc.ca/eng/new_team.asp.

10 Brodie, *Centre of Government*, 54.
11 See Orders-in-Council PC 2007-0004 to PC 2007-0008, 4 January 2007, in *Canada Gazette, Part I* 141, no. 4 (27 January 2007), 130–1.
12 Brodie, *Centre of Government*, 58.
13 The ten ministers of state later elevated to cabinet were Jason Kenney, Gerry Ritz, Christian Paradis, Jay Hill, Denis Lebel, Keith Ashfield, Peter Kent, Bernard Valcourt, Pierre Poilievre, and Greg Rickford.
14 Brodie, *Centre of Government*, 70.
15 Maxime Bernier, Helena Guergis, Bev Oda, and Peter Penashue.
16 Brodie, *Centre of Government*, 61–2.
17 Kenny William Ie, "Cabinet Committees as Strategies of Prime Ministerial Leadership in Canada, 2003–2019," *Commonwealth and Comparative Politics* 57, no. 4 (2019): 473; and John Ibbitson, *Stephen Harper*, 229.
18 Interview with CPC transition team official, 30 March 2022.
19 Ie, "Cabinet Committees," 467, 476–7.
20 Michael Wernick, *Governing Canada: A Guide to the Tradecraft of Politics* (Vancouver: On Point Press, 2021), 96.
21 Interview with Sean Speer, 9 June 2021.
22 Sean Speer, personal email, 28 June 2022.
23 Graham White, *Cabinets and First Ministers* (Vancouver: University of British Columbia Press, 2005), 148; and Donald J. Savoie, *Governing from the Centre: The Concentration of Power in Canadian Politics* (Toronto: University of Toronto Press, 1999), 128.
24 Interview with the Hon. Chuck Strahl, 30 June 2021.
25 Interview with DM 2, 17 March 2022.
26 Peter Aucoin, "Organizational Change in the Machinery of Canadian Government: From Rational Management to Brokerage Politics," *Canadian Journal of Political Science* 19, no. 1 (March 1986): 18.
27 Interview with DM 1, 16 June 2021.
28 Interview with Rachel Curran, 12 June 2021.
29 Interview with DM 2, 17 March 2022.
30 Interview with DM 2, 17 March 2022.
31 Interview with the Hon. Chuck Strahl, 30 June 2021.
32 Interview with PMO 1, 11 June 2021.
33 Interview with the Hon. Monte Solberg, 9 July 2021.
34 Interview with Minister 1, 30 July 2021.
35 Interview with the Hon. Chuck Strahl, 30 June 2021.
36 Interview with DM 2, 17 March 2022.
37 Interview with Hon. Tony Clement, 9 June 2022.
38 Interview with Andrew MacDougall, 10 June 2021.
39 Interview with PMO 1, 11 June 2021.
40 Interview with Darrel Reid, 7 June 2021.

41 Interview with DM 3, 22 March 2022.
42 Interview with Hon. Tony Clement, 9 June 2022.
43 Interview with the Hon. Chuck Strahl, 30 June 2021.
44 Interview with Darrel Reid, 7 June 2021.
45 Interview with Sean Speer, 9 June 2021.
46 Interview with Scott Streiner, 8 June, 2021.
47 Interview with Minister 1, 30 July 2021.
48 Wells, *The Longer I'm Prime Minister*, 195–6.
59 Interview with Darrel Reid, 7 June 2021.
50 See, e.g., Savoie, *Governing from the Centre*; Edward Greenspon and Anthony
    Wilson-Smith, *Double Vision: The Inside Story of the Liberals in Power* (Toronto:
    Doubleday, 1996); and Eddie Goldenberg, *The Way It Works: Inside Ottawa*
    (Toronto: McClelland & Stewart, 2006).
51 Interview with the Hon. Monte Solberg, 9 July 2021.
52 Interview with PMO 1, 11 June 2021.
53 Stephen Harper, "Stephen Harper's Full Eulogy for Jim Flaherty Funeral," CBC
    News, 16 April 2014, https://www.cbc.ca/news/canada/stephen-harper-s-full
    -eulogy-for-jim-flaherty-funeral-1.2612835.
54 Interview with Rachel Curran, 12 June 2021.
55 Interview with Ian Brodie, 4 June 2021.
56 Carson, *14 Days*, 155.
57 Interview with the Hon. Tony Clement, 9 June 2022.
58 Carson, *14 Days*, 156.
59 Interview with Rachel Curran, 12 June 2021.
60 The process is discussed in Jonathan Craft, *Backrooms and Beyond: Partisan
    Advisers and the Politics of Policy Work in Canada* (Toronto: University of Toronto
    Press, 2016), 72–80; and Jonathan Craft and Anna Lennox Esselment, "Stephen
    Harper's PMO Style: Partisan Managerialism," in *Open Federalism Revisited:
    Regional and Federal Dynamics in the Harper Era*, ed. Julie M. Simmons and
    James Harold Farney (Toronto: University of Toronto Press, 2022), 127.
61 Craft, *Backrooms and Beyond*, 72.
62 Interview with Bruce Carson, 14 June 2021.
63 Interview with Darrel Reid, 7 June 2021.
64 Interview with Guy Giorno, 23 June 2022.
65 PMO memo from June 2009, provided to the author courtesy of PMO, 6 March 2014.
66 Former senior government official speaking to a Master of Political Management
    class at Carleton University, 29 February 2016.
67 Interview with Rachel Curran, 12 June 2021.
68 Interview with DM 3, 22 March 2022.
69 Corporal Greg Horton, "Information to Obtain Production Orders," appendix
    B, sworn 15 November 2013, via "Read and Search the RCMP's Duffy-Wright

Documents," *CBC News*, 20 November 2013, https://www.cbc.ca/news/politics/read-and-search-the-rcmp-s-duffy-wright-documents-1.2434140.

70 Horton, "Information to Obtain."

71 G. Bruce Doern, "Evolving Budgetary Policies and Experiments: 1980 to 2009–2010," in *How Ottawa Spends, 2009–2010: Economic Upheaval and Political Dysfunction*, ed. Allan M. Maslove (Montreal: McGill-Queen's University Press), 28.

72 David Good, *The Politics of Public Money*, 2nd ed. (Toronto: University of Toronto Press, 2014), 114, 281.

73 Quoted in Good, *Politics of Public Money*, 115.

74 Auditor General of Canada, *Report of the Auditor General of Canada to the House of Commons, Chapter 1: Expenditure Management System at the Government Centre*, November 2006, 44, https://www.oag-bvg.gc.ca/internet/docs/20061101ce.pdf.

75 Auditor General, *Report: Chapter 1*, 44.

76 Auditor General, *Report: Chapter 1*, 34.

77 Canada, Department of Finance, *Budget 2007: Aspire to a Stronger, Safer, Better Canada* (Ottawa: Her Majesty the Queen in Right of Canada, 2007), 18.

78 Interview with Minister's Office 1, 13 June 2022.

79 Richard Van Loon, "Ottawa's Expenditure Process: Four Systems in Search of Co-ordination," in *How Ottawa Spends: The Liberals, the Opposition and Federal Priorities*, ed. G. Bruce Doern (Toronto: James Lorimer, 1983), 114.

80 Interview with DM 3, 22 March 2022.

81 Personal email from DM 2, 12 March 2022.

20 Justin Trudeau: A Cabinet That Looks Like Canada

JENI ARMSTRONG, ALEX MARLAND, AND DAN ARNOLD

Justin Trudeau has a unique perspective on cabinet government. Born in the early days of his father's tenure, he grew up surrounded by elite political circles and intimately familiar with the halls of government. This pedigree, combined with his own charisma and media sense, spurred his win over a Bloc Québécois incumbent to become a member of Parliament (MP) in 2008 and helped him secure the leadership of the Liberal Party five years later despite a relatively thin résumé. In the 2015 federal election campaign, his combination of positivity, charm, and trustworthiness propelled the party into power – the only time in Canadian history that a national party had gone from third-party status to a majority government in a single election. His first cabinet boldly emphasized gender balance, attracting headlines around the world. Trudeau claimed he would reverse a wave of centralization around the office of the prime minister that had blossomed under his father. Instead, his statecraft would revolve around his strong personal brand and a further consolidation of decision-making power.

This chapter focuses on the Liberal-majority government (2015–19), with some commentary about changes during the two Liberal minority governments that followed (2019–21, 2021–5). It examines the notable structural changes Trudeau introduced to cabinet, in contrast with those of his predecessor, Stephen Harper. This study draws on media reports, insider perspectives from two of the authors who were senior political staffers in the Liberal government,[1] and an extended interview with Michael Wernick, who was clerk of the Privy Council from 2016 to 2019.[2]

Justin Trudeau's Path to Politics and Management Style

Justin Trudeau has been in the public eye from the moment he was born. He completed degrees in English literature (McGill University) and education (University of British Columbia), and taught in private and public schools on the west coast. Thrust back into public life in 2000 when he delivered a poignant eulogy at his father's funeral, he engaged in public speaking, sat on the boards of not-for-profit groups, and, eventually, embraced partisan politics. He got involved with the 2006 Liberal leadership convention and, in 2008, was elected MP for Papineau (Montreal). The Liberals were coming off their worst election showing ever when he won the party leadership in 2013.

Just two years later, Trudeau was front-and-centre, leading the Liberal Party to an election victory in October 2015 and forming a majority government a month later. Stark differences from his predecessor emerged early on, in particular when it came to working with the media. Unlike Stephen Harper, who nurtured a fractious relationship with journalists, Prime Minister Trudeau initially made a point of making his ministry more accessible, including releasing his daily schedule. In late 2015, communications staffers and the parliamentary press gallery agreed on ways ministers could be scrummed after cabinet meetings. Known as "Cabinet outs," this practice had ceased under the Harper government, which refused to disclose the times of cabinet meetings.[3] Communications staff dutifully coordinated media interviews with ministers,[4] and the word around Ottawa was that policy decisions had indeed been devolved from the Prime Minister's Office (PMO) to ministers.[5] During this time, Trudeau was the subject of flattering media reports, including on the cover of the August 2017 edition of *Rolling Stone* magazine, which, in the wake of Donald Trump's election, asked, "Why can't he be our president?"

Another significant change in the early days involved the decentralization of executive appointments. An open application process for select positions, including Senate and Supreme Court appointments, was introduced. Because Prime Minister Harper had left nearly a quarter of Senate seats unfilled, this allowed Trudeau to substantially change the upper chamber's composition.

However, some practices in the new Trudeau government suggest that his early approach to statecraft offered more pragmatism than "real change" (one of the campaign slogans from the 2015 election). This included a lingering desire to control the message, to focus on the leader, and to engage in permanent campaigning. The PMO ran an election-style war room to respond to President Trump's erratic communications style,[6] and the Privy Council Office (PCO) was deeply involved with coordinating government publicity, including scripted messaging, event planning, and social media posts.[7] Trudeau's official photographer followed him relentlessly to capture behind-the-scenes moments and post a stream of images on Trudeau's social media accounts, with these images becoming more exclusive on occasions when photojournalists were barred from documenting events.[8]

The Prime Minister's Office

When it came to building the complement of staff who would work most closely with him, Trudeau turned to two trusted advisors: Gerald Butts and Katie Telford. Both had been with him since the earliest conversations about whether he should pursue the Liberal leadership. Butts, a close friend since university, had worked in and around politics for years, including serving as one of the top political advisors to Ontario Premier Dalton McGuinty. Along with future cabinet ministers Marc Miller and Seamus O'Regan, Butts was a member of Trudeau's wedding party. Telford, also a Queen's Park veteran, had run Trudeau's leadership campaign and went on to serve as national campaign manager during the 2015 election. They were installed as the new prime minister's principal secretary and chief of staff, respectively.

The prime minister told the caucus that any communication coming from Telford or Butts should be considered as coming from him.[9] This worked well when prompt decisions were needed but could also result in bottlenecking and files getting bumped; occasionally this required intervention from the clerk, who would explain to the PMO why a given item needed to be prioritized. Gradually, a number of PMO staff – many of whom shared Telford and Butts's experience working at provincial legislatures – were redeployed as chiefs of staff in underperforming ministers' offices. Platform commitments on openness and transparency (see "The First Cabinet") were put to the test: the Liberal government attempted to curtail opposition powers in the House of Commons, refused to release internal memos about making government more open and transparent, and abandoned its plan to make the PMO and ministers' offices subject to Access to Information laws. Select cabinet information was leaked while other information was shielded as a cabinet confidence,[10] and promises to avoid prorogation and omnibus bills also fell by the wayside.

The First Cabinet

The Liberal Party's 2015 election platform made substantive commitments aimed at changing the composition of cabinet. Diversity was a primary consideration: there would be an equal number of women and men in cabinet, plus the prime minister, and cabinet decisions would consider the different ways policies affect women and men (eventually, this approach was applied across government as "Gender-based Analysis Plus" and became a permanent part of the federal budget-making process). The platform promised that the Prime Minister's Office and ministers' offices would be subject to Access to Information, and a Trudeau government would both avoid prorogation and end the "undemocratic process" of omnibus bills, which the platform described as "legislative trickery." As well, a Prime Minister's Question Period would be created, a 45-minute period one day a week when only the prime minister would answer questions from opposition MPs. These commitments were buttressed by Trudeau's campaign comment that "we've reached the end point" on power concentrated in the PMO, and that he liked the "symmetry" of his ending a trend of centralization that his father was said to have started.[11]

Despite suggestions that Trudeau and his team were "having a hard time choosing from an 'abundance of talent,'"[12] decisions about the composition of his first cabinet were constrained by the limited ministerial or even parliamentary experience in the Liberal caucus, which had grown from 39 MPs before the election to 184 after. Trudeau and his transition team – which consisted of future senators Peter Harder (a former deputy minister in Ottawa) and Tony Dean (a former cabinet secretary in Toronto), future UN ambassador Marc-André Blanchard, senior PMO staffers Butts and Telford, former Trudeau chief of staff Cyrus Reporter, and others – ultimately prioritized gender balance and regional representation, while considering ethnicity, age, and political experience, as well as slotting MPs into portfolios based on their subject matter expertise and backgrounds. Eventually a cabinet roster of 31 (Trudeau and 30 ministers) was settled upon, of whom 18 had been elected to the House for the first time in October 2015. More than one-third (11) were rookie MPs who had never been elected to office at any level.

There was considerable fanfare when the cabinet was revealed. Trudeau and his future ministers arrived at the gates of Rideau Hall by bus, then walked to the induction together as a group. He announced that "government by cabinet is back," and attracted international headlines by explaining why there was an equal number of female and male ministers, a first for a Canadian federal cabinet: "Because it's 2015." He championed diversity by proclaiming he was happy to introduce "a cabinet that looks like Canada" – one that, in addition to the gender balance, included four Sikh ministers, two Indigenous ministers, and two ministers with disabilities. Notably, there were no Black Canadians in this first cabinet.

While the new cabinet was unveiled just 16 days after the 2015 election, more time was needed to properly staff each ministerial office, as the PMO insisted on vetting all chiefs of staff as well as key policy and communications personnel. Cabinet retreats became a regular feature in the first year and were held about three times annually until the coronavirus pandemic (COVID-19) struck in March 2020. Some retreats featured whole afternoons to discuss a single topic, such as abandoning electoral reform or reacting to Donald Trump's election. Guest speakers, such as British "deliverology" expert Sir Michael Barber, were invited to address the cabinet, and the party's pollster presented the latest public opinion research findings about the public mood, giving ministers a chance to reflect on the big picture. At times, ministers were given advice on how to better communicate the government's messages, whether through social media or by learning how to better "talk like people talk." In the first year, two cabinet retreats were held at luxury resorts and were criticized for their expense; for the third retreat, ministers shared rooms in student dormitories at Laurentian University in Sudbury.[13]

Cabinet meetings took place weekly. Ministers were impressed at the prime minister's ability to keep the agenda moving.[14] Nevertheless, Trudeau requested that the Privy Council Office install a timer with a light that would go off after a couple of minutes. Initially, ministers were unnerved by this, but the device prompted them to stick to a two-minute speaking limit, and those who agreed to a proposal simply said so without filling airtime. Less clear is how often the prime minister made time to meet with ministers one-on-one, or in smaller groups. While such meetings could be expected around large announcements such as the federal budget, one former political advisor noted that the prime minister had refused to meet with his foreign minister during Stéphane Dion's fourteen months on the job, despite repeated requests to do so.[15] Several other ministers from that original cabinet have since revealed that they rarely interacted directly with the prime minister and instead dealt with PMO staff.[16]

During his time as prime minister, Trudeau named ministers to cabinet (or reassigned ministers within cabinet) on more than two dozen occasions. In non-election years, cabinet shuffles were rare; they usually occurred only once or twice a year and tended to be small in scope. Both 2019 and 2024 were notable exceptions; each of those years featured at least seven cabinet shuffles, often to replace ministers who did not intend to run in the next election. His official photographer offered a rare glimpse at the complexity of cabinet formation, showing how the prime minister and his staff used magnets to map out how to organize cabinet selection (see image 20.1). The magnets were moved around the board several times before plans were finalized, and in the case of standard shuffles, staff typically worked out several different options that were then taken to the prime minister for decision. More dramatic rushed shuffles featured condensed deliberations. Following each election, there were discussions on potential structural changes – how big should cabinet be; which portfolios should be created, combined, or divided; should the prime minister appoint secretaries of state as Prime Minister Harper had done; and so on. One non-negotiable consideration was gender balance, which complicated the selection process. In 2015, the Liberal Party failed to elect a woman MP in Saskatchewan, Alberta, Prince Edward Island, and the three territories; and the one woman elected in Manitoba was removed from cabinet in the January 2017 shuffle. To maintain gender balance and regional representation, it became necessary to appoint a higher proportion of women from other provinces.

Described as "the platonic ideal of a Liberal cabinet,"[17] Trudeau's first iteration gave several key posts to political veterans, including public safety (Ralph Goodale), foreign affairs (Dion), immigration (John McCallum), Indigenous affairs (Carolyn Bennett), Treasury Board (Scott Brison), and government House leader (Dominic LeBlanc). Some fresh faces were assigned significant roles, signalling an effort to align new ministers' expertise with their new files. This included finance (Bill Morneau), justice (Jody Wilson-Raybould), international trade (Chrystia Freeland), health (Jane Philpott), environment (Catherine McKenna), defence (Harjit Sajjan), and science (Kirsty Duncan). Though the new cabinet was characterized as youthful,[18] the average age of incoming ministers was 51. A few ministers proved to have staying power and remained

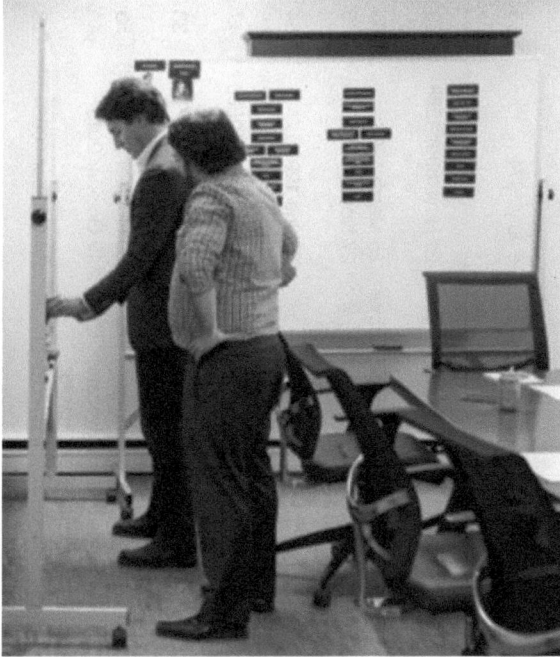

Image 20.1.   Prime Minister Justin Trudeau using magnets to plan his cabinet, 29 September 2021

Source: Adam Scotti.

in the same cabinet positions for years, but many would also be out of politics by the next election. Other than the prime minister, only one minister, Diane Lebouthillier in national revenue, remained in the same role through multiple elections. The portfolios, province, profession, date of each minister's first election as an MP, and age are presented in table 20.1. In addition to being prime minister, Trudeau was initially minister for intergovernmental affairs and minister for youth, roles he eventually shed.

Despite the media headlines around his "Because it's 2015" comment, gender parity among ministers did not result in true equality, given that five of the 15 women first named to cabinet in 2015 held junior minister of state roles, and many of the portfolios traditionally held by men (e.g., finance, defence, foreign affairs) remained as such. Furthermore, the commitment did not extend to ministerial chiefs of staff, the majority of whom were men. Trudeau's delivery of a gender-balanced cabinet nevertheless represented a first for Canada at the federal level, generating international accolades and setting an example that other national governments – such as New Zealand and the United States – later followed.

Table 20.1. Justin Trudeau's original cabinet, November 2015

Portfolio/title	Name	Province/ territory	Occupation/ profession	Date of first election to Parliament	Age
1. Prime minister + intergovernmental affairs + youth	Justin Trudeau	QC	Teacher	14 October 2008	43
2. Public safety and emergency preparedness	Ralph Goodale	SK	Business executive, broadcaster, barrister and solicitor, businessman	8 July 1974	65
3. Agriculture and agri-food	Lawrence MacAulay	PEI	Farmer	21 November 1988	69
4. Foreign affairs	Stéphane Dion	QC	Professor of political science, author	25 March 1996	60
5. Immigration, refugees, and citizenship	John McCallum	ON	Professor, economist, author	27 November 2000	65
6. Indigenous and northern affairs	Carolyn Bennett	ON	Physician	2 June 1997	64
7. President of the Treasury Board	Scott Brison	NS	Investment banker, businessman	2 June 1997	48
8. Leader of the government in the House of Commons	Dominic LeBlanc	NB	Lawyer, notary	27 November 2000	47
9. Innovation, science, and economic development	Navdeep Bains	ON	Professor, certified management accountant, financial analyst	28 June 2004	38
10. Finance	Bill Morneau	ON	Business manager, company head	29 October 2015	53
11. Justice and attorney general of Canada	Jody Wilson-Raybould	BC	Crown prosecutor, advocate, Indigenous leader, lawyer	19 October 2015	44
12. Public services and procurement	Judy Foote	NL	Broadcast journalist, director of public relations	14 October 2008	63
13. International trade	Chrystia Freeland	ON	Editor, author, journalist	25 November 2013	47
14. Health	Jane Philpott	ON	Physician	19 October 2015	54
15. Families, children, and social development	Jean-Yves Duclos	QC	Professor, economist	19 October 2015	50
16. Transport	Marc Garneau	QC	Engineer, astronaut	14 October 2008	66
17. International development	Marie-Claude Bibeau	QC	Director, executive manager, businesswoman	19 October 2015	45

Portfolio	Name	Province	Background	Date	Age
18. Natural resources	Jim Carr	MB	Musician, columnist, reporter, executive, administrator, provincial politician	19 October 2015	64
19. Canadian heritage	Mélanie Joly	QC	Director of public relations, lawyer	19 October 2015	36
20. National revenue	Diane Lebouthillier	QC	Advisor, social worker, business owner, municipal politician	19 October 2015	56
21. Veterans affairs + associate minister of national defence	Kent Hehr	AB	Lawyer, provincial politician	19 October 2015	45
22. Environment and climate change	Catherine McKenna	ON	Executive director, lawyer, negotiator, teacher	19 October 2015	44
23. National defence	Harjit Sajjan	BC	Police officer, military officer	19 October 2015	45
24. Employment, workforce development, and labour	MaryAnn Mihychuk	MB	Geologist, geoscientist, provincial politician	19 October 2015	60
25. Infrastructure and communities	Amarjeet Sohi	AB	Bus driver, actor, playwright, municipal politician	19 October 2015	51
26. Democratic institutions	Maryam Monsef	ON	Community activist and organizer	19 October 2015	30
27. Sport and persons with disabilities	Carla Qualtrough	BC	Mediator, athlete, lawyer	19 October 2015	44
28. Fisheries, oceans, and the Canadian Coast Guard	Hunter Tootoo	NU	Public servant, businessman, territorial politician	19 October 2015	52
29. Science	Kirsty Duncan	ON	Professor, lecturer, athlete, author, geographer	14 October 2008	49
30. Status of women	Patty Hajdu	ON	Executive director	19 October 2015	49
31. Small business and tourism	Bardish Chagger	ON	Executive assistant, community organizer, project coordinator	19 October 2015	35

Source: Library of Parliament.

Note: Presented in order of precedence (individual ministerial seniority).

Breaking from tradition, and in line with Trudeau's efforts to reduce partisanship in the upper chamber, there was no senator appointed to cabinet. Instead, a former public servant who had played a role in government transition (Peter Harder) was given a Senate appointment, with the title "representative of the government in the Senate." In the wake of Trudeau's 2014 decision to remove senators from the Liberal party caucus, ministers would need to lobby senators to ensure passage of the government's agenda. Other changes included eliminating the traditional title of regional minister which had been used by previous prime ministers to formally designate regional lieutenants (the role of Quebec lieutenant was resurrected after the 2019 election). Early in his government's tenure, PCO faced resource constraints brought about by the creation of so many non-traditional ministries, such as the establishment of a Youth Secretariat to support the prime minister's joint role as minister for youth.[19]

Ministerial Mandate Letters

An entire chapter in the 2015 Liberal platform was devoted to "fair and open government." To deliver on those commitments, the Trudeau government released some key documents, including a government manual for ministers prepared by PCO during the Harper era that it tweaked and made public. *Open and Accountable Government* established that cabinet decisions are led by the prime minister and outlined principles of ministerial responsibility and accountability, portfolio responsibilities, ministerial relations with Parliament, and standards of conduct.[20] The Trudeau government continued the practice of releasing *Guidelines on the Conduct of Ministers, Ministers of State, Exempt Staff and Public Servants during an Election*, but was slow to update *A Drafter's Guide to Cabinet Documents*. The other main documents that helped to shine a light on the work of cabinet ministers were ministerial mandate letters authored by the PMO and PCO, outlining the work ministers were expected to prioritize. By making the letters publicly available for the first time, the Trudeau government was both following the practice in place in several provinces and setting a national transparency standard. The lengthy letters clarified ministerial responsibilities, particularly on interconnected matters spanning several departments and whole-of-government initiatives. They underscored the prime minister's authority, and their public release formalized the instruments as directives to the public service.

Mandate letters initially appeared on the prime minister's website nine days after the first cabinet was sworn in. They featured feel-good messaging from the Liberal campaign platform, directives to uphold high ethical standards and to follow the PCO manual for ministers, and a stern reminder that across government, no relationship is more important than the one with Indigenous peoples. They became hotly anticipated marching orders whenever a new minister was installed, and were scrutinized by the media, advocacy groups, other orders of government, and the opposition, for clues on who could be held accountable on key files and hints on rising or falling government priorities. The mandate letters gave clear direction to ministers about their policy tasks, and encouraged coordination between them.[21]

The public service was reorganized to support the implementation of mandate letters. Tracking the status of commitments began with the creation of the Results and Delivery Unit (RDU) in PCO. The unit briefed the prime minister and the Agenda, Results, and Communications Cabinet committee using "dashboards, heat maps and short progress reports," and made progress by reviewing data in short "stock take meetings" with Trudeau,[22] which he reportedly valued. These meetings provided a chance to bring together relevant ministers and experts to have a frank discussion about an issue, often one that had encountered roadblocks along the way. Enthusiasm about mandate letters and their value in delivering political accountability eventually waned; after the 2021 election, it took nearly two months to provide ministers with a new set of letters.[23]

The experiment with releasing mandate letters came with a trade-off: relinquishing confidentiality meant blunt directives were no longer possible. While their release was a strong signal of ministerial priorities, they also acted as marketing tools designed to generate positive media coverage and placate interest groups looking for signs that the government is paying attention to their concerns. The laundry list of dozens of items made it implausible for everything to be actioned, particularly when new priorities arose. The missives were also subject to change at any given time. Letters were sometimes updated whenever a minister was replaced, as with the one to the freshly appointed minister of democratic institutions which backtracked on the Liberal Party's campaign promise to change the electoral system, but despite a sizeable shuffle in June 2023 most ministerial mandate letters were not updated to reflect new roles and responsibilities. Finally, ministerial priorities could shift without new letters being issued: in response to the Black Lives Matter movement in 2020, ministers set about examining policies within their mandates to find ways to minimize institutional racism, which did not require inclusion in a mandate letter to take effect.[24]

When made available publicly, mandate letters were a way for insiders and outsiders to assess a minister's performance. The Trudeau government's signature policies and achievements – from cutting taxes for the middle class to delivering more financial support for families to expanding the Canada Pension Plan to legalizing cannabis – all found a place in a relevant minister's letter. All mandate letters issued since 2015 were archived on Prime Minister Trudeau's official website, suggesting that – at least where these accountability tools are concerned – the government's commitment to more open and transparent government endured.

Cabinet Committees

Trudeau renamed and restructured cabinet committees from the outset, expanding the total number of committees from the seven that had been in place at the end of Harper's ministry.[25] The powerful Priorities and Planning Committee was immediately refashioned as Agenda and Results, later renamed as Agenda, Results, and Communications, and was chaired by the prime minister. Treasury Board, the oldest and only statutory cabinet committee, continued unabated, but the Operations Committee became Parliamentary Affairs, chaired by the government House leader. A new committee on Diversity and Inclusion was struck, and the environment and energy files were bundled together in a single committee. Progressive-sounding labels were applied to other committees, such as the committee on Inclusive Growth, Opportunities and Innovation, which was subsequently renamed the Cabinet Committee on Growing the Middle Class. Additional committees and sub-committees were added over time, to address issues around litigation management, reconciliation with Indigenous peoples, and ongoing problems with the Phoenix pay system for public servants. Notably, a Cabinet committee on Canada–US relations was established in 2016, abandoned in 2019, and then resurrected two days after the November 2024 re-election of US president Donald Trump. Chrystia Freeland, then deputy prime minister and finance minister, was named as chair of the reconstituted cabinet committee.[26] Two to four staff from PMO attended cabinet committees and cabinet, plus a representative from the Department of Finance, and occasionally, a ministerial staffer to assist a minister with a presentation.

The "Because it's 2015" commitment to gender parity was not reflected in the initial cabinet committee composition. Despite having equal numbers of men and women ministers to draw from, only three of 10 committees were chaired by women, and men constituted a majority of members on all but two committees (Diversity and Inclusion, and Open and Transparent Government).[27] Historically, women have been underrepresented on cabinet committees, and those who served have had limited political influence relative to men, which improved gradually under the Trudeau government.[28]

Following the 2019 election, cabinet returned with a total of seven permanent committees plus the Incident Response Group which was established the previous year to respond to national crises or international incidents with grave domestic implications. The new slate of committees came with slimmed-down titles as well; committees dedicated to Economy and the Environment, and Health and Social Affairs, are two notable examples where the brevity of titles belied the scope of responsibilities. Between the 2019 and 2021 elections, the composition of cabinet committees was relatively stable, perhaps reflecting the preoccupation of the government with managing the ongoing COVID-19 pandemic.

The number of cabinet committees grew slightly following the 2021 election, which saw the return of eight permanent committees and three sub-committees (on intergovernmental coordination, litigation management, and the federal response to COVID-19), plus the Incident Response Group. Among the permanent committees, political observers were confused by the creation of two cabinet committees on the economy, inclusion, and climate.[29] Labelled as "A" and "B" committees, these two groups had different memberships but identical mandates; an unnamed official described them as two parts of a super-committee, with the split intended to "accelerate the movement" of economic and climate platform commitments.[30]

Over time, Trudeau made good use of *ad hoc* cabinet committees, which were formed in response to emerging issues. These included a Committee on Refugees, created to address the goal of resettling 25,000 Syrian refugees in Canada, as well as committees to deal with defence procurement (later boosted to full committee status), wildfires in Alberta and British Columbia, and COVID-19. In early 2020, the Incident Response Group met regularly to discuss the federal response to COVID-19, Iran's downing of a Ukrainian passenger flight that killed 55 Canadian citizens and 30 permanent residents, and ongoing rail blockades across the country. The group was also convened in early 2022 to address the ongoing blockades and occupations in Ottawa and at international border crossings. A few months later, a task force comprised of 10 cabinet ministers was struck to resolve lengthy service delays in processing immigration and passport applications.[31]

That the Trudeau government also appointed many parliamentary secretaries – approximately one for every minister – is a function of executive creep, in which a high proportion of elected members are given formal roles in the government. This practice is driven in part by a need to assist busy ministers with their growing demands, and also by a desire by the head of government to exercise influence over caucus.[32] Despite promises to make parliamentary committees more independent, parliamentary secretaries were regularly assigned to act as cabinet sentries at committee meetings; after the Liberals were reduced to a minority government in 2019, they reinstituted voting privileges at parliamentary committees for these ministerial representatives.[33] Changes in the parliamentary secretary ranks usually followed cabinet shuffles and took into account feedback from ministers and chiefs of staff.

Shuffles, Resignations and Firings (2016–2019)

More than a dozen shuffles followed during the Liberals' majority government (table 20.2); one notable shuffle saw the division of Indigenous and Northern affairs into the portfolios of Indigenous services and crown-Indigenous relations. At each shuffle Trudeau sought to maintain gender balance. This included a series of changes brought about after months of private disagreement with the minister of justice and attorney general. Jody Wilson-Raybould had resisted PMO overtures to consider a special deferred prosecution deal for Quebec-based, multinational engineering firm SNC-Lavalin, whose executives had bribed Libyan officials to obtain lucrative public infrastructure contracts. That dramatic episode spilled into the public domain in February 2019 and revealed considerable discord within the highest levels of the Trudeau government, including the marginalization of Liberal backbenchers. Weeks of headline news and parliamentary committee investigations resulted in the resignations of the prime minister's principal secretary (Butts), the clerk of the Privy Council (Wernick), and two key ministers (Wilson-Raybould and Philpott). The resignations rank among the most explosive in Canadian federal history,[34] and among other critiques, raised questions about Trudeau's commitment to feminism.[35] Trudeau himself reflected that relations with Wilson-Raybould were unusually fragile due to a lack of "trust and faith" that existed with other ministers.[36]

The episode was evidence that despite the prime minister's sense that he was "accessible to and close to members of caucus and certainly cabinet,"[37] in practice, his leadership style often involved being inaccessible, instead delegating senior PMO staff to engage directly with ministers to work out details. At least one cabinet retreat included a presentation about how the government could better engage backbench MPs, some of whom had felt alienated by insufficient advance notice of government bills and frustration on occasions when cabinet voted against their private member's bills. In the wake of the SNC-Lavalin affair, an attempt was made to shore up support from disgruntled backbenchers by creating an office of caucus outreach in the PMO, along with a commitment that the prime minister would personally respond to any pressing issues or concerns presented by caucus within 48 hours.[38] On a more personal note, he also phoned Liberal MPs on their birthdays.

Partly because of the SNC-Lavalin affair, the 2019 election reduced the Liberals to a minority government. Trudeau increased the size of his cabinet to 37 members, with notable new faces including Anita Anand (public services and procurement) and Steven Guilbeault (heritage). Several ministers were assigned more important roles, including François-Philippe Champagne (to foreign affairs), Jean-Yves Duclos (to Treasury Board) and Patty Hajdu (to health). The only two ministers to lose their seats (Ralph Goodale and Amarjeet Sohi) hailed from Saskatchewan and Alberta, where the Liberals were shut out. To respond to this lack of representation and growing western alienation, the prime minister turned to Alberta-born Chrystia Freeland, a rising star of the first mandate. Freeland had been widely praised for leading Canada through the lengthy and contentious renegotiation of the North American Free Trade Agreement (NAFTA) and a series of trade disputes on steel and aluminium,

Table 20.2. Notable exits, entries, and new roles in Justin Trudeau's cabinet, 2016–25

Date	Results	Size of cabinet
31 May 2016	**Out:** Tootoo resigned to seek treatment for addiction issues	30
19 August 2016	**Notable new role:** Chagger added House leader to her duties, becoming the first woman and first racialized person to assume this role.	30
10 January 2017	**Out:** Dion and McCallum, who assumed diplomatic posts, plus Mihychuk **In:** François-Philippe Champagne (international trade), Ahmed Hussen (immigration, refugees, and citizenship), and Canada's youngest ever woman cabinet minister, Karina Gould (democratic institutions) **Notable new role:** Freeland moved to foreign affairs	30
28 August 2017	**Out:** Foote resigned following an extended absence from cabinet (on leave for personal/family reasons since April 2017) **In:** Seamus O'Regan (veterans affairs) and Ginette Petitpas Taylor (health) **Notable new roles:** Indigenous and northern affairs was divided, creating new roles for Philpott (Indigenous services) and Bennett (Crown-Indigenous relations)	31
25 January 2018	**Out:** Hehr resigned pending an investigation into allegations of sexual harassment	30
9 February 2018	**Out:** Gould temporarily stepped away from cabinet while on parental leave from March to May 2018 after becoming the first federal cabinet minister to give birth while in office	30
18 July 2018	A significant expansion and reorganization of cabinet gives many ministers new roles or additional responsibilities. **In:** Bill Blair (border security and organized crime prevention), former PMO staffer Mary Ng (small business, with the addition of export promotion), Pablo Rodriguez (heritage, with the addition of multiculturalism), Filomena Tassi (seniors, a re-established portfolio), and Jonathan Wilkinson (fisheries, oceans, and the Canadian Coast Guard) **Notable new roles:** International trade diversification was established, creating a new role for Carr; Joly moved to tourism and official languages; LeBlanc took on intergovernmental affairs, a portfolio previously handled by the prime minister	35

(Continued)

Table 20.2. (Continued)

Date	Results	Size of cabinet
14 January 2019	**Out:** Brison resigned from cabinet and left federal politics after deciding not to run for re-election **In:** David Lametti (justice and attorney general of Canada) **New portfolios:** Rural economic development was created (led by newcomer Bernadette Jordan); women and gender equality became a full department **Notable new roles:** Philpott moved to Treasury Board and digital government; Wilson-Raybould moved to veterans affairs	36
12 February 2019	**Out:** Wilson-Raybould resigned in the wake of the SNC-Lavalin affair	35
1 March 2019	A small reassignment of roles in response to Wilson-Raybould's departure. **New roles:** MacAulay to veterans affairs, Bibeau to agriculture and agri-food, Monsef picked up international development	35
4 March 2019	**Out:** Philpott resigned in the wake of the SNC-Lavalin affair	34
18 March 2019	**In:** Following Philpott's departure, Joyce Murray is sworn in as treasury board president	35
26 April 2019	**Out:** LeBlanc stepped away from cabinet to receive treatment for cancer	34
20 November 2019	A significant reorganization and modest expansion of cabinet following the 21 October 2019 federal election. **Out:** Goodale and Sohi, who were not re-elected; Carr, who was receiving treatment for cancer; plus Duncan and Petitpas Taylor, who both assumed House roles **In:** Anita Anand (public services and procurement), Mona Fortier (middle-class prosperity), Steven Guilbeault (heritage), Marco Mendicino (immigration, refugees, and citizenship), Marc Miller (Indigenous services), Deb Schulte (seniors) and Dan Vandal (northern affairs) **Notable new roles:** Freeland took on intergovernmental affairs and became Canada's deputy prime minister, a position that did not exist during Trudeau's first mandate; Chagger took responsibility for the newly created diversity and inclusion and youth; Champagne moved to foreign affairs; while formally out of cabinet, Carr continued to serve as special representative for the Prairies	37
18 August 2020	**Out:** Morneau resigned in the wake of the WE Charity scandal **Notable new roles:** Freeland became Canada's first ever woman minister of finance; LeBlanc returned to intergovernmental affairs	36

Table 20.2. (Continued)

Date	Results	Size of cabinet
12 January 2021	**Out:** Bains resigned from cabinet and left federal politics after deciding not to run for re-election, triggering a small shuffle **In:** Newcomer Omar Alghabra (transport); Carr (rejoined cabinet as minister without a portfolio, continued his special representative role) **Notable new roles:** Champagne (innovation, science, and industry), Garneau (foreign affairs)	37
26 October 2021	A significant reorganization and small expansion of cabinet following the 20 September 2021 federal election. **Out:** Jordan, Monsef, and Schulte, who were not re-elected; McKenna, who did not run again; plus Carr, Chagger, and Garneau **In:** Randy Boissonnault (tourism), Sean Fraser (immigration, refugees, and citizenship), Mark Holland (House leader), Gudie Hutchings (rural economic development), Marci Ien (women and gender equality and youth), Helena Jaczek (minister responsible for the federal economic development agency for Southern Ontario), Kamal Khera (seniors), Pascale St-Onge (sport), plus the return to cabinet of Petitpas Taylor (official languages) **Notable new roles:** Housing became a new portfolio, as did mental health and addictions, creating new roles for Hussen and Bennett, respectively; several ministers assumed new duties, including Anand (national defence), Duclos (health), Gould (families, children, and social development), Guilbeault (environment and climate change), Joly (foreign affairs), Mendicino (public safety), and Rodriguez (heritage)	39
31 August 2022	Jaczek and Tassi swap roles	39
26 July 2023	A significant mid-mandate reorganization of cabinet. **Out:** Alghabra, Bennett, Jaczek, and Murray (all of whom had decided not to seek re-election), plus Fortier, Lametti, and Mendicino **In:** Gary Anandasangaree (Crown-Indigenous relations), Terry Beech (citizens' services), Soraya Martinez Ferrada (tourism), Ya'ara Saks (mental health and addictions), Jenna Sudds (families, children, and social development), Rechie Valdez (small business), Arif Virani (justice and attorney general of Canada) **Notable new roles:** Anand (Treasury Board), Blair (defence), Fraser (housing, infrastructure, and communities), Gould (House leader), Holland (health), St-Onge (heritage)	39

(Continued)

Table 20.2. (Continued)

Date	Results	Size of cabinet
8 January 2024	**Out:** Gould temporarily stepped away from cabinet (parental leave until end of July 2024) **In:** In Gould's absence, Steven MacKinnon was sworn in as House leader	40
19 July 2024	**Out:** O'Regan resigned from cabinet, choosing not to run in the next election **Notable new role:** MacKinnon (labour and seniors)	39
19 September 2024	**Out:** Rodriguez resigned from cabinet to sit as an Independent MP, before entering the race to lead the Quebec Liberal Party	38
20 November 2024	**Out:** Boissonnault resigned from cabinet in the wake of controversy surrounding his former business activities	37
16 December 2024	**Out:** Freeland resigned from cabinet amid rumours of a cabinet shuffle that could have seen her removed from her role at finance **Notable new role:** LeBlanc (finance)	36
20 December 2024	Another large reorganization of cabinet, to fill vacancies from resignations and replace ministers who had signalled their intention not to run in the next election. **Out:** Bibeau, Fraser, Qualtrough, Tassi, and Vandal **In:** Rachel Bendayan (official languages), Élisabeth Brière (national revenue), Terry Duguid (sport and minister responsible for Prairies Economic Development Canada), Nathaniel Erskine-Smith (housing, infrastructure and communities), Darren Fisher (veterans affairs), David McGuinty (public safety), Ruby Sahota (democratic institutions and minister responsible for the federal economic development agency for Southern Ontario), Joanne Thompson (seniors) **Notable new roles:** Petitpas Taylor became president of the treasury board; MacKinnon moved to the newly reconstituted employment, workforce development and labour; internal trade was resurrected and given to Anand (LeBlanc held the role from July 2018 to November 2019); Anandasangaree added minister responsible for the Canadian Northern Economic Development Agency to his duties)	39
6 January 2025	Trudeau announced his intention to step down as prime minister and Liberal Party leader following a leadership race	39
19 January 2025	**Out:** Gould resigned from cabinet to run for Liberal Party leadership	38

Note: Not intended to be a definitive list

all instigated by US President Trump.[39] When the new cabinet was unveiled in November 2019, Freeland was appointed deputy prime minister and intergovernmental affairs minister; as deputy prime minister, her office was symbolically and strategically located in the same building as the PMO.

Cabinet in the West Block and the Age of COVID-19

The physical infrastructure hosting the political executive underwent some change itself. In 2017, Prime Minister Trudeau announced that the Langevin Block – a large building located across from the Parliament Buildings – would henceforth be known as the Office of the Prime Minister and the Privy Council, due to its namesake's role in advocating for an Indigenous residential schools system while minister of public works in the Macdonald cabinet.[40] The massive renovation of the Parliament Buildings required considerable planning, given that the cabinet room in Centre Block would be shut down and relocated to the upper floor of the West Block. PCO and PMO participated in space layout conversations with architects, such as sorting how to have food delivered without interrupting the flow of cabinet deliberations. The cabinet table has an oblong shape which enables a minister in a wheelchair to have a dedicated seat at the narrow part. In Centre Block, it was easy for journalists to intercept ministers, who could not walk to the House without passing media first. In West Block, a perimeter keeps journalists at bay, and a door was installed so that after a cabinet meeting, the prime minister could get to a private elevator without interacting with them. As well, there is now a generous lounge instead of the small anteroom in the Centre Block for political staff and public servants waiting to be summoned. The new cabinet room was in use for a little more than a year before COVID-19 prompted widescale changes in how Parliament operated.

The arrival of COVID-19 in Canada early 2020 brought with it a range of challenges. The post-election cabinet agenda was thrown off course by the need for a broad and coordinated government response. Cabinet meetings were held online, some of which lasted longer than seven hours, and massive new and untested government programs whizzed through cabinet and Parliament. The prime minister took centre stage in daily media availabilities outside his home at Rideau Cottage – sometimes referred to by pundits as "the morning show"[41] – to brief Canadians on the latest government developments, ranging from new financial supports to vaccine procurement to public health updates.

The pandemic necessitated widescale changes in how cabinet operated. The technology used by cabinet ministers needed to be upgraded to allow for more virtual meetings, as one example. Some of this work was already well underway. The move toward an "e-cabinet" had begun in 2016, involving new technology, more secure networks, and the ability for ministers to review cabinet documents on secure tablets. A group of ministers was involved in testing the

Image 20.2. Governor General Julie Payette leads Canada's first virtual swearing-in for cabinet ministers during a January 2021 shuffle

Source: Adam Scotti.

technology, including Qualtrough, whose visual impairment required accommodations that included providing her with documents and electronic devices formatted to a larger font. A small number of ministers, including younger ones, resisted transitioning away from scribbling remarks on sticky notes and paper copies of cabinet documents. As the pandemic progressed, most of the parties in the House of Commons agreed to temporarily adopt a blended sitting model that allowed for some in-person sittings, supplemented by virtual meetings. In January 2021, one year after the first confirmed COVID-19 case in Canada, the Trudeau government recorded the first virtual swearing-in for new ministers as part of a small cabinet shuffle (see image 20.2).

One of the cabinet's decisions during the pandemic was the allocation of over $900 million for WE Charity to run a student grant program, which was cancelled after controversy about the Trudeau family's ties to the charity. Bill Morneau, Trudeau's long-time finance minister, left cabinet following an admission that two years earlier he had accepted a family trip to Africa from WE Charity, though reports suggested the real reason for his departure was because he disagreed with the prime minister over pandemic spending and was frustrated about the interference of PMO staff on policy decisions.[42] Morneau's frustration with PMO and other key players was echoed in a June 2022 speech, in which the former finance minister suggested that when addressing economic challenges, "real solutions are more likely to be found around the boardroom table or in universities and think tanks than at the cabinet table."[43] This theme was echoed in Morneau's 2023 book, in which he spoke candidly about the prime minister's management style. He recalls that at the outset, Trudeau informed the cabinet that "all ministries would be considered equal in power and status."[44] From Morneau's perspective, as time wore on, Trudeau's emphasis on public performance over forging personal relationships with his ministers was a recurring managerial problem when problems arose, and the PMO exercised daily involvement in ministerial work, to the frustration of ministers. Wilson-Raybould levelled similar accusations in her memoirs,[45] as did Garneau.[46]

The WE Charity scandal was the latest in a series of investigations by the federal ethics commissioner – this one clearing the prime minister but implicating Morneau – and delivered another knock on transparency when Parliament was prorogued to avoid scrutiny by the Commons ethics committee. The government framed it as a necessary "reset" given its plans to address COVID-19.[47]

When Morneau stepped down, Freeland was once again asked to step up, becoming the federal cabinet's first woman finance minister in August 2020. She was tasked with managing Canada's recovery in the wake of a global pandemic that had ravaged the Canadian economy and fuelled a sharp increase in government debt. Freeland had developed such influence that she was dubbed the "minister of everything,"[48] harkening back to the power of C.D. Howe in the 1950s. In the days following the 2021 election, hers was the only name immediately confirmed to cabinet. Her special status was denoted by the prime minister when he announced, four weeks before the rest of cabinet was unveiled, that she would stay on as deputy prime minister and finance minister.

The prime minister placed considerable trust in a small inner cabinet. After the 2021 election that delivered another minority government to the Liberals, three of the highest profile cabinet posts – finance, foreign affairs, and defence – went to women, reasserting the Trudeau government's feminist inclinations. All three ministers rose within the ranks but followed different cabinet arcs. Freeland had competently managed a succession of portfolios, including international trade and foreign affairs. Mélanie Joly had faltered in heritage and was sent to tourism in a move widely regarded as a demotion,[49] but resurrected her role as a trustworthy Quebec adviser and was rewarded with foreign affairs after the election. Anita Anand was such a steady hand in procuring personal protective equipment and vaccines during the pandemic that she was promoted to take on culture change in the Canadian military, ultimately overseeing the Department of National Defence when Russia invaded Ukraine.

Cabinet itself was reshaped following the 2021 minority win. Despite the loss of two cabinet ministers who failed to win re-election (Maryam Monsef and Bernadette Jordan), cabinet grew to 39 ministers – nearly a third larger than the group named to cabinet when the Liberals formed a majority government. The new lineup saw eight new faces added and three ministers dropped, with many senior ministers assigned to new posts (about a third retained their previous roles and one, Pablo Rodriguez, returned to heritage, where he had been minister prior to the 2019 election). Media attention focused largely on the three ministers who were let go. Marc Garneau, an MP first elected in 2008 alongside Trudeau, was dropped from foreign affairs; Bardish Chagger, the minister of diversity, inclusion, and youth was out; as was Jim Carr who, in an attempt to bolster western representation around the cabinet table, had served as special representative for the Prairies. Harjit Sajjan, once seen by many as a rising star, remained but was moved from defence to international development, following a series of missteps in handling sexual misconduct allegations in Canada's military.

The 2021 restructuring also saw new portfolios added that reflected emerging challenges for Canadians. In response to rapidly rising house prices that made home ownership impossible for many Canadians, a new minister of housing role was created (headed by Ahmed Hussen), and in light of an ongoing opioid crisis and mental health difficulties brought on by the pandemic, a minister for mental health and addictions (Carolyn Bennett) joined the cabinet lineup. COVID-19 and natural disasters had focused attention on emergency preparedness and public safety, which became two separate roles. Gone from the new lineup was the curiously named and widely derided "minister of middle-class prosperity."[50] Mona Fortier, who went on to helm Treasury Board, was the only person ever to hold that title.

Cabinet Reset

The prime minister's interest in stability was perhaps most evident in 2022 when he struck a confidence and supply agreement with the New Democratic Party – an arrangement that held the promise of propping up the Liberal government until 2025. By summer of the following year– down in the polls and two years into a second minority government – Trudeau announced his largest mid-mandate shuffle yet, comparable in scope to the post-election shuffles. The communications rollout in July 2023 was like that of November 2015, with the entire ministry invited to Rideau Hall to swear their oaths irrespective of whether or not they were changing portfolios, followed by a group photo.

Pre-shuffle leaks emphasized that the reassignments would put strong communicators in key roles, to better deliver the government's message.[51] Following the shuffle, government sources shifted their framing slightly, suggesting that the primary aim was to put cabinet's strongest performers on files that need attention, particularly economic matters. Critics found neither explanation satisfying, arguing that this reset amounted to an admission that files had been mishandled, while some in the media pointed to the Liberals' flagging popularity, numerous ministerial missteps, a worsening affordability crisis, and the need to blunt the leadership aspirations of ministers interested in becoming the next party leader as more credible explanations for the sizeable shuffle. For his part, Trudeau spoke of "fresh energy" and the value of "having a renewed team with a range of new voices, with new skills and experience, (and) new challenges for our strongest ministers."[52] Around the cabinet table, the core team remained intact, including Freeland at Finance and Joly at Foreign Affairs. Seven ministers were dropped, seven backbenchers were appointed, and most other ministers changed portfolios. Notable ministers assigned new positions were Bill Blair (defence), Karina Gould (House leader), Ahmed Hussen (international development), Mark Holland (health), Marc Miller (immigration), Pablo Rodriguez (transport and Quebec lieutenant), Harjit Sajjan (emergency preparedness), Pascale St-Onge (heritage – the fifth consecutive Quebecker in that portfolio), and, surprisingly, the perceived demotion of Anita Anand (from defence to treasury board). Asked about this change in ministerial responsibilities, Anand said that "the prime minister asked me to be a member of his core economic team," an argument bolstered by later reports that, in line with a Budget 2023 commitment, she had asked her cabinet colleagues to find $15 billion in government spending cuts by the fall.[53] The biggest structural change was moving Housing into Infrastructure, leaving Sean Fraser as the new minister of housing, infrastructure, and communities. Fraser was seen as one of the government's rising stars, and the move signalled that Trudeau saw housing as an important issue, especially among young Canadians.

For the first time, Diane Lebouthillier was shuffled (to fisheries). Several other ministers had additional responsibilities tacked onto their roles. Government whip Steven MacKinnon would later be appointed House leader when Gould took parental leave, and then moved to labour and seniors when Seamus O'Regan stepped down.

Some of the ministers who were moved to the backbenches did not plan on seeking re-election, notably party stalwart Carolyn Bennett, but it is an open question as to whether they were removed from cabinet because they told the prime minister they did not plan to run or they chose not to run because they were removed from cabinet. The removal of Marco Mendicino from Public Safety was widely expected given multiple controversies, particularly his office's bungling of communications surrounding the prison transfer of serial killer Paul Bernardo, but David Lametti was surprised to be purged from Justice. The moves made way for new recruits and renewed energy, but failed to turn around growing public dissatisfaction with Trudeau and his government.

The cabinet reset harkened to the 2015 original focus on identity and diversity. Arif Virani (justice) became the first Ismaili Muslim to serve in that role. Rechie Valdez (small business) became the first Filipina in a federal cabinet. Ya'ara Saks (mental health and addictions) provided a voice for the Jewish community, as did Gary Anandasangaree (Crown-Indigenous relations) for Sri Lankan Tamils and Soraya Martinez Ferrada (tourism) for Chileans. The other new appointees were Jenna Sudds (families) and Terry Beech (the newly created citizens' services). These rookie ministers were generally younger than the departing ministers. Anandasangaree, Beech and Virani were part of the "Class of 2015," and had earned reputations as hard workers, appearing near the top of the internal "leaderboards" on door knocks in their ridings over the past few elections. The geographic breakdown stayed the same, so this shuffle seemed more about diaspora politics and priorities than regional ones. Some unnamed Liberal MPs complained about the changes, saying that by prioritizing tokenism over merit Trudeau had weakened morale in the caucus.[54]

By 2024, sunny ways had given way to gathering clouds. Lagging the Conservatives and leader Pierre Poilievre in the polls, the prime minister initially resisted calls to again shuffle his cabinet following a shocking June by-election defeat to the Conservatives in Toronto—St. Paul's, long considered a Liberal stronghold.[55] In September, the NDP abruptly cancelled the supply and confidence agreement, placing the unpopular Liberal minority government in a perilous state of regularly facing tests of confidence. That same month, another fortress riding fell, this time in Montreal, when the seat opened up by Lametti's departure was won by the Bloc Québécois.

In addition to the Liberal Party's persistent weakness in the polls—and perhaps because of it—2024 also brought several changes to the cabinet. O'Regan resigned in the summer, signaling his intention not to run in 2025 election; MacKinnon took on his responsibilities for labour and seniors following Gould's return from parental leave. In September, Rodriguez left cabinet to sit as an Independent so that he could pursue the leadership of the Quebec Liberal party; his responsibilities at transport and his role as Quebec lieutenant went to Anand and Duclos, respectively. In mid-November, following months of negative headlines surrounding his former business activities and shifting claims about Indigenous identity, Boissonnault stepped down from cabinet, with his duties temporarily assigned to Petitpas Taylor and leaving Alberta without a minister. In rapid succession, other ministers indicated that their time in federal politics would end in 2025: Bibeau, Qualtrough, Tassi, and Vandal all opted not to re-up.

In mid-December, Sean Fraser cited the desire to spend more time with his young family as his reason to leave cabinet, but his news conference was interrupted, and quickly overshadowed, by the explosive news that Chrystia Freeland was immediately quitting as deputy prime minister and finance minister. Her blistering resignation letter, issued on social media hours before she was to deliver the government's long-awaited fall economic statement, kicked off a whirlwind day that saw Karina Gould table the documents in the House without a speech, and Dominic LeBlanc hastily sworn in as finance minister. In her letter, Freeland said that she "no longer credibly enjoy(ed)" the prime minister's confidence. The shocking resignation came amid threats from the incoming Trump administration to impose tariffs of 25% on Canada and Mexico. News reports suggested that in an online video call days before, Trudeau had informed his finance minister that following the economic statement former Bank of Canada governor Mark Carney would be installed as her replacement, and that she would be shuffled to a role focusing on Canada-US relations, but without the usual public service and staffing supports. Freeland viewed this move as a demotion.

A sizeable shuffle took place on December 20, which some pundits labelled a "caretaker cabinet" given the increasing calls for the prime minister to resign and the prospects of the Liberal government nearing an end. The reorganization was prompted by a build-up of vacancies created by ministers who had resigned and others who would not be running in the next election (Table 20.2). In that shuffle, four veteran ministers were given new roles, and eight newcomers were welcomed into the fold. As with the July 2023 changes, attention was paid to gender balance, regional representation, and the incoming ministers' skills and interests. Rachel Bendayan, a former ministerial chief of staff who was elected in 2019, took on official languages while Nathaniel Erskine-Smith, who had run for leadership of the Ontario Liberals and publicly announced he would not run again federally, became the new minister of housing. The other new ministers included Élisabeth Brière (national revenue), Terry Duguid (sport and a regional economic development agency), Darren Fisher (veterans), David McGuinty (public safety), Ruby Sahota (democratic institutions and a regional economic development agency), and Joanne Thompson (seniors). This version of the cabinet included six ministers who were part of the original swearing in ceremony in 2015 (Duclos, Hajdu, Joly, Lebouthillier, MacAulay and Sajjan).

Prime Minister Trudeau made few public comments in the wake of Freeland's resignation. At the Liberal Party's year-end holiday party, he assured the crowd that "Like most families, sometimes we have fights around the holidays. But of course, like most families, we find our way through it." He was present for the swearing in of new members of cabinet but did not speak to the media, except for brief remarks following a cabinet meeting focused on Canada-US relations. The same day, the NDP issued a public letter in which they promised to bring forward a motion of non-confidence to take down the Liberal government. His office cancelled all his scheduled year-end interviews.

As the year drew to a close, Trudeau's future as Canada's 29th prime minister was in doubt. Individual members of Parliament, and eventually regional caucuses representing elected Liberals in Atlantic Canada, Quebec, and Ontario, called for his resignation. Heading into the holiday break the prime minister was said to be reflecting on his future.

On January 6, 2025, Trudeau met with the governor general to seek prorogation of the House until late March. The request was granted, and later that morning media were summoned to the front steps of Rideau Cottage where Trudeau announced that he would step down as prime minister and Liberal Party leader following a leadership race. The visuals of that moment were stark. Unlike the 2015 swearing in, which saw Trudeau surrounded by enthusiastic new ministers, he was alone at the podium. The era of "a cabinet that looks like Canada" concluded on March 9, 2025, when he submitted his resignation to the governor general and Mark Carney was sworn in as Canada's 24th prime minister—appointing a streamlined cabinet that included Freeland but did not uphold his predecessor's commitment to gender parity.

Conclusion

Prime Minister Justin Trudeau's approach to statecraft—while firmly rooted in his own personal appeal and an enduring centralization of power—evolved since the sunny November day when he and his first cabinet walked together up to Rideau Hall. His party's historic win in 2015 gave him an abundance of talent to choose from, but much of it was untested in parliamentary or executive roles. In some ways, this was a benefit: the collective lack of experience gave the new government the confidence to try new things in and outside of the House. However, he faced accusations that too much power was concentrated in his office; lost several key ministers along the way (with Freeland's stunning resignation setting in motion his own resignation announcement); and at times struggled to keep the government's agenda moving forward, especially during the final months of his tenure.

From 2019 on, the size of Trudeau's Cabinets remained relatively constant. Roughly an equal number of cabinet shuffles happened in Trudeau's last two minority governments as took place during his initial majority government. Two notable attempts to "reset" the composition of cabinet occurred in 2023 and 2024, at a time when the prime minister and his government were facing serious headwinds in the polls, with public support for Opposition Conservatives holding steady. From beginning to end, Trudeau's closest advisor remained: in 2023 Katie Telford became the longest-serving chief of staff to any Canadian prime minister since the role was created in 1979.

It will take years for scholars and observers to settle on Justin Trudeau's legacy. He exceeded the time in office of predecessors such as Mulroney, Borden, St-Laurent, Diefenbaker, and Pearson, and he capably steered cabinet and its committees through the monumental challenges wrought by a global pandemic. However, as his personal popularity declined, his desire to lead the Liberals into a fourth consecutive national contest was not enough to overcome an entrenched public desire for change. His time as prime minister, and his modern approach to statecraft, had come to an end.

NOTES

1   Jeni Armstrong was lead speech writer in the Prime Minister's Office from 2015
     to 2018 and director of communications to the minister of finance from 2018 to
     2020. Dan Arnold was director of research, advertising, and correspondence in
     the PMO from 2015 to 2021. Due to space limitations, some news stories are not
     cited, but are available from the authors upon request.
2   Michael Wernick, unstructured telephone interview, 23 June 2022. Relatedly,
     see Michael Wernick, *Governing Canada: A Guide to the Tradecraft of Politics*
     (Vancouver: University of British Columbia Press, 2021).
3   Laura Ryckewaert, "Hill Media, Liberals Settle on Cabinet 'Outs,'" *Hill Times*, 14
     December 2015, 19.
4   Pauline Dakin, "Scientists, Ministers Get Green Light to Speak under Trudeau,"
     CBC News, 6 November 2015, https://www.cbc.ca/news/canada/nova-scotia
     /scientists-ministers-get-green-light-to-speak-under-trudeau-1.3307679.
5   Susan Delacourt, "How Policy Is Being Made under the New Liberal Government,"
     Policy Options, 26 April 2016, https://policyoptions.irpp.org/magazines/april-2016
     /how-policy-is-being-made-under-the-new-liberal-government/.
6   Alexander Panetta, "The Trump Unit: Inside the PMO's NAFTA Squad," *CTV
     News*, 20 August 2017, https://www.ctvnews.ca/politics/the-trump-unit-inside-the
     -pmo-s-nafta-squad-1.3553537.
7   Alex Marland, "Strategic Management of Media Relations: Communications
     Centralization and Spin in the Government of Canada," *Canadian Public Policy*
     43, no. 1 (2017): 36–49.
8   Mark Gollom, "Limiting Access for News Photographers a 'Worrisome' Trend,"
     CBC News, 24 August 2016, https://www.cbc.ca/news/justin-trudeau-tragically
     -hip-canadian-press-photos-access-1.3732598#:~:text=The%20Tragically%20
     Hip%20concert%20promoters,trying%20to%20control%20their%20image.
9   Abbas Rana, "PM Instructs Cabinet to Attend All Caucus Meetings, Tells Grit
     Caucus Any Communications from Butts, Telford Should Be Considered as
     Coming from Him," *Hill Times*, 7 December 2016, 1.
10   Penny Collenette, "Are Cabinet Leaks Really a New Norm?," *Toronto Star*, 21
     October 2018.
11   "Justin Trudeau Would Loosen PMO Control, Reverse Trend Started by Father,"
     CBC News, 8 September 2015, https://www.cbc.ca/news/politics/canada-election
     -2015-justin-trudeau-interview-1.3219479.
12   Laura Ryckewaert, "Trudeau's Smaller Cabinet Could 'Frustrate' Numerous
     Liberal MPs in Long Term," *Hill Times*, 1 November 2015, https://www.hilltimes
     .com/2015/11/01/trudeaus-smaller-cabinet-could-frustrate-numerous-liberal-mps
     -in-long-term/34004.
13   Joan Bryden, "Federal Ministers to Share Student Dorms at Liberal Cabinet
     Retreat in Sudbury," *Global News*, 19 August 2016, https://globalnews.ca

/news/2891744/federal-ministers-to-share-student-dorms-at-liberal-cabinet-retreat
-in-sudbury/.

14 Aaron Wherry, *Promise and Peril: Justin Trudeau in Power* (Toronto: HarperCollins,
2019), 24.

15 Jocelyn Coulon, *Un selfie avec Justin Trudeau: Regard critique sur la diplomatie
du premier ministre* (Montreal: Québec-Amériques, 2018).

16 Benjamin Lopez Steven, "Former Trudeau Cabinet Minister Criticizes PMO over
Access to Prime Minister," *CBC News*, 29 September 2024, https://www.cbc.ca/news
/politics/former-trudeau-cabinet-minister-criticizes-pmo-over-access-to-prime
-minister-1.7337629; Bill Morneau, with John Lawrence Reynolds, *Where to from Here:
A Path to Canadian Prosperity* (Toronto: ECW Press, 2023); and Jody Wilson-Raybould,
Indian in the Cabinet: Speaking Truth to Power (Toronto: HarperCollins, 2021).

17 Wherry, *Promise and Peril*, 59.

18 Catherine McIntyre, "The Myth of Justin Trudeau's Youthful Government,"
Maclean's, 13 November 2017, https://www.macleans.ca/politics/ottawa/the
-myth-of-justin-trudeaus-youthful-government/.

19 Peter Mazereeuw, "Bigger Workload, Shorter Timelines a Growing 'Burden,' Says
PCO," *Hill Times*, 22 March 2017, https://www.hilltimes.com/2017/03/22/bigger
-workload-shorter-timelines-growing-burden-says-pco/99986.

20 Privy Council Office, *Open and Accountable Government*, Ottawa, 2015, https://www
.pm.gc.ca/en/news/backgrounders/2015/11/27/open-and-accountable-government.

21 Kenny William Ie, "Ministerial Mandate Letters and Co-ordination in the
Canadian Executive," *Canadian Journal of Political Science* 56, no. 4 (2023):
811-831.

22 Matthew Mendelsohn, "What We Do at the Results & Delivery Unit – and Why?,"
Government of Canada, 4 December 2017, archived 9 January 2024, https://web
.archive.org/web/20240109143633/https://open.canada.ca/en/blog/what-do-we-do
-at-the-results-delivery-unit-why.

23 Stephen Maher, "Canada's Cabinet Still Has No Official Marching Orders,"
Maclean's, 8 December 2021, https://macleans.ca/politics/canadas-cabinet-still
-has-no-official-marching-orders/.

24 Darren Major, "Trudeau Says Cabinet Will Look at Policies to Address Systemic
Racism," *CBC News*, 8 July 2020, https://www.cbc.ca/news/politics/trudeau
-cabinet-examine-systemic-racism-reform-1.5642003.

25 Ryckewaert, "Trudeau's Smaller Cabinet."

26 Laura Ryckewaert, "'Streamlining' of Cabinet Committees an Effort to Shore Up
Priorities before 2019, Say Strategists," *Hill Times*, 3 September 2018, https://
www.hilltimes.com/2018/09/03/biotechnology-243/156426.

27 "Cabinet Committees," *Hill Times*, 4 November 2015, https://www.hilltimes
.com/2015/11/04/cabinet-committees-2/34063.

28 Kenny William Ie, "Representation and Ministerial Influence on Cabinet Committees
in Canada," *Canadian Journal of Political Science* 54, no. 3 (2021): 615–36.

29 Colby Cosh, "The Mystery behind Trudeau's Two Climate Change Committees," *National Post*, 15 December 2021, https://nationalpost.com/opinion/colby-cosh -the-mystery-behind-trudeaus-two-climate-change-committees.

30 Nick Taylor-Vaisey and Zi-Ann Lum, "The Most Important Committees You've Never Heard Of," *Ottawa Playbook*, 6 December 2021, https://www.politico.com /newsletters/ottawa-playbook/2021/12/06/the-most-important-committees-youve -never-heard-of-495331.

31 "Prime Minister Announces New Task Force to Improve Government Services for Canadians," Prime Minister of Canada Justin Trudeau (website), 25 June 2022, https://pm.gc.ca/en/news/news-releases/2022/06/25/prime-minister-announces -new-task-force-improve-government-services.

32 Paul E.J. Thomas and J.P. Lewis, "Executive Creep in Canadian Provincial Legislatures," *Canadian Journal of Political Science* 52, no. 2 (2019): 363–83.

33 Rachel Aiello, "In a Backtrack, Liberals Move to Reinstate Parliamentary Secretaries' Power at Committees," *CTV News*, 11 December 2019, https://www .ctvnews.ca/politics/in-a-backtrack-liberals-move-to-reinstate-parliamentary -secretaries-power-at-committees-1.4726145?cache=.

34 Alex Marland, "The SNC-Lavalin Affair: Justin Trudeau, Ministerial Resignations and Party Discipline," *Canadian Studies*, no. 89 (2020): 151–77. See also Patrice Dutil, "Crisis of Cabinet Government," *Dorchester Review* 12, no. 1 (Spring– Summer 2022): 40–9.

35 Katherine Laidlaw, "Justin Trudeau's Feminist Brand Is Imploding," *Atlantic*, 12 March 2019, https://www.theatlantic.com/international/archive/2019/03/canada -trudeau-feminism-wilson-raybauld/584677/.

36 Wherry, *Promise and Peril*, 66.

37 Wherry, *Promise and Peril*, 57.

38 Abbas Rana, "'We're Really Getting Important Now,'" *Hill Times*, 25 March 2019, 1.

39 See, e.g., Emily Rauhala, "How Canada's Feminist Foreign Minister Cut a Trade Deal with Trump," *Washington Post*, 29 November 2018, https://www .washingtonpost.com/world/the_americas/how-canadas-feminist-foreign -minister-cut-a-trade-deal-with-trump/2018/11/29/5168f9b4-edba-11e8-8b47 -bd0975fd6199_story.html.

40 Kristy Kirkup, "Father of Confederation's Name Stripped from Prime Minister's Office Building," *CTV News*, 21 June 2017, https://www.ctvnews.ca/politics /father-of-confederation-s-name-stripped-from-prime-minister-s-office-building -1.3469526.

41 John Ivison, "It's Time to Cancel Trudeau's COVID-19 'Morning Show' and Get Back to Parliament," *National Post*, 21 May 2020, https://nationalpost.com/ opinion/john-ivison-its-time-to-cancel-the-justin-trudeau-covid-19-morning-show.

42 Christopher Nardi, "Morneau Quits after Rift with Trudeau," *Windsor Star*, 18 August 2020, 1.

43 Barbara Shecter, "Bill Morneau Says Business Community Was Unhelpful, Targets Political Divisiveness in Speech," *Calgary Herald*, 1 June 2022, https://calgaryherald .com/news/bill-morneau-says-business-community-was-unhelpful-targets-political -divisiveness-in-speech/wcm/6a8b95f1-f6ed-4ebc-80d0-0cc4388f2be2.

44 Bill Morneau, with John Lawrence Reynolds, *Where to from Here: A Path to Canadian Prosperity* (Toronto: ECW Press, 2023), 81.

45 Wilson-Raybould, *Indian in the Cabinet*.

46 *A Most Extraordinary Ride: Space, Politics, and the Pursuit of a Canadian Dream* (Toronto: Signal, 2024)

47 Kathleen Harris and Aaron Wherry, "Parliament Prorogued until Sept. 23 as Trudeau Government Reels from WE Charity Controversy," *CBC News*, 18 August 2020, https://www.cbc.ca/news/politics/liberal-government-trudeau -prorogue-government-1.5690515.

48 Trevor Cole, "Chrystia Freeland, Minister of Everything, Has Big Plans for Canada's Economic Future," *Globe and Mail*, 23 February 2022, https://www .theglobeandmail.com/business/rob-magazine/article-chrystia-freeland-interview -canada-economy-future/.

49 Graeme Hamilton, "Once a Rising Star, Mélanie Joly Demoted after Missteps Hurt Liberals in Quebec," *National Post*, 18 July 2018, https://nationalpost.com/news /politics/once-a-rising-star-melanie-joly-demoted-after-hurting-liberals-in-quebec.

50 Jennifer Wells, "Is the New Federal 'Minister of Middle Class Prosperity' for Real?," *Toronto Star*, 23 November 2019, https://www.thestar.com/business/opinion /2019/11/23/is-the-new-federal-minister-of-middle-class-prosperity-for-real.html.

51 Tonda MacCharles, "Insiders Reveal the Real Goal behind Justin Trudeau's Imminent Cabinet Shuffle," *Toronto Star*, last modified 21 July 2023, https://www .thestar.com/politics/federal/insiders-reveal-the-real-goal-behind-justin-trudeau-s -imminent-cabinet-shuffle/article_5f803be6-67ee-57d5-8b60-78d36214e87c.html.

52 Alex Boutilier, "Will Trudeau's Cabinet Shuffle Be Enough for Canadians Wanting 'Something New'?," *Global News*, 26 July 2023, https://globalnews.ca /news/9858641/trudeau-cabinet-shuffle-something-new/.

53 Catharine Tunney and David Cochrane, "Anand Says She Doesn't See Move from Defence to Treasury Board as a Demotion," *CBC News*, 27 July 2023, https:// www.cbc.ca/news/politics/anand-treasury-board-1.6919926.

54 Abbas Rana, "Some Backbench Liberal MPs 'Livid' with Trudeau's Cabinet Shuffle, Say PMO 'Couldn't Have Done a Better Job at Undermining Caucus Morale,'" *Hill Times*, 7 August 2023, https://www.hilltimes.com/story/2023/08/07 /im-so-pissed-off-some-backbench-liberal-mps-livid-with-trudeaus-cabinet-shuffle- saying-pmo-couldnt-have-done-a-better-job-at-undermining-caucus-mor/394422/.

55 Vassy Kapelos and Rachel Aiello, "Trudeau Cabinet to Meet Friday as Speculation Around a Shuffle Swirls," *CTV News*, 17 July 2024. https://www.ctvnews .ca/politics/trudeau-cabinet-to-meet-friday-as-speculation-around-a-shuffle -swirls-1.6967575.

Conclusion: The Mysterious Grammar of Canadian Statecraft

STEPHEN AZZI AND PATRICE DUTIL

Jean Chrétien thought he had seen it all. He entered Parliament in 1963, at age twenty-nine. Two years later, he was parliamentary secretary to the prime minister. After one year in that role and then another as parliamentary secretary to the minister of finance, he joined the cabinet of Prime Minister Lester B. Pearson in April 1967. Twenty-six years later, after serving in nine different portfolios, he was named prime minister, without a doubt the man best prepared for the position in Canadian history. The job had no mysteries to him, as he had seen leaders as different as Pearson, Pierre Trudeau, and John Turner in action and had observed John Diefenbaker, Joe Clark, Brian Mulroney, and Kim Campbell from close range. "The power really is with the prime minister," he casually offered in *Straight from the Heart*, his first volume of memoirs, published eight years before he reached the top of the proverbial greasy pole: "Backbenchers are frustrated because they think that all the decisions are made by the cabinet, but ministers feel a similar frustration.... There are no votes in cabinet.... There is a discussion, and then there is a decision. In theory the prime minister makes all the decisions." But Chrétien added a qualification: prime ministers who are not sensitive to their followers "will not survive long."[1] He was prescient; he suffered the fate he had foretold. Prime ministers in Canada are very powerful indeed – until they are not. It is not predictable.

They have one thing in common: every prime minister since 1867 has been the central figure in the Canadian polity. Many journalists and scholars have deplored the prime minister's dominance over cabinet, seeing it as a recent feature in Ottawa. Others – and this is eloquently shown by the neglect of prime ministerial studies – have considered that the role of individual prime ministers has been negligible and that the social and economic forces that pressed the national government were far more important. Yet, as this book demonstrates in chapter after chapter, the prime minister has been pre-eminent in making key decisions from the country's earliest days. John A. Macdonald chose ministers and deputy ministers, controlled the cabinet agenda, and made the key decisions when cabinet was hesitant. Every prime minister has followed suit. To proceed only by consensus is not to govern at all.

In the Westminster tradition, prime ministers are the most important actors in shaping the country's statecraft. They have moulded the institutional structure of government – the cabinet, government departments, agencies, and commissions – and in turn, those have provided the parameters of prime ministerial action. Prime ministers enjoy a wide range of discretion and they have demonstrated an equally wide range of approaches to their statecraft.

As the chapters in this book have shown, here are no strict rules to follow in Canadian statecraft. There are conventions and there are precedents, and then there are breakthroughs. There are also personalities, each vastly different from the other. For this reason, history is key to understanding the position as it is practised today, because it is founded on actions taken yesterday, last month, last year, and well over a hundred years ago. Statecraft amounts to a mysterious grammar of political ability conjugated with administrative competence as well as the soft skills of collegiality and the ability to convince and to win confidence.

The Political Test

The study of statecraft reveals how prime ministers win and lose. As obvious as it is elusive, political success is the ultimate test of statecraft in a democracy. By definition, individuals accede to the position of prime minister because they have won. They have found the means to be popular enough to be entrusted with the privilege of occupying the position. But that is the relatively easy part. They must then consistently show promise of future victories, as there is little patience for those who cannot demonstrate that quality. Every day is a plebiscite among caucus members and cabinet colleagues on whether the prime minister can win. The task for incumbents is always to remain sufficiently popular to convince a majority of parliamentarians to support them. The Progressive Conservative Party was so fraught by this fear that a nickname was given to its condition, the Tory Syndrome, but it also applies to the Liberal Party to some degree.[2] (It does not apply to the New Democratic Party, as it has never won the right to form government at the federal level. New Democrats have been tolerant of their leadership, even if victory is elusive.)

The task of winning has changed considerably since the late 1950s, first with the rise of television and of a more adversarial press, then with the onset of cable television and 24/7 television coverage, and finally with the advent of social media. Although not an object of study in this volume, the relationship with the media was tricky for all prime ministers, but it can be said that it was managed very differently until the Second World War, when prime ministers could reliably count on the support of newspapers owned by partisans. The spread of television in the 1950s and of an impatient and adversarial media during the 1960s made political success all the more unpredictable. Few prime ministers have had much patience for the media in this modern environment. Diefenbaker seemed at war constantly. Pearson had his troubles, even with the Liberal-leaning newspapers. Pierre Trudeau's approach was largely adversarial. Brian Mulroney was initially much more favourable, but he quickly reversed his views. Jean Chrétien did not seem to particularly care but made sure his staff was attuned to the evolving media environment. Paul Martin seemed to follow Chrétien's habits but was not as agile. Stephen Harper displayed an antagonistic attitude from the beginning, never believing that he would receive fair treatment from the Ottawa press corps. His successor, Justin Trudeau, also distrusted the media, but was never overtly hostile, and he and his staff swam with relative ease in the social media environment.

The charming era when media management consisted of the prime minister writing a few discrete personal letters and making phone calls to relatively friendly editors is long gone. Since the 1960s, prime ministers have hired media managers to engage with reporters on an hourly basis. Over the past decade, observers have captured the reality that prime ministers now engage in a permanent campaign that invariably consumes enormous amounts of time. They must constantly be concerned with how government positions can be articulated and how to respond almost instantly to comments and criticism.

The test of politics has tried the various personalities in office. Macdonald, Laurier, Diefenbaker, Mulroney, and Chrétien thrived on the campaign trail. Mackenzie King, Louis St-Laurent, Lester B. Pearson, Pierre Trudeau, and Paul Martin, all very good public performers in their best hours, did not relish elections. Mackenzie, Borden, Meighen, and Harper all seemed to hate every minute they spent trying to convince voters. Justin Trudeau seemed happy to be on the campaign trail all the time.

The prime minister's political position has been all the more significant in Canada ever since party leaders have been elected by the party membership. In 1919, Liberals chose a new leader, Mackenzie King, at a party convention; the Conservatives first did the same in 1927. This direct vote has weakened the capacity of ministers and backbench MPs to challenge prime ministers, as the party leader's mandate has come not from cabinet or caucus, but from the rank and file. The prime minister's status is reinforced by the behaviour of the Canadian electorate. Although ballots list the names of a riding's nominees (with their party affiliations since the 1970s), voters tend to think far less of the local candidate than of the party or leader when casting a ballot. This has long created an implicit mandate from voters, enhancing the prime minister's legitimacy. Still, widespread caucus dissatisfaction could always pressure party leaders into resigning. It certainly forced at least three prime ministers to step down: Mackenzie Bowell in 1896, Jean Chrétien in 2003, and Justin Trudeau in 2025. In 2015, the House of Commons passed the Reform Act, legislation introduced by Conservative Michael Chong to give members of Parliament a voice in the distribution of powers between a caucus and the party leader and a process to remove the leader. That procedure was triggered in full view of the public in February 2022, when the Conservative caucus voted to remove its chief, Erin O'Toole. That provision of the Reform Act has yet to be formally deployed against a sitting prime minister.

The Managerial Test

Prime ministers must demonstrate that they can command the administrative tasks of government: that they have the ability to direct people to respond in a timely way to issues that can emerge slowly as well as those that precipitate themselves onto the public agenda. Often, prime ministers are judged by the economic performance of the country, perhaps far more than they should be. Canada, as a trading nation, has consistently been rocketed by American prosperity or rocked by economic downturns that have sparked inflation or caused a depression in the price of commodities. There is little a prime minister can do to counter such continental (or even global) forces.

To manage, Canada's prime ministers have benefitted from a wide range of discretions and resources. They have often been directly involved, having assumed key portfolios over time. Macdonald set the precedent as minister of justice initially, then minister of the interior, as well as superintendent of Indian affairs; Mackenzie was his own minister of public works; Bennett was minister of finance for eighteen months. That practice of a prime minister holding a portfolio ended with Mackenzie King, but he retained the essential function of secretary of state for external affairs until 1946. (Surrendering the portfolio barely concealed the reality is that every Canadian prime minister has played a key role in the development of foreign policy since 1867.)[3]

Statecraft as an expression of public sector management is an elusive skill. It is never assured, and prime ministers must be agile in managing changing environments. Governments routinely fail the test and are then, as a result, defeated at the polls. Experience has not always paid off. Pierre Elliott Trudeau once observed that there was one puzzle he could not resolve:

> The longer that you are in the job of prime minister, the harder you have to work to do your job. With anything else … you get to know the ropes pretty well and it becomes easy. I feel the more you know, the more you have to know, and the more problems come at you. It is certainly not because I do not delegate.[4]

This book has certainly shown that delegation has been a constant for every prime minister. What has changed over the years is the growing scope and complexity of the government's activities. Undertakings by one department have had an increasingly profound impact on the business of other departments. This has required greater coordination among ministers and greater control over the messages they convey to the public, coordination and control that could be exercised only at the centre of government.

Because of the prime minister's central role, and because of the range of options open to a prime minister, governments tend to take on the managerial traits of their leader. This comes with a risk. The four men who succeeded Macdonald had neither the interest, the health, the skill, or the political luck necessary to win yet another election for the Conservatives in 1896 (though they did win the popular vote, they lost the majority Macdonald had secured in 1891). Borden's statesmanship was so fraught that he resorted to trickery to be re-elected in 1917, and his coalition was blown apart in 1921.[5] John Diefenbaker's ministry was indecisive and prone to strife, almost as much as its chief executive. Paul Martin's wide-ranging interests led to a cabinet that similarly pursued multiple priorities at the same time. Vulnerable on so many fronts, it was narrowly defeated in 2006.

Because the prime minister cannot do everything and cannot control everything, the selection of ministers is crucially important. Weak cabinets make for ineffective governments that cannot generate policy solutions to the problems of the age and are unlikely to win re-election. This was certainly the case in the Mackenzie government. Borden was hamstrung by weak ministers during the First World War, as were Mackenzie King in the 1920s and R.B. Bennett in the 1930s. The same could be said of John Diefenbaker's government, Pierre Trudeau's ministry in the late 1970s, the last four years of Harper's cabinet, and the final years of the Justin Trudeau cabinet.

Statecraft is in part about achieving a balance between decisions made by departments and those made by the centre. While prime ministers have always been at the centre of government, some also pressed for a *centralization* of government, by which we mean that some prime ministers strengthened the policy machinery at the centre, namely the Prime Minister's Office (PMO), the Privy Council Office (PCO), and the Treasury Board Secretariat. Prime ministers are key in managing centripetal and centrifugal forces. Effective prime ministers have given ministers an opportunity to shape the political agenda and to tailor government implementation. Macdonald and his successors until the Second World War met daily with cabinet members to collect their views. With the time demands on management of government and then of managing a growing state that was implicated in an ever-widening circle of negotiations, cabinet met less often as a whole. But it still met. During the Second World War, Mackenzie King created a committee system that has continued in various guises to this day. In recent decades, some prime ministers have made little use of full cabinet, but in large part that was because it was unwieldy, a necessity given the vast array of government activities. Cabinet cannot operate effectively when it has too many ministers. The forces that pushed for a larger ministry reached a zenith when Mulroney's cabinet reached forty ministers. Every subsequent prime minister has operated with fewer ministers.

The task of ensuring accountability, of ensuring that expenses are clearly tabulated, and that performance targets are met, but at the same time ensuring that managerial and service innovation are constant, is the pith and substance of statecraft. Thus, Treasury Board, PCO, PMO, and parliamentary committees have increased their scrutiny of departmental spending and management but must also ensure that the public service is motivated to be responsive.[6]

Power shifted in the Pierre Trudeau years but not necessarily towards the PMO. That centrical pull had always existed. Personal staff has been a constant source of support since 1867 and steadily gained more influence as time progressed. With time, personal influence grew into an institutional presence as the desks became the *Prime Minister's Office* that has occasionally drawn the ire of cabinet members, caucuses, and even party militants. To a large extent, power has moved towards the collective cabinet and away from ministers acting individually. Pierre Trudeau's goal was to reduce the power of unelected public servants in line departments and increase the power of ministers acting in concert. Given the changing nature of government as it sought to respond to a more complex policy environment, this was perhaps inevitable. No doubt it was also inevitable that some ministers would bristle at any suggestion that they need to win over colleagues to pursue policy agendas in their own portfolio. They complained off the record to reporters or later grumbled in their memoirs about undemocratic constraints on their freedom of action. These jeremiads have provided fodder for journalists and political scientists, ever alert, and rightly so, to any suggestion that democracy has been undermined. Yet there is nothing undemocratic about collective decisions made by a cabinet responsible to Parliament and supported by an array of officials who know that ultimate authority does not rest with them.

The powers of reward and coercion, namely the prime minister's ability to make and break ministers, draw much attention. The Crown (in the person of the governor general) appoints, promotes, demotes, and removes ministers, but does so only on the advice of the prime minister. The prime minister assigns duties to ministers (beyond those in the relevant legislation), sets the cabinet's agenda, and chairs its meetings. Decisions in cabinet are made by consensus, but that consensus is determined by the prime minister. Paul Hellyer, a minister in the governments of Lester Pearson and Pierre Trudeau, defined consensus in the Canadian cabinet as "one or more ministers, of whom the prime minister is one."[7]

Though often accused of being dictators, even the most powerful of Canadian prime ministers were never close to matching that definition. In theory, the prime minister has a free hand in hiring, firing, promoting, and demoting ministers, in other words of dictating what will be. In practice, there are strict constraints on the choices available. In making a cabinet, prime ministers have been sensitive to regional balance, including the tradition that every province, with the occasional exception of Prince Edward Island, and each of the largest cities should have at least one minister. The proportion of francophones and anglophones should roughly mirror that of the population as a whole. Every cabinet should include one anglophone from Quebec and one francophone from Ontario. For more than fifty years after Confederation, cabinets included representation from Catholics and each of the major Protestant denominations, though religious balance ceased to be a factor in selecting ministers long ago. Throughout the country's history, prime ministers have sought to include representatives of the main ethnic groups among the ministers. In recent years, gender balance has become an important consideration. Prime ministers typically appoint their main leadership rivals to the cabinet, usually in prominent roles. Prime ministers in Canada have been keen in ensuring a dosage of conservatives and liberals in their cabinets – regardless of their party labels. They achieved, for the most part, a balance that satisfied both sides, making life agreeable for the centrists who have dominated.

Ideological factions and petty personal jealousies have always mattered, and successful prime ministers have managed them effectively There is no doubt that Lester Pearson was relieved when Walter Gordon resigned from cabinet in 1965, but the prime minister was soon under considerable pressure to bring back the problematic former minister, because he was still enormously popular in the Liberal caucus, particularly in Ontario. Gordon was seen as the father of the party's 1963 election victory and the leader of a left-leading Liberalism.[8]

Many prime ministers have designated members of their cabinet as regional ministers, barons responsible for party organization and patronage in their designated geographic areas and for defending the interests of those places at the cabinet table. Canadian cabinets, in short, have not only been governing bodies but also tools to reconcile diverging interests within the country and the ruling party. This consideration imposes considerable limits on the prime minister's power to appoint and discharge ministers.

Ministers do play a role in the collective decision-making of cabinet. Prime ministers need to allow an open discussion of issues in cabinet (more likely in cabinet committees since the 1960s) and then choose the best policy option based on that discussion. Rarely do these decisions go against the cabinet consensus. Prime ministers would not last long were they repeatedly to override the verdict of their ministers. Often, prime ministers and a small number of ministers may reach a conclusion before a cabinet meeting. Other times, though rarely, prime ministers will have strong views and will have decided on an issue before they walk into the cabinet room. Until his last years, Mackenzie King was unyielding on issues of Canadian external affairs, as was Pierre Trudeau on many constitutional questions. Sometimes, ministers will have discussed an issue several times in general terms before circumstances force an immediate decision, which the prime minister will make without first meeting with cabinet. This was the case with Jean Chrétien's 2003 decision that Canada would not take part in the war in Iraq.

The institutions of government have had to adapt the accommodate the growth in the functions of government. The use of cabinet committees is one example. Committees could – and probably should – have been more widely employed immediately after the Second World War. St-Laurent's government amended the law to allow more issues to be handled by the Treasury Board and created a cabinet Legislation Committee, but otherwise made little use of standing committees. This was largely because the prime minister's efficiency rendered them unnecessary. His successor, John Diefenbaker, lacked St-Laurent's managerial competence and grasp of the machinery of government. As a result, cabinet became clogged with so much business that it ceased to function effectively. Lester Pearson, who followed Diefenbaker, was not much of an organizer himself but came to understand the need to funnel decisions through committees to lighten the load of the full cabinet. It was his government, not Pierre Trudeau's, that increased the role of cabinet committees and created the Committee on Priorities and Planning to better organize the work of cabinet. Trudeau expanded on these innovations, which have been kept, often in slightly altered form, by most subsequent prime ministers.

The number of standing committees has varied considerably since then. The Chrétien government had four steady committees; Paul Martin added many more, often with competing agendas; Justin Trudeau's government had up to ten working simultaneously. Since Lester Pearson's time, most prime ministers have chaired a central coordinating committee to make key decisions, a body originally called the Priorities and Planning Committee. For Joe Clark it was the inner cabinet, for Justin Trudeau the Agenda, Results, and Communications Committee. Kim Campbell and Jean Chrétien both opted against creating such a committee. Campbell wanted full cabinet to make the key decisions. In contrast, under Chrétien and Stephen Harper, cabinet did not act as a decision-making body, rarely, if ever, overturning a committee's conclusion.

The prime minister cannot do it all. The workload is overwhelming, even for those who are willing to delegate to cabinet colleagues. The key is to assemble capable ministers and then trust them to do their jobs. Both Alexander Mackenzie and John Diefenbaker were prone to suspicion, to the detriment of their governments. Arthur Meighen and R.B. Bennett were reluctant to make use of ministers and found themselves carrying a crushing load with little time to think. They did not learn the discipline of power. Effective prime ministers have understood that they cannot be involved in every file. They have chosen a few issues to focus on and have left the rest to the ministers. Most prime ministers, particularly since the Second World War, have concentrated on national unity and relations with the premiers, Canada-US relations, economic growth, and two or three pet subjects. Leaders who become involved in more issues inevitably find that their effectiveness wanes.

Although dependent on ministers, prime ministers are difficult to challenge. The individuals who have attained the position of prime minister have been admirable, diligent, and honest. They were possessed of magnetic personalities and a sense of vision, and extensive knowledge, decisiveness and political smarts, including an eagerness to solicit views. Pierre Trudeau earned widespread admiration for his vision and knowledge. Mackenzie King was valued for his political agility. Virtually every prime minister has won recognition for being the hardest working member of cabinet. This respect for extraordinary ability has increased the likelihood that ministers will defer to the prime minister. Prime ministers are often seen as rare pearls, and the temptation to change them has been in short supply in Canadian history. Mostly, they satisfied the vast majority of cabinet members who believed themselves lucky to sit, even if it was only on occasion, at the table with the prime minister.[9]

The record shows that ministers have been happy to leave the prime minister with the difficult tasks of setting the agenda, because those rare individuals had shown an ability to win elections. In a democracy, this is not a small point. Only the prime minister has the authority to coordinate the work of the government as a whole. Ministers cannot operate in isolation, as if their portfolios were watertight containers than do not leak into the responsibilities of other ministers. Building a cabinet is a task that requires considerable care. Prime ministers need an ability to spot talent. And they must ensure that ministers represent all or most of Canada's provinces (and regions within provinces), the two main language groups, and (for earlier prime ministers) the country's main religions. Rivals, real or potential, must be handled with care. They merit, and will often demand, portfolios that reflect their standing in the party and the country. It is crucial, too, to appoint the right ministers to the right portfolios. Placing Howard Green in External Affairs in thanks for past support and not for any knowledge of foreign policy, to give but one of the more spectacular examples, contributed to John Diefenbaker's downfall. Most recently, the appointment of Jody Wilson-Raybould to Justice was clearly a mistake for Justin Trudeau. The impact of her dismissal no doubt undermined his appeal among some voters.

The threat of reassignment and then resignation or demotion can hang over a minister's head, but for the most part, prime ministers easily survived the departures of high-powered ministers such as Alexander Galt, Israël Tarte, Frederick D. Monk, Sam Hughes, James Ralston, Chubby Power, John Turner, and Bill Morneau. But cabinets can be rocked by resignation, a subject not well understood. Mackenzie Bowell had little choice but to step down as prime minister after seven ministers walked out of his cabinet. The resignation of H.H. Stevens from R.B. Bennett's cabinet in 1935 had a devastating impact, as the renegade minister went on to take almost 9 per cent of the vote in that year's election, destroying the chances of a Conservative re-election. The resignations of Doug Harkness, George Hees, and Pierre Sévigny damaged John Diefenbaker's public standing and contributed to his electoral defeat in 1963. Lucien Bouchard's abandonment of the Mulroney government in 1990 helped spell the end of the Progressive Conservative Party. The 2019 departures of Jody Wilson-Raybould and Jane Philpott may well have cost Justin Trudeau's Liberals their majority in the Commons. The loss of Finance Minister Chrystia Freeland in January 2025 was fatal. Even the seemingly invincible Mackenzie King faced a major cabinet crisis in December 1947 when his reticence to involve Canada in the United Nations Temporary Commission on Korea was challenged by Louis St-Laurent, James Ilsley, Brooke Claxton, and at least half the cabinet. That event inevitably prompted him to consider retirement, which he did a few months later.

G.W. Jones has written that no British prime minister "threw out or forced the resignation of a man who had support enough to displace him."[10] Jean Chrétien fired Paul Martin, whose people then responded by pushing the prime minister from office, proving both that Jones's dictum does not hold true in the Canadian case and that the prime minister's power to dismiss ministers is not absolute.

Prime ministers and their staff lack the capacity to micromanage multiple departments, though in recent times the Prime Minister's Office has paid considerable attention to – and has exerted control over – public statements by ministers. There is plenty of evidence that party leaders are increasingly potent in selecting candidates of their choosing in local ridings. Since 2006, the PMO has also played an increasing role in choosing chiefs of staff and other aides for ministers' offices – a real and tangible expression of authority. The power and autonomy of individual ministers has depended on their ability, their political standing, their portfolio, and their relationship with the prime minister. Often portrayed as obsessive in his need to control cabinet ministers, Stephen Harper gave considerable leeway to several ministers, including Jim Flaherty, John Baird, Jason Kenney, and Peter MacKay.

A new wind of scholarship on cabinet government has emerged in Europe, as researchers have sought to understand the kinds of bargains that have been struck to shape governments. European countries have in the main adopted proportional representation methods to elect legislators, and as a result, rare are the cabinets that are composed entirely of members of one party. The work of these scholars inspires us to re-examine Canadian statecraft in light of their deliberations.

The very size of cabinet over time has certainly borne witness to these realities. At critical junctures in the evolution of the Canadian state, the growth and contraction of cabinet (and of its attendants) became telltales of prime ministerial approaches. One important study of European governments argued that the size of the cabinet depended on intra- and inter-party politics. Inter-party politics influenced the size of the cabinet because of the need of coalition parties to agree on division of ministerial portfolios, and increasing the size of the cabinet could at times smooth that process. Intra-party politics mattered because seats in the cabinet were an important tool to maintain party discipline. Such a situation seriously challenged a prime minister's ability to govern, as a diversity of ideological opinions within the cabinet makes coordinating work more complex.[11]

The strength of factions inside a government could also be measured by the sheer number of its members in cabinet.[12] In Europe the process of coalition negotiations is almost entirely expressed by portfolio allocations. Parliamentary support, in fact, depends on it. Numbers matter but, as some have pointed out, it is not strictly a question of counting. Another valuable measure can be the importance of the various portfolios being held.[13] Prime ministers, again, also have to consider the various factions of their parties.[14] In some cases, accommodations proved so difficult that the number of ministers was expanded to please as many people as possible.[15] The study of the selection of cabinet ministers provides an opportunity to observe how prime ministers practised their statecraft through trade-offs among policymakers, office-seeking individuals, and their concerns for electoral success.[16] One study looked at more than a thousand government bills in three parliamentary democracies (Denmark, Germany, and the Netherlands) over roughly a twenty-year period and found no evidence that ministers dominated the legislation they had proposed. In fact, their draft bills were changed systematically by legislative actors. The study also found that most policies were the product of some compromise between members of a coalition.[17]

There is little evidence of consistent and significant factionalism in Canadian cabinets. Political parties are rarely thoroughly uniform, and Canadian ones have not escaped the rule. They necessarily unite different perspectives on the role of the state and at times those differences have become belligerent. Stories of leftist or rightist factions are a staple of Canadian political history and can provide an exceptional prism by which to interpret a prime minister's statecraft. Obviously, the ideological leaning of key cabinet posts can be important clues. In Canada, the most influential have been finance, foreign affairs, and justice.[18] There has been occasion when prime ministers had to appoint teams of rivals. Macdonald brought together old *patriotes* and staunch loyalists and even Joseph Howe, the Nova Scotian independentist. Laurier's party was so split between imperialists and nationalists that he lost control in 1911. Borden was so unable to accommodate Quebec nationalists that he operated practically without policy input from that province. Pearson had some difficulty in reconciling Canadian nationalists and continentalists. Pierre Trudeau managed with some difficulty the tensions between business-friendly Liberals and those that leaned left, as did Jean Chrétien after him. But these are rare examples of where strong rival tensions shaped the statecraft of a prime minister. There is plenty of evidence that party leaders are increasingly potent in selecting candidates of their choosing in local ridings, thus reducing the chances of that a faction hostile to their leadership will actually challenge it.

Cabinet committees offer further clues to statecraft. In Canada, Kenny William Ie has examined them under Martin, Harper, and Trudeau and concluded that they were strategic.[19] He sees two patterns in the coordinating function of committees. First, there were smaller and fewer subject-matter committees with larger coordinating committees, most evident under Harper, and larger committees with more connections among ministers, most present in Martin's and Justin Trudeau's tenures. Second, distributions of ministerial influence within cabinet committee structures vary among committee periods but not significantly between these three prime ministers. To the extent that ministerial influence is a mechanism of placating ministers, it appears that prime ministers do not differ markedly in their understanding of how best to use this instrument.

Determining who is influential in the ministerial appointment process is important because it can illuminate the back-room bargaining that gives some individuals power other others in government and in caucus.[20] Prime ministers have many reasons to appoint certain people to cabinet and not to select others. Experience matters, though not all experiences have the same weight. In France, it seems that individuals who have shone in parliamentary committees attract attention and can gain an edge on rivals.[21] At other times, shuffles were necessary to stabilize and re-energize cabinet to ensure its survival.[22] These give clear clues to the way prime ministers engaged in statecraft.[23] Cabinet appointees tend to be experienced,[24] can be process oriented, purpose-driven (or activist), or technocratic and subject to constraints of all sorts.[25] Either way, there is some evidence to show that prime ministers usually proceed in selecting cabinet colleagues from a process of elimination.[26]

Matthew Kerby and Feodor Snagovsky identified four archetypes of political careers in Canada for the period 1968–2015 and found that MPs with a diversity of experiences are more likely to be appointed to cabinet, while MPs who served in opposition are just as likely to be named to cabinet as MPs who already have government experience.[27] Additional characteristics, such as previous ministerial experience, margin of victory, and their level of support for the prime minister, would also affect their likelihood of success in securing a cabinet position. Contextual political factors such as the governing party's strength in an MP's region, government majority size, and prime ministerial term are also posited to have an effect.[28]

Careful readers will have noted that we recorded the ages of cabinet ministers when governments were first appointed. This was mostly done out of curiosity, but it is not evident that age or profession has made much difference to cabinets in Canada or in other Westminster democracies. All the same, it is remarkable to note that most ministries since 1867 started with cabinets whose members were of average age of about fifty-three. Canadians clearly favour cabinet members who have tasted the experience of age. Almost all ministries were headed by prime ministers who were older than the average (notable exceptions were Meighen and King in the 1920s and Justin Trudeau in 2015).

Ireland is something of an exception, mentioned here only because of its thick Westminsterian roots, where family ties provide an advantage to those seeking a cabinet post.[29] In other Westminster countries there is no evidence that family histories have any significance.

More than sixty-five years after the appointment of the first woman minister, the impact of women on cabinet has yet to be well theorized. Elsewhere, some have argued that the presence of women has improved the duration and stability of cabinets. An important longitudinal study in Europe showed that liberal parties nominate the most women to cabinets, left-wing parties follow second, and conservative parties third. They also found that leftist parties had an edge somewhat before 2000, but this edge has disappeared, and liberal parties are now front-runners.[30] One study found that the presence of women made a difference only if women held important portfolios.[31]

Several studies in this volume have explored cabinet durability. The chapters on John A. Macdonald, Wilfrid Laurier, Mackenzie King, Louis St-Laurent, Lester B. Pearson, Pierre Trudeau, Brian Mulroney, and Jean Chrétien each examined various elements that could explain it. The literature on cabinet duration is split between those who seek to explain cabinet duration by pointing to various impersonal, structural, and cultural variables, and others who emphasize the importance of events.[32] In large part, it depends on the loyalty of ministers to the prime minister, and for that reason the nature of departures must be taken into consideration.

Cabinet shuffles can be real clues to the statecraft of prime ministers as they seek to address concerns about public approval, policy performance, scandals, or economic downturns. There is good evidence to show that the electoral calendar decisively shapes cabinet dynamics, but then again there is little comparative knowledge about why (and when) particular shocks affect government dynamics. An important clue to the evolution of statecraft is the nature of ministerial shuffles, an issue that has attracted attention elsewhere.[33] It is not clear if shuffles are advantageous to a prime minister or if, as some have found, they actually improved the performance and electoral success of a government. An important study of cabinet shuffles found them most likely in situations when the prime minister lost confidence in the ability of cabinet ministers to carry out missions. The second most likely scenario was when parliamentary and electoral popularity declined. The research also showed that prime ministers shuffled their cabinet as intra-party dissent increased and the prime minister's personal approval ratings began to lag behind the government's popularity.[34] The examples highlighted in this book would confirm this interpretation.

In coalition situations, researchers found that the chances of a shuffle rose whenever the popularity gap between the prime minister's party and the junior coalition partner narrowed. The same could be argued about factions in big-tent parties such as the Liberal and Conservative Parties in Canada. The common theme here is that prime ministers shuffle their cabinets whenever their intra-party, parliamentary, or electoral positions deteriorated and the prime ministers became identified as political liabilities among party members, coalition partners, and voters.[35]

Some prime ministers have focused cabinet's attention almost entirely on making key decisions to pursue priorities while leaving political success to chance (R.B. Bennett, Louis St-Laurent, Lester B. Pearson, Pierre Trudeau in his second ministry, and Brian Mulroney are good examples of such political trapeze artists). Others were more cautious, giving equal or greater emphasis to winning the next election (John A. Macdonald, Wilfrid Laurier, Robert Borden, Mackenzie King, and Jean Chrétien certainly rank high in this regard). Some (Arthur Meighen comes to mind, as does Stephen Harper's ministry after 2011) seemed to have ignored both.

Given this record of failure, the degree of freedom ministers have allowed prime ministers is remarkable. The politics of factionalism have been rare and rarely have been consequential in this country. The influence of regional ministers – always extremely difficult to measure – has probably been critical in ensuring a good distribution of government largesse, but in a quiet, back room sort of way.[36] The difference may just be the prime minister's ability to work with his carefully selected colleagues.

Managerial ability is also about working with the public service – that is, ensuring that bureaucrats remain responsive not just to the needs of the cabinet, but also to the needs of the voters. Prime ministers often come to office distrusting senior public servants, the officials who had advised the previous government. Often the clerk of the Privy Council needs to be replaced with a senior career officer who will work better with the new prime minister, because the public service needs to know that the government is serious about implementing its election promises. The corollary is also true: prime ministers can succeed only when they work through the public service. John Diefenbaker, for instance, eventually came to rely on Bob Bryce, the clerk of the Privy Council, but continued to distrust the bureaucracy as a whole, much to the detriment of his government.

Statecraft is also glimpsed through the evolution of portfolios. This is mostly a story of continuity: finance, defence, agriculture, and justice, for example, have proven constants. Experience shows that there were several prompts to expand the scope of government by creating institutions to look after new areas of government activity. In part, it reflected modernizing needs. The Canadian cabinet, for instance, originally featured a minister of public works who was responsible for railways, but within twenty years a separate portfolio of minister of railways was created. Such innovation could also be a response to new political demands being articulated by a faction of the governing party and eventually bargained into a new portfolio.[37] Competing ideologies within the Liberal and Conservative parties were accommodated with by the creation of new portfolios. The quality of the people appointed to them also sheds light on the realities of politics in a particular cabinet.

The Collegiality Test

Prime ministers are also measured by the style they bring to the job and, to a degree that needs to be raised, by the personality and collegiality they bring to the office. In other words, history matters in trying to understand the evolution of what Anthony Seldon has called the "impossible office."[38] Prime ministers must be open, supportive, even empathetic, to their colleagues around the cabinet table. Those who fail this regard do not survive long. Collegiality means the ability to make time and hear concerns, to involve members of caucus as much as possible in both formal and informal functions. It means showing concern for both the political and personal well-being of the MPs in the government's backbench. Cabinet members are more likely to step down because of a breakdown in communication than a genuine policy conflict with the prime minister or cabinet colleagues, more likely because of a scandal than because of a fear of losing a confidence vote in Parliament.[39]

Most prime ministers have made use of extensive soft power resources to pre-empt embarrassing resignations. Some prime ministers – John A. Macdonald, Wilfrid Laurier, Louis St-Laurent, and Brian Mulroney, for example – were beloved for their attentions. Macdonald succeeded brilliantly in leading politically, managing, and in being collegial, as did Laurier for much of his career. Macdonald died in office, leaving his cabinet members in tears, but Laurier was abandoned by several key players in the 1911 election and again in 1917. He had been leader since 1887 and remained in that position until his death thirty-two years later, because a majority of party members still thought he was the very incarnation of what they thought and what they felt. For the good of the Liberal party, he probably should have retired after his defeat in 1911. Others also did well in this regard. Mackenzie King, for all his private obsessions, cared about his fellow parliamentarians, as did Louis St-Laurent. Brian Mulroney was a modern master in the art; he held together a diverse coalition through fraught political times, largely through the force of his personality. The contrast with Arthur Meighen, R.B. Bennett, and Justin Trudeau, who lacked the basic ability to understand others, could not be more striking. In short, successful prime ministers spot, recruit, and promote talented individuals, and provide a working environment in which they can do their best work, all the time maintaining their trust. That is when Canadian cabinets function best.

In an earlier era, breaking ranks was common, so John A. Macdonald and other early prime ministers had no choice but to praise, persuade, pressure, and plead with their party's MPs. That need to keep caucus onside has continued into the more recent era of strict party discipline. When members have broken ranks, they have diluted the government's message and created the impression of a prime minister unable to lead, an image that can be politically fatal. Laurier's government was defeated by break-away Liberals. Chrétien's leadership was undone when many Liberal MPs let it be known publicly that they preferred Paul Martin as prime minister. Justin Trudeau suffered a similar fate. "In the parliamentary system, caucus is the most important piece of the puzzle," according to Brian Mulroney. "If you are the leader of a party in Parliament, you had better make it your business to ensure that your caucus is behind you all the time."[40]

The prime minister has considerable sway over the governing party's parliamentary caucus, but popularity is not a given, and relations with the caucus remain a key to success. A constitutional convention requires that government maintain the confidence of Parliament, meaning that MPs from the ruling party rarely break ranks in the Commons, and certainly not in large numbers, for fear of defeating the government and forcing an election. Since the 1970s, a party's candidates in a general election must secure the leader's signature on their nomination papers. As result, a prime minister enjoys a de facto veto over who can run under the governing party's banner. Backbench MPs who cross the prime minister might well find themselves removed from caucus and forced to run as independents or for another party in the next election. Prime ministers can also dispense a variety of rewards to MPs, including choice committee assignments, better office space, travel opportunities, and visits by the prime minister to the member's riding. If cabinet management is still a mystery, caucus management is a dark art. Now and then, caucus challenges have surfaced enough to provide a public view. Until Paul Martin, weekly meetings between the prime minister and the government caucus were restricted to parliamentarians. Martin asked that key PMO officials be present in particular caucus meetings. Stephen Harper's chief of staff was present at all meetings. Justin Trudeau resolved that his principal secretary and his chief of staff attend these meetings from the beginning. Each incremental step was denounced in parts, but the imposition of non-elected staff may have created a barrier between the prime minister and the caucus.

Cabinets are not clocks that can be wound up and then left to run. They require statecraft: diligent and continuous management with an eye for political advantage in order to win the next election. Some ministers may need little supervision, but others will always demand the leader's attention. A few ministers will prove unable to discharge their obligations. Others will succumb to the pressures of an exhausting job, tiring over time and becoming unable to administer their departments with vigour and imagination, or else becoming so arrogant that their hubris is easily visible to voters. Some ministers will decide to leave of their own accord, burned out by the demanding workload or frustrated by their inability to work with the centre. Many will need to be pushed out, though prime ministers are usually loathe to do so.

Prime ministers court trouble when they fail to recruit new talent and refresh the collegiality of cabinet. Macdonald suffered this in the last few years of his ministry. Borden, Meighen, and King in the 1920s had real trouble. Louis St-Laurent was the epitome of this phenomenon. Throughout much of his tenure, he replaced vacancies in cabinet by having ministers cover two portfolios. In his final four years in office, he recruited no new ministers. Although St-Laurent was not an egotistical man, by the end of his tenure he was leading one of Canada's most arrogant governments. The same could be said of Pierre Trudeau's cabinet in 1984, Stephen Harper's in 2015, and Justin Trudeau's ministry in its final days.

In looking for capable replacements, prime ministers often find a paucity of talent in the party caucus. Recruiting from outside Parliament can bring positive results, as it did when Mackenzie King recruited Louis St-Laurent and Lester Pearson, and when Lester Pearson urged Pierre Trudeau to run for Parliament and then brought him into cabinet. Often unpopular with backbenchers who have their eye on ministerial post, these appointments provide a necessary boost to the government.

Few prime ministers have engaged in succession planning. The objective here is not for prime ministers to choose their own successor, which is not their prerogative, but to recruit several potential successors and give them the experience necessary so that they might one day assume the top job. Most prime ministers do not think ahead to a day when they will no longer lead, and their parties suffer as a result. There are but two notable exceptions. Mackenzie King understood importance of preparing for the future, bringing into cabinet his two successors as Liberal leader, Louis St-Laurent and Lester Pearson. The latter shared King's sense of the importance of succession planning, advancing the careers of the next three Liberal prime ministers, Pierre Trudeau, John Turner, and Jean Chrétien. Pearson encouraged each of them, giving them important duties at a young age, particularly Turner and Chrétien, who both joined the ministry in their thirties. It is no coincidence that King and Pearson are the only two prime ministers to turn their governments over to a successor in the same party who was able to win a majority in the subsequent election.

What we do not know about prime ministerial government in Canada dwarfs what we do know; Laurier's words – the ones we cited at the very beginning of this book – still ring true, and the mysteries of statecraft have not all been dispelled. It is deeply ironic that we know so very little about the people and the office that without a doubt is the most influential and the most powerful in this country. There are no scholarly journals dedicated to the task and no research centres or think tanks that systematically publish or convene experts to consider their thoughts and actions. Publications on prime ministers are rare, a reflection of the decimation of political history in Canada that began in the early 1990s. Our ardent hope is that this collection of essays will rekindle the pursuit of better understanding the evolution of the many dimensions of cabinet government in this country and will inspire others to join the effort.

NOTES

1 Jean Chrétien, *Straight from the Heart* (Toronto: Key Porter Books, 1985), 53.

2 See George C. Perlin, *The Tory Syndrome: Leadership Politics in the Progressive Conservative Party* (Montreal: McGill-Queen's University Press, 1980).

3 See Patrice Dutil, ed., *Statesmen, Strategists and Diplomats: Canadian Prime Ministers and the Making of Foreign Policy* (Vancouver: University of British Columbia Press, 2023). Anthony Seldon, Jonathan Meakin, and Illias Thoms argue much the same point. They hold that the power of the foreign secretary, from the time of the Congress of Vienna to the beginning of the First World War, easily rivalled that of the prime minister, but that from that point to today, the prime minister has been ascendant. See Anthony Seldon, with Jonathan Meakin and Illias Thoms, *The Impossible Office? The History of the British Prime Minister* (Cambridge: Cambridge University Press, 2021), ch. 8.

4 "The Trudeau Interview: Stay and Fight Democratically," *Montreal Star*, 8 October 1977, B3.

5 See Patrice Dutil and David MacKenzie, *Embattled Nation: Canada's Wartime Election of 1917* (Toronto: Dundurn, 2017).

6 The point is speculative and almost impossible to document but is entirely plausible. The rationale is explained in Evert Lindquist, Ian Clark, and James Mitchell, "Reshaping Ottawa's Centre of Government: Martin's Reforms in Historical Perspective," in *How Ottawa Spends, 2004–2005: Mandate Change in the Paul Martin Era*, ed. G. Bruce Doern (Montreal: McGill-Queens University Press, 2004), 317–35.

7 Paul Hellyer, *Damn the Torpedoes: My Fight to Unify Canada's Armed Forces* (Toronto: McClelland & Stewart, 1990), 169.

8 Stephen Azzi, *Walter Gordon and the Rise of Canadian Nationalism* (Montreal: McGill-Queen's University Press, 1996), 147–50.

9 A new trend in this respect has emerged. Recent memoirs by Jody Wilson-Raybould and Bill Morneau have shown genuine doubt about the prime minister's capacity for judgment, management, and consultation. Morneau notably cast

doubt on Justin Trudeau's experience, and both former ministers deeply resented the constant presence and interference of staff in the Prime Minister's Office. See Jody Wilson-Raybould, *Indian in the Cabinet: Speaking Truth to Power* (Toronto: HarperCollins, 2021); and Bill Morneau, with John Lawrence Reynolds, *Where to from Here: A Path to Canadian Prosperity* (Toronto: ECW Press, 2023).

10 G.W. Jones, "The Prime Minister's Power," in *The British Prime Minister*, ed. Anthony King, 2nd ed. (Basingstoke, UK: Macmillan, 1985), 210.

11 Indridi H. Indridason and Shaun Bowler, "Determinants of Cabinet Size," *European Journal of Political Research* 53, no. 2 (2014): 381.

12 Alejandro Ecker, Thomas M. Meyer, and Wolfgang C. Müller, "The Distribution of Individual Cabinet Positions in Coalition Governments: A Sequential Approach," *European Journal of Political Research* 54, no. 4 (2015): 802–18.

13 Cristina Bucur, "Cabinet Payoffs in Coalition Governments: A Time-Varying Measure of Portfolio Importance," *Party Politics* 24, no. 2 (2018): 154–67.

14 See Josh Cutler et al., "Cabinet Formation and Portfolio Distribution in European Multiparty Systems," *British Journal of Political Science* 46, no. 1 (2016): 31–43. They found that portfolio distribution between government members conforms robustly to a proportionality norm, because portfolio distribution follows the much more difficult process of policy bargaining in the typical government formation process.

15 See Thushyanthan Baskaran, "Coalition Governments, Cabinet Size, and the Common Pool Problem: Evidence from the German States," *European Journal of Political Economy*, no. 32 (2013): 356–76.

16 Robert J. Pekkanen, Benjamin Nyblade, and Ellis S. Krauss, "The Logic of Ministerial Selection: Electoral System and Cabinet Appointments in Japan," *Social Science Japan Journal* 17, no. 1 (2014): 3.

17 Lanny W. Martin and Georg Vanberg, "Parties and Policymaking in Multiparty Governments: The Legislative Median, Ministerial Autonomy, and the Coalition Compromise," *American Journal of Political Science* 58, no. 4 (2014): 979–96.

18 Michael Laver and Kenneth A. Shepsle, "Coalitions and Cabinet Government," *American Political Science Review* 84, no. 3 (1990): 873.

19 Kenny William Ie, "Cabinet Committees as Strategies of Prime Ministerial Leadership in Canada, 2003–2019." *Commonwealth and Comparative Politics* 57, no. 4 (2019): 466–7.

20 Christopher Kam et al., "Ministerial Selection and Intraparty Organization in the Contemporary British Parliament," *American Political Science Review* 104, no. 2 (2010): 289.

21 Alexandra Cirone and Brenda Van Coppenolle, "Cabinets, Committees, and Careers: The Causal Effect of Committee Service," *Journal of Politics* 80, no. 3 (2018): 948–63.

22 John D. Huber and Cecilia Martinez-Gallardo, "Replacing Cabinet Ministers: Patterns of Ministerial Stability in Parliamentary Democracies," *American*

Political Science Review 102, no. 2 (2008): 169–80; and Daniel Diermeier and Randy T. Stevenson, "Cabinet Survival and Competing Risks," *American Journal of Political Science* 43, no. 4 (1999): 1051–68.

23 Torun Dewan and Rafael Hortala-Vallve. "The Three As of Government Formation: Appointment, Allocation, and Assignment," *American Journal of Political Science* 55, no. 3 (2011): 610

24 Judi Atkins, Timothy Heppell, and Kevin Theakston, "The Rise of the Novice Cabinet Minister? The Career Trajectories of Cabinet Ministers in British Government from Attlee to Cameron," *Political Quarterly* 84, no. 3 (2013): 362–70.

25 Miloš Brunclík and Michal Parízek, "When Are Technocratic Cabinets Formed?," *Comparative European Politics* 17, no. 5 (2019): 760.

26 Kaare Strom, Ian Budge, and Michael J. Laver, "Constraints on Cabinet Formation in Parliamentary Democracies," *American Journal of Political Science* 38, no. 2 (1994): 303–35.

27 Matthew Kerby and Feodor Snagovsky, "Not All Experience Is Created Equal: MP Career Typologies and Ministerial Appointments in the Canadian House of Commons, 1968–2015," *Government and Opposition* 56, no. 2 (2021): 326–44.

28 Matthew Kerby, "Worth the Wait: Determinants of Ministerial Appointment in Canada, 1935–2008," *Canadian Journal of Political Science* 42, no. 3 (2009): 594. See also Matthew Kerby, "Combining the Hazards of Ministerial Appointment and Ministerial Exit in the Canadian Federal Cabinet," *Canadian Journal of Political Science* 44, no. 3 (2011): 596; Samuel Berlinski, Torun Dewan, and Keith Dowding, "The Length of Ministerial Tenure in the United Kingdom, 1945–97," *British Journal of Political Science* 37, no. 2 (2007): 245–62; and Jörn Fischer, Keith Dowding, and Patrick Dumont, "The Duration and Durability of Cabinet Ministers," *International Political Science Review* 33, no. 5 (2012): 505–19.

29 One study examined the importance of family dynasties in Irish politics since the Second World War and found that politicians with a family history in Cabinet do enjoy an advantage in cabinet selection, and that this advantage cannot be attributed simply to greater electoral popularity. See Daniel M. Smith and Shane Martin, "Political Dynasties and the Selection of Cabinet Ministers," *Legislative Studies Quarterly* 42, no. 1 (2017): 131–65.

30 Daniel Stockemer and Aksel Sundström, "Women in Cabinets: The Role of Party Ideology and Government Turnover," *Party Politics* 24, no. 6 (2018): 663–73.

31 James Richard Martin, "Consensus Builders? The Influence of Female Cabinet Ministers on the Duration of Parliamentary Governments," *Politics and Policy* 46, no. 4 (2018): 630.

32 Gary King et al., "A Unified Model of Cabinet Dissolution in Parliamentary Democracies," *American Journal of Political Science* 34, no. 3 (1990): 846.

33 Indridi H. Indridason and Christopher Kam, "Cabinet Reshuffles and Ministerial Drift," *British Journal of Political Science* 38, no. 4 (2008): 621–56.

34 Christopher Kam and Indridi Indridason, "The Timing of Cabinet Reshuffles in Five Westminster Parliamentary Systems," *Legislative Studies Quarterly* 30, no. 3 (2005): 327.

35 Kam and Indridason, "Cabinet Reshuffles."

36 The political impact of carefully planned public investment is examined in Patrice Dutil and Byoungjun Park, "How Ontario Was Won: Spending the Economic Action Plan, 2009–2011," in *How Ottawa Spends, 2012–2013: The Harper Majority, Budget Cuts and the New Opposition*, ed. G. Bruce Doern and Christopher Stoney (Montreal: McGill-Queens University Press, 2012), 207–26.

37 Steffen Roth et al., "Government.com? Multifunctional Cabinet Portfolio Analysis of 201 National Governments," *Journal of Organizational Change Management* 32, no. 6 (2019): 621–39.

38 See Paul Barker, "The Canada Health Act and the Cabinet Decision-Making System of Pierre Elliott Trudeau," *Canadian Public Administration* 32, no. 1 (1989): 84–103.

39 John D. Huber, "Cabinet Decision Rules and Political Uncertainty in Parliamentary Bargaining," *American Political Science Review* 95, no. 2 (2001): 345–60.

40 Interview with Brian Mulroney, 17 December 2018, cited in Alex Marland, *Whipped: Party Discipline in Canada* (Vancouver: University of British Columbia Press, 2020), 85.

Contributors

Jeni Armstrong is a former political staffer in the Justin Trudeau government. She now teaches in the Clayton H. Riddell Graduate Program in Political Management at Carleton University.

Dan Arnold was director of research, advertising, and correspondence in the Prime Minister's Office between 2015 and 2021. He acted as pollster for the Liberal Party during the three Trudeau election victories. He is currently chief strategy officer at Pollara Strategic Insights.

Stephen Azzi is a professor of political management, history, and political science at Carleton University. He is the author of *Walter Gordon and the Rise of Canadian Nationalism* (McGill-Queen's University Press, 1999) and *Reconcilable Differences: A History of Canada-US Relations* (Oxford University Press, 2014).

Raymond B. Blake is a professor of history at the University of Regina and a fellow of the Royal Society of Canada. He has written and edited more than twenty books, most recently *Canada's Prime Ministers and the Shaping of a National Identity* (University of British Columbia Press, 2024) and *Where Once They Stood: Newfoundland's Rocky Road to Confederation* with Melvin Baker (University of Regina Press, 2019).

Frédéric Boily is a professor of political science at Campus Saint-Jean, University of Alberta. He specializes in Canadian political ideologies, specifically conservatism and populism. He is the author of several books, including *Trudeau: De Pierre à Justin. Portrait de famille de l'idéologie du Parti libéral du Canada* (Presses de l'Université Laval, 2019) and *Droitisation et populisme: Canada, Québec, États-Unis* (Presses de l'Université Laval, 2020).

Robert Bothwell is a professor of history at the University of Toronto. He is author of various books, the most recent being *Your Country, My Country: A Unified History of the United States and Canada* (Oxford University Press, 2015) and (with J.L. Granatstein) *Trudeau's World: Insiders Reflect on Foreign Policy, Trade, and Defence, 1968–84* (University of British Columbia Press, 2017).

P.E. Bryden is a professor of history at the University of Victoria, and a past president of the Canadian Historical Association. She writes on twentieth-century Canadian politics and is the author of, most recently, *"A Justifiable Obsession": Conservative Ontario's Relations with Ottawa, 1943–1985* (University of Toronto Press, 2012) and *Canada: A Political Biography* (Oxford University Press, 2017).

Patrice Dutil is a professor of politics and public administration at Toronto Metropolitan University. He is the author or editor of many books, including *Prime Ministerial Power in Canada: Its Origins under Macdonald, Laurier and Borden* (University of British Columbia Press, 2017) and *The Unexpected Louis St-Laurent: Politics and Policies for a Modern Canada* (University of British Columbia Press, 2020).

John English is a distinguished professor emeritus at the University of Waterloo and founding director of the Bill Graham Centre for Contemporary International History at Trinity College, University of Toronto. His major publications include *The Life of Pierre Elliott Trudeau* (2 vols., Vintage Books, 2007–10) and *The Life of Lester Pearson* (2 vols., Alfred A. Knopf, 1989–92).

Ben Forster is a professor emeritus in the Department of History at the University of Western Ontario. He is author of *A Conjunction of Interests: Business, Politics, and Tariffs, 1825–1879* (University of Toronto Press, 1986), as well as numerous articles on business, economic, and political life in mid- and late nineteenth-century Canada.

Larry A. Glassford is a professor emeritus in education at the University of Windsor. His main focus is the political history of Canada since Confederation. He is the author of *Reaction and Reform: The Politics of the Conservative Party under R. B. Bennett, 1927–1938* (University of Toronto Press, 1992), and a chapter-length biography of Ontario premier Mitch Hepburn in the *Dictionary of Canadian Biography*.

Ted Glenn is program coordinator for the Graduate Certificate Program in Public Administration at Humber College. He is author of *A Very Canadian*

Coup: The Rise and Demise of Prime Minister Mackenzie Bowell, 1894–1896 (Dundurn, 2022), *Embedded: Two Journalists, a Burlesque Star, and the Expedition to Oust Louis Riel* (Dundurn, 2020), and *Professional Communications in the Public Sector: A Practical Guide* (Canadian Scholars, 2014).

Mary Janigan is an historian and former journalist. She is author of *The Art of Sharing: The Richer versus the Poorer Provinces since Confederation* (McGill-Queen's University Press, 2020); and *Let the Eastern Bastards Freeze in the Dark: The West versus the Rest since Confederation* (Alfred A. Knopf, 2012)

Tom Kierans, O.C., LL.D., is a former investment banker who spent ten years as the CEO of the C.D. Howe Institute. He is a distinguished senior fellow at Massey College and the Munk Global Affairs Institute at the University of Toronto.

J.P. Lewis is a professor in the Department of History and Politics at the University of New Brunswick (Saint John). His major research interests are in cabinet government and provincial politics. His work has appeared in *Governance*, the *Canadian Journal of Political Science*, *Canadian Public Administration*, the *British Journal of Canadian Studies*, and the *Canadian Parliamentary Review*.

Alex Marland is Jarislowsky Chair in Trust and Political Leadership and a professor in the Department of Politics at Acadia University. He is the author of *Whipped: Party Discipline in Canada* (University of British Columbia Press, 2020) and *Brand Command: Canadian Politics and Democracy in the Age of Message Control* (University of British Columbia Press, 2016).

Asa McKercher is Steven K. Hudson Chair in Canada-US Relations and an associate professor in the Public Policy and Governance program at St. Francis Xavier University and a senior fellow of the Bill Graham Centre for Contemporary International History. His books include *Building a Special Relationship: Canada-US Relations in the Eisenhower Era* (University of British Columbia Press, 2024) and *Camelot and Canada: Canadian-American Relations in the Kennedy Era* (Oxford University Press, 2016).

Patricia I. McMahon is an assistant professor at Osgoode Hall Law School at York University, where she serves as the co-academic director of the Winkler Institute for Dispute Resolution. She is also the director of the Oral History Program at the Osgoode Society for Canadian Legal History, and the author of *Essence of Indecision: Diefenbaker's Nuclear Policy, 1957–1963* (McGill-Queen's University Press, 2009) and *The Persons Case: The Origins and Legacy of the Fight for Legal Personhood* (with Robert J. Sharpe; University of Toronto Press, 2007).

Lori Turnbull is director of and an associate professor at the School of Public Administration at Dalhousie University. Her research and teaching focus on parliamentary governance, political parties and leaders, elections, political ethics and public trust, and the relationship between ministers and the public service. Her book *Democratizing the Constitution: Reforming Responsible Government* (with Mark D. Jarvis and Peter Aucoin; Emond Montgomery, 2011) won the Donner Prize in 2011 and the Donald Smiley Prize in 2012.

Robert Wardhaugh is a professor of history at Western University. His books include *Mackenzie King and the Prairie West* (University of Toronto Press, 2000), *Behind the Scenes: The Life and Work of William Clifford Clark* (University of Toronto Press, 2010), and *The Rowell-Sirois Commission and the Remaking of Canadian Federalism* (with Barry Ferguson; University of British Columbia Press, 2021).

R. Paul Wilson is an associate professor in the Riddell Graduate Program in Political Management at Carleton University. He served as director of policy for Prime Minister Stephen Harper from February 2009 to June 2011.

Index

Please note: Page numbers in italics indicate illustrations. In subentries, "NAFTA" stands for North American Free Trade Agreement; "PCO," for Privy Council Office; "PM," for Prime Minister; "PMO," for Prime Minister's Office; and "P&P," for the Priorities and Planning Committee of cabinet. Pierre and Justin Trudeau are identified as "P.E. Trudeau" and "J. Trudeau," respectively. In entries for prime ministers, "statecraft of" is always the last subentry, regardless of alphabetical order.

THE INSTITUTE OF PUBLIC ADMINISTRATION OF CANADA
SERIES IN PUBLIC MANAGEMENT AND GOVERNANCE

Networks of Knowledge: Collaborative Innovation in International Learning, Janice Stein, Richard Stren, Joy Fitzgibbon, and Melissa Maclean

The National Research Council in the Innovative Policy Era: Changing Hierarchies, Networks, and Markets, G. Bruce Doern and Richard Levesque

Beyond Service: State Workers, Public Policy, and the Prospects for Democratic Administration, Greg McElligott

A Law unto Itself: How the Ontario Municipal Board Has Developed and Applied Land Use Planning Policy, John G. Chipman

Health Care, Entitlement, and Citizenship, Candace Redden

Between Colliding Worlds: The Ambiguous Existence of Government Agencies for Aboriginal and Women's Policy, Jonathan Malloy

The Politics of Public Management: The HRDC Audit of Grants and Contributions, David A. Good

Dream No Little Dreams: A Biography of the Douglas Government of Saskatchewan, 1944–1961, Albert W. Johnson

Governing Education, Ben Levin

Executive Styles in Canada: Cabinet Structures and Leadership Practices in Canadian Government, edited by Luc Bernier, Keith Brownsey, and Michael Howlett

The Roles of Public Opinion Research in Canadian Government, Christopher Page

The Politics of CANDU Exports, Duane Bratt

Policy Analysis in Canada: The State of the Art, edited by Laurent Dobuzinskis, Michael Howlett, and David Laycock

Digital State at the Leading Edge: Lessons from Canada, Sanford Borins, Kenneth Kernaghan, David Brown, Nick Bontis, Perri 6, and Fred Thompson

The Politics of Public Money: Spenders, Guardians, Priority Setters, and Financial Watchdogs inside the Canadian Government, David A. Good

Court Government and the Collapse of Accountability in Canada and the U.K., Donald Savoie

Professionalism and Public Service: Essays in Honour of Kenneth Kernaghan, edited by David Siegel and Ken Rasmussen

Searching for Leadership: Secretaries to Cabinet in Canada, edited by Patrice Dutil

Foundations of Governance: Municipal Government in Canada's Provinces, edited by Andrew Sancton and Robert Young

Provincial and Territorial Ombudsman Offices in Canada, edited by Stewart Hyson